THE TRANSPORT REVOLUTION FROM 1770

Studies in Economic and Social History

To Rosemary

Philip S. Bagwell

The
Transport Revolution
from 1770

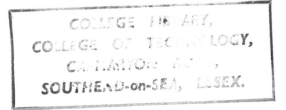
B. T. BATSFORD LTD London

First published 1974
Copyright © Philip S. Bagwell, 1974
ISBN 0 7134 1385 9 (hard cover)
0 7134 1386 7 (paperback)

Made and printed in Great Britain by
William Clowes & Sons, Limited, London, Beccles and Colchester
for the publishers,
B. T. Batsford Ltd, 4 Fitzhardinge Street, London W1H 0AH

Not for sale in the USA

Contents

List of Maps   *page*

List of Tables

List of Figures   *page*

Acknowledgement

In preparing this book I have been very conscious of the unstinted help generously given by many persons.

Professor G. E. Mingay read through the entire typescript, saved me from some pitfalls and gave much constructive advice. To my colleagues of the history staff and to students of the postgraduate seminar of the Polytechnic of Central London I am grateful for comments and criticisms made in discussions on aspects of this work. I also wish to thank the members of postgraduate seminars conducted by Professors A. H. John, T. C. Barker and Royden Harrison and the history staff and students of the Thames Polytechnic for inviting me to read papers on coastal shipping and the growth of motor transport and for questioning some of my judgements. Mr J. W. L. Forge not only read the typescript but also contributed three of the maps. Mr E. D. Wilkerson read through, with an expert eye, the chapter on coastal shipping. Mr R. Fitzgerald offered valuable information on tramways and canal traffic. Mr John Armstrong, making pioneering studies of the London Bills of Entry, provided information on the pattern of coastwise trade. In so far as the value of this book is enhanced by its diagrams and maps, this is largely due to the meticulous work enthusiastically undertaken by Messrs J. Bailey and G. Harrison. Dr W. Taylor gave of his expert knowledge of Scottish agricultural markets.

I wish to thank the Social Science Research Council for the award of a research grant which was of great assistance to me in preparing the chapter on coastal shipping.

The staff of many libraries and record offices have given their services most willingly. I am particularly indebted to those in the Public Record Office, the House of Lords Record Office, the British Museum Library, the British Railways Board Historical Records, the Institute of Transport, the Board of Trade Marine Library, the Isle of Wight Record Office and other County Record Offices, the secretarial department and office Manager of the National Union of Railwaymen and the editor of the *Railway Review* and the staff of the library of the School of Social Sciences and Business Studies of the Polytechnic of Central London.

I am very grateful to Mr Roger Hearn of B. T. Batsford for help in preparing this work for the press.

I wish to thank Mesdames P. Barbour and V. Nimmons for their valuable secretarial services.

None of the above is in any way responsible for any inaccuracies which remain in this account.

My biggest debt of gratitude is due to my wife, who amid the turmoil of catering for a family of five and giving a helping hand to neighbours, found the time and cheerful fortitude to type out an obscure manuscript on a temperamental typewriter.

Abbreviations

BTC	British Transport Commission
BTHR	British Transport Historical Records
Ec. Hist. Rev.	Economic History Review
GWR	Great Western Railway
HLRO	House of Lords Record Office
Jnl Ec. Hist.	Journal of Economic History
Jnl Ind. Econs	Journal of Industrial Economics
Jnl Inst. Tspt	Journal of the Institute of Transport
LMS	London Midland and Scottish Railway
LNER	London and North Eastern Railway
PEP	Political and Economic Planning
PP	Parliamentary Papers
PRO	Public Record Office
RC	Royal Commission
RCH	Railway Clearing House
SC	Select Committee
SR	Southern Railway
VCH	Victoria County History

Introduction

In his *Polite Conversation*, the satirist Jonathan Swift confessed that he preferred to begin journeys on Sundays because there would have been freshly said 'the prayers of the church, to preserve all that travel by land or water'. He was not alone among eighteenth-century writers in his keen awareness of the hazards of travel and in his concern to invoke every aid to a safe arrival. All the same, he was one of a very select company of people who could afford the luxury of time to travel. The vast majority of his contemporaries were villagers who rarely, in a lifetime, travelled further than a day's walking distance from home. Even in 1817 Hazlitt considered that country dwellers were 'out of the world', so different was their way of life from that of townsmen. For Robert Louis Stevenson, born in 1850, it was much easier and pleasanter 'to travel for travel's sake' than it was for either Swift or Hazlitt. Though his thoughts on the subject were expressed when using no faster means of transport than a donkey, he was at least able to reach the Cévennes with greater promptitude and certainty with the aid of steam locomotion than had been possible in the days when travellers were obliged to rely on either horse power or the force of the wind on sails to bring them to their destinations. In the 1970s the London–Dublin journey, which sometimes took Swift weeks to complete, could be accomplished in one hour and five minutes (from airport to airport) in a jet aeroplane. Using similar means, a traveller could be retracing Stevenson's steps in the South of France within three hours of leaving London. Very few of Swift's contemporaries possessed their own means of transport. In 1970 every seventh person in Britain was the owner of a motor car.

No apology is therefore needed for the title of this book. The changes of the last 200 years have constituted a transport revolution without parallel in previous ages. In terms of both the volume and speed of goods and passenger transport the achievements of the last two centuries have completely outclassed the painfully acquired gains of the whole of previous recorded history.

The scope of this book comprehends all the principal forms of transport within Great Britain. Earlier accounts have frequently failed to recognise the importance of coastal shipping in the overall provision of goods and passenger transport. An attempt has been made to rectify this omission and to give coastwise shipping its proper place, along with land, inland-waterway and air transport, in the complete pattern of British transport. Another relatively neglected aspect in the history of freight carriage has been the work of the carrier in the years before the coming of the motor car. In the past attention has often been focused on the dramatic improvements brought by the introduction of canals; but not all the new industrial areas were within easy access of navigable waterways. The extension of the turnpike system during the canal era increased the potentialities of road goods haulage. In this book the role of the carrier has therefore been given fuller consideration in chapter 2. No one form of transport can be considered completely in isolation. Much consideration has therefore been given to the impact of each form of transport on the rival media. No attempt has been made to cover ocean shipping or international air lines based on Great Britain. Any adequate treatment of these aspects would have added substantially to the length of an already lengthy book.

At the present time expenditure on all the different forms of transport absorbs at least a tenth of the national income. From the viewpoint of economic growth, the rate of economic progress can be significantly accelerated or retarded depending on the wisdom or folly of governments in the framing of legislation affecting transport. In the late eighteenth and early nineteenth centuries, when Britain became the workshop of the world, wasteful allocation of transport resources appeared to be no great handicap to the progress of the nation. In the second half of the twentieth century, with problems of inflation and the balance of payments looming large, any misappropriation of so large a proportion as one-tenth of the Gross National Product has far more serious consequences. Hence more space is devoted in the last two chapters to a critique of government policies since 1918.

In the last two centuries' history of these islands British inventiveness in transport has contributed much to the well-being of the population. From the construction of Brindley's Barton Aqueduct in 1761, through the pioneering work of Trevithick and Stephenson with the steam locomotive to Cockerell's hovercraft of modern times a magnificent roll of honour has been built up. But all too often the nation has been denied the full fruits of this inventiveness by the failure of government to provide the appropriate legislative environment for optimum development. Continuing public benefits from advances in transport will only be achieved if to a developing tradition of practical inventiveness is harnessed a statesmanlike wisdom in transport planning.

1
Inland Navigation in Britain
before 1830

I

In the eighteenth century the transport of goods depended on two principal sources of power: the wind and the horse. The harnessing of the wind was largely confined to coastal and estuarial shipping and will be considered in chapter 3. The full potentialities of horse power were realised on the inland waterways.

Using bridle paths, the greatest load that a pack horse could carry was between two and three hundredweight. A heavy waggon, moved by a team of horses employed on soft roads, was limited to a load of a ton, although the burden could be doubled if the road surface was macadamised. In the coalfield areas a horse harnessed to a waggon mounted on iron rails was able to pull eight tons. But the horse could be far more effectively employed on the tow path hauling as much as 30 tons in a river barge and on the more placid waters of a canal as many as 50 tons could be hauled by the one animal. It was an essential characteristic of the transport revolution of the eighteenth and early nineteenth centuries that by the application of capital and new technologies to river improvement and the construction of artificial cuts or canals the horse was employed to maximum advantage in the movement of goods.

II

The improvement of Britain's inland waterways was a continuous process dating back at least as early as the second half of the sixteenth century. Attention was at first directed to improving the navigability of the principal rivers by dredging, reinforcement of the banks, the elimination of meanders and the construction of sluices and staunches to control the water level. By an Act of 1571 powers were granted to the corporation of the City of London as conservators to spend money on the improvement of the river Lea.[1] Under powers granted by private Act of Parliament in 1698 the 'undertakers of the navigation of the rivers Aire and Calder' proceeded to deepen and straighten these two important waterways.[2] In the eighteenth century, under the stimulus of commercial necessity and growing discontent with the manifestly inadequate road network, the pace of improvement quickened. Under Acts passed in 1740 and 1792 a total of £11,500 was spent on widening and deepening first the upper and then the lower reaches of the river Medway. In the north, important works like the Mersey and Irwell Navigation (1720), the Weaver Navigation (1720 and 1760) and the improvements on the Wear (1716, 1747 and 1759),[3] helped on the rapid economic growth of the coalfields, the Yorkshire woollen and worsted industry and the Lancashire cotton industry.

But although river improvements helped to remove some of the worst transport bottlenecks they were far from being a complete answer to the growing needs of industry for the carriage of rapidly increasing quantities of goods. In any case, making rivers more easily navigable was not always a straightforward task. The consent of property owners to any alteration in the course of a river was not always forthcoming without long and expensive delays. Farmers sometimes objected to river improvements which, by cheapening the movement of food between regions, would reduce their profit from scarcity prices. The merchants in old-established market towns opposed the making navigable of rival waterways lest trade should be switched to newer markets with better transport facilities. Thus in 1725 the merchants of York objected to a bill for making further improvements on the Aire and Calder rivers because they believed that one consequence of the enactment would be a reduction in the volume of traffic on the river Ouse which served their city. Water mills and weirs were also substantial impediments to canal construction.

Moreover there were serious limitations to the benefits conferred by natural waterways however much they might be improved. Rivers stopped short at the barrier of watersheds and it was particularly unfortunate that the increasingly busy Midlands industrial area was perched on the central Pennine watershed, over 400 feet above sea level, with many areas quite inaccessible except by slow-moving land transport. Goods from this area had therefore to be hauled by pack horse or waggon either to Bewdley on the Severn, Winsford on the Weaver or Burton-on-Trent, depending on whether their destination was Bristol, Liverpool or the east coast. On occasion all traffic on waterways would be halted through floods making navigation dangerous or drought making it impossible. The river Severn has been known to rise 18 feet within five hours. On the other hand there were several occasions when Thomas Telford, the famous engineer, was surveyor for the County of Salop (1786–1800), when the depth of water in the river was less than 16 inches.[4] In 1796 the river was navigable for only two months out of the 12. One inevitable consequence of the delays caused by these natural impediments was the increase in opportunities for pilfering goods from riverside barges. So widespread were the thefts that in 1751 Parliament passed an Act 'For the more effectual prevention of robberies and thefts upon any navigable river, ports of entry or discharge, wharves or quays adjacent'.[5] Although there is no record of any offender being sentenced to death under the terms of the original Act, at least 13 persons were sentenced to transportation after 1752 when the maximum penalty for the violation of the law was made less severe.

No doubt the delays and inconveniences associated with river transport would have been tolerable if this means of conveyance of goods had been adequate for the needs of business. But in the second half of the eighteenth century there was a population explosion and a great increase in the volume of manufactures. During those 50 years, for example, the quantity of cotton raw material imported into Great Britain for manufacture rose by 15 times.[6] The rapidly expanding textile industry required increasing quantities of coal, and although the coastwise sailing brigs from Newcastle and Sunderland could meet the growing domestic demands of Londoners, the river navigations taking coal to the new cotton factories could not cope with the added burdens they were called upon to carry. It was the rapidly increasing volume of inter-regional exchange that made imperative the introduction of more sophisticated forms of goods transport.

III

The construction of the earliest English canals pre-dated many of the more important river improvements. The Exeter Lighter canal, cut by the Welsh engineer John Trew in 1564–6 and paid for by the Exeter Corporation, is in a class by itself in that it preceded by nearly two centuries the canals of the industrial revolution period. It is believed to be the first canal in England to employ pound locks.[7]

However, the cradle of the canal age proper was in the north-west around the estuary of the river Mersey and its two principal tributaries, the Irwell and the Weaver; it was Thomas Steers, sometime engineer of the Newry canal (1737–42), and his assistant, Henry Berry, who pioneered the improvements in this region.[8] The value of Liverpool's trade grew by more than three times in the 40 years between 1720 and 1760 when it was fast outstripping its rival, Bristol, in the development of the north Atlantic trade. But its continued expansion was dependent on the improvement of communications with its hinterland. Under an Act of Parliament of 1694 the river Mersey was made navigable as far as Warrington. But this was only a beginning. The growth of the very important salt trade to Ireland and northern Europe was completely dependent on the cheap transport of crude salt on the river Weaver and on the provision of cheap fuel from the Lancashire coalfield for the refining process. The main improvements in the river Weaver were completed—after much controversy—by 1733, and rock salt could thereafter be transported inexpensively to the Mersey; but the transport of adequate supplies of coal at reasonable cost required improvements to communications north of the Mersey estuary. Between 1754 and 1757, therefore, the Liverpool Corporation commissioned the construction of the Sankey Brook Navigation—an artificial cut and not simply a river improvement—under the able direction of Henry Berry, thereby making more easily accessible coal from at least a part of the Lancashire coalfield.[9]

It was in the same year that the Sankey Brook Navigation was completed that Francis Egerton, third Duke of Bridgewater, came into possession of his valuable Worsley Park estate. Utilising to the full the engineering experience of his agent, John Gilbert, and the dedicated energies of that self-educated genius, James Brindley, the Duke devised a plan to link the extensive coalfields on his estate to the rapidly growing markets in Manchester and Liverpool. Under the two Acts of 1759 and 1760 the first, ten-mile, stretch of the Bridgewater canal was opened between the coal mines at Worsley and Stretford in the suburbs of Manchester on 17 July 1761. The opening of this canal was as dramatic a turning point in the history of British transport as was the opening of the Liverpool and Manchester Railway on 15 September 1830. It was a remarkable demonstration both of engineering skill and of the economic potential of canals as a vastly improved medium for the movement of bulky commodities. The famous Barton aqueduct which carried the new canal 38 feet above the river Irwell; the successful crossing of the boggy Trafford Moss and the cutting of an elaborate system of tunnels to the coal workings at Worsley all revealed that inland water transport could be far more extensively used than had been previously thought possible. The reduction in the price of coal at Manchester from $7d$ to $3\frac{1}{2}d$ a hundredweight indicated the possibilities for reductions in transport charges that canals could provide.

Once the potentialities of canals had been demonstrated the construction of the main trunk routes followed in quick succession. By means of the Staffordshire and Worcestershire canal the Mersey was linked with the Severn at Stourport in 1772; the completion of the Trent and Mersey (Grand Trunk) canal in 1777 linked Hull and Liverpool; the opening of the Thames and Severn canal in 1789 brought through communication between the Thames estuary and the Bristol Channel and the completion of both the Coventry and the Oxford canals in 1790 joined the Trent and Mersey networks to the Thames. There were many deficiencies even after these important trunk routes were opened to traffic. More adequate trans-Pennine facilities were not available until the opening of the Rochdale (1804), Huddersfield (1811) and Leeds and Liverpool (1816) canals. The Grand Junction canal, providing a more satisfactory link between London and the Black Country, was not opened until 1805. Most of the Welsh canals were not built until the years 1794–1814. Although a part of the Forth and Clyde canal was opened as early as 1777 most Scottish canals came very much later, and the Caledonian, which joined the North Sea and the Atlantic, was not completed until 1822. By this time there were some 4,000 miles of navigable waterways in the British Isles (see maps 1 and 2).

Throughout the canal age it was most frequently the case that the local landowners and entrepreneurs, who had most to gain from internal improvements, took the initiative in calling promotional meetings, employing surveyors and providing a large part of the needed capital. The Duke of Bridgewater was merely the most famous of a long line of distinguished local sponsors of canals. There is space to cite only a few examples from among a great many. It was Lord Egremont (1751–1837) who placed an advertisement in the *Morning Post* on 17 May 1811 inviting those interested in the 'intended Surrey and Sussex canal' to a meeting at the White Hart Inn, Guildford, on the first of June following and who subscribed £20,000 of the original £90,000 capital of the Wey and Arun canal which was the outcome of these efforts.[10] In 1791 it was subscribers 'from within or near Rochdale' who provided most of the £200,000 initially required for the building of the Rochdale canal.[11] In the case of the Trent and Mersey (Grand Trunk) canal, 'most was local money', although nearly £11,000 of the initial £300,000 capital was subscribed by Londoners.[12] In Somerset the Chard canal was financed mainly by five wealthy men of the neighbourhood.[13] In 1786 nine-tenths of the shares of the Forth and Clyde canal were held in Scotland.[14] Two families, the Dadfords and the Sheasbys, provided practically all of the capital of the canals serving Cardiff, Swansea and Newport.[15] The funds needed for the construction of the Gloucester and Berkeley canal were 'provided by parties interested in the district that Gloucester supplies'.[16]

In the period of the canal mania between 1791 and 1794 the habit of canal investment became more generalised. Within those four years 42 new canals with a total capital of £6½ million—approximately one-third of all capital expended on canals up to 1830—were successfully launched. The sharply declining yield on consols—from 5·4 per cent in 1784 to 3·3 per cent in 1792—the low price of wheat in the three successive years 1786-7-8, with consequent discouragement of investment in enclosures, and the increasingly profitable return from earlier canal investments no doubt encouraged the more widespread and speculative character of canal investments in the early 1790s. Thus in the case of the Ellesmere canal project, launched in 1791–2, investors came from as far afield as Derby, Leicester, Northampton, Coventry and Birmingham.[17] In 1793, when the Crinan canal got its Act, three times as many of the shares were held in England as in Scotland. Farmers and local tradesmen also frequently purchased shares in local canals.[18]

Canal shares were generally of large denominations. Units of £200 were very common and it was exceedingly rare for capital to be raised in shares of less than £50. Hence, even in the time of the mania, investment was limited to the wealthier classes. The costs of construction almost invariably exceeded the original estimates of the surveyors. This was particularly true of those undertakings in the process of construction during the years of the war against France (1793–1801, 1802–15), when the level of wholesale prices practically doubled. The Rochdale canal, authorised in 1794, but not completed until ten years later, cost some £600,000, compared with an original estimate of £291,000.[19] But it was not only the unexpected rise in prices that sent the costs of construction of most canals soaring well above the anticipated cost. Miscalculation of the severity of the engineering problems involved could also escalate expenses. The formidable difficulties encountered in building the 5,415-yard-long Standedge Tunnel—the longest in the kingdom—rather than the fact that construction extended through the period of war-time inflation, was the principal reason for estimates of the cost of the Huddersfield canal being very wide of the mark.

When the original estimates were exceeded the canal management could either attempt to raise additional funds on the existing shares or they could borrow money from local banks or create a completely new type of security, the preference share, the payment of interest on which would be a first call on the resources of the company after interest on loans had been met. It was the financing of canals, rather than that of railways, which familiarised the capitalist with this type of security.

Only very rarely did the Government step in to contribute to the capital of canal undertakings. During the war against France William Pitt and his successors were concerned to defend the capital against invasion from across the Channel and to protect British shipping from the attacks of privateers. To further these ends nearly £200,000 of the taxpayers' money was spent before 1806 on the construction of the Royal Military canal which ran for 30 miles from Shorncliff in Kent, behind Dungeness, to the Rother, near Rye, in Sussex.[20] To provide safe transit across Scotland, increase ease of access to the Western Isles, and to enable ships to avoid the perilous journey through the Pentland Firth the Government loaned £50,000 to the Forth and Clyde, £74,000 to the Crinan and some £70,000 to the Caledonian canal. A great deal more government money was spent on the Caledonian, to make it a viable concern, during the years after Waterloo.[21]

In defence of the methods of promotion of British canals it can be argued that by allowing full scope to local initiative there was some guarantee that such works as were undertaken would be in response to a real need. On the other hand the absence of a central plan made infinitely more difficult the development of through, long-distance, communication. As the leading historian of Britain's inland waterways has aptly remarked 'canals were built, as they have remained, of all shapes and sizes'.[22] Although the typical narrow boat, measuring some 72 feet by seven, was able to pass along most British canals, its capacity was limited to some 25 to 30 tons and even with this relatively small consignment of goods it would have been unable to fit into the 64-feet long locks of the Droitwich canal. Other canals such as the Erewash could accommodate barges as long as 78 and as wide as 14 feet which could carry more than double the loads of the typical narrow boats; but because of the absence of a standard broad gauge for canals, carriers were precluded from exploiting the undoubted advantages of the long haul, by water transport, of large consignments of goods. As late as 1913 the canal carrier had the choice of three routes for the conveyance of goods between London and Liverpool; but on two of them he would have had to negotiate tolls with as many as nine separate canal companies, while, on the third, no less than ten companies were involved. The simplification and reduction of charges which became urgent when the railway challenge emerged, was made all the more difficult because of the legacy of localised, piecemeal, promotion. Unfortunately the boards of directors of British canal companies contained no counterpart to George Hudson, of the railway age, to bring together under one management, by the force of a dominant personality, a national system of waterway routes. Nor was there ever created a Canal Clearing House to facilitate the through conveyance of goods over the routes of independent companies in the same way that the Railway Clearing House did for the railways after 1842.

The opposition of the proprietors of older river navigation companies to the introduction of canals can be appreciated in the light of what happened once a rival artificial cut was opened to traffic. In a number of instances the most immediate effect of the opening of a canal was a reduction in the volume of traffic carried on the river because the newer form of transport was cheaper and more dependable. Thus the opening of the Duke of Bridgewater's canal in 1761 led to a reduction of tonnages carried on the Mersey and Irwell Navigation and the opening of the Grand Trunk canal in 1777 had the immediate effect of reducing traffic on the river Weaver from 13,917 tons in 1776–7 to 5,284 tons in 1779–80.[23] The switch of long-distance traffic from the roads was, however, far more complete than that from rivers for the reason that the cost differential in favour of the canal was greater. In 1813 there was no instance of the cost of canal carriage being above half the cost of land carriage. When the Grand Trunk canal was opened goods freights between Manchester and Lichfield were reduced from £4 to £1 a ton.[24] In 1792 goods carried from

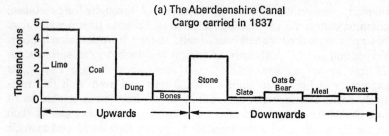

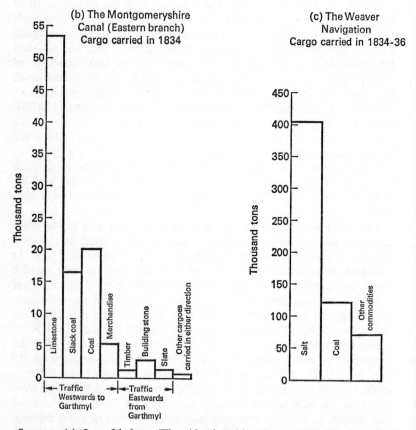

Sources: (a) Jean Lindsay, 'The Aberdeenshire Canal 1805–54', *Journal of Transport History,* vol. VI, 1963–4, p. 161. (b) E. C. R. Hadfield, *The Canal Age,* David & Charles, Newton Abbot, 1968, pp. 146–7, 150. (c) E. C. R. Hadfield, G. Biddle, *The Canals of North-West England,* David & Charles, Newton Abbott, 1970, vol. 1, p. 142.

Figure 1   Patterns of Canal Traffic

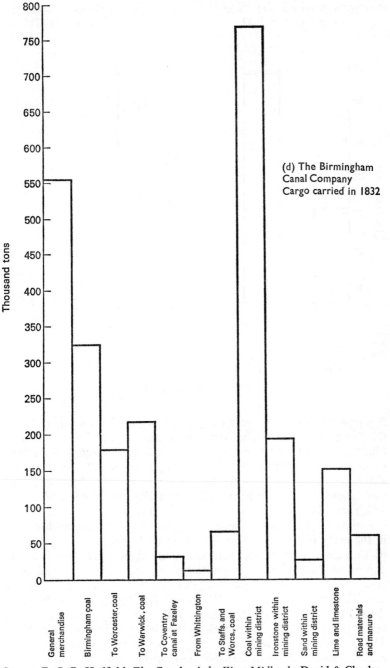

(d) The Birmingham
Canal Company
Cargo carried in 1832

Source: E. C. R. Hadfield, *The Canals of the West Midlands,* David & Charles,
Newton Abbot, 1966, p. 92.

Figure 1 (continued)

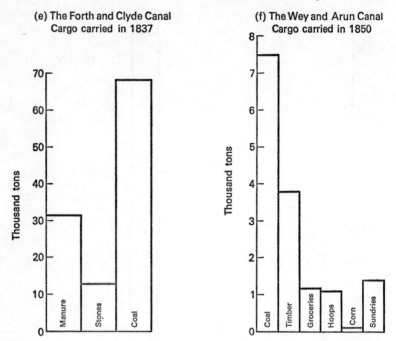

(e) The Forth and Clyde Canal
Cargo carried in 1837

(f) The Wey and Arun Canal
Cargo carried in 1850

Sources: (e) Jean Lindsay, *The Canals of Scotland*, David & Charles, Newton Abbot, 1968, Appendix IIIE. (f) P. A. L. Vine, *London's Lost Route to the Sea*, David & Charles, Dawlish/Macdonald, London, 1965, p. 152.

Figure 1 (continued)

Basingstoke to London were charged £2 by road but only 11s 7¾d by the Basingstoke canal. The transport of earthenware from Etruria to Manchester cost £2 15s a ton by road and 15s by canal. Tolls and carriers' charges taken together averaged around 2½d a ton-mile although charges on busy canals, like the Leeds and Liverpool, were well below this, while charges on canals like the Kennet and Avon, which served non-industrial areas, were higher.[25]

Estimates of the total tonnage of goods carried on British canals in the early 1840s vary from 30 million to 35 millon tons.[26] Because of important gaps in the evidence these figures are bound to be approximations. Some three-quarters of this tonnage was carried in an area bounded by the Tweed, the Thames, the Severn and the North Sea. The canals of Scotland, Wales and Southern England, between them, carried the remainder. Wales with 200 miles of canals, about seven per cent of the total, carried over eight per cent of the traffic.[27] The Scottish canals, with a similar mileage carried around seven per cent.[28] South and south-east England, with a greater mileage than

Wales and Scotland taken together, had little more than six per cent of the canal traffic and the 141 miles of canals of the south-west certainly took less than five per cent of the national total.[29]

Among the industries which benefited most from the creation of a canal network were those which were located the longest distances from the sea. Before the canal age their growth had been stunted because of the cripplingly high cost of land goods transport. The coming of the new waterways in the last quarter of the eighteenth century valorised Britain's industrial hinterland. From its opening in 1772 the Birmingham canal became an essential means of the industrial growth of the Black Country 'by bringing not only coal but pig iron for the foundries, limestone, articles for the manufacture of brass and steel, also stone, brick, slate, timber, etc.'[30] In 1760, before the Staffordshire potteries were connected by waterways to their source of supply of china clay in north Cornwall and their markets throughout the kingdom, the population of the 'five towns' employed in pottery manufacture did not exceed 7,000. By 1785 when the Staffordshire and Worcestershire and the Grand Trunk canals had both been open to traffic for at least eight years, three times as many people found employment in the industry. Indeed the canals were an important civilising influence in the area. On the occasion of John Wesley's first visit to Burslem in 1760 he was assailed with clods of earth—the traditional reception given to strangers. When he revisited the town in 1781 he was astonished to discover that 'inhabitants had continually flowed in from every side', the 'wilderness had become a fruitful field' and 'the country was not more improved than the people'.[31]

The Duke of Bridgewater was convinced that 'a good canal should have coals at the heels of it'. It was true of the large majority of canals in all parts of the kingdom that coals provided the 'bread and butter' source of revenue for the proprietors. On the important Leeds and Liverpool canal, although merchandise brought in more income than coal at the Yorkshire end, in Lancashire the position was reversed and in 1833 the canal supplied 270,753 tons of the total of 584,950 tons of coal consumed in Liverpool.[32] On the Forth and Clyde canal in 1837 the tonnage of coal carried exceeded that of the other principal items combined.[33] During the first three years of the Chard (Somersetshire) canal, between 1843 and 1845, coal tonnages amounted to nearly half the traffic.[34] There were, of course, a few canals where the carriage of coal was less important. On the Aberdeenshire canal, for instance, granite was for many years the principal item carried down to the coast.[35] For those canals which were linked to important ports timber was always a big revenue earner.

Most canals of South Wales 'were built upon the iron trade', both making possible the enormous expansion of the trade and benefiting from it. From 80,333 tons of iron carried on the Glamorganshire and

Monmouthshire canals in 1819 the total rose to 372,176 in 1839 and an estimated half a million tons in 1849.[36]

In the eastern counties the pattern was often of raw materials and manufactured goods carried inland, with agricultural produce carried to the sea for subsequent coastwise delivery to the large towns. On the Grantham canal, coal, coke, lime, building materials, groceries and clothing were carried inland, while corn, malt, beans, wool and other farm produce were moved in the reverse direction.[37]

The canals served agriculture both by distributing its products more expeditiously and cheaply and by carrying capital in the form of machinery and fertilisers to the farms. It was the carriage of corn on the Forth and Clyde canal that helped to avert famine in Western Scotland after the poor harvests of 1782 and 1783.[38] In November 1800 the Committee of the Grand Trunk canal being

'desirous of contributing their endeavours to relieve the distress of the Poor and labouring parts of the Community, by giving encouragement to a considerable Importation of corn ... Agreed, that all wheat, imported and brought upon this navigation after 25th instant, should be permitted to pass FREE OF TONNAGE, and all other dues for the space of two months.'[39]

Mr Clifford of Frampton Court, Frampton-on-Severn, used the Gloucester and Berkeley canal in the 1840s to bring supplies of oats from Stirling, clover and other seeds from Suttons of Reading and large quantities of imported guano to his Gloucestershire farm. Over a period of two and a half years in 1849–51 Clifford received, by way of the canal, more than 36 tons of this fertiliser, paying at the rate of 5s a ton for its carriage over the 20 miles from Bristol to Framilode.[40] The canals were also used on occasion for the movement of livestock. In the 1820s the London, Leith, Edinburgh and Glasgow Shipping Company operated cattle boats between Glasgow and Edinburgh on the Union canal charging at the rate of 1s 6d per head for fat cattle.[41] Thus the canals contributed handsomely to the improvement in agricultural techniques, the levelling out of regional differences in prices and the cheaper distribution of the food of the nation. Canals undoubtedly helped the enclosure movement by carrying timber to the farms for fencing purposes.

IV

On most canals the goods traffic reached its greatest volume many years after the arrival of the railway in the district. On the Leeds and Liverpool, the Leicester Navigation and the Kennet and Avon, maximum tonnages were carried in the late 1840s. On the Shropshire Union, the Staffordshire and Worcestershire and the leading Welsh canals traffic continued to grow for at least another ten years.[42] This resilience of canals in the early railway age was due in part to the railway companies' comparatively slow development of their goods traffic, an aspect of British transport history that will be dealt with more fully in chapter 5. Sometimes the greatest tonnage of traffic was achieved during the years in which a rival railway was being built. The Somersetshire coal canal carried its greatest quantity of coal in 1841 when the Great Western Railway was laying down rails in the district.[43]

Until 1845, unless they had obtained a special Act to enable them to do so, canal companies were not legally entitled to act as carriers since Parliament feared the creation of a transport monopoly. The work of transporting goods was therefore generally undertaken either by carrying firms of national repute such as Pickfords or Sutton, or by concerns independently established to carry on a particular canal or by local carriers from the nearby market towns. But since it was sometimes difficult to persuade those whose capital was geared to land carriage to switch to the new means of transport, groups of the canal's proprietors, or even the canal concern itself, sometimes undertook the carrying business. By 1845, with an outline railway network nearing completion, there was no longer any danger of canals monopolising goods transport. Parliament therefore allowed all canal companies to become carriers and also permitted their amalgamation in the belief that they would then be better able to compete with the railways.

The construction of over 3,000 miles of improved river navigation and canals between 1760 and 1830 was the leading influence in the creation of the new profession of civil engineer in Britain. What particularly taxed the ingenuity of men like James Brindley, Thomas Telford, John Smeaton, John Rennie and James Green was the difficulty of carrying water over the Pennines, across the Chilterns or up the Welsh valleys, the problem of preventing wastage of scarce supplies of lock water and the need to carry canals at great heights across the beds of rivers. During these 70 years, over 2,000 locks, at least 20 tunnels and as many inclined planes, many impressive aqueducts, and innumerable cuttings and embankments were constructed from as far north as Inverness to as far south as Bude.

When Brindley built his one-and-a-half-mile long Harecastle tunnel on the Grand Trunk canal before 1777 no such work had ever been undertaken in Britain outside of her coal mines. Because it was such a new kind of undertaking the work of construction occupied eleven years. By 1827, when Telford completed a parallel, but larger, tunnel at Harecastle in only three years, the members of his profession had gained much experience and a far greater expertise—valuable assets with which to meet the even more exacting demands of railway construction a few years later. The building of canals in the south-west presented its own variety of problems. When James Green and Thomas Shearn were asked to survey a route for the Bude canal in 1817 their special difficulty was how to carry the canal up the steep gradients towards the foothills of Bodmin Moor. Green's solution was succinctly expressed in his report to the canal committee:

'I propose to overcome the ascent from the sea to the summit level by means of inclined planes, up which these small boats may be readily passed by machines of a simple construction, moved by water. These machines may be executed at one-third the expense of locks, and worked with one third the quantity of water which locks would require, with a saving of more than four-fifths of the time in passing them.'[44]

Inclined planes such as were used on the Bude canal were also employed on the Torrington and Grand Western canals elsewhere in the south-west. They represented an important new development in engineering technology. James Green was also the first engineer to make successful employment of lifts on British canals when he constructed seven, with rises of between 16 and 46 feet, on the Grand Western canal, opened between Taunton and Tiverton in 1836.[45] These hydraulically operated lifts comprised tanks or caissons into which canal barges were floated and then raised simultaneously with the descent of a parallel lift. Through the successful development of such innovations as the inclined plane, the lift and the side-pond lock (to economise the use of water), British engineers' understanding of the laws of dynamics, hydraulics and mechanics was greatly enlarged.

Perhaps the most impressive engineering achievement of the canal age was Telford's Pont-y-Cysyllte aqueduct which carried the Ellesmere canal for a distance of 1,007 feet at a height of 127 feet over the river Dee. It was opened on 26 November 1805 with appropriate pomp and ceremony. Amidst cheers from thousands of onlookers a caravan of six boats passed along the aqueduct. In the first two boats sat the members of the managing committee; the band of the Shropshire Volunteers played in the third; the engineers and other staff with their families occupied the fourth and the last two boats were hauled empty. Many critics doubted whether the 11 piers, which were solid only for the first 70 feet up from the ground, would bear the weight of traffic. But the aqueduct, which Sir Walter Scott described as 'the most impressive work of art [he] had ever seen' stands complete to the present day.[46]

The practice of exporting British capital and engineering skill for the improvement of communications in other countries which was so notable a feature of the age of the railway was begun during the era of the canals. When king Gustavus Adolphus IV was eventually persuaded by his fellow countryman, Count von Platen, to authorise the

Map 1   English Canals, Showing Railway Ownership 1872

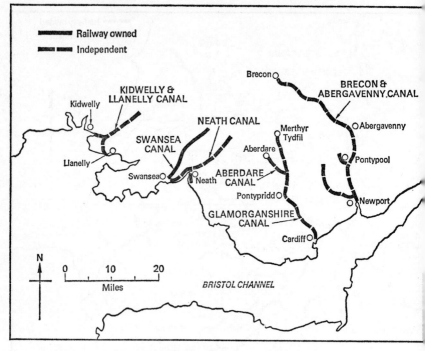

Note: Montgomeryshire Canal not shown.

Map 2   Welsh Canals, Showing Railway Ownership 1872

construction of a ship canal from Gothenburg to Stockholm the advice of Thomas Telford, the engineer of the Caledonian canal, was sought. For many years after 1808 Telford served as chief consulting engineer of the Gotha canal, taking over to Sweden not only assistant engineers and craftsmen skilled in the art of canal building but also iron lock gates, pumping engines and every kind of equipment needed for the construction of a great inland waterway.[47]

V

On most British canals the carriage of passengers was a feature of activity in some stage or other in their history: on very few did it continue over a long period as an important part of total commercial activity. In the exceptional cases where passenger traffic proved to be a big revenue earner the canal served a populous district and was blessed with easy gradients so that there were few locks to impede the relatively speedy passage of the packet boats.

The oustanding examples of canals as passenger carriers were to be

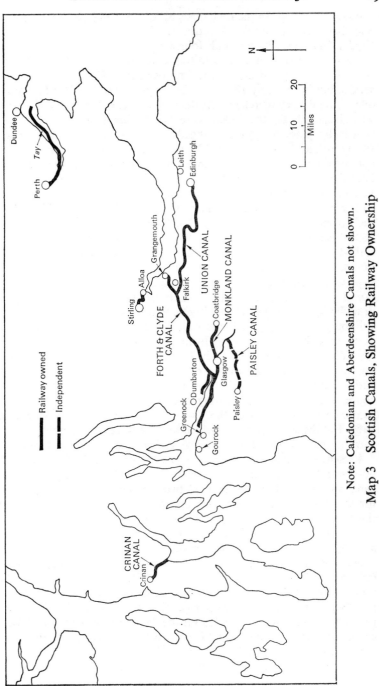

Note: Caledonian and Aberdeenshire Canals not shown.

Map 3   Scottish Canals, Showing Railway Ownership

found in Scotland. In the mid 1830s at least 800,000 passengers a year were being carried on five Scottish canals—the Monkland, Forth and Clyde, Glasgow, Paisley and Johnstone, an 11-mile-long, lock-free, canal which had been opened to traffic in 1811. At first little attention was given on this canal to the improvement of this branch of the service but in the early 1820s, on the suggestion of William Langmuir, one of the Paisley merchants on the committee, lighter passenger boats were installed. By the 1830s these boats were being towed at high speeds by pairs of horses changed every four miles of the route.[48] Penny-a-mile fares, comfortable accommodation, smooth passages and journey times that compared favourably with the mail coaches kept the travelling public loyal to the packet boats until Glasgow and Paisley were linked by railway in 1840.

The proprietors of the Forth and Clyde canal were also able to hold their own in the face of competition from faster coach services in the 1830s. New boats, modelled on those of the Paisley canal, were installed and journey times and fares were reduced, with the result that in 1836 nearly 200,000 passengers were carried. A traveller who experienced both the coach and passage-boat journeys from Perth to Port Dundas expressed pleasure at transferring 'from a rumbling old drag, badly horsed and worse driven, to a snug and warm cabin in the Edinburgh and Glasgow barge which went at the rate of 9½ miles an hour throughout the journey'. In this case the arrival of the railway— the Edinburgh and Glasgow—in 1842 did not kill the passenger traffic on the canal although it caused cabin fares to be reduced to 3s for the entire journey from Edinburgh to Glasgow. Some passenger traffic continued on the canal during the second half of the nineteenth century when this part of the business was leased to a private company. But the screw steamers which by then were being employed were carrying people on pleasure outings rather than on business trips.[49]

Passenger traffic was also of some importance in the industrial north-west of England: passage boats began to ply on the Bridgewater canal as early as 1767 but in 1774 two new boats were specially built for the Altrincham–Manchester run and each had a 'Coffee room at the Head, from whence wines, etc are sold out by the Captain's wife. Next to this is the first cabin, which is 2s 6d, the second cabin 1s 6d and the third cabin 1s for the passage.'

Services of this kind continued for a quarter of a century after the opening of the Liverpool and Manchester Railway, when the regular services closed down, though spasmodic passenger carrying occurred on other parts of the Bridgewater canal networks until 1924.[50] Passenger boat services were provided on the Manchester, Bolton and Bury canal for over 40 years after 1796 when the first packet boats linked the towns of Bolton and Manchester. From July 1833 to July 1834 over 64,000 persons found it convenient to travel by these means rather than by the rival coach services. However, when the railway was opened between Bolton and Salford in May 1838 business slumped and the passenger boats were sold off.[51] Another part of the English canal network on which passengers were carried for at least 40 years was the Wirral branch of the Ellesmere canal before 1840. Sir George Head, who travelled on the canals of the area in the summer of 1835, provides us with one explanation of the smaller volume of passenger traffic on the canals of the industrial north-west than was the case in Scotland. He conceded that in the Runcorn area this mode of transport enabled the traveller to 'glide tranquilly onwards through a continuous panorama of cows, cottages and green fields', but was obliged to admit that a 'very considerable drawback' of the voyage was that the water of the canal was 'black as the Styx and absolutely pestiferous' and that there was 'a compound of villanous smells past all endurance'.[52] The efficiency of coach services between London and the midlands and the establishment of a railway link with Birmingham as early as 1838 reduced the likelihood of successful passenger carrying on canals in this region. A series of lessees on the Grand Junction canal failed to make passenger services pay between 1801 and 1810.[53] Although occasional passenger services were provided on the Thames and Medway, the Kennet and Avon, the Gloucester and Berkeley and other canals of the south, the engineering difficulties often encountered in canal construction in the area made profitable packet boats unlikely. In south Wales, where the principal canals had numerous locks which greatly reduced the speed of transit, 'passenger carrying was rare' except on the six-and-a-half-mile-long Tennant canal.[54]

On the more important Scottish canals revenue from passengers must have made the difference between profit and loss. On the Forth and Clyde canal passenger fares brought in more than a quarter of the total revenue in 1828.[55] Revenue from passengers carried on the Paisley canal amounted to £9,000 in 1836.[56] Commuters' fares made a significant contribution to the finances of some of the canals south of the border also. The Manchester, Bolton and Bury canal obtained over ten per cent of its revenue from passengers in 1833–4.[57] On the Carlisle canal passengers brought in between a sixth and a tenth of the revenue in the 1830s.[58] Elsewhere in England and Wales they could not be counted upon to add significantly to the prosperity of a canal company. They could have contributed much more if at the time of their construction the dimensions of the canals had been larger and the banks of the canals had been more durably built. They might then have coped with the kind of fast-moving steamboat traffic which was found on the Caledonian, the Crinan and the Forth and Clyde canals. Steamboat services were tried out on the Ellesmere in 1819, on the Thames and Medway in 1824 and on the Gloucester and Berkeley in 1833, to mention only three examples, but these experiments were soon abandoned because of actual or anticipated damage to the canals' banks.

VI

Some canals were veritable gold mines before the arrival of railway competition from the 1830s onwards destroyed the opportunity for monopoly profits. These were the concerns which served industrial districts whose prosperity they helped both to create and enlarge. A list of share prices and dividends published early in 1830 shows that the seven most prosperous canals were the Loughborough Navigation, the Erewash, the Mersey and Irwell, Trent and Mersey, Oxford, Coventry and the Forth and Clyde. These all paid dividends in excess of 25 per cent and the market value of the shares stood at six or even eight times their nominal value.[59] In between these and another substantial group—principally found in southern England—which either paid no dividends at all or disappointingly low ones, were some very important concerns that did a large volume of business and paid well, though not extravagantly. At the beginning of the 1830's the Leeds and Liverpool's 20 per cent dividend on a toll revenue of £116,336 was not large enough to place it in the most profitable élite although the expansion of its business in the early 1840s did bring it into that category.[60] The Rochdale canal was in a similar class—with a traffic approaching half a million tons a year in the late 1820s and dividends not far short of five per cent it merits inclusion among the successful canals.[61] Although the canals of the south-west provided many opportunities for experimentation in engineering they did not bring a rich harvest of profits to their proprietors. The Chard canal, costing £140,000 to build (compared with an original estimate of £57,000) may be taken as a fairly typical example. It was unable to pay the full interest on the mortgage debt let alone bring any return to the ordinary shareholders.[62]

There is some substance in the charge that the shareholders of the most prosperous concerns were content, year after year, to draw monopoly profits, and that the public, and possibly they themselves, would have been better served in the long run if they had shown a greater far-sightedness and less avarice by re-investing their money in the widening and deepening of the canals, the enlargement and standardisation of locks and other equipment and the development of commercial arrangements for through traffic. Their properties would then have been in a better state to meet the competition of railways. The trustees of the Duke of Bridgewater's estate after 1802,[63] by their wise investment in dock improvements and their energetic pursuit of commercial agreements with river, canal and railway competitors, demonstrated what might have been done by other proprietors to ensure that, in the railway age, the canals continued to exploit their natural advantages as bulk carriers.

VII

More than 25,000 barges were being used on Britain's inland waterways in the middle decades of the nineteenth century. Living on board these boats was a floating population of no less than 50,000 persons, more than a third of whom were directly employed by the canal companies or the carriers. Of all the sizeable groups of wage earners in Victorian Britain this is almost certainly the one about which least was known by their contemporaries. It is not difficult to understand why this was the case, for the canal population was constantly on the move and, unlike the railway employees of later years, frequently had no land-based home. Overcrowding in the tiny cabins of the narrow boats seems to have been aggravated in the third quarter of the nineteenth century as railway competition for the carriage of goods increased. In the earlier years the typical arrangement was for the boatman to take one boy afloat with him to take turns with the steering, the leading of the horses, and the working of the lock paddles and gates. However, as railway competition intensified, the large firms which dominated canal carriage felt compelled to cut the boatmen's wages in order to stay in business. It then became impossible for the typical boatman to maintain a shore establishment and he was obliged to bring his entire family on board the boat.[64]

It was largely due to the efforts of George Smith of Coalville that Parliament was made aware of the need for legislation to make provision for the education of the canal boat children and the improvement of the sanitary conditions of the narrow boats. Through innumerable letters and articles in the Press and his two books *Our Canal Population* (1878) and *Canal Adventures by Moonlight* (1881), he made the facts known to the public and the legislature. But the problem was an exceedingly difficult one. Although the Canal boats Act of 1877 laid it down that each canal boat had to be registered with the nearest local sanitary authority, and although it permitted this authority to specify how many persons might inhabit its cabin, it made no provision for the appointment of inspectors. In consequence, as Smith made clear in his second book, the Act was largely ineffective and the overcrowding of the cabins and the illiteracy of their inmates continued largely unchanged. Even after the Canal Boats Act (Amendment) Act of 1884 had introduced stricter conditions of registration and had compelled the appointment of special inspectors, responsibility for the enforcement of the Act was assumed by the Local Government Board 'only with the greatest reluctance'.[65] It would be truer to say that the problem disappeared in the fullness of time rather than that it was solved by the intervention of Parliament. By 1938 there were only just over 600 children living in the narrow boats.[66] In so far as the canals fulfilled a decisive role in the transport revolution they did so at the expense of the canal boat people whose living conditions were more cramped and insanitary than those of the inhabitants of the back-to-back houses of the factory towns.

As essential to the working of traffic on canals which had tunnels without tow paths were a much smaller group of workers called leggers by the nature of their strenuous labour. The task of these men employed in the Huddersfield tunnel of the Huddersfield Narrow Cut canal was described by a contemporary:

> The operation of working the boats through is a singular one and performed by a description of labourers adventitiously hired for the purpose. As there is generally work to be had, a sufficient number continually present themselves, who having remained a few days or a week, or as long as it suits them, receive their payment, pursue their march and choose another occupation. These men from the nature of their service are called 'leggers' for they literally work the boat with their legs, or kick it from one end of the tunnel to another; two leggers in each boat lying on their sides back to back, derive a purchase from shoulder to shoulder and use their feet against opposite walls. It is a hard service, performed in total darkness, and not altogether void of danger, as the roof is composed of loose material, in some parts continually breaking in. Two hours is the time occupied in legging a boat through, and a legger earns a shilling for a light boat; after twelve tons he receives one shilling and six pence, and so on.[67]

But for all the arduousness of his labour the legger had one great advantage over the boatmen—he was not confined to one boat and he could, if he chose, set up his home in one of the cottages which stood by the entrance of the canal tunnel.

2
Road Transport before the Railway Age

When Tobias Smollett came south from Edinburgh in 1739 he found that there was 'no such convenience as a waggon' between the Scottish capital and Tyneside. Since he was too poor to hire a horse, he made an arrangement with a carrier to ride on one of his pack horses, sitting on a saddle between two baskets of goods.[1] No waggons were available in this part of the route to London because the roads were not in a fit condition to bear them and the farmers of the neighbourhood, who grew less wheat than did their contemporaries from the southern counties, consequently had less need to use them to carry heavy loads of grain. From time immemorial such ploughing and hauling as had to be done in the northern counties was performed by oxen as 'an ox's hoof splays slightly as it is thrust into the mud, and contracts as it is withdrawn, thus enabling the animal to keep going over soft ground in which a horse would soon be bogged'.[2] Whilst these conditions prevailed there was no urgent necessity to provide roads with a metalled surface in this part of the country.

It would be quite wrong to assume that roads elsewhere in the kingdom were necessarily much better. Sussex had a particularly bad reputation for poor communications. In 1750 the inhabitants of Horsham in Sussex petitioned Parliament for an improvement in the 'road' to London since it was suitable only for riding on horseback. Those wishing to drive a coach to the capital were obliged to go first to the channel coast before taking the only serviceable road via Canterbury.[3] In 1752 a correspondent, reporting to the *Gentleman's Magazine* after travelling from London to Falmouth by the main route through Exeter and Plymouth commented, 'You have such roads as the lazy Italians have fruits, namely what God left them after the flood.'[4]

Unless a journey was of vital importance the state of the weather was frequently a major factor in deciding for or against undertaking the risks it entailed. On 19 May 1746 Elizabeth Martin wrote from Lombard Street in the City of London to her cousin living in a Surrey village: 'The dry weather will make the roads so good that it encourages me to hope my Uncle and Aunt will give my dear cousins leave to make a visit this summer, which we have long had hopes of.'[5]

One reason why there were not higher standards of road-making in the eighteenth century was that the maintenance of most of the roads was still based on the provisions of the Highways Act of 1555, passed at a time when inter-regional commerce was on a small scale and the parish was still the effective unit of local administration. The Act provided that every person who held land to the value of £50 and every person 'keeping a draught of horses or plough in the parish' had to provide a waggon with oxen or horses to help with the movement of earth, whilst every other householder, labourer or cottager had to appear in person and work for four days each year unpaid (increased to six days from 1562) to keep the roads of the parish in repair.[6] The work was to be supervised by unpaid surveyors chosen annually from among the parishioners. Under an Act of 1670 those liable to this unpaid labour could make composition by paying 1s 6d for each day's labour due; 3s for the work of a man and a horse and 10s for the provision of a cart with two men. This concession brought little consolation to the labourer who was rarely in a position to pay for a substitute. Inevitably, therefore, most road work continued to be performed by conscripted labour. From 1776, if two-thirds of the ratepayers agreed, a parish could appoint a more permanent paid surveyor who was more likely to possess the necessary knowledge of road-building and of elementary accounts. But the outstanding defect of the Act of 1555—that the maintenance of the roads was to be left to local unpaid labour, often conscripted to the work during the busiest season of the farming year—remained as the principal barrier to improvement. Writing in his minute book on 12 June 1788, a Shrewsbury parish surveyor confided:

'I have found by ten years' service in the office of a surveyor that five hired labourers will do as much work as ten or twelve who come out upon the statute. They make a holiday of it, lounge about, and trifle away their time. As they are in no danger of being turned out of their work, they stand in no awe of the surveyor. It is a common saying amongst us that if a drop of sweat should happen to fall from any of them it would infalliably produce a quagmire. In short, statute work will never mend the roads effectually.'[7]

The system was unsatisfactory not merely because the labour employed was inefficient but also because the demand for road transport was changing. As the eighteenth century advanced and the inter-regional exchange of goods increased greatly in importance, road traffic became less and less local in character. So long as they remained the principal beneficiaries from their labours there was some sense in making parishioners maintain the roads. But once the roads took on the character of thoroughfares linking distant centres of population and industry it was unjust to expect farmers and labourers to work unrewarded mainly for the benefit of strangers. But once Parliament had committed itself to the policy of parish maintenance by the *corvèe* it was reluctant to change. It was not until Parliament itself had been reformed in 1832 and a new Highways Act had been passed three years later, that the system of compulsory unpaid labour on the roads was brought to an end. Thereafter it was the duty of parishes to levy a highway rate and to use the proceeds to pay both surveyor and labourers.

In the meantime governments in the eighteenth century sought to cover up the inadequacies of earlier legislation and to dodge the difficult question of road improvement by placing severe restrictions on the use of wheeled vehicles. Two leading historians of British roads were forced to the conclusion that the 'implicit assumption' of the vast mass of eighteenth-century road legislation was that 'the wheeled carriage was an intruder on the highway, a disturber of the existing order, a cause of damage—in short an active nuisance to the roadway —to be suppressed in its most noxious forms and where inevitable to be regulated and restricted as much as possible'.[8]

The surfaces of British 'dirt' roads being soft it was a principal objective of Parliament to prevent wheeled carriages from cutting up the roads and transforming them into quagmires. There were two approaches to a solution of this problem. Wheels must be made to act as rollers rather than as cutters of the road surface and the loads carried by waggons must be severely limited. An Act of 1753 forbade the use on the highway of waggons with wheel fellies (i.e. rims) less than nine inches wide, the penalty for the violation of the law being a fine of £5 or the forfeiture of one of the horses. A waggon builder who wrote to the *St. James' Chronicle* in January 1793 carried the purport of this legislation to its logical conclusion. He advocated the adoption of 16-inch fellies for carter's waggons since they would confer the inestimable benefit of 'rolling or smoothing a perfect flat surface thirty-two inches broad'.[9] There is no evidence that this plan was adopted since, given a passable road surface, the speed of a wheeled vehicle was in inverse ratio to the width of the fellies. Rather, farmers and carriers endeavoured to evade the law by altering the dish and angle of the wheels so that only a part of the felly was brought in contact with the road. Another form of evasion was by adding a narrow extra rim to the legal nine-inch one.

Ever since 1623 there had been laws limiting the number of horses that might be employed to pull a waggon, thus effectively limiting the size of the load. But in 1741 Parliament went further by forbidding loads in excess of three tons and giving turnpike trusts power to establish weighing machines and to fine waggoners £1 for each hundredweight by which their loads exceeded three tons.[10] Unfortunately, the weights recorded on these machines were as unpredictable as those revealed by weighing machines on seaside promenades in more recent times and were as frequently the cause of alarm and despondency. Mr Mann, a Hammersmith brewer, told a Parliamentary Select Committee in 1796 that

> 'Weighing machines are so uncertain in their operation that they are productive of the greatest vexation to persons employed in conveying the different necessaries of life and articles of merchandise, as it is a very common case that a load will pass at one engine when the same load at another will be subject to an increased toll.'[11]

Apart from the legislature, there were other interests which opposed the improvement in the nation's highways. Farmers, who know no other means of communication with the outside world than the dirt roads maintained by the parish, adjusted the marketing of their produce accordingly. Those who raised animals for sale had them driven to London and other markets 'on the hoof'. In the 1770s some 150,000 turkeys and 750,000 sheep were driven each year to Smithfield. The owners of these beasts were apprehensive that metalled roads would damage the animals' hooves and in 1710 Sussex farmers petitioned Parliament against the construction of stone-surfaced roads for this reason.[12]

II

In the course of the eighteenth century the interests in favour of the improvement of the roads grew along with the growth of commerce and manufactures. In the rapidly growing industrial districts of Lancashire and the West Riding manufacturers found that the payment of 10d a ton-mile[13] for the carriage of their raw materials and finished goods severely limited sales by reducing the area of the market. The way out of the road transport bottleneck was by the creation of turnpike trusts, many of which were established by merchants and manufacturers directly interested in improving the communications of their immediate neighbourhood. It was several 'Gentlemen, Merchants, Tradesmen and other inhabitants', users of the road from Liverpool to Prescot, who in 1725 took the initiative in establishing a turnpike trust to improve communications between the two towns.[14]

The first turnpike, which was built along a stretch of the Great North Road after 1663, was managed by the justices of the peace of the three counties of Hertfordshire, Huntingdonshire and Cambridge, through which it passed. But after 1706 it was normal for Parliament, by special Act, to give authority to an independent body of trustees to raise the necessary capital for road improvements, place bars or gates across the road and charge road users a toll within the limits prescribed in the Act. The money thus raised went to pay the surveyor, treasurer, clerks and labourers employed by the trust and to pay interest on the capital. At first the work of the paid labourers supplemented the unpaid labour of those who came 'out upon the statute', but many parishes found it more convenient to make composition to the turnpike trustees by paying a lump sum in lieu of services due. The number of trusts grew only slowly in the first half of the eighteenth century; but in the second half there was a rapid increase, over 1600 being formed before 1800. During the first thirty years of the nineteenth century no fewer than 2,450 turnpike Acts were passed by Parliament, some creating new trusts, some re-establishing old ones (powers were generally granted for twenty-one years only) and some consolidating smaller trusts into larger units. In the mid 1830s, at the beginning of the railway age, there existed 1,116 turnpike trusts in England and Wales managing some 22,000 miles of road between them, or averaging about nineteen and a half miles of road per trust. Since there survived at the same time 104,770 miles of parish highways the mileage of turnpikes was slightly more than one fifth of the total.[15] In the middle of the nineteenth century there were still many villages like the Raveloe of George Eliot's *Silas Marner*, 'nestled in a snug, well-wooded hollow, quite an hour's journey on horseback from any turnpike, where it was never reached by the vibrations of the coach horn, or of public opinion'.[16]

Even allowing for the payment of surveyors, treasurers, clerks and labourers and the occasional special dinners eaten by the trustees at the expense of the toll-payers, there can be no doubt that expenditure per mile on the turnpike roads greatly exceeded the outlay on the parish highways. In 1838 the expenditure of the trusts was £1¾ million or £51 per mile of road, whereas a mere £11 3s. was spent on each mile of the parish highways.[17]

It was due to the turnpike trusts that the road improvers had the opportunity they needed to test their theories. In the 1750s, the decade in which both Telford and McAdam were born, road-making in Britain was in a very sorry state. A critic of British roads in 1752 noted the methods of highway repair then being followed by the parish surveyors, and, clearly, did not have a very high opinion of them:

> They know not how to lay a foundation nor make the proper slopes and drains; they pour on a heap of loose huge stones into a swampy hole (as on the spungy hill near Honiton) which make the best of their way to the centre of the earth. In a word they try to fill up Curtius's gulph; and they might as well expect ... that a musket ball would stick on the surface of a custard.[18]

John Metcalfe (1717–1880), the blind carrier of Knaresborough, was the first of a great line of civil engineers to introduce improved methods of road-making. Between 1765 and 1797 he supervised the construction of some 180 miles of turnpike road in Lancashire and Yorkshire.

Of the best known road improvers Thomas Telford (1757–1834) was first to gain employment by turnpike trusts and recognition from the Government. As a former stonemason he emphasised the importance of a flat foundation or pavement of larger stones which, in the middle eighteen feet of the road were to be covered with closely packed stones roughly cubic in shape and small enough to pass through a two-and-a-half-inch ring. When these small stones had been compacted together by the weight of the traffic passing over them a final one-and-a-half-inch layer of clean gravel was added to the surface of the road. Although Telford's methods were criticised because of the unnecessary expense of the foundations and the disintegrating effect of frost and water on the gravel surface, his roads were an enormous improvement on their predecessors. Through his work as surveyor at Shrewsbury and surveyor of the London–Holyhead road after 1810 he made possible the acceleration of the Irish Mail and set an outstanding example to the parish and turnpike surveyors of more scientific methods of road-building.

John Loudon MacAdam (1756–1836), who ultimately came to have more influence on road engineering than did his eminent contemporary, considered that foundations were less important than an 'impervious and indestructible surface' combined with good drainage. He believed that the thickness of the road was immaterial provided these two essential conditions were fulfilled. His instructions were that the impervious surface was to be achieved by the compacting of small stones weighing under six ounces and capable of passing through a ring of two inches' diameter. Good drainage was to be achieved by raising the level of the road above the level of the ground on which it was built and by providing a camber of not more than three inches. He advised that if this procedure was followed the soil of the neighbourhood would serve perfectly well for foundations and unnecessary expense would be spared.

Early in 1816 MacAdam was appointed to the important post of surveyor for a large turnpike trust in the Bristol area. So rapidly did his method of road construction gain recognition that by February 1818 it had been adopted by 11 other trusts, managing over 700 miles of turnpike in 15 counties. Through the fact that his three sons all followed their father's profession the MacAdam family by 1823 supervised the road work of no less than 107 trusts with 2,000 miles of road.[19]

The great drawback of the turnpike system was that the trusts were local undertakings that improved roads within a strictly limited area. With the one important exception of the London–Holyhead road, on which some three-quarters of a million pounds of government money was spent in the 25 years after 1810, there was no master plan for the improvement of through routes such as the Corps de Ponts et Chausées followed for the main roads of France. Whether or not a road was rendered fully useable depended 'not on the needs of the users or on the national importance of this particular link but on the degree of enlightened self interest or public spirit of the squires, farmers and traders of the immediate neighbourhood'. The result was similar to the contemporary development of inland waterways—'a strange patchwork'[20] of improved and unimproved highways. The road engineers were fully aware of the disadvantages of the method of piecemeal improvements and the whole weight of their influence was lent in support of turnpike trust consolidation. In 1819 and 1820 MacAdam pointed out to the Select Committee on Turnpike Roads and Highways the advantages which would accrue from the amalgamation of the trusts and his views were partially adopted for the turnpikes of north London in 1826. In response to promptings from the municipal corporations of Hull, York and Newcastle, between 1823 and 1827 Telford prepared, for the Postmaster-General, a scheme for straightening important stretches of the Great North Road and consolidating the turnpike trusts on the route. But his plan was defeated by the marshalling of local vested interests against it, and the Great North Road Bill of 1830, which would have repeated for the London–Edinburgh route what had recently been achieved for the road to Holyhead, was given short shrift by the House of Commons.

Nevertheless, by the 1820s something more closely resembling a national network of roads was emerging in Britain. Despite their piecemeal development and their maladministration, the turnpike trusts had performed an invaluable service for the improvement of British transport. They made it possible for the roads to accommodate a greatly increased number of vehicles which could travel with relative safety at speeds two, or even three, times those of the pre-turnpike era. Even more importantly the roads now served national rather than predominantly local purposes.

III

One clear measure of the reality of the transport revolution during the turnpike era was the reduction of journey times between the principal centres of population (see map 4). Comparing the 1750s with the 1830s journey times on the main routes linking the principal cities were reduced by four-fifths; comparing the 1770s with the 1830s the times were halved. A newspaper advertisement for a London–Manchester coach in 1754 boasted 'However incredible it may appear this coach will actually arrive in London four days after leaving Manchester'.[21] Six years later Messrs Handforth, Howe, Glanville and

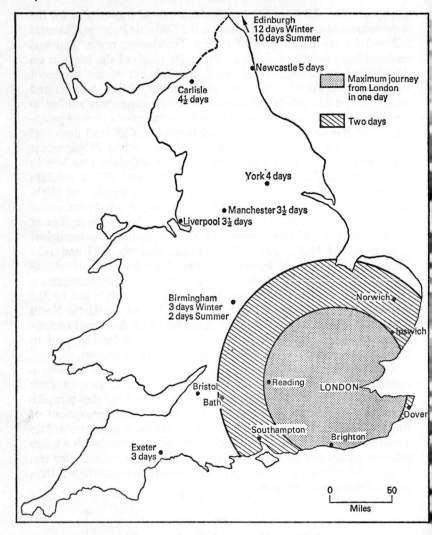

Map 4   Coach Journey Times 1750

Richardson's coach nevertheless completed the same journey in three days 'or thereabouts' and by 1784 competition between rival concerns had reduced the time taken to only half the 'incredible' four days of 1754. In the mid 1750s it took ten days to travel between London and Edinburgh in summer and 12 days in winter; by 1836 it only required 45½ hours.[22] In 1751 Tobias Smollett's Peregrine Pickle took two days to reach Oxford from London; in 1828 coaches, averaging a steady ten miles an hour, completed the journey in six hours. The 50-mile journey to Brighton would have taken Smollett's hero just as long as did the trip to Oxford but in February 1834 the *Criterion* coach, in a record-breaking dash to the coast, covered the ground in a mere three hours and forty minutes.[23] On the other side of the kingdom the journey from London to Carlisle which occupied three days in 1773 was completed in just over thirty-two hours in 1837.[24] These were some of the best performances. There were other routes where the increase in speed of travel had been much less impressive. A report on the performance of the Royal Mail coaches printed in 1836 showed that whereas an average speed of over ten and a half miles an hour was maintained by the Liverpool–Preston Mail, between Canterbury and Deal no more than six miles an hour could be managed.[25]

It was not only the speed but also the amount of travelling that increased dramatically in the age of the road transport revolution. The most impressive change was in the number of stage-coach services (Fig. 2 on page 44 illustrates their growth in a number of important cities). Taking ten of the leading urban centres of Great Britain—Birmingham, Bristol, Edinburgh, Exeter, Glasgow, Leeds, Liverpool, Manchester, Newcastle and Sheffield, the number of stage-coach services increased eightfold between 1790 and 1836.[26] The increase in travel was even greater than these figures would suggest, as in 1836 the typical coach was carrying nearly double as many passengers as was common in the 1790s, due to the more ample accommodation being provided for the 'outsides'. It would not be wide of the mark to claim that 15 times as many people were travelling by stage coach in the mid 1830s as were doing so 40 years earlier. In 1835 700 mail coaches and 3,300 stage coaches were in regular service in Great Britain.[27] Assuming an average of eight passengers per trip (though many coaches could carry up to 16 persons) and 2,500 trips per week, the number of individual coach journeys made in the course of that year must have been over 10 million. This compares with 30 million journeys a year by rail in 1845 and $336\frac{1}{2}$ million journeys by the same means in 1870.[28]

Some indication of the rate of growth of stage-coaching may be obtained from annual returns of stage-coach duty collected by the Inland Revenue. Between 1789–96 revenue from this source increased by only six per cent. Under a new basis of assessment, introduced in 1797, it rose by 17 per cent between 1798 and 1803. After another revision of the method of assessment in 1804, the revenue rose by an impressive 27 per cent between 1805 and 1814. The first years of peace after 1815 were times of trade depression in which stage-coach travel showed no marked signs of increase. Between 1823 and 1832, however, when the rate of tax remained unchanged there was a further 18 per cent rise in the revenue. Receipts reached an all time maximum

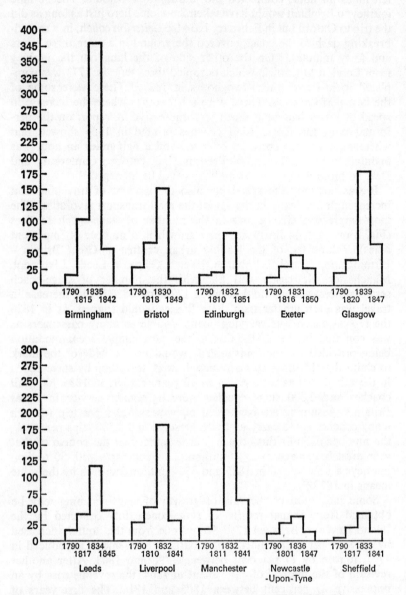

Figure 2   Development of Stage-Coach Travel 1790–1850: Number of
daily departures of Royal Mail and stage coaches

in 1836 but by the mid 1840s had fallen to less than half the levels of a decade earlier.[29]

The amount of road passenger transport in the years immediately preceding the coming of the railways was impressive. In 1836 some 26,000 persons travelled by coach between Bath and Exeter.[30] Eight years later 52,000 persons a year were using coach services which linked towns and villages in an area bounded by Torquay, Exeter and Falmouth.[31] In 1845 the coaches which ran between Edinburgh, Dundee and Aberdeen carried over 18,000 people despite the fact that 30,000 others preferred to use the coastwise steamers to reach the same places. At the same time more than 22,000 persons travelled by coach between Edinburgh and Perth.[32]

There were of course some parts of the country where innovation came much more slowly. The first advertisement for a stage-coach service in Cornwall did not appear until 1799 and it was not until 1820 that this single service between Exeter and Falmouth was extended to Penzance.[33] Up to as late as 1827 most of the roads in Wales were in such a poor state that the Post Office had found it impossible to insist on speeds faster than 5 m.p.h. from the post riders of the area.[34]

Increasingly after 1784 the Post Office was a powerful influence on the side of speedier and more reliable road transport. Until that date the Royal Mail was falling behind the stage coaches in respect both of dependability and speed, due to the fact that Ralph Allen, who had enjoyed a monopoly of the cross posts between 1720 and 1762, had arranged for the letters to be carried on horseback or by chaise by postboys who were not renowned either for their speed or their sobriety. John Palmer, a theatre manager of Bath, was one of many who experienced frustrations under the system established by Allen. In 1783 he complained to the Postmaster-General about the service between Bath and London. 'The coach diligence' he wrote, 'which left Bath at 4 o'clock on Monday evening would deliver a letter about 10 on Tuesday morning, whilst the post would not deliver a letter until Wednesday morning.' In the early 1770s, citizens of Bath (and elsewhere in the kingdom) who wanted to ensure speediest possible delivery sent letters by first class rather than second class mail. In the early 1790s they sent letters (illegally) by coach for 2s instead of legally (but slowly) by the Royal Mail for 4d.[35]

John Palmer claimed that by hiring coaches for short stages on the Bristol–London road he could bring the mail to the capital in 17 instead of the 18 hours then taken by the stage coaches. On 2 August 1784 he began the carriage of mail by stage coach from Bristol to London via Bath and kept his promise of outpacing the established coaches on the route. William Pitt the younger, the Prime Minister, fully appreciating the great advantages of the new plan,

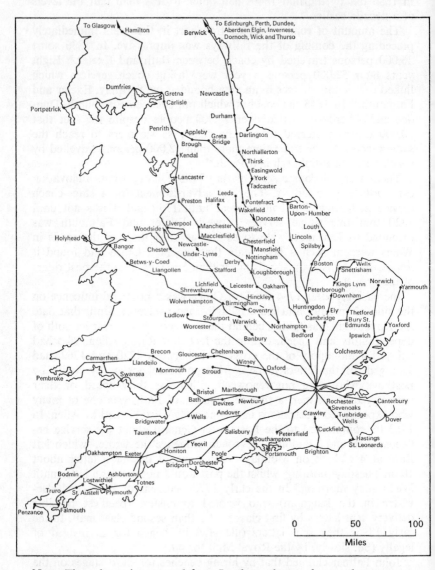

Note: Through services to and from London only are shown—the numerous cross-country and local Royal Mail routes between provincial towns are omitted.

Source: Route diagram in Bates, *Directory of Stage Coach Services*, 1836.

Map 5   Royal Mail Coach Services to and from London in 1836

soon authorised its extension to all the main post roads, and when the last main route, the Great North Road to Scotland, was given its mail-coach service in 1786 delivery times between London and Edinburgh were reduced from 85 hours to 60. Thereafter it was generally the Royal Mail coach on each route which maintained the best performance for speed and dependability.

This enviable reputation was achieved because of the high standards of construction and maintenance of the Royal Mail coaches. In 1787 the contract for the construction of coaches according to a patent of John Bezant (1786) was awarded to John Vidler of Millbank, proprietor of the largest coachworks in London.[36] By 1792, when the capital of the concern had grown to £30,000, 150 of these uniformly constructed coaches had been brought into service.[37] It was the policy of the Post Office that Vidler should hire out the coaches on the basis of $1\frac{1}{4}d$ per mile run rather than that he should sell them outright to the mail-coach contractors. It was believed that this was the only way of ensuring the highest standards of maintenance. Undoubtedly this part of the organisation was meticulously carried out:

> Every coach which set out from, and returned to, London, was immediately drawn by one horse from its terminal stables to the works at Mill bank, cleaned, greased, overhauled and sent back in time to go down to the country again. The servicing of the many coaches which did not end their journeys in London was also attended to under special arrangements.[38]

From 1792, when Thomas Hasker began his long tenure of office as Surveyor and Superintendent of the Mail Coaches, the influence of the Post Office on the dependability and speed of communication was felt from John O'Groats to Lands End. The instructions of Hasker to the mail guards were particularly stringent in the wake of poor harvests and consequent scarcity prices of grain. In a printed directive *To the Mail Guards* issued on 6 February 1800 he warned each guard that

> every minute should be used on the road and no one wasted at Calling Houses. I have ... to direct you at the peril of your situation and with the assurance that you should forfeit it if found out, that you do not quit your coach to go into any Public House, or stop at any place on the road. but where you have letters to leave or real coach business to perform, as from the dearness of corn and weakness of horses no time must be wasted; see to this, and if coachmen will stop, write me of their misconduct.[39]

By the end of the eighteenth century the construction and performance of stage coaches was the subject of much public controversy. The coaches Vidler built according to the Bezant patent were heavy and cumbersome vehicles with the main body placed high above the road in the mistaken belief that this eased the task of the horses. Because the carriage body was suspended by leather straps from heavy 'perches' linked to the front and rear axles, the four inside passengers were subjected at times to a severe pendulum-like jolting. In the 1790s to be 'coached' meant getting used to the nausea, akin to sea-sickness, which travelling in these vehicles induced.[40] At this time the Post Office contracts did not allow more than one outside passenger, but in a memorandum to the Postmaster-General written on 21 January 1804, Hasker wrote that another of the drawbacks of the Bezant patent coaches was that 'the outside passenger by riding on the present box without springs is so shook that the proprietors seldom obtain one except for a short distance'.[41] On the advice of Hasker, as early as 1792 the Postmaster-General employed Mr A. Walker, a man well qualified in mechanics, to examine a large variety of coaches and report on their suitability for the carriage of the mail. Walker found the Bezant coaches were perched too high up for maximum safety and efficiency and he was convinced that 'a vehicle with all the conveniences of the mail coach might be constructed that would not be above two-thirds of its weight, nor above two-thirds of the expense in materials and workmanship'. Changing long established tradition, however, was a formidable task, and he questioned who would have 'temerity enough to break in upon that phalanx of coach-makers, so formidable a body in this metropolis'. A few weeks later he wrote that 'neither the perch or Crane-neck are necessary in the mechanical construction of a four-wheel carriage'.[42]

In the early years of the nineteenth century two circumstances combined to induce the Post Office to make a radical change in the design of mail coaches. The first of these influences was the loss of revenue from passengers. The competition of the stage coaches with the Royal Mail was becoming keener, especially for journeys up to town from the provinces. Mail coaches left the provincial cities in the evening and, travelling through the night, brought their passengers and the post to the capital some hours before shops and restaurants were opened. The 'down' mail coaches which left the GPO at 8 p.m. kept their passengers more successfully since it was often found convenient to start a journey after the day's business in town had been completed. Coming to town, however, passengers seemed to prefer that travelling by day which not many of the Royal Mail coaches could offer. Since it was also the case that an inside seat in the 'Mail' cost more than it did in the stage coach there was an additional excuse for the passengers' desertion and a powerful incentive for the Post Office to search for an additional source of revenue from the mail coaches.

Obadiah Elliot's invention of the elliptical spring in 1804 (patented on 11 May 1805) was the second influence for change. The advantage of this device was that it enabled a carriage to be hung on springs without a perch and thus to be built less expensively—as Mr Walker had earlier asserted—but with the certainty of greater comfort for the passengers.[43] Thomas Hasker was quick to appreciate the potentialities of the new invention. In his memorandum to the Postmaster-General written on 21 January 1804 he urged that 'the mail coaches should be built on the new invented plan of the body, the coachman's boot and the boot behind the coach all to be joined together and play upon and lie on the horizontal springs'. Hasker's advice that 'Mr Vidler should as expeditiously as possible get the mail coaches built on the new horizontal spring construction, box, boot and body connected and the weight in no case to exceed 17 hundredweight' was followed by his superiors and it was not long before the new-style coaches were doing service on the roads.[44]

Elliot's elliptical spring and the redesigning of road vehicles which it made possible was as important in the history of stage-coaching as the introduction of the multi-tubular boiler in 1829 was in the history of the steam locomotive. Because the new coaches had a lower centre of gravity they could be drawn safely at faster speeds than their more top-heavy predecessors. Both because it was now much easier to climb to the top of the coach and because jolting was greatly reduced, more outside passengers could be accommodated. A law of 1806 gave recognition to these improvements by permitting ten 'outside' passengers in winter and 12 in summer in place of the previous all-the-year-round maximum of four.[45] Although on the Royal Mail the number of 'outsides' was limited to three—one seated beside the driver and two others with their backs to the driver and facing the guard—many other coaches took the opportunity of accommodating up to 12 on top. To say that Elliot's invention had resulted in a doubling of the number of passengers a coach could carry would be to make a conservative estimate.

One other significant consequence of the improvement of coach design and the achievement of faster time schedules was that by about 1820 it was quicker to travel by fast coach than on horseback. From this date the individual rider was much less frequently seen on the roads. If John Wesley had been making the world his parish in the 1820s instead of the 1770s he would have travelled by coach instead of on horseback.

It was the combined effects of better road engineering and the improvements in design of the stage coach which made possible the remarkable growth of passenger travel in the early nineteenth century.

IV

There was scope for the big business man in early nineteenth-century coaching. At a time when the majority of British industries were organised on a small scale the extent to which large firms had gained a foothold in the stage-coaching business was quite remarkable. Although there were said to be 1,476 coaches leaving London daily (exclusive of the short stage services within the greater metropolitan area) in the later 1830s, John Bates in his *Directory of Stage Coach Services* lists 342 as being the more important and permanent of the services provided in 1836. Of these no less than 275 were provided by the three largest proprietors, W. J. Chaplin (106), B. W. Horne (92) and E. Sherman (77). Although the dominance of the big firm was generally nothing like so complete in the provincial cities, in Bristol three men, R. Coupland, J. Weeks and C. Bessell, managed 21 of the 64 long-distance coach services starting from the city in 1815. In Birmingham R. M. Fletcher, Marshall and Co. and Waddell and Co., in Derby W. Hodgson and in Leeds Brothertons were all large firms enjoying a substantial share of the coaching business of their area.

Of the great coaching magnates of London William James Chaplin (1787–1859) had the most extensive establishment. His headquarters were at the 'Swan with two Necks' in Lad Lane where he had stabling for 200 horses. He also owned the 'Spread Eagle' and the 'Cross Keys' in Gracechurch Street, the 'White Horse' in Fetter Lane and the 'Spread Eagle' in Regents Circus where he had his West End office. He owned huge stables at Purley on the Brighton Road, Hounslow on the Great West Road and Whetstone on the Great North Road. In 1838 his coaching business, inns and hotels employed over 2,000 persons and 1,800 horses.[46] Benjamin Worthy Horne (1824–70) who operated from the 'Golden Cross', Charing Cross, also owned the 'Cross Keys' in Wood Street and three coaching inns in Holborn. In 1838 he joined forces with Chaplin in order to negotiate more success-ful terms with the London and Birmingham Railway. Edward Sher-man (1776–1866), who succeeded J. Williams as proprietor of the 'Bull and Mouth' at St Martin's le Grand in 1823, required 700 horses to run the 77 mail and stage-coach services he operated.

On the longer mail routes it was the custom for the contractors to provide the horses only for the 'high' or 'upper' ground of the route, viz. that part of it which was nearest to the proprietor's home base. For the 'middle ground' and 'lower ground' furthest away from the starting point the work was placed out to sub-contractors who paid up to 3*d* a mile for the privilege of carrying the coach further towards its destination. Thus Chaplin provided horses for only 350 miles of the 106 routes for which he was the main contractor.

Most frequently the principal source of capital for a stage-coach business was the revenue of an inn. Chaplin's father was an innkeeper and coach proprietor of a small establishment on the Dover road.[47] Horne's father was said to be the proprietor of several inns[48] and Robert Nelson's business was based on one of the best known inns of London, the 'Belle Sauvage' of Ludgate Hill. The sources of Edward Sherman's capital may well have been different from the general pattern. It is said that he came to London from Wantage in Berkshire with only half a crown in his pocket and that he worked as a boy porter in Oxford Market until he found employment on the Stock Exchange. There he struck up a friendship with Mr Levy, a wealthy farmer of turnpike tolls, who advanced him part of the purchase price of the 'Bull and Mouth' from which he entered the coaching trade.[49] Mrs Sarah Ann Mountain, proprietess of the 'Saracens Head', Snow Hill, London, whose coaches provided services on twenty-one routes, combined the management of a large hostelry with the business of coach maker. She built coaches for sale at around £120 or let them out to coach contractors at $3\frac{1}{2}d$ a mile.[50]

Running stage coaches could be a very risky business since coaches were frequently of defective manufacture and both roads and weather could be treacherous. Accidents brought losses through the need to compensate passengers and pay for the repair of the vehicles. The successful operator needed to have a detailed knowledge of the market value as well as the physical capabilities and weaknesses of horses; the condition of the roads; the toll charges on each route and the laws concerning the licensing of coaches and coachmen. He needed, above all, to be a firm but just manager of men.

The book-keeping side of a stage-coach business may be illustrated with reference to the London–Edinburgh route. In the 1830s the 400 miles between the two capitals was divided into 25 or more stages. If the coach was licensed to carry fifteen passengers it paid a passenger duty of £4 19s 3d per trip. The hire of the coach at $2\frac{1}{2}d$ a mile would come to £4, horses hired at 3d a mile to £4 19s 3d and turnpike tolls cost £6 12s. To this had to be added the wages of coachmen, guards and ostlers, the costs of maintenance, including oil for the lamps and grease for the axles, advertising charges and office expenses, including the wages of booking clerks, which together amounted to a further £12 per journey. The total expense to the proprietor was therefore £32. If fares were at the rate of 4d a mile inside and 2d a mile outside and all fifteen seats were hired for the entire journey the revenue would amount to £65 10s, or more than twice the expenditure. But many passengers only travelled a part of the way and where seats vacated were temporarily filled by short distance passengers it was not customary for fares of these casual customers to be entered in the waybill. By a tradition known as 'shouldering' the small change collected from such passengers was shared between coachmen and guards to augment their meagre wages. Average stage-coach takings on this long route therefore amounted to about £50 a trip. The profit of £15 10s had to be shared between a number of contractors and sub contractors who were responsible for maintaining the service on different stretches of the road.[51]

One source of uncertainty in the accounts was the income from fares. Quite apart from the adverse effect of inclement weather on the number of bookings, the charges made for both inside and outside seats fluctuated according to the intensity of competition from other coaches on the same route. Competition was at its fiercest on the road just before the even more formidable challenge of the railways appeared in many areas in the later 1830s. In 1834 fares between London and Birmingham fell to less than half their former level, the charge being reduced to £1 inside and 10s outside. Fares to Brighton were subject to more frequent changes than on any other main routes. The charge for an inside seat ranged from 25s to 10s. For a brief spell in 1837 the bargain-hunting traveller could ride down to Brighton for as little as 5s with the promise of a free lunch, with wine, at the end of the journey.[52] This intensity of competition was one of the reasons for the predominance of the large firms in the south-east, as they had greater resources with which to survive sudden reductions in income than did their smaller rivals. Nevertheless even the big firms felt the pinch of steam packet competition on the east coast in the 1820s and railroad competition more generally in the following two decades.

To coachmen and guards the greatest threat seemed to come from a quite different quarter—the professional informer. The laws concerning passenger duty, maximum seating capacity of coaches and the duties of Royal Mail guards—to mention only three areas of a happy hunting ground—were so complicated that they were often violated inadvertently as well as deliberately. Every extra short-stage customer meant more money in the pocket of coachman and guard as did every brace of pheasants illicitly carried in the mail guard's box at Christmas. But at the same time each violation of the law provided a further opportunity of profit to the diligent informer. In one big swoop in the Bath area in November 1825, the most notorious of the informers, Byers, reported thirty-four violations of the law which carried total liabilities to the offenders of £500 in fines. Byers' reward would have been up to half of this amount.[53]

The chief economic advantage of the improvement and extension of stage coach services was the speedier conduct of business. Before 1785, when the Royal Mail coaches first penetrated the Midlands, a London businessman who sent an order to a Birmingham firm by the post on Monday could not expect written acknowledgement that week. After 1785 a reply could be expected in two days. A new note of exactitude appeared in business transactions. This, no doubt, reflected the changing terminology of stage-coach advertisements in the press. In the earlier days coaches had 'set out' 'God willing', and had recklessly promised to reach their destinations in 'about two days' or 'on the same day' 'if the roads are good'. But in the heyday of coaching in the 1820s and 1830s they 'started' rather than 'set out' and arrived, as one irreverent wit remarked, 'God willing or not'. The records at St Martins le Grand show how concerned the Post Office was to put things right when God had shown his displeasure. In a book showing disbursements made in 1789 there is included under the date 9 February a brief note which reveals a man's dedication to duty in the face of great odds.

> To J. Steed for his journey to Glasgow directly after the snow in January to get the coach through in time, twelve days on the road going and returning and in consequence of the journey was so fatigued as not to be able to attend business for a considerable time (8 days on the whole), 20 days at 7s 6d per day, £7 10s.[54]

The new preoccupation with speed was reflected in the Post Office regulations for the changing of horses at the end of a stage. A footnote on a 'London and Brighthelmstone' (Brighton) mail-coach time-bill of 1812 reads 'Five minutes for changing four horses is as much as is necessary.'[55] Thomas de Quincey used a similarly brief space of time to make love to his 'Fanny of the Bath Road'—'the loveliest young woman for face and person that perhaps in my whole life I have beheld'—but confessed that because the Bath Mail 'timed all court-ship by the Post Office allowance', instead of being 'over head and ears in love' he ended up 'only over ears in love,—which still left a trifle of brain to overlook the whole conduct of the affair'. He also noted that anyone stopping at the same stage ten years later would have had but 80 seconds Post Office allowance instead of the 400 he had been granted in the year of Waterloo.[56]

The concern for promptitude and speed brought greater commercial benefits on the less spectacular stage-coach routes in the rapidly expanding industrial areas of Lancashire and the West Riding of Yorkshire. In the 1830s the industrial town of Leeds was served by a greater number of coaches than the city of York on the Great North Road.[57]

In an age when the taxes on knowledge put a severe limit on the printing and circulating of newspapers it was the guard of the Royal Mail who conveyed the news which in former days would have been brought at a far more leisurely pace by pedlars, packmen and wag-goners. In innumerable villages what the guard had said 'was repeated in the squire's drawing room, the vicarage parlour and the village inn'.[58] Long after the railway had reached the principal towns and cities of the kingdom, in the more remote parts of the country it was the coach which brought the latest news from the metropolis. As late as the time of the American Civil War (1861–5) many people of Launceston gathered round the White Hart Inn to await the arrival of the *Emerald* coach from Tavistock with the latest daily newspapers from Plymouth.[59] Mr Hardcastle lamented that although in his youth the 'follies of the town' crept slowly to the country, in his later manhood they travelled 'faster than a stage coach'.[60] The great increase in travel in the stage-coach era began the process of standardisation of manners, fashions and speech which was carried further forward by the railroad and the radio.

Despite the marked improvement in the speed and comfort of travel a journey by stage coach could still be a hazardous adventure. In inclement weather even the mail coach might fail to reach its destination. One day in the winter of 1814 thirty-three mail coaches due at the GPO failed to arrive.[61] When the Chartist leader, Julian Harney, made the long journey from London to Newcastle on the outside of a coach in December 1838 he was suffering so much from exposure at the end of the journey that his friends were obliged to put him to bed, although it was daytime and there was urgent business to transact.[62] When the Bath mail reached Cheltenham on the morning of Tuesday, 3 March 1812 the guard discovered to his horror that the intense cold had killed two of the outside passengers. A third died shortly afterwards.[63]

Although more persons used the stage coach than any other form of land transport it was often avoided both by the rich and the poor. the former generally preferred to 'travel post', using their own carriages and hiring horses at posting houses along the route. This was at least twice as expensive a way of travelling as by stage coach since the cost of hiring a pair of horses ranged from 1s to 1s 6d per mile in the early years of the nineteenth century.[64] Those travelling post were more frequently fleeced by post boys, innkeepers and ostlers than were those who went by coach. Sheridan's Lory arrived at Scarborough 'not worth a guinea' through having used up, not only his cash, but also some of his effects, en route.[65] Despite the expense of this mode of travel, government revenue from post horse duty and licences rose from an average of £140,000 a year in the 1790s to a peak of £241,500 annually in the 1820s.[66] It was evident that the improvement in the road surfaces required for the efficient running of the Royal Mail and the stage coaches also provided the opportunity for the well to do to travel more frequently in their own carriages and in hired gigs. On the road between Bristol and Exeter in the year 1835 nearly as many persons travelled post or by hired gig (83,200) as travelled by stage coach (87,000). A decade later the pattern of travel was much the same between Edinburgh and Dundee and in Surrey. Only in the more sparsely populated area of South Devon was the amount of posting down to as low as a quarter of the total of road passenger travel.[67] The Hon. John Byng found that one consequence of the growth of both posting and stage-coaching was that the innkeepers so concentrated on serving the customers these two types of transport provided that they had no time for that 'troublesome unprofitable intruder'— the tourist who simply wanted 'supper and a bed'.[68]

Thomas Rowlandson's painting of the *Kendal Flying Waggon* (1816) shown halted at a wayside inn is setting down and taking up passengers as well as goods. For the poor, travel with a stage waggon moving at no more than three miles an hour was often the only alternative to walking, for the fare by waggon might be as low as $\frac{1}{2}d$ a mile whereas the outside seat on a coach would cost at least four times as much. In the case of the carriers Russell and Co. of Falmouth it was understood that traveller's luggage would be carried and that sleeping space would be provided within the vehicle at night, but that when the party was on the move passengers would be expected to walk alongside the waggon except in inclement weather.[69] The man who was not prepared to walk or who needed to reach his destination more speedily could travel in a fly van where the charge was up to two pence a mile but the incidental expenses characteristic of stage-coach travel (e.g. tips to guards and coachmen) were largely absent. On the long and tedious journeys by waggon it was usual for the passengers to elect one of their number as chairman to negotiate stopping places with the waggoner and bargain with innkeepers over the charges for meals and beds when these were needed. It was a practice not uncommon amongst early travellers by stage coach.[70]

Another class of vehicle used by the poor was the caravan or long coach. Examples of these conveyances were to be seen on the Salisbury–London road from about 1750 onwards. Drawn by six horses and primarily designed for the carriage of goods, they were fitted with bench seats to accommodate a dozen persons. Their owners claimed a faster rate of travel than that of the common goods waggons.[71]

In the more remote country areas transport for the poor took on a bewildering variety. Thus the Welsh market cart was a primitive, unsprung, two-wheeled vehicle without any covering for the passengers.

V

The expansion of goods carriage on the roads after 1750 was not so spectacular as the growth of passenger traffic. Transport of goods by road was already well developed in the vicinity of the principal cities and towns before the coming of the industrial revolution. Thus when the volume of goods exchanged increased greatly in the second half

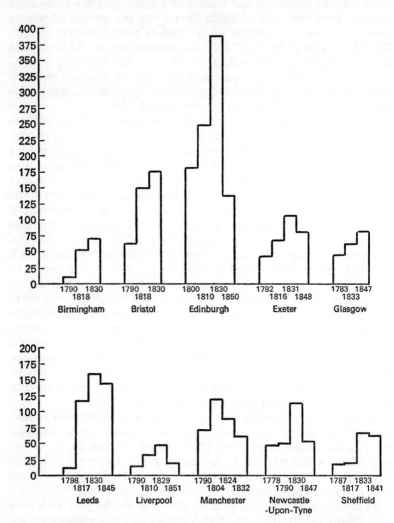

Sources: Bailey's Northern and *Southern Directories* from 1781; *Bailey's London, West and Midland Directories* from 1783; *Universal British Directory* from 1791 (reprint of 1790 edition); *Pigot's Directories* from 1814; *Holden's Annual Directory* from 1814; *Robinson's London and General Directories* from 1839; *Post Office Directories* from 1842; *Slater's General Directory* from 1848 and local directories for specific cities (or counties) and years.

Figure 3   Road Goods Haulage 1790–1850: Number of carriers in business

of the eighteenth century there was not so dramatic a change in the number of waggons and vans plying on the roads as there was in the number of stage coaches. In addition, the construction of a canal network took place simultaneously with the improvement of the roads and these newly available inland waterways took a larger share of the increased goods traffic than did the roads.

The example of London may be cited as an illustration of the magnitude of road goods haulage in the pre-industrial era. In 1680 Thomas Delaune found that there were 322 distinct carrier services operating from the inns of the metropolis and that goods were regularly being carted to places as far distant as Bristol, Exeter, Preston and York. No less than 16 carriers operated from the 'Belle Sauvage' on Ludgate Hill and as many plied from the 'Blossoms Inn', St Lawrence Lane. 'The Bear and Rugged Staff' at Smithfield and the 'Bull' at Bishopsgate were almost as popular; between them they constituted the headquarters of 23 more concerns.[72] But during the century following Delaune's survey the expansion of London's transport services proceeded at a leisurely pace, for as late as 1790 the number of carriers had only increased to 353.[73]

Nevertheless there was a great increase in the carriage of goods by road in the 40 years before the opening of the Liverpool and Manchester railway in 1830 even though the waggoners had to share the increase in business with coastal vessels and the rapidly multiplying number of canal barges. In 1823 London had more than twice as many carriers—735—as it had had in 1790.[74] Exeter had more than three times as many firms in 1831 as had been functioning in 1792.[75] Sheffield had 18 in 1787 and 68 in 1833.[76] The most spectacular growth was in the Birmingham area where the increase was more than fivefold in the 40 years from 1790–1830. In the case of the same ten cities whose stage-coach services have already been examined the number of carriers listed in local directories rose from just under 500 in 1790 to 1150 in 1830[77] (see fig. 3). Thus during the same period of time in which stage-coach services increased by some 800 per cent the number of carriers grew by only 131 per cent. It is worth remembering that in the shorter period 1801–1831 the population of the ten cities grew by 120 per cent. It is therefore the case that the number of carriers operating from the inns of the main cities barely kept in step with the growth in population. What put strict limits to the increase of land carriage in these years was the expansion of canal traffic and of coastal shipping. This is illustrated in the case of Liverpool and Glasgow (see fig. 3) where the number of carriers remained small despite the phenomenal growth in population. In the case of Glasgow the remarkable and early development of steamboat traffic on the Clyde and in Liverpool, the use of steam packets to carry goods (as well as passengers) on the Mersey and up the west coast

to the Cumberland ports, Annan and Glasgow reduced the opportunities for increased business for land carriers.

Since few carriers' accounts survive and in any case the measurement of weights was bewilderingly varied it is impossible to estimate
the total volume of goods carried on the roads in early nineteenth-
century Britain. What we do know is that the land carriage of goods
assumed greatest importance where topographical conditions made
the construction of canals expensive or virtually impossible and where
carriage by sea was circuitous and unduly risky. The south-west of
England was such a region. A traffic assessor made the (probably
generous) estimate that some 71,000 tons of goods a year were being
carried on the roads in the region between Bristol and Exeter in the
mid 1830s, and that, by comparison, only 10,000 tons were carried by
canal and 12,000 tons by sea.[78] A decade later along the route between
Carlisle and Edinburgh an estimated 39,100 tons of general merchandise (as distinct from coal, iron ore and lime) went by road compared
with 25,300 tons by canal and coastal steamer.[79] But between Edinburgh and the north-east coast ports of Scotland the land traffic was
only a quarter of the sea traffic—3,000 tons compared with 12,008
tons—because the sea route was faster and more direct.[80]

Unlike the business of stage-coaching, road goods haulage was
dominated by the small family business. This was more particularly
the case with the country villages rather than the larger towns where,
in some cases, big firms had obtained a foothold by the beginning of
the railway age. The organisation of the carrying trade in the Leeds
area provides a fairly typical illustration of the division of labour
between the smaller and larger firms. In 1822 163 firms were listed in
the directory of the town. Of this number 131 were small family
businesses trading between the centre of Leeds and the outlying towns
and villages. In the main part of the town there were 32 other concerns
operating on a larger scale and including Pickersgills; Scott, Carver
and Royston; Pickfords; Jackson & Co; Hobson Brothers and other
firms well known throughout the country for their predominance in
the long distance carrying trade to other large towns and cities.

On the other hand the carrying trade in and around Hull was completely dominated by small family businesses. In 1806 there were 74
of them listed as serving 73 towns throughout a wide area. That women
as well as men managed haulage businesses was shown by the inclusion in the list of Widow Bugg who carried goods between Hull
and Leven. By 1838 the number of carriers in the area had increased
to 125, visiting 105 different towns and villages; but the family unit of
management remained characteristic. The failure (or turnover) rate
was remarkably high. Only 24 of the firms functioning in 1838 had
been doing business under the same name 12 years earlier.[81] Much the
same pattern of quickly disappearing small firms was to be seen in

places as far apart as Bristol, Sheffield, Edinburgh and Glasgow. In Manchester, by contrast, where firms in manufacturing industry were well above the national average in size, the carrying trade began to be concentrated in fewer hands at an earlier date. Unlike the experience of other cities the number of firms decreased in the early years of the nineteenth century. From 106 in 1804 it fell to 87 in 1821 and 63 in 1832, when no less than 23 of the firms were styled as companies. Judging from the large number of places they served these must have been substantial concerns.[82]

If there were, perforce, limits to the quantity of goods the country carrier could bring from town there were certainly no limit to the variety of his consignments. In the 1730s and 1740s the Buckingham carrier William Eagles brought down from London canary wine, port, sack, leather, linseed oil, white lead, brushes, meat and mustard seed for the use of members of the Purefoy family at Shalstone. Mrs Purefoy from time to time instructed the carrier to settle her accounts with London tradesmen and she even used the carrier as intermediary when ordering a new set of false teeth from Mr William Corindon, 'Operator for ye teeth near the New Church in the Strand, London', in October 1737. Corindon sent down a wooden pattern which Mrs Purefoy returned with advice that the dental surgeon should 'take a bit off the two hind teeth' as marked on the pattern.

One reason why carriers failed to capture the business which went by coastal vessels or by canal barges (though many firms, including Pickfords, carried on both roads and canals) was that their charges were uncompetitive. Between 1692 and 1827 justices of the peace in Quarter Sessions had the power to fix road haulage charges within the county in which they served. In theory, therefore, there were as many different scales of charges as there were counties, but in practice freights were determined by the presence or absence of competition from rival carriers or the proximity to or distance from alternative water transport. Charges rarely fell below 10d a ton-mile although there were great variations as between different types of goods. For haulage to London in 1758 Yarmouth carriers charged 8s a ton for general groceries, 12s a ton for weighable linens and 1s a cwt for bales and butts of leather.[83] Such high charges were inevitable because of the slow pace of the cumbersome, canvas-covered, waggons drawn by four, six, or even eight, horses which did the bulk of the land haulage of goods except in areas where the packhorse was still widely used because of the poor state of the roads. In the second half of the eighteenth century it took four-and-a-half days for Manchester carriers to bring their waggons to London. Feeding and stabling as many as eight horses might account for as much as a fifth of the carrying firm's outlay and the proportion would be higher in years of poor harvest, such as 1800 and 1812, when the price of oats soared. Road tolls might account for another two-fifths of total expense and wag-goners wages at least a quarter more.[84] After 1815 the firm of Pick-fords began to exploit the opportunities for faster and safer road transport made possible by the better springing of vehicles. Their new 'caravan on springs and guarded' reduced the journey time from Man-chester to London to 35 hours.[85] Their example was gradually followed by other firms which introduced 'flying waggons' in greater numbers in the years after Waterloo. All the same, road haulage remained so expensive that a majority of the goods were despatched by water carriage until, by the early 1850s, the combination of an adequate basic railway network with a rational classification of goods by the Railway Clearing House, gave an increasing advantage to land carriage.

3
Coastal Shipping

On account of the remarkable length of coastline in relation to the land area the British Isles are particularly favourably placed for the development of coastal shipping. The eleventh edition of Baldwin's *London Directory*, published in 1768, names 580 places in England and Wales to which goods could be sent by water. Although it was necessary to use canal as well as sea to reach some of the places mentioned, the overwhelming majority were small seaports whose prosperity largely depended on the continuance of the coasting trade. The great economy of coastal shipping over land transport for the carriage of many types of goods was fully understood by Adam Smith, who wrote that 'it required only six or eight men to bring by water to London the same quantity of goods which would otherwise require fifty broad wheeled waggons, attended by a hundred men, and drawn by four hundred horses'.[1]

The transport of coal has dominated the business of coastal shipping for at least 350 years. At the end of the sixteenth century Shakespeare's Mistress Quickly kept a sea-coal fire in her Dolphin chambers and, ever since, the coal trade has figured largely in London's shipping. Between 1670 and 1750 the capital imported more than 40 million tons of coal. By the middle of the eighteenth century so much of it was burned that P. Kalm, who visited the city on his way to America, noted that the statues to James I and Charles I and Charles II 'looked just as if the image of a nigger or crossing sweeper . . . had been set up in royal costume'.[2] So completely did coal dominate coastal shipping that the trade in all other minerals taken together could not match it in volume. It was as true of the mid-eighteenth century as of the mid-nineteenth and mid-twentieth, that the tonnage of coal carried coastwise exceeded the weight of all other cargoes combined. Not only was it the case that, but for this trade, many thousands more would have gone cold in the winter months, but also a number of important industries would have been starved of one of their essential raw materials. Large quantities of coal were required in brickmaking, glassmaking, brewing and in the manufacture of salt, lime alum and a wide variety of metals.

Second only to coal in importance in the eighteenth century was the coastwise trade in corn. Daniel Defoe claimed that corn was brought

to London from 'all the counties of England near the sea coast'; but
the counties of East Anglia provided the greater part of the imports
of grain into the metropolis.[3] In 1735 for example Lynn supplied 62,410
quarters of all types of grain to the London market besides sending
over 10,000 quarters to Newcastle in exchange for coal.[4]

Four major centres of woollen cloth manufacture received an
important part of their supplies of raw wool through coastal shipping.
The West Riding gained some of its supplies through Hull; the West
Country depended upon the port of Bristol; Devon used Exeter and its
outport Topsham and the Essex bay and felt manufacturers depended
upon supplies coming through Colchester.

The British coasting trade was predominantly in raw materials and
agricultural surpluses—commodities of low value in relation to their
bulk which were unable to stand the high charges of land transport.
The more valuable manufactured goods, which required prompter
delivery, were more frequently sent by land or, increasingly after 1760,
by inland waterway.

Coastal shipping in the days of sail provided a means of transport
for passengers to a much greater extent than may be imagined, though
its use was generally confined to the period between April and
October inclusive when the risks of storms and wrecks were much
reduced. Perhaps the most frequented route was from London to the
Kentish seaside resorts, especially Margate and Ramsgate. In 1757
the fare by hoy (a kind of sloop) from London to Margate was only
2s, but by the end of the century it had risen to between 5s and 10s 6d,
depending on the type of accommodation.[5] Both Leigh Hunt and
Charles Lamb chose this method of getting to Margate at different
times in 1801 and it is clear from their accounts of the journey that the
vessels, which were of 80–120 tons, were well appointed below decks
and that meals were provided for the travellers.[6] According to one
Kentish source, as many as 18,000 persons used the hoys to reach
the Kentish resorts in 1792.[7] The Leith smacks made a regular practice
of taking passengers on their voyages to London; James Nasmyth, the
engineer, used the services of one of them to bring him to London
at the start of his career in 1829.[8] It was not uncommon for travellers
between the counties of the south-west and London to use sailing
vessels rather than road transport to make the journey as the fare by
water was so much cheaper. When William Lovett, the Chartist, came
to London to seek employment as a rope maker in 1821 he travelled
all the way by sea.[9]

Nevertheless there were severe limitations to the use of coastal
shipping in the days of sail. Although corn and coal carried coastwise
could help to eliminate local scarcities and thus even out regional
differences in prices, these beneficial results could only be achieved
if the winds and tides combined to make it possible. On 5 May 1782

Horace Walpole noted that 'an east wind has half starved London, as a fleet of colliers cannot get in'.[10] In consequence coals were selling at famine prices. It was not uncommon for the collier brigs from Tyneside to be held up for weeks together, with the inevitable result that the price of coal was too expensive for it to be purchased by the poor. Such times of dearth alternated with short periods of abundance—a sudden change in the wind to a more favourable quarter would bring dozens of brigs into the pool of London, flooding the market with coal and precipitating a collapse of prices. The limitations of coastal and cross-channel passenger travel in the days of sail were just as serious. It was a great inconvenience but, alas, a wholly unavoidable one, that travellers from Dublin could never be sure whether the voyage to Holyhead would take eight hours or more than three times as long. Between 5 October and 25 December 1818 there were eight occasions when the voyage was completed in less than eight hours but 14 others when it took over 24 hours.[11] On September 1727 Jonathan Swift, desirous of travelling to Ireland, waited five days at Holyhead for a favourable wind and had not been at sea an hour before a sudden adverse wind compelled the captain to put back to harbour.[12] But those who needed to travel between the Scottish and English capitals had the choice between the more expensive, but also more predictable, journey by coach and the cheaper, but less predictable, journey by sea. Where saving of time was all-important, therefore, the land route was chosen. In 1743 one of the Leith–London sailing packets took 20 days to reach only as far as Holy Island off the coast of Northumberland. By the end of the eighteenth century the clumsy, buff-bowed brigs formerly employed on this route had largely given place to the faster and more manoeuvreable smacks, but the voyage still had many uncertainties. In time of war there was the threat of attack from enemy vessels, as on 23 October 1804 when one of the Leith smacks, the *Britannia*, was attacked off Cromer by a large French privateer. The British ship sustained many shots through its canvas but inflicted more severe damage on the French vessel which eventually dropped astern, smarting from its wounds.[13] The danger of similar attacks inevitably predisposed travellers to take the safer land route at least for the next ten years while England remained at war with France.

II

If the tonnage of shipping entering British ports be taken as a measure of comparison, coastal shipping had a greater importance than the shipping engaged in trade with the colonies and foreign countries throughout the whole of the nineteenth century. In 1841 coastal shipping entries, at over 12½ million tons, excluding ballast, were

approximately three times the tonnage entering from foreign and
colonial trade (4,649,039 tons including ballast). It was not until 1906
that tonnages entering from overseas trade (66 million) for the first
time exceeded the tonnage of shipping entering from British ports.
What helped to maintain the supremacy of coastal shipping for so
long was the earlier and more thorough exploitation of steamships
in the coastwise trade than in the overseas trade. In coastwise shipping
steam tonnage exceeded the tonnage of sailing ships as early as 1866.
A similar turning point was not reached in the overseas trade until
seven years later.[14]

Although there was a substantial time lag between William Syming-
ton's successful experiment in steam navigation at Dalswinton in
Dumfriesshire in October 1788 and the launching of the first commercially successful steamboat, Henry Bell's *Comet*, on the Clyde
in July 1812,[15] subsequent developments in the use of passenger
steamboats were extremely rapid. In 1814, only two years after the
appearance of the *Comet*, no fewer than nine steamboats were
launched on the river Clyde alone.[16] By 1821 there were 188 steamships, aggregating 20,028 tons, in service in the coastwise trade of
Great Britain. By 1853 there had been a spectacular increase to 639
vessels (218,266 tons).[17] It is true that a handful of these ships were
exclusively confined to the carriage of goods, but the overwhelming
majority of them carried at least some passengers. When Queen Victoria came to the throne in 1837 there was no shadow of doubt that
the revolution in coastwise shipping which had taken place in the
previous 25 years was due to a quite unprecedented growth in the use
of the steamship for personal travel.

Because of the small size and low average horsepower of the
early steam vessel they were at first largely confined to the more
important river estuaries where they were employed as ferries, excursion boats or tugs. On the Thames the passenger traffic between
London and Gravesend grew with great rapidity after the *Margery* of
70 tons opened the service on 23 January 1815. By 1842 there were
16 steamboats employed on this route, landing and embarking over
1,141,000 passengers annually at the Town and Terrace Piers at
Gravesend.[18] On Tyneside the *Tyne Steam Packet* was ferrying passengers from Newcastle to Shields as early as May 1814 although
more important in the early history of steam navigation in this region
was the employment of steam tugs to tow vessels, especially collier
brigs, out to sea when the prevailing wind made it impossible to leave
harbour with the aid of sail alone.[19] On the Clyde, steamboats linked
Glasgow with the suburbs and the holiday resorts of the estuary. By
1822 there were six steam packets sailing daily between the city and
Helensburgh.[20] For many decades to come those commuting to work
in the Scottish commercial capital did so by steamboat rather than

by short stage coach or gig. Those seeking recreation on the beautiful banks of the river or at Rothesay or Dunoon used the same medium. On the Mersey, ferry services between Liverpool and Runcorn were started by the *Elizabeth* in 1815 and similar links to Birkenhead were established in March 1817.[21]

An event as important for the development of coastal passenger services as the Rainhill trials of 1829 were for the triumph of the steam locomotive, was the voyage made by Mr George Dodd in the 75-ton paddle steamer *Thames*, between 28 May and 12 June 1815, from Glasgow to London via Dublin. Until this time steamboats had rarely ventured into the open sea, but Dodd's 758-mile-long journey included treacherous passages through the St George's Channel and round the Lizard without serious mishap. At his ports of call his ship aroused intense interest, awakening mariners' understanding of the potentialities of steam navigation. The pilots from Wexford who caught sight of the trail of smoke from the *Thames*, mistook her for a vessel on fire and were disappointed in their hopes of exercising their right of salvage. Among other things, the voyage proved that it was possible for a steamer to sail 'direct in the wind's eye' to clear a lee shore or keep more closely to a time schedule, even though a heavy gale was blowing.[22]

Following Dodd's remarkable demonstration, entrepreneurs were emboldened to establish open-sea coastal steamship services. Even before his voyage, as early as June 1813, the *Rob Roy* provided a bi-weekly passenger service during the summer weeks between Glasgow and Belfast.[23] Summer services between Glasgow and Liverpool started in the following year. In June 1821 the London and Edinburgh Steam Packet Company employed the 400-ton *City of Edinburgh* and her sister ship the *James Watt* to carry passengers between the two capitals. They experienced competition from other steamers from the start.[24] Further up the east coast, earlier that same year, the Leith and Aberdeen Steam Yacht Company's vessel the *Tourist* began passenger services between Leith and Aberdeen, calling at intermediate ports.[25] On the south coast the Plymouth, Devonport, Portsmouth and Falmouth Steam Packet Company began regular summer sailings in 1823, its ships sometimes calling at Torquay and Cowes en route between Plymouth and Portsmouth.[26] A Brighton steamer, the *Swift*, had started weekly services to Ryde, Cowes and Southampton in the previous season.[27] By 1825 the steamers on the Cork–London station were also calling at Plymouth, Portsmouth and Cowes.[28] All the same, passenger services, apart from pleasure cruises, never achieved the same prominence on the south coast as they did in other regions, because coach services had the advantage of inner lines of communication, the passages round the Cornish coast were notoriously difficult and the arrival of the railways at Southampton in 1840, Brighton in 1841 and Folkestone in 1843 further emphasised the superiority of the land routes in this region.

In the early 1820s none of the steamship companies had sufficient confidence in the seaworthiness of their vessels to maintain sailings throughout the winter months. The 1823 season of the London and Edinburgh Steam Packet Company's vessels, for example, extended from 16 March to 12 November. It was not until 1829–30 that the company kept its ships in service in winter on this wind-swept east coast station.[29] What helped to persuade steam packet companies all round the British coast to establish continuous services was the bold decision of the Post Office to provide all the year round steam packets for the important Holyhead–Howth station from the end of May 1821, to maintain similar arrangements for the mail routes between Milford and Dunmore (for Waterford) from April 1824, between Portpatrick and Donaghadee from May 1825 and between Liverpool and Dublin from August 1826. Whatever may have been the shortcomings of the vessels employed in respect of creature comforts, there is no doubt of the superior regularity and punctuality of the sailings of the Royal Mail steamboats. Through the 1820s the Post Office established higher standards of efficiency which the steamship companies were at pains to emulate.[30]

British coastal passenger steamship services achieved their greatest extent and importance in the early 1840s when there were over 1,400 route-miles of regular sailings linking ninety ports and harbours.[31] From extremely busy arteries of water communication like the lower reaches of the Clyde and Thames, to the infrequent but vital links with remote ports like Lerwick in the Shetland Islands and St Mary's in the Isles of Scilly, the steamboat had become an essential link in the communications of the British Isles.

Since no national census of the volume of passenger traffic was ever taken in the nineteenth century it is impossible to give any precise figure of the number of persons who used this means of travel each year. But by adding together the estimates given by witnesses before parliamentary committees on railway and harbour bills it is possible to give some indication of the extent to which steamboats were used by the British people in the early years of Queen Victoria's reign. Apart from the estuarial services on the Thames and Clyde which carried at least a million and a half passengers each year and the short steam ferry services in the Mersey, the Humber, the Tyne, the Bristol Channel and the Solent, which probably accounted for as many more, steamers on the east coast at various points between Aberdeen and Margate carried about 250,000 persons annually. As late as 1849 only 5,792 passengers were booked by the North British Railway from Edinburgh to London in a year when 11,584 persons took the sea route. On the other side of the British Isles 53,456 passengers were carried between Glasgow and Liverpool in 1841 while, four years later, 15,000 persons were travelling by steamboat to the Merseyside port from Annan in Dumfriesshire. On the other hand the traffic round the south-west coast was less important. An estimated 12,000 persons sailed between Bristol and Exeter in 1836, a number which fell dramatically after the opening of the Taunton–Exeter stretch of the Bristol and Exeter Railway in May 1844.[32]

The popularity of passenger steamship services in the second quarter of the nineteenth century is explained by their much greater speed and reliability when compared with the sailing ship, and by their cheapness compared with coach travel. Margate hoys frequently took more than two days to reach London; but as early as 1818 the average time taken by the steamers was only eleven hours.[33] Whereas sailing packets took at least two days on the journey between Glasgow and Liverpool, steamships, by the early 1830s, were completing the journey in 24–26 hours. In mid-December 1834, at a time of the year when coastal sailing smacks rarely ventured out to sea, the steam packet *Manchester* made the return trip from Liverpool to Glasgow and back within 60 hours, an achievement for speed and turn-round considered quite remarkable at the time. Passenger fares for the single trip of 240 miles were only £1 5s, or less than $1\frac{1}{2}d$ a mile compared with $2d$ a mile for an outside seat on a coach or twice that amount for an inside seat.[34] Already by the early 1820s the inhabitants of the remoter parts of the kingdom were experiencing the advantages of more frequent and speedier contact with the more populous centres. Before the dawn of the steamship era it took three days, even with the most favourable winds, for sailing packets from Glasgow to reach Rothesay on the Isle of Bute. When winds were adverse it was thought 'not wonderful' for the journey to take as many weeks. In 1823 steamships were making the journey to Rothesay and back comfortably in a day. At the beginning of the nineteenth century sailing smacks made the journey between Edinburgh and Aberdeen only once in three weeks with a very uncertain time of arrival. From the summer of 1821 the steamships *Velocity, Tourist* and *Brilliant* between them maintained a thrice-weekly service with reliable hours of departure and arrival. Steamboat proprietors were in a position to undercut coach fares because each steamboat was able to carry many times the number of persons that could be accommodated on the most overcrowded stage coach. In 1833 the General Steam Navigation Company's steamship *Monarch*, employed on the Leith to London station, had berths for 140 persons, dining-room accommodation for 100 and room in the steerage for many more. By contrast the legal limit for a stage coach was four 'inside' and eleven 'outside' passengers.

There can be little doubt that it was for reasons of cost that so many persons chose to travel by steamboat rather than by coach even though the coach was generally quicker on the journey. It was, as a rule, much cheaper to take the sea route.[35] In the mid-1830s the deck passenger on the Leith–London packet paid £2 10s for his fare, including his food. Cabin passengers paid £4 4s, also inclusive of full board, for the two days and nights of the voyage.[36] The fare from London to Edinburgh, for the 'outside' passenger by coach was £3 10s whilst for the 'insides' it was £6 15s, both fares being exclusive of board and lodging. Moreover, for the long-distance coach traveller the payment of his fare was but the beginning of an extended agony, both physical and financial. His travelling costs were inflated by all kinds of incidental expenses. Ordinary inn charges for food and drink were: breakfast 8d to 1s; dinner 1s 6d to 3s 6d; supper 1s to 2s 6d; wine 6d a glass; tea 10d to 1s; porter 2d to 3d a glass. When a traveller stayed the night at an inn candles might be charged up at the rate of anything from 3s to 5s a night. These charges were considered a 'sighting shot' on the part of the innkeeper: if the guest submitted to this form of fleecing he was thought ripe for other forms of exploitation, and bills for fires and rushlights, stabling and carriage cleaning would follow in quick succession. The traveller was finally encouraged to contribute to the support of the local poor. He could well be excused for wondering whether he would not himself join the ranks of the destitute by the time his journey was completed. For it was not only at the inns that he had to dip his hands into his pockets. When each coachman had completed his stage of the journey his head would appear through the window and he would say 'I go no further gentlemen'. This would be the signal for the simultaneous dipping into the pockets of the inside passengers for the expected 2s tip.[37] The guard would not fail to give passengers a similar reminder at the end of his spell of duty. On a long journey such impositions inflated the cost of coach travel up to half as much again as the fare. By contrast the sea traveller, though sometimes unlucky enough to be subjected to physical agonies even worse than those of coach travel, had the great consolation that he was free from all further financial harassment once he had paid his fare and boarded his steamer.

Among the important reasons for the earlier commercial exploitation of steam power for water transport than for transport on land were the lower initial capital costs involved in starting a steam packet service than starting a railway. It could even be cheaper to establish a long-distance steamer service than it was to provide for stage-coach travel over the same distance. When the above mentioned *Thames* steam packet was built for the London–Margate service in 1815 it cost the nine proprietors a total of £4,050, or £450 each.[38] The steamboats *Superb* and *Robert Bruce* which provided the first reliable service between Glasgow and Liverpool, cost together less than £16,000. Many of the Clyde steamers were built by the small engineering firms of the locality, the cost of construction being met by friends and business associates and being divided up into sixty-fourths in the tradition of the ship-building industry. In the early years of the steamship boom their cost rarely exceeded the cost of the pioneering *Thames*. When the Post Office ordered two steamships of the most up-to-date design to man the Holyhead station in 1821 the cost came to less than £20,000. These low initial capital costs can be compared with the six- or even seven-figure sums required to launch a railroad. The capital expended on the Newcastle and Carlisle Railway up to the date of the opening of the line was £950,000.[39] The steamship proprietors had the enormous advantage over the owners of railways that they did not have to incur any track costs. They had the advantage over coach proprietors that they did not have to pay passenger duty or licence fees for their captains as licences had to be paid for coachmen (not to mention coaches and horses). It is true, that as the technology of marine engineering advanced and the simple side-lever engines gave place to the simple inverted and then the compound engines, and as first iron and then steel replaced wood in the construction of ships' hulls, the cost of construction soared and it became ever more difficult to establish a steamship service with small capital. Nevertheless steamship concerns, unlike railways, could start up by venturing remarkably small capitals, and by the ploughing back of profits, and the buying up of rivals could gradually enlarge the scope of their activities. In 1823 Charles Wye-Williams, with the assistance of a few business friends in Dublin and Liverpool, launched two steamers for the Dublin–Liverpool trade at a cost of £24,000.[40] These later became the first ships of the City of Dublin Steam Packet Company incorporated in 1828 with a capital which had been rapidly enlarged by further calls on subscribers and by mergers with other companies to £174,500[41]

The early history of the passenger steamship services is one of the keenest competition between small concerns anxious to capture a share of an increasingly popular means of transport. From the summer of 1831 on the east-coast route the ships of the London and Edinburgh Steam Packet Company were in fierce rivalry with the London, Leith, Edinburgh and Glasgow Shipping Company which in that year introduced the brand new steamers *Royal William*, *Royal Adelaide*, and *Victoria* to challenge the earlier established *Soho*, *James Watt* and *United Kingdom* regularly plying on the Leith–London station. The usurpers claimed of the *Royal William* that it was 'admitted by all to be unrivalled in the elegance and comfort of her accommodation' and that she had established 'a decided superiority in speed over all the other vessels'. When faced with this serious challenge, the rival company, in its newspaper advertisements. assumed an attitude of superior disdain. Of the *Soho* and *James Watt* it asserted that 'the well known character of these vessels supersedes the necessity of any comment as to their speed, safety and comfort'.[42] On the Cork–Milford station in 1826 the *Superb*, owned by a group of Cork businessmen, was at daggers drawn with the *Severn* of the St George's Steam Packet Company. The *Superb* solicited custom by parading a brass band through Cork; the *Severn* retaliated with the announcement that its deck passengers would 'get a loaf of bread gratis'.[43] Competition of this fierceness was accompanied by ruinous rate-cutting, followed by the inevitable truce. On the east-coast the London and Edinburgh Steam Packet Company was bought up by the General Steam Navigation Company in 1836.[44] The damaging rivalry between the City of Dublin Steam Packet Company and the St George's Steam Packet Company for the Irish Sea trade was soon brought to an end when a pooling agreement for an equitable division of the traffic was signed on 30 June 1826.[45] By the mid-nineteenth century the companies in the steam-packet business were often large concerns with a capital that went into six figures.

III

In the coastwise trades, as in the ocean-going services, steam power was adopted more slowly for goods than for passenger traffic. Until competition between the railway companies established new standards for speedy delivery there was not the same sense of urgency in the delivery of goods as there was to complete a, frequently unpleasant, passenger sea voyage. Furthermore, a much greater amount of capital had been invested, before the age of steam, in cargo vessels than in ships primarily designed for passenger transport, and men who had spent a lifetime in learning how to man sailing vessels were reluctant to change to a new-fangled medium. Moreover, the initial capital cost of building and equipping a steamship was greater than that for a sailing vessel of comparable size. In the mid-nineteenth century coal trade between Newcastle and London, a new screw-propelled steam collier cost around £10,000, but so numerous were the sailing brigs engaged in the same trade and so lengthy was their life-span that second-hand sailing vessels could be bought for £1,200 and the first cost of buying *six* new collier (sailing) brigs of 300 tons capacity each was no more than that of *one* new screw collier suitable for carrying 600 tons of coal.[46]

Nevertheless the distinction between the two types of coastwise traffic was often blurred. Few passenger steamships carried no merchandise and the master of a cargo steamer was generally willing to augment his ship's revenue by carrying passengers. This mixing of passenger and cargo transport was most apparent on the traffic of the Irish Sea where on the 'bargain' trips steerage passengers were accommodated along with the cattle and therefore got wet not only from the spray of the sea and the rain.[47]

Before the early 1850s, by which time the essential framework of a railway system had been constructed, coastal shipping was employed not merely for the movement of bulky low-value raw materials and farm produce but also for the transport of manufactured goods of high value in relation to their weight. In this transitional period between the appearance of commercially viable steamboats in the 1820s and the setting up of satisfactory conditions for the through transit of goods by rail some quarter of a century later, British businessmen were very open-minded as to which form of transport they used. Many of them resorted to a very mixed bag of road waggon, canal barge, coastal steamer and, where possible, railway, for different stages in the haulage of their merchandise. In 1836, Mr B. Redfern, a general merchant and factor of Birmingham, who did £20,000 worth of business annually with Scotland, sent his goods first by road waggon, then by canal *south* to London for transhipment by steamer to Edinburgh, as he found this cheaper than dispatching his goods all the way directly north by road waggon or partly by land and partly by canal to Hull and then the remainder of the journey by sea. Other Birmingham manufacturers sent their goods to Scotland via canal to the Mersey, by steamboat from Liverpool to Glasgow and then by canal to Edinburgh.[48] George Hudson, during his early career as a draper and furnisher at York (before he achieved renown as the Railway King) found it cheaper to have his Kidderminster carpets sent first to London for dispatch by steamboat to Hull before they were carried by inland waterway on the final stage of their journey to his warehouse.[49] The use of such a diversity of forms of transport greatly decreased when the railways, increasingly during the second half of the nineteenth century, were able to carry goods direct to their markets in a much shorter space of time than had been possible in the 1830s and 1840s. By this time coastal shipping had largely reverted to its traditional role; the movement of bulky low-value raw materials and farm produce.

Throughout the nineteenth century London's predominance over the coastal trade of the British Isles was unchallenged. Although the tonnage of shipping involved and the quantities of merchandise carried both increased until the First World War, the pattern of the trade was not dramatically altered. In 1824 of a total of 2,234,228 tons of mechandise imported, coastwise, into the capital, 1,870,425 tons, or 83·7 per cent, were coal and 312,653 or 13·9 per cent were food grains. The tonnage of all other commodities was remarkably small and took up less than $2\frac{1}{2}$ per cent of the imports into the region. Metals, rapidly rising in importance with the growth of engineering, amounted to 41,865 tons or 1·9 per cent of the total, leaving less than one per cent for all other items such as provisions, spirits and textiles.

In contrast with what she brought in from other British ports London sent out, coastwise, a much greater variety of produce, though foodstuffs, textiles and alcoholic beverages took the lion's share. Except for places within a short radius of the capital, food-stuffs could be supplied more cheaply by sea than by land. The quantity of tea (32,882 tons) consigned from London to other British ports in 1824 was more than double the amount of all other groceries combined. The 3,200 tons of wool loaded on outgoing ships completely dwarfed the small consignments of silk, cotton, yarn and flax, though the predominance of England's basic staple was rapidly shrinking. Without the wine, of which 143,299 gallons were sent out, the trade in alcoholic beverages would have been very small. Only 2,275 gallons of rum and 285 gallons of brandy left the Thames by sea that year (although an allowance must be made for an indefinite quantity smuggled round the coast).[50]

At the beginning of the twentieth century coal still completely dominated London's coastwise imports; the quantity entering the Thames, in 1905, 8,494,234 tons, having more than doubled over the previous 80 years[51] (see Fig. 4). At the same time imports of grain from British ports declined sharply in the last quarter of the nineteenth century so that in 1895 they amounted to 36,588 tons or little more than one tenth of the amount of grain brought in in 1825.[52] However there was, in compensation, a remarkable growth in imports of hay to feed the ever-growing horse population of the metropolis. The fodder was brought up the Thames in specially constructed flat-bottomed barges which carried 12-foot high hay-stacks on their decks. In the heyday of this traffic, just before the First World War, hundreds of vessels were employed in this trade which stretched from Harwich to the Pool of London. On occasions as many as thirty 'stackies' could be seen sailing up river. The trade was a profitable one for there was an assured return cargo of horse manure shipped from such harbours as the appropriately named Mucking, on the Essex shore of the Thames estuary, to the farms further up the Essex coast which supplied the hay.[53]

After the all-important trade in coal from Tyneside to London and the substantial early nineteenth-century shipments of grain the east coast trade in livestock and dead meat became important by the early 1830s. To overcome the severe disadvantages which sprang from the necessity of driving cattle and sheep 'on the hoof' from Aberdeenshire and Kincardineshire to Edinburgh and London, wholesale meat salesmen soon took advantage of steam navigation to bring the livestock more speedily to the two capitals without the damaging loss of weight associated with the land journey. By the mid

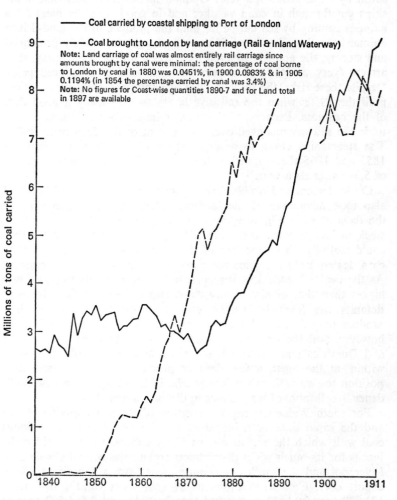

Coal carried by coastal shipping to Port of London

Coal brought to London by land carriage (Rail & Inland Waterway)

Note: Land carriage of coal was almost entirely rail carriage since amounts brought by canal were minimal: the percentage of coal borne to London by canal in 1880 was 0.0451%, in 1900 0.0983% & in 1905 0.1194% (in 1854 the percentage carried by canal was 3.4%)

Note: No figures for Coast-wise quantities 1890-7 and for Land total in 1897 are available

Sources: B.P.P. 1839–97, Annual Returns of Coal brought Coastways and by land to London for the Years 1837–96; B.P.P. 1871, XVIII, Report of Comm. E p. 159 and App. 125 to Report of Comm. E., *B.P.P.* 1909, XIII, App. 3, State 3; B.P.P. 1909, XXXIII, Pt. 1, App. 24 (to Eng. section), State 3; *The Coal Merchant & Shipper*, vol. XXVI (1 Feb. 1913), p. 111.

Figure 4   Quantities of Coal Carried to London by Coastal Shipping and by Land 1837–1911

1830s about 7,000 head of cattle and 10,000 sheep were being sent south by steamboat each year. Opinion in the trade was that if the ships got through in calm weather and in good time the meat from animals coming by sea cut better than the produce of the land-driven animals. On the other hand, if the sea voyage was unduly prolonged and stormy, the animals suffered from the sea air and the spray, they arrived 'very unsightly in appearance' and sold at a reduced price. Despite these risks, the trade in both live and dead meat grew rapidly until the 1850s when the railways began to take away a good deal of the business. Because of the greater importance of speed in this trade the railway managed over 95 per cent of the dead meat traffic. The steamships clung to a larger share of the livestock. Between 1856 and 1865 they carried 32·6 per cent of the total or an average of 5,340 animals a year.[54]

Cattle dealers and arable farmers in the western part of Scotland also took advantage of the facilities offered by the steamboat. In the days of sail, Wigtownshire cattle dealers paid farmers for their stock in bills because there was a long interval of time before they could realise cash by the sale of the animals in England. Travelling corn dealers used the same means of payment for the same reasons. As the dealers' trade was very precarious their bankruptcy rate was higher than that of almost any class, and because of their frequent defaults the Scottish farmers were reluctant to part with their produce for sale in such distant markets. With the coming of steam, however, and the opening of regular services between both Annan and Dumfries and Liverpool, the cattle and grain could be re-sold within, at the most, a few days of purchase, the dealer was in a position to pay cash to the farmer who in turn acquired a new confidence to sell more of his produce in distant markets.[55]

For south Wales the rapid expansion of steam navigation at one and the same time both increased the demand for the bituminous coal with which the region was so richly endowed and provided the means for its much wider distribution around the Bristol Channel, to Liverpool and the south coast, quite apart from a booming trade in export coal. Coastwise shipments of coal from Cardiff rose from 171,978 tons in 1833 to 826,044 tons in 1874 and 2,644,520 tons in 1911. Although this Welsh coal had superior thermal qualities, when seaborne it was unable to compete with the Newcastle coal in the London market because of the greater cost of the longer journey round the Cornish peninsula and along the English Channel.[56]

In the period between the end of the Napoleonic Wars in 1815 and the repeal of the Corn Laws in 1846 the population of the United Kingdom grew from 13 million to 20 million persons, but the importation of corn and meal from foreign countries was severely restricted because of the import duty. The development of steam navigation on the Irish Sea made it possible for Ireland to fill this important gap in the food supplies of the rest of the kingdom. Table 1 shows the remarkable growth in shipments over a 25-year period:

Table 1 *Quantities of corn and meal shipped from Ireland to the U.K. 1820–44 in tons*[57]

Year	Tons	Period/Average	Year	Tons	Period/Average
1820	206,804		1835	389,756	
1821	311,668	1820–24	1836	414,646	1835–39
1822	197,911	average	1837	414,280	average
1823	222,317	228,350	1838	462,859	393,965
1824	201,479		1839	288,276	
1825	338,082		1840	249,648	
1826	230,258	1825–29	1841	355,322	1840–44
1827	226,828	average	1842	303,883	average
1828	435,947	307,139	1843	402,789	344,927
1829	334,585		1844	367,993	
1830	338,335				
1831	353,951	1830–34			
1832	441,725	average			
1833	407,673	390,043			
1834	408,533				

The tonnage employed in the coastal trade between the United Kingdom and Ireland increased by 250 per cent between 1801 and 1849 but the increase was much more rapid in the period of predominance of steam than in the pre-steam era. The increase from 1801–26 was only 62 per cent, or two per cent annually. From 1827–49 it was 188 per cent, or eight per cent annually.[58] Although the increased passenger travel played a part in this rapid expansion the increase in shipments of farm produce was also of great significance.

With the disaster of the great famine 1845–7 and the opening of British ports to foreign corn from 1846, the cargo ships of the Irish Sea gradually changed their role from being suppliers of corn and meal to suppliers of livestock and livestock produce. From an average of under 200,000 head of cattle shipped from Ireland to the UK in the 1820s the number increased to over a million annually by the 1860s.[59] Steam shipping, with its reliable and greatly faster sailing times, had made the marketing of livestock across the Irish Sea a much more attractive proposition to thousands of Irish cattle breeders. The steamship also made it profitable for the first time to carry on a large business in the sale of Irish eggs in England and Wales. Before the establishment of steam navigation in the ports of Southern Ireland the price of eggs fluctuated sharply, depending on the progress of sailing vessels on the voyage to England, and the consequent glut or scarcity of supplies in markets such as Cork. With the greater regularity of sailing of steam vessels the Irish markets were at first in short supply and prices were higher. But with the greater certainty of sales more poultry were reared and a great expansion of the trade took place.[60]

IV

The rapid expansion of the passenger steamboat services round Britain's coasts had an important impact on other forms of transport. Long before the arrival of the railways gave the *coup de grace* to the long-distance coach traffic the activities of the steamship companies, particularly on the east coast, were causing alarm to coach proprietors. Mr Charles Collins, a coach proprietor on the London–Blackheath Road, told a parliamentary select committee in 1837 that, soon after the establishment of regular steamship services on the Kentish coast he had been obliged to halve the number of coaches he maintained on the route. 'The steam vessels', he said 'certainly took away nearly all our profit.' Formerly the coach proprietors had counted on making most money in the summer season: but this was just the time of year when there was the greatest competition from steamboats.[61] At that time the steamship fare charged for cabin passengers travelling from Hull to London was only 4s. The steerage fare was a mere 2s. The coach passenger duty payable per seat on coaches making the journey from York to London was double the cabin fare by steamer and the coach proprietor had other taxes to pay before he could begin to look for any profit.[62] Further north the revenue of the East Lothian, Berwickshire and North Durham turnpike trusts had all diminished 'in consequence of the steamboats'.[63] When, in 1838, the stage-coach proprietors of the Great North Road petitioned parliament for exemption from assessed taxes on guards and coachmen and from the stage-coach duties, they gave as their reason the 'improvements in steam navigation' which caused many persons visiting the north to prefer the journey by water rather than that by land.[64] In the heyday of the coaching age, Barnet, the first important stage on the Great North Road, found stabling for 800 horses. By 1845, principally because of the diversion of traffic to steamships, there were no more than 40 coach horses in the town and the value of property had fallen, in some cases, by more than half.[65]

Once a railway system had been created, the business of the steam-packets was increasingly threatened (except, of course, in the case of cross-channel and island services) and this sector of coastwise shipping began to fulfil a different role. The inevitable reaction to an

extension of the rail passenger services was fare-cutting by the steamship companies which endeavoured to dissuade their customers from
deserting to the railway. When through rail communication was
established to Edinburgh in 1846 the General Steam Navigation Company reduced steamship fares between the English and Scottish capitals for first class cabin passengers from £4 4s to £3 and for second
class cabin passengers from £2 10s to £1 15s. Three years later there
were further reductions to £2 10s and £1 10s, presumably because
the earlier changes had not arrested the passengers' growing preference for speedier journey by land. By 1885, fares, including the
steward's fee in the chief cabin, were down to 22s, and in the second
cabin to 16s. It was possible to buy a return ticket for as little as
24s 6d.[66] By this time all but the wealthier steam packet companies
had been squeezed out. The General Steam Navigation Company,
which gained its main revenue from the short sea routes on the
North Sea, kept a reduced passenger service on this station mainly
to act as a feeder to its more lucrative north European traffic. The
continued existence of a very cheap passenger service by sea, in
financial terms, if not in speed, highly competitive with the railroad,
helped to keep down rail fares on this and on other routes such as
that between Glasgow and Liverpool.[67]

After about 1830 the increased scale of both passenger and cargo
steamship and sailing ship services combined with the development
of the railways to make both urgent and profitable the construction
of new and improved harbours, jetties and piers. When steamships
began to ply regularly further out from Glasgow into the Firth of
Clyde in the 1820s, the want of a proper harbour at Largs, an
increasingly popular resort, was a great obstacle to further development of the traffic. In this case improvement followed the initiative
taken by Sir T. M. Brisbane, Bart., who secured an Act of Parliament and contributed shares, along with 30 other investors, for the
£4,275 needed for a new harbour, opened in 1832. The investment
yielded a steady six per cent return.[68] Partly in order to deal with
the emergent steam packet business to London, a new chain pier
was built at Newhaven (for Leith) in 1821. While the steam-packets
were small ships of under 200 tons it served its purpose very well;
but a decade later the more powerful ships coming into service drew
more than the maximum six feet of water available at low tide and
they were obliged either to await a favourable tide or to anchor out
to sea. The Duke of Buccleuch then sponsored the construction at
Granton of a new pier to which the steam-packets resorted. Meanwhile the cargo trade of Leith was developing rapidly and in 1847
the Government granted £135,000 for a new dock (the Victoria Dock)
which was opened in 1852.[69]

In the southern half of the kingdom piers were constructed at a large number of seaside resorts to cater for the growing steamship traffic. Southend was just one example where it was the building of a pier rather than a railway which gave the initial boost to popularity and rapid growth of population. Although the small town achieved notoriety with the visit of Princess Charlotte of Wales in 1801 the 'New Pier', built opposite the Royal Hotel in the following year, stood in water too shallow to accommodate the steamships which began to call from the season 1819 onwards. Visitors to Southend in those days needed to possess a stoical patience. When the steamers had sailed far enough inland for safety they often had to wait 'by the hour together' for the small vans, capable of carrying no more than 17 persons, to cross more than a mile of sand to their rescue. The alternative, much preferred by aspiring young maidens, but shunned by the older generation, was to be carried ashore on the backs of sailors. These romantic opportunities ceased in 1830 when steamers started to call at the second 'new' pier. Once the problem of landing visitors was resolved—at least for some years —there was 'a great increase' in the number of visitors coming from London, some 7,000 people making the sea voyage in 1834.[70]

As the railway became more ubiquitous in the second half of the nineteenth century it became clear that, if the coastwise cargo trade was to continue to grow, the efficiency of the vessels engaged in it would have to be improved by the enlargement of their carrying capacity, the adoption, where necessary, of steam power in the place of sails and the quicker turn round of ships so that shipping freights and delivery times would remain competitive with land transport. However, these innovations could not have been introduced without the enlargement and deepening of harbours.

Admittedly the even more rapid expansion of overseas trade was sometimes a more compelling reason for harbour improvement; but there is no doubt that the requirements of the coastwise trade were a significant and sometimes, decisive, influence on the side of modernisation and extension of berthing capacity. One area which from the 1820s experienced a very rapid growth in the coal trade was south Wales. To make possible the rapid increase in the quantity of coal seaborne from the Welsh valleys, river mouths were deepened and wet docks were opened at Llanelly in 1828, Cardiff in 1839, Newport in 1844 and Swansea in 1852.[71] Under the Harbours and Passing Tolls Act of 1861, the government authorised the Public Works Loan Commissioners to lend money at low rates of interest to harbour authorities carrying out works of modernisation and improvement. In the following twenty years nearly a million pounds was thus advanced to supplement local effort at Aberdeen, Belfast, Falmouth, Greenock and Newhaven and on Teesside and Tyneside

Table 2 *Public Works Loan Board: Capital advanced for harbour improvements annually.* (Years shown are April 1–March 31; all sums advanced under the Harbour & Passing Tolls Act of 1861 except where otherwise stated)

	England and Wales	*Scotland*
1878–9	2,500	42,500*
1879–80	70,000	30,000
1880–1	10,000	15,000
1881–2	7,000	23,000
1882–3	9,500	23,500
1883–4	8,500	10,000
1884–5	5,900	22,000
1885–6	47,100	30,000
1886–7	19,375+I.o.M. 6,000	7,400
1887–8	29,375+I.o.M. 12,000	31,600
1888–9	30,000+I.o.M. 12,000	16,000
1889–90	29,300	8,000
1890–1	7,000	11,000
1891–2	12,050	9,000
1892–3	34,000	18,000
1893–4	29,000	55,000†
1894–5	49,000	7,000
1895–6	44,000	19,000
1896–7	102,000	63,000
1897–8	1,000	20,000
1898–9	2,000	21,000
1899–1900	nil	4,000
1900–1	nil	4,000
1901–2	nil	500
1902–3	20,020	16,500
1903–4	12,000	3,500
1904–5	37,520	5,000
1905–6	37,770	35,800‡
1906–7	15,800	33,000
1907–8	24,940	15,000
1908–9	2,200	43,000
1909–10	9,000	48,000
1910–11	5,000	47,000
1911–12	10,000	26,000
1912–13	13,000	26,500
1913–14	7,300	27,000

I.o.M.=Isle of Man.
* 1878–9 figure for Scotland includes £10,000 given under Acts other than 1861 Act.
† 1893–4 figure for Scotland includes £30,000 given under Acts other than 1861 Act.
‡ 1905–6 figure for Scotland includes £1,800 given under Acts other than 1861 Act.

(see Table 2). In the same 20 years over £22 million of private and municipal capital was invested in new harbour works.[72]

On Tyneside, Teesside and the Wear the coastal trade in coal was the great all-pervasive influence for dock and riverside improvements. In Sunderland the leading developments in the harbour, paralleling the growth of coal shipments, is summarised as follows:[73]

Year	Works completed	Coal shipped in tons
1840	North Dock opened	1,318,497
1850	South Dock opened	1,718,427
1856	Sea outlet opened	2,204,898
1859	Administration of river and docks amalgamated	2,606,513
by 1883	Great development of coalfield; port improved	3,958,564

From the time the first iron screw collier vessel, the *John Bowes,* entered the Thames in July 1852 the proportion of coal coming from the north-east in steamships of this type rapidly increased. But because they cost more to build and run than the sailing brigs they replaced they could only be kept in service economically if they were able to discharge their cargoes quickly and complete 30 round trips between the Tyne, Tees or Wear and London each year, compared with the eight to ten trips which was the most that could be managed by the brigs. These innovations, however, provided a most powerful incentive to the authorities responsible for the ports of the north-east and on the Thames to provide modern cranes, deep anchorages and extended berthing space. As late as 1860 the River Tyne was not suitable for navigation by large vessels. The bar at the entrance was covered with only six feet of water at low tide and swift and dangerous currents swept round obstacles along the river banks like Bill Point and Whitehall Point. On either side of the harbour were the dangerous rocks known as the Black Midden at Tynemouth and the Herd Sands at South Shields. A significant milestone in the improvement of the shipping facilities of the region was the passing of the River Tyne Improvement Act in 1850, providing for a joint control over the river by the Admiralty and the four municipalities of Newcastle, Gateshead, Tynemouth and South Shields through a Tyne Improvement Commission.[74] Within the next 20 years the navigability of the river was transformed through a massive campaign of dredging. The quantity of earth removed from the river bed to widen and deepen the channel of navigation and increase harbour acreage rose from 496,402 tons in 1859 to 1,864,544 tons in 1862 and 5,273,588 tons in 1869.[75] Without these far-reaching improvements the more than five-fold increase of coal shipments from the Tyne—from 3,805,633 tons in 1850 to 20,299,955 tons in 1913—would have been quite impossible.[76]

Here was the supreme example of the truism that the continued growth of coastwise shipping was dependent on massive investment in major harbour improvements on the part of railway companies, river commissioners, the government and private investors. Port authorities which failed to meet the challenge provided by the larger steamships and lagged behind others in the investment of capital for the improvement of navigation in their district soon fell behind their more enterprising rivals. For a time coal shipments from the port of Blyth declined after 1873 because harbours on the Tyne could provide 'deeper water and better facilities' for the screw colliers. Only after the businessmen of the port were shaken out of their apathy by the decline in their basic source of livelihood was there a reversal of the downward trend. In 1883 they secured an Act of Parliament which provided for the appointment of commissioners for the management of Blyth harbour and thereafter 'a vigorous programme of improvements' was carried out. Following the opening by the North Eastern Railway of two new coaling berths in 1888 coal shipments doubled, topping the two million ton mark in the short space of three years.[77]

V

Throughout the greater part of the nineteenth century the conditions of employment of the merchant sailors who manned both passenger and cargo vessels were largely determined by the free play of market forces. Wages were fixed by individual bargaining though there were recognised rates of pay on each type of ship. Given the fact that passage times, even of steamships, were not precisely predictable, the limitation of hours of work was regarded as quite impracticable. On passenger vessels many of the journeys, as for example those from Glasgow to Liverpool or Edinburgh to London, took much longer than the nine, ten or 12 hours which at different times in the first half of the nineteenth century were regarded by landlubbers as constituting a normal working day.

Even on the regular-plying short-distance passenger packet boats wages were paid at infrequent intervals. Sailors employed by the crack City of Dublin Steam Packet Company on the Holyhead station in the 1850s were paid once in three weeks.[78] On cargo vessels payment was more commonly made at the end of each voyage. On the collier (sailing) brigs of the north-east captains received £8 9s, mates £5 6s, able seamen £4–£4 10s and cooks £5 to £5 10s, with the right to collect and sell the slush, i.e. the scum from boiled beef and pork. Apprentices, taken on for a period of five years, started at £8 and rose by £1 a year until their time expired.[79] Payment by the voyage meant that earnings were liable to fluctuate violently according to the season of the year and the state of the weather, but the typical collier brig rarely averaged more than ten trips annually. Even more unpredictable were the earnings of those who worked the collier brigs from the port of Sunderland. In 1854 a sliding scale of wages was adopted, varying with the freight charge per ton of coal carried to London. When coal was carried for 6s a ton, able seamen's wages were £3 15s a voyage; with coal at 12s a ton wages were £6 15s. Thus a man's yearly earnings fluctuated according to two variables; the state of the weather (and hence the number of voyages completed) and the state of the coal market. Men employed on the early screw colliers at this time were more fortunate. Though the rate paid them per voyage—£2 15s—was less than the payment per voyage to the men employed on the sailing vessels, their annual earnings at £80 8s were approximately double because the steamships could count on completing 30 round trips a year to the sailing ships' ten.[80] The great increase in the number of screw colliers in the third quarter of the nineteenth century served to aggravate the differential in earnings in the two types of ships. As both the speed and the carrying capacity of the steamships increased so the freights they charged were lowered. To stay in business the masters of the collier brigs were obliged to lower their freights in sympathy and to try and maintain their profits by reducing expenditure on maintenance and cutting down their wages bill (which usually took up a third of running costs).

Apart from questions of financial reward, the conditions of service varied enormously between the different types of ship in coastal service. Men employed in the steam packets could count on a more regular rhythm to their working lives. Times of payment as well as the duration of voyages were more predictable than they were on sailing ships. Because their main function was to carry passengers, the ships they worked were cleaner and more seaworthy and their living quarters more civilised. But the labour of able seamen as well as of firemen on these vessels could be very exacting. After their ship was tied up in harbour the crew of the City of Dublin Steam Packet Company's *Prince Arthur* were at regular intervals employed blacking the funnels, scraping the soot off the masts, cleaning the steam pipes, coating the ship's bottom or lending a hand to the painters. The crew was not even at liberty to do as it pleased on off-duty days. Against the date 26 December 1852 the master of the ship wrote 'Ship's company sent to church'.[81] On board the colliers which employed a majority of the sailors engaged in the English coasting trade living conditions were often grossly overcrowded and indescribably filthy.

Walter (later Viscount) Runciman, who owned a number of them, described what life was like in the crew's quarters under the topgallant forecastle. When the weather was the least bit rough the men's hammocks thumped against each other. A large part of the limited space available was littered with 'lumber ... ropes, blocks, tar barrels, water casks and all sorts of spare gear', while the stench from the anchor chain, 'covered with the mud and filth of the Thames' was 'intolerable until one became seasoned'. As the owners of collier brigs gradually lost out in the unequal struggle with the relentlessly efficient screw colliers and the wear and tear of their ships increased, it was the painter rather than the carpenter who was brought in to help keep up appearances because paint was less expensive than good, seasoned, timber.[82] One inevitable result of this skimping was that casualties among the ships were alarmingly high. The latterday vessels were described by one authority as 'a sorry fleet of floating death traps', an assertion borne out by the fact that no less than 675 collier brigs went to the bottom in the winter season of 1865-6.[83] Among sailors on this coast it was a common saying that 'if the North Sea were to dry up it would be found like a green field with Wilson's boats of Hull'—all of which were painted green.[84]

For the greater part of the nineteenth century collective efforts by the sailors to improve their wages and living standards were spasmodic and generally ineffective. In the packet service there is evidence that on 19 June 1861 eight men employed on the City of Dublin Steam Packet Company's vessel *Munster* made a collective protest against being obliged to work in the graving dock in Dublin after normal working hours on their ship and they were rewarded for their pains by being given the sack. Masters of the company's other ships were warned not to employ them.[85] In 1879 men employed on the Tyne, Wear and Tees formed the North of England Sailors and Seagoing Firemen's Union, but they failed to persuade the shipowners of the district to negotiate collective agreements. Eight years later one of the members of this union, J. Havelock Wilson, convinced of the ineffectiveness of an organisation which was confined to one region, established the National Amalgamated Union of Seamen and Firemen. In the trade boom of 1889-90 he succeeded in recruiting 65,000 members and in securing some improvements in wages; but the employers were adamant against any form of collective bargaining and set up the Shipping Federation for the express purpose of preventing it. The 'Federation Ticket' was only issued to those men who undertook not to refuse to work with non-union labour.[86] Shipowners also gave financial backing to William Collison's National Free Labour Association formed in 1893 to maintain a pool of 'free' labour available for filling the place of strikers. Quite apart from the employers' resistance to union recognition, many thousands of sailors remained completely untouched by trade unionism, being either self-employed or working closely alongside the ship's master. In this category were the small crews of the 'stackies' and 'stumpies' which plied between the East Anglian ports and the Pool of London and those who manned the sailing vessels out of Appledore on the north Devon coast.

Improvements in conditions on board ship were the product partly of changes in technology and partly the result of legislation. The design of coastal ships began to be modified in the early years of the twentieth century. Because of strong incentives for the quicker loading and discharge of ships and the requirements of the Merchant Shipping Acts of 1875, 1876 and 1890 in respect of the load line and for the better trimming of cargoes, holds were cleared of pillars and cantilever brackets were introduced.[87] At the same time the crews' quarters in the forecastle were raised to the level of the main deck with consequent benefits in improved lighting and ventilation. In the 1930s there were far more radical changes in design when the crews' quarters were moved to the stern of the vessel, well above the load line, while the forecastle head was confined to storing ship's equipment.[88] Although the tendency to move the bridge, funnel and crew's quarters has been attributed to changing economic and strategic conditions—the need for larger holds to facilitate the carriage of guns, steel plates and bulky machinery—it was also the outcome of the improved bargaining strength of the unions. It certainly made life at sea far more civilised.

The interventions of parliament in respect of the seaworthiness of ships were closely related to the occurrence of major disasters to shipping in the same way as the nineteenth-century legislation on public health followed closely in the wake of epidemics of cholera. Furthermore, as was the case with the railways, legislation designed to prevent accidents was at first primarily concerned to protect the lives of passengers rather than employees, as passengers were generally more articulate and they, or their next of kin, better able to exact compensation. After 1815 the demand for steam vessels was so great that there were neither sufficient well-qualified shipbuilders and engineers nor sufficient properly trained masters knowledgeable enough about steam engines to ensure safety at sea. The situation was summed up admirably by a Hull shipbuilder in 1839:

> Steam navigation has advanced more rapidly than men of experience and knowledge of machinery can be found to conduct it; hence we often find . . . in river packets in particular men advanced to the post of engineer who are mere automatons ignorant of the first principles of the machine over which they preside.[89]

The earliest steamboats put to sea without being subject to any government regulation as to the safety of their machinery, the number of passengers they were permitted to carry or the rule of the road they should follow when encountering other vessels. It took the destruction of the *Telegraph* steam packet at Norwich on 4 April 1817, and the death of many of its passengers through the explosion of its boilers, to persuade parliament to appoint a Select Committee on Boiler Pressures later that year. Although the Committee reported in favour of the appointment of inspectors to check the safety features of steamboats and a Bill was introduced to give effect to these recommendations, the House of Commons saw no occasion to panic and failed to give the measure its approval. The Bill's opponents pleaded that it was folly to legislate principally on the basis of one accident and that in any case steamboat proprietors were the best guardians of the safety of their own ships. But if Westminster did not recognise any urgency in the problem the shipping authorities on the Clyde soon did. Congestion of steamships on that river was so acute by the early 1820s and collisions and explosions so frequent that the Clyde Trustees were given power in 1825 to inspect steamboats and enforce regulations concerning the number of lifeboats they carried, how they were to be lit at night and how they should tie up when taking on and landing passengers. A Tyne Association of Steam Packet Owners assumed similar powers for the shipping of Newcastle and district from 1835 onwards. Meanwhile the Aldermen and Council of the City of London had found it necessary to limit the speed of steamboats plying in the Pool of London to half their normal rate because of the damage racing steamboats had inflicted on other river craft. Parliament did not stir again on the question until the number of shipwrecks reached alarming proportions in the early 1830s. It apparently required another major dramatic disaster, this time the sinking of the *Rothesay Castle* off Beaumaris on 17 August 1831, with the loss of over 100 lives, to convince the majority of MPs that a further enquiry into steamboat accidents was desirable.[90] Undoubtedly what persuaded the Commons to appoint a select committee on steamboat accidents later that year was the fact that an influential member of the House, Col. Sibthorp, had lost two relatives in the *Rothesay Castle*, and pestered the Government to take action.[91] Although, under Col. Sibthorp's chairmanship, the committee recommended such reforms as the professional examination of masters and mates, the registration of vessels and the introduction of masthead and other lights, its labours were as fruitless as those of its predecessor in 1817.

Some of the recommendations of Col. Sibthorp's committee were embodied in the Steam Navigation Act of 1846 which for the first time required all sea-going vessels to carry boats and to display lights, according to uniform regulations, after dark. At the same time parliament acknowledged the disadvantages of locally enforced 'rules of the road'—Liverpool's ships passed each other on the starboard side, ships registered elsewhere passed on the port side—and enforced a standard practice throughout the country. The Board of Trade for the first time obtained powers to receive reports on all accidents at sea and to appoint inspectors to check whether vessels were seaworthy. Gaps in the Act of 1846 were partly made good by the Steam Navigation Act of 1848 and the Mercantile Marine Act of 1850 and further legislation in the following year. By the mid-1850s passengers boarding a coastwise steamship were much better protected against disaster at sea than were their predecessors of the 1820s and 1830s.[92]

Insofar as sailors were employed on passenger vessels they too benefited from the better training of ships' officers and the more adequate provision of lights, lifeboats, etc. But most British seamen served on cargo vessels and the Board of Trade displayed a much greater reluctance to intervene in this branch of the merchant marine. In his famous book *Our Seamen. An Appeal*, which appeared in 1873, Samuel Plimsoll pointed out the outstanding abuses which made it inevitable that employment in the merchant navy was highly dangerous and second only to coalmining in terms of its annual mortality figures. Ships were sent to sea overloaded and with cargo piled so high on the decks that sailors were unable without great difficulty to reach the rigging in times of storm; cargo was carelessly, even dangerously, stowed; unseaworthy ships were sent from port over-insured so that, in the event of their sinking, they brought their owners a substantial profit; crimps entrapped drunken men into the service and kept them in their grip. Plimsoll gave further evidence of these malpractices when he spoke as a witness before the Royal Commission which was appointed to examine his charges in 1873. Eventually Parliament passed the Merchant Shipping Act in 1876 introducing a compulsory load line—the Plimsoll line—on all British registered ships and greatly strengthening the powers of the Board of Trade inspectors (first appointed in 1846). Although the Act had many shortcomings, it proved to be the most important legislative contribution to the improvement of the working conditions of the sailors employed round British and foreign coasts.

In at least one other respect the coastal shipping service was made less hazardous as an occupation before the First World War: the chain of lighthouses, lifeboats and rocket stations round the coasts of Britain was greatly extended and the quality of service provided vastly improved. Most of the early lighthouses were privately owned and, apart from the inadequacies of the kind of illumination provided, were sometimes administered with an eye more for the profit of the owners than the greater safety of ships at sea. The owners of the Skerries lighthouse on one of Britain's main trade routes near Anglesey, earned a net profit of £87,673 on total receipts from light dues paid by ships of £102,595 in the years 1827–33 inclusive.[93] From 1680 onwards the corporation of Trinity House had gradually taken over a number of privately owned lighthouses, but by an Act of 1836 it was given ownership of all lights round the coast of England and Wales as well as supervisory powers over those of Scotland and Ireland which were more directly administered by the Commissioners of Northern Lighthouses and the Dublin Ballast Board (from 1867 the Commissioners of Irish Lights). The corporation of Trinity House saw to it that money raised from light dues was devoted exclusively to the maintenance and improvement of the lighthouses and not, as had previously been the case, to a wide variety of other purposes like street lighting and paving as well. Meanwhile, in the first half of the nineteenth century candle lighting was replaced by, first, vegetable oil and then sperm oil lamps. In 1865 the first gas-lit high-candle-powered lighthouse was put in service in Dublin Bay. This example was followed by other stations round the British coast, although petroleum oil was more frequently used than gas as a source of power until, in the last two decades of the century, electric power began to be used, particularly after its successful installation at St Catherine's Point, Isle of Wight, in 1888.[94]

Where lights were inadequate or unavailing to prevent shipwreck the sailor's last hope was that there might be a rocket line or lifeboat to bring him safely ashore. Until the later 1830s his chances of being saved by life line were slim as the number of rocket stations were few and very indifferently manned. In 1858 control of rocket and mortar apparatus was assumed by the government and placed first under H.M. Customs and then, from 1857, under a department of the Board of Trade managing the Merchant Marine Fund. Under this new energetic direction the number of rocket stations increased rapidly from 198 in 1857 to 298 in 1886. Paralleling these improvements there was an impressive increase in the number of lifeboat stations established by the voluntarily supported National Institution for the Preservation of Life from Shipwreck (1824), renamed in 1854 the Royal National Lifeboat Institution.[95] Although the number of deaths from shipwreck remained distressingly high, many more lives were saved in proportion to the number of sailors employed in the 1880s than had been the case in the 1850s. In the nine years 1878–86 inclusive 5,592 lives were saved by lifeboats, 6,174 by rocket apparatus, and 96,360 by the boats of wrecked ships and by other ships.[96] The enormous wastage of the human resources of the industry was, at last, being substantially reduced.

4

The Foundation of the Railway System

I

The British railway system came into being through the efforts of the first generation of engineers to meet the needs of the rapidly expanding mining and textile industries. A modern railway has been defined as a publicly controlled means of transport possessing the four distinctive features of a specialised track, mechanical traction, the accommodation of public traffic and the conveyance of passengers.[1] The need for a more efficient method of carrying coal from the pithead to the waterside staith led to the development of a specialised track or railway; the need for a more efficient means of pumping water from tin and coal mines gave rise to James Watt's improvement in the steam engine in 1769; and the need of both cotton and coal industries for a more economical and rapid means of locomotion than the horse led to the adaptation of the steam engine to mechanical traction. Once the steam engine and the railway had been brought together the two other salient characteristics of a modern railway—the accommodation of public traffic and the conveyance of passengers—quickly followed.

Between 1574 and 1674 the quantity of coal carried coastwise from Newcastle to London rose by over 20 times.[2] As the best British forests became increasingly denuded to supply the navy and the charcoal industry of the Weald and Severn Valley the price of timber rose alarmingly. In the second half of the sixteenth century it rose at least twice as fast as the general rise in prices.[3] The increasing scarcity and high price of wood for domestic heating persuaded ever growing numbers of householders to use coal as a substitute. At the same time important industries such as brewing, salt-, glass- and brick-making either switched to the use of coal alone or used greatly increased quantities in the process of manufacture. The excessive cost of land transport meant that most coal sold in the market was carried by sea or by river. The business of marketing was largely confined to the spring and summer months when sailing vessels could expect with greater certainty to make the return journey to London, or other ports. From November to April the prospect of heavy gales on the east coast kept the sailing vessels in harbour at the same time as the rains and frosts transformed the land routes from the pits to the staiths into impassable quagmires. There were strict limits to the quantity of coal that could be stacked near the pit heads pending the improvement of the roads in spring. The staiths could easily take much greater quantities. What was urgently needed, then, was a satis-factory means of moving coal over land in winter. It was to remove this bottleneck that the wooden railway began to be introduced from the first decade of the seventeenth century.

At some date between October 1603 and October 1604 the first wooden rails were laid down at Wollaton in Nottinghamshire by Huntingdon Beaumont, lessee of coalpits from Sir Percival Willoughby, a substantial landowner of the district.[4] A few months later, in the course of 1605, the first wooden rails were laid down in the north-east coalfield at Bedlington in Durham. Before 1660 others followed in Shropshire and Scotland and at other places in the Severn Valley and the north-east. With the aid of these early wooden railways coal could be moved more speedily and cheaply to the sea or river bank. Un-doubtedly the need for them was greatest on Tyneside where coal production was expanding more rapidly than in any other part of the kingdom. It was estimated that some 20,000 horses were employed in the Newcastle coal trade in 1696 and that one group of pits at Whick-ham employed over 700 wains daily before the construction of railways made such a prodigal use of road transport unnecessary.[5]

At first the railway was given different names in the different regions of the country where it was employed. In the north-east the earliest lines were called *waggonways*. But it was the terms in use in Shrop-shire, *railroad* or *railway*, which ultimately gained general acceptance not only in preference to waggonway, but also to *groove*, the word used by Tennyson in *Locksley Hall* ('Let the great world spin for ever down the ringing grooves of change'), after his first railway journey had been made under cover of darkness and in ignorance of the nature of the track.[6]

Although the carriage of coal by wooden railway was greatly superior to the early methods of haulage, the wear and tear of the track made necessary the frequent renewal of the rails. At best, with light traffic, rails would have to be replaced within three years; with heavy traffic annual replacement was essential. The improvements in the methods of manufacturing iron during the latter part of the eigh-teenth century, particularly the patenting of the reverbatory furnace in 1766 and the puddling process in 1784, made it a feasible proposition first, to add a cast iron plate covering to the part of the wooden rail most exposed to wear and tear, and then to replace the wooden rail entirely by an iron one. A cast iron bar was laid on a wooden rail for the first time at Coalbrookdale in Shropshire in 1767. Rails made entirely of cast iron began to appear in the 1790s, their use being greatly encour-aged by the growth of iron production during the Napoleonic Wars and the increasing difficulty in obtaining imported timber because of war time interruptions to British shipping. More durable wrought iron rails began to be produced in 1808, by which time wooden rails

had practically disappeared. These were changes which were stimu-
lated by the scarcity prices of oats and hay and by the necessity to
make the most effective use of extensive horse power. By the first
decade of the nineteenth century, when the first experiments in steam
locomotive haulage were being conducted, the British Isles already
possessed an impressive total of 300 miles of railway track.[7]

Fortunately, from the viewpoint of the transport needs of the coal
industry, the Boulton and Watt patent for the manufacture of the
steam engine expired in 1800 and the early engineers, who were well
aware of the pressing need for improved methods of mechanical haulage of coal and tin, were free to adapt the steam engine to higher
boiler pressures and locomotive motion.

As a result of the boom in the tin-mining industry and the need
to pump water from the deeper workings there were probably more
steam engines in Cornwall than in any other county at the end of the
eighteenth century. Richard Trevithick (1771–1833), who made the
greatest contribution to the adaptation of the steam engine for tractive purposes, was born in the heart of the tin-mining area, the son of
the manager of Dolcoath mine and, in his early twenties, himself the
manager of a mine near Penzance. In 1800 he moved to Camborne
where on 28 December in the following year he tried out a steam road
carriage he had designed and built. Early one summer morning in
1803 he and his cousin drove another steam carriage at a speed of
eight miles an hour up Tottenham Court Road in London, acciden-
tally breaking down a garden fence at the end of the run.[8] These
exploits attracted the attention of Samuel Homfray, proprietor of the
Penydern colliery, near Merthyr Tydfil in Wales, who invited Trevithick to design a locomotive specifically for the $9\frac{3}{4}$-mile long railway
which ran from Penydern to Abercynon. Both there and at Torrington Square near Euston, London, where he ran the locomotive *Catch-
me-who-Can* round a circular track in 1808, the Cornish engineer
demonstrated the practicability of the steam locomotive. But his lack
of commercial acumen and the variety of his other mechanical interests
led to his ceasing his labours on the locomotive 'just when he should
have redoubled them'.[9] Nevertheless his achievements were impressive.
They were aptly summarised in a leading technical journal a generation
later:

> Trevithick was the real inventor of the locomotive. He was the
> first to prove the sufficiency of the adhesion of the wheels to the
> rails for all purposes of traction on lines of ordinary gradient, the
> first to make the return flue boiler, the first to use the steam jet
> in the chimney and the first to couple all the wheels to the engine.[10]

The problems which Trevithick had left to be solved were how to
strengthen the rails (which had frequently broken under the weight

of the early engines), and how to increase the power of the locomotive in relation to its weight so that it could outclass the best horses in speed.

Improvements in the railway track came gradually as wrought iron rails replaced the earlier cast iron variety in the 1830s and as refinements in design, such as the fish bellied pattern, first used extensively on the Liverpool and Manchester Railway in 1830, were more widely adopted. Apart from three designed by Trevithick, only 25 other locomotives had been built by 1823[11] and not one of them was decisively superior to horse traction. The slow progress in achieving a decisive breakthrough in the performance of the locomotive resulted in the Stockton and Darlington Railway using a mixture of stationary engines, locomotives and horse traction for working the regular traffic of the line after its opening in September 1825. Steep gradients precluded the use of locomotives on the Cromford and High Peak Railway in 1830.[12] The seal of the Newcastle and Carlisle Railway, opened in 1835, depicted a horse-drawn waggon, indicating that the triumph of the locomotive was not everywhere complete even ten years after the Stockton and Darlington line started in business.

Commercial conditions in Lancashire provided the occasion for the resolution of the outstanding uncertainties about motive power. The rapid growth of the cotton industry resulted in the population of Manchester increasing from about 20,000 in 1760 to an estimated 163,888 in 1824. Over the same span of time the population of Liverpool grew from 25,000 to 135,000. The customs receipts of Liverpool rose by at least eight times between 1770 and 1825.[13] In their prospectus, issued in 1824, the promoters of the Liverpool and Manchester railway complained that the merchants of the two cities were obliged to depend on the Mersey and Irwell Navigation and the Duke of Bridgewater's canal for the movement of their merchandise. 'These canal establishments' they wrote, 'were inadequate to the regular punctual conveyance of goods, at all periods. Strong in the enjoyment of their monopoly' they were charging 15s a ton for the conveyance of goods over the 30 miles, on occasion taking as long to get the goods through to Manchester as it did for the faster sailing ships to reach Liverpool from New York.[14]

In 1829, with their Bill safely through parliament and the greater proportion of the track already laid, the directors determined to settle once for all the disputed question of the mode of traction to be employed on the line. They offered a prize of £500 to the designers of a locomotive which did not exceed six tons in weight but which proved able to pull a load at least three times its weight, at a speed of not less than ten m.p.h. In the Rainhill Trials Robert Stephenson's *Rocket* was the only locomotive which complied with these conditions. Attaining a speed of 30 m.p.h., it gave a conclusive demonstration of the superiority of the steam locomotive. Through the introduction of the multi-tubular boiler the production of steam was enormously increased so that 'speeds were raised from about those of a carthorse to more than those of the fastest racehorse'.[15]

This technological triumph is one reason for regarding the opening of the Liverpool and Manchester Railway on 15 September as marking the beginning of the railway age. But this concern was also the first to combine *all* the features of modern railway mentioned in the opening paragraph of this chapter. As long ago as 1801 the Surrey Iron Railway had been open to the public use but it did not employ mechanical traction.[16] The Stockton and Darlington Railway, a quarter of a century later, did not fully qualify as it was not given over exclusively to mechanical traction and it carried few passengers. The Liverpool and Manchester Railway was unique in at least two important respects. From the date of its opening it was worked entirely with steam locomotive power and it was managed and run solely by the company which made all the arrangements for carriage of both goods and passengers.

II

What interested the investor after September 1830 was the $9\frac{1}{2}$ per cent dividend paid out with monotonous regularity by Britain's first inter-city railway company. An even higher dividend could have been distributed but this would have involved, under the terms of the Liverpool and Manchester Railway Act, a downward revision of charges. It so happened that in the years immediately following the opening of the new line other conditions also conspired to persuade the propertied classes that new railway projects offered the most promising rewards to the investor. The good harvests of the years 1832–5 helped the balance of payments and made credit easier. Conversions of Government stock to lower rates of interest in 1830 and 1834 reduced the attractiveness of this outlet for spare money. Railway shares seemed to offer more favourable prospects, with as much security as was found in Government funds.

In the years between 1825 and 1835 a total of 54 Acts had been passed authorising the construction of railways and resulting, by the end of 1838, in the opening of over 500 miles of track.[17] The most important component was the London and Birmingham Railway, opened in 1838, with its links via the Grand Junction Railway to Liverpool and the North Union to Preston.

Britain's economic growth was at its maximum rate in the 1820s and 1830s and there were ample funds available for investment. Under the impetus of the favourable financial conditions of the early 1830s the pace of railway promotion quickened. Between 1836–7 44 more

Acts were passed with the result that income-creating expenditure on railways rose from £1 million in 1834 to £9 million in 1839. It was the first British railway boom. The characteristics of the expansion are summarised in Table 3.

Table 3 *Number of companies, mileage and capital sanctioned by Railway Acts 1833–40*

Year	No. of companies sanctioned	Mileage sanctioned	Capital authorised (£ millions)	Railway share index (June 1840 = 100)
1833	4	218	5·5	69·3
1834	5	131	2·3	67·8
1835	8	201	4·8	71·1
1836	29	955	22·9	111·1
1837	15	543	13·5	81·4
1838	2	49	2·1	91·1
1839	2	54	6·5	79·9
1840	—	—	2·5	86·4

Source: R. C. O. Matthews: *A study in Trade Cycle History*, 1954, p. 107.

A violent trade recession in the USA in 1837 which depressed British exports to that country and a very poor harvest in 1838 with deficient harvests in the following three years pushed up the bank rate, severely reduced the availability of credit and undermined business confidence. In consequence there were very few new railway companies launched in 1838–9 and none at all in 1840. This does not mean that railway building came to a halt. On the contrary, these were years when the building of the more important lines, sanctioned earlier, was pushed ahead. London was linked by railway with Birmingham in 1838, with Bristol and Southampton in 1840, with Brighton in 1841 and with Dover in 1843. In Wales, Merthyr Tydfil was linked with Cardiff in 1841, and in Scotland a railway built right through the heart of the industrial lowlands connected Edinburgh with Glasgow, Greenock and Ayr in 1842. By 1844 there was a railway network of 2,000 miles, three-quarters of which had been built since 1839.

By 1844 the time was ripe for a great revival of promotional activity. Good harvests in 1842 and 1843, Peel's reduction of tariff duties, and the Bank of England's offer in January 1845 to make liberal advances on a wide variety of securities at the remarkably low rate of 2½ per cent were the preconditions of expansion. A fever of unbounded optimism in the future of railways swept the country. The railway mania of 1844–7 overshadowed in its magnitude the boom of a decade earlier.

Table 4 *Number of companies, mileage and capital sanctioned by Railway Acts 1841–50*

Year	No. of companies	Mileage sanctioned	Capital authorised (£ millions)	Railway share index (June 1840 = 100)
1841	1	14	3·4	83·8
1842	5	55	5·3	89·4
1843	3	90	3·9	98·2
1844	50	805	20·5	121·3
1845	120	2,896	59·5	149·0
1846	272	4,540	132·6	139·4
1847	184	1,295	39·5	117·1
1848	82	373	15·3	95·5
1849	35	16½	3·9	77·1
1850	3	6¾	4·1	70·4

Source: *Railway Returns*

Impressive though they are, the figures in the above table do not tell the whole story. Apart from Bills which gained the approval of Parliament there were as many as 600 other schemes which did not get as far as a first reading.[18]

At the height of the mania many extravagant schemes for railways were canvassed which stood little chance of ever becoming viable undertakings. These were the days of the 'traffic takers', employed by the promoters of new railways, to discover the potential traffic of the district through which the intended line would pass. Edward Watkin, a railway magnate, second only in importance to George Hudson the Railway King, gave a witty account of the kind of methods sometimes used by these early Victorian adventurers:

Between 1837 and 1845 inclusive, there were gentlemen who rode in their carriages and kept fine establishments, who were called 'traffic takers'. He stumbled over one of these gentlemen in 1844, who was sent to take the traffic on a railway called the Manchester and Southampton. It did not go to Manchester and it did not go to Southampton; but it was certainly an intermediate link between these places. This gentleman went to a place in Wilts where there was a fair, and there took the number of sheep on the fair day, and assuming that there would be the same number all the days of the year, he doubled or trebled the amount for what he called 'development' (Laughter) and the result was that he calculated that by sheep alone the Manchester and Southampton line would pay 15 per cent.[19]

Bearing in mind that much promotional activity was of this character it comes as no surprise to find that a substantial proportion of the railway building authorised in the mid 1840s was never carried out. A Parliamentary Select Committee in 1853 estimated that 'about 2,000 miles of railway involving an outlay of upwards of £40 millions have been sanctioned by Parliament and afterwards abandoned by the promoters without the leave of Parliament'.[20] Nevertheless the lines which *were* laid down as a result of projects launched during the years of the railway mania brought the total of route miles open to just under 7,500 by 1852. At least in respect of railways north of the Thames there is a remarkable degree of similarity between the railway map of 1852 and that envisaged by Dr (later Lord) Beeching under his 1963 scheme for the rationalisation of the railway network. By the early 1850s there were two through routes to Scotland; a relatively close network in the Midlands, Lancashire and the West Riding of Yorkshire; a line to Norwich and Yarmouth via Colchester, and railways through to the coast in both north and south Wales. The biggest remaining gaps were in the south and south-west and in mid-Wales. But, by and large, most promotional activity in the second half of the nineteenth century was for the construction of branch and feeder lines which pushed the total route mileage to 23,441 by 1912. The only major through route to be laid down after mid-century was the Great Central, an alternative route from London to the north, which was only completed in 1899 and was never very profitable.

III

After the superiority of the locomotive had been demonstrated on the Liverpool and Manchester Railway in 1830 the promoters of new lines had little difficulty in raising the necessary capital. Whereas in the 1820s the investing public had required a great deal of persuasion, through advertisements in the press and widely publicised promotional meetings, to place their savings in railway ventures, all that was normally required in the 1830s was the publication of a prospectus with invitations to the public to apply for shares. Applicants would then be sent letters of allotment indicating the number of shares to which they would be entitled, with a request that a deposit should be paid to the railway company's banker. The subscriber was thereafter able to exchange the banker's receipt for a scrip certificate which he held until the company gained its Act of Incorporation. Once Parliamentary authorisation had been obtained the investor could be called upon to pay instalments up to the full nominal value of his shares.[21]

Since the industrial north-west was the principal source of new wealth in Britain in the early decades of the nineteenth century it is scarcely surprising that this area provided most of the capital for the early railway projects. Very nearly half of the 4,233⅓ shares issued for the Liverpool and Manchester Railway in 1825 were taken up by citizens of Liverpool and Manchester. A thousand of the remainder were paid for by the Marquess of Stafford who, as chief proprietor of the Duke of Bridgewater's Canals, had a major stake in the prosperity of the area.[22] Over 78 per cent of the initial capital for the Manchester and Leeds Railway, opened in 1841, was held in the three counties of Lancashire, Yorkshire and Cheshire, more than half coming from Manchester alone. Lancashire supplied 98 per cent of the share capital of the Bolton & Preston Railway in 1837 and 96 per cent of that of the Blackburn, Darwen and Bolton Railway in 1845.[23] Outside the north-west, Lancashire capital was dominant in such widely scattered concerns as the Canterbury and Whitstable (1830),[24] London and Southampton (1840), Great Western (1841) and Eastern Counties (1841) railways.[25] With the development of the electric telegraph after 1846 and the predominance of its stock exchange, the London area grew in importance as a source of supply and marketing of railway capital. Although Lancashire capital was finding employment in railways all over the country from the early 1830s and although it could truly be said that there was a national market for railway capital by the mid-1840s, there were still the exceptions of railways mainly backed by local men of property. The subscription contract of the Furness Railway signed on 25 January 1844 reveals that the Duke of Buccleuch and the Earl of Burlington, the two principal landowners of the district, opted for £30,000 of the total of £56,500 initial capital of the new undertaking.[26] A little to the north, the Maryport and Carlisle Railway likewise was run 'entirely by local gentry and coalowners', apart from a 'freakish period' of some 15 months when it came under the control of George Hudson, the Railway King.[27] In the far north of Scotland in 1853 the 182 shareholders with a local interest in the newly launched Highland Railway contributed £48,710 of the £80,000 capital initially raised.[28] On the other hand with the more important North British Railway in 1844 the largest block of shares was held by Londoners.[29]

Although the construction of some of the less important lines was largely paid for by the local gentry it would be entirely misleading to suggest that this was a characteristic of the national pattern of railway finance. At least for the important group of companies which merged to form the Lancashire and Yorkshire Railway in 1847, it has been shown that nearly two-thirds of the capital came from trade and industry whereas the landed interest only subscribed eight per cent of the total.[30]

Despite the claim by a distinguished historian of transport that during the railway mania from 1845 ... the 'rage for shares infected

Source: Dyos and Aldcroft, *British Transport*, 1969.

Map 6   The Railway System in 1845

all classes from peer to peasant',[31] there is little evidence that wage-earners held any significant proportion of railway capital. A recent researcher has found that in the north-west 'the impecunious clerk ... was comparatively unimportant' as an investor and that there were likewise very few poor widows who were persuaded to risk their all on railway ventures.[32]

One result of the extravagant promotion of many uneconomic railways and excessive competition between companies in the years of the railway mania between 1845–7 was that the return on railway shares declined sharply. The average dividend on share capital which had been 5·48 per cent in 1845 fell to 3·31 per cent in 1850.[33] Both the Midland and the Lancashire and Yorkshire railways declared their lowest dividend—two per cent in each case—in 1850. In consequence the investor was no longer eager to subscribe to ordinary shares. He demanded the greater security offered by preference shares and debentures. By 1868 Henry Ayres was noting that

> The ordinary paid-up Share Capital, which ought to constitute the foundation upon which all the other descriptions should be secured, has been overwhelmed by the united claims of Preferential Shareholders, and the holders of Debenture Bonds, in many of our leading Railway Companies.[34]

In 1863 Richard Moon, the chairman of the London and North Western Railway—the largest railway company in Britain—lamented that there were 'no proprietors willing to come forward to make a railway. They are made by contractors, engineers and speculators, who live on the fear of the companies.' The contractors did indeed play a much larger part in railway promotion at this time. In the hectic days of the mania they had brought together huge armies of navvies with all the paraphernalia of shovels, planks, barrows, explosives, waggons and horses that went with railway building, and when the boom was over they were reluctant to disband resources so painstakingly assembled. But at the same time investors were far more reluctant to part with their savings, and the railway companies were short of funds. A bargain was therefore struck between the contractors and the companies. Parliamentary authorisation for new railway building was obtained and the contractors were offered continued employment provided they were willing to accept payment in the form of the mortgage bonds of the railway company rather than in cash. Thus the best known of all the contractors, Thomas Brassey, undertook building for the North Staffordshire Railway in return for payment of £45,000 in the company's bonds. Another contractor, E. L. Betts, was given £60,000 worth of the securities of the West End and Crystal Palace Railway for which he undertook the work of construction. Often it was only possible for the work of construction to continue through the cooperation of the banks. When the railway lacked the means of immediate payment the contractor would be given an 'acknowledgement under seal' that he would be paid at a subsequent date. These Lloyds Bonds—so called from the name of John Horatio Lloyd, the barrister who devised the way out of the impasse—enabled the contractor to obtain an advance from his banker and therewith to pay for the men and materials he needed to use.[35]

Such risky methods of building the 'contractors' lines' like the Metropolitan, the London, Chatham and Dover, the Metropolitan District and the Cambrian, were abruptly halted with the disastrous collapse of the leading London discount house of Overend, Gurney and Company in May 1866. But recovery was rapid. The railway capital market was more buoyant in the later 1860s and early 1870s when little difficulty was experienced in raising fresh funds. However, between the later 1870s and the first World War, the enormous growth in British overseas investment made it increasingly difficult for British railway companies to raise fresh capital, especially after 1905, except on markedly more disadvantageous terms. The evidence from at least two of the major companies, the North Eastern and the London and North Western shows that their capital accounts went increasingly in the red before 1914 to the detriment of some of the engineers' plans for modernisation of equipment.[36]

For all their vicissitudes British railways before 1914 never needed to call for government help in the raising of capital. Government funds were provided for railway building in Ireland but the Irish case was always considered a special one. The only instance of financing other than from private sources on the other side of the Irish Sea was Hull Corporation's contribution of £100,000 to the capital of the Hull and Barnsley Railway in 1862.[37]

IV

When comparison is made between the capital costs of railways in Britain, the USA, and the leading European countries it would appear that the British railway system was expensively and extravagantly built. An estimate of costs up to the end of 1884 gave the average cost per mile of line in Britain as £42,486 compared with £36,508 in Belgium, £27,704 in France, £21,236 in Germany and £11,000 in the USA.[38] Even when allowance is made for the fact that land was remarkably cheap in the USA (and sometimes given to the railway companies by the government) and that France and Germany were, at that time, less densely populated and less industrialised than was Great Britain, there can be no gainsaying the fact that the building of British railways was characterised by a wasteful use of time and resources.

It was certainly the view of many contemporaries that landowners held railway companies up to ransom before they would part with any portion of their property. J. C. Jeaffreson, in his life of Robert

Stephenson, published in 1864, wrote that 'any amount that could by any means be squeezed from the funds of a railway company under the name of compensation public opinion decided to be legally and honourably acquired'.[39] The chairman of the Eastern Counties Railway told a Parliamentary Select Committee in 1839 that his company had spent £600,000, out of a total of capital plus loans of £2,133,333, on acquiring the necessary land just to get the railway from London to Colchester—and the planned terminus of the line was Yarmouth! One of the landowners compensated by this company, Lord Petre of Ingatestone Hall, received £120,000 for land worth £5,000.[40] The Secretary of the London and Southampton Railway told the same Committee that he considered that on his line 'a great deal too much money' had been paid out to landowners in 'excessive compensation'.[41] The Chairman of the London and Croydon Railway cited the case of a family which owned 14 acres demanding £4,500 in compensation. The jury to whom the company appealed valued the property at £2,650.[42] On the other hand some landlords quickly appreciated that a nearby railway would increase, rather than lower, the value of their property and they were willing to settle with the railways on a reasonable valuation. Not so far from Croydon, the South Eastern Railway was acquiring land at an average price of between £80 and £90 an acre[43] and in Yorkshire the Leeds and Selby Railway's costs for land purchases did not greatly exceed the board's original estimates.[44] Overall estimates of the cost of land as a proportion of the railways' total costs have been attempted on at least two occasions. J. S. Jeans in 1887 estimated that, at an average cost of £4,000 per mile, the railways had paid about £76 million, or one tenth of their total capital, on acquiring some 235,000 acres of land. In 1952 Harold Pollins, after examining the finances of a sample of 27 companies, found that they had spent 13·9 per cent of their capital in purchasing land. He concluded that although British railway companies would obviously have benefited from buying their land more cheaply 'this would not have appreciably reduced the difficulties'.[45]

The method of obtaining Parliamentary authorisation for the construction of railways was very time consuming and wasteful of the companies'—and the nation's—resources. What was needed was an impartial tribunal to examine the need for railways in each area of the country and to decide on the particular routes the lines should follow. The Departmental Committee of the Board of Trade, presided over by Gladstone in 1844, made a strong recommendation that an independent body should be set up to vet railway projects so that unnecessary duplication of effort might be avoided. This proposal did not at all suit the railway interest, successfully mobilised by George Hudson. Gladstone's plan was quickly stifled. The result of the Government's shortsightedness was that a golden harvest was reaped by the solicitors who acted for the all-too-numerous railway companies promoted during the mania while a disappointingly meagre return was given to many of the shareholders. The situation in Westminster resulting from the failure of government to give a firm lead was the subject of frank comment by one of the most successful of the railway solicitors, George Burke, of Burke and Venables, who told the Lords' Select Committee on Railways in 1846 that the expense of getting some railway Bills through Parliament was 'quite frightful', because the supporters of rival schemes made objections to the 'minutest trifles' in order to wreck their opponents' plans. When asked 'Do you know what number of objections have been made by one party against a Bill?' he replied: 'I was guilty myself of taking 400 once and discussing them for 23 days upon minute matters.'[46]

The consequence of giving a free hand to every vested interest, however petty and sectional it might be, was to inflate the parliamentary costs of major railway undertakings. Because there were five competing schemes for a railway from London to Brighton £180,000 of shareholders' money was spent in wrangling over the respective merits of each. Eventually only one line was authorised and the chairman of the successful company admitted that 'a great deal of trouble and expense' would have been saved if an 'impartial board' had settled the question at an early date.[47] To get the first Bill for the GWR approved by Parliament cost the company £87,197 or about £775 per mile of line constructed.[48] But the supreme example of extravagance was the struggle of the Great Northern to obtain its Act in 1845–6. The company and its allies spent £433,000 on steering the Bill through Parliament. Allowing for the substantial expenditure of its opponents, it is safe to say that at least half a million pounds was expended in securing Parliamentary authorisation before the first sod of earth for the new railway could be cut.[49]

These are the outrageous instances which naturally find prominence in the literature about the railways; but how serious was the problem in the aggregate? J. S. Jeans estimated that, up to 1882, about £16 millions had been spent by the railways in securing Parliamentary powers and that this sum was no more than two per cent of the capital outlay of the companies.[50] Taking the longer span of time up to 1914 it seems unlikely that any larger proportion of total capital outlay went on Parliamentary expenditure.

Mr M. Robbins suggested that compared with a total investment of £1,100 millions on British railways before 1915 the 'picturesque episodes' of extortionate selling prices for land and inflated parliamentary expenses 'have no significance'.[51] It may be conceded that at the time of confident expansion, when Britain was the workshop of the world, wasteful expenditure on railway promotion seemed a small price to pay for the substantial economies in transport costs the railways made possible. In the longer view, however, the fact that this part of the capital expenditure of the railways was some 16 per cent (13·9 per cent on account of land, two per cent on account of Parliamentary costs) and was much greater than it need have been *was* of significance. By the end of the nineteenth century British manufactures were being elbowed out of European and American markets by the cheaper products of Germany and the USA. One reason why British goods were more costly was that ton-mile freight rates were higher in Britain than in Germany and America. Without an over-burdened capital structure British rates could have been lower. Furthermore additional funds would have been available for vital improvements in signalling, the braking of waggons and the introduction of electric locomotion.

V

By the beginning of the railway age the requirements of the earlier canal building had already brought into being a new class of civil-engineering contractor accustomed to organising the labour of another new class, the 'navigators' or 'navvies'. With the construction of the railways the contractors became, for a few years, the biggest employers of labour in the country and the armies of navvies they mobilised one of the largest categories of workers employed apart from agriculture and textiles. The work of constructing a railway line was usually the subject of an elaborate division of labour. In charge of the whole undertaking was the engineer who was directly responsible to the board of directors for the progress and successful completion of the line. He, in turn, issued instructions to the contractor who undertook the preparation of the whole of the necessary earthworks and buildings. On the great trunk routes responsibility for the work of construction was generally divided between a number of contractors in order to expedite the completion of the work although the key sections would be given to one of the leading firms such as Peto and Betts, Jacksons or Firbanks. In the case of the London and Southampton Railway, completed in 1840, the engineer Joseph Locke employed the famous contractor Thomas Brassey to build the important central stretch, 36 miles long, between Basingstoke and Winchester, whilst using the services of men of lesser reputation to complete other parts of the undertaking.[52] All the great contractors let out a part of their work, generally the more straightforward portion of the line, to sub-contractors who were men who possessed about £1,000 to £1,500 of capital and hired the services of a number of gangs of navvies.[53] The lowest rank of entrepreneur was that of 'butty man' or ganger, who under orders from the contractor or sub-contractor, undertook more limited assignments such as the removal of an agreed number of waggon loads of earth from a cutting. He paid the members of his gang and kept a 'cut' for himself. Some butty men acquired a well-deserved reputation for good management and craftsmanship in bricklaying, drainage work or other tasks and wise contractors made the maximum use of these specialised skills. Brassey was constantly advising his agents: 'let each man keep to his speciality'.[54]

Railway building undoubtedly provided the occasion for the growth of large-scale enterprise in the contracting business. Samuel Morton Peto, one of the largest contractors, was employing 14,000 men in 1850,[55] a larger number than the entire New Model army which fought at Naseby. On his death in 1870 Thomas Brassey left a fortune of £3,200,000, most of which had been acquired from his work as a railway contractor. Between 1844 and 1861 when some of the most important main lines were completed he was sole or joint contractor for 1,940 miles of railway, or approximately one sixth of the total till then built in Great Britain.[56]

The labour force was made up in part of skilled men including carpenters, bricklayers, masons and 'miners', whose pay in the 1840s rose to 5s a day in exceptional cases, and in part of the unskilled members of the butty gangs including trenchers, excavators and runners (those who carried the earth away in wheelbarrows), whose rates of pay were little more than half those of the craftsmen.[57] Amongst the unskilled the Irish predominated, especially in the north of England and the lowlands of Scotland. In the construction of railways further south redundant agricultural labour was more frequently employed. A witness before a Select Committee in 1827 declared that in any job where there was extensive excavation work he would 'not feel in the least surprised to find, that of 100 men employed in it, 90 were Irish'.[58]

A contemporary historian gave a very uncomplimentary description of the labour force that built the British railway network:

Rough alike in morals and manners, collected from the wild hills of Yorkshire and Lancashire, coming in troops from the fens of Lincolnshire, and afterwards pouring in masses from every country in the empire; displaying an unbending vigour and an independent bearing; mostly dwelling apart from the villagers near whom they worked; with all the propensities of an untaught undisciplined nature; unable to read and unwilling to be taught; impetuous, impulsive and brute-like, regarded as the pariahs of private life, herding together like beasts of the field, owning no moral law and feeling no social tie, they increased with an increased demand, and from thousands grew to hundreds of thousands. They lived but for the present; they cared not for the past, they were indifferent to the future.[59]

In some respects this is a misleading picture. A contemporary of the railway navvies, Robert Owen (1771–1858), was constantly asserting that 'a man's character is made *for* him and not *by* him'. The condition of the navvies illustrated more strikingly than did the lives of any other industrial group at the time the large measure of truth in Owen's maxim. One of the great contractors, S. M. Peto, denied that the labourers in his employment were an uncontrollable lot. He found them 'easily managed'. The engineer, I. K. Brunel, agreed. If well treated, he said, they were a 'very manageable' set of people.[60]

In those cases where the men's behaviour was anti-social the root of the trouble lay in the system of competitive tendering by the less affluent contractors anxious to climb the ladder of success. This system may well have ensured that the board of directors of the railway companies got the work done as cheaply as possible. But it also resulted in unduly low estimates and exceptionally early completion dates being quoted in frenzied efforts to secure contracts. To make what were regarded as acceptable rates of profit the contractors were then under the necessity of paring down expenses to the minimum. In the first place there was scope for economies in the kind of accommodation provided for the labourers. Where it was at all acceptable to the people of the locality, the men were crowded together in lodgings in the nearby towns and villages, as they were at Knaresborough in 1851 when the East and West Riding Junction Railway was under construction.[61] But often the workings were too remote or the local inhabitants too hostile for this to be possible. It was on such occasions that the humanity or the greed of the contractor became manifest. Thomas Jackson, who employed between three and four thousand men in the mid-1840s, was in the first of these two categories. He built large wooden cottages with two to three rooms, each cottage to accommodate one labourer and his family, and charged the uneconomic rent of between 1s 6d and 2s a week. By contrast the contractors who built the line between Carlisle and Glasgow were content to let men crowd into filthy, disease ridden, mud huts only 12 feet square. Not surprisingly human beings so accommodated tended to lose any sense of decency or self-respect.

Another way in which hard-pressed contractors could recoup losses arising from underquoting for contracts was to run 'tommy', or truck shops, compelling the labourers to accept at least a part of their wages, not in the coin of the realm, but in truck tickets expendable only in the contractor's store where the prices of food and other necessities were higher than in the nearest independent retail shops. There was every justification for Thomas Jackson's opinion that where this practice prevailed the men were 'most cruelly used'. It was often the case that the contractors made more profit from their truck shops than from the railway works they had undertaken to complete. Peto cited the case of one man who had made £1,400 in four weeks from his 'tommy shop'.[62]

That the labourers were on occasions unruly and violent in their behaviour arose from the unnecessary dangers that they were some-times called upon to face when at work. It happened that men's lives were put at risk because a contractor had allowed too short a time for the completion of the contract and therefore resorted to time-saving short cuts such as undermining dangerously large quantities of earth. When driving in charges of dynamite into hard rock expense could be spared if copper stemmers were used instead of the more costly, but safer, lead variety. The only drawback was that hammer-ing the copper stemmers could cause sparks, the premature explosion of the charge and the gruesome injury or death of the workmen involved.

The most notorious episode in the heroic age of railway building in Britain was the construction of the Woodhead tunnel in a bleak and remote corner of Cheshire between 1839–45. One of the surgeons who attended those employed in making the tunnel reported 32 men killed, with 23 cases of compound fractures, 74 of simple fractures and 140 serious cases resulting from burns and blasts. With charac-teristic exactitude Edwin Chadwick showed that the casualty rates amongst men making the Woodhead tunnel—over three per cent killed and 14 per cent wounded—were higher than those of the British armies engaged in the battles of the Peninsular War and at Waterloo.

Even at the time of the railway mania there was available a steam-powered mechanical excavator capable of moving 1,500 cubic yards of earth in twelve hours at a cost in fuel of only 12s per day.[63] Had machines such as this been employed in building British railways some of the loss of life associated with undermining might have been avoided. But it was not until the 1890s when the last main line railway, the Great Central, was being built that contractors found it worth while to employ any mechanical aids for the movement of earth, although Brassey used steam excavators when building the Grand Trunk railway in Canada in the 1850s because he found it difficult to secure labourers even at 7s 6d a day—50 per cent above the maximum rate paid in England.[64]

Many men's lives would have been saved it the government of the day had been prepared to follow the advice given by Edwin Chad-wick to the Select Committee on Railway Labourers in 1846. He urged that contactors should be made liable to pay compensation to injured workmen or to the next of kin of those killed even when it was the workman who appeared to be the one immediately responsible for the accident. He reminded the committee that in France, where this was the law, the accident rate had been greatly reduced. But although the committee expressed sympathy with the proposal, the government was not prepared to act and before long the numbers of labourers employed decreased rapidly and Parliament and the public soon lost whatever interest they once had in the problem of the railway navvies.

5

The Economic and Social Effects of Railways

I

Contrary to the original expectation, the opening of Britain's early railways had a more immediate impact on the pattern of passenger travel than it did on the goods traffic. With very few exceptions, whenever a new line was opened to traffic there was a spectacular increase in the number of persons travelling along the route served compared with the numbers previously using the road. After the opening of the Newcastle and Carlisle Railway throughout its entire length on 18 June 1838 eleven times as many persons travelled by train as had previously gone by coach.[1] Before the railway enabled the weavers and mechanics of Dundee to reach the seaside resort called the Ferry very few of them made the effort to reach it as the only means of travel was on foot or by one of the carriers' slow moving carts. In seven months of 1839, however, not less than 61,876 third-class tickets were sold on this short line.[2] By the mid-1830s parliamentary committees examining proposals for railway Bills took it to be axiomatic that, once a railway was opened, the number of persons travelling by train would be at least double the number who had previously travelled on foot, by coach or by any other road vehicle. The Leicester and Swannington Railway, which in the first half of 1843 gained only 5·1 per cent of its revenue from passengers, was an exception to the general rule that the first use to which the new railways was put was greatly to augment the volume of passenger transport.[3] In England and Wales as a whole there was a 20-fold increase in the number of persons travelling by train over the 30 years 1840–70.[4]

If at first some railways, exploiting travellers' preference for the speediest means of transport, charged the first-class passengers more than they would have had to pay making the same journey inside a coach, and the second-class passengers more than they would have been charged for an outside seat, it was not long before a majority of the companies decided to give railway fares the competitive edge over the charges for coach travel. Between Leeds and York, for example, the fare charged for a seat on the outside of a coach was 3s for a 31 mile journey occupying four hours. For the first few months the fare for the 80-minute train journey was 3s 6d, but this was soon afterwards lowered to 2s 6d to give the passenger by railway the advantages both of time and of cost.[5] It was a policy which contributed handsomely to the rapid increase in the volume of rail traffic. Initially also a cautious view was taken about the possibility of allowing children to travel at less than the full fare. In October 1831 the Liverpool and Manchester Railway, while allowing infants under three years of age to travel free, refused any concessions to children above that age.[6] At the same time, however, the Canterbury and Whitstable line allowed children under twelve to travel at two thirds of the adult fare and it was this policy of concessions to the under-12s which became generally adopted.[7] By the early 1840s half fares for the under-12s were generally available, making family rail travel more widespread and still further augmenting the volume of passenger traffic.

It took some time for the directors of the leading railway companies to accustom themselves to the idea that railway travel was appropriate for any other than the well-to-do classes. The poor were not encouraged to travel unless it was in search of work or to fulfil urgent family responsibilities. When he was asked in 1839, what plan the Great Western Railway had for the conveyance of third-class passengers, the company's secretary, Mr C. A. Saunders, answered:

'There has been no decision of the directors on that subject, but I think they will probably send carriages once a day, perhaps with merchandise: carriages of an inferior description, at very slow speed for the accommodation of those persons, and at a very low price; perhaps, too, it may only be done at night.'[8]

Like the Great Western, the London and Southampton at first made no provision for that type of traveller who had gone by carrier's waggon rather than by the outside of a coach, because it was cheaper. On this railway in 1839 'Each train' had 'a first class, corresponding to the inside of the stage coach; and a second class, in the absence of cushions, stuffings and other comforts, and in the exposure or partial exposure to the weather, corresponding to the outside.'[9] There was no hint of a third class. Where a company did decide to provide accommodation for the lower orders it was generally of the most primitive character. This was the case with the Manchester and Leeds Railway, whose board of directors decided in August 1838 that there should be three classes of carriage provided:

First class:	six inside—complete with everything which can conduce to comfort.
Second class:	to carry twenty-four passengers—divisions chair high—windows in door but none in panels—and no cushions.
Third class:	open boxes—no roofs, nor buffer springs.[10]

Robert Stephenson was taking what was then a moderately radical stand when he told the Select Committee on Railways on 2 July 1839 that there was 'a class of people who [had] not yet had the advantage from the railways which they ought, that is the labouring classes'.[11] Although the practice of providing third-class carriages on trains gradually spread it was not until the passing of Gladstone's Railway Act in 1844, with its clauses making the provision of third-class accommodation on at least one train a day in each direction through each company's network obligatory, that the labouring classes could count on penny-a-mile travel under the minimum conditions of comfort. Thereafter the number of third-class passengers increased more rapidly than did the numbers in the other two classes (see Figs 6 and 7). Between 1849 and 1870 the number of third-class passengers increased by nearly six times whereas the increase in second- and first-class travel was fourfold. The boost to third-class travel was further increased after 1874 when the Midland Railway abolished the second class and greatly improved the comfort of the third-class carriages. This initiative obliged other main line companies to follow suit so that by 1890 the difference in the standards of accommodation had been substantially narrowed. The companies had by then learned

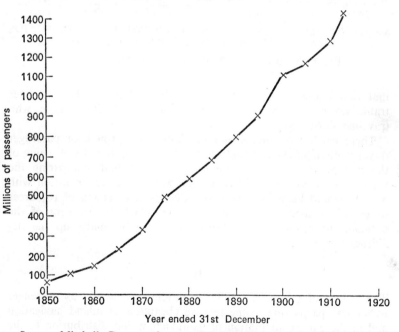

Source: Mitchell, Deane, Abstract of British Historical Statistics, 1962.

Figure 5   Growth of Railway Passenger Traffic 1850–1914 (Ireland not included)

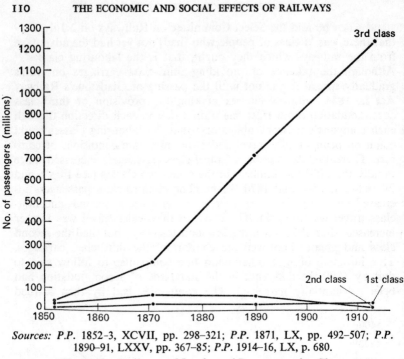

Sources: P.P. 1852-3, XCVII, pp. 298-321; *P.P.* 1871, LX, pp. 492-507; *P.P.* 1890-91, LXXV, pp. 367-85; *P.P.* 1914-16, LX, p. 680.

Figure 6   Railways: Number of Passengers by Class

that they could count on getting the lion's share of the passenger traffic revenue—it was 72½ per cent that year—from those who travelled third class.

There can be no doubt that the impressive growth of passenger travel made a significant contribution to the wealth and well-being of the nation. It is the estimate of Dr Hawke that, comparing the situation as it was in 1870 with a railway system in operation with what it would have been without railways, a diversion of resources to the older forms of transport costing about six per cent of the national income would have been necessary to make up the deficiency.[12]

II

The failure of rail goods traffic to develop as rapidly as passenger travel was partly due to the relative cheapness of inland navigation and to the earlier adaptation of manufacture and distribution to the transport facilities provided by the canal companies. In both the West Riding and the West Country, for example, the products of the woollen cloth mills were distributed through the canal network. The

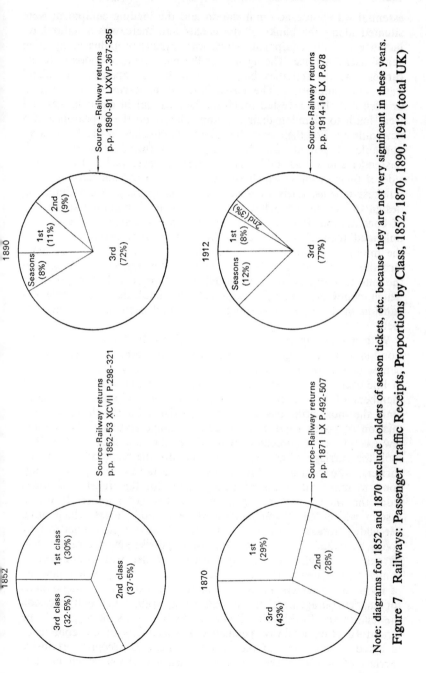

Note: diagrams for 1852 and 1870 exclude holders of season tickets, etc. because they are not very significant in these years.

Figure 7   Railways: Passenger Traffic Receipts, Proportions by Class, 1852, 1870, 1890, 1912 (total UK)

essential warehouse accommodation and the loading equipment were situated along the banks of the canals and there was a natural reluctance to scrap equipment which was capable of giving many more years' useful service. The agents for the movement of goods were the carriers, whose activities had grown with the expansion of inland water communication. The larger carrying concerns such as Sutton or Pickfords had invested much of their capital in canal barges and were loath to abandon their use immediately on the appearance of a new railway. For their part the railway companies in the 1830s were not able to provide for the simultaneous full expansion of both passenger and goods traffic. They therefore developed first of all that side of their business which was easiest to expand and promised the quickest returns. Early first-class passenger carriages were similar in design to the stage coaches and presented few unfamiliar difficulties of construction. For the most part passengers obligingly loaded and unloaded themselves. But apart from the coal waggons, familiar in the mining areas of the north-east and on other coalfields, the construction of rolling stock for the carriage of goods and livestock, and the business organisation of goods traffic presented new problems which could conveniently await solution until the remarkable expansion in demand for passenger travel had been in some measure met.

With a few important exceptions, such as the Great Western, the London and Birmingham and the Grand Junction, the railway companies of the 1830s were small concerns operating under fifty miles of line each. The average route mileage of the companies which were members of the Railway Clearing House in 1846 was 41 miles.[13] Only the most primitive arrangements existed for the through transmission of goods beyond the lines of a single company. With some few exceptions of companies which from the first themselves undertook the carriage of goods, it was generally the responsibility of the carriers, who paid a toll for the use of the railway companies' waggons, to make all necessary arrangements for the transfer of goods from the waggons of one company to those of another. It was a system which led to innumerable disputes and delays which often persuaded traders that it was still wisest to advise the carrier to take goods by canal or, where feasible, by coastwise steamer rather than by rail. Although the Railway Clearing House was established in January 1842 it was not until five years later that the first meeting of its goods managers' conference drew up a list of recommendations for the encouragement of through goods traffic. On that occasion the chairman, Braithwaite Poole, formerly goods manager of the Grand Junction Railway, persuaded the members of the conference to agree to the policy of the railway companies becoming exclusive carriers of goods on their own networks, a decision which in most

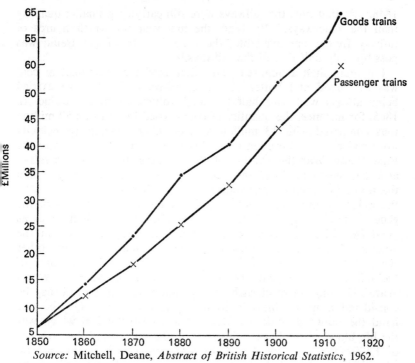

Source: Mitchell, Deane, *Abstract of British Historical Statistics*, 1962.

Figure 8 Goods Train Receipts and Passenger Train Receipts 1850–1914 (Ireland not included)

cases substantially reduced the cost of carriage. Other decisions of great importance included the acceptance of a common classification for goods, operative from 1 September 1847, and the division of goods receipts between the companies on the basis of mileage travelled on each company's lines.[14]

These decisive improvements in organisation, together with a revival of trade after the serious setback of 1847 resulted in a doubling of the railway companies' receipts from goods (including cattle, parcels and mail) in the short space of four years. By the end of 1852 receipts from goods exceeded receipts from passengers for the first time in the history of British railways.[15] The more business-like organisation of railway freight traffic also ensured the eventual eclipse of inland waterways as the principal medium for the movement of goods. It was in the early 1850s that the volume of goods carried by railway first exceeded the volume carried by the canals. There are no reasonably complete figures for canal traffic until 1888 but 40 leading companies carried an aggregate of nearly 20 million tons in

1848.[16] At that time the railways were still carrying a smaller quantity than the waterways.[17] By 1856, the first year for which figures of railway freight are available, the canals' share of the traffic was possibly only half that of the railways.[18]

For more than a hundred years after 1850 the movement of coal was the bread and butter of British railways, the tonnage carried being always well over half the total volume of freight traffic. In 1865, for instance, the quantity of coal carried by rail was 50 million tons compared with 13 million tons of other minerals (principally iron) and nearly 32 million tons of general merchandise.[19] Up to the First World War the volume of the railways' traffic in minerals— and that meant predominantly coal—increased at a faster rate than the traffic in general merchandise, so that whereas in the mid-1860s the weight of minerals carried was less than twice the weight of the general merchandise by 1912 it was over three and a half times as great (see Fig. 9).[20] Despite the remarkable preponderance in the volume of the mineral traffic it was less profitable than the other types of freight, earning only 45 per cent of the freight revenue of the railways in the years before the outbreak of the First World War.[21] The movement of such vast quantities of coal by rail may be considered a mixed blessing to the British economy. On the one hand the railways made available, at less cost, the fuel which was the life blood of the basic industries; on the other hand the presence of 1,400,000 mostly small capacity waggons, a majority but not all of which were required for the movement of coal, cluttered up the tracks, slowed the pace and increased the cost of movement of the more profitable general merchandise, thus contributing to the lack of competitiveness of British exports in world markets. The congestion of the railway network would have been even greater if the railway companies had had the same degree of success in displacing coastwise traffic in coal as they had in reducing the amount that was carried by canal. But it was not until 1867 that the volume of rail-borne coal brought into London exceeded the quantity carried by sea, and this preponderance was relatively short-lived. By 1898 the sea-borne total once more exceeded the quantity brought to the capital by rail as an ever growing number of Thames-side gasworks found it cheaper to depend upon the screw colliers coming from Tyneside and Teesside rather than the slow moving mineral train (see Fig. 4, p. 73).[22]

The railways' contribution to the prosperity of the coal-mining industry came, for the most part, indirectly, through their cheapening of delivery costs and the consequent vast extension of the use of coal in manufactures and in domestic heating; their influence on the expansion of the iron and steel industry was far more direct. With the exploitation of Nielson's hot air blast after 1828, the output

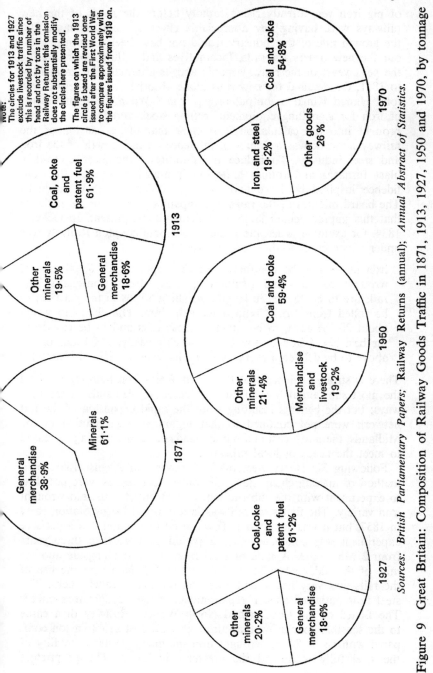

Note:
The circles for 1913 and 1927 exclude livestock traffic since this is recorded by number of head and not by tons in the Railway Returns: this omission does not substantially modify the circles here presented.

The figures on which the 1913 circle is based are revised ones issued after the First World War to compare approximately with the figures issued from 1919 on.

Sources: British Parliamentary Papers; Railway Returns (annual); Annual Abstract of Statistics.

Figure 9 Great Britain: Composition of Railway Goods Traffic in 1871, 1913, 1927, 1950 and 1970, by tonnage

of pig iron was already rising rapidly before the needs of the new railways were having any appreciable effect on total demand. But the growth rate of the industry would not have been sustained without the new orders for rails, locomotives and rolling stock. During the peak years of the railway mania and its aftermath, i.e. from 1844 to 1851, the demand for new rails alone absorbed 18 per cent of the total United Kingdom output of pig iron.[23] When the requirements of iron for signalling equipment, rolling stock and locomotives are brought into the calculation it is clear that the expansion of the railway network was a dominant influence on the growth of the iron and steel industry. To induce them to instal the most up-to-date blast furnaces and rolling mills the iron-masters needed the confidence inspired by large and sustained orders for their products. The board minutes of the railway companies provide ample evidence that this unprecedented large-scale demand was present. In October 1834, for example, when the London and Southampton Railway was under construction, its directors resolved:

iron masters to be contracted for the supplying of 6,000 tons of wrought iron rails and a suitable quantity of cast iron chairs. The rails are to be 15 feet in length, weighing 50 lbs to the yard . . . to be rolled from No. 2 refined wrought iron. The chairs to weigh about 20 lbs each, to be fitted to these rails and to be cast from the best No. 1 iron that will file and chip easily. 1,000 tons of the above to be delivered every two months from the date of contract.[24]

There is strong evidence that the south Wales iron industry received the most substantial boost from the increasing demands of the railways; but the benefits resulting from the rapid expansion of the rail network were not confined to that region, iron production in the Midlands, the north-east and the lowlands of Scotland being increased to meet the needs of local railways.

Following Sir Henry Bessemer's discovery, in August 1856, of a method of making cheap steel, the railway companies were not slow to experiment with the substitution of steel rails for the old wrought iron variety. The first steel rail was laid down at Derby Station early in 1857, but it was at Camden Town in north London that a decisive experiment was conducted over a period of more than three years from 2 May 1862. A mile of steel rails was laid alongside another mile of the older wrought iron variety at a point where the use of the rails was very heavy and equal on the two parallel tracks. The steel rails outlasted sixteen replacements of the wrought iron ones.[25] The Board of the London and North Western Railway then came to the sensible conclusion that although steel cost £15 1s a ton compared with £8 or £9 for wrought iron the much greater durability of the steel fully warranted the greater initial cost. The proprietors promptly approved the production of 10,000 tons of steel rails a year at Crewe[26] and other companies quickly adopted a similar policy of rail replacement.

The railways created an entirely new section of the British engineering industry. So important was the demand for locomotives, signalling equipment and rolling stock that at least a fifth of the engineering industry's output was going to the railways in the later 1840s. As early as 1839 export orders for British locomotives were so large that they created a temporary shortage of materials and rise in prices.[27] The impact of the railways was often to spread the engineering industry into counties hitherto regarded as predominantly agricultural in their economy. Thus the South Eastern Railway established its locomotive and carriage works at Ashford in Kent in 1845, and in Wiltshire the decision of the Great Western Railway to set up a similar establishment at Swindon in 1840 attracted no less than 14,000 men to the company's establishments there by 1905.[28] Elsewhere in the same county the construction of Saxby and Farmers' signal engineering factory at Chippenham in 1860 was followed by the end of the century by the arrival of two other firms in the same line of business.

Despite its outstanding early achievements, the later progress of railway engineering was unimpressive. Paradoxically enough one reason for the decline from early British pre-eminence in railway engineering was the dominance of the chief mechanical engineer over development policy in many of the larger railway companies. The manufacture of locomotives was undertaken mainly in the workshops of 15 of the leading companies. The railway engineers were great individualists who liked to be known for the distinctive features of the locomotives they designed. The consequence was that, with the one important exception of the products of the Crewe workshops of the London and North Western Railway,[29] there was insufficient standardisation of design for maximum economy of operation and considerations of engineering excellence took precedence over more mundane matters such as better cost accounting and the need for more adequate statistical data on the operating efficiency of the freight trains. All this does not mean that there were no improvements in the performance of the railways in the latter part of the nineteenth century. There were some important landmarks. The quick replacement of the wrought iron rail by the steel rail made possible the employment of weightier and more powerful locomotives. These were tried out extensively on the London and North Western Railway in the 1880s and 1890s and employed on the North Eastern Railways in the early years of the new century. The general substitution of coal for coke as locomotive fuel after 1870 made feasible higher steam pressures, greater speeds and heavier trains. The rapid spread of electric tramways in the ten years before 1914 encouraged electrification of some of the lines especially on the London Brighton and South Coast, the London and South Western and the Lancashire and Yorkshire Railways, although the mileage converted—314 out of 23,911 route miles of track—was very small.[30]

The experience gained in railway building was of undoubted benefit to the general advance of engineering expertise. The railway network at its fullest extension was at least five times as lengthy as the system of inland waterways. The number of bridges and viaducts to be constructed was correspondingly greater and the civil engineering profession learned from the mistakes of the railway pioneers. When the Chester and Holyhead Railway was built in 1845-6 a cast iron bridge of three spans, each 109 feet in length, was built to cross the river Dee. On 24 May 1847 one of the girders collapsed under the weight of a passenger train bound for Shrewsbury: it was something of a miracle that no more than five persons lost their lives. After this salutary lesson, with the notable exception of Bouch's Tay Bridge, few long-span bridges were built of cast iron.[31]

The impact of the railways on the brick-making industry was even more widespread than the stimulus given to mechanical and civil engineering. B. R. Mitchell considers that in 1845, with the frenzied railway building then in progress, as many as 740 million bricks may have been used for the numerous stations, bridges, aqueducts and embankments under construction.[32] Although demand was not sustained at this level in later years it was nevertheless true that opportunities for new employment were opening up in widely scattered parts of the country in the very same years in which commercial distress and unemployment were widespread. In particular brick-making was extended into the country market towns at a time when employment on farms was beginning to decline. During the age of railway building in Essex new brickyards were established in a dozen different centres as far apart as Wendens Ambo in the far north-west of the county to Brentwood on the verges of the metropolis in the south, and the numbers employed in brick-making rose from 860 in 1871 to 2,136 in 1901.[33] In Buckinghamshire the construction of the Great Western Railway, improving communications through the Thames valley, led to the opening of important brickworks in the neighbourhood of Slough in 1845.[34]

If brick-making became more widely dispersed as a result of railway building this was scarcely true of a host of other industries. The creation of a close railway network made possible a great extension of the market for all kinds of manufactured goods. Transport costs were so reduced that the manufacturing centre which was in a position to exploit the economies of scale was able to undercut the largely handicraft-based local centres of production. The economic life of towns and villages became less diversified. In the 1840s in all Essex towns, even the smaller ones, there were

fell-mongers, tanners, curriers, tallow-chandlers, soap boilers, dealers in British wines, breeches makers, boot makers, glovers, stay makers, mantua makers, hatters, sack makers, pattern makers, clock makers, tin men and many others, all selling goods made actually by themselves, or by their own workmen on their own premises.[35]

By the end of the nineteenth century, however, although the names of the trades had sometimes survived, the character of the business that went on behind the shop front had radically altered. Tradesmen had in many cases ceased to be craftsmen. They had become mere dealers, selling goods made in some remote manufacturing centre in an altogether different part of the realm or even in America or Germany.

One effect which the coming of steam transport—whether in the form of steamboats or of railways—had on British agriculture was to eliminate, more thoroughly than had been possible in the canal age, local differences in farm prices. Unenterprising farmers, working in close proximity to London and other large urban centres, could no longer count on obtaining near-monopoly prices for their hay and cattle in times of local scarcity. In the early 1840s Middlesex farmers resented the spread of the railway network because it resulted in lower livestock prices in the Southall cattle market.[36] But greater stability in agricultural prices was welcomed by enterprising farmers who appreciated the fact that they could plan for the future with greater assurance of steady prosperity. Improved communications enabled a larger proportion of the more perishable produce to be marketed than had previously been possible. James Smith, who farmed at Deanston in Perthshire in the 1820s, 1830s and 1840s, told a Parliamentary Select Committee in 1846 that there had been 'a very great agricultural improvement' of the lands proximate to recently opened railways. He cited one example of a 200-acre farm being worked on a six-course rotation and sending its produce 15 miles to the nearest market. In the pre-railway age it cost the farmer £142 16s 3d a year at 6d a ton-mile to send out 148 tons and bring in 346 tons of produce, fertiliser and machinery by road. On the railway, with charges averaging only a penny a ton-mile, transport costs were reduced to only £40 8s 9d a year. Hence the farm which was formerly worth £400 was worth £100 a year more after railway communication was established. Land in the vicinity of the Glasgow–Edinburgh railway line, which had been let at 5s an acre when produce had to be sent to market by road, was let at between 30s and 40s an acre soon after the railway became available.[37]

When they had to rely on road communications for the supply of fertilisers farmers were obliged to depend primarily on the soot, bones, marl, lime and chalk which were near to hand, as waggon transport charges were prohibitively high for long distance haulage. Although the canal network was utilised for the distribution of town manure and some imported fertilisers it was only when the more reliable and closer network of railways was available that large quantities of imported fertilisers, both natural and artificial, were purchased by farmers. In 1841 only 1,700 tons of guano were imported, but six years later, by which time the railway network had increased to over 4,000 miles, the quantity imported had shot up to over 200,000 tons.[38] In so far as domestic supplies of fertiliser were still relied upon the railway helped to make them more readily available. In 1857 the road and canal charges for the carriage of coal from the mines at Merthyr Tydfil in south Wales to the lime kilns at Quakers Yard were £5 a ton—sufficiently high to increase the price of the fertiliser beyond the means of many farmers. Rail charges were less than half this amount. Thus as the Taff Vale Railway extended its branches the farmers of the neighbourhood were better able to increase the productivity of their land.[39]

In the course of a few years the railways transformed the system of marketing livestock. The traditional method of supplying meat to the metropolis and other large centres of population was for the animals to be driven 'on the hoof' from the farms where they were reared by easy stages to the final fattening grounds near the main markets. Thus in the early 1830s 34 drovers guided 182,000 sheep a year from southern Lincolnshire to London while a further 52 men drove 26,520 oxen over the same route. It was an expensive and time-consuming routine. Over the 104 miles from Spalding to London the sheep lost an average of eight pounds weight per animal and the oxen three and a half stone. The estimated annual cost of the operation in drovers' wages and keep and loss of saleable meat in Smithfield was over £91,000.[40] When the rail link between London and Cambridge was opened and the greater part of the journey could be completed in less than a day the freight charge for the conveyance of the animals was above the earlier cost of droving, but this added expense was more than offset by the fact that under the new arrangements the beasts lost very little weight in transit. As the railway replaced the drove roads as the medium for transporting livestock to the centres of consumption so the location of the principal cattle and sheep markets changed. The gradual disappearance of the long-distance droving trade in Scotland in the 1850s and 1860s led to the emergence of new markets such as those at Lairg, Lockerbie and Lanark at the railheads near the rearing districts. In England the railway yards at Ludlow and Craven Arms dealt with the large numbers of cattle coming from north and mid-Wales and from Ireland.[41] Before railways greatly speeded up the marketing of live and dead stock there was little possibility of adjusting supplies closely to local preferences. For the first time from the 1840s onwards it was possible to sell different parts of the same carcase in entirely separate markets according to the dictates of customer demand.[42] The fatstock farmer could therefore expect a better financial return because less of his product was being wasted in the process of marketing.

Although there remained numerous examples of farms still cultivated with almost medieval backwardness, knowledge of farming improvements spread more rapidly in the second half of the nineteenth century than had ever been the case before. The railways greatly encouraged this enlightenment. On 15 February 1842 the directors of the Birmingham and Derby Junction Railway decided that, the following Friday being Derby market day, 'all persons travelling from Oakley and the intermediate stations to Derby to return the same day be supplied with a ticket to be called a *Market Ticket,* charged at the rate of fare and a half only'.[42] From 1838 onwards the shows organised by the Royal Agricultural Society drew each year even larger attendances as the spread of the railway network and the extension of facilities for third-class travel increased the opportunities for persons of humbler means to witness demonstrations of new farming techniques and to admire the finest products of livestock husbandry. When the Society's show came to Chelmsford in July 1856 up to 20,000 persons visited it in a single day. *The Times* reporter found it 'creditable to the farmers under whom the great body of men serve, that they paid the expenses of travelling by railroad to the show, as well as their wages, as if they had been working in their several vocations'. He was pleased to see 'the keen zest with which they (i.e. the labourers) enjoyed, with their wives and families, a spectacle they were so well able to appreciate'.[43]

After the census of 1871 the number of farm labourers decreased rapidly as the acreage under permanent grass increased at the expense of the area under wheat. Had the railways not been present 'to fan the spark of enterprise'[44] and open wider horizons of new opportunities for employment the miserably low wages of the farm labourers of southern and eastern England might well have sunk even lower than the eight shillings a week common in the later 1860s. As it was, cheap rail fares and spreading publicity were the means by which redundant agricultural labour was siphoned off to the mines of south Wales, the factories of Birmingham or to employment further afield in the United States or the British Dominions. The movement was of such large dimensions that there was an upward tendency of wages, a movement which encouraged some farmers to introduce labour-saving machinery.

Under the impact of the railways the transformation of Britain's fisheries was as great as the changes in her agriculture. In the early nineteenth century the fishing industry was widely dispersed, on a small scale and strongly localised, although the influence of London proved something of an exception as large quantities of fish were brought in to the capital daily from places as far away as Hastings. Most of the fish harvested from the North Sea, the English Channel or the Irish Sea had inevitably to be sold within eight or ten miles of the small harbours where they were landed. Although Manning-tree in Essex was noted for the fine quality of its whiting they were rarely marketed further away than Colchester, only eight miles distant.[45] But when railway links were established with important ports such as Wick, Hull and Lowestoft, the smacksmen who had frequented the small havens scattered all round the coast congregated within easy reach of the important railheads where special fish trains were provided to carry bulk supplies to the densely populated cities. The upshot was that the fishing industry of the later nineteenth century was concentrated in fewer centres than before.

Until the railways proved an irresistible magnet for the savings of the middle classes the investment habit was largely confined to members of the mercantile and landed interests whose opportunities for obtaining a secure return on their savings had been strictly limited. Apart from mortgages and personal loans, the man of property was largely restricted to consols, to the stock of the great trading companies and the high denomination stock of the canal companies. This situation was transformed in the second quarter of the nineteenth century. The new railways demanded a quite unprecedented volume of capital and in order to obtain it they were obliged both to lower the denomination of the shares and to increase the variety of the securities offered. One important consequence of the railway mania was the prospect of making a quick fortune, a prospect so alluring that a larger proportion of the national income was invested than had ever been the case before. In 1847 an estimated 6·7 per cent of the total addition to national wealth in that year was invested in railways while capital investment as a whole took over ten per cent. The significance of railway-building then was that it sparked off a permanent change in investment habits. Whereas before little over one twentieth of national income was annually invested, now the proportion was one tenth—a change which greatly accelerated the rate of economic growth.[46]

In the years before 1914 the middle classes of Britain found in the preference shares and debentures of the railway companies that degree of security in investment that landowners and merchants had found in East India Company stock or in consols a century earlier. The difference was that a great many more families were involved.

One typical nineteenth-century example may be cited. On the marriage in 1871 of T. H. Green, Fellow of Balliol College, Oxford, Trustees settled 11 different kinds of railway securities, yielding a guaranteed return of £600 a year, on Green and his wife. That was more than sufficient to give them a very comfortable living for the duration of their lives.[47]

What was the overall effect of the numerous influences outlined about on the economic progress of Great Britain? In recent years attempts have been made by historians of economic growth to measure the total impact of railways on the growth of the British economy. By comparing the actual costs of transport of passengers and freight by railway with the costs which would have been incurred if the older methods of transport had not been superseded it is possible to make an estimate of the social saving for which the railways were responsible. The conclusion reached by a leading historian of this school is that 'railways could not have been sacrificed in 1865 without the need to compensate for a loss of the order of ten per cent of the national income'. This estimate of a ten per cent boost to national wealth may be compared with Professor K. Fogel's estimate that railways' goods traffic alone boosted the economy of the USA by five per cent.[48]

While there is everything to be said for imparting a greater degree of exactitude in our understanding of economic history, one of the dangers inherent in the econometric approach to historical interpretation is that many influences which affect economic behaviour are not capable of precise measurement. The changes in marketing practices may be taken as one example. The availability of regular supplies by railway made it less important for traders to carry large stocks of goods or manufacturers to keep huge inventories of raw materials. Although by the second half of the nineteenth century there was little price competition between the railway companies, there was fierce rivalry in respect of the frequency of deliveries. The shopkeeper, merchant or manufacturer could therefore count on quick replenishment of a small level of stocks. His overhead charges for storage and warehousing were reduced. But whereas the savings enjoyed by tradesmen can be measured and balanced against the added cost of under-capacity running of freight trains, the indirect effects on business practices are far more difficult to assess. It is arguable that, under the new dispensation, traders were more amenable to frequent changes in fashion since they were in less danger of being caught out with large unwanted stocks of goods. The quickening of pace of transactions which came in the railway age provided an added stimulus to business innovation.

III

It would be very misleading to measure the impact of railways on British life solely by their effects on the costs of moving the goods which entered into domestic trade or by their influence on the number of passengers using public transport. Until, in some of their functions, they were superseded by motor cars, the railways were regarded as symbolic of the progressive spirit. Sponsors of railway companies were as often as not also supporters of parliamentary and municipal reform and free trade. The author of a survey of the Essex economy wrote in 1907: 'It was not easy to lay down rails in the soft Essex soil and a good deal of the country is still untouched by railroads and therefore quietly unprogressive in spirit.'[49] Significant in this comment is the 'and therefore'. Certainly it was the case that the arrival of the railway frequently provided the necessary stimulus for the introduction of other innovations. Another area 'quietly unprogressive in spirit' until the railway came was the Isle of Wight. But no sooner had the first sounds of a locomotive whistle been heard in the small village of Shanklin in August 1864 than the editor of a local newspaper grumbled that many of the visitors brought by the railway had had 'great difficulty in finding the beauty spots' and that not only improved signposting, but better roads and gas lighting, were urgently needed. Only two months later the same newspaper announced the formation of a gas company, 'the prospects of success being so very encouraging'.[50]

The spread of the railway network was accompanied by a greater promptitude in the conduct of business affairs. The railway was the instrument for the general acceptance of Greenwich time as a standard. From early in 1842 when the bare bones of a through railway network to many parts of the kingdom had come into being, the disadvantages of not having a standard time applicable to all parts of the kingdom were increasingly obvious. The Great Western time table of 30 July 1841 contained the disconcerting statement that 'London time is about four minutes earlier than Reading time, seven and a half minutes before Cirencester and 14 minutes before Bridgwater'. In January 1846 the Board of the recently constituted London and North Western Railway came up against this problem at its first meeting, as the following extract from the board minutes illustrates:

> A conversation ensued on the inconvenience experienced by having a different *time* for almost every place on the railway and the great advantage that would be almost universally felt if *London time* could be adopted throughout the whole line—The Grand Junction directors were requested to endeavour to introduce London time at the Manchester and Liverpool termini.[51]

As soon as the railway was opened through from London to Holyhead in 1848 the company enforced standardisation according to Greenwich time. Each morning an Admiralty messenger carried a watch bearing the correct time to the guard on the down Irish Mail leaving Euston for Holyhead. On arrival at Holyhead the time was passed on to officials on the Kingstown boat who carried it over to Dublin. On the return mail to Euston the watch was carried back to the Admiralty messenger at Euston once more. This was a practice which was taken over from the days of the mail coach and carried on until the outbreak of the Second World War, by which time the spread of telegraphy and the radio had long since rendered it superfluous.[52] Scottish independence was further undermined by the irresistible spread of the railway. The Caledonian Railway felt obliged, for reasons of business efficiency, to adopt Greenwich time from 1 December 1847.[53]

Although there are some outstanding examples of landowners as sponsors of important railway projects as were the Duke of Buccleuch and the Earl of Burlington in the case of the Furness Railway, many members of the landed aristocracy were (with some justification) apprehensive that the spread of railways would undermine their influence over rural society. The Duke of Wellington was at first opposed to the railroad on the grounds that it would encourage the lower orders to 'move about'. In his novel, *Sybil,* Disraeli portrayed the fears as well as the inconsistencies of the members of this class in the face of the new challenge:

'You came by the railroad?' enquired Lord de Mowbray mournfully, of Lady Marney.

'From Marham, about ten miles from us', replied her ladyship.

'A great revolution?'

'Isn't it.'

'I fear it has a dangerous tendency to equality', said his Lordship, shaking his head; 'I suppose Lord Marney gives them all the opposition in his power?'

'There is nobody so violent against the railroads as George', said Lady Marney, 'I cannot tell you what he does not do! He organised the whole of our division against our Marham line'.

'I rather counted to him', said Lord de Mowbray, 'to assist me in resisting this joint branch line here; but I was surprised to learn that he had consented.'

'Not until the compensation was settled', innocently remarked Lady Marney: 'George never opposes them after that. He gave up all opposition to the Marham line when they agreed to his terms.'

'And yet', said Lord de Mowbray, 'I think if Lord Marney would take a different view of the case, and look to the moral consequences, he would hesitate. Equality, Lady Marney, equality is not our métier. If we nobles do not make a stand against the levelling spirit of the age, I am at a loss to know who will fight the battle. You may depend upon it these railroads are very dangerous things.' [54]

In the same year in which Disraeli's novel appeared a prospectus was issued for a railway in the Isle of Wight. The scheme was vehemently opposed by the island's principal landowners including the Earl of Yarborough, the Lords Ashburton and Worsley, Sir W. Oglander and Sir R. Simeon. In a letter to the editor of the *Hampshire Telegraph* they wrote that whereas 'possessors of property to the amount of 76,000 acres' were against the projected line its only supporters were 'possessors of about 8,000 acres'. In their view, therefore, the case was conclusive that the proposal should be squashed: 'Our answer is we don't want your plan. It is not a question of which direction your lines may take; we say, and we have declared publicly that we don't require and we won't have *any* railways on this island.' Nobody appears to have suggested that it would have been more democratic to have counted heads rather than acres in order to determine the volume of local support for the scheme; in consequence the islanders had to wait a further 17 years for their first railway. [55] Thereafter change was rapid. In a few years, as the railways made the area extremely popular as a holiday resort, it was commercial interests rather than those of a small group of landowners which determined the future pattern of developments.

There is no doubt that the growth of the new form of transport contributed to the increasing secularisation of British society.

Since the overhead costs of running a railway were often more than half the total costs, the directors of the companies felt obliged to seize every opportunity of utilising more fully the resources at their command. From an early date there was a conflict between the promptings of conscience and the pressing claims of business on the vexed question as to whether or not trains should be run on Sundays. Many directors were subject to pressure from persons like Trollope's Mr Slope, who discovered, by looking into his copy of Bradshaw, that Barchester had three trains in and three out each Sunday, and therefore demanded that something be done to induce the railway company to 'diminish the evil'. [56] For a time the directors of the Canterbury and Whitstable Railway succumbed to such pressure. In May 1832 they resolved to 'discontinue the working of the railway on any day set apart for divine worship'. [57] Their contemporaries of the more commercially-minded Liverpool and Manchester Railway Board were less pliant. Although they had to face the resignation of one of the directors in consequence, they refused to stop the running of trains altogether on the Sabbath, resolving, as a compromise, that it was 'not desirable there should be any travelling by the railway on Sundays between 10 in the morning and 4 in the afternoon'.[58] No doubt, as Dr Grantly observed to Mr Slope, if the sabbatarians had succeeded in persuading the public not to travel on Sundays the companies would have stopped all Sunday trains; but they were largely unsuccessful in their efforts. Since, in the last resort, for the companies it was 'merely a question of dividends'[59] sabbath observance declined sharply in the age of the railway.

One way of filling empty seats in the passenger coaches and thus offsetting high overhead costs was to provide excursion tickets for organised groups of travellers. It has been claimed that Thomas Cook, the founder of the travel agency, was the originator of the railway excursion when he persuaded the Midland Counties Railway to issue cheap tickets to 510 Leicester temperance workers to enable them to attend a rally at Loughborough on 5 July 1841.[60] However, visitors to a church bazaar at Grosmont in August 1839 had been carried on a special excursion train provided by the Whitby and Pickering Railway. More than eight years before the first Thomas Cook excursion the Liverpool and Manchester Railway carried over 120 teachers of the Bennett Street Sunday School in Manchester to Liverpool and back for a total of £20, or 3s 4d each return, instead of the normal second class single fare of 3s 6d. This outing, which took place in June 1831, would appear to be the earliest example of a railway excursion in Britain, although it is not clear whether the party was carried in a special train or only in reserved carriages.[61] At first the number of opportunities for providing such travel bargains was strictly limited. The early impact of the steam engine was greatly to reduce the number of public holidays because the factory masters claimed that they could not afford to shut off steam just because it happened to be Guy Fawkes Day or the Prince of Wales's birthday. If the factories stayed open so did the banks. Before the age of steam the employees of the Bank of England had 47 individual days holiday each year, apart from Sundays. Under the combined influence of the evangelical revival and the implacable demands of the steam engine the number of days holiday fell to only four in 1834.[62] But with the further development of steam power in the form of the locomotive railway some redress was eventually forthcoming. There would have been little point in Parliament passing the Bank Holidays Act in 1871 had there not existed a railway system capable of carrying thousands of wage earners and their families to the seaside and back in a day at remarkably cheap rates.

It was above all the Great Exhibition held in London in the summer of 1851 which provided the greatest opportunity for the railways to promote excursion travel. The London and North Western

Railway alone brought 775,000 excursionists from the north of England to the metropolis for as cheaply as 5s return[63] and more than five million persons are thought to have used the railways to get to the exhibition. When Paris followed London's example in 1867, package tours to the exhibition in the French capital were offered by British railway companies. A week in Paris, including return travel from London, was offered to organised parties of 200 working men at 30s a head, the price including lodging, part board and entry to the exhibition.[64]

All the same, it was the British seaside resorts which before 1914 gained most in population and fame as a result of the arrival of the railway. While in Great Britain as a whole the population doubled in the first half of the nineteenth century the population of the seaside resorts quadrupled. Brighton grew with great rapidity after the railway reached the town on 21 September 1841. The first excursion train to reach London by the sea on Easter Monday 1844 was so popular that it required six engines to haul the 57 carriages over the 50 miles, a journey which took no less than four and a half hours to complete.[65] Subsequently both journey times and trains were (mercifully) shorter. Samuel Laing, the director of the London and Brighton Railway who did most to establish cheap excursions to the seaside, told a meeting of the company's shareholders on 26 January 1854 that he had been informed by Richard Mayne, chief constable of the metropolitan police, that since the introduction of the excursion trains the incidence of crime in London had 'greatly diminished'. Laing carefully avoided any consideration of the question of whether, in the meantime, the number of indictable offences had increased in Brighton. Everywhere the seaside towns strove hard to achieve rail links with London or the great industrial centres. When Torquay achieved this ambition in 1848 a public holiday was declared in the town. The railway did not reach Bournemouth until 1870, but in the following decade its population grew from 5,896 to 16,859 and by 1911 it was 78,674.

Although the companies attempted to keep passengers in their separate class compartments the railway was a great social leveller. A writer in the *Quarterly Review* in 1839 claimed that recent improvements in communications had helped to eliminate survivals of barbarism in manners and social customs since 'by the power of steam every nation is enabled to see without flattery, its own faults clearly reflected in its neighbour's mirror'. Within the last few years people had 'left hard drinking, attending prize fights, bull baits, wearing Belcher neck cloths, affecting to dress, nod, spit and meet each other like stage coachmen etc., etc.'[66] However rosy a view this may be with regard to the decline in uncivilised conduct there can be no denying the influence of the railway in starting that standardisation of language and speech which was carried more speedily forward by the influence of radio and television.

The Cambrian, Taff Vale, Chester and Holyhead and other railways of Wales were powerful agencies in the decline of Welsh speaking in the principality. Bi-lingual caution boards were in use at all stations and level crossings west of Mold Junction. One notice revealed the difficulty experienced by one Welsh-speaking clerk (who, no doubt, managed far better than would an English speaking clerk writing in Welsh!)

LIST OF BOOKING

You passengers must be careful. For have them level money for ticket and to apply at once for asking when will booking window open. No tickets to have after the departure of the train.[67]

The creation of a national railway network was one of the preconditions—together with technological changes in printing, the growth in literacy and the abolition of the taxes on knowledge—for the establishment of mass circulation daily newspapers. Before the railway age the circulation of such daily newspapers as had achieved a national reputation was puny by modern standards and was largely confined to the nobility, members of parliament, the wealthier clergy and the keepers of coffee houses and taverns who received their papers through the post. In 1830 only 41,412 copies of daily newspapers left London in this way.[68] The coming of the railways, however, provided an unrivalled opportunity for greatly extending the radius of circulation since towns and cities hitherto more than a day's coach ride from the metropolis could now be served in a few hours and newspapers could be distributed to all but the remotest parts of the realm within the day of publication. The Liverpool and Manchester Railway was the first to assist this widening of the market for daily newspapers. Its board of directors came to the remarkable decision in August 1831 to carry Liverpool newspapers to Manchester free of charge provided the printers brought the parcels to the departure platform and the wholesale newsagents collected them on arrival.[69] Although such liberality of treatment of the Press did not last long the railway companies were prepared to concede that there was a special case for carrying newspapers at charges substantially below those normally imposed for carrying other parcels of like weight, because there was a great value to the companies in having an assured *daily* consignment of merchandise. In 1866 the Superintendents' Conference of the Railway Clearing House, to which most railway companies belonged, agreed that, provided they were sent at 'owners risk', the standard charge for newspapers should be half the ordinary parcels rate.[70]

As early as 1848 potential demand was so great that the firm of W. H. Smith and Son chartered six special trains on as many different railways to get the newspapers through to Glasgow within ten hours of their publication in London.[71] When it is remembered that periodical publications, as well as newspapers, benefited from these arrangements the indirect educational advantages of the creation of a railway system can be more fully appreciated.

IV

When the opening of the Liverpool and Manchester Railway ushered in the new railway age in 1830 over three-quarters of the population of the British Isles were living in rural surroundings. By the time the railway network reached its maximum extent in 1920 more than three-quarters of the people inhabited large towns and cities. That urbanisation marched in step with the growth of the railway system was not coincidental. Until a framework of main line railways was completed mass production of manufactured goods and the strong localisation of industry characteristic of the later years of the nineteenth century were scarcely feasible. Some towns owed their very existence directly to the enterprise of a railway company; others would not have grown if the railway had not helped to provide access to markets for the goods which they produced and yet others had their character radically altered as a result of the extension of railway communications.

The outstanding example of a town which would have had no existence but for the railway is Crewe.[72] As late as 1841 no such place appeared in the national census of that year. Within the area occupied by the railway town at a later date there were the two small parishes of Monks Copenhall and Church Copenhall with a combined population of 747. The people of the neighbourhood had had, until recently, limited contact with the outside world because the condition of the roads, in the early nineteenth century, was primitive in the extreme, the ruts in the highways being 'excessive deep'. However the potentialities for development were present in the area. By the end of 1842 four routes converged at this point of the railway map establishing links with Manchester, Birmingham, Chester, and Liverpool. In 1841 the Grand Junction Railway started to build its locomotive and carriage works on the site since it was conveniently almost equidistant between Manchester and Birmingham and had good rail connections with other parts of the kingdom. The growth of the town under the paternalistic guidance of the directors of the powerful London and North Western Railway (which acquired the Grand Junction Railway in 1846) was thereafter very rapid. By 1901, the year in which it produced its 4,000th locomotive, Crewe had a population of 42,074. The railway company built the principal schools, established a Mechanics Institute, built four churches and over 800 houses and gave Victoria Park to the municipality in 1888.

Less spectacular was the development of Wolverton in Buckinghamshire, another town brought from obscurity to prominence through the decision of a railway company's board of directors. In 1838 the London and Birmingham Railway decided to establish its engine works on the site which was conveniently placed about half way between the two cities served by the company. For some years after 1838 all trains stopped at this place to change engines—a necessary procedure at a time when locomotives could not be trusted to cover the entire distance between the termini. Under this stimulus the population of the town grew from a mere 417 in 1831 to 2,070 20 years later. In 1860 the board of the London and North Western Railway, which had taken over responsibility from the London and Birmingham company in 1846, decided to concentrate the railway carriage building at Wolverton and the locomotive building at Crewe. This change did not stop the growth of the Buckinghamshire town which found employment for 4,500 men and boys in the railway carriage works alone in 1907.[73]

It cannot be said that there was no town of Swindon before the board of directors of the Great Western Railway decided in 1840, to establish its railway works in the vicinity for much the same reasons that had prompted their contemporaries of the London and Birmingham Railway board to opt for Wolverton two years earlier. At the time 'Old Swindon', with around 2,000 inhabitants, had some importance as a market centre but none in respect of manufacturing. When the railway works were opened at New Swindon in January 1843 only 423 men were employed, but over the next seventy years there was built up 'the largest undertaking in British industry',[74] engaging a labour force of over 14,000. Like Wolverton and Crewe, Swindon had its railway houses, churches and Mechanics Institute and the prosperity of the town was wholly dependent on that of the railway company which had been the main agency in its creation.

The development of Ashford in Kent, where the railway town grew up from 1845 alongside an old-established market town and centre of local manufactures, had characteristics similar to those of Swindon except that as a result of the smaller scale of operations of the South Eastern Railway its industrial requirements were similarly restricted.[75]

The railway workshops which sprang up in a predominantly rural environment can scarcely escape the historian's notice: those which emerged from an urban environment can more easily be overlooked. Stratford, in east London, fulfilled the same role for the Great Eastern

Railway as Ashford did for the South Eastern and provided as many men with employment. Gorton, in Manchester, employed more.

Dozens of other towns, though not the purposeful creations of railway companies to serve their own ends, as assuredly owed their rapid growth to the presence of good railway communications. The spectacular emergence of Barrow in Furness as a major industrial town after 1840 was associated with the expansion of iron mining and smelting in the peninsula. Nevertheless the historians of the town consider that the Furness Railway played 'a decisive role' in the opening up of the district which had in earlier years been 'remote and difficult of access'.[76] Middlesbrough, though not so geographically remote, was a parallel case in that the railway was an essential agency in the growth of the iron industry which built up the population and prosperity of the town.

The Redhill of to-day, familiar to thousands of London commuters, sprang up around two railway platforms, which were opened on 12 July 1841, amidst wholly rural surroundings, when John Rennie completed the original works of the London and Brighton Railway. Subsequently other railways passed through the district and it became convenient for locomotive superintendents to maintain a locomotive depot in the town which was at the same time growing increasingly popular as a residential centre for London businessmen.[77]

The railways' influence in opening up new urban centres continued right up to the First World War, and, if the underground railways are included, into the 1930s as well. In the late Victorian and Edwardian era the construction of branch lines helped to create or enlarge residential suburbs of large towns and cities rather than to establish completely new industrial towns. Thus on the eastern outskirts of London, branch lines were extended from Bethnal Green to Walthamstow in 1872 and to Chingford in 1873.[78] A building boom followed in these districts in the later seventies. After 1868 the Great Northern Line constructed a branch between Wood Green and Enfield with stations at Palmers Green, Winchmore Hill and Enfield (Chase). When its station was opened to traffic on 1 April 1871 Winchmore Hill was a small village, and there were no houses between the new railway and Wood Green, except a few old cottages on, or near, the high road and a few gentlemen's houses standing in ample grounds. Although subsequent development was delayed because of high interest rates in the early 1870s and the reluctance of local landowners to part with their property, building proceeded apace when cheaper money was available in the later 1870s and the mid 1890s and then the suburban sprawl of London was yet further extended.[79]

When railways helped to open up new towns in the 1840s and 1850s their role was almost entirely constructive: when the giant railway companies of the later nineteenth century extended their ownership of property within already existing cities their role was also partly destructive.[80] With the enormous growth of their passenger and goods traffic in later Victorian Britain the railways needed new or larger city termini and more extensive sidings, goods yards and warehouses. By 1900 the railways had acquired over five per cent of the central areas of London and Birmingham, more than seven per cent of the corresponding districts of Glasgow and Manchester and nine per cent of central Liverpool. These huge areas were acquired through the purchase and destruction of thousands of the meaner type dwellings which crowded the inner parts of the big cities. Tens of thousands of tenants were abruptly evacuated to prepare the way for the demolition gangs. The number thus dispossessed in London has been variously estimated at between 76,000 and 120,000 and there were similar upheavals in the other large cities.

Even when there was the possibility of purchasing a large factory rather than large numbers of individual homes, the railway companies still opted for the dwellings of the 'powerless and the poor',[81] because this was always the cheaper and less complicated alternative, especially where the buildings occupied by thousands of tenants were owned by one landlord. It was for these reasons that the Manchester, Sheffield and Lincolnshire Railway, when looking for a site for its central station in Manchester, carefully avoided Messrs Sharp, Stewart and Co.'s factory in Oxford Street. Similarly the Metropolitan Railway, in building an extension from Aldersgate to Moorfields, side-stepped Whitbread's Brewery. In building new stations, goods yards and stables in the centre of big cities, whilst carefully avoiding the displacement of large factories, the railway companies helped to create the urban ghettos of the late nineteenth century. After such an upheaval as the building of a new goods depot or the addition of more platforms to a railway terminus, more casual labour of goods porters, rulleymen and general labourers would be required, at the same time as the number of houses and rooms available in the vicinity had been reduced. It was all very well to suggest that those displaced should find new homes outside the city centre. The difficulty was, as one witness to the Royal Commission on Metropolis Railway Termini expressed it, that 'the poor man was chained to the spot'; he had neither 'the leisure to walk' nor 'the money to ride' to a more salubrious and less expensive spot.

'Money to ride' implied travelling at the normal third-class, penny-a-mile, rate. There was more hope of persuading the labourer to move out, at least to the cities' inner suburbs, if tickets at less than half this rate were made available. From the 1860s onwards, when the railway companies which served the great conurbations needed to raise more money for branches and extensions, Parliament sometimes granted them their extended powers only on condition that they helped to alleviate the problem they had been partly responsible for creating. They were required to provide workmen's trains at concessionary fares which were remarkably cheap. In the case of the Great Eastern Railway Act of 1864 the company was obliged to provide at least one workmen's train up to town before 7 a.m. and from town after 6 p.m. from Edmonton, Walthamstow and other specified stations to Liverpool Street at no more than one penny for the whole journey. In the event the company did more than the minimum required under the Act. By 1903 it was providing ten workmen's trains each day from a large number of stations at a penny for each journey, some of the stations being nearly 11 miles from Liverpool Street.[82]

In the early 1880s as the public conscience was increasingly aroused at the continuing disgrace of the slums, Parliament finally intervened in a more comprehensive fashion by passing the Cheap Trains Act in 1883.[83] When the 'Parliamentary Train' was introduced under the Railway Act of 1844 the railway companies were exempted from the payment of Passenger Duty on the third-class tickets they sold for such trains. From 1864 on when clauses instituting workmen's trains were included in Acts passed for the benefit of particular companies exemption from the duty was extended to these cases as well. Under the Cheap Trains Act Passenger Duty was repealed on all penny-a-mile (and cheaper) fares, but the companies, in return, were obliged to concede to the Board of Trade the right to determine when and where workmen's trains should be run. In fact the Act had the effect of making more general a practice which some railway companies had been extending partly on their own initiative. The year before it was passed an average of 25,671 workmen's tickets had been issued each day in the London area. Thirty years later about a quarter of all suburban rail passengers travelled with workmen's tickets. By this time, with the encouragement of Parliament, the railways had made something of a contribution to the dispersal into healthier districts of the people living in the grossly overcrowded city centres. But the continued existence of the slums a generation after the passing of the Cheap Trains Act makes clear that it would be wholly misleading to suggest that the housing problem could be solved simply by a policy of concessionary fares.

V

Although a brief account of the development of underground railways may appear to be out of place in a chapter devoted to the economic and social effects of railways, the case for its inclusion is that, but for the urban concentration consequent upon the growth of main line railways, the need for improved communications of this kind would never have arisen. The building of underground railways may also be seen, together with the introduction of workmen's trains, as a means of reducing the pressure on living accommodation in the centre of the city.

In a survey made as late as 1854 it was estimated that, to reach their place of work 88,000 Londoners used the horse buses, 54,000 the trains from the suburbs to the main line termini, 30,000 the river steamers and 52,000 their own or hired carriages. But no less than 400,000 still lived near enough to their work for them to make the journey on foot.[84] Nevertheless travel habits were changing rapidly and each year more thousands were depending on the railway and horse transport. By the early 1860s Londoners were complaining that the increase in horse-drawn traffic in the centre of the city and on the Thames bridges was causing an intolerable congestion. In 1863 *The Times* warned that 'the slightest addition to the ordinary traffic of the city would make the streets impassable'.[85]

One solution to the problem of congestion was to bring the railways nearer to the central parts of the city so that commuters could complete their journey to work on foot without addition to the congestion of vehicles in the narrow city streets. Victoria station was opened to traffic in October 1860, the South Eastern opened extensions to Charing Cross in 1864 and to Cannon Street in 1866 and the London, Chatham and Dover matched these developments with a railway to Blackfriars Bridge in June 1864.[86] Welcome as they were, these developments were only a partial answer to the mid-nineteenth-century traffic problem. Main line railway extensions within the London area were extremely expensive. Building the short extension from London Bridge to Charing Cross cost the South Eastern Railway £3,000,000— more than £1,000 a foot, and more than three times the cost of the line between Newcastle and Carlisle.[87] The commuter from Kent or South London who arrived at Victoria or Charing Cross still had a long way to walk if his place of work was in the City. Those who arrived at Paddington or Euston might well have an even longer distance to cover on foot.

It was to overcome these continuing deficiencies that London's first underground railway, the Metropolitan, was opened for traffic for the 3¾-mile stretch from Paddington to Farringdon Street in the City on 10 January 1863. The line was built on the 'cut and cover' principle. A deep trench was built (wherever possible along the route of existing roads to reduce cost and to avoid complications through possible subsidence) and then covered over with cast iron girders or brick arches. The problem of pollution exercised the minds of engineers in the 1860s as it did in the 1960s. In order to prevent the air in the underground stations and the third-class carriages becoming too unhealthy the ingenious John Fowler designed special locomotives (later known as 'Fowler's Ghosts') which, he claimed, would generate a sufficient head of steam at the beginning of the route to haul a train through to the other terminus without the need of a locomotive fire on the journey. The claim could not be substantiated. The line could not have been built without the financial support of the City of London and of the Great Western Railway which contributed £185,000 to the capital and serviced the line in its early years.[88] The unpleasantness of travelling underground in a tunnel of steam locomotive fumes did not deter over six-and-a-half million Londoners from using the line in the six months ending 31 December 1864. In the corresponding period of time four years later after an extension had been completed eastwards to Moorgate nearly 15 million people travelled by the 'Met'.[89]

Other underground lines constructed on the same 'cut and cover' principle but managed by different companies followed in the ensuing twenty years. The District Railway opened its route along the recently established Victoria Embankment in the summer of 1871. After long delays the Inner Circle, which linked most of the main line termini, was completed in 1884.

Meanwhile, in 1869, the Tower Subway Company, with J. H. Greathead as contractor, built a tunnel 1,350 feet long under the Thames, using a circular cutting shield of a kind patented by P. W. Barlow in 1864 to excavate the earth. Although the cable-operated railway worked in this tunnel for some months from 2 August 1870 was not a financial success and a pedestrian footpath took the place of the railway, the new method of tube construction was shown to be a complete success. The City and South London Railway, founded in 1884, used it to build the first financially viable tube railway between Waterloo and the Bank. When opened to traffic on 18 December 1890 it was the first underground railway to use electric power for traction. Subsequent extensions of the London underground network were built on the same principle. These included the Central London Railway Company's 'twopenny tube' from Shepherds Bush to the Bank opened on 30 July 1900 and extended westwards to Wood Lane on 14 May 1908 and eastwards to Liverpool Street on 28 July 1912.

Owing to the fact that many of the earlier underground railways had not been outstanding financial successes it was frequently the case by the 1890s that the very large amounts of capital needed for new construction were difficult to raise. The Hampstead Tube Railway which issued a prospectus for an underground link between Charing Cross and Hampstead in 1894 was obliged to obtain an extension of its parliamentary powers in 1897, 1898 and again in 1900 because of inadequate financial backing from the British investor.[90] C. T. Yerkes of Chicago, heading a syndicate of American financiers, came to the rescue. Between them they established in 1902 the Underground Electric Railways Co. of London which organised the building of the line later known as the Piccadilly and at the same time founded the Edgeware and Hampstead Railway Company to finance what became known as the Northern Line. By this time the role of the underground railways was changing. In the nineteenth century their main task had been to facilitate the movement of people within the central part of the metropolis. The newer lines opened in the decade before the First World War encouraged the growth of new suburbs. London Transport's jubilee booklet of the Northern Line issued in 1967 includes a photograph of Golders Green in 1904— a cross roads in open country. After the arrival of the first underground trains there on 22 June 1907 the district was rapidly developed as an outer London dormitory. When the plans of the Piccadilly and the Northern Lines, held back by the war, were completed in the 1920s the 'colonising' role of the underground was even more apparent.

No other part of Britain presented urban transport problems of the same magnitude as those of London. The pattern of Glasgow's passenger traffic was the reverse of London's. Most Glaswegians had their homes in the heart of the city and commuted to the suburbs daily to work. Owing to the excellence of the Clyde river steamboat services there was a less pressing need for a counterpart to London's underground and the city's first underground was opened as a cable line in 1896. In 1923 the municipality bought out the 6½-mile-long system and converted it to electric traction by 1935. Liverpool, not so profusely provided with river transport as Glasgow, established an overhead electric railway, principally to service the dock area, in 1893.

6

Road and Water Transport in the Railway Age

I

Mesmerised by the success of the Liverpool and Manchester Railway after 1830 many contemporaries considered that all earlier forms of transport had been completely outmoded. In the contest of horse versus iron horse the triumph of the new machinery was regarded as inevitable. With every mile of line added to the railway network more grass would spread over the turnpike roads while silt and weeds would rapidly block up the canals. One of the leading coach proprietors considered 'annihilation' as the most appropriate word to describe the prospects for his type of business in the railway age.[1] Modern historians of the railways have reinforced this impression of the rapid decay of alternative means of transport. In one of the best known recent studies coaches are referred to as being 'snuffed out' with 'dramatic suddenness' after the coming of the railway.[2] Much prominence is given to the fact that within five months of the opening of the line between Liverpool and Manchester only four of the 29 coaches which had operated between the two towns were still in business. Two years later only one remained.

But this experience was not typical of all parts of the country. A sharp distinction should be drawn between the prospects facing road passenger transport where the new railways ran roughly parallel to long-established through roads and the very different situation where the road traversed, or fed into, the route of the railway. Those who depict the coming of the steam locomotive as an unmitigated disaster for road transport select their evidence from cases where the railway simply duplicated pre-existing highways. But other examples can be cited to show that horse-drawn vehicles had still a very important part to play for many decades to come in the overall provision of transport services.

There was certainly little future in long-distance stage-coaching where the railway provided a much speedier means of travel along the same route. After the opening of the London and Brighton line on 21 September 1841 the coaching era for the road 'virtually died'. The Day Mail was taken off within a month; the Night Mail lasted only five months longer and of the 23 coaches on the road in 1839 only one, the *Victoria*, survived into the summer of 1845.[3] In the short run few towns suffered more severely from the arrival of the railway than did Doncaster, a major staging post on the Great North Road. In 1839 the town found employment for seven four-horse coaches, 20 two-horse coaches, nine stage waggons and 100 post horses; the total horse population was 258. In 1845, after the town had had railway links for five years, only one four-horse coach, three stage waggons and 12 post horses were still in service and the total number of horses had fallen to 60. One of the town's leading bankers told a Parliamentary Committee that trade had suffered 'most materially' and that the value of property had fallen between 25 and 30 per cent.[4] Within 15 months of the opening of the North Midland Railway to Derby in May 1839 36 coaches which plied, via Dronfield, to London were taken off the road, a charge which wrought 'dreadful havoc' with the incomes of innkeepers, horsekeepers and labourers on the route.[5]

On the other hand, where the new railway lines did not run parallel to established coach routes there were still opportunities for coaches to stay on the road and even to increase their business. After the completion of the main line of the London and Birmingham railway in 1838 there was an increase in feeder coach services bringing passengers to the stations along the line and enhancing the revenues of the Peterborough and Wellingborough Turnpike Trust by £100 a year.[6] Edward Sherman, who employed nine coaches on the London–Birmingham route before the railway was opened, had taken all but two of them off the road within a year of the start of through rail services, but, in March 1839 he admitted that those who had worked 'direct' coaches generally worked them 'to the station across' instead of going out of business altogether. Traffic 'on the cross roads from every part' to stations on the line including Denbigh Hall, Wolverhampton and Rugby, had substantially increased, so that quite as many horses would be employed in working from the towns and villages to the railroad as had been taken off the through road between London and Birmingham.[7]

The completion of the early skeleton network of railways by about 1840 provided innumerable opportunities for opening up new combined coach and railway routes for passenger traffic. People living in the lesser towns, away from the main mail coach and early railway routes, were able, in many cases for the first time in their lives, to visit London or one or other of the large urban centres. The establishment of a new light post coach service to Manchester from 13 May 1840 enabled the citizens of Derby to reach Liverpool easily in a day, the advertisement for the coach making clear that passengers on the coach would reach Manchester in time for the 4 o'clock train for Liverpool.[8] In April 1836 a new coach, which met the Leeds train at Selby brought passengers through to Scarborough by 6 o'clock the same evening.[9] In October 1840 another new coach service from Leeds met people from the London train and carried them through to the Lake District, thus cutting very substantially the journey time between the English capital and the towns of Cumberland.[10] The secretary of the Richmond and Lancaster Turnpike Trust considered that the opening of the Lancaster and Preston Railway on 25 June 1840 had improved the revenue prospects of the Trust as there would be more coach and other road traffic passing north of Lancaster.[11]

The transition from road to rail transport was in many areas a gradual process. There was certainly a marked continuity of tradition in the provision of passenger services. A resolution of the Committee of Management of the Liverpool and Manchester Railway of 29 June 1831 reveals the survival of the terminology and practices of the coaching age into the age of the railway: 'Ordered: that the guards of the Coach trains be provided with Horns and that they blow their horns as they approach the Gates.'[12] This instruction reminds us that one variant of the combined rail–coach service was the arrangement by which passengers made the first stage of their journey by coach to the nearest railway station, were then carried forward in the same coach on the railway train to the terminus of the line, and were horse-drawn a second time as they completed their journey by coach. Thus on 18 September 1840 the Traffic and General Purposes Committee of the London and Southampton Railway agreed to allow the *Subscription, Defiance* and *Telegraph* coaches to be carried by passenger train at half the rates normally charged for gentlemen's carriages.[13] Arrangements of this kind were destined to be very temporary in character, but they gave the coach proprietors time to adjust the pattern of their services from the long distance runs characteristic of the pre-railway age to the cross-country and feeder routes which were still covered by horse-drawn transport in the age of main line steam. By the time the railway companies had begun to abandon the practice of carrying coaches on the passenger trains there were often increasing opportunities for owners of horse-drawn vehicles to run cab services to and from the railway stations. A minute of the Board of Directors of the Birmingham and Derby Junction Railway was typical of similar decisions being made in all parts of the country where the new railway stations were being built:

Min: 1000. Read a letter of 25th instant from Mr. Jos. Edwards requesting that Mr. Jennings may stand with his car in the station yard at Hampton and drive passengers to and from the station. *Resolved*: that Mr. Edwards be informed that Mr. Jennings will be permitted to ply with a car between Solihull and the station at

Hampton with the facility for this purpose of standing in the station yard.[14]

Especially in cases where the station was situated an appreciable distance from the town it was intended to serve there was bound to be a continuing demand for road transport. Harrow was a case in point. In 1864 the *Harrow Gazette* was complaining that because of the inconvenient siting of the two nearest railway stations—Harrow and Sudbury—it took a longer time to travel from the town to either than it did to go the rest of the way by rail to London. From 1838, therefore, successive proprietors of the Kings Head Hotel, Harrow ran an omnibus to Harrow Station until in 1886 the LNWR took over the operation of the service.[15]

Some coach proprietors contrived to stay longer in business than others by exploiting the prejudices and weaknesses of their customers. Through the inexperience of some locomotive builders and the primitive character of early signalling arrangements early railway travel had its attendant dangers. There was a particularly bad spate of accidents in the summer and autumn of 1840 when coach proprietors made the most of their opportunity to proclaim the superiority of the old methods of travel. An advertisement in the *Derby Mercury* on 2 December 1840 reminded readers who were intending to travel from Derby to Nottingham that they still had opportunities afforded them of 'going by coaches combining safety and expedition with comfort and economy' and claiming that it 'must be evident to all that the Old Mode of Travelling is still the most preferable, and the only one to escape the Dreadful Railway Accidents, too awful to describe'.

Not every railway system was efficiently managed. Early in 1846 a Norwich newspaper doubted whether any other railway 'subjected passengers to such protracted journeys or greater inconvenience' than did the Norfolk and Eastern Counties. Travellers on the 5 o'clock evening train from London were not reaching Norwich until 3 o'clock the following morning and turkeys sent to London were arriving after Christmas dinner had been eaten.[16] Given such a poor railway service it is not surprising that since the average time taken by coach was $9\frac{1}{2}$ hours, some customers continued to use road transport until the rail services were improved.

Generally less successful were those coach proprietors who endeavoured to stay in business on the long-established routes by reducing fares. The proprietor of the *Criterion* coach which linked Sheffield with Derby, Birmingham and London reduced his charges in the autumn of 1839—but with little success from the viewpoint of retaining passengers. One of the most successful of the coach proprietors, B. W. Horne, had already concluded by 1838 that the public were 'more careful, on a large scale, about their time than about their money'. He confessed that even if he halved the coach fares to Chester he would not persuade people to travel by road now that they could make the journey in less than half the time by rail.[17]

In the early days of the railways it was the complaint of coach proprietors and all those who licensed road vehicles that they were unfairly taxed by comparison with the railways. A Parliamentary Select Committee summed up the situation in 1837 when it reported that 'all land travelling where the motive power is animal is heavily taxed, while land travelling, where steam is the motive power is comparatively lightly burdened; and the conveyance of passengers by steam in rivers or arms of the sea is free from every species of taxation'.[18] At that time there were no less than eight different taxes which affected horse transport, apart from turnpike road tolls. Stage coaches paid a licence duty and a mileage duty varying according to the number of passengers they were licensed to carry. There were assessed taxes on coachmen and guards and the horses they managed. Postmasters had to pay a licence duty of 7s 6d a year, besides paying duties on their horses and carriages, and there were assessed taxes on carriages and horses kept for private use. The passenger duty paid by the railways was at the rate of $\frac{1}{2}d$ per mile on every four passengers. The coach proprietors' grievance was that they were obliged to pay the mileage duty irrespective of whether, on any particular journey, they were carrying passengers or not, whilst the railways only paid duty on passengers actually carried. It worked out that whereas the railway proprietors paid $\frac{1}{8}d$ per mile of duty, stage coach proprietors paid double this amount and postmasters treble. Despite a strong recommendation from the Select Committee that the duty on coaches and on carriages let for hire should be abolished, Parliament made no alteration in the tax until 1842–3 when the licence duty on coaches was reduced from five pounds to three guineas a year and the mileage duty was lowered to $\frac{1}{2}d$ a mile irrespective of the number of passengers carried. Had the taxes been reduced at an earlier date it is very unlikely that such a gesture would have saved the long-distance coach services from extinction. A stage-coach proprietor, Mr Robert Gray, was frank enough to tell the Committee in 1837 that he did not consider coaches would be able to compete with the railways directly, even if all taxes were abolished. After the taxes were lowered in the early 1840s the decline in the revenue from stage carriages continued in both England and Wales and Scotland. In England and Wales it fell from an average of £211,729 per year for the five years 1845–50 to £197,614 per year for the five years 1850–4 and in Scotland for comparable periods the figures show a decline from £18,175 to £15,235.[19] Clearly the stage coaches were gradually fading away rather than being 'snuffed out'.

In April 1839 the well known coach magnate George Sherman expressed the opinion that after the railways had driven most of the coaches off the long distance routes 'there would be as much employ for horses as there ever was' through the 'extra ordinary quantity of omnibuses and cabs' that were appearing on the streets. For this reason he had found no difficulty in selling at good prices the horses he had taken off his coach runs.[20] As the century advanced the railways in fact were having to pay more for their cart horses. In 1872 the London and South Western were paying £54 17s for the same type of animal which had only cost them £44 10s five years earlier. The price obtainable for cast-off horses rose even more sharply, indicating that there was a growing demand for the animals to haul private carriages. The selling price of Great Northern Railway old cast-offs rose from £10 to £23, or by 130 per cent, between 1868 and 1872.[21] In the early 1870s Mr W. Banks, a commission stable keeper of Grays Inn Lane, London, told a House of Lords Select Committee that there was 'a wonderful demand for horses'. When asked

'Do you think that the establishment of railways has very largely diminished the number of horses that are used for the carrying trade, or that it has increased it?' He replied

'I should say that it has increased it. We thought that when railways first came in that we should have nothing to do, but it has not turned out so.'

'You think that the greater increase we have of railways, the greater will be the use of the horse?'

'Decidedly, because there is work to be done to and fro. The horses have to work in connection with the railways; for every new railway you want fresh horses; fresh cab horses to begin with: I know one cab proprietor, for instance who used to keep 60 horses and now has 120.'[22]

The increased demand for horses was certainly not confined to London: it was also strongly in evidence in the provinces. The advertisement and news columns of the *Sheffield and Rotherham Independent* between October 1838 and June 1842, when new railways were coming into the area, announced sales of horses on 13 separate occasions but also reported the establishment of new coach or omnibus services on eleven occasions. The truth of the matter was that 'Without carriages and carts the railways would have been like stranded whales, giants unable to use their strength, for these were the only means of getting people and goods right to the doors of houses, where they wanted to be.'[23]

Apart from carriages for hire there was a remarkable increase in the number of privately owned large carriages right through to the 1870s. From 30,000 in 1840 the number grew to 120,000 by 1870—a four-fold increase in 30 years. Over the same period of time the number of light two-wheeled carriages increased by six times to a total of 250,000. The growth of suburban rail networks and the opening up of tramway services combined with the increasing scarcity of stable and mews accommodation in the large towns after about 1870 checked the growth in number of large carriages. But the number of two-wheeled vehicles continued to increase, particularly in the smaller towns and country districts. By 1902 12 out of every 1,000 inhabitants in Great Britain owned some kind of private horse-drawn vehicle and it was not until 1926 that the number of car owners exceeded the number of persons who had owned horse-drawn carriages in 1870.[24]

II

The change in the pattern of road traffic consequent upon the coming of the railway was bound to affect the revenue of the turnpike trusts. At the same time the parish authorities which were still responsible until as late as 1894 for the condition of the greater part of the road mileage, had to provide for a heavier volume of road traffic and found it necessary to increase the burden of the rates.

In 1838, near the beginning of the railway age, there were 1,116 turnpike trusts and 7,796 toll gates and side bars in England and Wales. Between them the trusts managed some 22,000 miles of road compared with the 104,770 miles managed by the parish authorities.[25] The turnpike trusts were ill-equipped to meet the challenge of the railways. In the first place they operated on too small a scale to be economically run, the average turnpike road being under twenty miles in extent. Had the units of administration been larger they could have been managed more efficiently with considerably less than the 3,535 persons employed as treasurers, clerks and surveyors, not to mention some 20,000 pikemen. Secondly, they were in financial difficulties. Their total mortgage debt of over £7 million was four and a half times their annual income.[26] In consequence a growing proportion of total revenue was ear-marked to pay interest on previous borrowings while the residual sums available were becoming less and less adequate to meet the costs of road repairs and improvements. Thirdly, those concerns which were prosperous were understandably reluctant to join forces with their less affluent neighbours since this involved assuming responsibility for debts. Amalgamation of turnpikes to reap the benefits of large-scale operation therefore made slow progress.

The managers of many turnpike trusts at first viewed the spread of the railway network with equanimity rather than alarm. Where the railway did not run directly parallel to the road there was every likelihood that turnpike traffic would increase. Railways brought an enhanced appreciation of the need for speed in travel. Those who in former days would have walked considerable distances to join the nearest stage coach now demanded to be carried by short stage or chaise to the nearest railway station. In 1839 the Royal Commission on Roads sent a questionnaire to the turnpike trusts in England and Wales asking the officers whether they anticipated that the market value of their bonds would decrease as a result of the coming of the railways. Of the 1,107 who sent in replies only 226 considered that they would be adversely affected.[26] It is true that at this comparatively early stage in railway development there were important regions of the country such as Wales and the south-west which were still largely unaffected by the new means of communication. Nevertheless, even in areas which were witnessing the intrusion of the railway, there was no general despondency amongst those whose vested interests lay in the continuation of road travel. From Cheshire, the secretary of the Northwick and Kelsall trust, whose toll revenues had been increasing, commented: 'This road acts as a conduit to the railway, being at right angles with it'. From the Rugby and Lutterworth trust came the report: 'The road being a cross road and not a great high road, the tolls have materially increased'. Sir James McAdam, general superintendent of the Metropolitan turnpike trust, responsible for over 110 miles of road in north London, reported that the letting value of the tolls on the road between Hatfield and Reading had increased by £600 because this highway linked country market towns with important railway stations on the London and Birmingham and Great Western railways. On the Gloucester and Hereford turnpike bidding for the rent of tolls on the gate at Over, just across the river Severn, rose from £1,705 in 1841, the year the railway came to Gloucester, to a 'peak of £1,980 twelve years later'.[27]

Even though the gains might be short lived, there was extra revenue to be earned when nearby railways were in the course of construction. On the Stroud and Gloucester turnpike toll revenue increased in 1838 'in consequence of hauling materials for the construction of the new lines' to the Gloucestershire capital.

One development which helped to keep the toll revenues of the 'cross road' turnpikes buoyant was the increase in the number of Royal Mail short stages, especially after the introduction of the penny post in 1840. Despite the increasing use of the railway for the conveyance of the mail after the Post Office made its first contract of this kind with the Liverpool and Manchester railway on 4 November 1830, the number of horse-drawn mail carriages increased rather than decreased for at least a quarter of a century after

1830. In the second report of the Postmaster-General to the Post Office in 1856 it was stated that branch mail coaches communicating with railways conveyed the side mails over no less than 31,667 miles per day—a mileage greater than that covered by all the mail coaches immediately before the coming of the railways.[28]

It was, of course, a very different story where the turnpike and the railway ran parallel on inter-city routes. On the 106-mile-long Holyhead and Shrewsbury turnpike 'a very considerable proportion' of road travellers had deserted to the railway by 1839 and the trust lost £1,500 a year in revenue through the mails being transferred from coaches to trains. Because the Liverpool and Manchester railway ran parallel, tolls on the eight-and-a-half-mile-long Manchester Road turnpike which had been let for £1,680 in 1829 were only yielding £372 ten years later.[29]

It was the four-horse coaches which contributed more than any other type of vehicle to the revenue of the turnpike trusts. Each stage coach on the London–Manchester route contributed £1,700 a year to the income of the turnpike trusts on the route.[30] The decline of turnpike toll revenue by one third between 1837 and 1850 was largely due to the withdrawal of stage-coach services from the long-distance through routes. By the mid-1860s, by which time the branch lines of the railways were more extensive, it was no doubt true, as G. F. Newmarch, a witness before the Select Committee on Turnpike Trusts, asserted, that 'all turnpike roads had ceased to be national roads, and had become purely of a local character'.[31] But until more research has been done into the records of local trusts it is impossible to say whether or not the total *volume* of traffic on the turnpike roads rose or fell after the mid-1830s. The toll keeper in Dickens's *The Uncommercial Traveller* (1860) who was unable to get a living out of the tolls and whose house was 'all overgrown with ivy'[32] must surely have been living on one of the old long-distance coach routes rather than on one of the 'cross' roads leading to a railway station.

Even at the height of the coaching era, when they enjoyed a virtually unchallenged position, the turnpike trusts were accused of being too avaricious. In 1826 Theodore Hooke complained that 'turnpike roads were toll'd too often, like bad jokes'.[33] If this was true in the heyday of the coach, it was even more true after the rivalry of the railways began to eat into toll revenues. In an endeavour to make good the loss of revenue resulting from a decline in the stage-coach traffic some turnpike trusts raised additional toll gates especially on roads more frequently used by lighter carriages. On the road between Cirencester and Tetbury a new gate was erected 'in order to catch the passengers coming to the railway station'.[34] But such attempts to squeeze every penny from tradesmen and travellers could be self-defeating. The managers of at least one Sussex turnpike overplayed their hand in this manner. They had erected eight toll gates on the 17 miles of road between Frimwell and Hastings until total road charges had become so steep that it was less expensive, as well as faster, for the owner of a private carriage to leave his vehicle at home and travel by train.[35] Over-eagerness in toll exaction also swung opinion against the trusts and predisposed road users to favour a greater degree of public ownership of the highways. One consequence of farmers having to pay toll three times on the eight miles of road between Ledbury and Newent in Gloucestershire was that they viewed more favourably the alternative plan of paying a highway rate to a parish or a highway board.[36]

The remedy for the increasing indebtedness of many of the turn-pike trusts and their consequent inability to maintain their road network in a satisfactory state of repair lay in the consolidation of the trusts into larger units and their eventual transference to the control of public authorities. In 1826 north London set an excellent example with the formation of the Metropolitan Turnpike Trust uniting under one management the administration of 122 miles of turnpike roads formerly controlled by separate trusts.[37] In south Wales administration of turnpike roads reached a crisis in the years 1839–44. Pressure of population on the means of subsistence and the oppressive incidence of numerous tolls on the carriage of lime to hillside farms on the margin of cultivation (among other causes) pro-voked the Rebecca Riots of 1843–4. Some towns in the area were 'surrounded by toll gates like besieged cities', Rhayader having a toll gate on each side of the six roads entering the town.[38] The local population reacted by a systematic destruction of toll gates and toll houses and in 1844 Parliament endorsed the findings of a Royal Commission which recommended the consolidation of turnpike roads under county authorities. The Act to consolidate and amend the laws relating to turnpike trusts in south Wales, passed in 1844, merged all the trusts within each county under county road boards nominated by the magistrates in quarter sessions. It was an effective remedy. By the 1870s the turnpike roads in the six counties concerned were free of debt despite the fact that charges were lower than they had been before the uprising.

The rest of the country was slow to follow the examples of north London and south Wales. From 1806 on there were numerous par-liamentary enquiries into the turnpike system and there was no shortage of proposed remedies. In 1839, for example, the Select Committee on Turnpike Trusts urged that 'unions of trusts should be formed including all the roads in a district' of some 15 miles' radius. But no action followed this recommendation. It was politically impossible for a Whig parliament which had four years previously passed the Municipal Corporation Act to extend middle-class control over city administration, to transfer power over the roads in the counties to the magistrates who were generally Tory landowners.

In the event a series of stop-gap and piecemeal measures gradually decreased the number and importance of the turnpike trusts. In 1841 J.P.s in special sessions were empowered to order contributions from the highway rates to be made available for the repair of turnpikes where the trusts responsible were in financial difficulties. Where this happened the inhabitants of the vicinity complained that they were doubly taxed when they used the turnpikes—by the highway rate and by the toll. Under the Public Health Act of 1848 roads in some urban areas were acquired by local Boards of Health and the Local Government Act ten years later reinforced these provisions. In 1864 another parliamentary select committee recommended that the abolition of the turnpike trusts 'would be both beneficial and expedient' especially if the process of consolidation which, by then, had extended to Scotland as well as Wales, was accelerated.[39] But although 108 toll bars were removed in London that year[40] there were still over a thousand trusts functioning in Britain. It was not until the newly created Local Government Board took over responsibility for roads from the Home Office in 1872 that the dissolution of the trusts was hastened by the annually appointed parliamentary Committee on Turnpike Bills refusing to renew their powers. Meanwhile a special Act ended tolls in the London area in 1871. In the next two decades the number of turnpike trusts remaining sank rapidly from 851 in 1871 to 184 in 1881 and only two in 1890. On 1 November 1895 the last turnpike trust—on the Anglesey section of the Holyhead road—ceased to function.[41] It had been a tediously slow process.

The reform of the administration of the parish roads came just as slowly. Although the Highways Act of 1862 allowed J.P.s to combine parishes into highway districts, this scarcely helped to bring uniformity of practice. In the first place many parishes were loth to surrender control over their roads, and within twelve months, 900 of them had rushed to adopt the Public Health Act of 1858 which preserved their independence by enabling them to establish urban sanitary districts with control over the local roads.[42] In the following year, 1863, an alarmed Parliament found it necessary to enact the rule that new urban sanitary districts would only be permitted for towns and villages with more than 3,000 inhabitants. The retention of parochial privileges over roads was seen by many reformers in the late 1870s as quite untenable. In 1878 one parish had only two houses but was still presumed to be able to maintain its roads. In that year there were 787 other parishes with less than 50 inhabitants.[43] Even in those cases where parishes willingly surrendered their authority there was no guarantee of progress towards administrative uniformity. In some counties J.P.s adopted the poor law union area for the highway district but more frequently they chose the petty-sessional division or carved out a completely new area. From 1872, however, when the Local Government Board took over responsibility, the pattern gradually became more orderly. Under the Highways and Locomotives Act of 1878 quarter sessions were instructed, when altering or forming highway districts, to make them as far as possible coincide with existing sanitary districts. But it was not until 1894 that the chaos hitherto existing was finally sorted out. The Local Government Act of that year merged the old highway districts and highway parishes into the rural sanitary authority, the recently created county councils (1888) in the meantime assuming responsibility for the main through roads.

III

The reform of road administration came barely in time for the condition of the roads to be improved to meet the reawakening of interest in long-distance road transport in the last two decades of the nineteenth century.

In the 1880s horse-drawn coach transport experienced an Indian summer-like revival. The Post Office, disillusioned after 1884 with the terms offered by the railway companies for the carriage of the new parcel post, contracted with coach proprietors for the carriage of parcels on the London–Brighton route, an arrangement which came into operation in June 1887.[44] The venture was so successful that the experiment was soon extended to the London–Chelmsford and other routes. At the same time there was a revival of interest in four-in-hand coaching, primarily as a recreational activity. 'Four-in-Hand' clubs sprang up in London and the provinces and G. G. Harper began his prolific writing of the 'Roads' series of chatty historical guides (*The Holyhead Road, The Brighton Road*, etc.)

For the less well off, like H. G. Wells in the 1890s, the bicycle was the great emancipator from the restraints of city life. According to Beatrice and Sidney Webb, who were persistent cyclists, what the bicyclist did for the roads, between 1888 and 1900, was 'to rehabilitate through traffic and accustom us all to the idea of our highways being used by other than local residents'.[45]

The British bicycle industry had its origin in the late 1860s. In 1868 an Englishman, R. B. Turner, who had invested money in a factory for the manufacture of velocipedes in Paris, visited his uncle, manager of the European Sewing Machine Company in Coventry, to persuade him to make the machines, the demand for which was currently too great for the Parisian firm to meet. Since the trade in sewing machines was slack at that time, the uncle obliged, the name of the firm was changed to the Coventry Machinists Company (capital £5,000) and the manufacture of 'boneshakers' soon provided employment for many of those who had earlier lost their jobs in the silk industry in the city.[46] In the following year James Starley, a foreman of the company, invented the Ariel bicycle, generally known later as the 'penny-farthing' or 'ordinary', a machine which achieved considerable popularity. But it was the Rover safety bicycle with rear-wheel chain drive, first produced in Coventry in 1885, that 'set the fashion to the world'[47] and greatly extended the bicycle craze. The introduction of the pneumatic tyre by J. B. Dunlop in 1888 considerably increased the comfort of cycling and helped to make the new means of recreation socially acceptable to women. The mid-1890s were boom years for the industry.

Bicycle manufacture had important repercussions on other forms of transport. Men who had invested their money in it were naturally leading advocates of road improvements and they campaigned energetically for the removal of the 12 m.p.h. speed limit. They achieved a measure of success when the Locomotives on Highways Act of 1896 raised the limit to 20 m.p.h. and abolished the 'three persons in attendance' rule—both changes which benefited the nascent motor-car industry. The manufacture of cycles requiring the production of high quality precision components, paved the way for the growth of both automobile and aircraft industries, many of whose pioneers had served their apprenticeships in bicycles.

One form of transport whose development was stifled by the combination of highway inefficiency and public and Parliamentary prejudice was the steam carriage. It will be recalled that Trevithick's first experiment in steam locomotion was carried out with a road vehicle as early as 1801. His pioneering efforts were followed by the appearance of many other similar contrivances through the century. There is no doubt that Goldsworthy Gurney's steam carriage of 1827 and many of its numerous successors were reliable machines and less expensive to run than stage coaches. Their viability was attested by the House of Commons Select Committee on Steam Carriages in its report of 1831 and by many individual witnesses. But the odds against their commercial success were overwhelming. Despite the evidence of T. Telford and J. MacAdam to the contrary, opinion was widespread that the iron wheels of steam carriages did more damage to the roads than did horses' hooves. Turnpike trusts, whose administration was often dominated by landed gentry with strong interests in the continued use of horse transport, imposed oppressive tolls. On the Liverpool and Prescot road Mr Gurney's carriage would have been charged £2 8s compared with the 4s charged to the fully loaded stage coach. On the Ashburnham and Totnes Road steam carriages were required to pay £2: coaches were let through the gates on payment of only 3s. In 1867 the railway interest in the House of

Commons (i.e. MPs who were directors or managers of railway companies) numbered 162, or well over one third of the total membership of the House. Even though it may be conceded that the 'active' railway interest was limited to no more than 45 MPs, given the nineteenth-century faith in the efficacy of railways, it is unrealistic to imagine that Parliament was likely to bestir itself to secure a fairer deal for a rival means of transport.[48] Parliamentary intervention was, in fact, designed solely to curb the freedom of the road locomotive. The famous 'Red Flag' legislation of 1865 made it obligatory for every road locomotive to be preceded at a distance of 60 yards by a man carrying a red flag. If a traveller on horseback or riding in a carriage chose to raise a hand the locomotive was obliged to come to a halt. By an amendment to the law passed in 1878 Parliament could prohibit the use of locomotives on roads entirely in any district where it was held that damage to road surfaces would result. By the time the 'Red Flag' legislation came to be repealed in 1896 it was the petrol-driven motor car that benefited from the removal of restraints rather than the by now outmoded steam carriage.

IV

As the proportion of the population of Great Britain living in large towns and cities rose from under a half at the beginning of the railway age to over three-quarters by the end of the nineteenth century the problems of urban transport assumed an ever-growing importance. During the second and third quarters of the century an attempt was made to meet the rapidly expanding demand by the provision of horse-drawn short stage and omnibus services. In the last quarter of the century and the first two decades of the twentieth there was a rapid expansion of the tramway network.

The consolidation of the turnpike trusts and the subsequent switch to municipal and county management of the roads undoubtedly paved the way for the expansion of local public transport services. Thus the formation of the Metropolitan Turnpike Trust in 1826 made more feasible the introduction of omnibus services in North London. Short stage services began in the Manchester area as early as 1824 and by 1850 there were 64 buses serving local routes in the city.[49] The first horse bus services in Leeds linked Headingley with the main line railway station in the late 1830s. A decade later eight bus routes were being operated. A much more rapid expansion of the city's transport services came in the 1870s and 1880s with the number of daily bus departures rising from 634 in 1879 to 1,200 ten years later. Thus many years before the first tramway line was laid the city had a very extensive network of bus services.[50] It was the same story with the cities and towns of the north-east. Trade directories of the region reveal no trace of long-distance coach services in the 1860s but a sharp increase in the number of short stage and local omnibus services.[51]

In view of the establishment of a basic network of main line railways by 1850 it may at first seem surprising that the development of street tramways did not take place in any serious way for a further 20 years despite some short-lived experiments in the early 1860s. The explanation lies partly in the mid-century chaos of local administration and partly in the tactical errors committed by the pioneers of the tramway. This new form of transport was developed in the USA fully a decade earlier than in Great Britain and it was an American citizen, G. F. Train, who was the promoter of the Birkenhead Street Railway Co. Ltd. which opened a $1\frac{1}{4}$-mile-long tramway route from Woodside Ferry to Birkenhead on 30 August 1860.[52] Within the next 12 months Train backed three experiments with horse tramways in London. The first, the Marble Arch Street Rail Co. Ltd., opened a mile-long route from the junction of Edgware Road along the Uxbridge Road to Porchester Terrace on 23 March 1861—the first tramway in London. The second was another short line which ran from the north entrance of Westminster Abbey to the Western boundary of St Margaret's parish. It started operations on 15 April. The third concern, the Surrey Side Street Rail Co. Ltd., was opened to traffic from 15 August, providing an eight-minute service between Westminster Bridge and Kennington Gate. All three concerns were ordered to close within a year of their opening because both the Metropolitan Road Commissioners and the Lambeth Vestry considered that the rails, which protruded above the level of the street, were dangerous to other forms of traffic. Of the three, the Kennington line was best sited for commercial success and carried over 700,000 passengers in nine months. The other two were injudiciously sited in more fashionable streets, were unpopular with local inhabitants and attracted far less traffic.[53]

With one or two exceptions such as the horse tramway opened on Ryde Pier, Isle of Wight, on 29 August 1864, the remainder of the decade of the sixties was devoted to building railways rather than tramways. However, the reform of local government administration and the manufacture of a more suitable type of rail for street use both helped to bring a revival of interest in tramway in the 1870s. The Tramways Act of 1870 permitted the construction of trams by local authorities, companies or private individuals. It did not allow the local authorities actually to work the lines though they were permitted to acquire them by compulsory purchase after a period of 21 years and at seven-year intervals thereafter. Thus the tramways of the 1870s were built and operated by private enterprise. The principal drawback of this system was that just at the time when electric

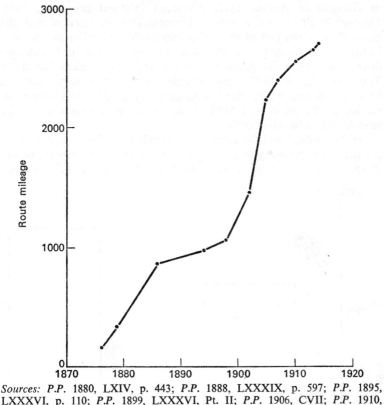

Sources: *P.P.* 1880, LXIV, p. 443; *P.P.* 1888, LXXXIX, p. 597; *P.P.* 1895, LXXXVI, p. 110; *P.P.* 1899, LXXXVI, Pt. II; *P.P.* 1906, CVII; *P.P.* 1910, LXXX; *P.P.* 1914, LXXVII, pp. 949–51.

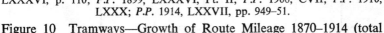

Figure 10   Tramways—Growth of Route Mileage 1870–1914 (total UK)

traction was becoming a worthwhile proposition in the later 1880s, tramway proprietors were discouraged from switching from horse to electric power because their leases were running out and they could not be sure that they would profit from the heavy capital expenditure which would be needed. However, there were sufficiently strong incentives for the installation of horse tramways since the cost of horsepower for a tram was only half that for a bus carrying the same number of passengers and the pace of horse buses in towns was slowing down because of the growing congestion of traffic. Hence there were good reasons for using horsepower as economically as possible.

In Scotland promotion quickly followed the passage of the Tramways Act. Edinburgh got its Act in 1871 and the first trams appeared in Glasgow in August 1872. Aberdeen followed two years later. Meanwhile there was a spate of promotions in London and the provinces. By the end of the 1870s there were 321 miles of tramway in the United Kingdom. At this stage the cars were almost all horse-drawn. But after the passing of the Use of Mechanical Power on Tramways Act in 1879 steam locomotion was increasingly applied. In England and Wales there were as many as 532 steam trams in service in the peak year 1894.[54] They were most commonly to be seen in the industrial north.

On 29 September 1885 Blackpool provided the first example of an electric street tramway in Britain: but it was another ten years before there was a general move to replace the older modes of traction.[55]

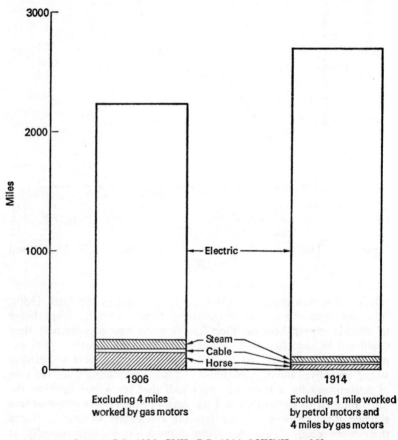

Source: P.P. 1906, CVII; P.P. 1914, LXXVII, p. 950.

Figure 11   Tramways—Lengths Worked by Various Means of Traction (total UK)

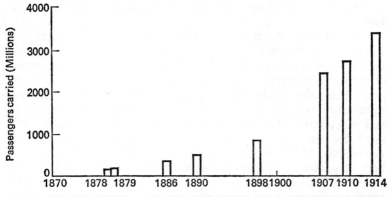

Sources: *P.P.* 1878, LXVI, p. 661; *P.P.* 1880, LXIV, p. 443; *P.P.* 1888, LXXXIX, p. 597; *P.P.* 1895, LXXXVI, p. 110; *P.P.* 1899, LXXXVI, Pt. II; *P.P.* 1906, CVII; *P.P.* 1910, LXXX; *P.P.* 1914, LXXVII, p. 949.

Figure 12   Tramways: Millions of Passengers Carried (total UK)

The passage of the Light Railways Act in 1896 encouraged the local authorities to make the change by providing them with a cheaper and speedier procedure—by submission of plans to the Light Railway Commissioners of the Board of Trade—than had existed under the Tramways Act of 1870. The route mileage then rose sharply to 1,064 in 1898 and 2,703 in 1914, by which time horse traction was employed on only 4% of the route mileage and steam haulage had practically disappeared. By this time the local authorities owned more than two-thirds of the network. Electric tramways provided the cheapest-ever form of mass transportation for urban residents and the increase in the number of passengers carried from 151 million in 1879 to 3,426 million in 1913–14 reveals that the public was not slow to seize the new opportunities for travel. The figure for passenger journeys just before the First World War was 74 times the estimated population of the United Kingdom. When it is remembered that there were more than twice as many tram journeys as there were train journeys in 1913[56] and that millions of British subjects did not live within sound of the tram bell though they did hear the whistle of the steam locomotive, the importance of the tram as a means of getting to and from work in the urban areas can be better understood. A number of municipally owned tramway undertakings provided some remarkable travel bargains right up to the Second World War. The maximum day fare on the Glasgow trams in 1937 was 2½d or just over a third of a penny per mile.[57] The London County Council Tramways issued '2d All the Way' tickets for off-peak travel and an 'All Day Ticket' costing 1s which gave the enterprising schoolboy the chance to travel the 160 miles of the council's network in 24 hours.[58]

To the Edwardian man of property tramway companies provided a more attractive outlet for the investment of spare funds than did the stocks of many of the railway companies. By 1914 the capital of the nation's tramways was £75 million.[59] In the 1880s the nominal value of the share capital was more than double that of the loan and debenture stock but with the growth of municipal ownership investors preferred the fixed interest bearing securities and by 1914 more than three-quarters of the capital was in the form of loans and debentures. Although fares were cheaper in the electric tram era than they were in the days of the horse trams the percentage of net receipts to total capital outlay rose from 3·97 in 1879 to 6·95 in 1913–1914, a substantially better return than that earned by the railways. While tramway company shares were commonly for denominations as low as £1 the characteristic debenture stock was for units of not less than £10.[60]

V

It is understandable that the 'smarter' businessmen of early Victorian times should have regarded canal transport as appropriate only for the requirements of their more easy-going and less enterprising contemporaries. A pamphleteer of the late 1840s perceived that there was 'an air of assumption and parade about a railway' which dazzled and deceived the superficial observer. It was 'the very type of enterprise, energy and efficiency whereas the canal appeared to be 'the embodiment of quiet, plodding undisguised sluggishness'.[61] The belief that in every facet of transport the railway was superior to the canal was sustained throughout the greater part of the nineteenth century. The railway companies were not above fostering such an illusion. For some years before the First World War the Railway Companies Association employed the talented author, Mr Edwin A. Pratt, to propagate the view that any attempt to bolster up the canals as an alternative form of transport to the manifestly superior railways was wholly misguided. In no uncertain terms Pratt denounced the proposal

> that the resources of the country should be employed, to the extent of many millions of public money, not in support or further development of the form of transport which has so well established its economic superiority, but in the revival of an earlier and inferior form of transport, and one that ... is in no way suited to the geographical and physical conditions of our country.[62]

And yet a properly planned and maintained system of canals was, and is, fully capable of competing with railways for the carriage of a wide range of bulky commodities. Except in conditions of difficult terrain or water shortage, the upkeep of a waterway and the labour costs of moving goods along it are less than those of a railway. Both the initial cost and depreciation of canal barges are below those of railway waggons, and the same unit of tractive power can haul a greater weight of cargo on a canal than it can on rails. The history of the inland waterways in Great Britain and overseas demonstrates that where canals have been given the opportunity to exploit these inherent advantages they have been able to undercut railroads for cheapness of transport. As a result of enterprising and efficient management the Bridgewater Canals were still carrying more than two-thirds of the goods traffic between Liverpool and Manchester a full 20 years after the supposedly all-sufficient railway had first linked the two cities.[63] After 1860 the proprietors of the Aire and Calder Canal, by spending £600,000 on such improvements as the lengthening and widening of locks and the introduction of steam-tug haulage, boosted the traffic of this important waterway from 1,098,140 tons in 1858 to 2,412,062 tons in 1898.[64] It was the conviction of a prominent businessman from the potteries as late as 1872 that wherever navigations were free (i.e. independent of railway control) as between termini they could 'not only hold their own against the railways but beat them both in rate and in time of delivery'.[65]

All the same it would be misleading to suggest that there was not a sharp decline in the relative importance of canals as goods carriers after the coming of the railways. Whilst it is not possible to agree with such sweeping statements as that 'the downfall of the canal industry in the face of the competing railway was as swift as its meteoric climb to prosperity',[66] it is true that from carrying more goods than the railways in the mid-1840s the canals sank to a situation in which they carried only just over one tenth the tonnage carried by their rivals in 1898. In the ten years between 1888 and 1898, while the tonnage of goods carried on the canals rose from 36,300,000 tons to 39,350,000, or by $8\frac{1}{4}$ per cent (largely as a result of the opening of the Manchester Ship Canal in 1894), the railways' tonnage had risen from 281,747,439 to 378,593,085 or by $34\frac{1}{4}$ per cent.[67] At the close of the nineteenth century, while the more important independent canals were holding their own, the non-industrial and railway-owned canals were losing ground to the railroads. Furthermore most canals were by this time fulfilling the more humble role of local feeders of traffic to the main line railways rather than acting as the principal arteries of trade as they had been in the first half of the century.

That canals did not have a more important part to play in the movement of goods before 1914 was in large part due to the mistakes in government policy. Through 'a want of foresight' which the members of the Royal Commission on Canals in 1909 believed to be 'not unusual' in the management of affairs in Britain, the organisation of the canals was, in the early days, allowed to pass into the hands of a multitude of small authorities most of which lacked adequate resources to meet the later challenge of the railways. Secondly, in the critical years 1845–72 government failed to prevent the absorption of key sections of the canal network by the railway companies so that the necessary consolidation of canal management was made far more difficult. The crucial damage was done in the course of the railway mania. In the one year 1846 over 200 Bills with provisions for uniting railways with canals were presented to Parliament. Not all of these became law, but those which were enacted provided for the acquisition of 774 miles of canal by the railway companies. By 1865 37 out of 109 canal undertakings with 1,271 miles of a total of nearly 4,000 miles of navigable waterways had been amalgamated with the railways. By 1883 the independence of the canals had been still further whittled away, more than one third of the mileage having passed under railway control[68] (see Fig. 13).

The irony of the situation was that by 1845 members of Parliament were becoming dimly aware that the railway monopoly might well extend to the canals and that such a development would be harmful to public interests. But their convictions were not sufficiently strong to overcome their strong preference for a policy of, at all costs, encouraging free competition. The Select Committee on Railways and Canals Amalgamation in 1846, whilst urging that a 'searching enquiry' should be conducted by those Parliamentary committees considering Bills for the amalgamation of railways with canals, nevertheless did not consider it wise altogether to refuse parliamentary sanction for such measures.[69] In the event the 'remedy' resorted to only aggravated the disease. The undoubted intention of Parliament in passing the Canal Carriers Act in 1845 was to increase the competitiveness of canals and to prevent the monopolisation of transport facilities by the railways. The effect of the Act was the opposite of that intended. Besides allowing canal companies themselves to act as carriers it also authorised them to be lessees of other canal companies. However, by this time a number of railway companies had already acquired canals and had therefore changed their titles by adding the words 'and canal' before the concluding word 'company'. As 'canals' therefore such railway companies were legally entitled to further strengthen the railways' stranglehold over the canal system by leasing or purchasing hitherto independent canal companies. It was not until 1873, under the Railway and Canal Traffic Act that a firmer stand was taken against railway and canal amalgamations. The Act forbade such mergers except under the express authorisation of Parliament. But by then it was too late.

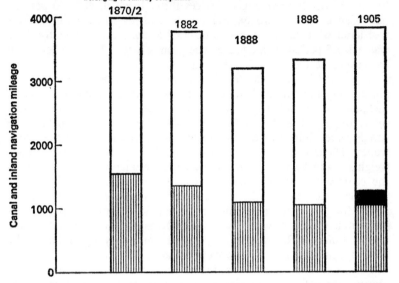

Note: The 1870/2 total mileage of 4,000 is only very approximate. Incomplete collection of statistics for 1870/2, 1882 and 1888 (incomplete for the NON-railway-owned or controlled mileage only) accounts for the apparent rise in total canal mileage in 1898 and 1905 which belies the fact that total mileage actually declined over the whole period 1870–1905.

Sources: 1870 *B.P.P.* 1872, vol. XIII, Pt 2 (S.C. on Railway Companies Amalgamation), App. T, p. 971, and Evidence, Q.7490; 1882 *B.P.P.* 1883, vol. XIII (S.C. on Canals), Appendices p. 215 and pp. 222–8 (position as of 31 December 1882); 1888 *B.P.P.* 1890, vol. LXIV (Board of Trade Returns), p. 751; 1898 *B.P.P.* 1900, vol. LXXV (Board of Trade Returns), p. 861; 1905 *B.P.P.* 1907, vol. XXXIII, Pt 2 (R.C. on Canals and Waterways), p. 6 (the non-railway-owned mileage includes only the nagivations on which a record of traffic was kept).

Figure 13   Great Britain: Proportion of Inland Navigation and Canal Mileage Controlled by Railway Companies

In the new situation of the co-existence of railways and canals the most rational arrangement would have been for each form of transport to have carried out those tasks for which it was best suited. There was no question of the superiority of railways for passenger transport and of the canals for the cheap movement of low-value, bulky materials. But in the absence of an over-riding authority such as the Corps de Ponts et Chaussées, which had powers over transport policy in France, to encourage the flow of goods into appropriate channels, such a sensible diversion of labour was scarcely ever achieved in Britain. A rare exception was the arrangement made in 1843 between the Glasgow and Paisley Canal and the Glasgow, Kilmarnock and Ayr Railway by which the canal agreed to abandon to the railway the passenger services through which 400,000 persons had been carried annually, and for the railway to give the canal a free hand with the heavy goods traffic.[70] Much more frequently there was a brief period of intense competition followed by the absorption or leasing of the canal by the railway.

In the battle between the rival forms of transport the canal engineers and the Midland traders maintained that the conflict was an unequal one in that the railways could afford to undercut the canals by recouping their losses from the passenger receipts, whereas the canals were obliged to depend solely on the receipts from the goods traffic. Then, once the canal had been forced to surrender, goods freights could be raised once more to a remunerative level. In 1846 the chairman of the Birmingham Canal Company, Mr Robert Scott MP, claimed that the Birmingham and Gloucester Railway carried goods for 'a considerable time' at a loss, in order to strengthen its bargaining position with the rival Worcester Canal, and that the Grand Junction Railway followed a similar policy to subjugate the Birmingham and Liverpool Junction Canal.[71]

Whenever Parliament investigated the canal problem there were always complaints from traders, engineers or the directors of the canal companies that the railway companies were guilty either of neglect of the canals that had come under their control or of a deliberate obstruction of the carriers' boats, and that it was for these reasons that the canals were not carrying a larger proportion of the goods traffic. In 1872 the Civil Engineer, E. J. Lloyd, accused the Midland Railway of allowing the Ashby-de-la-Zouch canal to get 'gradually worse and worse' so that the carriers found the passage through it increasingly difficult.[72] When the General Manager of the Midland Railway was accused, in 1908, of doing nothing to improve the condition of the canals owned by his company he replied that their sole obligation was to maintain them in the condition they were in when taken over. Questioned as to whether this was a very creditable objective, he was obliged to agree that 'the policy of simply maintaining a system of canals in the pristine condition in which it was fifty years ago was not likely to be conducive to great improvement'.[73]

The unfortunate pattern that emerged was that railway companies controlled parts of through canal routes but rarely owned all the canals on any important trade link (see maps 1–3, pp. 27–9). Faced with the choice between encouraging the traffic to go all the way by rail or part-

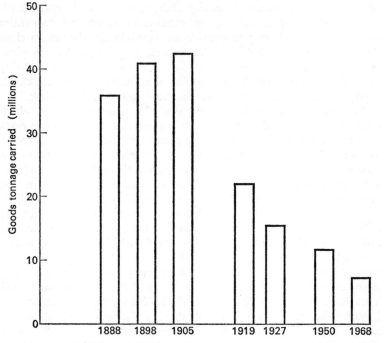

Note: Totals for 1950 and 1968 comprise only tonnages conveyed over canals owned by the British Waterways Commission.

Sources: B.P.P. 1907, vol. XXXIII, Pt 2, pp. 5–7; *B.P.P.*, Reports of the British Waterways Board (annual).

Figure 14   Total Tonnage of Goods Carried on Canals in Great Britain

ly by rail and partly by canal, they showed an understandable preference for the simplicity of the all-rail route. In 1909 the Canal Commissioners summed up the situation tersely when they wrote that 'the cases in which railway companies have a more or less strong positive interest in pushing the trade on canals belonging to them are exceptions to the rule'.[74] The obstructions to canal traffic of which they were accused largely sprang from this cause. A common accusation made against the railways was that they took an excessive time to carry out repairs to the canal banks, a task which involved closing the canal to traffic. The London and North Western Railway was said to have chosen the busiest season of the year to close down the Huddersfield canal for the repair of a tunnel and the canal banks.[75] Whereas it was in the interest of the independently owned canals to keep the waterways free of ice, the railways had a less pressing incentive to maintain navigation on their canals. One of the managers of the Trent Navigation Company charged the Great Northen Railway with allowing the Nottingham canal to be frozen up for an entire week without bothering to provide ice breakers and horses to clear the route.[76] In 1855 the Great Western Railway installed drain pipes in a field near Brimscombe station in Gloucestershire, thus diverting water from springs which had supplied the Thames and Severn canal. Navigation along this route was therefore impeded for a time.[77]

Apart from such pettifogging physical obstructions to traffic, which were, in any case, often temporary in character, a far more serious obstacle to the full utilisation of the canals was the commercial policy of the railway companies. The ton-mile rates on railway-owned canals were frequently substantially higher than they were on the independent canals. Since the railways owned vital links in the through canal networks it therefore became difficult, if not impossible, for carriers to quote through rates which were competitive with the railways. When they were independent the Aire and Calder, the Calder and Hebble and the Rochdale canals, which formed the waterway link between Leeds and Manchester, were fully competitive for most forms of goods traffic with the railways. In order to destroy their competition, the London and North Western, Lancashire and Yorkshire, the North Midland and the Manchester, Sheffield and Lincolnshire railways jointly obtained a lease of the Rochdale canal and raised the tonnage on Manchester packs to a prohibitively high level, thereby effectively destroying any possibility of cheap through freights on the waterway.[78] In 1872 the through freight on iron goods carried from South Staffordshire to London by canal was 4s 6d a ton, but of this sum the Birmingham canal, which was controlled by the London and North Western Railway, received 1s 6d for ten miles while the independent canals received only 3s for the remaining 146 miles of the route.[79] Had the canals been independent throughout, and had they charged on the ten miles at the same rates as on the 146, freight rates from the Black Country to London would have been reduced by more than a quarter. One of the most damaging practices of the railways, the levying of 'compensation' tolls, often arose as a direct outcome of their taking over leases of formerly independent canals. Some leases were negotiated as a result of the panic of canal proprietors acting under the belief that their undertakings were doomed to extinction through railway competition. In these cases the sums subsequently payable each year by the railway might not be excessive. But where the lease was agreed as a result of the railways' desire to buy off canal opposition the rent paid could well be formidably large, as in the case of the Manchester and Leeds Railway's lease of the Middle Branch of the Calder and Hebble canal for £40,000 in 1843.[80] The London and North Western Railway not only frequently refused to concede through rates on the Birmingham canal but also charged heavy 'compensation tolls' on the traffic entering their system of waterways to make good the sums they had undertaken to pay out to the original proprietors of the canal. One consequence of this policy was that although the traffic of the Birmingham canals reached the impressive total of 7,181,022 tons in 1898 only 1,446,052 tons of this was through traffic.[81] Railway control had resulted in the canal acting principally as feeder and distributor of goods whose long haul was by goods train.

In fairness to the railways it must be emphasised that they were often landed with a situation which was not of their own choosing. At the height of the railway mania the proprietors of some canals lost all sense of proportion and, in a state of extreme despondency, begged the railway companies to buy them out, guarantee a minimum return on capital in return for a control of the management or a lease on the canal. At a time of rosy optimism for all railway undertakings it is scarcely surprising that railway directors took the opportunity offered them of eliminating their principal competitors since they believed they could well afford the price being asked. It seemed a little hard that they were subsequently held responsible when the traffic on the canals continued to fall under their management. Railway acquisition was at times the only alternative to immediate closure. In 1908 the General Manager of the North Eastern Railway said of the Boroughbridge and Ripon canal that if his company had not taken it over 'it would have been a ditch long ago'. To send the coal traffic by the canal instead of by rail would double the length of the journey and, in any case, very few cargoes were being offered for carriage on the return route from Ripon.[82] At the same time the General Manager of the Great Western Railway showed that although the Kennet and Avon, Wiltshire and Berkshire and Somersetshire Coal canals served similar territory, the Kennet and Avon had been kept in reasonably good repair at considerable cost to the railway whilst the other two, which were independently owned, were 'virtually derelict'.[83]

The canals' failure to keep what they regarded as their rightful share of the goods traffic was partly the result of their own shortcomings. Many of their managers were too complacent in the face of the railway challenge. Those who were more aware of the dangers often pursued mistaken policies. Instead of improving the competitiveness of their properties they spent money in futile attempts to oppose the railway bills when they came up for consideration by Parliamentary committees. The Basingstoke canal first spent money in opposing the London and Southampton Railway Bill and then, when this attempt misfired, reduced its toll charges only a few days before the Basingstoke–Nine Elms rail link was opened on 10 June

1839.[84] The impecunious Stroudwater Navigation spent £212 12s 6d between 27 June and 15 August 1865 in a vain attempt to stop the authorisation of the projected Severn Junction Railway.[85] It was not only railway companies that were guilty of exploiting a strong strategic position to profit their shareholders at the expense of the traders and the general public. The Oxford canal and the Birmingham canal (before, as well as after, it came under railway control) took full advantage of their location as vital links in through canal routes. Sir F. B. Head, Chairman of the Grand Junction Canal Company, found that they had been 'actuated by the common narrow feelings of mankind, an anxiety to gain as much as they can without looking to the fatal consequences of such policy'.[86] It was through a policy of high tolls that the Oxford canal was able to declare a dividend of 34 per cent in 1833. If the railway companies were unscrupulous they had merely learned from the experience of the canals. T. H. Farrer, Permanent Secretary at the Board of Trade, watched it happen. He noted that 'the weapons which the canal companies themselves framed and invented as against one another, have passed into the hands of the railway companies'.[87]

The outstanding weakness of the canals' position in the second half of the nineteenth century was their failure to amalgamate and standardise their equipment and their charges so that a greater volume of through traffic would be carried by inland waterway. It is true that the pusillanimity of Parliament in allowing vital links of the system to pass into the hands of the railways made the task far more difficult. But canal management was far too parochial in outlook. In the absence of a firm leadership in Westminster what was lacking was an outstanding leader with the energy of a George Hudson and a vision of a national system of inland waterways fulfilling a major role in the transport services of the nation. The canal companies made at least two attempts to establish their own organisation. The Canal Association, formed in 1843, was joined by most of the companies[88] but had no effective voice either in Parliament or in negotiations with the railways. In 1856 the Canal Association of Great Britain had as its first secretary T. Wilson, a principal agent of the prosperous Aire and Calder canal. Its aims were stated by him to be '(1) To watch any Bills in their passage through Parliament that may affect the general interests of the navigation, not particular interests, and (2) To meet once a year for the purpose of consulting on improvements in canals and their managements'.[89] The one major attempt by the canal interest to bring under one management a large number of concerns ended in complete failure. In the course of 1865–6 E. J. Lloyd, the engineer of the Birmingham canal, led an attempt to amalgamate the whole of the independent canals south of Staffordshire and north of the Thames, including such major concerns at the Grand Junction, the Oxford and the Coventry canals, in order to get 'a joint outlet to the Thames'. The reason given for the breakdown of the negotiations was that it was believed that the railway companies, which held important links in the projected system, would have interfered with the arrangements for through rates and would have frustrated attempts at standardising equipment.[90] Nevertheless one does not get an impression of a very determined effort on the part of the canal companies to overcome their difficulties.

When a major campaign was conducted in the years before the First World War to promote the fuller utilisation of Britain's canals the initiative came from commerce and from the municipalities rather than from the canals' own management. Naturally it was those comunities furthest removed from the sea that had the greatest interest in the improvement in communications to the ports. As early as 1883 the Wolverhampton Chamber of Commerce carried a resolution recommending 'that the government should take some steps to emancipate English canals from the control of the railways'.[91] Four years later the Birmingham city council appointed a special committee to investigate the possibilities for the improvement of the waterways to Bristol, London, Liverpool and other major ports. On 28 March 1888 the committee reported its concern that the industries of the area were 'very seriously affected by the high rates of carriage by rail to the sea'. It recommended that the enlargement of the Birmingham and Worcester canal and other main waterways should be undertaken by 'a public trust which would be more likely to ensure and preserve the interests of the town and secure the lowest possible rates to traders and consumers' than would a private company which might 'ultimately be absorbed or controlled in the matter of rates by the railway interests'.[92] After many other councils and chambers of commerce had shown a similar concern the annual meeting of the Associated Chambers of Commerce in 1905 unanimously resolved.

That the improvement and extension of the canal system of the United Kingdom should be carried out by means of a public trust, and, if necessary, in combination with local public trusts and aided by a government guarantee, and that the executive council be requested to take all reasonable measures to secure early legislation on the subject.

It is not difficult to explain why there was such an upsurge of interest in the canals in late Victorian and in Edwardian times. During the Great Depression (1873–96) there was mounting evidence of the effectiveness of foreign competition in manufactured goods. When British manufacturers investigated why they were losing markets they concluded that one of the reasons was that transport costs were higher in Britain than they were in Europe and America. Sir John

Brunner, the well-known chemical industry magnate, informed the Royal Commission on Canals that in Belgium the ton–mile freights for chemicals were only half, and in Germany only two-thirds, of those charged in Britain.[93] There were plenty of British businessmen who felt they had good reason to be angry with the railway companies which suddenly raised freight charges on a large range of items on 1 January 1893 under powers given them in the Railway and Canal Traffic Act of 1888 and the Railway (Rates and Charges) Order Confirmation Acts of 1891 and 1892. By contrast, there was optimism concerning the potentialities of canals. The outstanding success of the Manchester Ship Canal—after a long period of incubation and initial financial difficulties—was the subject of much favourable comment. It was rightly believed that the opening of the canal had served to keep down railway freights on traffic between the east coast ports and Lancashire.[94]

Although it was sometimes conceded that the scope for a canal revival was greater in countries like France than it was in Great Britain, the better-informed businessmen could not help noticing that, in the principal countries of Europe, the period of neglect of canals in the middle decades of the nineteenth century had given place in the 1880s and 1890s to a renewed interest in their improvement and greater utilisation. Under a law passed in France in 1879, 2,250 miles of canal and 2,500 miles of river were widened and straightened and an additional 870 miles of canal were cut. The main network of waterways was nationalised and the equipment and facilities standardised so that boats with a capacity of 300 tons could be used throughout the system. In the 16 years following the start of the programme freights were reduced and the tonnages carried increased by 90 per cent. It is true that these improvements cost the state the equivalent of £2¾ million a year, equal to 0·21 pence per ton-mile of goods carried and that the railways were forbidden to charge less than 20 per cent above the canal rates, but both manufacturers and farmers felt the benefit of cheaper freights for the haulage of raw materials and farm produce.[95]

These were some of the reasons which prompted the Associated Chambers of Commerce to sponsor Canal Bills in Parliament in 1904, 1905 and 1906 and which finally persuaded the government to appoint the Royal Commission on Canals, the most thorough enquiry into any aspect of transport made in Britain in the twentieth century.

The Report and Minutes of Evidence of the Commission, published over the years 1906–10 filled twelve massive volumes of Parliamentary Papers. The evidence given by businessmen reinforced the accusation, made by witnesses before the Select Committees in 1872 and 1883, that the railways had allowed the canals under their control to suffer from insufficient maintenance and high tolls levied on traders. Mr Walter Somers of Halesowen, a manufacturer of forgings, asserted that the London and North Western Railway had allowed the Birmingham canal, which it controlled, to become silted up so that whereas formerly thirty-ton barges could navigate it with ease now it was increasingly difficult for twenty-ton barges to get through. The result was that traders had been driven to use the railway and the traffic on the No. 2 section of the canal had decreased by over 50 per cent in the previous 40 years.[96] It is true that the commissioners were informed of other instances where the railway companies had energetically promoted canal traffic. The Caledonian Railway was a case in point: since the Forth and Clyde canal, which it owned, passed through the territory of its great rival, the North British Railway, it encouraged the maximum use of the waterway routes. But, as the commissioners noted in their report, the cases in which the railways had a strong positive interest in developing the use of the canals were 'exceptions to the rule'.[97] They concluded that, as a general rule, the railway companies 'had little desire to do more than their barest legal duty'[98] in maintaining the canals for which they were responsible.

As for the future, the commissioners agreed with the Chambers of Commerce that it was improbable that, under unaided private management, the canals would be able to stop the steady drift of traffic to the railways. In their report they stated: 'We are convinced, then, that private enterprise cannot be expected to take the improvement of canals in hand, because, as things stand now, there is no prospect of adequate remuneration, except perhaps in a very few cases.'[99] For this reason they urged that the English and Welsh waterways should be nationalised and placed under the control of a Government-appointed Waterways Board controlled by not less than three and not more than five commissioners who would have power, with the sanction of the Treasury, to issue new capital stock or to raise loans guaranteed by the state. The money thus raised would be used to improve $533\frac{3}{4}$ miles of mainline waterway, the routes constituting the 'Cross' and forming through links for heavy traffic between the Thames and the Mersey and the Humber.[100] Forty-five years later the Board of Survey of Inland Waterways in 1954 came to a somewhat similar conclusion as to the canals which had a sufficient promise of a large volume of traffic to warrant their widening and deepening. The 336 miles classified by the Board under Group I—'waterways designated for improvement'—were included within the Royal Commission's 'Cross'.[101]

The commissioners of 1909 may be excused feeling a sense of frustration that after their extremely protracted labours the government of the day did nothing to implement the main recommendations of the report. From the viewpoint of the canal enthusiasts it was unfortunate that in the years immediately following Parliament was preoccupied with problems of industrial strife and with the contentious issues of Irish Home Rule and the power of the House of Lords. No time was made available for lesser issues like the management of the canals. In addition, the railway interest, through the pen of E. E. Pratt, strongly questioned the wisdom of spending the £15 million proposed for improvements to the canals of the 'Cross'. With the outbreak of war on 4 August 1914 the railway-owned canals came under the management of the Railway Executive Committee, acting for the government. By the time the independent canals were taken over by the Canal Control Committee of the Board of Trade on 1 March 1917[102] they had already suffered a serious loss of traffic to the railways. When the war ended Britain's inland waterways had a much less significant role in the movement of goods than they had had five years earlier.

7
Government and the Railways 1830–1914

Almost alone amongst modern industrial nations Britain left the development of her railways to private enterprise, largely untrammelled by government interference. In 1850 Dionysius Lardner, an early authority on railway questions, observed that the case of the railway companies 'was in several respects peculiar':

> The spirit of the laws and traditions renders the state averse from interference in commercial enterprises, and somewhat reserved even in the exercise of that control over them, which would seem to be indispensible to the general interests ... Powers of an unusually extensive and durable character were therefore readily granted to all railway companies in this country.[1]

This liberality towards private capital was in marked contrast with what happened in Belgium, where a decision was reached on 1 May 1834 that the main line railways should be built and operated by the state, and with the situation in France where, under the railway law of 1842, the routes which railways were to follow were determined by government engineers and the private railway companies were granted leases to work the lines for a strictly limited number of years and under stringent conditions.[2]

But although private enterprise was given its head to a greater extent in Britain than elsewhere, government could not entirely escape involvement in railway matters from the very outset. Before they could proceed with confidence in the building of their lines the railway companies needed the authority of parliament to acquire land, if necessary by compulsory purchase. To attract the necessary capital it was an advantage to be able to offer the investor the benefits of limited liability which came with incorporation by private Act of Parliament. By long tradition magistrates had fixed the charges made by public carriers and Parliament had regulated the tolls charged by canal companies; so that the inclusion, in private railway Acts, of clauses which laid down maximum charges for the conveyance of various classes of goods provoked little opposition, especially as it soon became apparent that the charges were fixed at too high a level in any way to cramp the enterprise of the companies. Beyond these minor areas of interference, however, the companies were left to their own devices throughout the 1820s and 1830s.

In defence of the non-involvement of Parliament in major matters of railway regulation it has been argued that as Britain was the pioneer of the railway as a means of transport, her MPs had no exact precedent to follow and could not be expected to anticipate the drawbacks of free enterprise in railway building and operation. Certainly the expectation was that, as with other forms of business, competition would keep down charges and confer maximum benefits to both traders and the travelling public. When considering bills for railways, MPs followed the only precedent they knew—the procedure followed in the case of canals. A common feature of this earlier legislation was that carriers were to be allowed unlimited right of access to the waterway to compete with each other in the carriage of goods and passengers, provided only that they paid to the canal company the tolls stipulated in its Act. In 1854, Edward Cardwell, President of the Board of Trade, made clear to the House of Commons what principles of railway policy had guided his predecessors in office in the thirties: 'When the railways were originally made, the theory of the law was ... that a railway is open to any person who chooses to travel upon it with his engine and carriages, paying the toll which Parliament has sanctioned to be taken'.[3]

Although many businessmen in the earliest years of railway construction considered this theory unexceptionable, its weaknesses were recognised by at least one MP as early as 17 May 1836. James Morrison MP, in a speech in the House of Commons, warned his colleagues that each private railway Act gave to the company it incorporated 'a substantial monopoly in as much as no company that might be formed at any future time for making a new canal or a new railway between the same places could come into the field under equally favourable circumstances'. Hitherto, in the case of the roads, effective competition had existed, since any coach proprietor or carrier who paid the necessary tolls was at perfect liberty to undercut existing charges. Thus the public was protected against extortion. But the railways were a different case. It was going to cost over five million pounds to link London and Liverpool by rail and it would clearly be 'all but impossible', because of the prohibitive expense, 'to bring a rival establishment into the field'. Parliament ought, therefore, to reserve the right to revise the railway companies' charges from time to time and to lease the lines for a limited period of years rather than to grant, in perpetuity, outright ownership of the routes.[4]

It was not long before Parliament recognised the futility of endeavouring to maintain, on the railways, the same kind of competition which existed between carriers on the roads and on the canals.

In 1839 the Select Committee on Railways reported that the early intention to open railways to all carriers could not be implemented:

> The intention of Parliament cannot be carried into effect; the payment of legal tolls is only a very small part of the arrangement necessary to open railroads to public competition; any person with the mere authority to place an engine or carriages on a railway would be practically unable to supply his engine with water, or to take up or set down his passengers . . . The safety of the public also required that upon every railway there should be one system of management under one superintending authority. On this account it is necessary that the company should possess a complete control over their line of road although they should thereby acquire an entire monopoly.[5]

After this Parliament abandoned the attempt to enforce a policy of making lines available to all who could provide the means of locomotion. Henceforth on each route the railway company had a monopoly of haulage.

Early in 1844 the young Gladstone was doubtful whether competition between the railway companies would keep down prices 'in the same sense and with the same assured results which they could in other matters'. The uncomfortable fact was that the vastness of the capital required to be invested, and the circumstance 'that the parties advancing it were limited in number, made arrangements between rival lines easy of accomplishment'. The likely consequence of Parliament allowing competing lines would be 'an increase of the evil' and 'a mere multiplication of monopoly'.[6] Both the Select Committee and the young president of the Board of Trade showed a keen appreciation of the distinctive characteristics of railway finance. The tendency to monopoly in railway management was apparent from an early date. In the 1830s there were two examples of 'end on' amalgamations of companies whose lines abutted on each other— the merging of the Wigan branch and Preston and Wigan railways in 1834 and the Grand Junction company's acquisition of the Warrington and Newton line in the following year—and one of a company, the Great North of England, buying up a branch line of a neighbouring concern, the Croft branch of the Stockton and Darlington Railway. However, these small mergers were straws in the wind compared with what was in the offing when Gladstone made his assessment of the situation in February 1844. The Midland Railway, created that year, resulted from the merging, not of lines which fed into each other and formed part of a continuous link, but of two companies, the Birmingham and Derby Junction and the Midland Counties, which had provided alternative routes for the traffic between Derby and Rugby.[7] It may therefore be considered the first example of a regional monopoly, even though initially the region was a small one.

Since it proved futile to expect that monopoly would be avoided and the public demand for cheap transport satisfied merely by the sanctioning of competing lines, the case was all the stronger for sifting proposals for new railways in order to prevent undue wastage of national resources. Gladstone had this objective very much in mind when he persuaded Parliament early in 1844 to agree to the setting up of a departmental committee of the Board of Trade to make recommendations on future railway policy. Under his energetic leadership as president, the committee pursued its task with vigour, presenting no less than six reports within the year. Among the important recommendations of the third report was the following:

> Each line should be viewed as a member of a great system of communications binding together the various districts.
>
> Hitherto bills had not been examined systematically and at large with reference to public interests. The committee entertain the opinion that the announcement of an intention on the part of parliament to sift with care the particulars of railway schemes, to associate them with the public interest will produce very beneficial effects in deterring parties from the attempt to entrap the public by dishonest practice.[8]

Before Gladstone left the Board of Trade early in 1845 an instrument was created which could have carried out this far-sighted recommendation. At the Board of Trade a reconstituted and enlarged Railway Department (formed in 1840) was given the new title of Railway Board with responsibility for implementing some of the recommendations of the departmental committee. At its head was Lord Dalhousie who saw eye to eye with Gladstone on the necessity of planning railway development with a view to the public interest. The Board examined all proposals for new railways or the amalgamation of existing companies 'with the object to securing the best lines of communication for the country at large and for the whole of the district'. It sought to prevent the construction of inferior or unnecessary circuitous routes' or 'the mobilisation of several capitals when the business could have been equally well or even better performed by one'.[9] Dalhousie went even further. He 'proposed a scheme by which the country was partitioned out amongst the great companies'.[10] Unfortunately the recommendations of the Board were generally either ignored or rejected. On the key question of the Oxford, Worcester and Wolverhampton Railway Bill Peel took the side of the Great Western Railway instead of supporting the proposals of the Board. Dalhousie was 'incensed' at this decision. He felt that there was no point in continuing the pretence that the

Board vetted railway Bills if its decisions were set aside by ministers of the Crown. Peel agreed. By the end of July 1848 the Board itself was dissolved and the whole experiment, which never had enough support, either moral or financial, from the Government, was brought to an end. Although the consequences were serious from the viewpoint of an economical and efficient planning of Britain's future railways, Dalhousie's team had been working under great difficulties. Because of the flood of Bills being submitted at the beginning of the railway mania it was grossly overworked. Keen parliamentarians, including Peel, distrusted its powers, maintaining that, in principle, the final decision on railway matters should rest with the parliamentary committee rather than with the members of an 'independent' board.[11]

In default of a Government board determining the pattern of Britain's future railway network there remained another alternative, that of public ownership. In the spring of 1844 Gladstone favoured this proposal, at least under certain conditions, in respect of the lines to be built in the future. The fifth report of the Departmental Committee on Railways, over which he presided, agreed to a number of resolutions, with regard to new railways. The second of these read, in part:

> That if, at the end of a term of years to be fixed, the annual divisible profits upon the paid up share capital of any such line of railway shall be equal to a percentage to be fixed, or so soon after the expiration of the said term as the said percentage shall have been reached, it shall be the option of the government either, first, to purchase the line at the rate of a number of years purchase to be fixed of such divisible profits, or, secondly to revise the fares and charges on the line, in such manner as shall, in the judgement of the government, be calculated to reduce the said divisible profits ... to the said percentage.[12]

In the railway Bill which he helped to draft shortly afterwards Gladstone included the proposal that Parliament, 15 years from the date of the Bill's enactment, should have power to buy up the railways opened after 1844 on the basis of 25 years' purchase of each company's distributed profits to a maximum of ten per cent per annum.

As soon as the Bill was made public the railway interest mobilised a quite unprecedented opposition to its nationalisation proposals. On the occasion of the second reading in the House of Commons Gladstone made 'a slashing speech, hitting out right and left'.[13] He affirmed that 'no Bill coming before Parliament had ever been more grossly misstated in the appeals made to the public to raise opposition against it' than had his. Its 'great opponents' were 'the parlia-

mentary agents and solicitors' of the railway companies 'who knew
how to get up an opposition in the House'. He vowed that he would
'not shrink from the contest' with these insidious influences.[14] Nevertheless, within the next few weeks he completely changed his tune.
The 'universal railway world'[15] had declared itself against his proposals and his leader, Sir Robert Peel, instead of coming to his
defence in Parliament, went out of his way to praise the railway
directors—'I must say that so far as regards the practical superintendence of our railways, it has been conducted in a manner which
reflects the highest credit on the managers'.[16] After a bustling deputation of railway directors, solicitors and secretaries, representing
over £50 million of railway capital, called upon him in Downing
Street, Peel gave way. In the committee stages, 20 clauses, which concerned detailed provisions for state purchase, were withdrawn from
the Bill. In their place less precise provisions for a possible state
purchase after 21 years (in place of the original 15) were inserted.
Although, formally speaking, the opportunity for state purchase
remained, the battle for an effective public control of the railway
system had been lost.

It is probable that however skilfully the Bill had been drafted,
opposition to it in some quarters would have been vociferous. The
fact that it had many loopholes and inconsistencies merely made the
task of its opponents an easier one. Perhaps its greatest weakness was
that the state purchase provisions only applied to lines opened after
1844, thus exempting the more than 2,000 miles of line already
opened to traffic before 1844 from the same degree of control. In the
event the chief importance of the Railways Act of 1844 lay in its
provisions for the Parliamentary Train. On all future railways the
companies were to provide covered-in third-class accommodation on
at least one train a day travelling in each direction. The minimum
speed of travel was to be 12 miles an hour and the cost for the third-
class passenger was not to exceed a penny a mile. For its part, the
government undertook to remit the passenger duty on third-class
travel.

Having abandoned, or at least relegated to the distant future, the
policy of public ownership, Parliament toyed once more with the
idea of entrusting to a government body the task of supervising the
railways. Following a recommendation of a Select Committee on
Railway Acts Enactments in 1846, that 'no project for the construction of a new railway should be allowed to be brought forward till
it had been considered by a government Board', an Act for Constituting Commissioners for Railways was passed later in the same
year. It provided for the appointment of five Commissioners of Railways, the President (£2,000 a year) and two others (£1,500 a year
each) of whom were paid, while the remaining two were unpaid.

The powers with respect to railways that had been exercised by the Board of Trade were transferred to the new commissioners who were also to report on projected railway schemes 'if so directed by Parliament'. However, Parliament failed to give any such direction. Although an attempt was made by the commissioners to persuade the government to give them a clear definition of their duties, they were unsuccessful, and the Bill which would have defined their powers was never passed. The reasons for their disappointment are not difficult to discover. The Bill appointing the commissioners had an easy passage through Parliament in 1846 when a flood of railway Bills was awaiting the attention of members in committee, and it seemed to make sense that some controlling body should sift the numerous projects and eliminate the most extravagant. But in the following year came the financial panic which brought the railway mania to an end and reduced the flood of Bills to a mere trickle. In 1846 219 Acts for new lines of railway were passed: by 1850 there were only five. Over the same span of time the miles of new line authorised slumped from 4,538 to eight. In the wake of bank failures, the collapse of share values and industrial depression, the cry of the exponents of laissez-faire in the Commons, such as Col. Sibthorpe and J. Hume, was for an end to government 'extravagance' (by 1850 the sum involved was a mere £10,000). At first the Commons were content simply to reduce the commissioners' expenditure, but in August 1851 the final blow came with the passing of the Act to Repeal the Act for Constituting Commissioners of Railways. Thus the five-year-long experiment was ended.[17]

In default of either a Railway Board or Railway Commissioners to exercise any say in the planning of new lines or the regulation of established ones, the Parliamentary committees, which had never ceased to exercise their rights to examine railway Bills, now had virtually unchallenged power. In view of the importance of their task it is worth recalling their merits and their limitations. It was said in defence of the committee system that at least some of the members of each committee possessed an intimate knowledge of the locality to be served by the projected railway and could therefore give expert judgement on the extent of local need and expose any bogus claims of the promoters. The disadvantages of the system were acknowledged by Sir Robert Peel in 1846:

> For what was the species of enquiry they delegated to the ordinary committees of the House? Why, they referred each Bill to the consideration of five gentlemen. No reference was made by the tribunal so constituted to the general interests of the country. They merely considered the probable amount of traffic on the projected line—whether in all respects the expectation of its promoters would

be probably realised, whether the estimates of expense would, or would not, be probably exceeded. They thus reviewed only the individual merits and prospects of each scheme.[18]

According to another expert of the day, Mr Ricards, the Speaker's counsel, it was only 'through the medium of opponents'[19] that the public were heard at all against railway Bills. It was, therefore, as a more recent authority has expressed it, only 'through the fluke of opposition',[20] that the point of view of the public at large was in any way considered.

The network of railway lines which resulted from this method of authorisation was unnecessarily close in some areas and unduly sparse in others. In 1854 Cardwell, the President of the Board of Trade, summed up the situation when he said that over the past 22 years railways had 'grown up at haphazard rather than upon any system of well devised legislation'.[21] The main line companies which had clearly emerged by the 1850s sought, for the remainder of the century, to keep a dominance over what they regarded as 'their' territories. Branch lines were often constructed and expensive amalgamations approved more with a view to prevent encroachment by a great rival company than in the expectation of large profits. The buying up of the financially weaker lines and the consolidation of the great monopoly systems continued. With each new spate of amalgamations Parliament gave renewed consideration to the question of legislative control.

By 1852 railway property had recovered sufficiently from the disastrous years 1847–50 for there to be a revival of interest in the promotion of new lines but, above all, in the amalgamation of existing ones. Before Parliamentary committees in 1853–4 were proposals for the amalagamation of the London and South Western and Brighton lines; in Scotland the merging of the Caledonian and Edinburgh and Glasgow Railways; the grouping into one organisation of the three companies which actually joined forces to form the North Eastern Railway in 1854; and, most important of all, proposals from the London and North Western Railway for the union under one control 'of a raised capital of £60 millions—between one quarter and one fifth of the railway property of the kingdom—with an annual revenue of £4 millions and an extent of communication of upwards of 1,200 miles, or more than one sixth of the railways of the United Kingdom'.[22]

These alarming indications of the elimination of competition within large areas of the country prompted the House of Commons to appoint a Select Committee on Railway and Canal Bills on 9 December 1852. The evidence heard by this body over the ensuing six months showed clearly, that both outright amalgamation and less formal alliances were increasing. Included in the latter were pooling arrangements, such as the Octuple Agreement between the eight main line companies which shared the traffic between London and Edinburgh and Glasgow from 1850, and understandings to avoid ruinous price cutting such as had been reached between the five principal transport concerns linking Liverpool and Manchester. The Select Committee urged Parliament in general to ban the outright amalgamation of railway companies though it favoured understandings for the encouragement of through traffic. Its views were clearly stated in the words of its Fifth Report:

> That working arrangements between different companies for the regulation of traffic and the division of profits should be sanctioned, under proper conditions and for limited periods; but that amalgamation of companies should not be sanctioned, except in minor or special cases, where it clearly appears ... that the true and only object of such amalgamation is improved economy of management, and consequent advantage to the public.[23]

The Railway and Canal Traffic Act of 1854 which followed had more to do with the encouragement of through traffic in goods and the railway companies' 'obligation to carry' than it did with the question of monopoly. Only indirectly, through the clause which forbade companies 'to make or give any undue or unreasonable preference' did it make any serious contribution to sustaining competitive services. What soon became apparent was that Parliament was quite happy to disregard the Cardwell Committee's recommendations that monopoly groupings ought to be confined to 'minor or special cases'. It could hardly be claimed that the formation of the North Eastern Railway by the merging of the Leeds Northern, York and North Midland and York, Newcastle and Berwick Companies in 1854 or the fusion of five other companies to form the Great Eastern Railway in 1862 were of 'minor' importance.

The most comprehensive investigation into the general principles of public policy for railways since Gladstone raised the question in 1844 was conducted by the Royal Commission on Railways in 1865–7. Through the editorial columns of *The Economist*, just before the commission began its hearings, Walter Bagehot argued that since in the long run 'railways did not thoroughly compete with each other' but rather sought 'to combine and settle their charges against the public', they ought to be more closely under the 'superintendence and correction of the state', possibly through a system of leasing the lines as was the practice in France.[24] Although, in his evidence to the commission Edwin Chadwick advocated that the government 'should resume its duties and functions towards the public' by purchasing the railways for the state, and one of the commissioners, Sir Rowland

Hill of penny-post fame, wrote a special report advocating a system of leasing, the majority of the commission were unimpressed. Those who signed the majority report considered that, for all the extravagances associated with railway promotion in Britain, railway building had been 'probably far more rapid than could have taken place under any other conditions'. They came to the general conclusion that it was 'inexpedient ... to subvert the policy which had hitherto been adopted of leaving the construction and management of the railways to free enterprise of the people under such conditions as parliament may think fit to impose for the general welfare of the public'.[25]

Having rejected any idea of a major change of course in Government policy the commission was content to recommend reforms in detail. It stressed the need for both a standardisation of the railway companies' accounts and the fullest publicity being given to their charges. In urging that the companies 'should be bound by law to provide means of conveyance, and to convey, all articles tendered to them', the 'obligation to carry', spelt out in Cardwell's Act in 1854, was further strengthened. Amalgamation of companies, it was considered, should not be allowed to take place unless and until Parliament had had the opportunity of determining the conditions under which it was to take place.

Less than five years after the royal commission had seen no need to depart in any substantial way from a laissez-faire policy the amalgamation movement again loomed large. In 1872 Bills for amalgamation or for working arrangements affecting every important railway company in England and most of those in Scotland awaited the attention of Parliament.[26] But it was the scheme for the union of the 427 miles of line of the Lancashire and Yorkshire Railway with the 1,500 route miles of the country's 'senior line', the London and North Western, which aroused the greatest concern and controversy. Plans of such moment could not be left to the usual procedure of parliamentary committees. In February 1872, therefore, the government announced the appointment of a joint select committee of both houses on amalgamation of railway companies. Of all the committees which examined railway questions before the First World War it was, perhaps, the best qualified, and partly for this reason, its cautiously worded, almost complacent, report, which appeared at a time when trade was booming, was reassuring to the railway companies and many railway users.[27]

All 12 members of the committee agreed that competition between railway companies existed 'only to a limited extent' and that it had proved impossible to maintain it by means of legislation. They found that combination between railway companies was increasing and was 'likely to increase whether by amalgamation or otherwise'. The marginal subheadings of their report—'Amalgamations inevitable and perhaps desirable', 'Past Amalgamations have not brought with them the evils that were anticipated'—show that they were much less alarmed about possible disadvantages to the public from the growth of monopolies, than were the members of earlier committees. In any case, they argued, the railway companies did not have the field entirely to themselves. It was noted that 'effectual competition by sea' still existed and that there was still some competition by river and canal, though only to a limited extent. It was recommended that these competing forms of transport should be protected by Parliament preventing railway companies obtaining control over public harbours and that acquisition of canals by railway companies should be more stringently checked. The interests of the public would best be secured through the appointment of a Railway and Canal Commission which would have the task of securing through communication, establishing a uniform classification of goods, and compelling the companies to exhibit their books of charges.

One prominent witness, Captain H. W. Tyler, RE, who had been a railway inspecting officer of the Board of Trade for 19 years and was also a director of the Grand Trunk Railway of Canada, took a far less complacent view of the spread of monopoly control than did those who questioned him. In a memorandum[28] to the Committee he pointed out that 12,414 miles of the 15,537 miles of railway which were open to the public at the end of 1870 were in the hands of only 28 companies. He claimed that although it was once true that 'competition had counteracted some of the conditions in which company interest was antagonistic to public interest', this was unlikely to be the case in the future. The alternatives, as he saw them, were that 'the future monopolies must either be managed by the state in the interest of the general public or must be managed by the monopolising companies in the interests of their own shareholders'. Company management had been 'sometimes disastrous, frequently inefficient, constantly wanting in the means of properly conducting its business and of securing safety': state management, ably administered, would be more economical and more efficient and would have no other possible object than the common good. He was sure that under Government ownership there would be a 'reduction and equalisation of rates' and a 'vast accession of traffic' which would afford 'an unparalleled stimulus to the manufactures, commerce and general prosperity of the country'. The committee was not impressed with these arguments. Its views on the subject of public ownership were confined to one short paragraph of a 50-page report. It could see 'no present necessity' for the 'full and prolonged enquiry' which would be needed before such a major change of policy could be introduced.

One short-run consequence of the publication of the report was the rejection by the House of Commons of Bills for the amalgamation of the London and North Western with the Lancashire and Yorkshire Railway and the Glasgow and South Western with the Midland. Another was the passage of the Railway and Canal Traffic Act in 1873 establishing a Railway and Canal Commission of three persons to carry out the through traffic, 'obligation to carry' and other provisions of Cardwell's Act of 1854. Neither the Act nor the work of the commission had much to do with the wider questions of railway management.

Although outright mergers of railway companies occurred less frequently after 1872 the process of eliminating competition continued, mainly by other and less direct means. Working unions, leasings, working agreements, arrangements for securing uniformity of rates, charges and services, and agreements for the pooling of receipts multiplied during the ensuing 40 years. Perhaps the best known of the arrangements of this kind was the working union of the South Eastern and London, Chatham and Dover railways formed in 1899 after more than 30 years of extravagant rivalry between the two companies for the traffic of Kent.[29] Some outright mergers also took place. The Great Western, for example, absorbed the Bristol and Exeter in 1876 and the South Devon in 1878 and the Midland took over the London, Tilbury and Southend line in 1912.

By the time the next major parliamentary enquiry into the question of monopoly was conducted, just before the First World War, MPs, traders and the public were not prepared to take so complacent a view of the railways' performance as had the earlier generation in the 1870s. As had always been the case previously, it was the announcement of important proposals for agreements between large companies for the elimination of competition which stirred parliament into action. In 1907 two of the giants operating north of London, the Great Central and the Great Northern, announced a working agreement for the sharing of their net receipts. When both the Railway and Canal Commission and the Court of Appeal turned down these proposals, the two companies devised a scheme for a working union under which 'almost all the railways in Eastern England from the Humber to the Thames'[30] would have been placed under one control. The plan was dropped only when it became apparent that it would be strenuously opposed both within the House of Commons and outside. About the same time the Midland, Lancashire and Yorkshire and London and North Western boards negotiated a comprehensive pooling agreement for the division of traffic.

Traders were not unnaturally alarmed at these developments. Through their MPs they persuaded Asquith's government in 1909 to appoint a departmental committee of the Board of Trade to discover:

what changes, if any, are expedient in the law relating to agreements among railway companies, and what, if any, general provisions ought to be embodied for the purpose of safeguarding the various interests affected in future Acts of Parliament authorising railway amalgamations and working unions.

Witnesses giving evidence to the committee revealed a growing awareness of the decline of competition and growing doubts as to whether it was worthwhile to attempt to resuscitate it. Mr W. F. Marwood of the railway department of the Board of Trade, confirmed that there was no active competition 'in the sense of a competitive cutting of rates from time to time' although there were still some areas where the rates charged for the use of the shorter of two routes between the same two termini were the same as for the longer. He reported that until recently there had been competition in respect of facilities, competitive rebates being offered on collection and delivery charges. But even these survivals of a competitive world had disappeared after January 1907, when an agreement made by the leading companies for their removal came into effect. He illustrated the growth of monopoly control by showing that whereas in 1872 sixteen companies with 9,522 miles of track controlled 85 per cent of the total mileage, in 1907 no more than thirteen companies, with a combined mileage of 14,022, owned 88 per cent of the total.[31]

Some of the most eminent railwaymen who appeared before the committee confirmed an assessment made by Bonar Law a few months earlier in the House of Commons, that not only was much of the competition that survived 'utterly wasteful', but also there was 'a strong movement on foot' amongst the managers to put an end to it.[32] Sir J. Owens, General Manager of the London and South Western Railway, for example, declared that

To the extent to which lines not absolutely necessary in the public interest have been made, railway capital has been unduly increased and a permanent burden has been placed on the greatest carrying industry in the country. In this manner competition, which parliament has thought well to foster, has been from its very inception a disadvantage'.[33]

In its final report, published in 1911, the committee endorsed these conclusions. It was admitted that competition only existed 'exceptionally or spasmodically' and that it would have to be accepted that 'the era of competition between the railway companies was passing away'. In declaring that the growth of cooperation was 'likely to be beneficial both to the companies themselves and, if properly safeguarded, to the public also'[34] the committee adopted a viewpoint strikingly different from that adopted by all previous enquiries. Nevertheless it was one which was shared by Winston Churchill,

President of the Board of Trade, who believed that there was 'no real economic future ... for British railways apart from amalgamation of one kind or another'.[35]

Since no fundamental change of policy was recommended by the committee and since Parliament was, in any case, preoccupied with other more pressing matters such as the Agadir crisis, the Parliament Bill and the widespread industrial unrest, it is not surprising that no legislation of major importance followed the publication of the report. But the issue was by no means dead, and within two years a Royal Commission was appointed to look once more into the whole question of the relationship between the railways and the state. This new body had insufficient time to finish its labours before the outbreak of the First World War brought into operation the Regulation of the Forces Act of 1871 through which the railways came under the direct control of the government working through a railway executive committee of the general managers of the ten leading railway companies. When the war ended there was to be no return to the competitive systems of the years before 1914.

II

One of the most frequently repeated accusations made about the railway companies was that when determining freight charges they discriminated unfairly between one type of customer and another or that they gave preference to traders in one district as against another. Since the fixed, or overhead, costs of railways amounted to as much as half of their total costs the companies' principal concern was to collect as much revenue as possible to offset these high and largely irreducible charges. While railways were still fighting for their supremacy over roads, canals and coastal shipping in the first half of the nineteenth century, there were relatively few complaints about excessive or discriminating charges. It was a different story once the railway companies had established a virtual monopoly of long-distance inland carriage. The aggrieved trader, having no possibility of transferring his custom to an alternative means of transport, concentrated his criticism on the railway company which was 'charging what the traffic would bear' and on Parliament for allowing the practice to continue.

The early private railway Acts included clauses specifying maximum charges for the different types of goods grouped into a primitive classification. The freight charges allowed, as well as the classification, varied from company to company, but included in each case the three elements of a charge for the use of the track, another for locomotive power and a third for the actual conveyance of goods. Although Parliament fixed an upper limit for freight rates it did nothing at this stage to prevent discrimination in charges below the maximum laid down. The establishment of the Railway Clearing House in 1842 and the drafting, by its goods conference in 1847, of the first general classification of goods, paved the way for a standardisation of practice in the grouping of goods by class; but did not ensure a common pricing policy. Through the Railway Clauses Consolidation Act of 1845 Parliament simplified matters by combining into one, charges formerly made separately, for track, locomotion and carriage while, at the same time, through an 'equality clause', forbidding undue discrimination in charge between one customer and another for the carriage of similar consignments of goods over similar distances. However, these clauses of the Act were so hedged around with conditions that they were inoperative.

The case for more effective legislation concerning the railway companies' rates and charges seemed stronger in the early 1850s as the number of amalgamations and pooling agreements multiplied. Although the Railway and Canal Traffic Act (Cardwell's Act) of 1854 sidestepped the issue of public ownership it attempted to lay down the conditions under which traffic was to be conveyed. In particular no railway (or canal) company was 'to make or give any undue or unreasonable preference or advantage to or in favour of any particular person or company or any particular description of traffic in any respect whatsoever'. Consignors who sought redress could take their case to the Court of Common Pleas which had power to determine what constituted 'undue preference' and could impose fines of up to £200 on companies which defied its injunctions. The railways' customers were no more satisfied with the way the companies treated them after the passage of Cardwell's Act than they had been before 1854. The new measure said nothing about charges for the collection and delivery of goods and the companies merely lumped these together with the charge made for conveyance, without specifying how much of the total sum demanded was for terminal services and how much for the actual rail transport. A further weakness was that companies were still under no obligation to publish their charges, so that the customer was often completely in the dark as to what had been charged to others for like services. If he brought his complaint to court he would experience the law's delays and would discover that the railway companies could afford to employ the most skilful lawyers.

After the pace of amalgamation again quickened in the early 1870s and another Select Committee examined afresh this aspect of railway administration, a new body, the Railway Commission, was set up under the Railway and Canal Traffic Act of 1873 to take over from the Court of Common Pleas the responsibility for hearing complaints about undue preferences and unreasonable rates and to arbi-

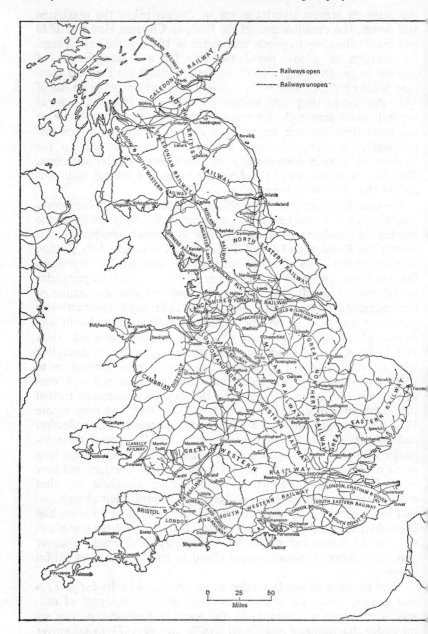

Railways open
Railways unopen

Source: Report of the S.C. on Railway and Canal Amalgamations, 1872.

Map 7   The Railway System in 1872

trate in disputes between the companies. At the same time the companies were put under legal obligation to publish their rates. But the new three-man commission was not as powerful as many railway reformers would have wished. It had uncertain status. Initially it was appointed for a period of five years only; thereafter it was reappointed annually until 1888, when it finally achieved permanence. The indecision about the life and role of the commission was an undoubted stumbling block to its full effectiveness. According to a contemporary authority it had 'power enough to annoy the railroads but not power enough to help the public effectively'.[36]

In the meantime two of the railways' most important groups of customers, the farmers and the city merchants and traders, were becoming more effectively organised through the Chambers of Agriculture and the Associated Chambers of Commerce. From the later 1870s English wheat farmers experienced sharply falling incomes as an increasing volume of imported grain depressed the domestic prices. Arable farmers were bitter that the railways charged less to carry foreign or colonial wheat from the ports to the great conurbations than they did to farmers located nearer the markets. In 1879 home-grown wheat carried by rail from Doncaster or Wakefield to Leeds was charged 5s a ton more than was the imported variety, carried the longer distance from Grimsby to Leeds.[37] Although they were generally more prosperous than the wheat farmers, livestock and dairy farmers complained of a like discrimination in favour of the foreign producer. Consignments of meat carried all the way from Liverpool to London were charged 25s a ton while from stations in Cheshire along the same route, but nearer the metropolis, the rate was as much as 40s a ton.[38]

The railway companies' case was that if they had not made substantial concessions to foreign shippers they would have lost the traffic in imported produce altogether since the customer would have found it cheaper to extend the sea journey so that supplies could be unloaded nearer the ultimate market. In order to meet their overhead costs the railway companies would then have to charge more to their domestic customers who would be in a worse situation than before. They also argued that the lower rates on imported produce were for large consignments carried the long, uninterrupted, haul from the ports to the great urban markets; if domestic producers cared to bring equally large consignments for the long haul they would be quoted exactly the same rates as were charged on the foreign produce. English farmers were unimpressed by these arguments. Had they followed the companies' advice, the payments they would have had to make to send their consignments first to the port terminal would have more than offset any subsequent advantage gained from the cheap long-distance rates.

Many manufacturers and traders had similar grievances against the rail companies. Mr T. Marsden of Barnsley told the AGM of the Associated Chambers of Commerce in 1888 that:

> every trader was aware that at each seaport the railway companies kept two books—one for inland commerce and one for goods imported into the country. He might say briefly that nearly one third more was charged to the English trader than to the foreigner.

In 1881 the government bowed to the storm sufficiently to appoint a Select Committee on Charges for the Conveyance of Goods on Railways and Canals, to hear both the railways' and the traders' explanations and proposals. Both farmer and merchant witnesses were united in opposition to the low international through rates of the railway companies. In its report the committee recommended that the Railway Commission should be placed on a permanent basis and given greater powers and that the railway companies should be compelled to adopt a uniform classification of goods and adhere to strict limits imposed by the Commission when determining their terminal charges. It was not until 1888 that the government implemented any of these recommendations. Under the Railway and Canal Traffic Act of that year the Railway Commission was given a new name— the Railway and Canal Commission—and a permanent existence. The railway companies were given six months in which to prepare both a revised classification of goods and a new schedule of maximum rates and charges. Fixing an agreed classification, with eight categories of goods, proved relatively easy since the practice of the Railway Clearing House provided invaluable guidelines. But agreement on maximum charges was far more difficult of attainment. It took 85 meetings of the special commissioners appointed by the Board of Trade to hear over 4,000 objections made by traders to the railway companies' proposals for new rates. But when this immense task was completed the Board of Trade submitted to Parliament 35 Provisional Orders with schedules of maximum rates and these were then given the force of law in the Railway (Rates and Charges) Order Confirmation Acts of 1891 and 1892. The new scales of charges were to come into operation on 1 January 1893.

There remained, for the companies, the gargantuan task of working out and publishing actual charges to be levied on each of the thousands of varieties of goods from each of some 7,000 stations in the British Isles to each other station with which there were through booking arrangements. The five months allowed the companies to complete the new schedules proved to be quite inadequate. By 1 January 1893 the new rate books contained only the new class rates. There had been insufficient time to determine replacements for the old special rates and therefore, to cover themselves against any possible loss, the companies decided to raise all rates in this category to the maximum permitted by the Board of Trade. In consequence on 1 January 1893 hundreds of traders were shocked to discover that they were being charged half as much again as they had been paying previously for similar services. The result was an avalanche of protests to the Board of Trade and the outright refusal by many thousands of traders to settle their accounts with the railway companies. In haste, the government appointed a select committee of the House of Commons to consider the accusations of overcharging made against the railways and to hear the companies' defence. On this occasion the President of the Board of Trade was on the side of the traders. He declared that the railway companies would have to be 'brought to their senses'. In 1894, in the face of the opposition of the Railway Companies Association, Parliament passed the Railway and Canal Traffic Act which provided that if any trader complained that the rates he had been charged since 1 January 1893 had been unduly raised, the burden of justifying the increase to the Railway and Canal Commission rested with the railway company.

The unfortunate outcome of these months of tedious labour was that it proved impossible in practice for the companies to raise their rates above the level of 31 December 1892. It also made them most reluctant to pass on to the traders any economies in operating costs lest, at some future date, costs rose again and it then proved impossible to effect a corresponding increase in charges. An important indirect effect of the Act of 1894 was a hardening of the companies' attitude to demands from the railway trade unions for improved working conditions and rates of pay. Yielding to these demands would have meant raising operational costs which it would have been virtually impossible for the companies to recover by charging more to their customers. When, following the first national railway strike in August 1911, the unions achieved improvements in the wages of some of the railwaymen, the government felt obliged to promise the companies that if they could show that their running costs had increased through meeting the demands of labour, special legislation authorising increases in charges would be forthcoming. Less than two years later the railways were allowed to raise their freight charges by an average of four per cent to offet the increase in their wages bill which had been an indirect outcome of the strike.

Before the First World War the railway companies received most of the blame for freight rates on British railways being generally higher than they were in Belgium, France, Germany or the USA. This was not entirely just. The 600,000 privately owned railway waggons of the collieries, iron works and other companies, lacking as they did any standardised pattern of construction or capacity, cluttered up the tracks, slowed the pace of goods trains and hence increased the costs of rail goods services. Only after 1947, when the privately owned waggons as well as those of the railway companies were taken over by the Railway Executive under the Transport Act of that year was there a possibility of effecting substantial economies in haulage costs.

In so far as it paid the railway companies to quote preferential rates to foreign, as against domestic, farm produce and manufactures the fault lay with the government for allowing such policies to continue. The railway directors could not be blamed for endeavouring to maximise the return on capital invested. Nor could they be blamed for having as their primary concern company, other than national, interests. While select committees in Britain were deliberating on how best to curb the railways' granting of undue preferences, the Minister of Public Works in Imperial Germany sent a directive to the various state railways instructing them that it was their duty, in the national interest, when establishing a schedule of freight charges, to quote preferential rates in favour of the products of domestic farm, as against foreign, produce, and preferences also to the domestic manufacturer who was to have his necessary imported raw materials carried at low rates from the ports and his finished products carried to the markets at cheaper rates than those charged to foreign manufacturers.[39] Given a different political climate, more receptive to enhanced measures of public ownership and control, similar priorities in rate fixing could have been followed in Britain. But before 1914 Parliament still adhered to the belief that the nation's railways were best run by private joint stock companies and it proved impossible both to retain commercial incentives and to meet the complaints of those domestic traders who were sometimes the victims of a policy of 'charging what the traffic would bear'.

III

Just as Public Health and Nuisance Removal Acts in the nineteenth century followed closely serious outbreaks of cholera, so it was often the case that legislation to promote the safety of railway travel was prompted by newspaper reports of gruesome railway accidents. It is true that the Regulation of Railways Act of 1840—the first Act to make any reference to railway accidents—was prompted more by concern about monopolistic practices than railway fatalities. It did, however, sanction the appointment of Board of Trade inspectors who were to examine the works of new railways before they were opened to traffic, and it did require the companies to send the Board of Trade returns of traffic 'as well as of all accidents attended with personal injury'. On 25 January 1841 Sir Frederick Smith, G. R. Porter and S. Laing, the first three railway inspectors, reported to Mr Labouchere, Vice-President of the Board of Trade, the severe limitation of their powers under the Act of the previous year:

The present Act establishes the principle of a Government inspection of railways previously to their being opened for public traffic; but if this principle is to be maintained, it is indispensible to give the Government power to prevent the opening of the railway in case the conditions considered as essential for the public safety are not complied with. As matters stand at present, the Government has the responsibility, without any of the power which ought to accompany it. The public naturally look to the Government inspection as a guarantee that the line is in a fit state to be opened, while in point of fact, the line may be opened in defiance of the representations of the government and its inspector.[40]

The report recommended that the Board of Trade should be notified at least a month before the intended opening date of any new line of railway and that the inspectors should have power to postpone the opening where public safety made such action necessary.

As if to underline the importance of what the inspectors had written there were more fatal accidents in 1840 and 1841 than in the entire previous decade—29 passengers killed compared with only five in the 1830s. This was partly due to the fact that by the early 1840s there was a skeleton national network of lines whereas in the 1830s the railways were largely disconnected with each other. With a greater amount of through running of trains the risks of accidents were greater. Certainly the alarm that was caused gave the government the confidence to introduce in 1842 a new measure, the Regulation of Railways Act, which Mr Labouchere declared to be necessary because of the occurrence of several accidents.[41] The Act gave the inspectors the powers they had demanded, to withold permission for the opening of new lines until the proper standards of safe working had been ensured. It also obliged the companies to report to the Board of Trade within 48 hours all accidents attended with serious personal injury. Even those accidents which did not involve personal injury had to be notified.

This was as far as Parliament was prepared to go, at least for the next quarter century, in restraints on the railway companies' freedom to organise their own businesses. Early Victorian MPs were of the opinion that a greater amount of interference by the legislature would only serve to diminish the sense of responsibility of the railway companies. Robert Lowe expressed the concensus in the 1850s when he declared that they had 'given the preference to the commercial element in the matter' of railway operation and they should therefore be consistent and trust to the companies' business sense to keep down the accident rate. Lord Campbell's Act of 1846 which made the companies liable to pay compensation to passengers (but *not* to railway servants) injured or killed in a railway accident, was not inconsistent with the broad principles of government policy since it could be maintained that the knowledge that large sums would be payable would act as a spur to management to keep accidents down to the minimum.

In the aftermath of the railway mania of 1845–7 railway dividends slumped. In 1850 they averaged only 3·31 per cent compared with 5·48 per cent in 1845. The Cardwell Committee of 1854, searching for an explanation of the increased number of accidents which had 'recently occurred', found that an 'operative cause' of the 'defective condition of the railways ... has been the smallness of the dividend paid to the unguaranteed shareholders, their pressure on the directors and the consequent endeavour of the board to carry retrenchement to the utmost limit'. It warned that 'true economy is not promoted by the neglect of necessary repairs'. It recommended that a code of regulations for working the railways should be devised and that in each company one of the directors, with high professional qualifications, should be personally responsible for the safe working of the line.[42]

As the volume of railway traffic increased in the boom years from 1853–7, so did the number of fatal accidents. In the five years from 1853–7 inclusive, an average of more than fourteen passengers a year were killed compared with an average of less than ten a year between 1848–52. The public were less concerned with the proportion killed compared with the numbers travelling, than they were with the actual number of fatalities. Major disasters such as those at Staffen on 5 October 1853 when fifteen were killed and at Lewisham on 28 June 1857 when 12 more passengers met their deaths, intensified the demand for government interference to secure safer working of trains. In the House of Commons on 24 February 1857 Mr Bentinck moved the appointment of a Select Committee 'to enquire into the causes of accidents on railways and into the possibility of removing any such causes by further legislation'. Although another member, Mr Hadfield, 'did not think it possible to devise any means by which the watchfulness of the railway directors for the prevention of accidents could be augmented',[43] the majority of members thought otherwise and a committee was soon at work hearing evidence.

Although important railways had been functioning in some cases for more than a quarter of a century, the government was able to exercise very little control over their operation. Significantly the Rt. Hon. Robert Lowe, President of the Board of Trade, admitted that once lines were open to traffic his department's powers of compulsion were 'altogether gone'. The Board did not even possess any legal powers of enquiry after an accident. It was a 'mere act of courtesy' on the part of the companies that the Board's inspectors were allowed on the railway at all to make enquiries into the cause of an accident. However, the minister was 'entirely against interference' by the Board of Trade in matters of railway operation. He was content to suggest that inspectors should be given full powers of enquiry and that their findings should be given immediate publicity.[44] The committee largely endorsed Lowe's proposals. Apart from recommending that the Board of Trade inspectors should be given full legal powers to investigate the causes of accidents and should report to Parliament with the minimum of delay and suggesting that it be 'imperative on every railway company to establish a means of communication between guard and engine driver', it opposed any further interference by the Board in matters of railway operation. But despite the modesty of the committee's recommendations, Parliament did not see fit to act on them until more than ten years later.

Only in 1868 did Parliament make an important departure from the principle of non-interference with the details of railway working. Section 22 of the Regulation of Railways Act of that year made it obligatory on each railway company to provide 'an efficient means of communication between the passengers and the servants of the company' in the case of all passenger trains where the distance between stops exceeded twenty miles. In deciding which particular method to impose on the railways John Bright took the advice of the railway companies' general managers, sanctioning the bell and cord system designed by T. E. Harrison of the North Eastern Railway, despite the doubts expressed by the Board's own inspecting officers. The choice was an unfortunate one. The method proved so unreliable that the Board of Trade sanction was withdrawn in January 1873, less than four years after it had been imposed. It was not until 1890 that provisional approval was given by the Board to the system under which the pulling of a cord worked the train's continuous brakes, and not until the end of the century that this much safer method of bringing a train to a halt was in general use.

In the one year 1868 there were no less than eight collisions of trains on the British railway network. None of these need have happened if the block system of signalling, for many years in use on the Prussian railways,[45] had been in operation. (Under this plan each line was divided into sections, and no train was allowed to enter a section until the 'all clear' signal had been received from the end.) This spate of avoidable accidents persuaded Mr Shaw-Lefevre, the President of the Board of Trade, to issue a circular to railway companies requesting that they should give their 'most serious attention' to the introduction of the block system and warning that 'a grave responsibility' would rest upon the directors if they were too dilatory in taking action.[46] Two years later the Select Committee on the Law of Compensation commended to the careful consideration of the railway companies, not only the block system, but also continuous brakes and the interlocking of signals and points. Its recommendations would have carried more weight had it not been for a difference of opinion between two of the Board of Trade inspectors, Col. Yolland favouring an extension of the powers of his department while Capt. Tyler preferred to rely on the pressure of public opinion on the companies.[47]

In 1870 65 passengers were killed in railway accidents in Britain. This was nearly 50 per cent more than in any previous year. Parliament was shocked into passing in the following year the Railway Regulation Act—described by a contemporary as 'the most important step taken in the cause of safety on railways'.[48] At last the Board of Trade inspectors were given the enlarged powers which the Select Committee on Railway Accidents had considered essential 14 years earlier. The Companies were required to send in more detailed returns of all accidents including, for the first time, cases involving the injury or death of railway servants. The original Bill contained a clause which would have obliged the companies to submit returns of progress made with block signalling and interlocking signals and points, but after receiving a deputation from the Railway Companies Association on 14 March Mr C. Fortescue, the President of the Board of Trade, was persuaded to withdraw it. But the more ample information he received about accidents after 1871 enabled him to increase the pressure on the companies. In a circular letter dispatched on 18 November 1873, for example, he warned that 'methods of working and mechanical contrivances, the value of which had been thoroughly ascertained' had been 'too slowly introduced'. Under the Regulation of Railways Act of 1873 the companies were required to make the annual return on progress in interlocking and block signalling which Fortescue had originally hoped to receive from 1871.

Out of a total of 281 accidents on British railways in the years 1870 and 1871 no less than 113 were caused through want of interlocking. Quite clearly the companies had been dilatory in introducing safety devices.[49] In the House of Lords Earl de la Warr considered that the companies had been given the kid glove treatment for too long. In 1873 he introduced a Bill which would have made compulsory the installation of block signalling and interlocking signals and points on all lines by 1878; but he failed to persuade his fellow peers that such drastic action was needed. He was induced to accept the compromise of a Royal Commission on Railway Accidents in 1874. By the time its members had put 43,443 questions to 336 witnesses, more than two years had passed, and the report did not appear before February 1877. Although the commissioners were unanimously of the opinion that the companies should continue to have unimpaired responsibility for the safety of passengers, they did recommend that the Board of Trade should have powers to compel the adoption of the block system and the interlocking of signals and points unless there were 'exceptional circumstances' which rendered such intervention unnecessary. They also considered that the case for the installation of continuous brakes had been substantiated. But still Parliament hesitated. In 1878 it could not be persuaded to do more than require of the companies under the Railway Returns (Continuous Brakes) Act, bi-annual returns on the progress they were making with the fitting of continuous brakes on locomotives and rolling stock.

An important reason why Parliament did not bestir itself further for another ten years was that, under the searchlight of greater publicity, the railway companies made steady progress with the introduction of safety measures. Returns made to the Board of Trade reveal that whereas in 1877 only 13 per cent of the locomotives and 19 per cent of the carriages employed on British railways were fitted with continuous brakes, in 1889 79·5 per cent of the engines and 76·0 per cent of the carriages were so fitted.[50]

Once again it required a major disaster to persuade Parliament to do something more than merely require periodic returns from the railway companies. Progress with safety measures had been substantial, but not energetic enough to prevent the catastrophe which killed 78 persons, including 22 children, and seriously injured 260 others at Armagh on 12 June 1889. There would have been no disastrous end to this Sunday school outing if Earl de la Warr had passed his bill in 1873, for there would have been no 'accident' if the train had been fitted with continuous brakes and the track had been worked on the block system of signalling. Within a week of the Armagh disaster new legislation was promised. Within three months the Regulation of Railways Act, 1889, making compulsory the introduction of the block system, interlocking signals and points and continuous brakes on passenger trains, had passed through all its stages. This was the last important measure concerning the safety of railway passengers to be passed before the outbreak of the First World War.

IV

From 1846 onwards the railway companies were liable to pay compensation on account of passengers who were injured or killed in a railway accident. Between 1 January 1848 and 31 December 1857 the South Eastern Railway paid a total of £61,897 compensation on account of passengers whose injury or death was the result of an accident for which the victims had not been responsible. In 1853, as a result of legal actions, the Lancashire and Yorkshire Railway paid out £3,000 to the executors of C. A. Carrati, and £2,000 to those of Mr Fitton, besides three other payments of £1,000 and one of £1,050.[51] It is true that the amounts annually disbursed never amounted to more than one per cent of the annual outlay of any railway company. All the same, the knowledge that such large individual sums might become payable in the event of faulty working of the lines kept the general managers on the alert to avoid undue risks with passenger trains.

There was no such strong incentive to protect the lives of the companies' employees. When a passenger was killed the railway company in whose train he had been travelling was held to be fully liable. When a railwayman was killed at work the company managed to escape liability because of the doctrine of 'common employment'. The relatives of the dead railwayman had no legal claim to compensation because it was held that the death occurred as a result of the negligence of a 'fellow servant' of the company—such as the foreman or the locomotive superintendent—rather than that of the company itself. It is not entirely surprising therefore, that nearly 3,000 railway servants were killed at work during the years 1872–5 inclusive, compared with 155 passengers killed in railway accidents over the same span of years.[52]

The practice of the companies on the occasion of the injury or death of their servants was ably summarised by Capt. W. O'Brien, the General Manager of the North Eastern Railway when questioned by a member of the Select Committee on Railways on 16 June 1870:

'Does your company pay any compensation to their servants when an injury occurs to them through an accident?'

'If it is an injury, and if a man is fit for work, we try to keep him in our service, but if it is death, we pay a certain sum of money, in proportion, to his relatives. We treat it as a case of charity; the man has no legal claim on us . . .'

'What sums of money do you pay the relatives when death occurs?'

'It varies in every case.'

'Can you give at all an idea of what the amount is?'

'It has grown up without any question at all. A sum of £10 is given where there is no particular case of distress. Where there is a case of a family it comes to this, that we employ the children and put them into our service, and give them employment rather than a sum of money.'

'But otherwise it is a small gratuity?'

'Yes.'[53]

Of the great companies, the North Eastern Railway, for whom Mr O'Brien worked, was one of the best employers. He rightly pointed out that in accepting the doctrine of common employment his company was 'on a footing with all other employers of labour' at the time. The big difference, of course, was that in less dangerous occupations the human consequence of the doctrine were less serious. But in the nineteenth century railway employment ranked third on the list of dangerous trades, being surpassed only by coal mining and the merchant service. The Royal Commission in 1877 recognised that the railwaymen were an exceptional case and that the law worked unfairly and to their disadvantage:

> Railway servants have some grounds for seeking exceptional measures for their protection, from the fact that owing to certain incidents of the law of Master and Servant, the law of liability on which Parliament has relied for the safe working of railways is practically a dead letter as far as they are concerned. We recommend that in any action against a railway company for compensation for the death or injury of a servant through the defendant's negligence, the officials whom the company entrusts with executive authority shall no longer be deemed to be merely the fellow servants of their subordinates.[54]

However, the commissioners largely nullified any good that they might have achieved by this recommendation through their mainly uncritical acceptance of laissez-faire doctrines. They were 'decided in the opinion ... that it is undesirable to interfere with railway labour otherwise than by the operation of general laws'. Furthermore they gave unqualified endorsement of the railway companies' claim that 'nine out of ten of fatal accidents to railway servants' were attributable to their 'misconduct or want of caution'.[55] If 90 per cent of the fatalities were the result of the railwaymen's own folly the case for amending the law was considerably weakened.

Since November 1871, however, the Amalgamated Society of Railway Servants, the first enduring trade union for railway men, had made safety at work one of its foremost preoccupations. Two officials of the union, F. W. Evans and E. Harford, appeared as witnesses before the Commission—the first time that railwaymen trade unionists had appeared before any parliamentary enquiry on railway matters. Through the initiative of the branches of the ASRS a petition, signed by over 10,000 railwaymen, was submitted. In contradistinction to the assertion of the railway directors the petitioners maintained that 'a very large proportion' of the 765 railwaymen killed and 3,618 injured in 1875 'were so killed and injured from causes within the power of the companies to prevent'. It was because the hours of work were excessive, the number of men employed insufficient, the working space cramped or inadequately lit at night, and safety appliances grudgingly introduced on account of their cost, that men were killed or maimed unnecessarily. The introduction of employers' liability to pay compensation in cases of injury or death would, they believed, greatly reduce the casualty rate.[56]

The Employers' Liability Act of 1880, which was the outcome of this (and other) agitation, did not meet entirely the demands of the union because those railway companies which organised provident societies for their employees were given the opportunity to 'contract out' of some of its most important provisions. While the majority of the companies, to their credit, chose not to take advantage of this loophole in the Act, three of the largest, the London and North Western, Great Eastern and London Brighton and South Coast preferred to maintain their own arrangements for compensating their workmen. In the next 17 years it was, regrettably, all too easy for the union to show that on these three companies' lines the accident rate was higher and the compensation payments lower than was the case with the companies not contracting out.[57] In 1897 Joseph Chamberlain's Workmen's Compensation Act removed the anomaly and made all the companies liable to pay the compensation determined by courts of law rather than by the rules of companies' provident societies. In 1875 one in every 334 men employed in the railway service was killed at work: in 1899 the proportion had fallen to one in 1,006.[58] It would be naïve to claim that the improvement was simply due to the legislation of 1880 and 1897: but it would be equally naïve to deny the truth of assertion made by the petitioners of 1875 that the introduction of employers' liability would make the companies more careful of railwaymen's lives.

The first direct legislative interference with the conditions of work of railwaymen concerned their hours of work. But to begin the government needed to know the facts. Before 1887 no systematic efforts were made by the Board of Trade to gather information on the hours worked by railwaymen, but between 1887-90 three sample surveys were conducted. Events in Scotland provided the occasion for a much more thorough enquiry. There is no doubt that the principal cause of the bitterly fought strike on the Scottish railways in the winter of 1890-91 was the excessive hours worked by goods guards and shunters at a time of booming trade and congested railway yards. When the strike was over, Mr F. Channing, MP, the railwaymen's spokesman in Parliament, demanded an enquiry. The House of Commons, in its resolution, agreed that 'the excessive hours of labour imposed on railway servants constituted both a grave social injustice and a constant source of danger'.[59] Thus over sixty years after the Liverpool and Manchester Railway was opened, Parliament appointed the Select Committee on Railway Servants' Hours of Labour which made the first major investigation into the working lives of railwaymen.

The report of the committee confirmed that there were 'too many cases' where 'excessive hours were habitually worked without adequate reason 'and that 'no sufficient effort' had been made by the companies to deal with the problem.[60] In view of the fact that the

railwaymen witnesses were not agreed on the remedy for long hours—
some wanting a legal limit to the working day while others preferred
to trust to union negotiating strength—it may seem remarkable that
any legislation followed, especially as the companies' spokesmen were
unanimously opposed to state interference. But the Government was
anxious to show the electorate, to whom it was about to appeal, that
it was concerned to remedy an abuse; and thus the Railway Regulation
Act of 1893 saw the light of day. It was a very modest start to government interference between the companies and the men. Although it
did not apply to railway clerks or to the men employed in railway
workshops, it gave the Board of Trade power, in cases where the
hours of work of other railwaymen were found to be 'excessive', to
demand that the offending companies should provide revised work
schedules. The term 'excessive' was not defined in the Act, but an
incentive was now given to union officials to persuade the President
of the Board of Trade to adopt their definition of the term. Although
some small gains were achieved it was not until just before the outbreak of the First World War that railwaymen's hours of work were
reduced to something approaching those of men in other major
occupational groups.

   In the meantime the unions' agitation for improved safety measures
continued. In 1893 the railroad unions in the USA persuaded Congress to pass a law for the compulsory introduction of automatic
couplers on all rolling stock in order to reduce the heavy casualties
among shunters. Richard Bell, General Secretary of the (British)
Amalgamated Society of Railway Servants went to America in 1899
to see for himself how successful congressional intervention had been.
The halving between 1893 and 1898 of the accident rate amongst
shunters employed on American railroads[61] undoubtedly helped to
persuade the House of Commons to agree to the appointment of a
Royal Commission on Railway Accidents in 1900 and to the passing
of the Railways (Prevention of Accidents) Act later in the same year.
Parliament was not to be stampeded into forcing the railway companies to introduce automatic couplers on all their rolling stock, as
practical difficulties were considered too formidable. But the Act
did empower the Board of Trade to compel the companies to use
'any plant or appliance' which was calculated 'to reduce danger to
persons employed on a railway' or to disuse any plant or appliance
whose use was considered dangerous. Within the next few years the
Board's intervention resulted in such improvements as the better
lighting of shunting yards, the introduction of either-side brakes and
the more adequate labelling of goods waggons and the protection of
point rods and signal wires. Through these and other changes fatal
accidents sustained by railwaymen fell from one in 334 employed in

1875 to one in 1,006 in 1899, while fatal accidents to shunters fell from one in every 156 in 1894 to one in every 444 in 1913.

Throughout the nineteenth century the directors and general managers of the railway companies generally refused to recognise the trade unions as negotiating agents. They were about to claim that the majority of railwaymen were non-unionists and that therefore individual, rather than collective, bargaining over working conditions was appropriate.[62] However, in 1907, under the stimulus of an 'All Grades' campaign for improved wages and shorter hours, the membership of the principal union, the ASRS, rose from 70,130 to 97,561 within a year and the membership of the two other principal unions, the Associated Society of Locomotive Engineers and Firemen and the Railway Clerks Association was also increased. Under threat of a strike the general managers were persuaded by Lloyd George, President of the Board of Trade, to accept a plan under which Conciliation Boards, comprising representatives of the employers and workers in the operating, but not the clerical or workshop grades, determined basic conditions of service apart from matters of discipline. It so happened that when the various Conciliation Boards of the main line railways met to make their awards the country was suffering from a trade recession. Inevitably the decisions erred on the side of caution and retrenchment. In 1911 the average weekly wage of all railwaymen at 25s 9d a week was a penny *less* than it had been in 1907 although prices, in the meantime, had been rising. Dissatisfaction with the Conciliation Boards' awards and the determination on the part of the unions to achieve recognition by the companies led to the first national railway strike in August 1911. When the strike was over the Prime Minister, Asquith, appointed a Royal Commission to examine the working of the conciliation scheme. Under pressure from the government, the railway companies at last agreed that union officers should be eligible for membership of the men's panels. In the elections for the new Conciliation Boards which quickly followed trade union nominees were elected to represent the men. Although formal union recognition by the employers had yet to come a big step forward had been taken towards collective bargaining on the railways.

8

The Development of Motor Transport
1885–1939

I

Britain pioneered the development of the steam locomotive: she lagged behind Germany, France and the USA in the development of motor transport. In Germany Nikolaus Otto devised the four-stroke internal combustion engine as early as 1876, Karl Benz constructed a successful petrol-driven motor car in 1885 and Gottlieb Daimler, working quite independently of Benz, produced another in 1886. Three years later the Parisian engineers, René Panhard and Emile Levassor, acquired the right to use the Daimler patents in France and completely reorganised their factory to concentrate on the production of motor cars. Their second vehicle, made in 1894, represented the first serious attempt to get away from the pattern of the horse-drawn carriage. It is true that, in England, Edward Butler produced a motorised tricycle as early as 1885 but modifications, taking four years to complete, were needed to make it at all reliable and the inventor lacked the capital for commercial production. It is generally agreed that the first British-built motor car was that made by John Henry Knight of Farnham in 1895, more than two years after an American, Frank Duryea, assembled the first motor car made in the USA.[1]

The development of the British motor industry is summarised in Fig. 15.

It has often been asserted that the principal reason for the slower growth of the industry in Britain than on the European continent or in America was the existence, before 1896, of legal restrictions on the use of self-propelled vehicles on the public highways.[2] There was of course the much publicised Red Flag Act—The Locomotive Act of 1865—which imposed on all 'road locomotives' a speed limit of four m.p.h. in country districts and two m.p.h. in towns. A man carrying a red flag had to walk not less than 60 yards ahead of the 'locomotive' to warn pedestrians of the grave threat to their safety. After the passing of the Highways and Locomotives (Amendment) Act in 1878 the safety man no longer had to carry a red flag and was expected to walk only 20 yards in front of the vehicle. But the speed limits remained and local authorities had the right to ban all 'locomotives' from public highways for a period of up to eight consecutive hours out of the 24.

The state of many of the roads in 1890 was also such as to deter faint-hearted motorists. They were covered with a heavy layer of dust in summer and were quagmires of mud in winter.

However, experiments in the manufacture of self-propelled vehicles continued despite the seemingly formidable obstacles to their use, and almost as soon as a campaign was launched for the repeal of the repressive legislation the law was substantially modified. In October 1895 Sir David Salomans, an early motor enthusiast and mayor of Tunbridge Wells, began the softening-up process by organising a Motor Car Show (with no less than five vehicles, three at least of which were imported) in the Agricultural Show ground of that town and followed this up by founding the Self Propelled Traffic Association —the first of the motoring associations—two months later. Before another two months had passed Salomons had led the first deputation of motoring interests to a minister of the crown and was pleasantly surprised to learn from Henry Chaplin, President of the Local Government Board, that a new Bill to amend the existing law was already at an advanced stage of preparation. He was even more pleasantly surprised when he was asked, a few days later, to give advice on the wording of the Bill.[3] If anything more was needed to give the aura of respectability to the movement for reform it was provided by the Prince of Wales's (later King Edward VII) attendance at the motor exhibition staged by H. J. Lawson's Motor Car Club at the Imperial Institute in London in May 1896, just at the time that Parliament was debating the new Bill.[4]

The Locomotives on Highways Act of 1896 at first greatly pleased Salomons and his friends. It raised the speed limit on vehicles of up to three tons to 14 m.p.h., but it gave the Local Government Board power to reduce this if it was considered advisable. The Board promptly reduced the limit to 12 m.p.h., and imposed other driving regulations which impeded motorists' freedom of action.[5] However, it was certainly not the case that this new law seriously impeded the progress of the motor industry in Britain any more than did its predecessors. By this time many firms had embarked on motor-car manufacture. It was the immature state of development of automobile engineering rather than repressive legislation which explained the humiliating fact that at the beginning of the twentieth century 200 times as many French cars were sold in Britain as British cars were sold in France.[6] In a memorandum to the President of the Local Government Board, written in 1896, Salomons, who was a knowledgeable engineer as well as a keen driver, predicted that it would take 'some years' before a really sound system of locomotion came into existence. He considered that 'a large number of . . . motor toys' would appear on the roads but that 'no type extant would survive in a practical country like England'.[7] To celebrate the passing of the 1896 Act Lawson organised

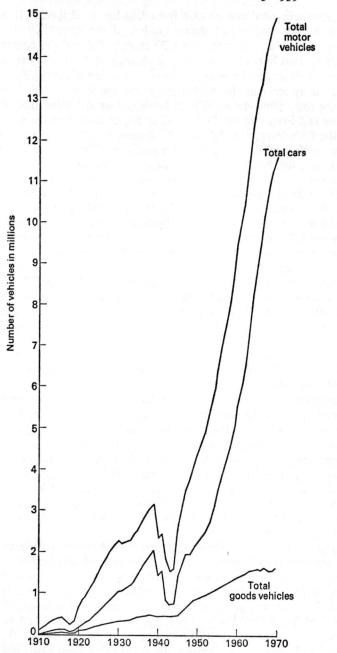

Source: Basic Road Statistics, published annually by the British Road Federation.

Figure 15   Total Motor Vehicles, Cars and Goods Vehicles in Use
in Great Britain, 1910–70 (1970 projections are provisional only)

an 'Emancipation' run of cars from London to Brighton. It was to have been a magnificent demonstration of the potentialities of the motor car. Alas, only ten of the 33 starters finished the course. The affair 'started in confusion, ended in chaos, and confirmed the average person's view that the motor car was a most ingenious toy'.[8]

In many respects the British motor car industry started off on the wrong foot. Since automobile technology lagged behind that of Germany and France in the 1890s the key requirement was the possession of the Daimler patent rights. F. R. Simms, a skilled engineer coming from a Warwickshire family with a tradition of interests in the profession, was the first to appreciate their importance and in May 1893, in association with his cousin and one other person, he founded the Daimler Motor Syndicate Ltd with a capital of £6,000 to buy up and use the German patents in Britain. But although the Simms-Welbeck cars made by the new firm were technically sound, Simms lacked the commercial acumen so necessary to make the new model profitable. Thus it came about that in 1895 a small syndicate headed by H. J. Lawson bought the patent rights from Simms for £38,000, mainly as a speculative venture and in the belief that it could establish a corner in motor-car patents and hold up to ransom all firms in the new industry.[9] The subsidiary companies which Lawson formed, ostensibly for the purpose of manufacturing cars, were 'little more than excuses for public issues to provide the money to buy more patents'. As the members of the syndicate were largely ignorant of automobile technology, in so far as they did sponsor actual manufacture they encouraged eccentric and spectacular developments rather than those less immediately profitable but, in the long run, of sounder worth. The group's grip on the patents was finally broken only in 1901 through the success of an action brought against them by the Automobile Material Protection Association, an organisation set up with the express intention of breaking Lawson's hold on the industry.[10] Thereafter entry into the industry was untrammelled by legal restrictions. Lawson's involvement in the industry served to deter the more cautious of the well-to-do classes from investing money in cars. They were all too well aware of his earlier disastrous speculations in the bicycle industry.

The nature of the early market encouraged individualistic methods of production and helps to explain the lack of standardisation and large-scale production of cars in Britain before the First World War. During the first 20 years of the industry's history it was broadly true that 'automobilism as a sport was mainly for rich men'.[11] Like Toad of Toad Hall the younger gentry who predominated as early owners of the new means of transport were 'possessed' by the 'new craze' and were mesmerised by 'the magnificent motor car, immense, breath-snatching . . . with an interior of glittering plate glass and rich morocco'.[12] In the view of the writer of a letter to *The Autocar* in 1901 there were a good many drivers who liked to 'show off, cutting in quickly, through traffic, as though going to a fire'. Such customers wanted high-powered cars made to their own specifications; manufacturers complied with their wishes. The firm of Napier, for example, through its selling agent S. F. Edge Ltd, quoted 'a price for the frame and all the driving mechanism . . . but without any body'. The superstructure was constructed according to the particular requirements of the purchasers just as had been the practice in the earlier coaching trade. The numerous small firms in the industry vied with each other in the excellence of workmanship of their cars so that they might attract orders from the discerning motorist. Thus the firm of Talbot Motors advertised that every part of a Talbot car was 'produced from the very best material known for that specific part, regardless of cost'.[13] One consequence of the adoption of these methods of business was that manufacturers required the payment of a deposit—amounting to at least ten per cent of the final price—on the receipt of an order. Another was that there was a time lag of several months between the receipt of the order and the delivery of the car. A third was that relatively few cars were made. D. Napier and Sons, one of the largest firms in the industry before 1914, produced but 8,582 vehicles of all kinds between 1906-24.[14] It is scarcely surprising that those business and professional men who were won over to the idea that a car would be useful for their work were inclined to be impatient with the uncertainty of delivery dates characteristic of the British industry and that they purchased the more rapidly produced French cars which, before 1915, could be imported free of duty.

By the standards of the second half of the twentieth century progress in the technology of the motor car was painfully slow. In the famous thousand miles reliability trial round England in the summer of 1900 only 23 of the 65 vehicles entering satisfied all the tests. Nineteenth-century car brakes only held vehicles facing downhill: they lost at least 80 per cent of their effectiveness when the object was to prevent the car moving backwards.[15] The untrustworthy hot tube system of ignition was not supplanted by magneto ignition until 1901. In the pioneering days starting was a very tricky business. In the 1900 editions of its catalogue the Daimler company boasted that the starting of the motor was 'only a matter of a few minutes' and proceeded to give detailed advice to the owner on how to activate the engine:

It is first necessary to heat the tubes. This is accomplished by lighting a small quantity of methylated spirit below the burners. In the space of half a minute, the burners are sufficiently heated to vaporise the petrol. The latter is now fed to the burners from the supply tank. If the tank is placed at a low level the petrol is forced out of the tank by means of air pressure created by a hand pump, which causes the oil to flow both to the burners and to the float chamber.... With gravity feed engines it is only necessary to open the supply cock. As soon as the ignition tubes are at red heat the motor is started by means of the detachable starting handle which fits on the end of the crank shaft. A few revolutions of the starting handle draws in the first explosive charge after which the motor will continue to work.[16]

The harassed businessman might be excused from concluding that such antics were all very well for gentlemen of means with time on their hands, but that it was quicker for him to hop into his gig, say 'Gee up' to his horse, and be well on his way while the car's ignition tube was still reaching the required temperature. Inevitably, until the teething troubles of the new industry were overcome—as they were in the course of the first decade of the new century—the market for motor cars was largely confined to those of the wealthy leisured classes who were possessed of an adventurous spirit.

In many respects the British engineering industry was ill-equipped to meet the new challenge of motor-car manufacture. It was certainly less appropriately organised to this end than was its counterpart in the United States. The individual family firm still dominated the scene. In the manufacture of motor cars as in the earlier manufacture of steam locomotives, individuality of design and excellence of workmanship was rated higher than the achievement of quantity production and cheapness. As late as 1922 the President of the Institution of Automobile Engineers commented that with many British car designers 'the capturing of records' was 'of greater importance than the capturing of orders' and that there was 'too much originality of design prevailing for commercial production in Great Britain'.[17] As long ago as 1841 the engineer J. Whitworth had introduced his system of standardised screw threads, but other members of his profession were slow to follow his example in other aspects of production.

A variety of explanations has been offered for the slow adoption of standardised production techniques in the British motor industry. On the one hand it has been asserted that the backwardness of the machine tool industry and the small scale of operations of the firms manufacturing components prevented the firms that assembled motor cars from producing on a large scale.[18] In 1913, the year in which the first of his cars was produced, W. R. Morris discovered that the component manufacturing firms were 'not big enough to take the orders he wished to place with them'. Although the engine-manufacturing firm of White and Poppe at Coventry was already supplying several well-known car firms, their scale of operations was very small compared with that of American contemporaries. Morris found that in the USA he could buy for £25 the same type of engine the Coventry firm were supplying for £50.[19] On the other hand Britain's slow start is blamed on the lack of commercial acumen of the motor manufacturers. The editor of *Autocar* wrote of the ignorance shown by heads of firms of the production methods and achievements of their rivals.[20] Morris was exceptional in visiting America to learn the reasons for the industry's success there. As late as 1924 Mr H. Kerr Thomas, a member of the Institute of Automobile Engineers, was confessing that standardisation was 'a very weak point' with English car manufacturers. Although the Dunlop wheel works at Coventry already had a very large output for cars of the 12-horsepower class, and although these were 'all of approximately the same weight and more or less the same size', the adoption of mass production methods in the factory was handicapped because there was a difference in number and size of the bolts which secured the wheels to the hubs. He was amazed to find that with wheels of similar size for similar horse-powered cars the three attaching bolts were differently positioned.[21] F. W. Lanchester was the one important early exception to the general run of motor manufacturers. As early as 1895 he decided 'that production could only be conducted on a system of interchangeable parts'.[22]

II

The state of the engineering industry of Great Britain at the close of the nineteenth century had important repercussions on the capital structure of the young motor industry. The production of cars in the early experimental years required comparatively little capital. No large outlay on heavy equipment and machinery was needed and production techniques were comparatively simple. This was particularly the case with firms like Humber, Rover and Morris which started life as cycle manufacturers. Lord Nuffield's biographers do not state how much William Morris's first partner, Cooper, contributed when the two men started manufacturing motor cycles in 1902, but it cannot have been more than a few hundred pounds. After the partnership broke up two years later, Morris had little difficulty in returning Cooper his share of the capital and he was able to make a new start with the aid of 'a small loan' from the bank and the patient confidence of the component suppliers. Thereafter, apart from £4,000 contributed by the Earl of Macclesfield in 1912, up to the First World War the firm was largely self-financed through the ploughing back of (initially small) profits.[23] The paid up capital of the Lanchester Engine Co. Ltd, through which F. W. Lanchester produced his remarkably efficient and sophisticated 10–12 h.p. cars from 1901 onwards, was only £25,000, supplied mainly by a small group of men who had already worked together in the Whitworth Cycle Co.[24] The Wolseley Tool and Motor Co. of 1901, which became one of the largest firms in the business before the First World War, had a capital at the outset of £40,000, divided into £30,000 in ordinary shares of £1 each and 10,000 five per cent cumulative preference shares of the same nominal value.[25] On the commercial motor side the Guildford firm of Dennis Bros., a private company, had a capital of only £12,500 in 1901, £7,500 of the total being held by the Dennis family and the remainder by another Surrey family, the Hartmans. Growth in this case came entirely through the ploughing back of profits. By 1912 the capital stock had risen to £49,000, the two families still owning all the company's assets.[26] Public capital issues for the entire industry only amounted to £264,000 between 1899–1964, inclusive. Thereafter there was a rapid expansion to a peak of £1,104,000 in the one year 1906 followed by a relative decline over the years 1907–12 until a new peak of £1,443,000 was reached in 1913.[27]

Most of this financing was for small-scale production and experimentation in the construction of improved models. Financing large-scale production was a very different matter. Owing to the small scale of operations of component firms, those motor manufacturers who had, for the most part, passed the experimentation stage and were thinking in terms of larger outputs were largely precluded from investing heavily in specialised equipment for car assembly because they felt obliged to engage in the manufacture of their own components. Of his firm's difficulties in 1905 F. W. Lanchester wrote that 'owing to the fact that no ancillary trades had then developed we had to do *everything* ourselves, chassis, magnetos, wheels, bodywork, etc., everything except the tyres'.[28] The situation of this firm was typical. The historians of the industry concluded that because 'the first British manufacturers were forced to make a high proportion of their own parts and components, their capital requirements were appreciably greater than they would have been if they could have relied more on component suppliers with capital equipment of their own'.[29] What it amounted to was that whereas in the USA the progress of the components industry was such that Henry Ford was able to invest heavily in special purpose machinery for the mass production of the model T after 1908, it was at least 15 years later before any British firm was able to concentrate resources to anything like the same extent.

Because the introduction of large-scale production was delayed in Britain the field was still wide open for any small group of capitalists with access to a few thousand pounds of capital to try their luck in the industry. But the mortality of firms was severe and the waste of valuable enterprise and resources deplorable. The turnover rate of firms is summarised in Table 5:

Table 5 *Number of firms making motor cars in Britain to 1914*

Date	Number founded	Existing in 1914	Failed pre-1900	Failed 1901–5	Failed 1906–10	Failed 1911–14	Total firms existing at end of period
To 1900	59	21	6	18	12	2	53
1901–5	221	22	—	59	112	28	197
1906–10	49	24	—	—	13	12	109
	64	46	—	—	—	18	113
Total	393	113	6	77	137	60	

Source: S. B. Saul, 'The Motor Industry in Britain to 1914', *Business History*, vol. V, December 1962, p. 22.

Some concerns squandered their scarce capital on eccentric and unrealistic experiments; others lacked adequate marketing outlets and publicity; the Argyll Motor Company foolishly raised a palatial factory, fronted by a marble colonnade, and shortly afterwards paid for its folly by bankruptcy.

With a total output of only 34,000 of all types of motor vehicle in 1913 there was no possibility of the industry making a major contribution to Britain's exports. However, in proportionate terms the pre-war performance was better than the inter-war one. Over 11,000 cars and chassis (valued at £4,314,000) were sold overseas in 1913, nearly one third of the national output.[30] This compares favourably with an export of only 14 per cent of private cars and 22 per cent of commercial vehicles produced in 1937—the year in which the industry achieved its best export performance before 1946.[31]

Despite all the uncertainties and the precarious and short-lived character of many pioneering firms, employment in the motor-car industry rose impressively from 54,000 in 1907 to 160,000 in 1914. It was already a characteristic that average earnings in this branch of engineering were above the average of those of other engineering workers and well above the national average of all trades. In the automobile industry just before the First World War average earnings of skilled and unskilled taken together were 40s 8¾d a week compared with a national average in manufacturing industry of 33s.[32]

Owing to the obscure origins and brief life of many of the early firms and their involvement in cycle, aircraft and other manufactures, besides the production of motor cars, it is impossible to give a general picture of the rate of profit in the automobile industry. Certainly the better-known firms expanded their capital resources at a rapid rate and earned a handsome return on their investment. D. Napier and

Sons, with assets valued at over a quarter of a million pounds in 1909, achieved a net profit that year of £28,485. In 1910, the firm's best pre-war year, profits were raised to £67,072.[33] The firm of Wolseley, another big producer, had its most successful year in 1903 when it paid a dividend of 10 per cent. Thereafter, owing to difficulties with carburettor design, small losses were made until 1908 when the firm's activities became increasingly profitable.[34] Compared with the well-known successes, the number of obscure failures was many times greater as Table 5 above makes clear.

III

On balance the interruption caused by the First World War held back, rather than encouraged, the progress of the motor industry. The firm of Daimler (by then amalgamated with BSA) was fortunate in receiving large orders for ambulances, staff cars and trucks. Even so the management was not able to specialise sufficiently to make the fullest use of large-scale methods of production since factory space had also to be set aside for the manufacture of aeroplane engines, tractors, tanks and shells.[35] Most other firms which survived the war were engaged primarily in the manufacture of arms and munitions. Wolseley made armoured cars, light aircraft and gun sights[36]; the Morris concern concentrated on the manufacture of munitions[37] and the promising pre-war expansion of Guy, a commercial motor firm, was cut short through the factory being 'virtually taken over for armaments production' while commercial contracts were abandoned.[38] By contrast, the American industry enjoyed almost uninterrupted production with only one slight setback in output in 1918.

The British industry would have received greater benefit if the War Office had been convinced of the value of motor transport before 1914 or had been more completely converted to its advantages in the course of the conflict. But the British Expeditionary Force possessed only 827 motor cars and all except 80 of these had been requisitioned. G. Holt Thomas, who made many visits to the Western Front in August 1914, was amazed to see lorries labelled Maples, Harrods, Millenium Flour, etc. 'with their owners' names on just as they were commandeered from the streets of the cities of England'. It is true that by the time of the armistice the army possessed 56,000 trucks, 23,000 motor cars and 34,000 motor cycles, but these numbers were smaller than would have been produced for civilian use if the peace-time trend had continued after 1914.[39] Selected types of truck which were considered suitable for army use were subsidised from government funds at the rate of £100 per vehicle both in the immediate pre-war years and during the war; but it is doubtful whether the policy was of lasting benefit to the commercial motor industry

because it was mainly the heavy types of vehicle that were subsidised, whereas the greatest domestic shortage was in light vans.[40]
Furthermore, shortly after the armistice the majority of War Department vehicles were sold off at knock-down prices and were eagerly
purchased by aspiring ex-army officers, keen to establish themselves
in the road haulage business. The development of new commercial
motor types was thus delayed because of this immediate post-war
glut of vehicles.

Because of the shortage of materials there was little opportunity
for continued manufacture for the domestic market while the war
continued. In any case the coalition government encouraged the most
economical use of the existing stock of commercial vehicles. On 18
February 1918 it set up the Road Transport Board whose task it
was 'to increase the efficiency of existing transport facilities without
increasing the number of vehicles on the roads'.[41] Although there
were protests at the continued presence of a large number of high-
powered private cars at the Ascot race course each year there was
a far more economical use of buses and trucks.

Indirectly the automobile industry felt some benefit from the
circumstances of the war. Thousands of servicemen learned how to
drive and maintain army trucks and staff cars and, on demobilisation,
rapidly spread knowledge of the new means of transport in the commercial community and amongst the general public. With more
qualified drivers and mechanics available, shops and factories found
it easier to make the switch from horse-drawn to motor transport.
The duty of $33\frac{1}{3}$ per cent *ad valorem* on foreign motor cars and
motor cycles, imposed by Mr McKenna in 1915, mainly to prevent
scarce shipping space being taken up by 'luxury' motor vehicles, was
retained when the war ended—with one brief interruption from
1924–5—and enabled British car manufacturers to enjoy a secure
domestic market in the years of peace. Although standardisation was
not so much directly applied to car production during the war, it was
increasingly adopted in the armaments industry which also utilised
machine tools and new steels and alloys to a much greater extent
than ever before. Knowledge of these new technologies was transferred to the expanding car industry in the 1920s.

IV

No sooner had the 1914–18 war ended than the motor industry of
Great Britain experienced a frantic speculative mania reminiscent in
its extravagance of the railway mania of 1845–7. For a few months
of 1919 and 1920 unbounded optimism prevailed. With the managers
of the many new firms that sprang up enthusiasm was more in
evidence than farsightedness. There was an even greater waste of

resources than there had been in the earlier promotional booms of 1906-7 and 1912-13. What happened in the early years of peace led *The Economist* to comment that few industries in the country presented 'such a deplorable picture of wasted capital' as did the motor industry.[42] Between 1919 and 1922 issued capital for motor production rose from £46,703,000 to £96,220,000,[43] the number of firms rose by 50 per cent[44] and 40 new makes of car were placed on the market.[45] The most ambitious project of the time was the launching of a £6 million (over-subscribed) stock issue by Harper Bean Ltd for the purpose of buying up a financial interest in other car companies.[46] The venture was wrecked on the rocks of the 1921 slump and many of the over-enthusiastic investors of 1920 were left without a penny in 1922. The extravagance of the post-war boom was reflected in the motoring periodicals. The issue of *The Motor* dated 10 November 1919 and selling for 6*d*, contained 548 pages, including 144 pages of reading matter and 404 pages of advertisements. Perhaps the most fraudulent venture of the boom was the *Speedy* car, the full-page advertisement for which in a popular daily newspaper aroused the suspicions of *The Motor*'s editorial staff. It was found that the 'factory' in South London was 'little more than a shack' and that only two cars were in the process of assembly. Far more substantial was the company's office in Holborn Viaduct to which customers' cash deposits were to be sent.[47] An editorial in *The Motor* prevented many would-be investors from being defrauded on this occasion; but the number of companies wound up between 1921 and 1925 exceeded the number launched by 35.[48]

The basis of the post-war boom was the extreme shortage of passenger cars in relation to demand. As there had been a much reduced production of these vehicles in more than four years of war the second-hand market flourished in the months following the armistice. Light cars that were priced at £185 to £195, new, in 1914 were selling for £3–400, second hand, in 1919. New editions of the same make of car were being priced at £500. A surcharge of £100–£200 for quick delivery was 'demanded and cheerfully paid'. Not surprisingly dozens of new manufacturing concerns sprang up almost overnight.[49]

When optimism gave place to gloom in the economy in the latter part of 1920 and the number of unemployed rapidly shot up to over two million, few of the firms in the industry were in a strong position to weather the storm. The profits of eight 'representative' motor firms in 1920 had amounted to £926,000, or 13 per cent of their capital. A year later they made a loss of £229,000.[50] However, these larger firms soon got out of the red. It was the great discrepancy in resources between concerns like Daimler, Wolseley and Morris, whose manufacturing capacity had been inflated by war industry production, and the numerous small firms that entered the industry in 1919 and 1920, which led to disaster for many. Those firms which had a vastly increased productive capacity in 1919 placed large orders with founders, stampers and component manufacturers. The smaller car firms, recently established, discovered that to obtain supplies at all they too would have to take the big risk of placing large orders at inflated prices. No sooner had their components been delivered, however, than the bottom fell out of the car market. This was one reason for the number of car-manufacturing firms falling from 88 in 1922 to 31 in 1929.

A more important reason was the emergence of a British manufacturer with a similar understanding of the potentialities of the car market to that shown by Henry Ford in America a decade earlier. At the outset of the post-war slump, in common with other car makers, W. R. Morris suffered severe setbacks. The output of cars from his factory fell from 276 in September 1920 to 74 in January 1921 and profits gave place to heavy losses. In this emergency Morris alone appears to have had a true insight into the market. His selling philosophy was expressed at the time:

'We have never waited for the public to ask for a reduction: we get in with the reduction first. Is it quite sufficiently realised in this country that every time you make a reduction, you drop down on what I may call the pyramid of consumption power to a wider base? Even a £10 price reduction drops you into an entirely new market.'[51]

The price reductions in the two-seater Morris Cowley in 1921 and 1922 were of a far more impressive character. In February 1921 the price was reduced from £465 to £375; in November of the same year it was still further reduced to 285 guineas. By the time of the autumn motor show of the following year the same vehicle was selling for only £225. Far from landing the firm in bankruptcy as many had predicted, the new policy brought unprecedented prosperity. The number of Morris cars of all kinds sold rose from 387 in 1919 to 3,076 in 1921 and 55,582 in 1925. By the end of 1922 the £168,903 of external debts incurred by the firm since the war had been entirely wiped out. Faced with price competition of this magnitude there was little chance for many of the smaller producers to survive. The initiative taken by Morris in 1921–2 led to a fall of 25 per cent in the average of car prices between 1924 and 1929 and to the beginnings of mass production in England. The famous Austin Seven appeared in 1922 and was soon in quantity production.

The picture at the end of the 1920s was very different from what it had been at the beginning of the decade. Eighty-one makes of car produced in 1920 were out of production within the next eight years.[52]

In 1929 the three firms of Morris, Austin and Singer were respon-sible for three-quarters of all the cars manufactured. Twenty-eight other firms shared the remaining quarter of the output.[53] The reduction in the number of firms had partly come about through mergers. Morris bought up the Wolseley firm in 1926; the American firm of General Motors acquired the Luton firm of Vauxhall in 1928 and Humber joined forces with Hillman later in the same year. There were many amalgamations of car assembly firms with the firms manu-facturing components. Thus Morris bought out the Coventry Works of Hotchkiss et Cie and the Osberton radiator factory and other component-making firms in 1923.[54]

Despite the growth of concentration in the industry and the be-ginnings of mass production the number of motor vehicles on the roads of Britain in 1925 was only a million and a half. Fourteen years later there were twice as many, but this was still only a fifth of the 15 million registered in 1970 (see Fig. 15). It was broadly true up to the outbreak of the Second World War that car ownership in Britain was largely confined to the middle and upper classes and to commercial firms.

One reason for the failure of the industry to expand more rapidly before the later 1940s was the car manufacturers' underestimation of the size of the potential market. Figure 16 shows that in 1926 the Society of Motor Manufacturers and Traders, which included all the principal car makers, considered that persons with incomes below £450 a year (equal to £1,500 in terms of the value of money in 1971) could be ruled out as potential car owners and that the possible market among those whose incomes exceeded £450 was only 835,000 including 175,000 belonging to owners of more than one car.[55] Four-teen years after this estimate was made there were 2,034,000 private cars on the roads of Britain. The significance of the manufacturers cautious estimate—no doubt influenced by widespread experience of over-investment and over-production relative to demand in 1919–21 —is that production plans correspondingly erred on the side of caution. Scale production was scarcely attempted by many of the firms still in business in 1938. The six largest producing groups were turning out 40 different types of engines and in the case of 26 of these less than a thousand units were being manufactured annually.

Large-scale production would have been more profitable if Britain had achieved a major breakthrough in the export markets before 1939. This did not happen. Although the number of private cars and chassis exported rose from 4,290 in the average of the years 1920–22 to 70,578 in the average of the years 1936–8, yet it remained the fact that in the best of the inter-war years, 1937, only 14 per cent of the nation's output of private cars was exported; and although 22 per cent of the production of commercial vehicles went abroad this

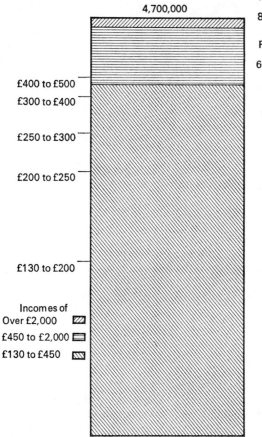

4,700,000

Potential owners
of 2 cars
87,700=175,000
cars

Potential owners
of 1 car
660,000=660,000
cars

Not car owners
3,940,000

£400 to £500

£300 to £400

£250 to £300

£200 to £250

£130 to £200

Incomes of
Over £2,000

£450 to £2,000

£130 to £450

Source: Society of Motor Manufacturers and Traders, *The Motor Industry of Great Britain* (1926 edition).

Figure 16   Number of Incomes in United Kingdom above £130 p.a.

was small by comparison with the achievement of 1950 when five times as many cars and nearly eight times as many commercial vehicles were exported as had been exported in 1937.

In the inter-war years Britain still enjoyed the privilege of preferential tariff rates in many Commonwealth markets. In Canada, for example, imported British cars paid a duty of 15 per cent compared with 25 per cent or more paid by other importers. In New Zealand the corresponding figures were ten per cent and 35 per cent.[56] In 1937 over 85 per cent of British cars exported went to Commonwealth countries and in no single year since 1919 had foreign countries ever

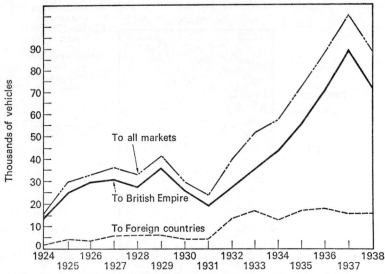

Source: Society of Motor Manufacturers and Traders, *The Motor Industry of Great Britain* (1939 edition).

Figure 17   Export of Motor Vehicles to Empire and Foreign Markets

taken as much as a quarter of the vehicles sent overseas.[57] (see Fig. 17). All the same, sales to countries like South Africa and Australia could have been several times larger if more consideration had been given to customers' needs and if the British Government's fiscal policy had encouraged rather than depressed the production of cars in the higher horsepower range. On the occasion of the British Empire Exhibition held at Wembley in 1924 the Institution of Automobile Engineers, taking advantage of the presence in London of a large number of its members from Commonwealth countries, arranged a special conference on Commonwealth markets in a meeting hall on the exhibition site. Following the reading of a paper by Mr F. A. S. Acres on 'The Requirements of the Colonial Market', Mr L. A. Legros from South Africa bluntly declared that he would not look twice at more than nine out of the 58 British-made cars exhibited although he was tempted by all four of the Canadian vehicles on show. The trouble with the majority of the British cars was that beneath the body of the car and, in some cases, as low as eight inches from the ground, there were 'hanging brake levers which could be damaged or removed by a small obstruction on the road or track, thus putting the brakes out of action without attracting the driver's attention'. At least up to that time, most British car makers, when designing their vehicles, had failed to take into account the inferior quality of roads in many overseas markets.[58]

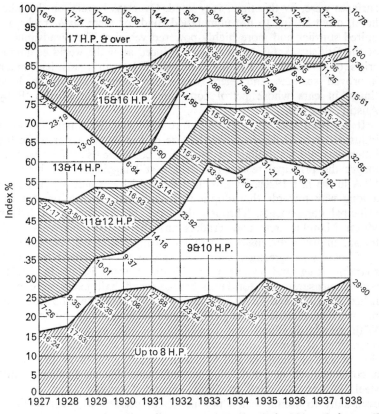

Source: Society of Motor Manufacturers and Traders, *The Motor Industry of Great Britain* (1939 edition).

Figure 18   Percentage Share of Sales of Selected Horsepower Groups

From 1 January 1910 British-made motor cars were subject to an annual tax directly related to their horsepower. Cars of 26 to 33 horsepower, for example, were taxed four times as heavily as were cars of under six and a half horsepower. Ten years later a simpler scale of £1 tax per unit of horsepower was substituted and remained in force for a quarter of a century. The effect of this system of taxation was to reduce the importance of the hitherto predominant medium-powered car of 11–14 h.p. and to give a great impetus to the production of low-powered vehicles in the 8–10 h.p. class. Fig. 18 shows that cars of up to 10 h.p. which comprised less than a quarter of the output in 1927 formed over 62 per cent of the total produced in 1938. Manufacturers' concentration on the making of 'baby' cars no doubt helped sales very greatly in the domestic market since British road surfaces were, by this time, very good. Overseas buyers, on the other hand, often having to use unmetalled roads or mere farm tracks, required sturdier and more highly-powered vehicles. The disadvantages of the British taxation system were reduced after the world economic crisis of 1929-32 as by this time many foreign roads had much improved surfaces and there was more interest shown, in hard times, in cars whose petrol consumption, like that of the 'Baby Austin', was low.

It has been said of the years before 1914 that the American motor industry 'grew to fifteen times the size of her British sister while the latter was out scrabbling for parts and components'.[59] This was no longer the principal reason for Britain still lagging well behind the USA in the late 1920s. By this time the British car industry had gone a long way towards the adoption of standard specifications for the principal components. Through the work of the Society of British Motor Manufacturers and Traders and the British Standards Institution, uniform dimensions were increasingly adopted. As early as 1915 there was agreement on measurements for pneumatic tyre rims; sparking plug and magneto specifications were issued in 1917;[60] agreed measurements for lamp brackets and ball joints were published in 1923 and in the following years came specifications for piston rings, electric lighting cables, and valves for pneumatic tyres.[61] With standardisation went consolidation and growth in scale of operations of firms manufacturing components. With the amalgamation of Lodge Brothers and Co. with Bernard Hopps in 1913 came a concentration of spark plug manufacture. Joseph Sankey's sheet steel business, founded in 1908, expanded rapidly after the war, eventually to dominate the production of pressed steel car bodies.[62] Thus, in the 1930s, the reason for the diversity of types of motor car manufactured in Britain was the production and marketing policies of management, which preferred to make a large variety of types of car to suit the preference of middle-class purchasers, rather than to concentrate on the production of a much more limited range of models of a less costly type likely to have some appeal to the better-paid working man.

V

British motor transport in its pioneering days had a greater impact on social life than it did on the economy. The country's roads were in no fit state to accommodate the noisy new vehicles with their solid rubber, or even metal tyres. The chief concern of many witnesses before the Royal Commission on the Motor Car in 1906 was the great nuisance caused by the huge clouds of dust, sometimes rising up to 40 feet in the air, stirred up by the pleasure-seeking motorist 'hogging' along quiet country roads. Lord Montagu of Beaulieu considered that dust was 'the cause of nine-tenths of the unpopularity of motor cars'.[63] The authoress, Miss E. Everett-Green, of Albany near Guildford, who had been a car-owner as early as 1897 but later reverted to horse transport, complained that the dust 'simply ruined everything' in her garden and that 'all the strawberries and grapes were spoiled'.[64] Cottages and market gardeners whose properties fronted on roads popular with motorists were angry that the quality of their crops, and hence the saleability of their land, had fallen sharply. Estate agents reported a decline in property values on the more fashionable motoring routes. On the London to Portsmouth road the fall was in the order of 25 to 35 per cent.[65] There was much animosity towards what was regarded as 'a fashionable amusement'.[66] Capt. Sant, Chief Constable of Surrey, felt that class hatred was being aggravated by the use of the motor car. 'Five very respectable working class sort of men' were walking ahead of him on the road when a passing car 'kicked up a most fearful cloud of dust', smothering them all from head to foot. One of the fellows then turned round to the other four and angrily demanded, 'Look here mates, how long are we to stand this?' Capt. Sant considered the comment 'rather ominous'.[67] He was not alone in his views about the social impact of the motor car. The government's chief industrial adviser, Mr G. R. Askwith (later Lord Askwith), considered that the manifestation of wealth in the form of ostentatious expenditure on motor cars was one of the reasons for the current industrial unrest.[68]

The origin of the disrespect with which early motorists were sometimes regarded lay partly in the frequency with which they fell foul of the law. Although the Motor Car Act of 1903 raised the speed limit to 20 m.p.h., many of the vehicles then being manufactured were fully capable of double this speed. Constant violation of the law by (mostly well-to-do) motorists gave the police, who were mainly recruited from the working classes, their first big opportunity to assert their authority over the hoi polloi. They organised speed traps for the unwary motorist with a zeal for duty much above the ordinary. The more responsible members of the upper classes were concerned that they were being let down by the more reckless of their contemporaries. Their anxiety was reflected in the dressing-down given by Badger to Toad:

> 'You're getting us animals a bad name in the district by your furious driving and by your smashes and your rows with the police. Independence is all very well, but we animals never allow our friends to make fools of themselves beyond a certain limit, and that limit you've reached.'[69]

The ardour of the Sussex police in endeavouring to curb 'speeding'

Source: Dyos and Aldcroft, *British Transport*, 1969.

Map 8   The Railway System in 1914

was the immediate occasion for the establishment of a new organisation of motorists, the Automobile Association, in 1905. This initially
comprised a group of motoring enthusiasts who had been victims of
police traps on the Brighton road. A party of cycling 'scouts' were
sent to take up positions a suitable distance in advance of the police
traps so that by displaying brightly-coloured discs from the roadside,
members approaching in their cars could be warned of the necessity
to reduce speed if they were to avoid prosecution. Shortly afterwards
some of the scouts were themselves prosecuted for obstructing the
police in the execution of their duty and, in consequence, the disc
warning system was soon abandoned. Instead, the scouts were instructed to salute members they met on the roads unless they knew
of the presence of a police trap in the vicinity. Members were at the
same time advised to stop any scout who failed to make the respectful
salute and the opportunity would then be provided for the scout to
'tip the wink' to the motorist. The practice of the scouts saluting
members continued long after the occasion for it had disappeared
with the abolition of the speed limit (except in built-up areas) in 1930.
It was not until the enormous growth in numbers of motor vehicles
on the roads made it impossible for the scout both to salute members
and to drive with safety that the practice was discontinued in 1961.[70]

That serious animosity to the motor car and the motorist was comparatively short-lived was partly due to the genius of Lloyd George
who, through the Finance Act of 1909, introduced a petrol tax of 3*d*
a gallon, and an annual vehicle licence the cost of which increased
progressively with the horsepower rating of the vehicle. The proceeds
of these taxes were to go into a Road Fund to be administered by a
Road Board established under the Development and Road Improvement Act passed later in 1909. For the first time substantial sums of
money became available for dealing with the new problems of road
construction and maintenance brought into being by the motor car.

The immediate preoccupation of the Road Board when it began
to function from 1 January 1910 was 'the alleviation of the intolerable
and injurious nuisance arising from the mud and dust'. Its members
decided that the 'condition of the road crusts' was 'the most urgent
problem' and that they would spend money to make the most of
existing roads rather than embark on the construction of completely
new ones.[71] It greatly aided their task that important experiments in
road surfacing had been conducted in recent years. Purnell Hooley,
considering the need in the motor age for road surfaces impervious
to water, discovered that a mixture of tar and slag resisted wear
better than tar and stone, and christened the new material 'tarmac'.[72]
The surveyor of the Buckinghamshire County Council was one of
the earliest of his profession to appreciate the merits of the new
material, and in March 1904 he surfaced a small stretch of the

London–Bath road with it.[73] The Report of the Royal Commission on Motor Cars made reference to such experiments but the commissioners considered that they had 'not been on a sufficiently large scale or carried on long enough' for any firm conclusion to be drawn as to their value. By April 1911, however, the Road Board was sufficiently convinced of the durability and imperviousness of tarmac to issue to all local authority surveyors standard specifications for its constituency and methods of application.[74] The importance of Road Board grants and loans in the attack on poor road surfaces and the dust problem cannot be underestimated. In the four years preceding 31 March 1914 £1,900,574 of a total of £2,268,433 granted to local authorities and £388,462 of a total of £403,362 loaned to them was spent on 'improvement of road crusts'. The small sum that was left from the total had to suffice for road widenings and straightening, diversions and reconstruction and improvement of bridges. The uncomfortable fact was that before the introduction of the County Councils Act in 1888 the maintenance of the roads had been sadly neglected. The arrival of the motor car and the creation of the Road Board undoubtedly helped to speed up their improvement; but it was a long job which had only just been started by the outbreak of the First World War. In the case of Nottinghamshire, whose surveyor, Purnell Hooley, was fully conversant with the new road surfacing techniques, only 40 miles out of the county's 408 miles of main road had been completely covered with tarmac by 1918 although another 167 miles had been covered in the centre of the road only.[75] If this experience is at all typical it is not difficult to understand why the main concern of county surveyors after the war was still to concentrate on the improvement of road crusts. Progress in road surfacing depended on the rapid expansion of the gas industry and a continued high rate of production of pig iron. A million and a half tons of tarred slag were produced in 1920—sufficient to cover only 900 of the 28,000 miles of main roads in the country. As late as 1922 the President of the Institute of Automobile Engineers considered that the words 'a coat of tar covers a multitude of sins' aptly described the condition of many of the nation's roads.[76]

Fifty years before Britain's first motorway, the M1 (from London–Birmingham) was opened in 1959, the motoring interest both within Parliament and without rejected a government proposal that special roads without speed restrictions should be built for the exclusive use of motorists. A leading spokesman, Joynson Hicks MP, expressed his opposition to 'taking the motorist and placing him on the heights of fame with a special road to himself'. He was afraid that once special roads were opened there would be an increasing outcry to forbid the car driver access to the ordinary roads or at the least to refuse any relaxation of the speed limit of 20 m.p.h.[77]

Except in the case of some city and country bus services, the commercial use of motor transport was small before the First World War; during the first 20 years that it was available the internal combustion engine was used mainly for pleasure driving. By 1914 the motor car had generally displaced the carriage and four; it had not yet displaced the horse and gig. Censuses conducted on behalf of the Road Board in the counties in 1912 revealed that horse-drawn traffic still predominated but that the motor cars greatly outnumbered motor vans and lorries.[78] In London the big switch from horse-drawn omnibuses to motor buses came between 1905-8. There were only 20 motor buses at work in the whole of the metropolitan area in 1905: by March 1908 there were over 1,000.[79] By 1913 only six per cent of the passenger vehicles plied for hire in London were horse-drawn. But the capital was still using horse-drawn transport for the carriage of goods. At the same time as the horse bus had almost disappeared from the streets only 12 per cent of trade vehicles were motor-powered.[80] Some contemporaries welcomed the arrival of motor vehicles in the streets of the cities for at first they eased traffic congestion. A traffic census in Fleet Street on a typical working day in 1907 revealed the passage of 3,236 buses, 995 of which were motor-powered. On a similar day in the spring of 1912 2,770 buses, nearly all of larger capacity than the vehicles of five years earlier, and nearly all motor-powered, were sufficient to carry the traffic.[81]

Many doctors were to be found among the early users of motor cars. Dr Bruce Porter, who said he was the first London doctor to use a car professionally, claimed that 'on several occasions he had saved life by having a motor car'.[82] His contemporary, C. B. Lockwood, a surgeon of St Bartholomew's Hospital, London, found that a car was more reliable and punctual for use within 30 miles of the capital than were either horse-drawn vehicles or the local trains. His reason for making the change from other forms of transport was the same as that which motivated millions of the next generation: 'I can go when I like, get there when I like and come back when I like'.[83]

In the second half of the twentieth century the motor car was regarded by many as the great contaminator of the environment: at the close of the nineteenth century it was seen by sanitary engineers as a public benefactor. The annual conference of Municipal Engineers, meeting in Birmingham on 28 September 1898, resolved:

That this conference of Municipal Engineers assembled in connection with the congress of the Sanitary Institute ... is of opinion that the introduction and use of efficient motor vehicles should be encouraged by county, municipal, urban and other authorities, in view of the fact that the extended use of such vehicles would contribute to the general improvement of the sanitary condition of our streets and towns, and this meeting recommends the Council of the Sanitary Institute to make known this opinion as widely as possible.[84]

No doubt the sanitary engineers, in coming to this decision, were of like mind to the above-mentioned Dr Porter who considered 'the amount of irritation to the nose, throat and eyes in London from dried horse manure' was 'something awful'.

The growing motor industry was already having some impact on employment in transport and servicing before the First World War. The first number of *The Commercial Motor* which appeared on 16 March 1905 contained a cartoon depicting a down-and-out Londoner watching a passing motor car. The caption read: ' 'Opeless, 'ungry and not an 'orses 'ead to 'old'.

VI

The adaptation of the internal combustion engine for commercial use came more slowly than its use for pleasure driving for a number of sufficiently good reasons. The sight of many broken-down private cars on the roads in the first decade of the new century must have been an effective deterrent to businessmen who gave some consideration to the claims of motor transport. It was not until 1907 that the first Commercial Motor Show was staged in London, and as late as 1913 only about 11,000 of the 33,000 motor vehicles produced were for commercial use. Most of these were buses or taxis. The early commercial vehicles were unpopular with shopkeepers and shoppers alike because of the noisy clatter they created. It was said of the typical motor van of Edwardian times that 'it barked like a dog and stank like a cat'. At first it was uncertain whether the motor van or the steam or electric powered vehicle would replace horse-drawn transport. As late as November 1918 Harrods, the London store, used nothing but electric-powered vehicles—80 of them—for their in-town deliveries, since they had been found very much cheaper to run and to maintain than petrol motors.[85] For passenger transport the steam bus rivalled the motor bus for many years. In 1907 there were 40 steam buses in service in London and seven years later the National Steam Car Company was manning six London bus routes.[86] It was not until 19 November 1919 that the last steam buses, which plied between Dulwich and Shepherds Bush, were taken off the London streets.[87]

It was high running costs rather than the conservatism of transport users that explains the slow progress of motorised goods transport until the 1920s. The most expensive, and in many cases, most vulnerable, part of the equipment of the early commercial motor vehicle was its tyres. The cost of upkeep of the solid rubber tyres used on a four-wheeled London bus in 1906 was 4d a mile. This expense could be met from the revenues of a well-patronised passenger vehicle: it was uneconomical in the case of most goods vehicles. It was not until 1916 that both Goodyear in the USA and Dunlop in Britain patented the new cord pneumatic tyre which made possible a decisive reduction in the maintenance costs of wheels. The new product had a working life four times the length of its canvas-covered predecessor. By 1932 the cost per mile of the *six* tyres of the typical London bus was down to 0·10d per mile.[88] Economies of this scale were needed to persuade business firms that it was cheaper to use motor transport than it was for them to retain their horses. Although a number of railway companies opened up bus services before 1914 they had scarcely begun to use mechanical transport for goods delivery service. The London and North Western experimented with motorised goods delivery in the City of London but discovered that the motor van's advantage in speed could not be exploited because of traffic congestion in the narrow streets. The company possessed only 67 mechanical vehicles of all types (motor, steam and electric) in 1918 compared with 4,650 horses and 6,694 horse-drawn vehicles.[89] At that time the combined motor lorry fleets of all the railways of Great Britain only amounted to 191 units compared with 32,657 horse-drawn vehicles.[90]

By contrast the spread of motorised commercial passenger services was much more rapid. Edinburgh's first (privately operated) motor bus services began operations as early as 1898, but this experiment and others which followed it early in the new century were short-lived, and it was not until 1914 that the corporation began to operate a bus service of its own.[91] The oldest municipal bus undertaking with a continuous history started services at Eastbourne on 12 April 1903.[92] By the end of 1906 the number of provincial motor bus services was 'mounting into the hundreds'[93]; but they were more abundant in the rural areas and the smaller towns where there was a more obvious need for public transport than there was in the larger towns and cities where tramways, mostly municipally owned, provided frequent and remarkably cheap passenger services. Very often bus services started to make good deficiencies in railway transport. The Crosville Motor Company, for example, took advantage of the fact that railway passengers between Chester and Ellesmere Port had to change trains and were subject to annoying delays, to open its first bus service between the two towns in 1910.[94]

Apart from the great fleet of motor vehicles owned by the London General Omnibus Company before 1914, the largest fleets of buses were held by railway companies. In this the Great Western Railway led the way. At the half-yearly meeting of shareholders held in August 1903 the chairman of the company said

'We have been considering the cases in which independent persons

run motor-car services along the roads to our railway stations. We
do not see why we should not feed our own railways ourselves by
means of motor cars. We have therefore given instruction for the
purchase of five motors which will each carry twenty two passengers.'[95]

The intention was that the new motor buses should act as 'feeders to
the system'[96] of railways and this was precisely the task performed
by the company's first motor bus service opened between Heston and
the Lizard on 17 August 1903. The Board of Directors was so impressed
by the success of the new venture that at its meeting on 8 October
1903 it decided to purchase no less than 25 Milnes–Daimler omnibuses
at a total cost of £19,541 to enable new services to be opened in the
following spring and summer season.[97] Besides new ventures in the
West Country the company established a new bus route between
Slough and Beaconsfield from 1 March 1904[98] and was soon operating
buses in the west Midlands and in north Wales as well. The growth of
traffic was impressive. Between 17 August 1903 and 31 December
1906 1,357,000 miles were run and 3,023,281 passengers were carried.[99]

Other railway companies, including the North Eastern, the London
and North Western, the Cambrian, the Great Eastern and many
others opened numerous services before the outbreak of the first
World War. In Scotland the Great North of Scotland Railway opened
a service between Ballater and Braemar as early as 2 May 1904 and
before 1912 was linking Aberdeen with Newburgh, Cluny and Mid-
mar, Huntley with Aberchirder, Fraserburgh with New Aberdour and
Strathdon with Alford.[100] The railway companies' motives for establishing bus links with railway routes were the development of holiday
traffic (as in the GWR Cornish services); as 'feelers' to ascertain the
possibilities of establishing light railways at a later date—the Rural
Transport (Scotland) Committee in 1919 described their ventures as
'the natural pioneer of the railway'; and as more flexible extensions of
the railway companies' services into areas whose topography precluded
the laying down of railway tracks except at prohibitive cost. It is
significant that the railway bus services were complementary to rather
than competitive with the older-established railway services.

After the armistice of November 1919 progress in the technology
of the commercial motor was delayed in consequence of the governments decision to sell some 60,000 WD lorries through the War
Disposals Committee at bargain prices. Motor manufacturers faced
with this sudden glut of supplies were content to continue production
of pre-war designs rather than take the risk of trying to sell new
models at inflated prices. Not until 1923–4, when some of the ex-army
vehicles were wearing out and demand was picking up after the
depression of 1920–21, was there any appreciable progress in this part

of the industry. At the beginning of the 1920s delivery services were still performed mostly by horse-drawn vehicles rather than motor vans as the latter were still not regarded as dependable in all types of weather and road conditions. Many commercial motors of those days were as fickle as the British weather and drivers needed great experience and patience to circumvent their wiles. In the winter of 1919–20 the drivers of the Crosville buses eased the problem of starting by pre-heating the petrol in tins before pouring it into the tank![101] The innovations and improvements of the next ten years made commercial vehicle operation far more reliable and much less complicated.

The general replacement of solid by pneumatic tyres on vans and lorries began in 1924 and was virtually complete five years later; the fully enclosed driver's cabin became commonplace over the same span of time and these two improvements made possible long-distance motor road haulage. Overnight long-distance delivery services spread rapidly in the 1930s helped by the gradual introduction of the light-weight chassis. The unreliable chain drive had virtually disappeared by 1930 and compression ignition, brought in from 1928, greatly eased the problem of starting the engine.[102] The carrying capacity of vans was all the while increasing as more and more articulated vehicles of the kind pioneered by Guy and by Thornycroft in 1922 took to the roads.[103] The change from petrol to diesel oil after its introduction in 1928 was somewhat slower. The Tilling–Stevens group of companies did not make the change until 1931 and it was not until 1933 that the Scottish Motor Traction group placed an order for 250 Leyland diesel oil engines.[104]

The combined effect of all these innovations was to increase greatly the acceptability of the motor vehicle for road goods services and to add to the frequency and comfort of motorised passenger services. The number of goods vehicles grew from 62,000 in 1919 to 488,000 in 1939. The number of buses and coaches increased less dramatically from 40,118 in 1926 to 53,005 in 1938 but the vehicles were more effectively utilised at the end of this period.

Bus operation during the first ten years of peace was a highly competitive business and expansion was at first far more rapid than was the case with goods haulage. For a time the field was wide open for the enterprising freelance with a modicum of capital and a familiarity with local needs. W. J. Crosland-Taylor who lived through these adventurous times recalled the procedure:

'The technique of starting a new route was amazingly simple. First of all one travelled over it in a car and decided the places of the fare stages and their mileages. Then we worked out the time table and fare table for one bus, say three or four trips on a week day, and a late one on Saturdays, allowing times for meals for the crew. Handbills were printed announcing the date of starting and the details of the service. These we distributed at every home within half a mile of the route, and at the appointed hour the service was just launched and was very soon made use of. It was just as easy as that.'[105]

What made it so easy was that throughout the 1920s local authorities licensed the vehicles but not the services, so that all that it was necessary for the operator to do was to obtain permission to run his bus. After that he could run anywhere within the licensing authority's area. In some districts where the local authority had not adopted bye-laws no licence of any kind was required.

Given these remarkable opportunities for development, it is not surprising that the number of motor transport undertakings in Great Britain rose from 331 in 1916 to 3,962 in 1929-32 or that the amount of capital invested increased from £9 million to £55 million over the same fourteen years.[106] Nevertheless the life of most bus undertakings was very short because of the fierce competition in the industry in the early 1920s. In the Folkestone and Ashford area of East Kent nine firms competed for business, bringing down the Folkestone–Hastings fare from eightpence to a penny and driving seven of the firms into bankruptcy within two years.[107] In these years of 'war to the knife' the methods used to eliminate a competitor were sometimes completely unscrupulous. 'Cutting in' and 'hanging back' to steal customers from established enterprises were widespread practices. When Crosville's service between Chester and Ellesmere Port was challenged by the entry of a new competitor in 1919, the senior company designed an exact replica of the rival bus, complete to the same coloured livery, and ran it immediately in front of the offending intruder who was soon obliged to concede defeat. When a new rival emerged four years later Crosville turned the tables on him by fitting a powerful fire pump engine into the bus that had the job of beating off the new challenger. Although the revamped vehicle had a voracious appetite for petrol it possessed an unsurpassed acceleration and was thus soon instrumental in persuading the gadfly company to come to terms.[108]

Such goings-on satisfied the sporting instincts of the more adventurous of the operators, extended the scope of bus services and for a time gave the public the blessing of remarkably cheap public transport. But there were attendant disadvantages. If there was an abundance of service in the profitable rush hours, off-peak buses were few and far between. With fares cut to the bone maintenance was skimped and road travel became more hazardous. Other vehicles were inconvenienced by the antics of rival operators. The unscrupulous competition between the independent operators and the London

General Omnibus Company which erupted in the capital in 1922 and 1923 led to the passage of the London Traffic Act in the following year which limited the number of roads over which buses might run and imposed strict time schedules and safety regulations on the bus operators. Although the Act did not bring about an immediate cessation of chaotic competition, in 1927 the 'General' reached an agreement with its principal rival on the division of traffic. Six years later the London Passenger Transport Act of 1933, by transferring all bus, trams and tube undertakings to the London Passenger Transport Board, brought all competition in passenger transport in the capital to an end.

For the country as a whole the period of cut-throat competition was ended when, in each district, Road Traffic Commissioners, appointed under the provisions of the Road Traffic Act, 1930, introduced a system of licensing of bus and coach routes and their operators.[109] Even before Parliament intervened there had been a noticeable trend towards amalgamation of bus companies. Between 1920 and 1928, for example, the National Omnibus and Transport Company (generally known as The National), by following a policy of opening up new depots in the towns of the West Country, and pioneering new services, came to control some 861 vehicles on 342 routes.[110] The Midland Red, from its secure base in Birmingham, built up an equally impressive empire. As far back as the First World War the Southdown, East Kent and Maidstone and District companies had reached an 'area agreement' for the avoidance of competition on each other's territory. By 1942 consolidation of ownership in the bus industry had advanced very much further. Tilling and British Automatic Traction Ltd owned 22 major concerns of the standing of the Western National Omnibus Company with a capital of £2 million, while the British Electric Traction group controlled 26 others, including such important companies as Southdown Motor Services and Ribble Motor Services.

Helping the process of consolidation was the participation of the four main line railway companies (LMS, LNER, Southern and Great Western) in ownership of bus and coach undertakings in 1928. An attempt had been made by the railways in 1921–2 to obtain legislative powers to invest in motor transport undertakings, but on the advice of the newly created Ministry of Transport the Government refused its support and the proposal was dropped. Six years later, however, it was manifest that earlier expressed fears about a railway monopoly of inland transport were unfounded and that the short-distance passenger revenue of the railways had been considerably eroded by the competition of the buses. In 1928 therefore four separate Railway (Road Transport) Acts were passed authorising the railway companies to invest in road motor transport enterprises. By 1932 they had invested £9 million in existing road transport undertakings and were in a position to share in the earnings of an increasingly important sector of the transport industry.[111]

In the meanwhile there had been a rapid growth in motor coach services which restored to long-distance road passenger travel something of the importance it had lost some 80 years earlier when the principal through rail routes had been completed. This was a development which only began after the First World War. During the railway strike of September–October 1919 Elliot Bros. of Bournemouth opened an experimental weekend express service between Bournemouth and London. In the next year a regular timetable of weekly services was operated, to be followed in 1921 by a daily and then, later in the same year, a twice daily, service in each direction.[112] However, Elliot's 'Royal Blue' coaches booked passengers between terminals only. There were no scheduled stops en route. The modern long-distance coach service has been described as 'a motorised reincarnation of the original horse drawn mail coach, regularly operated to a published timetable, with stage to stage fares, and individual bookings, single and return'.[113] The first service of this kind was provided by Greyhound Motors Ltd of Bristol from 11 February 1925 between Bristol and London. For the next two years these long-distance coach routes were generally only manned in the summer months because of the absence of satisfactory methods of heating, but between 1927 and 1929 other railway companies' London suburban stations lost between 20 and 40 per cent of their long-distance passenger traffic to motor coaches. Although the coach journeys generally took twice as long as the journeys by rail, fares were lower and travellers from the Greater London area could pick up their coach from a nearby stop instead of having to make the longer journey to the main line railway terminal. By the summer of 1930 334 daily long-distance coach services were being run from London, including eleven to Scotland.[114]

J. B. Priestley, who started his *English Journey* in 1932 by coach to Southampton, found this form of travel 'determinedly and ruthlessly comfortable'. But his assertion that it had 'annihilated the old distinction between rich and poor travellers' because it offered 'luxury to all but the most poverty-stricken' may be questioned. The poor who travelled by coach still had to make their own way to and from the coach stations. The rich could drive from door to door.

In a different class were the extended coach tours provided for recreational purposes. In 1910 Chapman's of Eastbourne pioneered with a tour into North Wales and found the venture so popular that they made increased provision for this kind of holiday, including a 21-day tour to John O'Groats and back, before the First World War for a time put a stop to these interesting experiments. However, the post-war revival was rapid. The total tour days provided by the large firm of Crosville rose from under 50 in the 1920s to 995 in 1939.[115]

VII

By the 1930s motor transport had a much greater impact on the economy than it had in 1913. Capital investment in road vehicles came second only to 'plant and machinery' in total capital formation (in terms of 1930 prices) in the period from 1920–38 and rose from £29 million in 1920–21 to £40 million in 1929. After a fall to £29 million in the slump of 1932 it rose again to a new peak of £58 million in 1937.[116] Expenditure on roads increased from £26·4 million in 1920 to £45·8 million in 1925 and £65·6 million in 1938.[117] C. H. Feinstein estimated that the combined investment in roads and motor vehicles accounted for 6·7 per cent of total investment in the inter-war years.[118] Over the 20 years 1856–75, when most of the main lines had already been opened and the railway mania was past, investment in railways averaged 19·1 per cent of gross domestic capital formation.[119] Thus even when railway investment was well past its peak it took up nearly three times as large a part of British domestic capital investment as did the road and motor investment in the years before the 1939–45 war. From this point of view the economic impact of the motor car was nothing like as great as that brought about by the railways.

In 1939 an estimated 282,000 persons were employed in the manufacture and servicing of motor vehicles. This figure does not include those employed in road construction and maintenance or those employed as drivers, either by private contract or on public service vehicles. In 1946 there were at least 750,000 employed as motor-vehicle drivers and it would be legitimate to assume that not many less were so employed in 1939. Thus, if this group is added to the numbers employed in the manufacturing and servicing of vehicles and allowance is also made for the work force employed in road construction and maintenance—some 80,000 men in 1946—more than 1,100,000 of the 1939 insured working population of 15½ million persons, or seven per cent of the labour force, was employed directly or indirectly in motor transport.

An important secondary effect of the development of the motor industry in Great Britain was the stimulus given to mass production techniques in other branches of the engineering industry. The firm of Lucas, for example, which by 1939 had established a virtual monopoly in the manufacture of electrical components of the motor car and employed 20,000 persons, was fully committed to assembly line techniques of production.[120] The motor industry, more than any other, provided suitable conditions for the increased use of special purpose machines. The output of the largest car-manufacturing firms in the 1930s was large enough to permit the use of flow techniques with machines of this type arranged in sequence.[121]

By the late 1930s the demands of motor car production had a very substantial impact on other branches of British industry. In 1938 car manufacture absorbed 526,027 tons of iron and steel, or nearly eight per cent of the national output of pig iron. This was well below the 28·6 per cent of pig iron output used in the construction of the permanent way at the height of the railway mania (1844–51), but it was, nevertheless, a valuable antidote to depression in the heavy industries at a time when recovery was sluggish.[122] The principal reason for the growth of crude rubber imports from an average of 23,400 long tons a year in 1920–4 to 101,210 long tons in 1934–8 was the rapid growth in the production of tyres, which accounted for three quarters of the imports in 1929 and 62 per cent in 1939 (when remoulding of old tyres had assumed a greater importance).[123] The car industry's consumption of other products was only marginally significant; for example, the 13,000 tons of copper used in 1939 represented less than three per cent of imports.[124] The motorists' demand for petrol and oil did not make any significant difference to Britain's balance of payments before the Second World War. Motor fuels accounted for only 3·7 per cent by value of all imports in 1920–4. By 1934–8 their share had still only risen to 4·6 per cent. It was not until 1955 that they amounted to as much as one tenth of total imports.[125]

In the early days of the motor industry it proved to be a decided advantage to locate both car and component factories near the source of supply of skilled labour in the Birmingham, London or Clydeside regions. By the 1930s, however, when manufacture was concentrated in the hands of a few large firms producing a limited range of car models, the highly paid skilled labour of Birmingham became 'an actual deterrent to location'. For the mass assembly of motor cars a large reserve of unskilled labour was preferred. In 1925 Henry Ford chose his 500-acre site for new development at Dagenham, rather than Coventry or Birmingham, partly because he wanted easy access to European markets but also because he knew that large supplies of unskilled labour were within easy reach. In 1939 three of the industry's six main producers—Vauxhall, Ford and Morris—were located outside the west Midlands, traditional home of the motor industry.[126]

In 1914 motorists were a very privileged group. Only one person in every 232 in Great Britain owned a car. By 1922, when there was one motor vehicle to every 78 persons, car ownership had become much more commonplace. By 1938 car ownership was widespread, with one car to every fifteen persons, but because of the small extent of hire-purchase sales and the low average weekly wage, it was still largely confined to the middle classes. Many businessmen and better paid professional workers were no longer dependent on public transport. In so far as the wage earners had acquired a greater mobility it was through the motor cycle rather than the motor car. The 1920s, rather than the 1930s, saw the peak of popularity of this type of vehicle whose numbers rose from 287,739 in 1920 to 724,319 in 1930 before decreasing rapidly to 418,000 in 1939.[127] By the time the war with Hitler began the motor cyclists were a more homogeneous group and comprised mainly adventurous teenagers or working men. The decline in registrations of motor cyclists in the 1930s must have been due mainly to former owners buying up the increasing numbers of second-hand cars that were coming on to the market.

In many respects the decade of the 1930s was the golden age of the motor vehicle in Britain. For car owners life was enriched through the greater opportunity of visiting distant friends or of recreation in the countryside. Knowledge of the nation's cultural heritage grew as an ever-increasing number of country houses were opened to the public and an ever-growing number of motorists discovered them. Organisations such as the Royal Automobile Club provided guides and road signs to make their discovery easier. The pattern of social life was rapidly changing. The English Sunday became much less an occasion for church going and much more an opportunity for a drive out of the smoky cities into the open country or down by the sea. At the same time the rapid multiplication of bus services greatly increased the mobility of those who were not car owners. By 1933 the annual number of passenger journeys by bus and tram exceeded 9,450 million. Since the 4,032 million tram journeys were a quarter more than they were in 1913, the motor bus had been responsible for the increase of over 5,000 million journeys in the space of twenty years.[128] The person without private transport was better served by public transport in the 1930s and 1940s than had ever been the case before or was to be the case in the decades which followed. After the Second World War, as the number of privately owned motor vehicles soared upwards from 2½ million in 1945 to 15 million in 1970, tramways practically disappeared, branch railway lines were closed and many uneconomic bus services were withdrawn. The low income earners and the pensioners were then often less mobile than were those of the previous generation.

For the first time since the great days of the long-distance mail coach the main roads of Britain sprang into life once more. But in place of the splendour of the old coaching inns of the county towns there came the less pretentious roadside cafés. A special correspondent of *The Times* who made a 'fortuitous, figure of eight, four-day journey by car over the body and shoulder of England' in August 1936 got the impression that 'a fever of mobility had seized the population'. In former times to watch the people of England relaxing on a bank holiday you visited the railway station; now you took to the road.

By the mid-1930s the expansion of long-distance road goods transport had given rise to a class of men—the long-distance transport drivers—as separate and distinctive as the stage coach drivers of a century before. The working life of these men centred round the 'pull in' roadside, all-night cafés of which there were hundreds on the country's main arterial roads. These were the focal points of a new type of social life where messages were given and taken, drivers changed shifts, the performance of the vehicles was compared and the issues of the day disputed over cups of strong tea and plates of jammy pastry. The all-night café had a pioneering, improvised appearance reminiscent of the all-purpose store of frontier America in the 1890s. Its name was generally informal :'Joe's', 'Pete's' or 'Jack's Snacks'. Thirty-five years later it had changed very little. The mechanical piano had given place to the juke box but the familiar name of the café and the light-hearted banter between proprietor and lorry driver that went on inside it had altered very little.

The motor car undoubtedly brought the country and town closer together, thereby hastening the standardisation of dress, speech and social customs. In remote villages people who had not been able to obtain their newspapers until the late afternoon or even the day following publication were now supplied almost as soon as their urban contemporaries. The same bus which carried its quota of townsmen seeking the pleasures of the countryside carried back the farm labourers and their wives for an afternoon's shopping and a visit to the cinema. Horizons were widened. Aldous Huxley believed that the motor bus had done more towards the disappearance of the village idiot than all the lectures on eugenics. The more the bus networks spread the more difficult it became to justify a lower standard of domestic and civic amenities in the country village than was to be found in the nearby town.

Unfortunately the greater accessibility of the countryside was not always accompanied with a lively concern for the preservation of its amenities. In July 1928, no doubt with the roadside hoarding and the ugly petrol station very much in mind, Stanley Baldwin prophesied that if 'improvements' continued to be introduced as rapidly as was then the case 'all the beauty and charm of the towns and villages' would be destroyed within 50 years.[129] The Restriction of Ribbon Development Act of 1935 was intended to check the octopus-like spread of house building from the towns to the surrounding country districts brought about by the increased use of the motor car. However, the authors of the Scott Report on rural land use wrote in 1942 that the Act 'had broadly speaking failed to restrict ribbon development'.[130] One of the chief objections to the new ribbon settlements was that they had 'no centres, no sense and no communal spirit. They were composed of little more than individual motor cars come

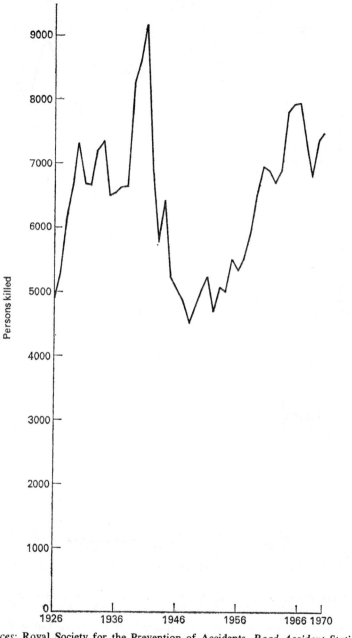

Sources: Royal Society for the Prevention of Accidents, *Road Accident Statistics*; British Road Federation, *Basic Road Statistics*, 1971.

Figure 19   Number of Persons Killed on Roads in Great Britain
1926–70

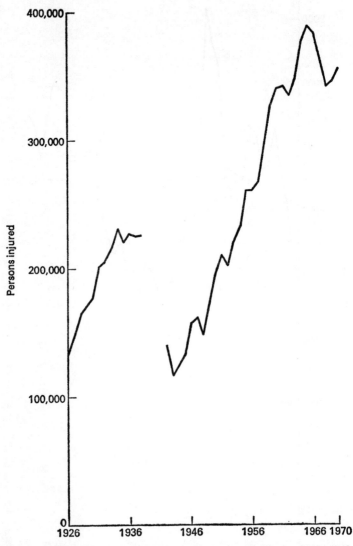

Note: No statistics for the whole 12 months are available for 1939, 1940 and 1941.

Sources: Royal Society for the Prevention of Accidents, *Road Accident Statistics;* British Road Federation, *Basic Road Statistics,* 1971.

Figure 20   Number of Persons Injured on Roads in Great Britain 1926–70

to rest.'[131] It was not until after the Second World War that the development of the countryside was more effectively controlled.

An even more serious indictment of the motor car was that its use led to an unprecedented destruction and maiming of lives. The 120,000 persons killed on the roads of Great Britain between 1918 and 1939 equalled in number the entire strength of the British Expeditionary Force in France in 1914. In addition there were a million and a half others who in war time would have been classified as 'wounded'. In the 1930s the casualty rates were much higher in relation to the number of vehicles in use than they were in the 1960s, when the public had become much more traffic conscious. The number of those killed on the roads in 1934, when $2\frac{1}{2}$ million vehicles were in use, was higher than in 1964 when there were $12\frac{1}{2}$ million. The reforms of L. Hore-Belisha introduced in 1934, including the introduction of pedestrian crossings, improved road signs and stricter speed limits, helped to check the increase in casualties by improving road discipline. But the number of road deaths remained obstinately above the 6,500 limit each year. More determined efforts to tackle the problem were only undertaken after 1950.

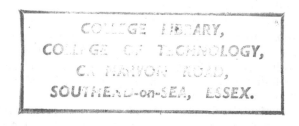

British Transport Policy, 1914–39

I

In the quarter of a century covered by this chapter there were momentous changes both in the means of transport and in its organisation. The emergency of war accelerated the process of consolidation of railway management and also led to government control over canals and coastal shipping. During the years of enthusiasm for reconstruction in 1917–19 the coalition government for a time considered the continuance of comprehensive control over transport through a specially created new department of government. But the Ministry of Transport which finally emerged was but a pale shadow of the all-embracing Ministry of Ways and Communications at first envisaged by the Prime Minister, David Lloyd George. After 1919, therefore, each major form of transport was left to develop separately in response to demand and the investment of private funds. At least until the 1930s, government control was substantially extended only in the case of the railways.

Because transport developments followed this pattern, it seems wisest to consider the measures of wartime control and the plans for postwar reconstruction in sections one and two and then to deal with each major form of transport—railways, commercial and private motoring, highways, coastal shipping, canals and air transport in six other separate sections. At the same time the repercussions of the important developments in motor transport on older-established means of communication will not be neglected. In the concluding section the consequences of the failure to devise a comprehensive transport policy in the immediate postwar years will be summarised.

II

One of the characteristics of British railway operation before 1914 which was frequently the subject of critical comment was the profligate use of capital and manpower. It was the feature of the transport situation which most impressed Lloyd George. He told a delegation of railway trade union leaders in March 1918 that in pre-war days there had been 'a gigantic waste . . . attributable to competition, with an excess of trains serving one district merely because there were three or four companies competing for custom' while, in other districts, where single companies held the field to themselves, there was often 'a shortage of facilities'.[1] An outstanding example of wasteful multiplication of effort was to be seen at Carlisle. The seven railway companies which served the city in 1913 owned no less than nine freight yards with the result that a large part of railway activity in the area comprised the shunting of wagons from one yard to another.[2]

A country at war could not afford such extravagance. After 4 August 1914 it was imperative that the transport resources of the nation should be directed towards the sole objective of military victory. Inessential deployment of equipment and manpower had to be avoided. But a precondition for the elimination of waste was a greater measure of public control over all forms of transport. In the case of railways all that was needed was to bring into operation the Regulation of the Forces Act of 1871 which empowered the government to take over the management of the railway system in the event of war. Three years before the outbreak of the First World War, Lord Haldane, Secretary of State for War, had asked the leading railways to prepare plans for a unified system of operation and the General Managers of the twelve leading companies formed themselves into a Railway Executive Committee for this purpose. When the Government took over responsibility for the railways at the outbreak of war it did so through the REC which was issued with military and strategic directives but was given a free hand to carry them out. It was indirect government control of a unified railway system rather than outright nationalisation. In return for exercising a first claim for the use of the nation's railways the government guaranteed to the companies their net revenues of 1913. This was a good bargain from the viewpoint of railway management and the shareholders since the last year of peace had been an exceptionally busy and profitable one. However, the wear and tear on railway equipment was exceptionally heavy in wartime and in 1915 the cabinet recognised this fact by agreeing that the companies should be given additional allowances to cover the cost of repairs and renewals. In the following year it was further provided that all railway capital was to be guaranteed a minimum four per cent return and that all stocks were to be guaranteed at 1913 levels.[3] Between 4 August 1914 and 21 December 1918 the Treasury paid out £95 million in fulfilment of these promises over and above payments made for the movement of troops and military supplies.[4]

That important part of the canal network—1,025 out of 2,500 miles —which had passed to railway management before 1914 was subject to government control through the REC from the outbreak of hostilities. It was not until March 1917 that the remaining, independently owned, undertakings were brought under the direction of a Canal Control Committee of the Board of Trade. Since road goods motor transport was in a very early stage of development before 1914, war-time governments at first felt little need to regulate the use of commercial motor vehicles. But growing shortage of shipping space and the need to conserve petrol supplies led to the establishment of the Road Transport Board in February 1918 with powers to organise the most economical use of commercial motors. Although in the summer of 1914 a considerable number of ships were requisitioned for naval and military use, coastal shipping in general escaped wartime controls until June 1917, when the Home Trade branch of the Ministry of Shipping was formed with the main task of checking the decline of coastwise traffic which had occurred because railway freight rates had been kept at artificially low levels.[5]

Thus by the early summer of 1918 the Government was in a position to marshal the services provided by railways, canals, coastal shipping and commercial motor transport to meet the needs of a nation at war.

Despite the fact that 184,000 railwaymen out of a total of 650,000 employed in 1914 enlisted in the armed forces, British railways had to carry fifty per cent more goods traffic and a continuing large volume of passenger traffic during the years 1914–19. The London and South Western and Great Eastern Railways between them carried 17½ million servicemen in the course of the war and 60 per cent of the Great Northern's passenger traffic was made up of soldiers and sailors on their way to the front or coming home on leave. These remarkable results were achieved with a substantially smaller body of equipment than the railways had possessed in August 1914. By the end of the war the army had commandeered 30,000 waggons and 700 locomotives for use in France and the companies were not able to make adequate replacements, for many of their workshops were employed in the manufacture of war material. In fact the railways were 80,000 waggons below peacetime strength in November 1918. That the railways did so well was partly due to the patriotism of the men and women who kept the traffic moving by working longer hours. But it was also due to the introduction of the common-user scheme for railway waggons through which empty running of waggons was reduced from 60 per cent in October 1913 to 20 per cent six years later. The saving in running costs from this cause alone was nearly half a million pounds annually. In 1918 the Select Committee on Transport in its report on wartime operations praised the 'high efficiency' of railways under the unified direction of the REC.[6]

The Canal Control Committee had less success in its task of trying to achieve a better utilisation of the country's inland waterways. This was principally for the reason that it was appointed too late to restore the loss of business on the independent canals which had occurred during the first two and a half years of war. By March 1917 30,000 men, or nearly half the total canal staff, had enlisted into the armed services. Although in the course of 1918 valiant efforts were made to divert the carriage of wheat and coal from the hard-pressed railways on to the under-utilised canal network, traders were reluctant to use the slower means of transport. The total tonnage of goods carried on the inland waterways fell from 31,585,909 tons in 1913 to 21,599,850 in 1918. Most of the traffic lost in the early months of the war was never regained.[7]

The Home Trade branch of the Ministry of Shipping had even less success than did the Canal Control Committee in diverting traffic from the railways on to water. The expenses of the coastal liner or tramp steamer operator rose faster than did those of their contemporaries in other forms of transport in wartime. Insurance premiums soared because of the risks to coastal shipping from enemy action, and coal bought by shipowners was more expensive than that bought by the railways. The high prices and high interest rates payable by traders persuaded them to order small consignments of goods by rail rather than large consignments by sea so that their insurance and warehousing costs were reduced to the minimum. Not surprisingly, therefore, net tonnages of all coastwise shipping entrances fell from 35 million tons in 1913 to 20 million tons in 1919 and coal shipped coastwise fell from $20\frac{1}{2}$ million to 13 million tons over the same period.[8] The obverse of the decline of coastal shipping was congestion on the railways, a congestion so great that on 18 August 1919 the war cabinet directed that a subsidy should be given to traders using coastal shipping to divert traffic from the overloaded rails.[9] The directive came not a day too soon. Food was rotting on the quaysides, waiting for goods trains to carry it to the markets. The turnaround time for ships was lengthening each month. The average discharge time for five vessels in the port of London in 1913 was 32 days; in 1919 it was 165 days. The Minister of Shipping declared that the country was not getting more than 40 or 50 per cent efficiency from its shipping. It was a striking illustration of the interdependence of the different forms of transport and the futility of considering one means of transport in isolation from the others.[10]

III

Even before the war there was widespread recognition of the fact that the era of competition on the railways was virtually at an end. Successive war cabinets recognised that when peace was signed there would be no return to the independent company administrations characteristic of the years before 1914. On 5 September 1916, Walter Runciman, President of the Board of Trade, informed the railway companies by letter that government control of the railways, including all the financial arrangements made since 4 August 1914, would continue for two years after the cessation of hostilities.[11] Thus the government had given Parliament time to devise a new transport policy for the nation once the war had been won.

There was undoubtedly need for rethinking in this important area of government policy. New forms of transport were emerging. The war had demonstrated the potentialities of the internal combustion engine for both land and air transport. Over 100,000 motor vehicles had been used by the British army in France. What part would the motor vehicle play in the transport services of peacetime Britain and what would be the policy of government towards the growth of the new industry? Was air transport for passengers a viable proposition in postwar Britain and should it develop under a state monopoly or free enterprise? Should the decline in use of the canals be allowed to continue? How imperative was it for the government to ensure an important role for coastal shipping in the movement of goods and passengers? In the face of the challenge from new forms of transport should Parliament seek to protect the traffic of the railways or allow unrestrained competition to determine its volume? These and many other questions required answering in the period of postwar reconstruction.

For some time in 1918 and 1919 it appeared that ministers of the Crown supported a policy of nationalisation of transport. Lloyd George told A. G. Walkden, the able general secretary of the Railway Clerks' Association, who led a deputation from the TUC in March 1918 to demand 'full nationalisation' of railways and inland waterways after the war, that he was in 'very, very complete sympathy' with such proposals.[12] Nine months later, in the course of the general election campaign, Winston Churchill told the Dundee Chamber of Commerce that it was the intention of the government to nationalise the railways. At the same time Lloyd George drafted an election manifesto to similar effect. Although this document was watered down by Bonar Law to the vaguer promise that there would be 'development and control in the best interests of the state ... of the railways and means of communication', the electorate had some excuse for thinking that the coalition government favoured a policy of public ownership for transport.[13]

There were other pointers suggesting that a major change of public policy towards transport was in the offing. In 1918 the Report of the Select Committee on Transport concluded: 'From a purely technical point of view, it appears therefore to be desirable that there should be unification of ownership'.[14] In December 1918 Sir Sam Fay, one time general manager of the Great Central Railway and in recent months Director General of Movements and Railways, submitted to the cabinet a scheme for a Transport Authority. This was to be a public body composed of the representatives of the railway and dock companies, the Board of Trade, the trade unions and commercial, agricultural and industrial bodies. It was to buy up, through the issue of new public stock, the capital of the country's railways and canals with all their subsidiary undertakings, including steamships, hotels, etc. For administrative purposes the railways and canals were to be divided up into five regional groups, but the Transport Authority was to have full power 'to take over, manage and control' them in the public interest.[15]

Lloyd George had got to know Sam Fay well since November 1906 when he had adopted his (Fay's) proposals for a conciliation scheme for settlement of industrial disputes on the railways. Once more, a dozen years later, the railway manager's views matched those of the Welsh statesman. The Premier determined that something like Fay's plan should be adopted as reconstruction policy for transport. The only question in the aftermath of the coalition election victory of December 1918 was who to entrust with the implementation of these ambitious plans?

One obvious candidate was Sir Eric Geddes, the elder of two brothers who had entranced Lloyd George in the dark days of the war by their singing of Welsh songs.[16] He had impressed the Premier by his decisiveness, energy and organising ability. Recruited from his peacetime job of deputy general manager of the North Eastern Railway, he had been appointed successively Deputy Director General of Munitions Supply, Director General of Military Railways and Inspector General of Transportation for the British Army in France, Director General of Military Railways and Inspector General of Transportation in all Theatres of War, Controller of the Navy and First Lord of the Admiralty, before being given a seat in the cabinet as Minister without Portfolio in the autumn of 1918. His task in France had been to reorganise military transport on the Western Front after the disasters of the Somme. The carnage in this battle arose not only because of the mud but also because each stage in the movement of war material was under a different authority, with consequent confusion and delays. He had rapidly brought order out of chaos and had earned the nation's gratitude.

At the end of 1918, therefore, the Prime Minister entrusted Eric Geddes with the task of drafting a Bill for a new Ministry of Ways and Communications and of using the two years' grace of continuing government control over the railways through the REC to devise a transport policy for postwar Britain. Lloyd George was anticipating sweeping changes and a comprehensive reform. In a message to the parliamentary draughtsman Geddes gave what he called a 'rough outline' of his leader's wishes. The Bill was to be drafted

sufficiently widely to permit of the existing functions of any other government department in conection with railways, light railways, roads (including traffic control); canals; docks; harbours and shipping; electric power, tramways and road vehicles being taken over. . . . In addition to the above, the Bill should provide for the Ministry of Ways and Communications increasing its control and regulations over all these means of transit and also for working any one of them; or of leasing and working any one of them under the control of the state.[17]

The minister-designate then took his six principal lieutenants—mostly recruited from his transport staff in France—to a series of discussions in Harrogate early in February 1919 to agree on a policy submission to the cabinet and to consider amendments to the first draft of the Bill. A close associate of Sir Eric Geddes in earlier days, Sir Ralph Wedgwood of the North Eastern Railway, rightly distinguished the new transport chief's outstanding concerns as 'a passionate hatred of waste and disorder' and 'a passionate devotion to efficiency'.[18] On his own admission, Geddes went to Harrogate 'with an open mind' as to the best means of achieving these prime objectives.[19] Some of his team had far more definite views and set about their task with a high idealism. In the memorandum which he drafted for submission to the cabinet, Major-General Baird expressed the forthright opinion that

In a highly organised modern state, living in an era of fierce international competition, the movement of men and materials is a matter far too vital to be left to private enterprise, necessarily acting in private interests, subject to the more or less haphazard system of control hitherto in force . . . The railways, however, though forming the main artery of communication, are only a part of the national transport system and in order to obtain the maximum of efficiency, every conceivable means of transport must be co-ordinated and adopted so as to give the best service possible.

A new department of government was needed

not merely devoted as in the past to functions of criticism, regulation, conciliation and arbitration, but definitely charged with the inspiration and control of the development of a public service comprised in all methods of commercial movement of men, animals and materials in the Realm . . . The interdependence of all means of communication has been proved. National conditions forbid their reversion to the competitive conditions which prevailed among them before the war.[20]

Returning to the realities of Westminster the team met determined and persistent opposition to the new proposals. There was, first, the resentment of those ministers who saw in the creation of a new government department the loss of a part of their authority. Major-General J. E. B. Seely of the Air Ministry opposed Geddes' plan to take over responsibility for civil aviation.[21] Sir Albert Stanley, from the Board of Trade, wrote to the minister-designate that the proposal to take over electric power supply was open to 'grave objections' and that the municipal authorities would object strongly to their tramways being subject to control by those railway interests which, it was assumed, would dominate the new ministry.[22]

When the proposals came before the cabinet on 19 February Sir H. Llewellyn Smith took exception to the plan to give Geddes responsibility for merchant shipping—hitherto the concern of the Board of Trade. Sir Albert Stanley supported his objection with the warning that 'the shipping interest was very powerful and there was no doubt that it would add greatly to the difficulties of getting the Bill through if this clause were retained.' Despite Geddes' plea that there was no provision for taking over anything but the existing powers of the Board of Trade, the First Lord of the Admiralty was unappeased. He reminded his colleagues that 'there was no vested interest in the House of Commons so powerful as the shipping interest'. After Llewellyn Smith had noted that traders would object to the new ministry assuming powers over coastal shipping since something between one third and one half of the railway rates were more or less affected by the coasting trade, the cabinet decided that the offending clause should be excised from the Bill. This was not all. At the same sitting the cabinet decided that 'the power to convey passengers and goods by air' should also be deleted. Control over electricity generation would have gone the same way had it not been for the intervention of Lloyd George who suggested that Geddes should 'come to an arrangement' with the Board of Trade which was drafting proposals concerning control of electric power transmission. Responsibility for tramways was, however, entirely relinquished after R. Munro, the Secretary of State for Scotland, had warned that Glasgow corporation would raise 'the strongest opposition' to any curtailment of its powers over its transport services.[23]

Before this momentous cabinet meeting dispersed Austen Chamberlain, the Chancellor of the Exchequer, raised the crucial question as to 'whether it was right that the Bill should provide for the possible purchase of railways by the state'. He thought it 'a mistake to insert these powers before the government had made up their mind'. Lloyd George only salvaged this part of the Bill by urging that it was essential to keep it as a conciliatory gesture to the labour movement. 'If the government could say that they had in mind a proposal to make the railways state property it would be much easier to deal with the menacing industrial trouble. They would be able to say to the men that they were imposing a burden on the community if they persisted with their demands.' When Geddes reminded the cabinet that the powers specified were being granted for a period of two years only and that they were no greater than those conferred on government under the Defence of the Realm Act, the rest of the cabinet agreed to let these vital clauses stand.

Meanwhile the Bill was subject to attack from other quarters. The parliamentary council advised that it conferred 'such autocratic powers' on the new minister that it would be difficult to get it through Parliament. Certainly the House of Lords would 'kick at it' because of the clauses which empowered the minister to take over transport industries by Order in Council. It was undoubtedly an aspect of the bill which reflected Geddes' experience as transport dictator on the Western Front rather than any understanding of long cherished parliamentary traditions.[24]

On 10 March a deputation from the Federation of British Industries brought Geddes a resolution of unanimous opposition to any plans for railway nationalisation. He told them, no doubt with sincerity, 'I hope the railways will not be nationalised. I fear they may be, but I hope not'.[25]

The final blows came when the Bill was considered by Parliament at different times between 26 February and 1 July 1919. In the debate on the first reading, Sir W. Joynson-Hicks, for long the spokesman for the motoring interests, declared that 280 MPs had, that day, joined a private committee 'to promote the use and development of the roads in Great Britain'. Its members, he said, were all 'gravely suspicious of the roads being put under railway control'.[26] T. P. O'Connor quoted a resolution of the Shipping Committee of the House of Commons which strongly objected to dock and harbour undertakings passing into the possession of the state.[27] On the day before the third reading of the Bill, the members of these two private committees interviewed Bonar Law who agreed to insert new clauses making explicit the exemption of dock and pier undertakings from control by the new ministry and watering down earlier provisions concerning the roads.[28] Meanwhile, in committee, Mr. Shortt, the Home Secretary, yielded to strong pressure from rank and file Conservative members. On 6 May he suddenly announced the complete withdrawal of clause four—which gave the minister power to nationalise the different forms of transport.[29] It was reminiscent of Gladstone's surrender of the original state purchase clauses of his Railway Bill in 1844. Geddes' Bill would have been even more severely mutilated in committee had it not been for the consistent support given him by Labour members. On the other hand, at least one alteration made by the House of Lords had much to commend it. It was that the new department should be called the Ministry of Transport instead of

The Ministry of Ways and Communications. The Bill as passed on the third reading was very different from what J. R. Clynes called the 'robust proposals' of February. A senior member of the Commons, Sir F. Flannery, did not exaggerate when he declared that the Bill had 'sustained about as much alterations as ... anyone, even the most experienced in this House, can remember any Bill to have sustained and yet to have survived'.[30]

It has often been claimed that nationalisation had no chance of adoption in 1919. But the indications are that there would have been a wide degree of acceptance for a much stronger measure than the one Parliament eventually produced. At least some of the railway managers, including Sir Sam Fay, would have accepted public owner-ship, given a satisfactory settlement with the shareholders. The *Railway Gazette* approved the new principle contained in the original Bill that the government was to be made 'responsible for the initiation and development of transport'.[31] Even *The Times* conceded that if the transport undertakings of the country were to be worked as practi-cal monopolies it was 'clear that the state must control'.[32] General P. A. M. Nash of Sir Eric Geddes' staff may not have been so wide of the mark when he wrote to his chief on 22 January 1919 that 'state control in some form or other was inevitable and the railway companies recognised this state of affairs and were waiting for the government to move'.[33] It was the swamping of the House of Commons in December 1918 with a large majority of members bent on freeing the country, at all costs, from the trammels of Government control over the economy, that made Lloyd George more of a prisoner on his own government benches and induced him to abandon many of his idealistic plans for the better ordering of British transport.

The coordination of transport—the carriage of traffic by that form of transport whose real economic costs are lowest—has been generally accepted as a worthwhile objective. The significance of the abandon-ment of many vital clauses of the Ministry of Ways and Communica-tions Bill was that one important means of achieving this objective had been jettisoned. There is no guarantee that with public ownership each form of transport will be used to optimum advantage, since these ends can only be achieved by an accurate costing of alternative means of transit and the adjustment of charges to match costs. Unified ownership and control is, however, a most important precondition of coordination and the avoidance of wasteful duplication of services. In 1930 the Royal Commission on Transport recognised this truth when it reported that 'without unification—however it may be accom-plished—no attempt to bring about complete coordination would be successful'.[34]

Having abandoned effective overall control of the various means of transport in 1919 Parliament subsequently drifted into a piecemeal

approach, dealing with the problems of railways, roads, coastal shipping and airways when they became so acute as to demand attention.
Thus although lip service was constantly paid to the need for transport
coordination and the Royal Commission, appointed in 1928, was even
briefed to suggest how Parliament might promote the 'coordinated
working and development' of road, rail and water transport, no comprehensive transport policy was attempted before the outbreak of war
in 1939 made one essential for national survival.

When the Ministry of Transport Bill became law on 15 August
1919 it gave to Sir Eric Geddes, as Britain's first Minister of Transport,
the powers over railways formerly exercised by the Railway Department of the Board of Trade, besides less substantial powers over
canals and roads. A new feature of the Act was the establishment of a
Railway Rates Advisory Committee which the minister was obliged
to consult before introducing any changes in freight charges or passenger fares. Geddes soon pressed these clauses of the Act into service.
During the war the state had made a profit of some £20 million on
the railways since net revenue exceeded the guaranteed revenue
promised the companies. As soon as the wartime emergency traffic
disappeared, however, the government was out of pocket, having to
pay the railway companies a total of £126 million out of the taxpayers'
pockets in the period 1919-21 inclusive. The principal reason for this
state of affairs was that, although passenger fares were increased by
50 per cent in 1917, freight charges remained unchanged through the
war despite the fact that wholesale prices had risen to three times
their 1913 level by the beginning of 1920. Inevitably traffic had been
drawn away from those forms of transport—coastwise shipping and
road vehicles—whose charges had been increased to match rising
costs. But the new railway traffic was not paying its way. In the course
of 1920 therefore the Railway Rates Advisory Committee approved
applications for increases in freight charges of between 75 and 100
per cent, a move which diverted some of the coal and other bulky
goods traffic back to coastwise liners and tramps.

IV

Once the new Ministry of Transport had been established there was
every reason why railway questions should be given prior consideration. To many members of the House of Commons transport policy
was railway policy. There was, as yet, little appreciation of the
commercial importance of the motor vehicle. From the Treasury
point of view it was a matter of financial urgency that future arrangements for the railways should be settled as soon as possible. Geddes
himself was very conscious of the dateline of 15 August 1921, at
which time REC administration was due to end.

It was not until 24 June 1920 that Sir Eric Geddes told the House of Commons that the cabinet had finally decided against the nationalisation of the railways. However, this was but a belated formal recognition of the situation which had existed ever since the committee on the Ministry of Ways and Communications Bill had struck out the whole of clause four on 6 May 1919. For some months before he made his Commons announcement Geddes had been engaged in drafting plans for a regional grouping of railways under private ownership, and the publication of the government white paper *Outline of Proposals as to the Future Organisation of Transport Undertakings in Great Britain and their Relation to the State* (Cmd 787), later in the summer of 1920, made clear what these plans were. The railways of the nation were to be merged into seven regional groupings, viz.: the Southern, Western, North Western, Eastern, North Eastern, London and Scottish within which competition would be eliminated by the absorption of each smaller company into the monopoly company of its area. It was proposed that freight rates and fares should be fixed so as to bring to the combined companies a net revenue 'substantially equivalent' to that obtained 'on some pre-war basis'. Clearly officials in the new ministry had no conception of the inroads into railway revenue about to be made by a growing volume of road transport, for it was anticipated that 'with due care and economy' the railways would be able to 'improve on their pre-war return'. The government was to take a share of the expected surplus revenues and was to amass a Development Fund for the purpose of assisting backward areas 'to develop light railways' and to make resources available for 'other appropriate transport purposes'.

The government plans for the railways were subject to prolonged criticism and controversy in the Press, behind the scenes in the Ministry of Transport and in Parliament. The railway companies 'concurred generally in the principle of grouping' since, as they stated, 'a scheme very similar was under consideration ... before the war'.[35] But there were differences on the precise delimitation of the regions. By the time the ministry drafted a memorandum on the Railway Bill for the cabinet the seven groups were reduced to six through the elimination of London as a separate region. After complaints from Scottish MPs that a separate Scottish region would not be self-supporting, the railways north of the Tweed were regrouped with those south of the border, reducing the number to five. By the time the Railway Bill became law on 19 August 1921—four days after the ending of REC control—there remained the four regional groups: Southern, Great Western, London and North Eastern, and London, Midland and Scottish—familiar to railway travellers in the inter-war years (see map 9, p. 248). The final grouping was the result partly of political bargaining and partly of anticipated business

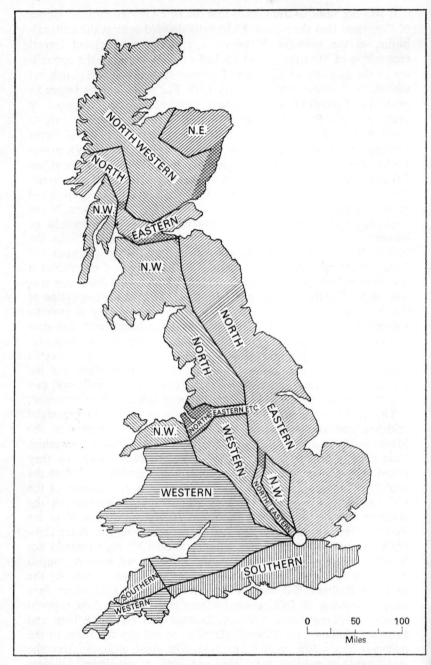

Source: W. E. Simnett, *Railway Amalgamation in Great Britain*, 1923.

Map 9   Railway Grouping in 1921

trends. Before 1914 the North Eastern Railway, monopolising transport between Tyne, Pennines and Tweed, enjoyed a prosperity founded on the busy basic industries of coal, iron and steel and ship-building. The Great Eastern, spread through largely non-industrial East Anglia, had been less profitable. It was anticipated that, merged together in the new LNER, the old North Eastern would help to 'carry' its weaker neighbour to the south. The depression on Tyneside and the movement of population and industry into Essex produced a situation almost the exact reverse of that anticipated. A similar miscalculation was made about the part that would be played by the formerly very profitable Taff Vale Railway in the enlarged Great Western system. Severe depression in the Welsh coal industry compelled the GWR board to look elsewhere for its shareholders' dividends than in the Welsh valleys.

One of the most novel of Geddes' proposals for the new Bill was the plan for railway workers' representation on the boards of directors of the new companies. With the events of the September 1919 national railway strike fresh in his memory, Geddes wrote to the members of the cabinet that 'by so introducing workers into the inner councils of the railway ... they would see for themselves when the economic level was being reached and would thus be educated to ease onerous conditions of service in the interests of economy and not to press their wage claims beyond what was reasonable for the industry to bear or to an extent which would kill trade by high charges'.[36] The cabinet raised no serious objection to the plan. But industry and railway management were adamantly opposed. Geddes had regretfully to report that the general managers of the railway companies 'would unitedly oppose the inclusion either of officials or of wages grade men on the boards of management'.[37] Although activists in the NUR had been advocating various forms of workers' control for some years, J. H. Thomas, the union's general secretary, was unenthusiastic. He struck a bargain with the general managers. If they would agree to drop their plan for district wages settlements such as were the rule before 1914, and would accept statutory enactment of the Central and National Wages Boards for the settlement of wages and working conditions of railwaymen, he would agree to drop the demand for workers' representatives on the boards of directors.[38] Reluctantly Geddes reported to Parliament a few months later that 'the proposal for workers' representatives has been abandoned as such representation is no longer desired by the trade unions representing the men'.[39] It was not so much that the activists amongst the railwaymen had abandoned the principles of workers' participation as that they did not wish that the small trade union minority on the boards should be saddled with responsibility without power. As it happened, Part IV of the Railways Act 1921, which brought statutory enforcement of the Central and National Wages Boards, was one of the new measure's most successful features. That labour relations were, generally speaking, remarkably peaceful on the railways between 1920 and 1939 was partly due to this scheme for the equal representation of unions and management for negotiating wages and working conditions.

One of the main tasks given to the Railway Rates Tribunal under the Act was to devise a new classification of goods to replace the eight-category classification in use since 1894. This task was completed in 1923 when the new 21 class classification was introduced. No fundamental change was made in the basis of grouping mineral and merchandise traffic. The low number categories (now 1-6) continued to be set aside for minerals and other commodities of low value in relation to their bulk, while classes 7-21 included general merchandise, the highest class of which, 21, included goods of greatest value in relation to their bulk. The Railway Rates Tribunal was expected to approve 'standard charges' for all classes of traffic at such levels as to ensure the standard revenues for the railways as a whole. These were to be the companies' actual charges in contradistinction to the *maximum* charges previously laid down by the Railway and Canal Commission. However the railway companies were permitted to quote exceptional rates not less than five per cent or more than forty per cent below the standard charges, without reference to the Railway Rates Tribunal. In 1921 it was hoped that the standard rates would apply for the vast majority of transactions and that they would replace the multiplicity of exceptional rates prevalent before the war. It was imagined that the clauses in the Act permitting deviation from the standard charges would be only infrequently invoked. The rapid growth of commercial motor transport destroyed all such illusions. In order to meet the new road transport competition the railways resorted to special agreements much more frequently than had been anticipated. By 1938 80 per cent of the rates charged were exceptional ones.[40]

Old ways of thinking about railways as transport monopolies were reflected in the Railway Act's continuation of the companies' 'obligation to carry'. Each railway was still to be legally obliged to accept all commodities offered for carriage and to publish information about the charges to be made for the conveyance of the different types of goods. Undue preferences in railway charges were still disallowed. Any trader who considered he was the victim of an unjust discrimination in charge had the right to appeal to the Railway Rates Tribunal.

At first substantial working economies were predicted from the grouping of the pre-war railway companies. Savings of up to £20 million a year were forecast as a result of standardisation of equipment and the avoidance of wasteful competition. But the more experienced railwaymen were sceptical of the gains of amalgamation. H. A. Walker, the respected general manager of the London and South Western Railway, wrote to Sir Eric Geddes on 4 May 1921 hoping that in the minister's speech introducing the Bill he would 'not make too much of the economies that would result from grouping'. Apart from the fact that many general managers felt that the figures had been 'placed much too high' he considered that 'if too much value was attached to them it would make it very difficult ... to deal with labour'. This would be 'unfortunate to say the least of it'.[41] Geddes took the hint. The wording of the *Memorandum on the Railways Bill*, published later that summer, was much more guarded: 'Opinions will always differ as to the estimate of economy possible, but no difference of opinion is known to exist as to the fact that valuable economies can be effected'.[42] The caution was not misplaced. Nobody really knew how much would be saved as a result of railway amalgamation since 'there had been no investigation into the economics of railway operation either by the Government, the companies or independent observers'.[43]

The Act can be criticised for having the defects of a half-way measure. This can be illustrated with reference to much needed technological innovation and standardisation of equipment. The incentives to introduce economies of scale in the production of railway material cannot have been as great with the existence of four independent boards of directors as they would have been if the railways of the country had been under completely unified direction. A reform dear to the heart of Britain's first Minister of Transport was the standardisation of rolling stock and the elimination of the privately owned wagon. Back in 1918 the Ministry of Reconstruction Advisory Council on the Standardisation of Railway Equipment ruefully reported that the tare (i.e. unloaded weight) of the standard eight-ton waggon, built to Railway Clearing House regulations, was as much as 70 per cent of the load, compared with 40–45 per cent in the case of the waggons of other countries. It was 'in the national interest to carry out standardisation of railway plant', including all the principal parts of waggons and locomotives. Under Section 13 (5) of the Ministry of Transport Act, 1919, the minister had 'power to make regulations prohibiting or restricting the use on railways of privately owned waggons'; but more than 600,000 privately owned waggons of every conceivable shape and capacity continued to clutter up the rails for a quarter of a century more. There was not even agreement on waggon-nomenclature. On 7 May 1920 Sir J. F. Aspinall, Consulting Mechanical Engineer to the Ministry of Transport, confessed that

the difficulty of identifying particular classes of waggons belonging to the railways was very much increased by the fact that waggons of practically similar construction were known by different names . . . It was extraordinary to find that on some railways . . . the Traffic Department may use one set of names and the Control Department of the same railway a third set, for the same vehicles.

A first step was obviously that 'all the railway companies should be asked to standardise the nomenclature of their waggons'. It is true that by the end of 1920 a sub-committee of the Railway Companies' Association, with the help of Aspinall, reached agreement on specification for a 12-ton waggon and that more of these larger capacity standardised vehicles were then made by the four main line companies; but the sub-committee found, to their distress, that because 'existing cranes, lifts and sidings were very varied in dimension' it was often impossible to use the more economical rolling stock.[44] Thus the tedious sorting out of an enormous variety of waggons, a process

Table 6 *Expenditure and receipts of main line railway working 1913–38* (£,000)

Year	Total expenditure	Receipts		Total	Net receipts
		passenger	goods		
1913	75·7	54·5	64·3	119·8	44·1
1920	232·0	109·4	126·9	238·9	7·0
1921	226·8	105·9	109·6	217·8	−9·0
1922	174·8	101·8	115·6	219·3	44·5
1923	166·0	94·1	109·8	205·8	39·8
1924	166·9	95·1	106·4	203·4	36·5
1925	165·0	94·1	103·7	199·7	34·6
1926	154·0	85·1	85·0	171·9	17·9
1927	160·6	90·3	110·4	202·4	41·8
1928	144·1	82·0	103·1	186·9	37·7
1929	146·9	80·0	106·5	188·2	41·3
1930	143·3	76·8	99·3	177·7	34·4
1931	132·6	71·3	90·3	163·1	30·5
1932	125·2	67·1	81·2	149·6	24·4
1933	123·1	67·4	80·8	149·6	26·5
1934	126·8	68·6	85·5	155·6	28·8
1935	127·4	70·0	86·2	157·7	30·3
1936	130·6	72·2	90·2	164·0	33·4
1937	136·1	75·2	94·6	171·4	35·3
1938	137·7	75·3	87·8	164·7	27·1

Source: *Railway Returns*, 1913–38

which Aspinall compared with 'the perpetual piecing together of a jig-saw puzzle with all the disadvantages of waste work',[45] continued right through the inter-war years.

The financial results achieved by the four main line companies in the inter-war period are summarised in Table 6 and the traffic in Table 7.

Table 7 *Railway traffic 1913–37 (,000 tons)*

	1913	1924	1933	1937
General merchandise (classes 7–21)	67,755	60,943	42,479	50,319
Minerals (classes 1–6)	71,067	65,393	43,117	58,683
Coal	225,601	209,161	165,452	188,149
Number of passenger journeys (including season ticket holders, millions)	1,549·8	1,746·9	1,575	1,819

Source: *Railway Returns*, 1913–38

Although both the number of passenger journeys and the number of passenger miles travelled in 1938 were greater than in 1920 they were only marginally so. In order to try and fend off competition from bus services and private cars the railways increased the number of reduced-rate tickets. The most important innovation in this respect was the introduction of three-day return tickets at single fares in 1935. In 1938 about 85 per cent of passenger receipts were derived from reduced fares. In 1924 the proportion had been only 34·4 per cent. The result of this policy was that average receipts per passenger mile fell from 0·86 pence in 1921 to 0·67 pence in 1938.[46] Here was the most important reason for the decline by more than a quarter in passenger receipts between 1921 and 1938. Where the railways lost custom was on the shorter distance travel on local, stopping trains. The greater convenience of bus, trolley-bus and private car transport for these journeys lost the railways an estimated 250–300 million journeys a year by 1937. From the railways' point of view the distressing fact was that whereas the number of land passenger journeys increased by 48 per cent between 1920 and 1938 practically all this increase was due to bus, coach and private car journeys.

The railways' declining freight receipts had two principal features: the loss of merchandise traffic to the road hauliers for distances of up to about 75 miles and the loss of coal and other mineral and bulky goods traffic because of the decline in business activity. For shorter-distance door-to-door transport commercial motor vehicles had the immense advantage over the railways that they provided a more flexible service. With the improvements in tyres, ignition systems, brakes and tare-to-load ratios, the operating costs of road haulage firms fell by at least a third in the inter-war years. One result of Parliament virtually abandoning the original proposals for general transport legislation and resorting to the piecemeal approach of the Railways Act of 1921 was that the wages and working conditions of railwaymen were protected by legislation whereas those of road transport workers were not. In March 1923 the weekly wage rates of railway porters were 160 per cent above their (admittedly low) levels of 1914. The national average rise for all trades was only 67 per cent. In 1932 the lowest basic wage paid on the railways was a not very adequate 40s. But this figure was well above the *maximum* weekly rates paid to bus drivers and lorry drivers in many parts of the country. Mr G. Stirk, Traffic Commissioner of the East Midland Area under the Road Traffic Act, 1930, reported that in his area there were 'over 900 "Jitney" bus operators who had built up their reserves by paying very low wages ... sometimes as low as 25s for drivers and 15s for conductors'.[47] Until these substantial differentials in earnings were narrowed through the effects of the licensing clauses of the Road Traffic Act and the gradual increase in the bargaining strength of the Transport and General Workers Union, road operators' costs and charges were inevitably far below those of the railways.

For many decades coal traffic had been the principal money spinner for the railways. It generally brought in about a fifth of all railway receipts. The fall in the quantity of coal mined—and carried—was thus a very serious blow to the companies' prosperity. The decline in revenue from this source was almost wholly due to the decrease in demand as a result of the depression in the basic industries and not at all due to road competition.

The Railways Act was a measure more appropriate for the nineteenth-century railway age than for the twentieth-century era of motor transport competition. This characteristic was most apparent in respect of pricing policy. A salient reason for the disappointing commercial performance of the railways between the wars was that railway charges, in the nineteenth century tradition, were based on the value of the cost of commodities carried. Road transport charges, on the other hand, were closely related to the cost of service. Under the Act the railways were restrained from charging less than the road hauliers for merchandise in the profitable classes 7–21 but were also unable to raise substantially charges for heavy traffic in classes 1–6, where road competition was virtually non-existent.[48] Road hauliers had no legal obligation to publish their charges and they were not subject, as the railways were, to an 'obligation to carry'. Hence all that the astute road operator needed to do was to visit his nearest railway station, study the railway's charge for a comparable order, and then to underquote this railway rate just sufficiently for him to capture the business. Furthermore, the road operator was perfectly free to provide services only on those routes which were profitable to him; the railway company, by contrast, was under obligation to forward goods to any station in the United Kingdom, irrespective of whether or not it was a profitable undertaking.

Once the plan for a comprehensive transport policy was abandoned in 1919 there was an insuperable barrier to any effort to direct traffic into the most suitable channels from the viewpoint of technology and the economy of operation. Whereas the nation's railways were effectively organised into no more than four major concerns fully capable of organising a rational distribution of traffic, road goods transport was practically without any kind of organisation. In the 1920s there was 'not even the machinery to prevent spasmodic drastic undercutting of rates'. Such arrangements as there were for the use of commercial motor vehicles were 'parochial, haphazard and inefficient'.[49]

A consequence of the railways' meagre financial returns was their failure to invest adequately in modernisation. Although gross investment amounted to £283 million between 1920 and 1938, this was an insufficient sum even to cover proper depreciation and replacement, especially in respect of the permanent way. The net result was thus a disinvestment of £125 million over the 19 years. The seriousness of this shortfall only became apparent after 1945 when to the underinvestment of peacetime was added the effects of wartime shortage and 'making do'. The general inadequacy of inter-war investment masked some important exceptions. The Southern Railway invested nearly £14 million in the electrification of more than a quarter of its rail network in the 1930s with very beneficial effects on the reliability of train timings, the frequency of services provided and the volume of passenger traffic carried. As a general rule, whenever a rail service was electrified—and this applied in the Manchester area and on Tyneside and Merseyside as well as in the south-east—there was a substantial increase in passenger travel. On the long-distance routes which still relied on steam traction, journey times were slashed as more powerful and efficient locomotives were pressed into service. On the London–Edinburgh run the journey time was cut by two and a quarter hours. But despite these and other notable innovations, the railways' commercial policy and technical performance were ill-suited to match the challenge of newer forms of transport.

From the late 1920s onwards the government came to the aid of the railway companies with a series of patchwork measures. As soon as it became apparent that road transport was likely to make serious inroads into the revenue of the railways, one of the leading objectives of the main line companies was to participate in road goods and passenger services. For this they required parliamentary authorisation.

Early in 1922, before the grouping of companies under the Railways Act had been completed, the London and North Western and Midland Companies proposed to introduce a Bill to give them extended road powers. The Minister of Transport, therefore, appointed a small Committee, chaired by J. H. Balfour Brown KC, 'to enquire and report whether it is desirable that the railway companies should have general or limited power to carry goods by road and, if so, what, if any, conditions should be attached to the exercise of this power'. In the first of three reports three of the Committee noted that if the railways' request were granted 'the power of the railway workers' unions' would be increased. In the case of another strike, like the national railway strike of 1919, 'this would create great problems for the government'. All the same, the three signatories considered that, subject to certain safeguards for the avoidance of railway and railway union monopoly, the companies should be given their Bill. However, other members of the Committee, led by Mr L. S. Shrapnell Smith, a leader of the road interests, were entirely against any such concessions to the companies and said so in separate reports to the minister.[50] On 9 March 1922 the cabinet agreed to the Bill going forward subject to its possible amendment before the third reading.[51] But by the time it reached the House of Commons Select Committee on Private Bills on 4 May the Minister of Transport had yielded to the road lobby and he therefore sent his lieutenant, Sir George Beharrel, to speak against it. Beharrel expressed fears that the railway companies would not be able to earn their standard revenue on the rails if they started to carry goods by road at lower rates than those charged by the road carriers. The railways should compete by improving their own services rather than by entering the sphere of road transport. 'In the main', he said, 'the railway development is on the steel track and not on the road.'[52] When he learned of the onerous safeguards the ministry proposed to insert in the Bill, Mr H. P. Macmillan KC, counsel for the companies, decided to proceed no further with it.

By 13 July 1927 when a deputation from the four main line railways and the Metropolitan Railway was interviewed by Mr W. Ashley, the new Minister of Transport, road competition had intensified. It now seemed somewhat unrealistic to answer the companies' demands for extended road powers with talk of the dangers of railway monopoly. Three days later the minister concluded a lengthy report to the cabinet by expressing the view that the railways were 'entitled to support from the Government'. On 9 November 1927, after some delays through the pressure of other business, the cabinet agreed.[53] The four Bills giving the companies 'power to own, work and use in any district to which their system affords access, road vehicles for the conveyance of passengers and goods' or the right to enter into agreement 'with any company, body or person owning, or running, road vehicles for hire or as public service vehicles', were passed in July 1928. The Companies used their powers under the Railway (Road Transport) Acts principally to buy financial interests in the larger bus companies, such as Southdown Motor Services, Crosville and Scottish Motor Traction. By 1931 they had an interest in 19,500 buses out of 41,500 on British roads. In goods cartage they purchased Pickfords and Carter Paterson but their share of this side of the business was much more restricted. By 1938 they owned only 10,000 goods vehicles out of a total of nearly 495,000. Their wisdom in taking these steps is questionable. They did not effectively control the policies of the bus companies in which they acquired an interest: and although the goods vehicles were used more directly as feeders to the railway, the £15 million invested in the two forms of road transport might have brought in a better return if it had been invested in further schemes for electrification of lines.

Two other concessions from government followed in 1929. Passenger duty, to which the companies had been liable since the days of the stage coach's pre-eminence, was at last abolished. Under the Local Government Act, railway properties were de-rated to the extent of 75 per cent, on condition that the sums saved went into a Freight Rebates Fund for reducing freight rates on some classes of traffic.

In 1931 the Weir Committee[54] recommended a major extension of main line electrification on the third rail system. The railways' share of the capital cost was estimated at £260 million, the rest of the capital being provided by the Central Electricity Board. It was estimated that £17½ million would be saved in operating and maintenance expenses, thus providing a profit of seven per cent on the entire undertaking. However, as the work would require twenty years to complete, the net return, after deductions for interest charges, would be no more than two per cent. These estimates were on the conservative side since they made no allowance for the expansion of passenger traffic which, experience showed, followed on electrification. The report could not have appeared at a worse time. The national budget was unbalanced and the Treasury and the May Committee were demanding rigid economy in government expenditure. In any case many leading railwaymen were more interested in improving the performance of the steam locomotive than in making an exhaustive enquiry into the economies of electric traction. Consequently a very promising scheme was still-born. It was one of the great missed opportunities of the 1930s.

The railways were helped in the 1930s by two important Acts controlling road transport, the Road Traffic Act, 1930 and the Road and Rail Traffic Act, 1933. These will be considered in the next section of this chapter.

The depression years of the early 1930s hit the main line companies so severely that by 1935 they were pleading for a government loan to help them out of their difficulties. The largest part of the £32 million that was lent them in response to this appeal went on the Southern Railway's electrification schemes.

Despite the introduction in 1933 of a policy of 'agreed charges' under which the railways were given freedom to contract with traders to provide transport services on the basis of annual payments, by the closing years of the decade the companies felt a growing resentment against the strait-jacket of the rate-fixing provisions of the 1921 Act. In 1938 they launched a 'Square Deal' campaign in which they demanded the same degree of freedom in their pricing policy as was employed by road transport interests. Although the Minister of Transport agreed that they had a strong case the war intervened before new arrangements could be worked out.

V

In the first nine months of 1919 bus proprietors and municipal tramway authorities were in a state of continual uncertainty about future plans for development. Few new bus services were started and little capital was being invested in trams. Col J. A. Pickard, head of the Traffic Department of the new ministry, reported that in the provinces the transport industry was 'almost entirely stagnant pending the declaration as to what was to be the future policy of the Ministry'.[55] Sir Eric Geddes set out his views for the future in a letter to Lord Inverforth. In general there was 'no intention that the state should undertake the management of road transport services' where these could be run 'by a commercial undertaking on commercial lines'. Where, however, there was a 'national necessity' for such a service but no private entrepreneur was forthcoming to provide it, the policy would be '(a) preferably to assist private enterprise to establish the service or (b) to inaugurate state services'. Efficiency was to be the prime objective. It would be the policy of the Ministry of Transport 'to fix proper economic rates for carriage by rail, road or water so that traffic would tend automatically to take its proper channel'.[56]

However, the minimum prerequisite for fixing 'proper economic rates' for the different forms of transport was a national body with sufficient power to ensure that charges levied for goods and passenger carriage corresponded as closely as possible to the real costs of providing those services. The sober reality was that after the cabinet and Parliament had decimated the original Ministry of Ways and Communications Bill the Minister of Transport lacked adequate powers to achieve the ends he was seeking. He and his successors were therefore reduced to tackling the problems of road transport in a piecemeal fashion—and in virtual isolation from developments in other forms of transport—as they became particularly acute, in the same way as they dealt with the problems of the railways.

It was the situation in London that first demanded attention. For at least two generations, and long before the arrival of motor transport, there had been dire predictions that if the number of vehicles using the streets of central London continued to increase traffic would grind to a halt. More recently, in 1905, the Royal Commission on London Traffic warned that unless the 'standard of movement' of traffic within the city was improved 'the life and growth of the metropolis would be slowly, but no less surely, strangled by the choking of the great arteries of traffic'. The difficulty was that 'there did not exist . . . any municipal or other authority having jurisdiction over the whole area, and possessed of sufficient power and resources to enable it to deal satisfactorily with the problem of locomotion'.[57]

Within a few months of the armistice the problems pinpointed by the Royal Commission fifteen years earlier appeared in an aggravated form as buses and other commercial vehicles reappeared on the streets of the metropolis. One of the first decisions of the newly appointed Minister of Transport was therefore to set up an Advisory Committee on London Traffic, under the chairmanship of M. Kennedy Jones, to make recommendations on how congestion in the streets might be eased. In its report published on 1 January 1920, it urged that 'unless the existing powers are grouped and placed in the hands of one authority, authorised as a result of its technical experience, or the technical experience it can command, to lay down the lines on which London traffic shall extend and develop, it seems that no real reform is possible'. The remedy lay in appointing a London Traffic Authority with power to control the whole of greater London public transport services and all other forms of traffic.[58] At the same time the House of Commons Select Committee on Transport (Metropolitan Area), recommended 'as a vital measure of the most immediate necessity', the creation of a supreme traffic board 'to coordinate routes and services of all systems of transport, regulate all traffic and street repairs, etc.'[59]

In the light of these unequivocal recommendations the Minister had no excuse for delay. He drafted a Bill for the setting up of a London Traffic Authority and presented it to the cabinet. However, the Bill appeared just as the postwar boom burst. It involved 'a charge upon the state funds and, in view of the financial situation, it was not possible to proceed with it'.[60] Londoners had to wait 12 more years for the supreme traffic authority that had been recommended since 1905.

In the meantime, however, the London County Council had to continue to grapple with a problem aggravated by the appearance in 1922 of a large number of independent 'pirate' bus operators. In a resolution passed on 16 May 1922 it warned the government 'that the difficulty of reaching a settlement of the traffic problem as a whole would be enhanced by any steps taken by the Government . . . assisting particular traffic undertakings operating in London . . . without recognising the essential community of the traffic interests of the entire area'. Within another two years the speed of traffic in the streets of central London was down to only half what it had been in 1919.[61]

In 1924 a Court of Inquiry was set up under the Industrial Courts Act to examine the causes of a tramway and bus workers' strike in London and the merits of the men's claim for better wages. It was obliged to recognise the impossibility of paying adequate wages to the tramwaymen or busmen while the unrestricted competition of the 'pirate' buses was allowed to continue. Briefed to report on a wage dispute, it felt impelled to make strong comments on London's transport policy:

'In our view, no satisfactory and abiding solution of the difficulties of the tramway undertakings can be reached unless the tramway industry is considered in relation to the wider problem of passenger transport in London. We are also of opinion that the best interests of the public would be served if all services of passenger transport were so regulated that instead of being largely competitive they were complementary.'[62]

The London Traffic Act of 1924 which was the outcome of these pressures for reform was not the comprehensive remedy for which Lord Ashfield, chairman of the underground group, and other transport experts had campaigned. It gave the Minister of Transport, through the commissioners of police, the right to restrict bus operations to certain streets within the greater London area and to require proprietors to provide bus services throughout the day and not simply during the traffic rush hours when operation was most profitable. Although 'approved routes' were now established the licensee had complete liberty to run on as many (or as few) routes as he chose provided he could sustain the pretence of a comprehensive service. Nevertheless the 195 independent bus proprietors in London disliked the Act. In 1925 they formed themselves into the Association of London Omnibus Proprietors to undercut the fares of the London

General Omnibus Company which provided the largest number of services. Despite the 'General's' buying up of many of the independent concerns in 1927, a great deal of wasteful competition continued, to the detriment of the underground combine, the tramway undertakings and to the travelling public which had to put up with overcrowded conditions in peak periods and inadequate service at other times of the day.[63]

After 1924 the experiment of partial regulation of public service motor transport through the London Traffic Act provided an instructive example for the government to follow in more general legislation or to modify or reject.[64] The London and Home Counties Traffic Advisory Committee, set up under the Act, kept the Ministry of Transport informed regarding the adequacy of the measures taken. But this was information about the London area only. The demand was intensifying for a more general enquiry into transport policy.

It was during discussions on the Railway (Road Transport) Bills in the winter of 1927-8 that Wilfred Ashley, the Minister of Transport, suggested in a memorandum to the cabinet that there was a strong case for the appointment of a Royal Commission to consider the co-ordination of all forms of transport.[65] Meanwhile, increasing concern about the impact of commercial motor transport on the railways' finances was being shown in the provinces. At a meeting of the Manchester Chamber of Commerce held early in February 1928 the view was expressed that 'too much of the heavy transport was being diverted to the roads, that the roads were gradually being made impassable and that an enquiry should be made into the whole question'.[66]

Later in 1928 the Government appointed a Royal Commission, under the chairmanship of Sir Arthur Griffith Boscawen, to consider the problems raised by the growth of road transport. The Commission's terms of reference were:

to take into consideration the problems arising out of the growth of road traffic and, with a view to securing the employment of the available means of transport in Great Britain (including transport by sea and by ferries) to the greatest public advantage, to consider and report what measures, if any, should be adopted for their better regulation and control, and, so far as is desirable in the public interest, to promote their co-ordinated working and development.

Influencing the policy of the cabinet and the activities of the commission was the alarming increase in the number of road accidents. The number killed rose sharply from 4,856 in 1926 to nearly 6,700 in 1929. In the crowded streets of Britain's cities there was profound disquiet as the lives, particularly of children and old people, were increasingly sacrificed. In the Metropolitan Police area of London alone the number of fatal accidents rose from 960 in 1927 to 1,230 in 1928.[67] To the embarrassment of the government, which was not ready for legislation, Lord Cecil of Chelwood introduced his own Road Vehicles Regulation Bill in the House of Lords in July 1928. It received widespread support. Typical of those who spoke for it was Lord Buckmaster who declared that the proposals in the Bill for driving tests, differential speed limits for different classes of vehicles, and heavier penalties for offending drivers, were intended 'to avoid the use by rich people of their comforts and conveniences so as to interfere with the comforts and conveniences of those who are poor'.[68] The government reacted by asking Boscawen to advance the date for the publication of the Royal Commission's report—or at least that part of it which concerned road safety. However, before there was time to frame a government Bill the Baldwin administration was defeated in the general election of June 1929.

In the following month the first of the commission's three reports was published, stating unequivocally that legislation on the subject of road safety was 'greatly overdue'. The new Minister of Transport, Herbert Morrison, urged the cabinet to give priority to a Road Transport Bill because he could see that if the Labour Government did not act quickly Lord Cecil would insist on passing some measure in the House of Lords and would then 'throw upon the government the onus of refusing to proceed'. He was also persuaded by Sir Cyril Hurcombe of the Ministry of Transport that it would be a good idea to combine in one enactment safety measures and the more stringent system of licensing public service vehicles he had long favoured.[69]

The most important feature of the Road Traffic Act of 1930 was the complete overhaul of the system of licensing public service vehicles. In some areas licensing had been the responsibility of the police, in others it was the local authority, and in yet others it was possible for a bus or coach operator to initiate a service without any authorisation. Under the Act these diverse arrangements were abolished and all public service vehicles had to be licensed by the Area Traffic Commissioner. The country was divided into 13 traffic areas—11 for England and Wales and two for Scotland—with a full-time paid Commissioner in charge of each. Each operator was thenceforward required to hold three licences. The public service vehicle licence was required as a certificate of the fitness of the vehicle and was issued after its inspection by a qualified motor engineer. The drivers' and conductors' licences were issued subject to the operator paying rates of wages and employing his staff for hours 'not less favourable than those commonly recognised by employers and trade societies'.[70] The Road Service licence was required before the operator was allowed to run a bus or coach service on any route. Of the three the Road Service Licence was undoubtedly the most important since it was the means by which entry into road passenger service was regulated. In issuing licences the Commissioners were guided by four main considerations mentioned in Section 72 of the Act. They included the suitability of the routes to be served, the extent to which the proposed routes were already covered by existing services, the extent to which there was a public demand for the service and 'the needs of the area as a whole ... and the co-ordination of all forms of passenger transport including transport by rail'. The fares charged had to be reasonable; there was to be no deliberate undercutting of the services provided by other operators and time-tables had to be publicly displayed.

In justifying the Bill's clauses abolishing the speed limit for private cars (though keeping a revised speed limit for commercial vehicles) Herbert Morrison considered that there was not one member of the House of Commons who observed the existing limit of 20 m.p.h., operative since 1903. He held it to be indefensible for MPs 'to try to enforce a law which they themselves had no intention of observing'.[71] A majority of the House agreed with him. He also had the backing of the police: 37 out of the 58 chief constables felt that endeavouring to enforce a speed limit was inadvisable. The Act made no provision for driving tests. The police had approved a proposal made by a Ministry of Transport committee back in 1922 that every applicant for a driving licence should be asked to give a verbal declaration as follows: 'I hereby declare that to the best of my knowledge I am not suffering from any disease or physical disability which would be likely to cause the driving of a mechanically propelled road vehicle by me to be a source of danger to the public.' However, the House of Commons in committee defeated by 57 votes to 30 a proposal that provision for driving proficiency tests be included in the Bill, Lord Erskine declaring that 'driver's tests are no use'.[72] Section 4 of the Act made it compulsory for each driver to hold a licence which he would be given on payment of 5s and on making a declaration of physical fitness.

The Royal Commission made a thorough investigation into the working of compulsory motor insurance in Denmark and Massachusetts—the only states known to have introduced it—but it made no decisive recommendation for its introduction in Britain. It was quite otherwise with the hospitals whose management was still dependent on voluntary contributions for finance and who were finding it increasingly difficult to cope with the rapidly growing number of road casualties. Their spokesmen were strong advocates of compulsory payments from the 'guilty' party in road accidents to the costs of treatment of the injured. Morrison eventually accepted this viewpoint and Section 35 of the Act made provision for compulsory third-party insurance and for payments to be made to hospitals where treatment arose from road accidents.

Throughout the 1920s Britain's road signs were in a muddled and chaotic state. H. H. Piggot, of the Ministry of Transport, admitted to the Royal Commission that 'the man travelling on a very unimportant by-road had got just as much right of way as the man on the first class main road'. This dangerous situation, which was 'a frequent cause of road accidents' arose because there was still no official road traffic code.[73] By 1930 the Ministry had done a great deal towards sorting out the tangle. In Section 48 of the Act it was laid down that traffic signs were to be of 'the prescribed size, colour and type' and local highway authorities were given power to remove private road signs which confused the driver.

The Road Traffic Act has been criticised on the grounds that it abandoned 'the discipline of the market' in respect of the number and frequency of bus and coach services and the fares they charged. It is claimed that the administration of the Act 'discouraged change and introduced inertia into a highly competitive and adaptable industry'.[74] The Traffic Commissioners, in deciding whether to authorise a service, followed the principles of priority, protection and public need in that order of importance, thus giving the secure foothold to the established operator, however inefficient, and making new entry into the industry very difficult.[75] That the Act abandoned the discipline of the market is undeniable. That there was a failure to improve services and efficiency is highly questionable.

The Act undoubtedly encouraged the process of consolidation in the bus industry. The number of bus operators declined from 6,486 in 1931 to 4,789 in 1937. Over the same years the percentage of buses owned by operators with 100 or more vehicles each rose from 47 to 61 and the total number of buses in service fell from 52,648 (1930) to 49,372 (1937). But, at the same time there was an increase in the comfort and seating capacity of the vehicles. The seat-miles run in 1937 were a record, showing an increase of nearly 28 per cent over 1931. Receipts per vehicle-mile rose steadily through the 1930s. Despite consolidation the small man was by no means completely elbowed out. There were still 1,850 operators who owned only one vehicle each in 1937.[76] Another major consequence of the Act was that it helped to arrest some of the drift of passenger traffic away from the railways, especially over the longer distances.

The Ministry of Transport files for the years after 1930 reveal the very unequal conditions of work as between railwaymen and bus workers. Under the Road Traffic Act the Traffic Commissioners had no power to oblige bus operators to pay adequate wages or limit hours of labour. They could, however, decline to authorise services where labour conditions were unsatisfactory. The Transport and General

Workers or other unions then brought actions before the Industrial Court. Early in 1932 there were women bus conductors in Northumberland and Durham who were paid 12s 6d for a 65 or 70 hour week. These were exceptionally bad instances. But in 12 of the 15 cases brought to the Industrial Court before August 1936 bus companies were found to be employing staff an excessive number of hours at rates of pay well below the average in the industry; and the companies involved included important concerns such as Thames Valley Traction and the City of Oxford Motor Services.[77] Eventually Parliament recognised that the earlier legislation was ineffective in securing a fair deal for the half-million road transport workers employed in passenger and goods transport. In May 1938 Ernest Brown, the Minister of Labour, introduced the Road Haulage Wages Bill whose purpose he defined as 'to help a rapidly growing modern industry towards settled self-government as regards wages'.[78] When the Bill became law later that summer it brought into being Area Wages Boards and a Central Wages Board representing both sides of the industry, with effective power to determine conditions of employment. Thus it took twenty years for bus workers to achieve a machinery of wage negotiation of a kind used by railwaymen since 1919. During those two decades many bus operators had increased their passenger traffic at the expense of the railway partly because they enjoyed a substantial wage-cost advantage over the rival form of transport.

Some MPs had grave doubts about the abolition of the speed limit in 1930. As road casualties mounted in the next few years these doubts spread to many others. In 1934 7,343 persons were killed on Britain's roads, a slaughter not to be exceeded in peacetime until 1964. Parliament responded by passing the Road Traffic Act in 1934, re-introducing a speed limit (but at 30 m.p.h. in place of the earlier 20 m.p.h.) in 'built up areas', introducing driving tests and empowering local authorities to create regulated pedestrian road crossings after approval by the Ministry of Transport. Thereafter Belisha beacons—named after Leslie Hore-Belisha, the Minister of Transport responsible—appeared in rapidly increasing numbers, and for a time road casualties were stabilised.

It was not until 1933 that Parliament extended the system of licensing and control to the road hauliers. The existence of many more smaller concerns than was the case with buses made the task of framing legislation more difficult. In April 1932 the ministry was stirred into action by pressure from the railway trade unions, the railway companies and by business.

Later in January 1932 Mr P. J. Pybus, the Minister of Transport, received a deputation from the four main line railway companies who were concerned about 'the seriousness of their position as a result of road competition'. They asked that 'a scheme of licensing goods vehicles should be introduced by public legislation on lines which were recommended by the Royal Commission'.[79] On the following 7 April, at the request of J. Ramsay Macdonald, the Prime Minister, Mr Pybus received a deputation from the NUR, ASLEF and the Railway Clerks' Association. The minister was handed a lengthy memorandum on transport policy agreed by the executives of the three unions. They were realistic enough to recognise that 'for relatively short distances, or in areas where no railway service was available, the use of motor vehicles may be the more expeditious and economical means of transport,' but they maintained that road transport did 'not bear its fair share of the expense involved in its operations'. To ensure the optimum utilisation of each form of transport they proposed the formation of a National Transport Board which would have power to acquire and operate canals, coastal shipping and 'aerial navigation' as well as railways.[80] Less than three weeks later, a meeting of the Associated Chambers of Commerce passed a resolution calling for 'a removal of the disabilities and restrictions which made it difficult for railways to compete efficiently with their rivals'.[81]

These were among the pressures which persuaded Mr Pybus to ask Sir Arthur Salter to preside at a conference of road and rail representatives to examine the state of the law regarding road and rail goods transport under the following terms of reference:

(1) To investigate the facts concerning the total costs of the highway system, the incidence of those costs and the contributions of the different classes of users of mechanically propelled vehicles.
(2) To consider and report on the nature and extent of regulation which, in view of modern economic developments, should be applied to goods transport by road and by rail.
(3) To make such further recommendations as they are able to frame designed to assist the two sides of the industry to carry out their functions under equable conditions which adequately safeguard the interests of free trade and industry and
(4) To report by the end of July.

In what the Minister of Transport described to the cabinet 'as a most valuable and unanimous report'[82] the Salter Conference recommended that taxes on heavier goods vehicles should be increased so that their contribution to the revenue more fully covered the cost of the damage they inflicted on the roads. Because the scale of road tax on commercial vehicles had been fixed 'before the development of the heaviest type of vehicle in considerable numbers', it stopped at the level of five tons. Thus the ten-ton vehicle paid no more duty than one half its weight and the existing tax scale gave 'a preferential advantage to just that type of vehicle which the evidence showed to involve disproportionately high road expenditure'.[83] As a matter of general principle the Conference agreed with the final report of the Royal Commission on Transport that it was 'not in the national interest to encourage further diversion of heavy goods traffic from the railways to the roads' and therefore it recommended a comprehensive system of goods vehicle licensing. Its members were also unanimous in their dislike of the unfettered competition of a large number of small concerns. With regard to wages and conditions of service of the employees of the road haulage industry they wrote

> The less favourable conditions obtaining over a part of the haulage industry are due to the greater number of individual units in that industry. In justice to the employees and also in the interests of both the railways and of those hauliers who are struggling to maintain satisfactory wage rates and conditions of work, it is of the utmost importance that an end should be put to the abuses in these respects which have so far attended the organisation of the industry in so many small units.[84]

The granting of licences to road hauliers, therefore, should be 'conditional upon the observance of proper conditions as to fair wages and conditions of service'.

In commending the report to the cabinet as a basis for legislation the minister endorsed the view of the railway companies that the overloading of road goods vehicles was 'frequent, gross and notorious' with the result that there was 'much general inconvenience through noise and vibration'. He therefore considered that 'the root of the rail–road problem' was 'the equitable taxation of commercial road transport in relation to the use which it makes of, and the value it derives from, the highway system'.[85]

The Road and Rail Traffic Act, 1933 followed closely the recommendations of the Salter Committee. Part I of the Act incorporated the kind of proposals it had made for the licensing and regulation of goods motor vehicles. Henceforward no person was permitted to carry goods commercially except under licence. Regular road hauliers required a public carrier's or 'A' licence; those who used their vehicles partly for their own purposes and partly to carry for others required a limited carrier's of 'B' licence; and those whose vehicles were used exclusively in connection with their own business qualified for a private carrier's or 'C' licence. The Traffic Commissioners appointed under the Act of 1930 were responsible for administration and were able to control entry into road haulage through the fact that the licences were of a strictly limited validity: two years for the 'A', one year for the 'B' and three years for the 'C' variety. The licensee had to comply with the conditions of Section 93 of the 1930 Act (the fair wages clause) in respect of the drivers he employed, and his vehicle had to come up to Ministry of Transport standards of serviceability. Whereas those who were in business at the time the 1933 Act was passed were granted their licences, future applications for 'A' and 'B' licences would be examined by the court of the licensing authority in relation to the state of public demand for services and the existence, or otherwise, of alternative means of transport. Only if the applicant could demonstrate a specific need for his services would the licence be granted. The general assumption made by the commissioner was that duplication of services was wasteful.

Part II of the Act was designed to put the railways in a better competitive position in relation to their competitors on the road. With the consent of the Railway Rates Tribunal they were allowed 'to make such charges for the carriage of merchandise of any trader, or for the carriage of any part of his merchandise, as may be agreed between the company and the trader'. These were the 'agreed charges' by which the four main line companies hoped to win back traffic which had been taken by the road hauliers.

Part III of the Act set up a Transport Advisory Council whose task was 'to give advice and assistance to the Minister of Transport in connection with ... his functions in relation to means of and facilities for transport and their co-operation, improvement and development'. The new body gave influential advice to the minister on policy for the support of coastal shipping as well as land transport and its reports were of great value in determining transport policy in time of war. The Salter Committee's recommendations for steeper rates of taxation on the heavier road haulage vehicles were implemented in the Finance Act of 1933.

If it was expected that the effects of the Road and Rail Traffic Act would be to lead to the coalescence of hauliers into bigger groups, such expectations were not generally realised. Although there was some tendency on the part of the larger undertakings to purchase other haulage firms with a view to economies in management and operation, in general the individual haulier avoided being absorbed by other haulage operators. When the ministry assessed the nation's resources just before the Second World War it found that even the 350 largest firms could muster between them only 10,000 vehicles, an average of under 30 vehicles per firm.[86]

The survival of hundreds of small firms makes it difficult wholly to accept the claim of the critics that the Road and Rail Traffic Act 'checked the growth of a highly competitive industry'. The charge has been made that 'greater stability was achieved at the cost of preventing the expansion of new enterprise in the industry, thus impeding the offering of lower rates and improved services to the consumer'. It is certainly true that it was much more difficult to enter the road haulage industry after 1933 than it was earlier. There were fewer 'A' and 'B' licence holders in 1938 than there were in 1933. The critics of the Act have argued that the Reports of both the Royal Commission and the Salter Conference were unduly influenced by the views of the railway companies and the larger road haulage firms, which were feeling the pinch of unrestrained competition. After 1933 it was necessary for the consumer to prove to the Traffic Commissioner the need for additional services before the new licences would be forthcoming. It is claimed that the system cramped initiative because it prevented the ambitious haulier from venturing into an expansion of his business by exploiting the advances in technology of the commercial vehicle and attracting custom by a superior service after he had embarked his capital.

However, the fact that the number of 'A' and 'B' licensed vehicles actually shrank from 150,740 in 1935 to 147,322 in 1938 reflects an improvement rather than a deterioration in services provided. The capacity of trucks increased, the substitution of pneumatic tyres for solid tyres made possible increased speeds and decreased maintenance costs, while improved organisation meant that there was less empty running. At the outbreak of the Second World War the productivity of the Road Haulage industry was noticeably greater than it had been six years earlier.

The London Passenger Transport Act saw the light of day in the same year as the Road and Rail Traffic Act was passed. Though enacted by Macdonald's National Government it was largely the work of Herbert Morrison, Minister of Transport in the second Labour Government of 1929-31. Unfortunately the London Traffic Act of 1924 had largely failed to solve the problem of congestion and inadequate accommodation for rush-hour traffic. When the Minister of Transport instructed the London Traffic Advisory Committee to report on the situation in north, north-east, east and south-east London it found that there was no way out of the impasse of inadequate services 'so long as . . . competitive methods were pursued'. The difficulty was that the underground railways 'were not prepared, or were not in a position to raise, the capital necessary for substantial schemes of extension or improvement'. One of the worst areas of congestion was around Finsbury Park and districts north. The Transport Advisory Committee pressed the underground railways to extend the tube from Finsbury Park in the direction of Southgate but they were met with the statement

'We cannot afford it. We cannot contemplate an expenditure of £800,000 to £1,000,000 per mile to extend this Tube with unlimited competition going on on the surface. Give us some protection; show us that if we extend the Tube we will have an opportunity of making a return on our outlay, then we will do it; but as long as you, the Traffic Committee and the Ministry of Transport allow this unlimited competition, it is impossible for us to raise the capital to do this kind of work.'

The Committee's solution, endorsed by the ministry, was the establishment of 'a pooling arrangement between the various tramway undertakings, the underground railways and the omnibuses'.[87]

The London Passenger Transport Act, 1933, followed the broad principles of policy advocated by the London Traffic Advisory Committee. The Act gave the new London Passenger Transport Board of seven persons the responsibility of making provision for 'an adequate and properly co-ordinated system of passenger transport for the London Passenger Transport area' and for taking steps, where necessary, for 'extending and improving the facilities for passenger transport in that area'.[88] London Transport stock to the value of £113 million was issued in exchange for the capital of the five railways, 14 municipally owned tramways and 61 bus undertakings acquired by the Board, which from 1 July 1933 held a monopoly of transport in the London area, except for taxis and private cars. All receipts from traffic originating in the London area were pooled.

Under the able leadership of Lord Ashfield and Frank Pick, both of whom were transferred from the Underground Combine to the LPTB, the work of co-ordinating services, pooling receipts, standardising equipment, services and charges went on apace. In the latter 1930s it proved possible to make substantial extensions to the tube railways—something that it had not been found possible to achieve in the 1920s. By the outbreak of war London's transport services—provided by the biggest monopoly undertaking of its kind in the world—were the envy of many other countries.

VI

In the course of the 1920s and 1930s Britain developed a national highway policy. It was a change which was forced upon government through the rapid growth in the number of motor vehicles using the roads. When a London motoring enthusiast, once known to the author, drove his $3\frac{1}{2}$ h.p. Benz from London to Glasgow and back to visit an international exhibition in the Summer of 1901 he met but one other motor car on the road in the entire journey, although the 12 m.p.h. speed limit made the enterprise a prolonged one. By 1914 there were 388,860 motor vehicles on British roads: by 1938 there were over three million.

The eminent engineer Sir George Gibb reminded a government committee on Local Taxation in 1914 that there were still rural districts in England which 'obstinately refused to steam-roller their roads'. Their method of repair was the time-honoured one of throwing down metal from time to time and leaving it to the traffic to work it in. There was, by that time, a manifest conflict of interest between the growing number of motorists and the local authorities. The road user was arguing that the condition of the roads ought not to be dependent on purely local standards and that there should be some central authority to secure a minimum standard of maintenance on all roads used for through traffic. The local authorities, on the other hand, were saying 'Our roads are quite good enough for us; they carry the agricultural and local traffic of the district and we will not raise the standard of maintenance to meet the demand of "alien" traffic at the expense of our local taxpayers'. The law as it stood in 1914 provided no real answer to this dilemma. County Councils were held to be responsible for the maintenance of the 'main' roads within their frontiers of jurisdiction but there were wide differences of interpretation. In Huntingdonshire 93 per cent of the roads were classified as 'main'; in Hertfordshire it was 74 per cent; very surprisingly in Middlesex it was only nine per cent.[89]

Work had begun on the reform of road administration just before the outbreak of the First World War. On 30 April 1914 the Road Board sent a circular to all highway authorities, other than the London County Council and the County Boroughs, inviting their help in the compilation of a new classification of roads. The highways in each authority's area were to be divided into 'First Class', 'Second Class' and 'Other' roads. By August 1914 proposals had been received for placing 23,137 miles of road, or 14 per cent of the total mileage, into the first class.

This work was resumed soon after the cessation of hostilities. Under section 17 (2) of the Ministry of Transport Act, 1919, the minister had power to classify Britain's roads and to defray from public funds up to one half of the salary and establishment charges associated with their maintenance. One of the first tasks of the Road Department of the newly established ministry was to issue guidelines to the local authorities on the principles to be followed in road classification. From the information subsequently obtained from the localities, the Roads Advisory Committee of the Ministry of Transport issued a provisional road classification in March 1921. Of the 152,154 miles of road in England and Wales, 17,587 miles were placed in Class 1 and 10,655 in Class II, the remainder being 'unclassified'. Of the 24,899 miles of road in Scotland 4,447 miles were in Class I, 3,276 in Class II and the remainder unclassified.

Whilst this sorting out had been in progress the government set aside nearly £10½ million for the construction of new arterial roads, £4 million of which came from the Road Fund. Unfortunately most of the detailed proposals were stillborn through the onset of severe economic depression in 1921 and the drastic curtailment of government expenditure initiated by the National Economy Committee—the 'Geddes Axe'.[90]

Meanwhile under the Roads Act, 1920, a new Road Fund was established to take over the monies accumulated in Lloyd George's Road Improvement Fund since 1909. The collection of motor taxes was transferred from the customs and excise to the local authorities and cars were taxed according to their horsepower measured by their cylinder bore.

Government economy drive notwithstanding, the number of cars using the roads increased with great rapidity, making it impossible for the administration to turn a completely blind eye to the question of road improvement. Ministry of Transport road censuses revealed that the tonnage of motor vehicles passing Sankey Bridge on the A55 between Liverpool and Manchester rose from 8,250 tons a day in 1922 to 11,610 tons a day in 1925. At Findon, on the A24 London to Worthing road, the increase over the same short span of time was from 1,920 tons to 3,600 tons, and at Greymoorhill, just north of Carlisle on the A7 to Edinburgh, the increase was from 1,920 tons to 4,330 tons.[91] However, in the 1920s the Government did very little to encourage basic road improvements such as widening and straightening through routes: the bulk of the expenditure still went on the improvement of road surfaces. Throughout the years to 1934, as Table 8 shows, receipts from vehicle and petrol taxes were exceeded by road expenditure.

The change from a situation in which the expenditure on highways exceeded vehicle and fuel taxes to one in which receipts exceeded expenditure was the result of two main influences. The first was the success of the railway interest in persuading the Ministry of Transport that the motorist was inadequately taxed in relation to the benefit he received from the use of the roads. This resulted in the introduction of a petrol tax of 4d a gallon in 1928, increased to 6d and then 8d in 1931; a tax on diesel fuel at 8d a gallon from 1935; increases on both types of fuel tax of a penny a gallon in 1938; and increased registration duties on commercial vehicles in 1935 and on private cars in 1938. The second influence was Winston Churchill's 'raiding' of the Road Fund from 1926 onwards and Neville Chamberlain's winding up of the Road Fund as a separate entity in 1937.

The process of clarifying responsibility for road maintenance was carried a stage further under the Local Government Act, 1929, which made County Councils responsible for all Class 1 and Class 2 roads besides 'county' roads and bridges.

With added financial burdens placed on their shoulders the County Councils looked with a more critical eye at the ribbon development which accompanied the growth in numbers of the private car. More

Table 8 *Costs of road upkeep and receipts of motor taxation 1921–1937, annual expenditure on highways and receipts of motor taxation in £,000s*

Year	Annual exp. on highways, G.B., including 'loan' charges but excluding loans	Receipts of motor vehicle taxation less rebates and refunds	Receipts of petrol tax	Total tax receipts	Proportion of col. (4) to col. (1)
	1	2	3	4	%
1921–2	46,161	10,042	—	10,042	21·8
1922–3	45,165	11,480	—	11,480	25·4
1923–4	46,713	13,124	—	13,124	28·0
1925	51,763	15,190	—	15,190	29·3
1926	55,156	16,961	—	16,961	30·8
1927	56,257	18,685	—	18,685	33·2
1928	58,980	23,000	—	23,000	39·0
1929	58,092	25,002	12,982	37,984	65·2
1930	57,760	25,586	15,043	40,649	70·5
1931	66,509	27,086	15,909	42,995	64·5
1932	68,384	27,277	29,277	56,544	82·8
1933	58,949	27,637	25,310	52,947	89·6
1934	56,710	28,357	40,408	68,765	123·3
1935	57,101	31,473	42,300	73,777	129·0
1936	58,547	29,186	45,129	74,315	126·7
1937	—	30,999	47,801	78,800	—

Source: G. Walker, *Road and Rail*, 1947, p. 31.

and more villas were being built to front the main arteries leading into the urban areas. A joint conference of the County Councils Association, the Council for the Preservation of Rural England and the County Surveyors Association, held in January 1935, noted that not only did this kind of urban sprawl spread road congestion and the risks of accidents, but also that the cost of providing approach roads, electricity, gas and water services to the widely dispersed dwellings was greatly increased.[92] The Government reacted by passing the Prevention of Ribbon Development Act in 1935 which banned building within 220 feet of the middle of a classified road without the sanction of the highway authority.

The drawback of the road clauses of the Local Government Act, 1929, was that although County Councils were given responsibility for maintaining the principal roads there was no guarantee of uniformity of standards of maintenance. Thus the quality of a road on a through route might suddenly deteriorate as the motorist crossed the county boundary.

A solution to this problem was found in the Trunk Roads Act, 1936, under which 4,500 miles of major roads were transferred from the county authorities to national administration through the Minister

Source: *Keesing's Contemporary Archives*, 1936.

Map 10   Trunk Roads 1936

of Transport (see map 10). The purpose of the Act was to secure a proper standard of design and greater uniformity of widths, surfaces and layout.

In his book *Anticipations*, published in 1900, H. G. Wells wrote of the 'highly mobile conveyance' of the future which would travel at 'a reasonably controlled pace on the ordinary roads and streets' but which would have 'access for higher rates of speed and long distance travelling to specialised ways restricted to swift traffic and possibly furnished with guide rails'. As mentioned in chapter 9, this concept of specialised motorways was also aired by Lord Montagu of Beaulieu when he gave evidence before the Royal Commission on the Motor Car in 1906. However, the pre-war motoring lobby was strongly opposed to motorists being treated as a separate caste. In 1917 the idea was revived by councillors of the Borough of Southwark in London who sent a memorandum to the Prime Minister recommending the construction of 'new main roads built primarily for motor transport and laid out on new lines'. One of these would be a straight highway from London to the north passing near, but not through, Luton, Northampton, Coventry and Birmingham. The proposal was given a very cool reception. The comment of a leading official of the Road Board was that the scheme was 'visionary and impracticable'.[93] The idea reappeared seven years later in 1924 as a private member's Motorways Bill for toll roads to be constructed on the major trunk routes of the kingdom. But it was opposed by the influential Sir Henry Maybury, Director General of Roads at the Ministry of Transport, and failed to win parliamentary approval.

Proposals for motorways came into the limelight again in 1937 when Dr Todt, Inspector General of German Highways, invited the British Parliament to send a delegation to Germany to examine the construction and use of the new *autobahnen* there. No less than 224 persons, including 57 members of both Houses of Parliament—a deputation 'in size and representative character almost without parallel in the history of international relations'—visited Hitler's Reich in response to the invitation. They were impressed by what they saw and by the fact that the accident rate had fallen on the new roads. They urged the adoption of a similar scheme for Britain 'without delay'.[94] In consequence of the very favourable report of the delegation, the chief engineer of the Ministry of Transport was instructed to make a survey for a London–Birmingham motorway in the summer of 1938. His estimate for a $93\frac{3}{4}$-mile concreted dual carriageway with a ten-feet-wide central grass reservation and two outer grass margins, each fifteen feet wide, 'for future extra traffic lanes', was £6$\frac{3}{4}$ million, or approximately £72,000 per mile. (The actual cost of the M1, built some twenty years later, was over ten times the amount per mile of the estimate made in 1938, although, in the interim, prices had

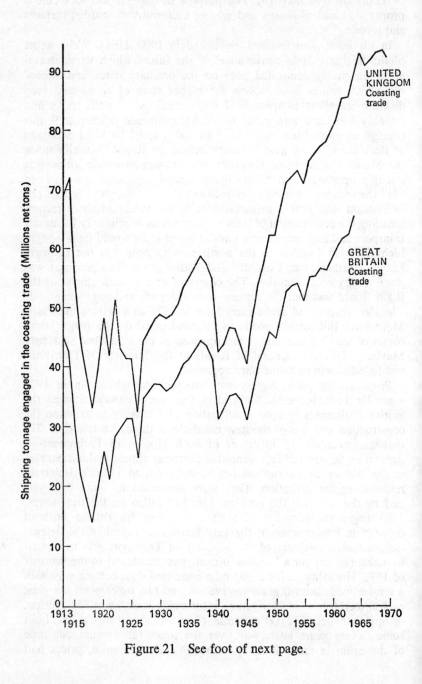

Figure 21   See foot of next page.

risen to three times their former level.) No more than 2,900 vehicles were expected to use the motorway in the course of 24 hours but it was hoped that with a revenue from tolls of £1,000 a day most of the cost would be met from the motorist.[95] Rearmament, the Munich crisis and the Second World War ensured that the engineer's file collected dust for nearly two decades.

VII

The fortunes of British coastal shipping between the wars were affected by the administrative decisions of the cabinet and the Ministry of Transport rather than by legislation specifically designed to benefit coastwise trade. Although the measures taken did not hit the head-lines they were of vital importance to the prosperity of this part of the nation's transport system.

Arrivals and departures of coastwise shipping in Britain declined from nearly 44½ million tons in 1913 to little more than 14 million tons in 1918, but they increased rapidly to 25 million tons in 1920 as a result of the government's decision to impose a belated increase in railway freight rates. In the severe trade recession of 1921 clearances fell back to just short of 21 million tons but quickly recovered to top the 30-million-ton mark in 1924. Progress continued into the thirties. Business held up remarkably well in the slump. Only in 1930–31 was there a setback, though the decline in tonnages employed was less than three per cent. The best inter-war year performance was in 1937 when, at 43⅓ million tons, the aggregate of arrivals and departures of ships in coastwise trade was only a little over a million tons below

---

Note: The shipping tonnage charted represents the total of vessels arrived and departed (each about 50 per cent of the total) with cargo and excludes all coastal shipping movement in ballast. The charted tonnage is the total of commonwealth and foreign shipping. Prior to the late 1950s (excepting World War Two) foreign tonnage in the coasting trade was small and generally less than two per cent of the total, but in the 1960s this proportion increased sub-stantially. Including Irish Republic tonnage with that of the commonwealth, foreign shipping tonnage comprised 1·3 per cent of the coasting trade in 1913, 1·6 per cent in 1938, 0·7 per cent in 1946, 4·6 per cent in 1957, 11·8 per cent in 1960 and 20·4 per cent in 1970.

Prior to 1 April 1923 the coasting trade of the Irish Republic and Northern Ireland–Irish Republic trade is included in the UK total; the figures for 1913–23 are separated from those after 1923 on the graph by a dotted line.

Sources: Annual Abstract of Statistics; B.P.P., Trade and Navigation Returns (annually), 1913 to date; Chamber of Shipping of the United Kingdom, Annual Reports 1920/1 to date (Table of Movement of Shipping in the General Coasting Trade of the UK).

Figure 21 Shipping Tonnage Engaged in the Coasting Trade of the United Kingdom 1913–70

that of 1913. In 1934 coastal shipping accounted for as much as 32 per cent of the total entrances and clearances of the sea-borne trade of the UK.[96]

Over 33 million tons of merchandise were carried coastwise in 1935, a figure which nevertheless seems dwarfed by the 271 million tons carried by rail. At first glance it would appear that ships carried only one-eighth of the volume of domestic trade carried by the railways. But whereas the average railway haul was no more than 56 miles, the average haul of the coastal steamer was as much as 250 miles.[97] Measured in ton-miles, therefore, the contribution of coastwise shipping to domestic transport was about half as great as that of the railways. Furthermore, the rail-borne traffic included much of the water-borne transport twice over; once when carried from the point of consignment to the port of shipment and again when carried from the port of discharge to the internal destination. The total capital investment of the 65 leading concerns in British coastal shipping was less than £20 million. It would therefore be safe to claim that, with only about one fiftieth of the nominal capital of the railway companies, coastal shipping firms were doing at least half of their goods haulage work even though their importance for passenger transport was, of course, very much less.

The coastal trade was organised by two types of firm; the liner companies and the tramp shipping concerns. In 1935 41 liner companies, with their 281 steamers of 208,176 gross tons, plied according to regular sailing dates and maintained 308 services, exclusive of the links between the Clyde and the Western Islands of Scotland. The 330 tramp shipping firms owned a total of 971 steamers of 543,095 gross tons.[98] They earned a living by picking up trade wherever it was to be found and had no regular times of sailing, though they often concentrated on one type of business, viz. coal or wheat. By the mid-1930s amalgamation and large-scale operation had progressed more rapidly in the liner trade than it had in tramp shipping. Five leading liner companies—Coast Lines, the Isle of Man Steam Packet Company, the Clyde Shipping Co., the Tyne–Tees Shipping Co. and the Belfast Steamship Co.—owned 52 per cent of the tonnage employed in this branch of the trade. By contrast the five largest firms in tramp shipping—Clarke (Stephenson) and Associated Companies, W. Cory and Co., France, Fenwick and Co., W. Robertson and Co. and Richard Hughes and Co.—controlled only 34 per cent of the tramp tonnage.[99] Whereas the typical vessel engaged in the liner trade was owned by a large concern with capital in excess of half a million pounds, the typical coastal tramp was owned by a small firm with less than one tenth of the capitalisation. There were 94 firms in tramp shipping that owned only one vessel apiece.[100]

In the inter-war years the coal trade dominated British coastal shipping as it had done for centuries. In 1934 it comprised 60 per cent of the tonnage of all commodities carried coastwise[101] and the proportion grew in the remaining years of that decade as the demand from the public utility companies generating gas and electricity gathered momentum. In January 1938 209 of the 580 coal-laden ships entering the Thames were employed by just four concerns, the Gas Light and Coke Co., the Commercial Gas Co., the Wandsworth Gas Co. and Fulham Borough Council. The improvement in coastal carryings in the later 1930s was almost entirely due to this expansion in gas and electricity generation based on coal supplies drawn mainly from the north-east.[102]

Apart from coal, the commodities carried coastwise were very diverse, although foodstuffs and bulky materials predominated. The liner ships carried 'fish and grain from Aberdeen, jute goods and potatoes from Dundee, beer and paper from Leith, paint, ropes and heavy goods from Newcastle, manufactured steel from Middlesbrough, oil cake and fruit from Hull, foodstuffs and manufactured goods from London, manufactured goods of all kinds from Liverpool and Manchester, heavy cargo and chemicals from Glasgow, linen from Belfast and livestock and dairy produce from the other Irish ports'.[103] The tramp steamers carried slate from north Wales, cement from the Thames and Medway, tin-plate from Swansea, china clay from the Cornish coast to the ports on the Severn and Mersey estuaries, stones and clay from Port Clarence and other ports on the Tees, from Inverkeithing and from Penmaenmawr to Dagenham and other centres of the manufacture of tarmac,[104] salt from Cheshire, pig iron, steel rails, steel billets, grain, sugar and timber from ports as far apart as Barrow and Bristol, Hull and Inverness. A very important part in the trade with Ireland was played by the steamers of the GWR and LMSR. The service between Holyhead and Dublin was maintained by the LMS with six powerful steamers providing two sailings a day in each direction and bringing to England in 1921 92,872 head of cattle, 98,367 sheep and lambs, 21,791 pigs and 9,520 horses.[105]

By the 1930s most of the coastwise liner companies had agreed to a comprehensive schedule of rates for the major traffics they customarily carried. The rates were based on the railway classification scale with a differential in favour of the water route. In 1929 the coastal shipping interests became alarmed when the government derated railway property to the extent of 75 per cent on condition that the sums saved went into a Freight Rebate Fund for reducing charges. They could see that they might well be underquoted again by the railways, as they had been in the later years of the war, to the detriment of their traditional traffic. However the railway companies proved amenable to compromise. In all the major ports of the U.K. local conferences between the representatives of the railways and the coastal liner companies reached agreement on scales of charges which would give each form of transport a share in the traffic. By 1938, however, when these amicable arrangements had been in force for nearly ten years, all parties were of the opinion that they would have 'to be extended to embrace the road haulage and canal companies before they could become a useful part of any general scheme of coordination'.[106]

The method of rate-fixing followed by the tramp steamers was more akin to that of the small-scale road hauliers than to the railways' system of varying the rates directly with the value of the merchandise carried. Tramp freights involved 'making an ad hoc bargain for each separate consignment'.[107] Often, if overhead costs could be covered on the outward voyage, the tramp owner would be content with remarkably low payment for any cargo he could acquire for the return journey. However, when the railways were allowed to make agreed charges with the traders under the Road and Rail Traffic Act of 1933 the tramp owners became alarmed. They exercised the right, given them under Section 39 of the Act, to point out to the minister that coastal carriers might be placed 'at an undue or unfair disadvantage'. Profitable negotiations with the railways followed. In due course the two parties reported their agreement to the ministry. No doubt influenced by the threatening clouds of war, they found it desirable

> to establish as great a degree of coordination as possible among the various forms of transport that engaged in the carriage of goods, so as to ensure that each form of transport is used to the greatest national advantage and that, through coordination, each form of transport will tend to carry those traffics to which it is best suited.
>
> The railways recognise the national importance of preserving coastal shipping and have given an assurance to coastal tramp shipping that it is not their intention to use any relief from their existing rates control to embark upon a policy of cut-throat competition with coastal shipping, with the recognition that this would be calculated to defeat the common object of coordination.[108]

It is highly probable that this agreement saved many tramp shipowners from bankruptcy. Although the liner companies, for the most part, made acceptable rates of profit, it was otherwise with a large number of the tramp shipping firms. In the autumn of 1938 the Chamber of Shipping of the UK reported to the Ministry of Transport that in the case of the 48 owners replying to a circular, their net profits between 1930-37 were less than total depreciation, reckoned at five per cent of original cost, and that, in consequence, many vessels remained in the coastal trade until they were 'well over twenty years of age'.[109]

One reason why coastal shipping did not obtain a larger share of domestic goods traffic was that port charges were often prohibitively high and arrangements for the loading and unloading of cargo sometimes primitive in the extreme. Although the typical coastal steamer of the inter-war years only occupied a berth for one day the port charges were frequently still calculated on the basis of the nineteenth-century sailing vessel's stay of 30 days. It was also unfortunate that charges did not discriminate between vessels on regular services and those which only entered a port once in 25 years. Some ports had modernised their methods of charging—to the benefit of all types of shipping. At Southampton tonnage rates varied according to the length of time the ship spent in port and at Leith rates were substantially reduced on vessels which exceeded eight visits in the year. But these were honourable exceptions.[110] In respect of the loading and unloading of vessels in some English ports the situation was said to be like 'baling out a cistern with a teaspoon'.[111]

Britain tended to lag behind her near continental rivals in the technology of shipbuilding for the coastal services. Mr. P. McCormick, a Belfast shipowner and one of a deputation calling on the President of the Board of Trade on 26 April 1939, declared that disappointment with the government was 'bitter and deep' because of its failure to protect the industry from the competition of the Dutch-built and owned motor vessels. However, at no time between 1919 and 1939 did foreign-owned vessels account for as much as two per cent of tonnage of vessels entering and leaving British ports in the coastal trade. The liner companies were scarcely affected at all and resisted the tramp owners' clamour for a return to something like the old Navigation Laws because they feared retaliation in foreign countries—such as the Netherlands—which allowed unhampered participation of British ships in their coastal trade.[112] It was the tramp steamers, especially those which frequented the ports between Cardiff and Boston, which most felt the pinch of foreign competition. It was said of the small, highly efficient, Dutch motor vessels that 'they can get anywhere a duck can swim'.[113] They thus brought new life to small ports such as Norwich and Felixstowe. The small motor ship certainly had a shallower draught than did the steamship of comparable tonnage, its fuel consumption was little more than a third of the oil-fired steamer, it could carry more cargo in relation to its deadweight and required fewer men to man it because no stokers were needed.[114] The difficulty, from the British point of view, was that in the relatively depressed years of the 1930s the many small tramp shipping firms lacked the capital to invest in the more efficient craft. Because the problem only affected a section of the coastal shipping industry the government felt no compulsion to introduce a 'scrap and build' loan scheme which would have helped the tramp owners.[115] What the Government did do was to advise all local authorities of 'the desirability of securing that, as far as possible, heavy goods, such as coal, road and building materials and materials used in works of civil engineering... should be brought, if carried coastwise, in British ships'.[116]

The benefits of sympathetic administration by the Ministry of Transport and the 'live and let live' policy of the railways were experienced by more than 300,000 soldiers who were picked up from the Dunkirk beaches during the last days of May 1940. Their lives were saved because British coastal shipping had been enabled to recover from its deep depression of 1919. The industry of the 1930s gave employment to over 12,000 men. Their services proved indispensable in the great national emergency in the first summer of the war.

The peacetime working conditions of many sailors on British coastal tramps were inappropriate for those destined for such great deeds as the Dunkirk evacuation. On 16 February 1939 the members of a TUC deputation told the President of the Board of Trade that the hours of duty in the tramp shipping industry were 'probably without parallel in any other organised industry'. Carefully collected information showed that the average hours of duty for officers exceeded 80 per week and that 'hours of duty in excess of 100 per week were by no means uncommon'. Since there was no approved manning scale for coastwise shipping 'the active personnel engaged in a number of ships in the tramp section of the industry was grossly overworked'. Broadly speaking, conditions in the liner vessels, with their regular sailing times and generally superior accommodation, were much better. For all coastal vessels the Board of Trade issued a new set of instructions in September 1937 which established much higher standards of accommodation and manning. But they only applied to vessels subsequently constructed. Inevitably progress in this aspect of the coastal shipping service was slow.

VIII

Wartime government supervision of Britain's inland waterways was brought to an end on 31 August 1920, almost a year before the railways were returned to private management. In the following two decades of peace the contribution of inland waterways to British transport services was a rapidly shrinking one. Tonnage carried fell from 22 million tons in 1919 to 15½ million tons in 1927 and 13 million tons in 1938. The decline in business on the railway owned and controlled canals was steeper than it was on those independently owned. The 'narrow cut' canals which could only accommodate the slow-moving narrow boats suffered most severely from the competition of road transport and railways.

Although canal transport did have its backers in the inter-war years they were not sufficiently influential to counter the belief that its decline was inevitable and not unduly to be lamented. Following the return of canals to private ownership in the summer of 1920 the government appointed a committee under the chairmanship of Mr N. Chamberlain to examine the possibility of implementing the Royal Commission's Report of 1909 in favour of the development of the 'Cross' network linking the Humber, Severn, Mersey and Thames. An interim report the committee published in February 1921 favoured major improvements in the navigation of the Trent to make it possible for boats of 300 tons capacity to reach Nottingham. The main report, published three months later, was influenced by the severe economic recession and the growing demand for economy in government expenditure to oppose plans for nationalisation (Ernest Bevin dissenting) on the grounds that the cost would be too great. Instead it was suggested that a Waterways Board should supervise the merging of canals into seven regional groups with a Board of Management in charge of each. But the government of the day was too preoccupied with the crisis in Ireland and the drive for economy to develop a positive policy for British canals. Nor did any change in government policy result from the Report of the Royal Commission on Transport in 1930 which revived the proposal for public trusts to be appointed to take over the management of the waterways of the 'Cross'.

In default of a government initiative to promote better facilities for through bulk haulage on the main waterway routes the decline in carrying business was largely unavoidable. Even the prospects for canal and road haulage cooperation were limited. On many canals the difficulty was that there were no lay-bys 'where the boat could be got out of the fairway in order to give up its load'. Little initiative was shown by the canal companies in constructing approach roads to the towpaths.[117] Owing to the depressed state of Britain's basic industries the railways had less traffic to spare for carriage on the canals which they owned or controlled.

By and large the drawbacks of differing canal gauges and lock sizes which were inherent in the independently promoted canals of the nineteenth century remained to retard the development of large consignments of through traffic in the inter-war years. But there were some successful amalgamations. In 1929 the Grand Junction Canal joined forces with the Warwick and Birmingham, the Warwick and Napton, the Regents Canal and the Birmingham and Warwick Junction to form a new concern, the Grand Union Canal. When three more independent waterways were brought into the new enterprise in 1932 more than 300 miles of canal were under unified management. On the initiative of the corporation of Nottingham, and following the advice of the Chamberlain committee, major works of improvement were carried out on the Trent, with the result that traffic conveyed over the Trent Navigation grew from 375,803 tons in 1927 to 675,377 tons in 1939, an increase of 73 per cent.[118] On three other navigation systems capable of carrying large consignments of traffic there was a similarly impressive growth of business in the period:

	1928	1936
Gloucester and Sharpness Canal	257,758 tons	460,318 tons
Severn Commission	120,688	283,977
Sheffield and South Yorkshire	451,235	771,264[119]

On the other hand where the canals were narrow and no capital was available for their improvement the sharp decline in business was inevitable. There were some closures of hitherto important canals. Except for some six miles to Chalford, the Thames and Severn Canal was closed to traffic in 1927 and the closure of the Grantham canal came in the following year.

In the light of the depressed condition of the heavy industries during most of the inter-war years it is difficult to envisage anything other than a decrease in canal traffic whether or not large sums had been spent on modernisation. The sad decline in the use of the nation's inland waterway assets was as much due to the general mismanagement of the British economy as it was to lack of initiative on the part of the managers of individual undertakings.

IX

Once the cabinet had rejected Sir Eric Geddes' plan for control over air transport to be exercised by the proposed Ministry of Ways and Communications, those seeking to promote air transport in Britain were left very much to their own devices. It is true that in January 1919 a new Civil Aviation Department was set up within the Air Ministry, but its powers were extremely limited. At late as 30 October 1935 Mr F. C. Shelmerdine, Director General of Civil Aviation, told an audience of transport experts that air transport had 'grown up quite independently of government control' and that 'government had not hitherto regulated these services or required any statistics concerning them'.[120]

The early history of air transport in Britain is a story of repeated optimistic ventures in the development of new services which almost invariably ended in financial failure. The first regular air service in Europe pre-dated the First World War. In September 1911, to celebrate the coronation of King George V, Mr Graham White, by arrangement with the GPO, provided an airmail letter service between Hendon and Windsor. The service was withdrawn after 21 flights. Regular passenger services did not begin until after the armistice.

From 10 January 1919 until the late summer of the same year, No. 1 Communication Squadron of the RAF began a regular London (Hendon) to Paris (le Bourget) air service for passengers and mail. This was sometimes used by British statesmen involved in the peace negotiations which preceded the signature of the Treaty of Versailles. It was not until 1 May 1919, when the Air Navigation Regulations under the Air Navigation Act, 1919, came into force, that civil aviation was officially permitted in Britain. Thereafter a number of experimental services were operated during the summer months. Among the first was the North Sea Aerial Navigation Company's Scarborough–Hull–Harrogate service, maintained with Avro 504K aircraft, and the same company's Hull–Leeds–London (Hendon) service using Blackburn Kangaroo planes. However, the first regular daily air service within the British Isles was provided by Avro Civil Aviation linking Manchester, Southport and Blackpool between 24 May and 30 September 1919.[121]

In 1920 the main developments were in the short routes to the continent with S. Instone and Company competing with Daimler Airways and Handley Page Ltd for the still very limited passenger traffic between London and Paris. The internal air services were seen principally as feeders of traffic to the international ones. At first the coalition government took the view that these private ventures should be self-supporting. In the House of Commons on 15 December 1919 Winston Churchill boldly asserted that 'it was not the business of government to carry civil aviation forward by means of a great expenditure of public money'. However it was not a policy that could be sustained in the face of developments on the European continent. In every country with developing air services the government subsidised them to the extent of at least two-thirds of the cost of operation throughout the 1920s.[122] Just over four months after the Churchill statement the Weir Advisory Committee on Civil Aviation recommended that the British government should give direct financial assistance to the new airlines. As if to underline the realism of the Weir Committee Report, all British air services ceased operation on 28 February 1921 because of financial difficulties. Flights were resumed on 19 March when Handley Page Transport received a 'temporary' subsidy on its London–Paris service. Just over a year later the subsidy to British airlines was fixed at a maximum of £200,000 a year for three years, the division of the global sum between the companies being fixed on the basis of 'payment by results'. In 1924 this arrangement was followed by a grant of £1 million, spread over ten years, given to the newly-formed Imperial Airways, a company established through the merging of Instone Air Lines, the British Marine Air Navigation Company, Daimler Airways and Handley Page Transport.

Although most of the subsidy went to the new empire air routes a small proportion was earmarked for domestic air services.

Despite token financial assistance from government, none of the domestic air routes operated was a paying concern in the 1920s. There were numerous reasons for their failure to break even in these years. Aircraft technology was still at a very immature stage of development when the First World War ended. The typical civil aeroplane of the early 1920s had a single engine of under 500 horsepower, a maximum speed of 115 m.p.h., a normal range of 300 miles and seating capacity for no more than six passengers.[123] Only in the course of the 1920s did instrument flying control begin to be introduced. As late as 1932 radio control was described in tones of wonderment as 'a remarkable system whereby the movements of machines are accurately charted and by means of which pilots may receive instructions and advice whilst in the air'.[124] Other innovations of the decade included electric engine starters, the metal propeller and retractable undercarriages, all of which contributed to the ease and safety of air travel but came into general use only in the 1930s.[125]

With aircraft of such limited technical capabilities air travel of the 1920s lacked the reliability of surface transport. A pioneer of British aerodynamics, F. Handley Page, considered it 'a tribute to the unquenchable optimism of airline organisers that they should ever have entertained the hope of out-manoeuvring the British climate'.[126] Particularly in the northern half of the British Isles there were weeks in winter when 80 per cent or more of the scheduled services had to be cancelled because of bad weather. In 1926 only 84·5 per cent of scheduled flights were completed.[127] Since the cheapest air fares at 4d a mile were at least four times the cost of rail travel the principal reason for passengers choosing to go by air would be the promise of a shorter journey time. But if the promise was uncertain of fulfilment the traveller would opt for the greater reliability of rail travel, and the load factor, and hence the financial return, of the air service would decline. Initially the Air Ministry only provided wireless services for the international air routes and air pilots on domestic routes were largely without information about the weather. A consequence of the competitive system under which numerous airlines sprang quickly into existence and as quickly disappeared was that the Air Ministry was at a loss to know where to establish its information centres. In the later 1920s it hit upon the idea of operating mobile wireless stations until more permanent ones were established in the mid-1930s.[128]

Air transport in Britain would have become more of a viable proposition had it proved possible to secure substantial Post Office contracts for the carriage of mail. But it was not until 20 August 1934 that the first official airmail services were provided within the British

Isles. The routes covered then included those between London and Glasgow, London and Belfast, Liverpool and Plymouth, and Birmingham and Cowes.[129] That no earlier development of permanent airmail services occurred was due to the absence of any decisive advantage in speed for distances under 200 miles and the slow development of night-flying. Most British mail is posted in the early evening and transported overnight to its destination. But night-flying was very exceptional in Britain until well into the 1930s. There was a prolonged controversy through the preceding decade on the issue of the degree of illumination needed for safe night-flying: one school of thought maintained that the entire route ought to be illuminated 'so that the pilot was never out of sight of a beacon or lighthouse even in unfavourable weather'.[130] The management of Imperial Airways was of this persuasion. The more far-sighted view was that, with the development of instrumental flying and wireless aids, it was only necessary for the airports to be lit up. But until this second view prevailed the vast majority of aircraft remained grounded at night, increasing the companies' overhead costs and reducing to some 600 hours per year the average flying time of the typical aircraft.

One consequence of the dissipation of capital resources into a number of small, short-lived, airlines was that municipal authorities were reluctant to spend money on the construction of aerodromes, whilst such non-municipal aerodromes as were established were often inadequately equipped and of brief existence. At the end of 1929 Britain had only four municipal airports compared with Germany's 80. Twelve years after the armistice a leading exponent of air travel complained that there was 'no regular means of air communication with the great industrial north'.[131] It was a vicious circle. Airline promoters hesitated to open up new services because of the absence of airports or their inadequacy; municipalities failed to see why they should spend ratepayers' money in building the airports when the prospect of a profitable return appeared to be so meagre.

Since the technology of aircraft production was advancing rapidly in the early postwar years machines became obsolescent at an alarming rate. As one contemporary expressed it, the rate of progress was 'so rapid as to be almost a disadvantage'.[132] Large concerns, such as Imperial Airways, could meet this difficulty by setting aside large sums as an obsolescence reserve: the smaller concerns characteristic of domestic air services could not.

Because the airline industry was still establishing itself and air travel was not so safe as travel by rail, insurance premiums were exceptionally high. G. Holt Thomas, a pioneer of air transport in the 1920s, was paying premiums of 20 per cent of the value of his aircraft.[133]

Undoubtedly the crux of the matter was that air travel lacked decisive advantages over the speedier forms of land transport. The proportion of total journey time spent in the air compared with that taken up by land travel to and from airports was, generally speaking, too small for the advantage of the aircraft's superior speed to be fully exploited. In 1935 F. C. Shelmerdine estimated that on an air journey of a mere 100 miles travelling time was split up as follows:

Road journey to and from airports	40 minutes
On and off loading aircraft	10 minutes
Aircraft manoeuvres, allow	15 minutes
100 miles by air at 160 m.p.h.	37 minutes
Total	1 hour 42 minutes
	average speed: 58·8 m.p.h.

Although with double the air journey average speed could be raised to 86 m.p.h. and with treble the distance to 101 m.p.h., the crucial question was 'does the passenger save enough time to save money?' In many cases it would appear that the answer was 'No'. On 51 of the 92 air stages regularly operated in 1935, with an average of 60 miles a stage, the speed of the journey averaged only 45 m.p.h. At the same time there were 55 British trains averaging 58–63 m.p.h. on their scheduled routes.[134] Only where the surface journey involved crossing a stretch of water, as on the routes to Northern Ireland and the Western Isles, was air travel decisively faster. Unfortunately, from the viewpoint of the financial return of the airlines, the volume of passenger and goods traffic on the longer distance routes where the aeroplane was able to exploit its advantages of speed was too small to make the operation of air services profitable.

Air transport in the 1920s was 'still a relatively unsafe mode of travel'. Between August 1919 and August 1924 one person was killed for every 5,719 passengers carried. This compares with one in 145,557 killed on BEA flights in 1957–8.[135] In the course of the 1930s there was a rapid expansion in the number of domestic air services in Britain. In 1932 services were established between Blackpool and the Isle of Man, Portsmouth and the Isle of Wight and Romford and Clacton-on-Sea. In 1933 no less than 18 services were maintained by 13 companies. In 1934 there were two more companies in operation and the number of services rose to 34. The peak of inter-war activity came in 1935 with 19 companies providing 76 services, covering 5,810 route miles and 121,559 passengers carried.[136] The conditions which favoured this rapid expansion included the greater potentialities and performance of aircraft which increased the advantages of air travel in comparison with surface transport. Four-engined aircraft in regular use on some of the routes provided safer flying than was possible a decade earlier. In 1932 some Imperial Airways machines

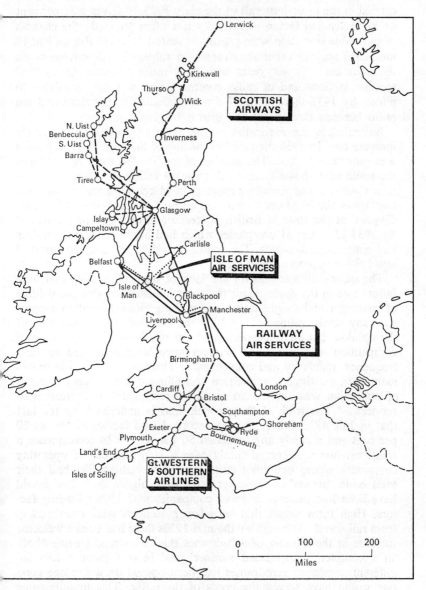

Source: R. E. G. Davies, *A History of the World's Airlines,* 1964.

Map 11   Railway Group Domestic Air Services 1939

could carry up to 38 passengers—more than six times the number carried in the typical aircraft of the early 1920s.[137] Given a 50 per cent or more loading factor—admittedly not often attained—the chances of profitable operation were greatly increased. By 1932 Britain had 12 municipal and 43 other aerodromes—a substantial improvement on the situation only six years earlier. A more adequate network of weather stations and of radio control towers was now available to pilots. By 1937 there were 27 direction-finding installations and ten radio beacons throughout the British Isles.

Nevertheless the expansion of the early 1930s was an extremely insecure one. In 1936 the rapid expansion of the four preceding years was suddenly checked. The number of services fell from 76 to 54 and the route miles flown from 5,810 to 4,019 within the year. The Cadman Committee of Enquiry reporting in March 1938 and echoing the findings of the Maybury Committee a year earlier, expressed 'extreme disquiet' at the state of British domestic and overseas air services.[138] By 1937 12 of the 31 companies which had begun scheduled services had gone out of business. The routes served by those which survived into 1939 are shown on map 12.

The outstanding reason for the lack of financial success and high failure rate in the domestic air transport industry was that the volume of passenger and freight traffic was nothing like sufficient to support so many small companies. In 1937 the Maybury Committee was of the opinion that air transport would not pay its way whilst 'wasteful competition' continued and services were 'unduly limited in their frequency, regularity and convenience'. There would be no improvement until cut-throat competition was eliminated and some measure of restriction was applied 'to avoid indiscriminate multiplication of services'.[139] The truth of these conclusions is underlined by the fact that in July 1935 five companies recorded load factors as low as 20 per cent and scarcely any exceeded 50 per cent.[140] In consequence a small revenue was spread thinly over a large number of operating companies whose operating costs formed something like half their total costs. Inevitably passenger fares were higher than they would have been had there been fewer companies with higher loading factors. High fares meant that very few passengers were drawn away from rail travel. Although by the mid-1930s there had been a welcome increase in the number of aerodromes this development came about 'in a completely haphazard manner', and in one instance four indifferent municipal aerodromes had been opened up where one good one would have served the needs of the traffic. This muddle came about because 'the licensing of aerodromes was regarded as an administrative act unrelated to the probable requirements of the air service'.[141]

Not long before the outbreak of the Second World War govern-

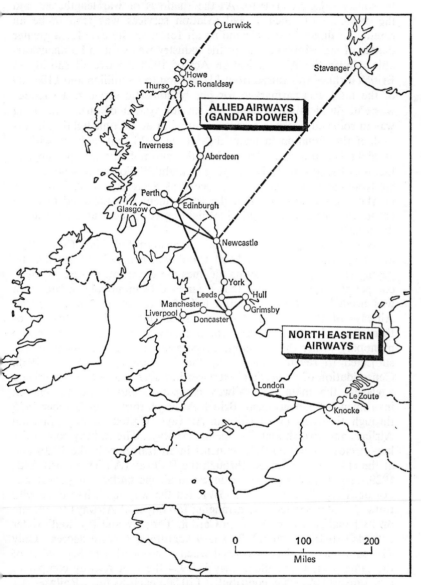

Source: R. E. G. Davies, *A History of the World's Airlines*, 1964.

Map 12   Independent Domestic Air Services 1939

ment policies were beginning to resemble much more closely those so brusquely rejected in 1919. As the shadows of war lengthened and the existence of efficient civil aviation services was seen to be an essential adjunct to the expanding air force, so the case for a greater degree of state involvement in the industry was seen to be unanswerable. Under the Air Navigation Act of 1938 the overall subsidy to British airlines was raised from £1½ million to £3 million and £100,000 of the total was earmarked for purely domestic services. To reduce wasteful duplication of capital a stricter system of airline licensing was introduced. Despite recent advances in aerodrome lighting it was said of the situation in many districts in 1938 that 'nobody will fly at night because there are no facilities and nobody will put up any facilities because there is no flying at night'.[142] To end this bottleneck Sir Kingsley Wood, in his first speech as Secretary of State for Air, in May 1938 announced that the government was prepared to make grants to help establish full night-lighting equipment at certain aerodromes.[143]

As early as 1923 the Civil Air Transport Subsidies Committee, under the chairmanship of Lord Hambling, had pointed out that by paying subsidies to competing air lines the government was, 'in effect, competing with itself' and that a large-scale monopoly organisation was needed to ensure optimum use of government funds. Imperial Airways of 1924 was the 'chosen instrument' for the application of these funds in the case of overseas services; but this was a private monopoly rather than a public corporation and its management was subjected to severe criticism by the Cadman Committee in 1938. Consolidation of domestic air services however was left to two private agencies: the main line railway companies and a second 'chosen instrument' of Government, British Airways, formed in October 1935 through the merging of Hillman Airways, United Airways, Spartan Airlines and British and Continental Airways. The railway companies kept a close watch on developments in air transport in the 1920s and at the close of the decade, through the Railway (Air Transport) Acts, 1929, they acquired powers to invest in airline undertakings.[144] It was not until April 1933 that the GWR led the way (as it had done with railway motor services) by arranging for Imperial Airways to operate on its behalf a service between Cardiff, Torquay and Plymouth (later extended to Birmingham). The new venture was not a success. Only 714 passengers had been carried when it was ended in September of the same year. Undaunted, early in 1934 the four railway companies and Imperial Airways contributed £10,000 each to form Railway Air Services. This new company opened up air routes principally over the territory of the GWR and the LMS. By the end of 1938 only five airlines whose services, in any case, offered little threat to the railways' business, were outside the railway companies' control. Inevitably the railways were accused of buying up airlines so that the flights would be slower than their star expresses. But the Cadman Committee in 1938 considered that the railway companies were making 'a useful contribution to civil air development' and that Section 10 of the Railway (Air Transport) Acts provided 'adequate safeguards' against the destruction of the public interest.[145]

In the meantime the government's second chosen instrument, British Airways, had developed in directions largely other than those originally envisaged. It concentrated its energies in opening the new routes to the European continent and in July 1936 it sold its internal services to two companies, Northern and Scottish Airways and Highland Airways, which merged just over a year later to form Scottish Airways. In 1938 Chamberlain's Conservative government did not consider it in the national interest that there should be competition between Imperial Airways and British Airways on the overseas routes. The British Overseas Airways Corporation, established under an Act passed on 4 August 1939, merged the two concerns in a form of organisation which had already been applied successfully in another area of transport—Greater London—since 1933.

Had the war not intervened it is highly probable that the kind of solution which was adopted for the overseas air services would have been applied to domestic air transport before very long. Railway Air Services incurred deficits in each financial year. They failed to achieve even a 50 per cent load factor and in 1934 were down to as low as 12·6 per cent. Only a thorough-going consolidation of rival companies would have made the company a viable proposition and this was never undertaken.

The most that can be said in favour of the government's air transport policy in the years 1919–39 is that it put no obstacles in the way of the numerous small companies which pioneered air travel in Britain. But when comparison is made with the growth of Lufthansa in Germany or KLM in Holland the shortsightedness of the crucial decisions of the coalition and succeeding governments becomes all the more apparent.

X

In the 25 years surveyed in this chapter the concept of transport coordination—the carriage of traffic by that form of transport whose real economic costs are lowest—was never far from the centre of public discussion. In the emergency of the First World War government was under exceedingly strong pressure to eliminate waste in the use of the railway, canal, road and coastal shipping resources it controlled. Although the coastal liners and tramps were underutilised and control over commercial vehicles was only belatedly introduced, the nation's principal means of carriage—railway waggons and passenger coaches—were more economically used under unified management than had proved possible under purely company control in the years before 1914.

This experience was recalled by the advocates of reform during the months when 'Reconstruction' and 'Homes fit for Heroes' were the principal topics of government statements and informed political discussion. The Conservative landslide in the 'coupon' election of December 1918 and the onset of severe trade recession in the second half of 1920 combined to stifle ambitious proposals for a new Ministry of Ways and Communications (later altered to Ministry of Transport) with comprehensive control over all the principal forms of transport. Thus the opportunity created by the wartime emergency of introducing a more rational planning of future transport developments after the armistice was allowed to slip by. Instead, successive governments devised ad hoc measures to deal with each crisis—rail deficits, traffic congestion in towns, the financial failure of airline companies, etc.—as it arose. Nevertheless, in the 1930s circumstances were compelling the adoption of a more positive approach to transport problems and a more comprehensive view of their solution. Typical of the 1920s was the Railways Act, 1921, which was not concerned with other forms of transport than the railway. More characteristic of the 1930s was the Road and Rail Traffic Act, 1933, which, as its title suggested, was concerned with the impact of the two principal forms of transport on each other but which also contained provisions for the protection of a third form of transport, coastal shipping. Although in the early 1920s, for largely doctrinaire reasons, transport developments had been left to market forces, between the passing of the London Passenger Transport Act in 1933 and the establishment of the British Overseas Airways Corporation under an Act passed on 4 August 1939, leading opinion in both the main political parties was becoming committed more and more to an increased degree of public control over the principal forms of transport. Even if the Second World War had not intervened it is safe to predict that public ownership would have advanced much further by the end of the 1940s than was the case in 1939.

10

British Transport Developments, 1939–70

I

In the first six years of this period, when Britain was at war, the two main political parties cooperated in forging a transport policy for the nation. But no sooner had the wartime emergency passed than the differences in transport policy began to be emphasised. In the quarter-century which followed British transport was subjected to a greater degree of politically-motivated interference than at any previous period in its long history. When the Labour Party was in power the emphasis was towards a greater degree of public ownership; in periods of Conservative rule the private sector was encouraged. Hence the railways and the commercial motor transport and civil aviation industries were subjected to sudden, and frequently damaging, changes in their spheres of operation and forms of management. (Policies for canals and coastal shipping were less affected by political changes.) Inevitably much time and energy were taken up in restructuring management to the detriment of efforts directed towards the improvement of productive efficiency. Of the 21 years from 1948–68 inclusive 'approximately thirteen were spent waiting for major Transport Acts of Parliament ... and in reorganising after them'. Apart from the war years, which are the subject of the first part of this chapter, there have been three main phases of transport policy since 1945. Between the Civil Aviation Act of 1946 and the Transport Act of 1953 there was a short-lived experiment in more comprehensive public ownership; from the Transport Act of 1953 to the Beeching Report, *The Reshaping of British Railways*, 1963, denationalisation and the restoration of competition were the outstanding features of policy; finally during the two Labour Governments of 1964–6 and 1966–70 the expansion of the private enterprise sector was checked and some new forms of public ownership were established through the Transport Act of 1968. Each of these main phases will be the theme of one section of this chapter. Two other important aspects of transport—the expansion of private motoring and its consequences, and the progress of coastal shipping—being less directly influenced by the changing balance of political forces at Westminster, will be dealt with in separate sections.

II

The experience of the First World War had taught British statesmen at least one lesson: a much greater degree of control over public transport than had been exercised in the years 1914–16 would be essential if any future war effort was not to be frustrated through delays in the mobilisation of manpower and supplies. Hence more comprehensive plans for government control over the different forms of transport were worked out before 3 September 1939 than had been the case before 4 August 1914. As early as 23 March 1937 the Committee of Imperial Defence ruled that in a period of war or national emergency the Ministers of Transport should be responsible for the 'provision, allotment and coordination of transportation services'.[1] On 24 September 1938, nearly a full year before the outbreak of war, Mr L. Burgin, as Minister of Transport, set up a Railway Executive Committee of six men under the chairmanship of Sir Ralph Wedgwood of the LNER, to direct, in an emergency, the activities of the main line railway companies and the London Passenger Transport Board so that supplies and services essential to the war effort and the life of the community would be maintained.[2]

In April 1939 the Minister of Transport issued printed instructions to the general managers of the railway companies advising them of the arrangements which would come into force in the event of the outbreak of war. The minister would issue instructions on broad lines of policy to the Railway Executive Committee which would be responsible for the detailed administration of the railways 'as a unified whole'. When war was imminent these arrangements came into force under the Emergency (Railway Control) Order of 1 September 1939. This gave the minister immediate authority to take over direction of the main line railways, the London Passenger Transport Board and a few other less important railways and docks through the REC as intermediary.

So that the REC should have complete control of all the waggon resources on the railways another order under the Defence Regulations requisitioned the fleet of 563,000 privately owned waggons. These, together with the railway companies' own stocks, gave the REC command of a pool of 1,252,000 waggons to be deployed according to need and irrespective of previous ownership or limits of operation.[3]

As the war clouds gathered in Europe in the course of 1938 the ministry gave some thought to the kind of contribution which commercial motor vehicles might make to transport services in a national emergency. The Regional Transport Commissioners (appointed under the Acts of 1930 and 1933) were instructed to revise their districts so as to coordinate them with the existing railway network and to organise the sub-districts round railheads. But the difficulty was that the road haulage industry was still a 'highly individualistic' one and, in consequence, direct operational control over 200,000 firms with half a million vehicles was regarded as an 'administrative impossibility' in 1939. As he was completely in the dark as to the volume of goods which could be carried in a given span of time by the existing stock of commercial vehicles and as he was assured by the general managers that the railway companies would have no difficulty in carrying the increased volume of traffic which would arise in wartime, the minister decided to use petrol rationing as the main instrument of control. In an emergency each road transport region was to be allocated 75 per cent of its normal peacetime requirements for petrol. Two-thirds of these reduced wartime supplies were to be distributed to the owners of the goods vehicles.

To manage the coasting trade Coastal Shipping War Control Committees, comprising representatives of local shipowners, were set up at the principal ports in the course of 1938. They were expected to ensure that the shipping resources of their area were deployed to the best advantage according to information on the national shipping situation received from the Headquarters Organisation in the Mercantile Marine Department of the Board of Trade. Control over the movement of ships was to be exercised through voyage licences rather than through the requisitioning of vessels. The more drastic method of control would undoubtedly have given rise to administrative difficulties because of the extensive subdivision of ownership of the vessels.

Only in respect of canal transport did the National Government of the late 1930s fail to appreciate the lessons of the First World War— when the independent waterways were uncontrolled for over two years with the consequent loss of manpower and transport potential. In 1939 the possible contribution of canals to the total transport effort of the nation was not seen as important enough to justify requisitioning of boats or government management of that part of the canal network not controlled through the REC.

Although more thought had been given to the structure of government control of transport than was the case in 1914 the preparations made proved inadequate to meet the strains of war, particularly in the winters of 1940–1 and 1941–2. Before September 1939 the General Managers had expressed every confidence in the ability of the railways to carry all the extra traffic which might be expected as military campaigns developed. When the Minister of Transport hinted that bottlenecks might arise through the diversion of many imports from the vulnerable east coast ports to the more secure ports of the west, the Chairman of the REC thought it impossible to envisage all the contingencies and advised that the best course would be to 'await the event'. In consequence no new strategic lines, sidings or other railway works, in anticipation of a different pattern of traffic, were constructed before the outbreak of war. Instead, priority was given to air-raid precautions on which £4 million was spent in the last months of peace. No attempt was made at the ministry 'to fit together the complicated jigsaw puzzle of war-time demand for transport as a whole and to compare this with transport capacity'.[4]

The short-run result of the railways' over-confident claim that with their excess peacetime capacity they could meet all additional demands for transport in wartime was that too much traffic which should have been sent by canal boat, coastal steamer or motor lorry was consigned to the rail. The great increase in wartime railway traffic is summarised in Table 9:

Table 9 *Railway traffic and capacity, 1938–45*

Traffic	1938	1943	1944	1945
Number of passenger miles (m.)	18,993*	32,273	32,052	29,231
Total freight traffic (m. net ton-miles)	16,266	24,358	24,444	22,023
Merchandise (7–21) and livestock (m. net ton-miles)	4,980	9,659	10,275	8,850
Minerals and merchandise (1–6) (m. net ton-miles)	3,182	5,356	4,902	4,303
Coal (m. net ton-miles)	8,104	9,343	9,267	8,807
Capacity available for traffic				
Locomotives	18,460	19,303	18,915	18,728
Passenger coaching vehicles	40,793	38,404	37,305	36,025
Waggons:				
(1) railway owned	644,789	654,302	637,115	609,256
(2) requisitioned	563,000	553,890	545,829	529,443

* September 1938 to August 1939.
Source: Railway Clearing House, *Tables of Statistical Returns Relating to the Railways of Great Britain, 1938–46* (1947).

Comparing 1944 with 1938 it can be seen that freight traffic rose by nearly 50 per cent and passenger traffic rose by 68 per cent, although the number of locomotives rose by only 2·3 per cent and passenger coaching vehicles available *decreased* by 8·6 per cent. Clearly the railways were being put to far more intensive use than had been the case in peacetime. In 1943, for example, the freight-train load per train mile had risen to 153·6 tons compared with 121·9 tons in 1938 and the average passenger train load had more than doubled in the same period. The stock of locomotives, wagons and passenger carriages was being strained to breaking point. By the end of 1943 one of the four main line companies was running nearly 500 locomotives which in peacetime would have been on the scrap heap.[5] From the point of view of the Coalition government, however, the most serious transport crisis came in the winter of 1940–1 rather than in December 1943. In these earlier winter months there were many occasions when trains were not available to move essential war supplies. The REC had failed to make adequate allowance for the greater length of haul often needed for imports diverted to the west coast ports. In addition, damage to railway property from enemy action was almost as extensive in the six months ending 31 December 1940 as it was in the remaining four and a half years of war.[6] Although there were again shortages of locomotives and rolling stock in the following winter of 1941–2 they were less severely felt. Thereafter the intervention of the Ministry of War Transport (established in May 1941) greatly improved transport planning and resulted in higher load factors of railway waggons and commercial road vehicles alike. Although, inevitably, more time was spent in the repair sheds as the equipment passed its period of normal usage, productivity when in service was greatly enhanced. Furthermore the REC put in hand a much needed doubling and quadrupling of tracks on the busiest routes, besides constructing loop lines and sidings, stations and halts serving war factories.[7]

From the longer-term point of view the over-optimism about the ability of the railways to carry an abnormally large wartime traffic had very serious consequences for their competitiveness when the challenge of motor transport was renewed after 1945. As pointed out in the previous chapter, the four great railway companies were, on balance, disinvesting capital in the inter-war years. When to this peacetime net disinvestment there is added the excessive wear and tear and the huge arrears of replacement characteristic of the war years it is not difficult to understand why Britain's railways entered the second half of the twentieth century in very poor physical shape.

These great disadvantages could have been more rapidly offset if the financial arrangements made between the government and the railway companies had been worked out with more regard to the future viability of the railways as an investment and with less regard to the railway shareholders' and the taxpayers' pockets. In 1938, the last full year of peace, only one of the four main line companies had paid a dividend on its ordinary shares and that was limited to one half per cent. Under the agreement signed between the Chamberlain government and the railways in February 1940, there was to be a pooling of all the receipts of the London Passenger Transport Board and the four main line railways and a government guarantee of a combined net revenue of £39·5 million, a figure based on actual earnings of the railways in the more prosperous years 1935-7 and the revenue of the LPTB for the year ending 30 June 1939. If the controlled undertakings earned more than the guaranteed minimum they were allowed to keep an additional £3½ million. Over and above this they could keep half any other revenue accruing to the pool up to a maximum of £56 million—the standard revenue of the Railways Act of 1921 plus the sum needed to pay interest on LPTB 'C' stock. These terms were exceptionally favourable to the shareholders and within three weeks of their publication the price of railway shares rose by £200 million on the stock market.[8] The agreement was completely revised in September 1941 when it was realised that the earlier policy of making the railways carry all that they possibly could would have to be modified. Under the new arrangements, backdated to 1 January 1941, the net revenue of the controlled undertakings was limited to £43·5 million, any surplus above this going to the government after sums had been set aside to cover arrears of maintenance. The outcome of these two agreements is summarised in Table 10:

Table 10 *Net financial return of the controlled under-takings, 1940–46*

Year	Net revenue of pool (£m.)	Surplus over fixed guarantee accruing to the Government (£m.)
1940	42·8	—
1941	65·1	21·6
1942	89·1	45·6
1943	105·6	62·1
1944	90·3	46·8
1945	62·5	19·0
1946	32·2	−11·3

Source: *Government Control of Railways: Financial Returns, 1940–46.*

The railway shareholders did exceptionally well while the boom in railway traffic continued. Through the years of war they received some £9 million a year more than they had in the last years of peace. The government benefited to the tune of £143 million net over the years 1941-6. The travelling public and the nationalised railways in the postwar years were the losers. The Coalition government made depreciation allowances to the railways at historic cost rather than replacement cost. In consequence the sums flowing into the Exchequer from the intensive use of railways in wartime were helping the general relief of taxation rather than being earmarked for postwar investment in a modernised railway system. Illustrative of the backlog of maintenance and replacement was the fact that in 1945 124,000 waggons were undergoing or awaiting repair. Two years later the situation was even worse. No less than 203,000 waggons, or 16·6 per cent of the total, were out of service. In 1939 the comparable figure was 3·2 per cent.[9]

In contrast with the railways, the road transport industry was under-utilised in the first two years of war. Early government hopes that a system of petrol rationing would suffice to ensure the optimum deployment of commercial vehicles went unrealised. As the official historian of wartime transport noted, 'the fuel rationing system did not stop hauliers seeking the best paying rather than the most essential traffics'.[10]

In the winter of 1940-1 it became steadily more difficult to obtain the services of enough vehicles of the right type at the right time. From May 1940 onwards a succession of Committees at the Ministry of Transport and (after May 1941) the Ministry of War Transport was occupied in working out a solution to the road transport problem, but opposition came from 'almost every quarter in turn'. At first the Road Haulage Consultative Committee, set up in the Autumn of 1940, recommended that the Ministry should 'charter' a number of road goods vehicles to carry goods on behalf of the government whilst leaving the running and management to the owners of the vehicles. But the road haulage interests suspected that the scheme was a first step to outright nationalisation and they opposed it vigorously. However, two winters of rail transport bottlenecks persuaded the cabinet that a more effective government control over road transport was imperative and therefore a Road Haulage Branch was set up within the Ministry of War Transport in February 1942. Within the year the steady fall in the stocks of petrol helped to convince Lord Leathers that, as Minister of War Transport, he must take direct control over the 25,000 vehicles which were regularly engaged in road haulage work for distances of over 60 miles. By March 1943, when this scheme became fully operational, some of the well-organised larger firms had been taken over as whole units while arrangements were made to hire the trucks of other concerns at weekly rentals. In 1944, the year of maximum war effort, some 30,000 vehicles out of a total of 411,000 registered as engaged in general haulage were directly employed by the Ministry to carry over 40 million tons of traffic in the merchandise and minerals categories. Without their help it is doubtful whether the overstrained railways could have coped with this extra burden. In particular the supply of lorries near the west coast ports was inadequate to deal with the greatly increased volume of goods to be carried. Without the requisitioning of fleets of vehicles from other areas the ports could not have been cleared.

In daylight hours the government requisitioned lorries could reach their destinations more speedily than had been possible in days of peace. There were remarkably few private motor cars on the roads. In 1939 over two million of them and over 400,000 motor cycles had been licensed for use. By 1943 petrol rationing had reduced the number to 718,000 cars and 124,000 motor cycles. Apart from the movement of troops and munition workers, this was one of the principal reasons for the enormous growth of rail passenger travel in wartime.

Coastal shipping was of vital importance to the war effort because it was available to move traffic just at those seasons of the year when the railways were pressed most severely. The job of the nine Coastal Shipping War Control Committees in the regions was to ensure that essential cargoes were given priority of movement and that the necessary tramp or liner shipping was available at the right time. In liaison with the Inter-Company Rolling Stock Control at Amersham and the Ministry's Central Transport Committee, steps were taken to relieve rail transport bottlenecks by providing alternative coastal transport. After Dunkirk, 105 of the 320 cargo liners employed in coastal shipping were requisitioned by the services. Because there were fewer business units with which to negotiate and because the machinery of Government control was more complete and effective, coasters were able to play a notable part in relieving railway transport in the early stages of the war whereas poorly organised road transport was not. In the view of the official war historians, railways alone could not have carried that additional traffic of coal, sulphate of ammonia, sugar beet and scrap iron which the coasters carried.[11] Nevertheless coastal shipping suffered serious disadvantages compared with land transport. Losses sustained through enemy action were proportionately greater. No less than 172 vessels, of 343,700 deadweight tons, were lost through this cause; and between April 1941 and August 1945 a further 86 vessels were lost at sea from causes other than enemy action. Air and sea attacks and the effects of blackout delayed shipping movements. Round trips of collier vessels between Tyneside and London, which took between six and seven days to complete in peacetime, took twice as long in the war years. For all these reasons it is not surprising that the tonnage of goods carried coastwise declined from 26,881,200 tons in 1942 to 23,123,300 tons in 1944 as the organisation of both railway and road transport improved.

Immediately on the outbreak of war the 1,300 miles of canals owned or controlled by the railway companies were brought under the direction of the REC. The independently-owned canals, of double this mileage, were at first left to their own devices. War transport plans had not been drawn up in the expectation that there would be a shortage of carrying capacity on the railways and canals were assigned a somewhat residual role in the carriage of goods. However, the Ministry of Transport quickly discovered both that the railways were less able to cope with an inflated volume of wartime traffic than the general managers had predicted, and that the shift of imports from east coast to west coast ports was seriously undermining the revenues of the canal companies. In June 1940, therefore, the government decided to give a subsidy of 50 per cent of tolls to canal carriers on condition that tolls were pegged. At the same time, carriers were not allowed to raise freight charges without the consent of the ministry.

After the transport crisis of the winter of 1940–41 the government strongly suspected that the canals could be put to better use. It therefore asked Mr Frank Pick, who already had a distinguished record of service for London transport, to investigate the possibilities for their fuller utilisation. He recommended that the government should assume a more complete control over all inland waterways and that government departments should consign a larger volume of their traffic along these channels. By order issued between July and October 1942 18 canal companies and 42 carriers were brought under the control of the Ministry of War Transport. The six Regional Canal Committees which had been established on the outbreak of war were strengthened by the inclusion of representatives of the 'supply' departments of government and of the trade unions with the intention of ensuring a fuller utilisation of the nation's waterways.[12]

The best that can be said of all these measures was that they caused the decline in canal traffic to be less severe than would have been the case if they had not been taken. The canal network was found to be too inflexible to meet the changing patterns of wartime transport demand. By contrast, rail and road services could be adjusted more rapidly. The canals suffered through the neglect they had sustained in peacetime and through the failure of government to exercise effective control over them until more than two years of war had passed. By this time many skilled men who had built or manned canal boats had enlisted in the armed services. Thus canal tonnage carried declined from 13 million tons in 1938 to 10 million tons in 1946. The fall in carryings was as much as 16 per cent between December 1943 and December 1944 when the improved organisation of road and rail transport was beginning to take effect.

Summing up the part played by each of the principal means of transport in the movement of all types of goods in 1944, a year of peak wartime effort, we find that railways, with nearly 142 million tons, carried over 64 per cent of the traffic; road transport, with approximately 45 million tons, carried 20 per cent; coastal shipping's share was 23 million tons, or ten per cent, while the share of the canals was only 11 million tons, or just under five per cent of the total.[13]

On his appointment as Minister of War Transport in May 1941, Lord Leathers declared that 'the organisation of our national economy for the maximum war effort demands that the entire transport systems of the country should be considered as a unit'. This objective took two years to achieve. But throughout the last two years of war the Ministry was exercising control over the whole of inland transport to an extent 'hitherto unparalleled'. The department achieved a high reputation for carrying out a task of great size and complexity with complete success. It was an experience which was invoked to reinforce the arguments of those who were advocating a unified and publicly-owned transport system as a priority for postwar planning.

III

The Labour Party's victory in the general election of July 1945 was of decisive importance for the future of British transport. The policy of the party had been set out in the statement *The National Planning of Transport,* approved by the annual conference in 1932, in Herbert Morrison's pamphlet *Britain's Transport at Britain's Service,* published in 1938, and in the election manifesto of July 1945 *Let us Face the Future.* Although few details were spelt out in these documents, the party was committed to the appointment of a National Transport Board on the lines of the London Passenger Transport Board. It was intended that the railways, canals, docks and long-distance haulage undertakings should be acquired by the Board, compensation being paid to the former owners. It was claimed that the objective of coordination of transport services by rail, road, air and canal could not be achieved without unification under one central authority. The TUC was committed to similar policies: the 1945 congress at Blackpool approved a report entitled *The Public Operation of Transport* which was more precise and clearly worded than the above-mentioned publications of the Labour Party. The report declared that

First, each of the seven separate services which together comprise internal transport (i.e. rail, canal, road haulage, road passenger, ports and docks, coastwise shipping and internal airways) must be operated at the highest level of operational efficiency.

Second, the transport services of the country must be operated as one system and must be so developed and so utilised that each separate service shall, as one complementary part of national transport, carry the traffic most appropriate for it, while transport as a

whole must be capable of being used as an instrument in the carrying out of Government policies of national development and full
employment.

As was the case with the Labour Party's statements, details were
lacking on the administrative policies which would be adopted to
secure these very worthwhile objectives.

The Transport Act of 1947—the first public Act to which it had
been possible to give such a simple and comprehensive title—was
described by *The Economist* as the Attlee Government's 'biggest
venture into nationalisation'.[14] In terms of the size of the assets
acquired, the complexity of the issues and the extent of the opposition
to the original proposals, this was certainly the case. The Act established the British Transport Commission to which all railways (including their steamships, hotels and all other ancillary undertakings),
canals, all privately owned railway waggons and some road haulage
and road passenger concerns were transferred on 1 January 1948.
Admittedly their powers were much wider, but in one sense the four
men appointed to the Commission by the Minister of Transport, Mr
Alfred Barnes, were responsible for continuing the kind of policies
pursued by the Central Transport Committee of the Ministry of War
Transport between 1941 and 1947. The duty in each case was to ensure
that all transport resources were used in 'mutual support and co-operation'.[15] In the words of the Act, the Commission had the duty of
'providing, or securing the provision of an efficient, adequate, economical and properly integrated system of public inland transport
and port facilities within Great Britain'. As both *The Times* and *The
Economist*[16] conceded, there were strong arguments for unified and
concentrated control of broad policy for the principal means of transport. But many of the benefits which could have sprung from the
creation of the Commission were undermined as a result of other
clauses in the Act setting up separate Executives for Railways, London
Transport. Docks and Inland Waterways, Hotels and Road Transport
(from June 1949 split into Road Haulage and Road Passenger Executives). The personnel of these executives was appointed directly by
the Minister and not by the BTC, thus giving them an independence
of outlook towards the four members of the Commission which was
not generally compatible with policies of transport integration.

The powers formerly possessed by the Railway Rates Tribunal were
transferred to a newly established Transport Tribunal whose approval
was required before any changes could be made in freight rates and
fares. Significantly, the Minister retained the power to forbid increases
in charges whenever he considered such action to be in the public
interest. In addition the old nineteenth-century legislation, forbidding
railways to give undue preference or discriminate between one type

of customer and another, was not repealed. Thus the Commission might be prevented from acting in accordance with purely commercial considerations in the pricing of transport services. At the same time it was given no clear direction as to whether the railways and road undertakings were to be run as a service or as purely business undertakings. It could be implied from Section 3 sub-section 4 of the Act that cross subsidisation was permissible and that over some ill-defined period of time the Commission was to pay its way:

All the business carried on by the Commission . . . shall form one undertaking, and the Commission shall so conduct that undertaking and, subject to the provisions of this Act, levy such fares, rates, tolls, dues and other charges, as to secure that the revenue of the Commission is not less than sufficient for making provision for the meeting of charges properly chargeable to revenue, taking one year with another.

It was not until the passage of the Transport Act of 1968 that the vexed question of unremunerative services and the role of public transport as a social service was seriously tackled.

In respect of road transport the Transport Act made a half-hearted compromise between the policy of complete public ownership and that of free competition. After an 'Appointed Day' to be announced by the Minister (1 February 1950 was the date chosen) all 'A' and 'B' licence holders were to be restricted to a sphere of operations not more than 25 miles from their bases, the business of long-distance road haulage for hire (with some exceptions in the case of unusual consignments) being the monopoly of the vehicles managed by the Road Transport Executive. In the original Bill 'C' licence holders, i.e. those who carried goods solely on their account, were to be limited to a sphere of operations within forty miles of their base. The road haulage industry's opposition to all these proposals was prolonged and strident, from the publication, on 16 July 1946, of the Road Haulage Association's booklet *The Challenge of Tomorrow's Transport: the Road Hauliers' Reply to the TUC,* to the collection of 600,000 signatures to a petition against the Bill and a sustained lobbying of MPs throughout its passage through Parliament. Even the Co-operative Movement was unhelpful. According to Herbert Morrison, there was 'a distinct lack of enthusiasm'[17] in the wholesale and retail societies about any curtailment of their 'C' licence powers. Partly because of their opposition, the clauses which limited the range of operation of 'C' licence vehicles were removed from the Bill. It was a most serious blow to the Commission's prospects of achieving one of its prime objectives— 'a properly integrated system of transport'. The number of vehicles with 'C' licences was nearly two and half times the number with 'A' or 'B' licences, as Fig 22 shows. With a large majority of road goods

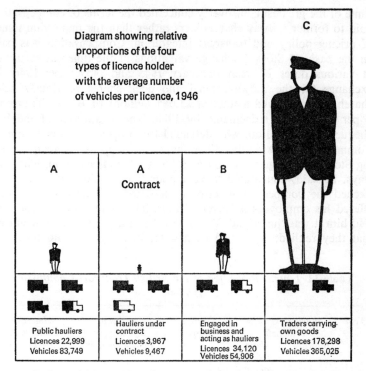

Source: Society of Motor Manufacturers and Traders, *The Motor Industry of Great Britain* (1947 edition).

Figure 22

vehicles beyond its control the possibility of allocating each form of transport to its most appropriate sphere of operations was enormously reduced.

Because monopoly powers were granted to the Commission in respect of the railways and to a lesser extent in canals and some road transport services, the Act set up a Central Transport Consultative Commitee for Great Britain and a number of area Transport User Consultative Committees to consider complaints and suggestions for improvements from transport users. Although these were valuable public safeguards, there is no doubt that they also came to constitute obstacles to the streamlining and rationalisation of the Commission's assets. They upheld the importance of loss-making local railway lines and bus routes as necessary social services at a time when the Commission was trying to fulfil its statutory duty of paying its way 'taking one year with another'.

While the Bill was making its tortuous progress to the statute book some of the greatest controversy concerned the terms of compensation paid to former railway shareholders rather than the more vital issues of pricing policy and transport integration. Compensation was paid on the basis of Stock Exchange valuations of the different securities at various dates between February 1945 and November 1946. In exchange for the railway, canal and dock shares previously held, shareholders received a total of £1,065 millions of British Transport 3 per cent stock, redeemable by 1988. The Chancellor of the Exchequer, Hugh Dalton, who defended the proposals in the House of Commons on 17 December 1946, taunted the opposition for questioning Stock Exchange valuation as a basis for compensation. The railways, he said, constituted 'a very poor bag of physical assets'. He likened the compensation terms to the story of the employer who offered his employees a barrel of beer. They had drunk it and had told him it was 'just right'. When he asked them what they meant by that they replied: 'If it had been a bit better you would not have

Table 11 *Financial position of the British Transport Commission 1948–62*

Year	Working surplus or deficit		Central charges	Surplus or deficit after central charges	Interest contained in central charges
	railways	whole undertaking			
	£m.	£m.	£m.	£m.	£m.
1948	+23·8	+40·8	45·6	−4·7	42·3
1949	+10·6	+28·1	48·8	−20·8	43·9
1950	+25·2	+37·6	51·7	−14·1	44·9
1951	+33·3	+48·1	48·0	+0·1	44·8
1952	+38·7	+54·5	50·1	+8·0	46·0
1953	+34·6	+57·6	53·4	+4·2	50·4
	+166·2	+266·7	297·6	−27·3	272·3
1954	+16·4	+42·9	54·7	−11·9	52·4
1955	+1·8	+26·6	57·2	−30·6	53·8
1956	−16·5	+4·5	58·9	−54·7	54·7
1957	−27·1	−3·7	59·8	−70·1	61·9
1958	−48·1	−28·1	60·9	−104·8	72·4
1959	−40·3	−12·59	61·2	−99·5	82·8
1960	−67·7	−47·8	64·6	−133·4	92·7
1961	−86·9	−53·4	68·6	−160·2	102·8
1962	−104·0	−69·2	74·4	−182·6	110·7

Source: *Annual Report and Accounts*, British Transport Commission, 1948–62. From 1957 allocation does not include interest on accumulated railway losses and on new borrowing. Both these items were transferred to a special account.

Source: H. Pollins, *Britain's Railways an Industrial History*, 1971

Map 13   The Railway System in 1952

given it to us, and if it had been a bit worse we would not have drunk it.' It was an apt parallel with the situation of the former railway shareholders. Although the interest they would be receiving was lower than that received by the more fortunate stockholders in the best years of the 1930s, it was higher than the railways yielded in depressed years like 1932 and 1938 and likely to be higher than the railway companies would have been able to earn once motor car competition gathered momentum in the postwar years.

The British Transport Commission's financial position during the 15 years of its existence is summarised in Table 11. In the first six years of the life of the Commission a working surplus was earned and in 1951-53 inclusive a surplus was achieved after making deductions for central charges, the principal element of which was interest paid on British Transport Stock issued at the time of nationalisation. At the end of 1950 there was an accumulated deficit, after meeting central charges, of £39·6 million, but three years later this had been reduced to £27·3 million, mainly because of the growing success of the Commission's road haulage business—British Road Services earned surpluses totalling £15·1 million in the years 1948-53 inclusive. From the beginning of 1954, when the greater part of the Commission's profitable road haulage business was 'hived off' to private enterprise under the terms of the Transport Act of 1953, the most promising growth sector of the whole undertaking was removed and it was no longer possible for the Commission to keep within manageable distance of solvency. As Table 11 reveals an overall surplus was achieved by the Commission during the last three years of operation of the Road Haulage Executive. By contrast, from the beginning of 1954, the rapidly expanding long-distance road haulage business, now under private management, was undermining the Commission's finances by competing with the railways instead of strengthening them through cross subsidisation.

The Commission's big loss-maker was the railways. Only in 1952 did they make an overall surplus after payment of their share of the central charges. The financial position of the railways within the BTC is shown in Table 12.

The railways' rapidly increasing deficits in most years after 1955 might suggest a correspondingly sharp fall in passenger and freight traffic. In fact the estimated passenger mileage was slightly higher in 1961 than it was in 1948, and although freight traffic declined, it remained above the level of 1936. Certainly the fall in business was not so steep as the worsening financial situation suggested. The railways' traffic experience is summarised in Table 13.

Before the reasons for the railways' growing difficulties after 1952 are examined it is worth recalling their positive achievements in the first five years of nationalisation. In 1952 with 40,000 fewer employees,

Table 12 *British Railways: receipts and expenditures 1948–62 (£m.)*

Year	Passenger receipts	Freight receipts	Total gross receipts (incl. misc. receipts)	Total working expenses	Current operating return	Central charges allocated to railways	Overall return
1948	122·6	180·5	346·3	322·5	23·8	31·9	−8·1
1949	114·0	178·9	335·7	325·1	10·6	34·2	−23·6
1950	106·6	198·9	351·3	326·1	25·2	36·2	−11·0
1951	107·0	227·9	348·9	351·6	33·3	33·6	−0·3
1952	111·9	250·5	416·3	377·7	38·7	35·1	3·6
1953	114·8	263·1	434·7	400·1	34·6	37·4	−2·8
1954	116·6	272·8	449·3	432·9	16·4	38·3	−21·9
1955	118·1	274·2	453·9	452·1	1·8	40·1	−38·3
1956	127·5	284·1	481·0	497·5	−16·5	41·2	−57·7
1957	138·9	288·5	501·4	528·6	−27·1	41·9*	−69·0
1958	138·0	259·1	471·6	519·7	−48·1	42·6	−90·7
1959	140·0	242·7	457·4	499·4	−42·0	42·8	−84·8
1960	151·3	267·3	478·6	546·2	−67·7	45·2	−112·9
1961	157·5	236·8	474·7	561·6	−86·9	48·0	−134·9
1962	161·1	224·9	465·1	569·1	−104·0	52·1	−156·1

* From 1957 allocation does not include interest on accumulated railway losses and on new borrowing. Both these items were transferred to a special account,

Source: *Annual Reports and Accounts*, British Transport Commission.

1,500 fewer locomotives and 100,000 fewer waggons, they carried 12 million tons more merchandise than in 1948 and 19 million tons more than in 1938. In 1952 the ton-miles carried per engine-hour worked were the highest achieved to that date and were 11 per cent better than in 1948 and 31 per cent better than in 1938.[18] There were sub-

Table 13 *British Railways traffic 1948–62*

Year	Passenger journeys (m.)	Estimated passenger miles (m.)	M. tons total	Total	Net ton-miles		
					Merchandise	Minerals, etc.	Coal and coke
1938	1,237	18,993	266	16,266	4,980	3,182	8,104
1948	1,024	21,022	273	21,457	6,949	4,926	9,582
1949	1,021	20,902	280	21,848	6,913	4,990	9,945
1950	1,010	19,953	281	22,136	6,925	5,029	10,182
1951	1,030	20,561	285	22,902	7,078	5,164	10,660
1952	1,017	20,459	285	22,392	6,818	5,207	10,367
1953	1,015	20,578	289	22,766	6,790	5,261	10,715
1954	1,020	20,712	283	22,089	6,542	5,059	10,488
1955	994	20,308	274	21,353	6,087	5,075	10,191
1956	1,029	21,113	277	21,473	6,008	5,217	10,248
1957	1,101	22,591	274	20,880	5,944	5,067	9,869
1958	1,090	22,150	243	18,426	5,231	4,263	8,927
1959	1,069	22,270	234	17,711	5,376	4,331	8,004
1960	1,037	21,547	249	18,650	5,706	4,840	8,104
1961	1,025	21,061	238	17,591	5,553	4,289	7,749
1962	998	19,772	228	16,104	5,200	3,600	7,304

Source: *Annual Report and Accounts*, British Transport Commission.

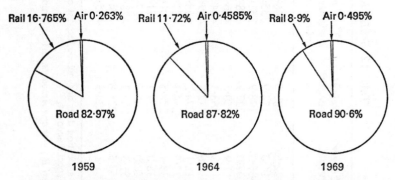

Source: British Road Federation, *Basic Road Statistics*, 1971, p. 14.

Figure 23   Great Britain: Internal Passenger Traffic—Share of Passenger Traffic Carried by Road, Rail and Air Transport, 1959, 1964 and 1969 (calculated on a basis of total passenger mileage)

stantial achievements in respect of standardisation of equipment. In place of the 400 different patterns of locomotive inherited from the railway companies in 1948 the Railway Executive designed 12 standard types. A far more efficient railway system was in the making.

All the same, there can be no mistaking the railways' falling traffic and nearly stagnant productivity in the late 1950s and early 1960s. A major change of role was required and for a large variety of reasons the railways failed to match up to it. The British railways network

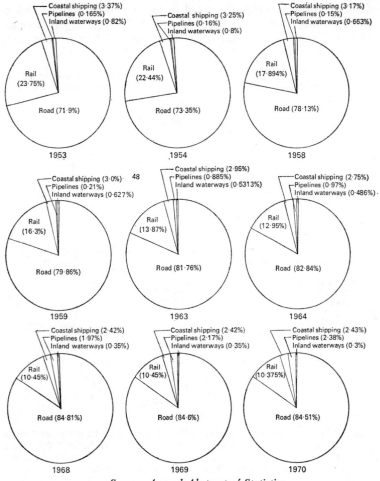

Source: Annual Abstract of Statistics.

Figure 24   Great Britain: Goods/Freight Transport—Share of Goods Traffic Carried by Road, Rail, Coastal Shipping, Inland Waterways and Pipelines, calculated on a basis of total tonnage

had been constructed in Victorian times when the efficiency of road transport was no match at all for the all-pervasive railway. In consequence many lines were built to link small towns and villages where the amount of traffic was often insufficient to cover working expenses even in the days before motor transport. That the nineteenth-century legacy was still very much present in the second half of the twentieth century was the subject of comment by the British Transport Commission in 1961:

> Stations are still so closely spaced as to serve, on average, a radius of only about 2½ miles. In association with this, and largely because of it, the waggon is still the predominant unit of freight movement.

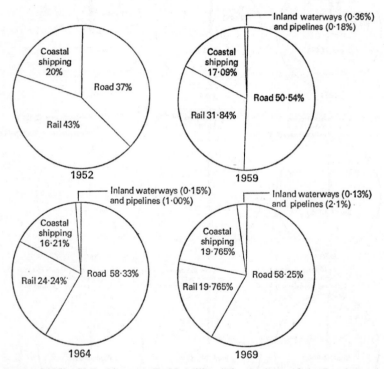

Sources: 1952—K.F. Glover & D. N. Miller, 'The Outlines of the Road Goods Transport Industry', *Journal of the Royal Statistical Society*, Series A (General), vol. 117, Pt 3, 1954, p. 318. Note: the inland waterway and pipeline shares for 1952 are numerically so small as not to be given.

1959, 1964, 1969—British Road Federation, *Basic Road Statistics*, 1971, p. 14.

Figure 25   Great Britain: Goods/Freight Transport—Share of Goods Traffic Carried by Road, Rail, Coastal Shipping, Inland Waterways and Pipelines, calculated on a basis of total ton-mileage

On the passenger side, enormous train mileages are run to provide local stopping services between stations which are still spaced with little regard to the competition from buses or the ever-growing availability of private transport.[19]

Already in the summer of 1950 the Commission showed an awareness of the very substantial long-term changes that were needed, the slimming process that was required to adapt the railways to the new conditions of the later part of the twentieth century. In a statement issued on 27 July 1950 it declared that the object of policy would be 'the development of road and rail transport according to the traffic for which each is specially suitable and efficient'. Rail transport was (and is) best suited for traffic forming complete trainloads, or serving private sidings, or carried long distances in regular quantities and at regular time intervals, or large consignments of minerals where handling costs are less than by road, or grain and feeding stuffs for which the railways provided bulk storage. Road transport on the other hand, was (and is) best suited for local haulage, cross-country haulage, for removals requiring skilled packing and handling, and for loads restricted by the railway gauge.

To ensure that the railways fulfilled this role, however, their equipment needed to be modernised; dead-wood in the form of under-utilised track and uneconomic marshalling yards, depots and local stations, had to be removed from the system. (At the same time fully adequate public motor transport services were needed in replacement, where there was a social need.) While the elimination of surplus capacity was a relatively inexpensive process, the vital task of providing the railways with essential new equipment, such as diesel or electric locomotives, new colour signalling systems, welded rails and large capacity steel waggons with continuous brakes, required large amounts of new capital. The Commission's failure to acquire this in sufficient quantity at the right time and at low rates of interest was one of the principal reasons for the railways' failure to retain or capture that proportion of the traffic which, given modernisation, was suitably theirs. The Commission was unable even to maintain the level of investment at which it started in 1948. Early in 1949 it proposed that, by 1952, railway investment should be 43 per cent higher than it had been in 1948. But, due to the restrictions imposed by the government, it fell by about one fifth. Railway investment did not reach pre-war levels until 1956. This was not because there was less capital to go round. The railways' proportion of UK capital investment was falling. In 1948 it had been 4·4 per cent; in 1951 it was only 3·3 per cent.[20] A basic reason for the railways' decline was that far more capital was being invested in roads and road transport than in railway transport, as Fig. 26 makes clear. This situation of capital starvation must be seen in the light of the backlog of investment due to the war and to pre-war depression. The government's policy, under the Transport Act, 1953, of hiving off the profit-making road haulage section of the Commission's activities largely destroyed any prospect of financing any proportion of railway modernisation through cross-subsidisation.

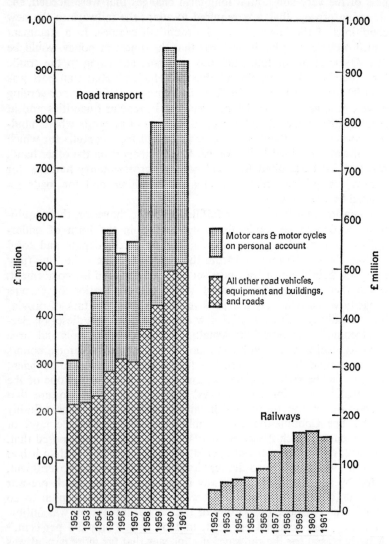

Source: British Transport Commission, *Annual Report and Accounts,* 1962.

Figure 26   Road and Rail Transport: Investment Expenditure 1952–61

To the extent that this source of funds was no longer available, money had to be borrowed through loans on less advantageous terms.

It was not only the funds but also essential raw materials and skilled manpower that were in short supply. The Commission had to compete with the motor car industry and with other branches of the engineering industry for the inadequate supplies of steel that were available in the early 1950s. The government was often more concerned that the output, including output for exports, of the motor car industry was increased than that the railways were properly equipped. In 1952 the Commission was allocated 20 per cent less steel than the amount it had requested. As a result, the construction of new rolling stock was postponed and it was found necessary to resort to the 'wasteful expedient' of repairing life-expired carriages to carry summer peak traffic and patching up condemned, small-capacity freight waggons. Between 1949–52 nearly £600,000 was spent on this kind of 'make do and mend' because the larger sums needed for more fundamental re-equipment were not available.[21] Shortages of both funds and equipment slowed down the introduction of welded rails and the electrification schemes were held up partly because the BTC had been 'unable to get the technical staff on whom they had been banking'.[22]

The Commission's deficits would not have been so large and its debts would not have risen so alarmingly had it been able to meet rising costs of materials and labour with promptly applied increases in charges. The Commission had to wait eleven months for the introduction of its first Passenger Charges Scheme in 1951 because of lengthy consideration of its merits and defects by the Transport Tribunal and the Consumers' Consultative Committee. The delay cost the Commission £100,000 a day. This was only one example among many.

Probably even more serious was the delay of a decade in the abandonment of other important restraints on the railways' charging policies—a legacy of the pre-1914 days of railway monopoly. The early Reports of the Commission reveal awareness of the need to abandon the old methods of charging based on the value of goods and to substitute a system of charging according to costs. The *Draft Outline of Principles proposed to be embodied in a charges scheme for Merchandise Traffic* which it published in 1951 put the value of the merchandise last in the list of considerations which would determine the freight to be charged.[23] However, it was not until the passing of the Transport Act of 1953 that the Commission was freed from its responsibility to publish special rates agreed with traders and from its obligation to avoid unfair rates and undue preferences.

It would be quite misleading to suggest that the railways' shortcomings after nationalisation were solely due to governments' failure to make sufficient capital available for modernisation. The slow progress made in transforming the character of the railways' physical assets was partly the result of the faulty organisational structure of the British Transport Commission. The original concept of the nationalisation plan was that the Commission should own and direct the entire undertaking but that the direct management of the various undertakings, railways, docks and inland waterways, etc., should be the responsibility of the Executives named in the Act. According to M. R. Bonavia, who knew the workings of the Commission from the inside, the whole plan 'bristled with practical difficulties'. The biggest obstacle to smooth working was the fact that the Commission did not appoint its own agents; the members of the Executives were appointed by the Minister of Transport and not by the Commission.

The complications which sprang from this faulty organisational structure were most manifest and most damaging in respect of policy for locomotive power. Within four months of the vesting date for public ownership, i.e. by April 1948, Sir Cyril (later Lord) Hurcomb, the chairman of the Commission, wrote to the chairman of the Railway Executive advising the appointment of a committee, including a representative of the BTC, to examine as a matter of some urgency the relative advantages of diesel and electric locomotion. The Railway Executive delayed the appointment of the committee for eight months, did not bring in a member of the BTC staff, and presented a leisurely report nearly three years later, in October 1951. In the meantime the RE pushed ahead with the ordering and/or manufacture of steam locomotives on standardised patterns. The result was that although the committee recommended that large-scale experiments with both diesel and electric traction should be undertaken 'steam traction continued on the main lines practically without let or hindrance until the change in management',[24] i.e. the abolition of the Railway Executive at the beginning of 1954. The crux of the matter was that the Executive contained a number of devotees of steam whereas the members of the Commission were searching for a more modern alternative. The decision to continue with steam traction, according to one interpretation of what happened, 'was taken more or less by default . . . because the steam interests were all set to jump in with the utmost vigour, whereas a certain amount of fact finding was necessary for alternative forms of traction'.[25] Other fundamental differences of approach developed in the course of the years 1948–53 when the Railway Executive was functioning. Whereas the Commission was very mindful of its central task of developing an integrated system of transport with railways, road transport and canals each forming a part of a single whole, the Railway Executive concentrated on developing a national system of railways according to its own concepts. Each body jealously guarded what it regarded as its proper sphere of activity. The Executive resisted the desire of the BTC to take too close an interest in their proceedings by an ingenious device. While continuing, as directed by the BTC, to supply the latter with copies of their Minutes, the Executive produced what were, in effect, a second set of Minutes entitled *Memoranda of Decisions at Meeting*, which were issued on coloured paper and reserved for internal circulation. They were generally known to the staff as the Green Minutes whilst the White Minutes were those prepared for submission to the BTC.[26]

What becomes clear, in the light of these differences, is that although the allocation of a larger share of capital to the BTC would have brought an earlier and more substantial increase in the productivity of railways, it is doubtful whether the improvement would have been as great as that achieved in the 1960s, when there was greater unanimity on the merits of diesel and electric traction.

While the Railway Executive was in the process of welding the resources of four main line railway companies into a national undertaking the Road Haulage Executive was engaged in its formidable task of establishing a large national road haulage business. Under the terms of Part III of the Transport Act, 1947, long-distance road haulage firms were allowed until 30 June 1948 to reach voluntary agreement on the sale of their assets to the RHE while compulsory acquisition orders had to be served on the remaining firms by 1 October 1948. (Originally also the RHE had responsibility for the creation of a nationally owned system of bus services, but this work was transferred to a new organisation, the Road Passenger Executive, in 1949.) Throughout 1948 and 1949 the staff of the newly created RHE set about their task with considerable enthusiasm. Early in 1950 Maj.-Gen. G. N. Russell, the chairman of the organisation, wrote that it was 'impossible to convey the atmosphere of thrill and adventure that pervades the activities of those who, starting with virtually nothing, have set about building the biggest road haulage undertaking in the world'.[27] It was not until early in 1951 that Lord Hurcomb, chairman of the BTC, was in a position to claim that the organisation of British Road Services by the RHE was 'broadly complete'. In under three years some 2,900 separate road haulage concerns comprising about 40,000 vehicles, based on 1,000 depots or sub-depots, and employing 75,000 persons, had been merged into a national undertaking. Of the BRS share of road transport vehicles, 11,000 had been acquired as a result of voluntary negotiation while of the remainder, 23,000 had been acquired compulsorily and approximately 11,000 through the acquisition of the former subsidiary companies of the railways, of whom Pickfords and Carter Paterson were the largest. Although BRS had a monopoly of the business of road haulage *hiring* for distances over 25 miles it controlled less than one eighth of road

Table 14 *Ownership of road freight vehicles, 31 December 1951*

	No. of vehicles	Av. capacity per vehicle (tons)	Approx. total capacity
A. Publicly owned			
Railway delivery services	27,000	3·75	100,000
BRS	44,000	7·0	310,000
B. Privately owned			
'A' and 'B' licence	119,000	5·0	585,000
'C' licence			
2½ tons and under	665,000	1·25	850,000
over 2½ tons	140,000	5·25	750,000
Total	995,000	4·45	2,595,000

(N.B. The number of vehicles attributed to the BRS is some 3,600 greater than that estimated by the National Board for Prices & Incomes in 1971.)

Source: B. R. Williams, 'Nationalisation and After', *Jnl Inst. Tspt*, vol. 25, No. 1, November 1952, p. 15.

haulage capacity for all types of goods transport. Even in long-distance haulage its vehicles were greatly outnumbered by the 'C' licence lorries and vans which were subject to no limit in the range of their operations.

The new Executive took over a very mixed bag of physical assets. According to the road transport correspondent of *The Times* it was 'compelled to acquire many vehicles in bad condition, some with poor premises and some with none'. The Acton Society described one road haulage depot very much in the image of a junk yard:

> An old railway carriage, dumped about 50 years before, was used as an office; close by was a bathing cabin which the old owners had made their private HQ. No washing or lavatory amenities were available, and female clerks were given 2*d* a day to use public facilities.[28]

On the other hand the large firms, such as Pickfords, which were taken over were nationwide in their scope and generally had better amenities for their staff.

In place of this variegated pattern of big and small undertakings, the RHE formed about 200 BRS depots with an average of 174 lorries in each. A nationwide service was in the making. How efficient was it? Towards the end of 1950 *The Economist* claimed that the publicly owned road haulage industry had given 'a very creditable performance' bearing in mind the immensity of the task of transferring property from some 2,900 separate owners to one organisation.[29] Professor P. E. Hart, using statistics of tonnage hauled per vehicle per worker, considered that labour productivity in BRS fell in the early 1950s.[30] But if capacity ton mileage, excluding empty running, be taken as a more satisfactory yardstick, then productivity in 1951 was $5\frac{1}{2}$ per cent higher than it was in 1950. And although productivity fell in 1952 it rose again in 1953 to a level seven per cent higher than in 1950. Perhaps the greatest benefit conferred by BRS was that for the first time a comprehensive network of trunk services, nationwide in extent, had been created. The very satisfactory performance in respect of capacity utilisation was the result, in part, of the creation of a teleprinter network linking the principal BRS depots.[31] According to R. Wilson, who had some responsibility as a member of the BTC for the success of road haulage, the BRS was 'vastly more efficient than the little businesses it swallowed up'. He was prepared to concede that the independent operator 'worked harder, saved more time and used more personal initiative' but he considered these advantages were outweighed by those of the BRS which 'brought big economies, reduced empty running, put maintenance on a scientific basis, raised the standard of management by employing better brains at the top, and saved effort generally'.[32]

With the exception of the one year, 1950, BRS made a profit on each year's trading from its inception in 1948 until its dissolution at the end of 1968 as Table 15 indicates.

In 1953, the last full year of operation before the substantial dispersal of its assets under the Transport Act of that year, BRS achieved a record turnover of £80·2 million, a record profit of £8·9 million and a record rate of return—over 12 per cent—on its net assets. It was possible to cite a worsening financial position as a reason for the reorganisation of railway management. No such argument was possible in the case of the Road Haulage Executive.

The disturbing changes resulting from, first, nationalisation (1948-53) and then denationalisation (1953 onwards), in the road haulage industry, had important repercussions on the broader plans of the BTC for transport integration. Until the size and deployment of its road vehicle assets became clear in the early 1950s the Commission could make but tentative plans for the dovetailing of its rail and road goods services. But no sooner had the way been cleared and a pattern of road goods transport organisation successfully achieved than there came a change of government in 1951 which brought with it a radical change in direction of transport policies. At the very time when some of the preconditions for transport integration were at last achieved, the hasty dismemberment of the BRS road transport assets was begun. Henceforward the deployment of transport resources would be deter-

Table 15 *British Road Services: trading 1948-68*

Year	Turnover (£m.)	Profit (£m.)	Net assets (£m.)	Rate of return %	Vehicles
1948	14·3	1·1	22·9	5·2	8,208
1949	38·9	1·4	46·3	3·2	34,894
1950	62·5	−1·1	68·6	−1·6	39,932
1951	78·6	3·3	70·1	4·7	41,265
1952	77·6	1·7	72·3	2·4	39,325
1953	80·2	8·9	73·0	12·2	35,849
1954	72·7	8·7	(71·2)	(12·2)	25,442
1955	55·8	4·3	(52·8)	8·1	17,570
1956	48·5	1·8	37·7	4·8	16,377
1957	50·3	2·8	39·7	7·1	16,312
1958	49·5	2·0	42·1	4·8	15,976
1959	52·5	3·1	43·2	7·2	15,911
1960	55·5	1·8	44·2	4·1	16,184
1961	57·9	3·4	45·2	7·5	16,066
1962	60·3	3·7	45·8	8·1	16,040
1963	64·2	4·7	45·8	10·3	16,075
1964	71·1	7·3	48·0	15·2	15,765
1965	79·9	7·0	64·1	11·1	18,346
1966	89·2	4·9	74·0	7·0	19,247
1967	90·7	3·0	85·0	3·7	18,210
1968	102·0	3·8	89·0	4·4	18,931

N.B. Asset figures for 1954-5 are estimates due to the fact that the Road Haulage Disposal Board, set up under the Transport Act 1953, was selling BRS road vehicles at this time. The RHE ceased to function after 1954.

Source: *National Board for Prices and Incomes Rept. No. 162: Costs, Charges and Productivity of National Freight Corporation*, App. A, Cmd 4569 of 1971.

mined to a much greater extent by the influence of private enterprise competition rather than public enterprise planning.

In contrast with the controversy which raged over policy for railways and road transport there was less disagreement between the main political parties concerning plans for the future of civil aviation. One reason for this greater consensus was that in the days of the wartime coalition both parties had agreed to the appointment of a committee, chaired by Lord Brabazon, whose task was to prepare plans for the postwar development of civil aviation. Both parties also supported the recommendation of the committee that British air services should be equipped with British-built planes, powered by turbine engines of the most up-to-date design. From being relatively backward in civil aircraft design in the 1930s Britain would 'leap frog' ahead of all her rivals in the late 1940s.[33] The setting up of a separate Ministry of Civil Aviation by the caretaker government of Winston Churchill in 1945 was bound to increase official interest in the speedy expansion of peacetime civil air services. There was hardly likely to be any disagreement about the future of the British Overseas Airways Corporation since this had been established as a state-owned enterprise by the Conservative government in 1939. There was some difference of emphasis in policy for the development of the routes outside the sphere of influence of the BOAC. Both the caretaker government and the Attlee governments favoured the creation of two corporations, one to provide domestic and European services and the other the service to South America. But whereas the Churchill administration favoured mixed enterprise with both state funds and private investment providing the necessary capital, the Attlee government in its White Paper *British Air Services* (Cmd 6712, December 1945) opted for 100 per cent state ownership.

The rationale of the new Labour Government's policy as spelt out in the White Paper was that full national ownership and control would 'make it possible, as costs of operation are progressively reduced, for the taxpayer to receive some benefit in return for the assistance he is required to provide during the initial period of state-aided operation'. Furthermore it would be Government policy to require the air corporations to employ British-made planes. In this way an enormous stimulus would be given to the domestic aircraft industry which would contribute to the much-needed export drive. Under the Civil Aviation Act, 1946, two new state-owned corporations, British European Airways and British South American Airways, were brought into being to start operations on 1 August 1946. (BOAC began its operations as a commercial enterprise on 1 April 1946.) It was not long before the policy of creating a separate corporation for the South American services was seriously questioned and the BSAA was merged with BOAC on 1 August 1949.

Throughout the period 1946–70 BEA dominated the business of providing scheduled air services within the British Isles. Through the 1950s nearly one quarter of the Corporation's total revenue came from the provision of domestic air services. Of this domestic revenue about 40 per cent came from the first-class and tourist passengers using the trunk routes between London and Manchester, Glasgow, Edinburgh and Belfast. The rest of BEA's passenger transport revenue came from tourist-class traffic on the subsidiary routes to the Channel Islands, the Isle of Man and the Scottish Highlands and Islands. Whereas by the later 1950s the European trunk routes paid their way both in themselves and in their most important role as feeders to other European services, the main and subsidiary routes within the British Isles were frequently unprofitable. The difficulty with the flights north of Glasgow and Edinburgh was the small size of the passenger market; the snag in the case of the Channel Islands and the Isle of Man was the great seasonal fluctuations in traffic. Twenty times as many people flew to Jersey and Guernsey in the month of August as made the same journey in February.[34] For the greater part of the year, therefore, a distressingly large proportion of the Corporation's capital assets was under-utilised. The early progress of BEA's domestic services is summarised in Table 16:

Table 16 *BEA domestic services, 1946-52*

Year ending	No. of pass. carried	Passenger load factor	Mail tons	Freight tons	Load ton-miles
31 March 1947	224,334	59·9%	526	809	2,433,000
31 March 1948	361,311	53·2	792	988	4,137,000
31 March 1949	370,841	62·7	1,175	1,216	4,935,000
31 March 1950	397,089	61·8	1,281	1,556	5,911,044
31 March 1951	431,676	55·3	1,653	2,179	7,314,618
31 March 1952	486,203	62·9	2,576	2,393	8,288,992

Source: BEA, Annual reports and accounts.

Until the financial year ending 31 March 1951 the Corporation carried more passengers on its domestic than it did on its continental services but with passengers to the continent increasing from 352,423 in 1949-50 to 507,910 in 1950-51 the pattern of traffic took on the characteristics common throughout the 1950s and 1960s with UK internal services playing a relatively minor role in the airline's activities.

Between 1947 and 1953 inclusive BEA made an aggregate loss of £11·9 million, after making allowance for depreciation, but before payment of interest on loans. Broadly speaking it was the operation of the domestic routes of a social service character that prevented the Corporation from getting out of the red earlier. In 1950-1, for example, it lost £1 million on its domestic services but was able to show a profit of £200,000 on its continental services.[35] However, a far more important explanation of early losses is to be found in the large investment programme that was needed in the first decade of the Corporation's life. By the terms of the Civil Aviation Act, 1946, BEA took over eight pre-war domestic airways which between 1939 and 1946 were managed by an Associated Airways Joint Committee. The aircraft assets of Highland Airways Ltd, West Coast Air Services Ltd and the other six concerns acquired were a very varied bunch, largely unsuitable for efficient postwar operation. Moreover, many of the aircraft were of American manufacture and the Civil Aviation Act made it obligatory for the new corporation to equip its fleets with British planes. London Airport was under construction in the

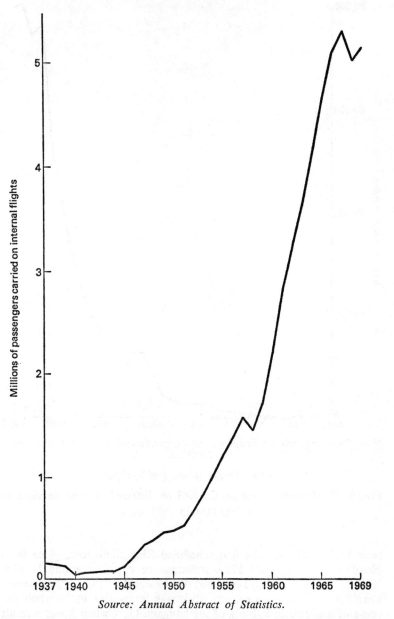

Source: Annual Abstract of Statistics.

Figure 27 Volume of Passenger Traffic on Internal Airline Services
in Great Britain 1937–69

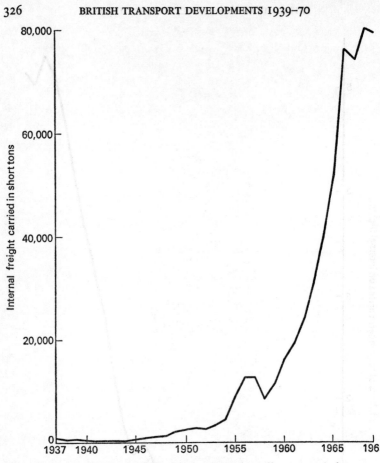

Note: Domestic freight tonnage excludes domestic mail tonnage. 1 short ton= 2,000 lbs.

Source: Annual Abstract of Statistics.

Figure 28   Freight Tonnage Carried on Internal Airline Services in Great Britain 1937–69

later 1940s and until the first scheduled BEA flight took place from Heathrow on 16 April 1950, maintenance costs were unduly high because the work had to be carried on elsewhere and under improvised conditions. Night maintenance work was impossible at Northolt because of inadequate lighting of the hangars. Only when newer aircraft such as the 'Elizabethan', with a seating capacity of 47 and a cruising speed of 234 m.p.h., took over from the 'Viking' (27 seats and cruising speed of 196 m.p.h.) in increasing numbers from March 1952 was it possible to achieve the higher payloads which offered a prospect of profitable operation.[36]

BEA never completely monopolised air transport in Britain. By the terms of the Civil Aviation Act, 1946, private airlines were not allowed to compete with the scheduled air services of BEA, but charter services could function on other routes. In the financial year 1946-7 no less than 69 private British airlines offered chartered services mainly financed and manned by 'enthusiastic war time pilots'.[37] The companies were financially extremely insecure; within eighteen months 30 had disappeared. However, Lord Swinton and other Conservative spokesmen on aviation policy urged the Labour Government to allow more scope for the private operators within Britain, and in 1948 Lord Pakenham, Minister for Civil Aviation, agreed to the appointment of a committee under the chairmanship of Lord Douglas of Kirtleside to advise on the limits of independent airline operation. In the House of Lords on 26 January 1949 the Minister expressed agreement with the Douglas Report recommendations to extend the operations of the private airlines. He conceded that although BEA was steadily expanding its services 'it would place an unjustifiable burden on them and on the taxpayers if they took over all these routes at the present time'. Meanwhile he 'did not wish to deny the benefits of such facilities as the charter companies were prepared to offer'.[38]

The policy of greater liberality to the private companies was operated through the Air Transport Advisory Council which had been established under the Civil Aviation Act, 1946. Operators wishing to open up a new service applied for a licence from the Council which was guided on policy by a Directive sent them by the Minister on 26 January 1949. Although it was declared to be the intention that 'scheduled air services to and from the U.K. and internally should normally be undertaken by the British Corporations', as an 'interim policy' associate companies would be allowed to operate, provided that their fares and freight rates on routes also operated by BEA and BOAC were not undercutting those of the corporations. The Council was warned that 'Associate arrangements that would hamper the development of the corporations' services should not be recommended'.[39]

Despite all these limiting conditions, the Minister's statement marked an important turning point in civil aviation policy. It was the thin end of the wedge in the growth of privately operated air services in Britain. In 1949 the Air Transport Advisory Council received 231 applications to run new services. It rejected 146 of them. In 1951 it approved 117 out of 149.[40] In his Lords' statement on 26 January 1949 Lord Pakenham noted that existing charter services were doing only three per cent of the volume of business undertaken by the corporations. By 1959 independent operators were responsible for something like 25 per cent of the air passenger mileage of British-based concerns.[41]

So long as Lord Pakenham's directive guided policy the corporations were not greatly disturbed by the growth of the private sector. When Silver City Airways (later merged with British United Airways) started a car ferry service between Lympne and Le Touquet in 1948 BEA decided that it would not be diverted from its principal effort of improving its scheduled passenger services by the development of such a sideline.[42] The first Annual Report of BEA disclosed 'We have not sought to offer our own aircraft for charter work on any substantial scale, but we have acted as intermediaries in arranging charters for the charter companies'.[43] While air transport was at a stage of rapid expansion there was scope for a division of labour. The corporations concentrated on improving the reliability, speed and comfort of the regular scheduled passenger services; the private companies specialised in chartering, in round tours and in car ferrying.

Principally because the advantage in travelling time by air was marginal for distances under about 250 miles (except in instances where the surface journey included a sea voyage) air passenger travel was of small importance compared with rail or road travel. Even in 1959, when the number of passenger journeys by air within the British Isles had risen to 1,234,000, they were only a tiny fraction of the 1,101,000,000 passenger journeys made by rail.

IV

The general election of 25 October 1951, which resulted in the formation of a Conservative Government, was of great significance for the future of British transport. The victorious party's election manifesto had made unequivocal promises: 'Publicly owned rail and road transport will be reorganised into regional groups of workable size. Private road hauliers will be given the chance to return to business, and private lorries will no longer be crippled by the 25 mile limit.' The new Government lost no time in implementing these pledges. Within a month of the election, in the House of Commons debate on the Address, Sir David Maxwell Fyfe, the Home Secretary, announced that standstill orders had already been issued to the Road Haulage Executive obliging it to postpone, for at least six months, agreement pending for the purchase of between 80 and 90 private haulage firms. On 8 May 1952 the Government's White Paper *Transport Policy* (Cmd 8538) was published, without prior consultation with the BTC, forecasting legislation which would impose on the Commission a duty to dispose of the greater part of its road haulage undertaking and to decentralise the administration of the railways. In justification of the proposed changes it was argued that

In spite of efforts made by the BTC and its executives. integration of its road and rail services into a co-ordinated whole has made little progress and shows little prospect of developing into much more than working arrangements between separate transport entities. Even if integration in the fullest sense were practicable it would result in a huge unwieldy machine, ill adapted to meet with promptitude the varying and instant demands of industry.

The Transport Act, which received royal assent on 6 May 1953, contained two outstanding features. The first was the plan for the return to private ownership of the road transport assets of the RHE: the second was the plan for decentralising the administration of the railways through the setting-up of regional railway boards and the abolition of the Railway Executive.

The road haulage clauses of the 1953 Act masked the triumph in Parliament of the road lobby which, since the 1920s, had superseded the railway interest as the major pressure group with great influence on transport policy. Through the Road Haulage Association, the British Road Federation and other organisations of the commercial motor industry a steadily intensified campaign had been waged for the removal of restraints on private road haulage operation. The Act was a major victory for these forces. Undoubtedly 6 May 1953 was a red letter day in the history of the commercial motor industry.

To enable the BTC to dispose 'as quickly as is reasonably possible' of all property controlled by the RHE a Road Haulage Disposal Board of six persons, nominated by the minister, was established under the Act. The new body was to sell 'transport units' ranging from single vehicles to an upper limit of 50 vehicles, a task which was to be completed 'without delay and on the best terms available'. The BTC was allowed to retain some 4,200 vehicles, including those of the road undertakings formerly owned by the railways, e.g. Carter Patersons and Pickfords. At the same time the restraints imposed by the Transport Act of 1947 on the range of operation of 'A' and 'B' licence commercial vehicles were completely removed as from the end of 1954. Thereafter lorries could be plied for hire beyond the 25-mile limit to which they had been confined since January 1948. To compensate the BTC for the loss of capital assets which would arise from selling at 'knock down' prices vehicles which had been purchased new, a once-for-all graduated transport levy was made payable in 1954 on all road vehicles of over $1\frac{1}{2}$ tons unladen weight.

Although the road haulage clauses of the Act were generally welcomed by commercial motoring interests they were unpopular with the BTC and some businessmen and transport experts. In its 1952 Annual Report the Commission stated that it had not been consulted before the Bill was published but it had made it clear to the Minister that it was 'completely opposed' to the road haulage provisions because of the 'disturbing effect ... the proposals were likely to have upon the efficiency of their services, upon their finances, and their staff'.[44] The journal *Modern Transport* condemned this part of the Act as 'purely destructive and wholly unjustified by the progress which has been made over the last four years by the RHE'.[45] A survey of firms made by Professor A. A. Walters and Mr Calford Sharp in the Birmingham area revealed that although the smaller firms welcomed the Act, some of the larger concerns expressed satisfaction with the nationwide service provided by BRS and were doubtful whether they would find an organisation sufficiently large to handle their traffic after the Road Haulage Disposal Board had completed its task.[46]

There was a stronger case for reorganising the management of the railways, though not necessarily along the lines laid down in the Act. The BTC was itself aware of the need for change. At the end of 1951 it submitted to the Minister proposals for a simplification of the Commission's structure which provided for devolution of authority to regions, combined with the development of road/rail freight traffic under a single commercial management. (This was the policy eventually adopted when the National Freight Corporation was established under the Transport Act of 1968.) However, the Minister held no discussions with the Commission on its proposals and instead went ahead with his own plans. The Transport Act, 1953, required the BTC, 'within twelve months of the passing of the Act, or such longer time as the Minister might direct' to submit a scheme for the reorganisation of British railways including the abolition of the Railway Executive and the setting up of area authorities. Only the London Transport Executive was to remain untouched. In the event the Minister intervened first. By the BTC Executive's Order, issued on 19 August 1953, all the executives, with the exception of that for London Transport, were abolished as from 1 October 1953 and their functions transferred to the Commission. The BTC's own plans, as approved by the Minister, were eventually published as a White Paper, *Railways Reorganisation Scheme* (Cmd 9191), in July 1954. The new structure (which, in the event, lasted only until 1963 when the BTC was abolished under the Transport Act of 1962) was as follows:

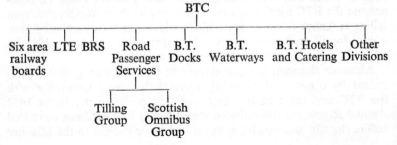

BTC
—
Six area | LTE | BRS | Road | B.T. | B.T. | B.T. Hotels | Other
railway | | | Passenger | Docks | Waterways | and Catering | Divisions
boards | | | Services

Tilling | Scottish
Group | Omnibus
Group

The most justifiable part of the 1953 Act was that concerning railway charges. The keynote of the new measure was, after all, 'competition', and it was therefore only logical that, in order to allow the railways to compete with road transport, existing restrictions on their charging policy, some of which dated from as far back as the Railway Clauses Consolidation Act of 1845, should be abolished. All the traditional restraints about equality of charges, undue preference, etc. were swept away and, subject only to satisfying the Transport Tribunal, the Commission was now at liberty to frame its charges on a completely new set of principles.

What was the effect of the Transport Act of 1953 on the viability of the BTC as an undertaking and the progress of the different forms of transport? The most immediate and damaging effects were to be seen in the road haulage business. The morale of the staff of British Road Services was adversely affected. The situation of those in charge of this large enterprise has been forcefully depicted by Mr Pryke:

> Having successfully accomplished the immense and exhilarating administrative task of taking over nearly 3,800 separate firms and 42,000 vehicles, and having welded them into a unified organisation, they were now faced with an equally enormous, but this time heart-breaking task of destroying their handiwork.[47]

The denationalisation of road haulage was a process speedily completed. The disposal of vehicles did not begin until January 1954 and was virtually complete two years later. Because the organisation was not able to reduce its white collar staff as rapidly as it did its drivers and maintenance workers, it was left, for a time, with a top-heavy and less productive labour force. Between the end of 1953 and the end of 1956 output per man-hour fell by over ten per cent. Owing to the effects of the Suez crisis it fell still further in 1957. Thereafter came recovery, and by 1959 productivity was higher than ever before.[48] Profits slumped from £8·7 million, equal to 12·2 per cent on net fixed assets, in 1954, to £1·8 million, or 4·8 per cent, in 1956. In the meantime the Government had second thoughts on the advisability of continued sales of BRS vehicles. On 11 July 1955 Mr Boyd-Carpenter, the Minister of Transport and Civil Aviation, told the House of Commons that as the main objects of the Act had been achieved and 15,688 road haulage vehicles of the Commission's fleet of over 42,000 vehicles had already been sold and other sales were in the offing, the government were considering allowing the Commission to retain 8,000 vehicles originally intended for disposal. These were mainly employed in long-distance work and 'rendered efficient service to industry'.[49] The Transport (Disposal of Road Haulage Property) Act of 2 August 1956 gave effect to this intention. The Road Haulage Disposal Board was abolished. The Commission was allowed to retain over 10,000 vehicles instead of the 3,500 envisaged in the 1953 Act. From 9 September 1956 the vehicles controlled by the Commission were operated through five companies: British Road Services Ltd (general haulage); BRS Pickfords (special traffic and some contracts); BRS (Contract) Ltd; BRS (Parcels) Ltd; and BRS Meat Haulage Ltd. With the exception of BRS (Parcels) Ltd these proved financially viable undertakings.

The effect of the abolition of the operational limits for 'A' and 'B' licensed vehicles was less damaging to the business of the BTC and to the railways in particular than was the growth in the number of 'C' licences. Whereas the combined total of 'A' and 'B' licences rose from 158,400 in 1954 to 238,000 in 1968, or by just over 50 per cent, the number of 'C' licences increased from 834,200 to 1,263,000, or by 66 per cent. In the 21 years following the end of the Second World War the number of 'C' licences multiplied four times: 'A' and 'B' licences rose by only 63 per cent. It is therefore arguable that the Labour Government, by conceding an unlimited range of operation to 'C' licence vehicles, did more damage to the prospects of a policy of transport integration than did the Conservatives in abolishing the 25-mile limit for 'A' and 'B' licence operators under the Transport Act of 1953.[50]

The BTC's obligation to draft a plan for the reorganisation of railway administration and the need to establish the six regional Railway Boards after 1954 tended to divert talent and resources away from the vital tasks of improving the railways' technical efficiency. In 1968 Sir Stanley Raymond, on the point of retiring from the Chairmanship of the British Railways Board, complained that in 21 years of service to public transport nearly half his time had been devoted to 'organisation, reorganisation, acquisition, denationalisation, centralisation and decentralisation'.[51] Decentralisation of railway operation was carried too far after 1953. One consequence of giving greater powers to the regional boards for the organisation of their traffic was 'a ridiculously cross-purpose working of empty waggons'.[52] According to A. J. Pearson, who was a member of the railways' administrative staff at the time, decentralisation often had to be changed as soon as it was introduced; it was 'so obviously inefficient'.[53] Under the policy of decentralisation the railway workshops were controlled by the regions. This made it more difficult for the much needed policy of specialisation to take place.

The important work of giving effect to the 1953 Act's valuable provisions concerning railway rates and charges was much delayed through the activity of the Transport Tribunal. The Commission handed its draft scheme to the Tribunal in March 1955 after discussing it with the Traders' Co-ordinating Committee and other representative bodies of railway users. But the public enquiry before the Tribunal lasted 44 days and no less than 21 counsel were employed by the Commission between July 1955 and March 1956. It was not until 1 July 1957 that the new charges scheme could be put into operation. Classification by value, the obligation to avoid undue discrimination, bans on agreed charges, all disappeared. In their place consignment weight and loadability, together with an elementary form of route and terminal differentiation, became the main criteria for determining charges. The larger and more manageable the load and the longer the distance it was to be carried the lower would be the charge per ton-mile. At last, from the summer of 1957, the railways were free to charge rates which would help attract the kind of traffic they were best suited to carry and to deter consignments more suitable for road transport.[54]

One casualty of the reshuffle of public transport management was the Modernisation Plan for the railways prepared by the Commission in 1954 but not published until the following year.[55] It is arguable that the plan would have been produced earlier and, more importantly, that it would have been more carefully researched and more realistic in its recommendations, if it had not been for the competing claims on the time of the members of the Commission. There is much evidence that the Plan was hastily conceived and ill thought out 'and that it was accepted by the Ministry and the Government on the grounds that anything was better than nothing'.[56] The Commission stated that the main objective of its proposals was 'to exploit the great natural advantages of railways as bulk transporters of passengers and goods and to revolutionise the character of the services provided for both, not only by the full utilisation of modern equipment but also by purposeful concentration on those functions which the railways can be made to perform more efficiently than other forms of transport'. The outstanding innovations proposed were the substitution of diesel and electric traction for steam power, the introduction of modern track and signalling equipment, the complete overhaul of freight services by a modernisation of the rolling stock and methods of organisation and the transformation of stations and passenger rolling stock. The original estimate was that the plan would cost £1,240 million over fifteen years but in 1957 this was revised to £1,660 million. Re-appraisals of the plan by the Commission took place on two occasions, in 1956 and 1959, the second being published as a White Paper, *Re-appraisal of the Plan for the Modernisation and Re-equipment of British Railways* (Cmd 813).

By the end of the 1950s it was apparent that modernisation had not fulfilled the optimistic hopes that had been expressed about it five years earlier. As Tables 12 and 13 reveal, in 1959 the net ton-miles of goods traffic carried reached the lowest level since nationalisation and the overall deficit on operations at £84·8 million was lower only than that of 1958. The reasons for this disappointing outcome are complex and varied. For more than a century the railways' biggest revenue earners had been coal and coke. Owing to industrial depression in the heavy industries and the switch to new sources of power the quantity of coal and coke carried on the railways fell sharply. Between 1954 and 1959 ton-mileage declined from 10,488 million to 8,004 million, a decline of more than one fifth in the most important commodity trade of the railways. However, the decline in mineral traffic was proportionately almost as great. The 1950s was a decade of very rapid structural change in the economy when the nation's reliance on the old basic industries was greatly reduced and new light industries were supplanting them. What was happening during these years was described by the Geddes Committee on Carriers' Licensing in the following terms:

A substantial part of the fall in the total volume of rail traffic arises from a decline in the transport needs of traditional rail users. The growth in road transport equally owes much to the development of industries for whose work road is specially suitable. In the overall change which has taken place there must have been an element of transfer of traffic from rail to road, but this element is probably a minor part of the whole.[57]

A second important reason for the disappointing results of the Modernisation Plan was that in 1955 there was less obvious scope for economy than there had been in 1948. At the time of nationalisation the easiest economy to introduce was the reduction in the railway labour force—reduced from 625,000 in 1948 to 577,000 in 1954— and the closure of the more obviously unremunerative stations and depots. But this early phase had been largely completed by 1955 and the economies in operational costs envisaged in the Plan through the employment of new locomotive power, more efficient rolling stock and track and signalling improvements, required heavy additional capital outlay and would only yield dividends over a longer span of time. The locomotive and freight rolling stock changes brought about during the late 1950s illustrate this predicament of the Commission. In 1955 steam was still king on British Railways. Three years later diesel locomotives, which were to produce the most spectacular gains in productivity, were responsible for less than ten per cent of the train mileage. But after that date progress was very rapid. By the time of the Beeching Report in 1963 steam power had ceased to be the main form of traction and by 1968 Britain was ahead of France and Germany in displacing old forms of locomotive power. It was an advance achieved at damaging cost to the Commission's finances. Because of the haste with which the operation was mounted big mistakes were made. As many as 32 of the 64 diesel locomotives supplied by the North British Locomotive Company—a firm which was shortly after bankrupted—had to be scrapped as useless soon after delivery. The remaining 32 required expensive modifications before they could be used.[58] The overdue electrification of the London–Birmingham line and the Glasgow suburban services was also costly and at the same time disruptive of existing steam services, with consequent losses in punctuality and passenger goodwill. In its report for 1959 the Central Transport Consultative Committee reported that 'unpunctuality of trains causes the greatest number of complaints by passengers'.

The Modernisation Plan stated that the number of railway waggons would be reduced from 1,100,000 in 1954 to 750,000 in 1974 and that turn-round time would be cut by 30 per cent. But by the end of 1961 the number of waggons had only been reduced to 940,000 and the average turn-round time was 15 per cent worse than in 1954, principally because of inadequate cooperation between the regional boards. Whereas the Plan noted that there were conclusive arguments for concentrating railway freight at a smaller number of goods depots, progress made was slow. In the seven years 1954–61 the number of freight depots was cut by only 12 per cent.[59]

Quite apart from the important social reasons for the retention of many of the branch lines it is a mistake to assume that their earlier closure could have made anything but a marginal contribution to the balancing of the Commission's accounts. In the 1950s savings from closures were little over £4 million annually. In 1958 the Commission's overall deficit was £105 million. Closure would have come more rapidly had it not been for the hope that dieselisation would reduce operating costs and boost revenue. There was every justification for a degree of optimism. In 1957 it was found that movement costs per train were reduced by 63 per cent where passenger stopping services were dieselised. On 22 important schemes there was an average increase of passenger receipts, following dieselisation, of 34 per cent. The trouble was that as private motoring increased the gains in branch-line revenue did not prove lasting.[60]

A much more important reason for the unbalanced accounts of the Commission was the unrealistic state of the railways' capital debt and the heavy burden of interest payments arising from it. Since nationalisation the railways had been required to make their contribution to the Central Charges—principally the interest on British Transport 3 per cent stock. But by the close of the 1950s the old physical assets of the railways were shrinking as a result of the policy of closures. However, there was the additional obligation to pay high rates of interest on the money borrowed for modernisation. Before 1948 the railway companies were able to cushion the adverse financial effects of years of trade depression by cutting dividends on ordinary stock. No loophole of this kind was available to the BTC which had no equity capital. By the early 1950s the situation had deteriorated so seriously that the railways were having to find revenue to pay interest on funds borrowed to meet deficiencies in their interest payment of previous years. In the average of the years 1956–62 interest charges amounted to the equivalent of two-thirds of the BTC's total deficits. In most European countries the railways' accounts had for many years been balanced by a process known as 'normalisation' i.e. by the state's making good any deficiency in receipts where the railway had been required to maintain a service for social reasons. This policy was not adopted in Britain until 1968.[61]

After the passing of the Transport Act in 1953 the BTC's 2,000 miles of inland waterways passed from the control of the Docks and Inland Waterways Executive to the newly created British Transport Waterways. The change in name and style of management made little appreciable difference to the business of British canals. Under the Executive's management the volume of traffic carried rose from a post-war level of ten million tons to a peak of $12\frac{3}{4}$ million tons in 1953. Even at this higher level of activity the work performed—approximately 200 million ton-miles a year—was less than 1/100th of that of the railways. In the early 1950s coal accounted for about half the tonnage carried on both canals and railways; but whereas the average canal haul was only 14 miles the average haul on the railways was 56 miles. Apart from coal, the commodities carried on the canals, in order of importance, were petroleum, grain and flour, timber, chemicals, iron and steel. It was still advantageous to use the waterways for large, bulky consignments where there were favourable conditions of trans-shipment. In 1951 a BTC statement identified the main cargoes which were waterborne inland as 'traffic imported and for shipment in the ports connected with the inland waterways, particularly where overside exchange between ship and barge occurs, and trunk haul to river or canal waterheads with subsequent delivery by road'.[62] The Commission's statement was issued before the undermining of the policy of transport integration following the 1953 Act and before the impressive growth of road haulage by articulated diesel trucks. The new lorries of the 1950s could easily carry a load of 15 tons single-manned a distance of 150 miles in a day and distances and loads were rapidly increasing. Compared with this achievement of 2,250 ton-miles per day, a pair of narrow boats with two men in charge and with a total cargo of 55 tons covered about 35 miles in a day or a ton mileage of 960—less than half the performance of the motor vehicles.[63] Commercial motor developments were making it clear that continued commercial viability would only be possible on the canals and rivers where larger boats, or trains of boats, with correspondingly large consignments of goods were able to navigate.

In 1954 the Conservative government asked Lord Rusholme to head a Board of Survey to find out whether all possible steps were being taken to ensure that the maximum economic advantage was being derived from the canal system under the Commission's control. In its report, published on 12 April 1955, it recommended that 336 miles of inland waterways should be further developed, that a further 994 miles should be kept serviceable and that 771 miles which cost the Commission £200,000 annually had not 'sufficient justification to justify their retention for navigation'. The Rusholme survey was essentially an internal investigation sponsored by the BTC. The Bowes Committee, which reported in the following year, was an independent body appointed by the Minister of Transport. It reached conclusions broadly similar to those of its predecessor. The inland waterways were divided into three categories: Class 'A', the big barge navigations which were worth developing, Class 'B', mainly the narrow canals which nevertheless carried some commercial traffic and were worth maintaining in their existing state and Class 'C' waterways which had no further use as commercial navigations. A new departure in the Bowes Committee report was the greater emphasis given to the amenity value of the canals. It was urged that a special body should be appointed to look into the future of the Class 'C' waterways including their possible development for recreational purposes. In 1959 the Government followed Mr Leslie Bowes' advice and appointed a Redevelopment Advisory Committee which submitted several confidential reports to the Minister of Transport over the next three years.

While there was much public discussion on the future role of Britain's inland waterways there was a growing reluctance on the part of business firms to make use of them. The total tonnage of goods passing over the waterways decreased by 8 per cent between 1954 and 1962; the ton-mileage fell even more—by 13 per cent. The decline in traffic was reflected in mounting deficits on BTC waterways: the shortfall of receipts in 1954 had been a modest £153,000; by 1962 it had mounted to £1,068,000.[64]

Following the Conservatives' general election victory on 8 October 1959 the Minister of Transport in the new government, Mr Ernest Marples, appointed a Special Advisory Group under the chairmanship of Sir Ivan Stedeford, and including Dr Richard Beeching (later Lord Beeching) as one of its members, to examine the organisation of the BTC. Although the group's recommendations were not made public, it is believed that they were more critical of the structure of management of the Commission than was the Select Committee on the Nationalised Industries which was making its investigations at about the same time.[65] It is likely that they influenced the Prime Minister, Mr Harold Macmillan, who made a statement of the Government's intentions in the House of Commons on 10 March 1960. He declared that the reorganisation envisaged would include 'decentralisation of management so that individual undertakings, including the Regions of British Railways, should as far as practicable, be made fully self-accounting and responsible for the management of their own affairs'.[66] In December 1960 the government's intentions were elaborated in a more guarded fashion in a White Paper, *Reorganisation of the Nationalised Transport Undertakings* (Cmd 1248). Nevertheless there was a broad hint of future plans. 'The activities of the British Transport Commission,' it was asserted, were 'so large and diverse' that it was 'virtually impossible to run them effectively as a single undertaking.' The Transport Act 1962 gave legislative effect to most of the proposals contained in the White Paper.

The new Act largely completed the process of dismemberment begun nine years earlier. The Transport Commission was abolished and its assets transferred to separate and independent Boards for British Railways, London Transport, British Transport Docks and Inland Waterways. Road transport, hotel and other assets were to be managed by a Transport Holding Company. The new organisational structure is summarised as follows:

Minister of Transport

—Nationalised Transport Advisory Council

British Railways Board	London Transport Board	British Transport Docks Board	British Waterways Board	Transport Holding Company

Regional Railway Boards

British Road Services	Tilling (Buses) Group	Scottish Omnibuses Group	Hotels	Road Freight Shipping Service	Thos. Cook & Sons Ltd	Other Holdings

The Transport Holding Company was the first example of a publicly owned enterprise which had a holding company structure.

The big change from the situation which had existed between 1948 and 1962 was the absence of a unifying authority of any kind such as had been exercised by the British Transport Commission. The National Transport Advisory Council, appointed by the Minister, was no substitute. It could 'advise' and make recommendations to the Minister 'on questions relating to the co-ordination or any other aspect, of the nationalised transport undertakings'. But as it had no executive powers there seemed much less likelihood of any serious effort being made to integrate the different transport services.

In introducing the Act to the House of Commons Mr Marples, the Minister of Transport, stressed that each of the new Boards would have a large measure of independence, with responsibility for its own capital debt and financial performance. They would have much more commercial freedom than was allowed in the days of the British Transport Commission. Many of the most important features of the Act were consistent with this new approach. Although the London Transport Board was an exception, all the other Boards were given blanket powers under Section 43(3) to 'take and recover such charges for their services and facilities, subject to such terms and conditions, as they think fit'. The Boards also had power to use any surplus land in their possession for commercial development (Section 11 (2)) and construct and operate pipelines (Section 12 (a)). But commercial freedom was not carried through, its logical conclusion when there was any possibility of nationalised industries competing with private industry. The Boards could engage in manufacture to meet their own requirements for equipment but 'creeping Socialism' was to be barred. Under Section 13 they were forbidden to diversify production or to sell to customers other than the new Boards. Thus neither the Holding Company, British Rail or London Transport had power to sell petrol or spare parts for cars at parking sites or bus depots.

The limitation on the manufacturing and selling freedom of the nationalised undertakings was nothing new. Successive Ministers of Transport since the mid-1950s had directed the switching of orders for new equipment from the publicly owned to privately owned concerns. Seventy-five per cent of new locomotives were built in British Railways Board workshops in 1957. Only 39 per cent were so built in 1962. In respect of manufacturing activities Sir Brian Robertson, Chairman of BTC, told the Select Committee on Nationalised Industries that 'We have had a considerable amount, if I may say so, of pressure brought to bear on us from several quarters on this matter', and explained that this meant industry on one side and the trade unions on the other.[67]

BTC's capital debt 1962	£2,450m.
To be written off	475
Capital debt remaining	1,975
Railways' debt	1,575
Other public transport	400
Railways' debt made up of:	
interest-bearing capital	900
debt carried in suspense	675

Source: Speech of Mr Marples, *Hansard*, 5th series, vol. 649, 20 November 1961, Col 942.

It was consistent with the new commercial principles which imbued the Act that there was a realistic scaling-down of capital debt. The changes effected in this important sphere are summarised in the table on p. 339.

The Treasury was made responsible for the debt written off; the £900 million of interest-bearing capital was the cost of new equipment since modernisation began; the £675 million left in suspense represented the Government's optimistic hope that at least some of these written-down book assets of the pre-1956 railways might some day earn interest. In many respects Sections 36-40, which dealt with these changes, were the most constructive and helpful parts of the Act. There is nothing so depressing to morale as to work in an organisation which is hopelessly 'in the red'. From 1963 British Rail could start with a clean slate.

The early 1960s have often been described as the Beeching Era of British railways. On 1 June 1961 Dr Richard (later Lord) Beeching was brought in from the board of Imperial Chemical Industries to serve as chairman of the British Transport Commission during its closing months. When the 1962 Transport Act came into operation on 1 January 1963 Dr Beeching was appointed chairman of the new British Railways Board. His resignation at the end of May 1965 ended a comparatively brief spell of only four years' service to public transport. They were years of rapid and momentous change.

The Beeching Report, *The Reshaping of British Railways*, which was published early in 1963 was based on a traffic costing survey made in 1961. This was an investigation with the limited aim of finding out which parts of the railway system were profitable financially and which were not. At the same time as Dr Beeching was organising his important investigation other enquiries were in progress into Rural Bus Services and into docks and harbours. What was lacking was that kind of comprehensive survey of transport made by the Royal Commission between 1928 and 1930. Within the limits of his too narrow brief Dr Beeching made as thorough an investigation into the costs of railway operation as had ever been made. The difficulty was that the Report covered one facet of the transport problem only and gave little consideration to the repercussions of proposed changes in railway policy on the costs of alternative forms of transport. The Report revealed that one third of the route mileage of railways carried only one per cent of the total passenger miles and only one and a half per cent of the freight ton-miles (pp. 62-4); that a mere 118 stations, out of 2,067 dealing with freight, carried 52 per cent of the traffic (pp. 72-3); that on half the route miles traffic density was so low that it scarcely sufficed to cover the basic costs of covering the route, i.e. track and signalling, without any allowance for operating costs, and that on the other half there was enough traffic to cover route costs more than six times (p. 10). As much as £131 million of the total losses of £172 million were accounted for in 1961 by stopping passenger trains and general merchandise traffic.[68] The profitable business of the railways was the carriage of coal and train loads of goods carried from siding to siding and the transport of passengers by express trains linking major conurbations. Much emphasis was given to the railways' surplus capacity in relation to traffic demand. Of the total of 18,500 gangwayed coaches available for fast and semi-fast services only 5,500 were in use all the year round: most of the remainder were used only in holiday and other peak periods (p. 15). At least 348,000 of the 848,591 waggons on the books were surplus to real need (pp. 46–8).

The remedy Dr Beeching proposed was a drastic one. Over 5,000 route miles, and 2,363 stations out of some 7,000, would be closed to passenger traffic. Stations receiving coal would be reduced from 5,000 to 'a few hundred'. Every encouragement would be given to traffic carried in full train loads and the number of liner trains would be expanded. The Report did not completely ignore the social consequences. Under the heading 'Total Social Benefit' the comment was made: 'It might pay to run railways at a loss in order to prevent the incidence of an even greater cost which would arise elsewhere if the railways were closed. Such other costs may be deemed to arise from congestion, provision of parking space, injury and death, additional road building or a number of other causes.' However, the stringent costing exercise which was applied to the railways was not applied to the effect on the community of greater congestion of roads by heavy commercial vehicles. Apart from the general statement 'It is not thought that any of the firm proposals put forward in this Report would be altered by the introduction of new factors for the purpose of judging overall social benefit' and the concession that an exception would have to be made in the case of commuter services in the big cities, there was no attempt to consider the effects of the far-reaching changes proposed on the transport system as a whole, let alone amenity considerations. Dr Beeching stuck to his brief and these questions were outside it. In the House of Commons, Jeremy Thorpe warned that if the Minister of Transport was to follow the Report and 'decide railways policy in isolation from transport problems generally' it would be 'like a judge making up his mind on the evidence of one expert witness'.[69]

Following the Beeching Report the process of pruning the dead wood of the old railway system and introducing modern equipment and operating methods was greatly accelerated. The waggon fleet, which still numbered 862,640 at the end of 1962, was down to 637,608 two years later, a reduction of 24·9 per cent. Over the same two years, 4,000 new steel waggons, including coal waggons with a capacity of over 20 tons, were brought into service.[70] Even in 1962 virtually all suitable merchandise waggons had been fitted with continuous vacuum brakes enabling nearly half the freight train mileage to be covered by express trains.[71] Between 1961 and 1968 waggon turn-round time improved by 25 per cent and ton-miles carried per ton of waggon capacity improved by as much as 90 per cent.[72] The London Midland electrification was held back for some years after 1961 because of Mr Marples' reluctance to authorise the additional expenditure, but elsewhere, where plans could be completed, the increase in passenger traffic was very encouraging. On the Southern Region's Kent coast lines the increase of passenger revenue exceeded the 50-60 per cent anticipated.[73] Following the eventual completion of the London–Manchester–Liverpool electrification in April 1966, there was 'a dramatic increase in train speeds of up to 100 m.p.h. and an upsurge of 50 per cent in passenger receipts and 65 per cent in passenger journeys, some of which were recaptured from air'.[74] In the early 1960s British Railways were over-manned in relation to route mileage and traffic carried by comparison with other European railway systems. This was no longer the case by the end of the decade. The number of staff employed fell by more than half between 1963 and 1970 when there were only 273,063 persons on the books (compared with 641,000 in 1948).[75]

Before leaving the service of the British Railways Board Dr Beeching was responsible for the publication of one other report, *The Development of the Major Trunk Routes*, published early in 1965. This concerned the 7,500 route miles of the surviving total of 16,000 route miles which were the main arteries of rail traffic. Even on this limited part of the track, so it was argued, there was an unnecessary duplication of facilities and in order to ensure the most economic utilisation of lines it was proposed that new investment should be concentrated on a mere 3,000 miles of the system. Traffic from those parts of the 7,500 miles of the trunk routes which were under-utilised would then be transferred to the highly modernised nucleus where it would be carried in swift-moving and highly profitable liner trains. The whole exercise was based on estimates of what traffic would be available in 1984 rather than on that which existed in 1964. Although it was denied in the report that the failure to select a route for intensive development implied its subsequent abandonment, there was a strong suspicion among Dr Beeching's critics that this was the next step intended. However, between the preparation of the report and its publication the Conservative government was defeated in the general election of 15 October 1964 and Mr J. Fraser, who became Minister of Transport in the new Labour administration, soon indicated that there was going to be a second look at the question of rail closures. By 1 June 1965 Dr Beeching had left BRB to return to ICI.

At one of his last Press conferences, held on 16 February 1965, Dr Beeching said that full implementation of the trunk-line proposals would bring about savings of between £50 million and £100 million a year. If these plans were coupled with the closures recommended in the Reshaping Report British railways could run 'at a good profit'. On 20 December 1967 Mr John Morris, on behalf of the Ministry of Transport, stated that 84 per cent of the passenger train withdrawals and 72 per cent of the station closures listed in the 1963 Beeching Report had been implemented. There were also some startling improvements in operating efficiency. In 1969 127 express trains daily were averaging over 75 m.p.h.; this was a greater number than were averaging 60 m.p.h. in 1939. Freight charges fell substantially. Between 1957 and 1968 the charges for general goods traffic declined by 35 per cent. For all goods, other than coal and coke, the fall was in the order of 28 per cent over the same period of time. Although part of this change was due to a change in the composition of the traffic—more oil and cement (with low charges) were carried in place of the higher-priced coal—the main reason was the concentration on train loads rather than wagon loads and on longer hauls. By these means charges for petroleum products fell by 43 per cent between 1962 and 1966 and charges for cement fell by 15 per cent.[76]

Despite these impressive gains in productivity, the profits anticipated by Dr Beeching did not materialise, the two years 1969 and 1970 being the only exceptions, as Table 17 illustrates.

Table 17 *British Railways Board financial results, 1963–70*

Year	Passenger receipts £m.	Freight receipts £m.	Total gross receipts £m.	Total working expenses £m.	Current operating return £m.	Interest £m.	Overall surplus or deficit £m.
1963	161·8	235·4	468·7	550·2	−81·6	59·9	−135·6
1964	167·2	233·0	474·1	541·6	−67·5	60·8	−123·3
1965	173·5	225·5	472·6	545·7	−73·1	63·2	−134·8
1966	179·4	216·9	470·4	542·1	−71·7	65·0	−135·5
1967	179·7	194·8	445·9	536·1	−90·6	66·5	−153·0
1968	185·2	204·3	463·7	547·1	−83·4	67·3	−147·4
1969	205·4*	195·4	539·2	491·7	48·6	41·5	14·7
1970	227·8*	208·2	571·5	530·2		42·2	9·5

* In 1969 and 1970 Passenger receipts do not include 'Social Service' grants from the Government of £61 million.

Source: BRB Annual reports and accounts.

A significant change which occurred during these years was that in 1969 and 1970, for the first time since 1852, the railways' receipts from passenger traffic were greater than receipts from goods. This was largely due to the success of new fast inter-city services. The principal reason for the poor financial performance of the railways was the decline in freight traffic. The biggest drop was in the carriage of coal and coke, which had provided the railways with the greater part of their freight for over a century. Between 1957 and 1968 railway carryings of these fell from 167 million tons to 123 million, a reduction of over a quarter. At the same time the average length of their haul fell by 13 per cent due to electricity power stations, whose rail haul of coal and coke was only half the national average, taking a greatly increased proportion of the total amount rail-borne.[77] Dr Beeching had forecast a decline in this traffic but had been wildly over-optimistic in the ability of liner, merry-go-round and company trains to more than make up the deficiency. The physical performance of the railways in the period 1963-70 is summarised in Table 18:

Table 18 *British Railways traffic, 1963-70*

Year	Passenger journeys (m.)	Estimated passenger miles (m.)	Total (m. tons)	Freight Net ton-miles (m.)		
				Total	Coal and coke	All other freight train traffic
1963	938·4	19,230	292·8	15,398	7,805	7,593
1964	927·6	19,874	291·6	16,052	7,470	8,582
1965	865·1	18,713	283·9	15,429	7,005	8,424
1966	835·0	18,453	275·2	14,825	6,868	7,957
1967	837·4	18,089	250·3	13,609	5,997	7,612
1968	831·1	17,835	263·4	14,693	6,277	8,416
1969	805·2	18,400	255·5	15,258	6,307	8,951
1970	823·9	18,895	270·6	16,394	6,247	10,145

Sources: Annual reports and accounts British Railways Board *Annual Abstract of Statistics*, 1971.

While the organisation and activities of British railways were being radically reshaped the pattern of domestic air transport organisation was changing more gradually. The Conservative party's belief in the suitability of competition as a policy for all types of transport found reflection in the encouragement given to private airlines in the 1960s. The principal instrument of change was the Civil Aviation (Licensing) Act, 1960, which established a new air service licensing procedure and which ended the exclusive right of the state-owned corporations to operate scheduled air services. It was maintained that there were large loopholes in the licensing rules operated by the Air Transport Advisory Council in the 1950s, by which approved private airlines became 'associates' of BEA, helping to fill in gaps in the scheduled services, and were provided with some of their capital by the state-owned corporation. From 1961 any private airline could apply for a licence to run a service even on the old-established scheduled routes of BEA and BOAC. The only general guideline the new Air Transport Licensing Board had in deciding whether or not to sanction new services was the vaguely worded aim, stated in the Act, 'to further the development of civil aviation'. Seizing the new opportunities open from 1961, a great deal of capital flowed into the private airlines from a variety of sources. By the end of the 1960s a leading shipping company, British and Commonwealth Shipping, owned 92 per cent of the share capital of by far the largest of the private airlines, British United Airways, with assets of £22 million. The remaining eight per cent of the share capital was owned by Eagle Star Insurance. Although official policy was to encourage competition, some of the smaller companies found it impossible to stay in business and the tendency towards amalgamation was a very strong one. By 1963 the Air Holdings Group, which controlled BUA, was responsible for about two-thirds of the traffic flown by private airlines.

The private companies secured most of their business in the package tour and charter trade and in trooping. The air corporations refrained, at the request of the Minister of Civil Aviation, from keeping aircraft specifically available for charter work, with the result that BEA's share in this rapidly expanding business was less than 1/30th of that of the private airlines. The other big business of the private air lines was in trooping, where they enjoyed a complete monopoly. On the scheduled services BEA still enjoyed a great predominance throughout the 1960s. Immediately these scheduled services were thrown open to competition in 1961, BUA and Cunard Eagle, with some other smaller companies, applied to the Air Transport Licensing Board for authority to run on the main domestic routes parallel to BEA but not those to the highly unprofitable Scottish Highlands and Islands. After a mammoth public hearing spread over 18 days, applications were refused on the 'lower' traffic routes between London, Manchester and Liverpool, but once-daily flights conceded on the longer flights to Glasgow, Edinburgh and Belfast. Cunard Eagle's appeal for a more frequent service was rejected by the appeals Commissioner in October 1963 on the grounds that it would undermine the viability of the BEA's services. Nevertheless on 9 March 1964 the Minister reversed the decision of the nine members of the Board and the Commissioner and allowed the private company more frequent services. This was one of the reasons for the continued unprofitability of BEA's domestic services. Despite these discouragements, the corporation made overall profits in every year from 1955–70 inclusive with the exceptions of 1962–3 and 1968.

Between 1960 and 1970 the number of passengers carried by air on domestic routes more than doubled from 2,240,000 to 5,366,000. Of these totals BEA carried 1,425,484, or 60 per cent, in 1960 and 3,148,751, or 59 per cent, in 1970. At the end of the 1960s BEA and its 'associated' companies were holding their own on the scheduled domestic air routes but they were responsible for a shrinking proportion of total passenger carryings, principally because of the great increase in the number of private charter flights. Whereas the independent companies had been responsible for only ten per cent of total passenger journeys in 1960 ten years later their share had increased to one quarter. Between them BEA and the private airlines carried relatively insignificant quantities of freight. From 22,796 short tons in 1960 there was an increase to 71,257 short tons in 1970.[78]

The results of 13 years of Government encouragement of competition, changes in the efficiency of different forms of transport and the growth of new industries with new patterns of demand may now be considered. In the movement of freight the decision made in 1953 to remove all restraints on the range of operation of road haulage vehicles and the simultaneous decision to sell off the majority of BRS vehicles led to a huge upsurge in the number of commercial vehicles licensed for use. The total grew from 922,700 in 1952 to 1,520,000 in 1964. What was particularly noteworthy was the growth of long-distance road haulage and the increase in numbers of heavy lorries, as Table 19 indicates.

Table 19 *Goods carriage by commercial vehicles of 3 tons and over unladen weight*

Year	Number of vehicles	Traffic carried m. ton-miles	1952–62 increase %
1952	89,000	84·3	
1958	157,000	306·7	
1962	292,000	573·2	597
1970	422,000		

Sources: *Annual Abstracts of Statistics*. Ministry of Transport, *Survey of Road Goods Transport*, 1952. K. F. Glover, 'Statistics of the Transport of Goods by Road', *Jnl Roy. Stat. Socy*, vol. 123, series A, 1960, p. 107.

The increase in the proportion of vehicles of three tons and over to the total number of commercial vehicles is shown in Fig. 29. In long-distance haulage it was the 'C' licensed vehicle which predominated. In the mid-1950s 55 per cent of the tonnage and about half the ton-mileage of goods hauled by road for distances of over 40 miles was carried in vehicles of this class.[79] Inevitably, therefore, the 'C' licensee's

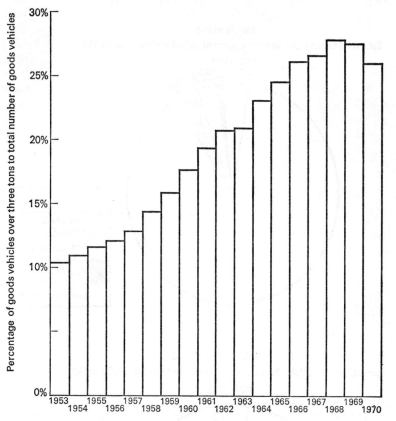

Note: The total number of goods vehicles is that of general goods vehicles and haulage tractors and excludes agricultural and crown vehicles.

Source: Annual Abstract of Statistics.

Figure 29   Percentage Proportion of the Number of Goods Vehicles over Three Tons to the Total Number of Goods Vehicles in Great Britain 1953–69

costs dominated the market for road freights and since the public road carrier could not generally charge more than it would cost the ordinary trader to do the job himself the railway was hardly able to do otherwise. It was the British Railways Board's inability to raise freight charges beyond this ceiling which made it so much more difficult for it to make this side of its business pay its way.

If for some types of traffic the road haulier and 'C' licence operator were able to undercut the railways, one reason for this, apart from the greater flexibility of road transport, was that in many cases main-

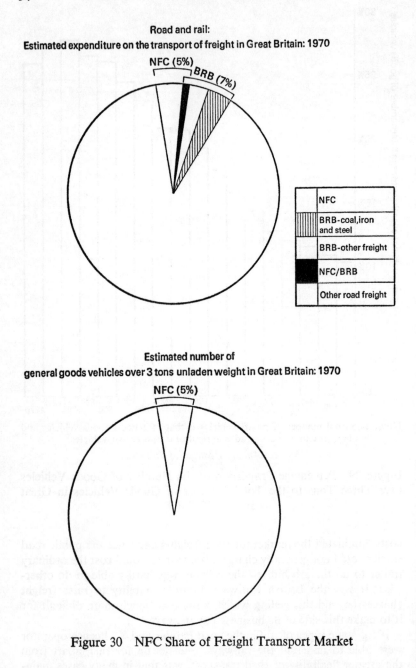

Road and rail:
Estimated expenditure on the transport of freight in Great Britain: 1970

NFC (5%)
BRB (7%)

	NFC
	BRB-coal, iron and steel
	BRB-other freight
	NFC/BRB
	Other road freight

Estimated number of
general goods vehicles over 3 tons unladen weight in Great Britain: 1970

NFC (5%)

Figure 30   NFC Share of Freight Transport Market

tenance work on the vehicles was skimped, lorries were overloaded and their drivers employed for excessive hours. During the Commons' debate on the Beeching Report, Mr Marples, the Minister of Transport was criticised for not subjecting road transport to the same kind of thorough investigation recently made of the railways. In October 1963, therefore, he asked Lord Geddes, a shipowner, businessman and chairman of the British Travel Association, to head a small committee to investigate the commercial vehicle licensing system. The Report, entitled *Carriers' Licensing*, appeared in June 1965. In checks on a sample of 15,000 lorries taken from all parts of the kingdom 'a shocking state of affairs' was revealed, particularly as 'advance warning was given' of the survey in the towns affected. It was found that the legal position was such that it could hardly fail to tempt operators to overload vehicles and that in practice many lorries carried more than is safe. The statutory limits on drivers' hours were widely disregarded and 'the system of enforcement through the examination of records, quite inadequate'.[80]

It must be emphasised that very often it was the convenience, rather than the cost, of road haulage which influenced most traders to prefer that form of transport to rail. In 1966-7 the Edwards Committee of the Ministry of Transport, surveying the behaviour of a sample of 750 firms, found the effects of the relative prices on the mode of transport selected was small. There was a great similarity in the charges made by railway and public road hauliers for many consignments of less than 10 tons. More than half the 'C' licence operators did not know what their road costs were. Speed of delivery was the decisive influence. 'C' licence vehicles delivered 60 per cent of their total consignments on the same day, compared with the road hauliers' 30 per cent and the rails' 10 per cent. No doubt the 'C' licence vehicles had a higher proportion of short hauls than did the public hauliers and the railways, but the traders' experience of quick collection and delivery on the shorter runs no doubt created a habit of mind inimical to the 'hard sell' activities of railways and BRS in the post-Beeching era.[81]

The pattern of distribution of traffic which emerged therefore is as shown in table 20, p. 350.

The changing distribution of freight transport is also shown in Fig. 30. Outstanding among the changes of this era was the decline in the railways' proportion of the goods carried from nearly a quarter to only a tenth; the dominance of the road haulage business, whose share of freight transport rose from less than three-quarters to more than four-fifths; the virtual elimination of canals as commercial goods carriers; the resilience of coastal shipping which, for a brief period in 1966, carried a greater ton-mileage of goods than did the railways; and the emergence of a new carrier, the pipeline, of growing importance

Table 20 *British domestic freight transport, 1938–70*

	1938	%	1952	%	1960	%	1966	%	1970	%
Total (m. tons)			1,498		1,920		1,920		1,976	
Road			900	72	1,192	80	1,615	84	1,670	85
Rail	266		300	24	249	17	214	11	205	10
Coastal Shipping	35		40	3	43	3	52	3	48	2
Inland Waterways	13		10	1	10		8		6	
Pipelines					4		31	2	47	2
Total ton-miles (000s millions)					61·1		76·1		83·3	
Road	8–10		19	37	30·1	49	44·8	59	50·8	61
Rail	16·3		22	43	18·7	31	14·8		16·4	20
Coastal Shipping			10	20	11·9	19	15·5	20	14·2	17
Inland Waterways					0·2		0·1		0·1	
Pipelines					0·2		0·9	1	1·8	2

Sources: K. F. Glover, 'Statistics of the Transport of Goods by Road', *Jnl Roy. Stat. Socy*, vol. 123, Ser. A, 1960, p. 107. K. F. Glover and D. N. Miller, 'The Outlines of the Road Goods Transport Industry', *Jnl Roy. Stat. Socy*, vol. 117, Ser. A, 1954, p. 318. *Annual Abstract of Statistics*, 1971, p. 217. Figures for road and coastal shipping in 1938 are estimates.

not only for petroleum but also for an increasing number of chemical and other products.

V

The Labour Party's general election victory 15 October 1964 resulted in a change of priorities in transport policy which by the end of the decade brought new encouragement to the public sector without appreciably curtailing the freedom of the private operator. In its election manifesto the party had promised 'to draw up a national plan for transport covering the national networks of road, rail and canal communications, properly co-ordinated with air, coastal shipping, and port services'. It was, nevertheless, significant that there was no mention of the renationalisation of road haulage and no promise to re-establish an organisation such as the British Transport Commission with centralised public ownership of some of the principal means of transport. To that extent, in socialist terms, the programme was a retreat from that of the mid-1940s.

In matters of transport the great monument of the Wilson Labour Government of 1964–6 and 1966–70 was the Transport Act of 1968. It cannot be said, as was sometimes said of the previous Labour Government's 1947 Act, that it was a hastily prepared measure. It was preceded by the publication of no less than six White Papers (*Transport Policy*, Cmnd 3057 of 27 July 1966; *British Waterways*, Cmnd 3401 of 7 September 1967; *Railway Policy*, Cmnd of 6 November 1967; *Transport of Freight*, Cmnd 3470 of 16 November 1967; *Public Transport and Traffic*, Cmnd 3481 of 5 December 1967; and *Trans-*

port in London, Cmnd 3686 of 2 July 1968), which gave a substantial foretaste of what was to come. They were the products of teams of experts that Mr J. Fraser, the Minister of Transport, and his successor from 23 December 1965, Mrs Barbara Castle, had brought in to aid the permanent members of the department. The Act, with its 161 clauses and 18 schedules, established an all-time record for length in a measure of this kind. It had three main objectives. The first was described by the Minister as building up 'a new relationship between road and rail' so that they should 'no longer be seen as rivals—almost enemies—but should complement each other'.[82] Since the party had abandoned the idea of renationalising long-distance road haulage a new medium of extending the publicly owned sector of the industry and of making it more attractive to the trader had to be found. The National Freight Corporation, which was created for this purpose, was given the duty in conjunction with the Railways Board,

(i) to provide, or secure or promote the provision of, properly integrated services for the carriage of goods within Great Britain by road and rail, and

(ii) to secure that, in the provision of these services goods are carried by rail whenever such carriage is efficient and economic.

All the undertakings previously associated in the Transport Holding Company together with the British Railway Board's Roadrailer and Tartan Arrow interests and the allied road collection and delivery service (grouped into National Carriers Ltd), were brought under the new Corporation's umbrella. In addition the BRB's freightliner services were transferred to a new subsidiary company, Freightliners Ltd, in which the NFC would hold a 51 per cent share and the BRB 49 per cent. The essential aim of this major reorganisation as stated in the White Paper, *Transport of Freight,* Cmnd 3470, was for the NFC Board 'to set the framework within which its various subsidiaries will operate, rather than to operate them'. This was advisable because 'freight transport is not a single indivisible industry, and flexibility is therefore essential'. In its first Annual Report the Corporation described itself as 'a new and strange animal belonging to no accepted classification, being neither wholly road or wholly rail'.[83] Although the NFC was a large organisation with a capital of £100 million, a labour force of 66,000 and an annual turnover (in 1969) of £170 million, it was responsible for only five per cent of the freight traffic of the nation, measured in terms of annual expenditure, as Fig. 30 illustrates. However, its prospects for growth lay in the development of container services. The government cherished the hope that the new corporation, with its streamlined modern image, would be the exemplar and pacesetter for long-distance goods haulage and that its share of the market would rapidly expand. Doubts were expressed by the opposition in the House of Commons about possible confusion between the roles of railway and road transport under the new dispensation. But the White Paper (Cmnd 3470 p. 4) had made clear what the division of labour was to be. The NFC would 'take commercial responsibility for all the movements which originate by road, leaving the BRB responsible for both the marketing and operation of freight traffic—full train loads, company trains and waggon load traffic—originating by rail'.

The government's plans for the development of the NFC must be seen in conjunction with those for 'quality control' of 'large goods vehicles' i.e. those of about 5 tons unladen weight 16 tons gross weight, contained in Part V of the Act. Under clause 67 these heavy lorries were not to be allowed to carry goods for distances of over 100 miles, or more than ten tons load of certain bulk cargoes, without a special licence, the authorisation of which both BRB and the NFC might oppose on the grounds that the goods might be better carried by rail. The licensing authority was to refuse the application of the road haulier if the rail service offered to the consignee of the goods was 'not less advantageous' than the road transport service. Opposition to Part V of the Bill on the part of the Road Haulage Association was particularly strong because the fate of 100,000 heavy vehicles was at stake. The result was that a two-year time lag was allowed before this part of the Act was to come into force. This saved the day for the road haulage interests. Before the operative date arrived there had been a general election in which the Conservatives, pledged to repeal this part of the Act, had been victorious.

Linked with the policy of 'quantity control' set out in Part V were the proposals contained in Part VI for the increase in taxation on heavy commercial vehicles. Although it had been the case ever since 1933 that the revenue raised from the taxation of motor vehicles exceeded the sums spent on roads, it was widely believed that the financial cost of damage to roads caused by heavy commercial vehicles exceeded their contribution to the treasury in the form of road tax and licence fees. The Bill provided for steeper payments to be made by heavy goods vehicles of 3 tons and over unladen weight. The licence fee for lorries would be £50–190 a year while articulated vehicles would pay between £70 and £210 a year, the size of the fee being proportional to the weight of the vehicle in each case. An extra fee varying from 1s to £5 a mile was to be chargeable where 'abnormal' heavy loads, requiring police escorts, were carried by road. All these proposals for increased taxation of the giants on the road were dropped during the Committee stage in the House of Commons. Since the second reading of the Bill, the 1968–9 Budget had been approved, increasing the rates of vehicle excise duty and fuel oil duty and it was considered unjustifiable to subject operators of heavy commercial vehicles to a double penalty.[84]

Mrs Castle followed the recommendation of the Geddes Committee on Carriers' Licensing to the extent of including in the Bill clauses for the ending of licensing of vehicles of 30 cwt and under, unladen weight. This was a new freedom which applied to over 900,000 vehicles, mainly traders' delivery vans. For vehicles above this unladen weight she did not follow the advice, given in 1965, that all licensing should be ended. The Minister considered that one effective way to tackle the problems of the overloading of lorries and the overworking of drivers disclosed in the Geddes Report would be to institute operators' licences conditional on the proper maintenance of the vehicles and the limitation of drivers' hours to a maximum of 11 per day and 60 per week. In the interests of road safety and to ensure that the legal working hours were not exceeded, the Minister of Transport was given power to have tachographs—time-recording instruments—fitted to the cab of every commercial vehicle. The limitation of the driver's working day applied to coach and bus as well as lorry drivers.

A second major new departure in the 1968 Transport Act was the introduction of 'social service grants' to the railways to enable the unremunerative lines to be kept open where real hardship would be caused by their closure. As deficit followed deficit with monstrous regularity in the late 1950s and early 1960s the Board repeatedly pointed to the branch lines' losses as a major component of the general imbalance. Thus in its annual report for 1965 it emphasised: 'The Railways can never become wholly viable without further action to relieve them of social burdens which, if they must be met, should be financed from sources other than railway revenue'. A policy of deliberate subsidisation of unremunerative services, which it was considered essential in the national interest to maintain, had been followed in France since 1916 and it was the general practice in the European Common Market (EEC) at the time Mrs Castle's Bill was being debated.[85] British governments had had power under the Transport Act 1962 to make good in a general way the deficits incurred by the railways, but the deficits arose from interest charges as well as from the provision of unremunerative services, and the subsidies were not linked to any specific item in the railways' accounts. The 1968 Act broke new ground in obliging BRB to show the finances of the uneconomic services separately in the accounts. The grants were for a period of three years with the possibility, but no certainty, of renewal.

Since the most important immediate reason for the railways' deficits was the heavy burden of interest charges (the 1962 Act had reduced the size of the capital debt, but new capital for modernisation had

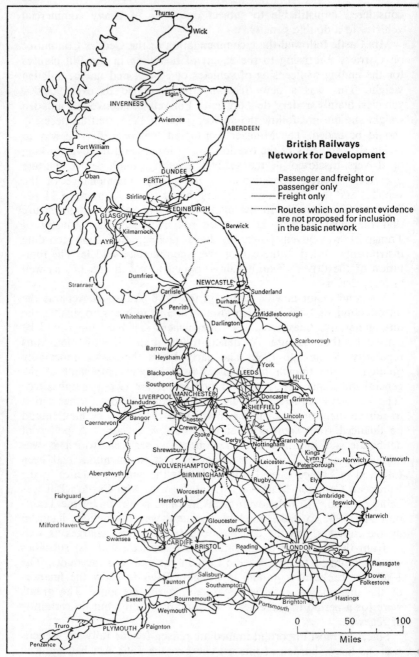

**British Railways
Network for Development**

—— Passenger and freight or
passenger only
— Freight only
········· Routes which on present evidence
are not proposed for inclusion
in the basic network

0   50   100

Miles

Source: H. Pollins, *British Railways and Industrial History,* 1971.

Map 14   The Railway System in 1967

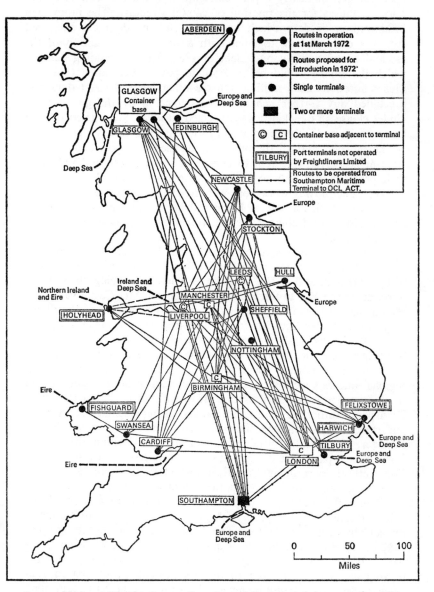

Source: National Freight Corporation, Annual Report and Accounts for 1971.

Map 15   British Rail: Freightliner Services 1972

been charged at nearly 6 per cent annually), the Act contained important clauses for the revision of capital structure. The more than £700 million of debt which had been 'suspended' under the 1962 Act was extinguished, together with a further £557 million of the original commencing capital debt of 1962. The outstanding debt on which the Board would be expected to pay interest after 1969 was thus reduced to £300 million. On the other hand the Act definitely precluded any further general deficit-financing by the government. Under clause 38 the Board was expected either to cover its costs from its revenues or to borrow money at interest to meet any deficiencies.

The railways and all the other nationalised transport undertakings were at last given free rein to engage in manufacture and selling of their products, not only to nationalised concerns, but also in outside markets. The railway workshops were free to manufacture locomotives and rolling stock for sale at home and abroad and petrol and spare parts could be sold and repairs undertaken at publicly owned garages and car parks.

A third major objective of the Act was 'to make it possible for public passenger transport to survive both in the cities where it is being strangled, and in the rural areas where it is being starved'. In introducing the Bill to the House of Commons, Mrs Castle gave as a reason for not re-creating a British Transport Commission the differences in character between freight and passenger transport. Freight transport, she declared, had to be organised 'on national lines' whereas 'passenger transport is much more closely linked to local community life and has important local social implications'.[86] To ensure that regional interests were served, Parts II and III of the Act empowered the Minister to establish Passenger Transport Areas with a Passenger Transport Authority, composed mainly of representatives of local government but with one sixth of their number nominated by the Minister, responsible for all forms of transport within the region. There was a particular obligation to integrate road and rail services. The Authorities could instruct their Passenger Transport Executives to maintain uneconomic services, the cost of which was to be met from local authority funds. Where railway services were concerned the Minister could reimburse the PTA the losses it incurred in maintaining socially necessary services. The Act provided for the setting up of a National Bus Company to acquire the Transport Holding Company's interests in bus companies and bus-manufacturing concerns in England and Wales and to operate through locally based subsidiaries. In 1969, when it commenced operations, the NBC controlled 93 bus companies grouped into 44 operating units which employed 21,000 vehicles and 87,000 staff. The company's activities were managed by regional boards whose areas are shown in Map 16.

The Minister gave VIP treatment to Scotland which was provided

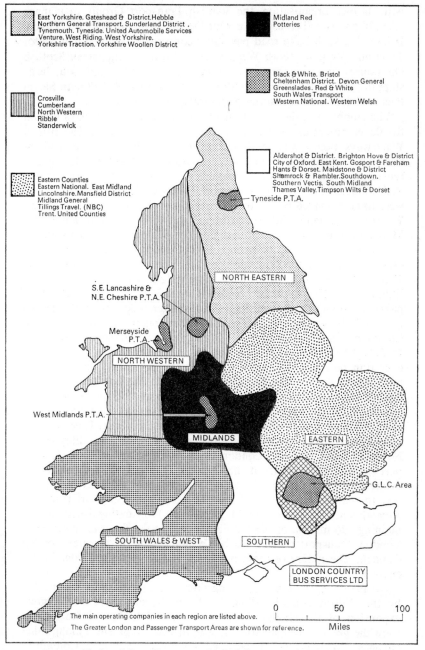

East Yorkshire. Gateshead & District.Hebble
Northern General Transport. Sunderland District .
Tynemouth. Tyneside. United Automobile Services
Venture. West Riding. West Yorkshire.
Yorkshire Traction. Yorkshire Woollen District

Crosville
Cumberland
North Western
Ribble
Standerwick

Eastern Counties
Eastern National. East Midland
Lincolnshire.Mansfield District
Midland General
Tillings Travel. (NBC)
Trent. United Counties

Midland Red
Potteries

Black & White. Bristol
Cheltenham District. Devon General
Greenslades. Red & White
South Wales Transport
Western National. Western Welsh

Aldershot & District. Brighton Hove & District
City of Oxford. East Kent. Gosport & Fareham
Hants & Dorset. Maidstone & District
Shamrock & Rambler.Southdown.
Southern Vectis. South Midland
Thames Valley.Timpson Wilts & Dorset

Tyneside P.T.A.

S.E. Lancashire &
N.E. Cheshire P.T.A.

Merseyside
P.T.A.

NORTH EASTERN

NORTH WESTERN

West Midlands P.T.A.

MIDLANDS

EASTERN

G.L.C. Area

SOUTH WALES & WEST

SOUTHERN

LONDON COUNTRY
BUS SERVICES LTD

0   50   100

The main operating companies in each region are listed above.
The Greater London and Passenger Transport Areas are shown for reference.

Miles

Source: National Bus Company, Annual Report and Accounts, 1971.

Map 16   National Bus Company: Regional Boards 1971

with its own organisation, the Scottish Transport Group, to manage all publicly owned transport, except the railways, north of the Tweed. It included such large road passenger concerns as the Scottish Motor Traction Company (both Western and Central Companies), Scottish Omnibuses and the three groups of W. Alexander and Son, large shipping firms like David MacBrayne Ltd and the Caledonian Steam Packet Co., as well as insurance and travel companies.[87]

The emphasis in the Act's clauses concerning the Waterways was on the development of their use for recreation and amenity. The British Waterways Board was continued in being but its work was split in two. The Commercial Waterways division was responsible for the remaining canals and river navigations which continued to carry industrial traffic. The 'Cruising Waterways' of over 1,000 miles in length were to be managed by a separate division of the Board and an Inland Waterways Amenity Advisory Council was to be set up to advise the Minister on the future extent and value of this part of the network.

Outside the scope of the mammoth Transport Act was the organisation both of London Transport and of the Air Corporations. The Transport (London) Bill which largely followed the lines of the White Paper, *Transport in London* (Cmnd 3686), had a much easier passage through Parliament than did its larger predecessor, the Transport Bill. It was unopposed on its second reading in the House of Commons on 17 December 1968 and received the royal assent on 25 July 1969. The big change here was the transference of authority over transport in the Greater London area from the London Transport Board to the Greater London Council. A London Transport Executive was established with its chairman and other members appointed by the GLC. The undertakings managed were broadly the same as those run by the Board except that the Green Line (Coach) and Country Bus services were transferred to a new subsidiary of the National Bus Company, London Country Bus Services Ltd. A large part (nearly 90 per cent) of the London Transport Board's debt was extinguished but the new London Transport was expected to pay its way thereafter. A few weeks later, however, the Transport (London) Amendment Act passed on 11 December 1969 extinguished the remaining £26 million of the old debt. Even so the financial position of London Transport remained a big headache for the Greater London Council. The nature of these problems will be examined later in this chapter.

No major legislation concerning domestic air transport was passed by the Wilson administration. In the mid-1960s there was a great expansion of the air-tour business from which the private airlines were the greatest beneficiaries. It was this development, among other changes, which prompted the appointment in 1967, of a Committee under Sir Ronald Edwards, chairman of the Beecham group of Com-

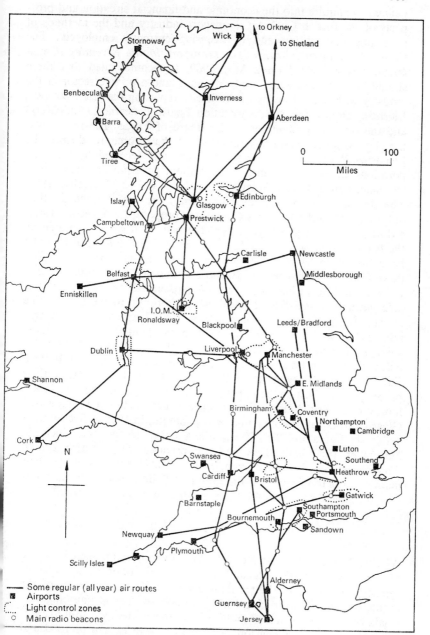

Source: N. J. Graves, T. J. White, *Geography of the British Isles*, 1971.

Map 17   Domestic Air Services 1970

panies, 'to enquire into the economic and financial situation and prospects of the British Civil Air Transport industry and the methods of
regulating competition and of licensing currently employed'. The
Committee's report, *British Air Transport in the Seventies* (Cmnd
4018), was published on 2 May 1969. It recommended that there
should be a public sector, a mixed sector, and a private sector in the
industry with a Civil Aviation Authority replacing the Air Transport
Licensing Board, the Air Registration Board (concerned with safety)
and the regulatory functions of the Board of Trade. The report was
popular with the private airlines which had come to dislike the
Licensing Board, but was less enthusiastically received by the Corporations and the government. The Labour government's plans were
announced in a White Paper (Cmnd 4213) on 12 November 1969.
The idea of a 'mixed economy' for air transport was accepted but they
did not agree to the Edwards Committee proposal for a 'second force'
airline sharing 'a significant part' of the scheduled routes operated by
the two corporations. Throughout the sixties BEA continued to make
heavy losses on its social service routes and it was expected to offset
these from its profits on the European routes. This it generally did.
Its fares and operating costs were lower than the somewhat comparable government-subsidised 'local service airlines' in the U.S.A. The
average BEA domestic revenue rate in 1961–2 was 5·1d a passenger
mile which was 5 per cent lower than the United States domestic
average of 5·4d a passenger mile.[88] In the summer of 1963 BEA
reduced summer fares on the routes between London and Belfast,
Edinburgh or Glasgow to a 2d-a-mile rate.[89] This boosted their
passenger carryings at the expense of the railways. In the late 1960s,
however, as British Rail cut its journey time between London and
Glasgow from seven hours and twenty minutes in 1965 to five minutes
under six hours in 1970, it was BEA's turn to feel the pinch. In
November 1970 both BEA and the private airline British United
Airways estimated that they would have 800,000 empty seats on their
main services to Glasgow, Edinburgh and Belfast. Railway electrification in England and sectional strife in Ulster were having their effects.[90]

VI

As Fig. 25 (p. 314) illustrates, coastal shipping maintained its share
of the movement of merchandise in domestic trade in the quarter
century after 1945 far better than did the railways. In terms of the
tonnage of goods carried the contribution of coastal shipping was
small, ranging between 2·43 and 3·37 per cent of the total. But average
hauls by ship were much longer than they were by rail or road and
thus in terms of ton-miles of goods carried the coasters' share, varying between 17·09 and 24·24 per cent, was a much more impressive

one. One reason for the steady progress of the industry was the absence of the kind of political interference which characterised the history of rail and road transport after 1945. In a statement made to the House of Commons on 15 November 1945, Herbert Morrison, Lord President of the Council, declared that the Labour Government did not propose the nationalisation of the shipping industry. When Labour returned to power in 1964 there was no change from this policy. All the postwar Transport Acts, whether initiated by the Conservatives or by Labour, contained clauses designed to protect the private enterprise coastal shipping industry from the undercutting of its freight charges by the publicly owned railways. Thus under Section 53 of the Transport Act of 1962 the coastal shipping industry was given the right to appeal to the Transport Tribunal against unfair long-distance freight charges proposed by the railways and under Section 150 of the Transport Act of 1968 a Railways and Coastal Shipping Committee was set up as a permanent body to endeavour to harmonise railway and shipping interests. The experience of the war had convinced all parties of the desirability of maintaining an efficient coastal shipping service.

The changing size and composition of the shipping employed in the United Kingdom coastwise trade is summarised in Table 21:

Table 21 *Steam and motor vessels employed in the coasting and home trades*

Year	Liners		Tramps		Tankers		Total	
	No.	Gross tonnage (000s)	No.	Gross tonnage (000s)	No.	Gross tonnage (000s)	No.	Gross tonnage (000s)
1950	374	449	758	623	83	49	1,215	1,121
1955	353	464	674	659	108	65	1,135	1,188
1960	292	388	506	514	140	111	938	1,013
1965	251	356	409	443	120	104	780	913
1970	170	309	310	338	107	104	587	757

N.B. Coasting and home trades (i.e. trade with near continental ports) are not shown separately in the statistics. The same vessels which were predominantly employed in the coasting trade were, on occasion, employed also on the short sea lanes to the European continent.

Source: Chamber of Shipping of the United Kingdom, *Annual Reports.*

The outstanding trends revealed in the above table are the halving of the tonnage of tramp shipping, the more gradual reduction in the liner tonnage and the increase by more than 100 per cent in the tanker tonnage engaged in the coastal service. These changes reflected the decline in the general commodity trade, the sharp fall in the quantity of coal carried, the emergence of containerisation and the increased consumption of oil and petroleum in motor transport.

In six years of war there had been little opportunity to modernise the fleets employed round Britain's coasts and the heavy casualties suffered through enemy action at sea resulted in those vessels which survived being employed for a longer span of years than would otherwise have been the case. But in the later 1950s and through the following decade the process of replacement of old steam ships by modern motor and diesel vessels was accelerated. The average age of coastal liners in service fell from 14·7 years in 1964 to 12·3 years in 1970. The revolution in tanker design ensured an even quicker rate of replacement for this class of vessel: whereas the average age of tankers in service in 1964 was 15·4 years by 1970 it had fallen to only 8·4 years. The newer vessels which were coming into service in the 1950s and 1960s had a larger carrying capacity, greater speed and quicker turn-round time than did their predecessors. The average size of coastal liners in 1969 was 170·1 gross tons, or 50 gross tons larger than the average of 20 years earlier. Over the same 20 years the average size of coastal tramps rose from 83 to 109 gross tons.[91] There were many fewer ships in service in 1970 than there were in 1945 but they were capable of undertaking a larger volume of business.

Although figures of tonnages of coastal shipping arriving at and departing from British ports give only an indication of trend of the volume of merchandise carried coastwise they show two distinct movements in the post-war years. The first is a substantial increase in the net tonnage of shipping in the coastal trade passing through the ports. Although it was not until 1949 that the 1937 pre-war peak of 43,379,000 tons combined arrivals and departures was surpassed, by 1955 there had been an increase to 47,886,000 tons and by 1970 a further rise to 73,162,000. The second tendency was for the proportion of foreign registered tonnage engaged in the British coastal trade to increase. From a mere 1·6 per cent in 1938 it rose, at first slowly, to 2·4 per cent in 1950 and then much more rapidly to a postwar peak of 23·3 per cent in 1966.[92] Among the more important reasons for foreign encroachment in the traffic round Britain's coasts were the earlier modernisation of Belgian, Dutch and French shipping in the short sea and complementary coastal trades, the importation and coastwise distribution of road-building materials from Normandy and the occasional importation of coal.

After 1945 Britain's fleet of coastal vessels continued to specialise in the movement of bulky, low-value commodities of the kind traditionally included within classes 1-7 of the Railway Clearing House Classification of Goods. But the composition of the traffic changed dramatically in the 1960s. Of the 29½ million tons of merchandise carried coastwise by tramp vessels in 1948 nearly 25 million tons were of coal and coke.[93] Of an estimated 28 million tons of coastwise cargo carried in 1960 nearly 21 million tons were still the products of British coal mines.[94] Thereafter, with the rapid decline of the household consumption of coal and the discovery of North Sea gas in 1965, coal and coke shipments declined sharply. By 1970 they had fallen to only just over 14 million tons. Growing in importance were shipments of oil, road-building materials, other minerals and timber.[95]

The ability of the coasting companies to maintain, let alone develop, the services of goods transport depended very heavily on the aggregate level of costs at the ports concerned. It was frequently the case that the coaster was in a position to undercut the railways and even the 'C' licence road haulage operator in terms of rates per ton-mile for the actual sea voyages. But these advantages were frequently nullified by high port terminal charges or antiquated methods of unloading ships.[96] The small coasting company whose trade was between high cost ports was at a decided disadvantage when compared with the larger concern with a more diversified business. This was one reason why the amalgamation movement in coastal shipping acquired a new momentum in post-war Britain. By the 1950s one firm, Coast Lines Limited, dominated the business. Formed in 1917, when the old firm of Powell, Bacon and Hough Lines Ltd changed its name, it acquired several important companies, including the City of Dublin Steam Packet Company, Laird Line Ltd and the Buras Steamship Company in the immediate aftermath of World War I, but absorbed a number more, including the Tyne-Tees Shipping Company Ltd, the Aberdeen Steam Navigation Company Ltd, and the North of Scotland, Orkney and Shetland Shipping Company Ltd during or after World War II.

One means by which coastal shipping was able to retain its share of domestic merchandise traffic was through containerisation, which may be defined as the bulking of general cargo before it reaches the ship. Although long-distance ocean traffic lends itself to the greatest economies in this field and has been the subject of the most far-reaching changes in organisation, containerisation was of particular importance in the Anglo-Irish trade. Pioneer container ships operated between Larne in Northern Ireland and Preston on the Lancashire coast as early as 1954, but the more widespread development came some ten years later.[97] Containerisation in coastal shipping greatly reduced port costs and also encouraged changes in freight rate policy. Traditionally coastal freights had been influenced by the railways' policy of charging what the traffic would bear, i.e. making freight rates directly proportional to the value of commodities carried. With bulk handling, roll-on/roll-off and container cargoes becoming increasingly important, more emphasis was given to loadability as the main factor determining freight charges. In this respect coastal shipping companies were marching in step with the railways in the later 1960s.

In part the competitiveness of coastal shipping with railway transport was maintained through the inferior conditions of employment of merchant seamen as compared with railwaymen. With the important exception of the staff employed on British Railways cross channel ferries, sailors worked longer hours and for less pay than did the men and women who were in the employment of the British Railways Board. In 1965 the average weekly hours worked by sailors was 61; for railwaymen it was 48. At the same time, even allowing for 'hidden' wages in the form of 'free' board and lodging on board ship, the wage rates of seamen were inferior to those of railwaymen.[98]

In the later 1960s one of the biggest challenges to the prosperity of British coastal shipping came from the rapidly growing pipeline network. 1969 saw the completion of the 245-mile-long United Kingdom Oil Pipeline project linking main oil installations on the Thames Estuary and on Merseyside with regional distribution depots in Greater London, Birmingham and Nottingham. It was a development which threatened seriously to curtail the carriage of oil coastwise—the most rapidly expanding part of the coastwise commodity trade in the early 1960s. In the same year in which the oil pipeline project was completed nearly 400 miles of trunk pipelines were laid for the Gas Council—a major contribution to the availability of cheap natural gas which was rapidly supplanting coal as fuel for domestic heating.[99] Coal, which had been for centuries the main commodity carried coastwise, was now subject to rapidly shrinking demand.

Confronted with these significant developments it is not surprising that leading firms in coastwise shipping began to diversify their investment into other forms of transport. Thus in the early 1970s the firm of Coast-Lines was negotiating a merger with P. and O. Lines and spreading its interests into road haulage as well as ocean shipping. It seemed probable that the future survival of the coastal shipping industry lay in its closer linkage with other types of transport.

The outstanding development in coastal passenger transport after 1945 was the remarkably rapid progress of the hovercraft, from Christopher Cockerell's experiments with coffee tins in the 1950s, to the first commercial service across the Dee estuary between Rhyl and the Wirral Peninsula in July 1962. Four years later, Seaspeed, British Rail's hovercraft division, started scheduled services between Southampton and Cowes and for a short time between Portsmouth and Cowes. The latter service was discontinued when a Portsmouth to Ryde service was opened in 1968. Other services between Bournemouth and Swanage, across the Humber and on the Clyde either preceded the services to the Isle of Wight or quickly followed them. The great advantage of the new medium was that of speed. On the Portsmouth–Ryde service a journey time of 10 minutes for the five-mile crossing compared very favourably with the 25–30 minutes of the more conventional diesel-powered ferries. The hovercraft's main drawback was that it was not so reliable for sailing in all types of weather as the traditional craft they are eventually likely to supersede. On the Dover–Boulogne route 18 per cent of Seaspeed sailings were cancelled because of bad weather. Cancellations in the calmer estuarial waters of the Clyde or Spithead were naturally less frequent, but improvements were needed before the hovercraft could claim to provide as reliable services as those already provided by the slower ferry boats.[100]

VII

In his famous report *Traffic in Towns*, published in 1963, Professor Colin Buchanan wrote that 'for personal and family use, for the movement of people in mass, and for use in business, commerce and industry, the motor vehicle has become indispensable'. The British people, he claimed, were 'inextricably committed'[101] to the motor vehicle. At least in respect of the private motor car it was a commitment that had arisen in the previous ten years. Before the Second World War the motor car was mainly the plaything of the well-to-do and the professional classes. In 1939 there were only two million private cars on Britain's roads, representing one car to every 24 persons. Because of wartime conditions there were fewer than a million and a half private cars in 1945. Ten years before the Buchanan Report, with petrol rationing only just ended, the total had crept up to $2\frac{3}{4}$ million, or one car to every 20 persons. But by 1963 there had been a threefold increase over the previous decade—with nearly $7\frac{1}{2}$ million cars there was one vehicle to every 7 persons. It looked very much as if the private car had come to be regarded as 'indispensable'. By the end of the 1960s there was no doubt about it; with $11\frac{1}{2}$ million private cars in use there was one such vehicle to every 4·7 persons.

In 1953 when the author came to live in a north London suburb the motor car was still not completely dominant. Private car ownership was limited to the occupants of one house in every five. Milk was delivered by means of a horsedrawn cart. In the delivery of bread there was a choice between a horsedrawn van and a motor van and support was given to the former for horticultural reasons. Ten years later horse transport had disappeared from the neighbourhood and car ownership had extended to three-quarters of the households.

But even in the early 1950s the total value of road transport and travel in Great Britain, at £1,160 million, was about three times the value of rail transport and travel was equivalent to about one tenth of the national income.

The foundations of the modern mass production motor car industry were laid in the immediate post-war years when governments gave the highest priority to the expansion of British exports in order that essential food and raw material imports could be purchased. In war-time, car production for civilian use virtually stopped. In 1943 only 1,649 cars left the assembly lines. In the later 1940s the problem for British car manufacturers was not how to sell their cars but how to produce them quickly enough. The pre-war industry's export perform-ance had been disappointing. There could be few complaints about the achievement in the immediate postwar years. Nearly three-quarters of the output of private cars was exported in the late 1940s and early 1950s. With the aid of priority allocations of steel—in contrast with the low priority given to the railways—output of cars rapidly soared, so that by 1949 the 412,000 cars produced exceeded the production of 1937—the best pre-war year. Capital investment was 'swift and heavy'.[102] By 1955 car production had leapt upwards to 900,000 vehicles a year. After setbacks in the two following years output topped the million mark in each of the years 1958–60.

With production of such a magnitude both the adoption of thorough-going mass production techniques and the merging of smaller con-cerns into the giant corporations were given every encouragement. The largest firms in the business concentrated on producing very large numbers of a few popular models. More than a quarter of a million Austin A40s were sold between 1947 and 1950. Another best seller, the Morris Minor, appeared in 1948. To make the most of the oppor-tunity for mass sales provided by full employment and rising living standards and to ward off the challenge of the American-owned Ford Motor Company, the historic firms of Austin and Morris merged to become British Motor Corporation in November 1951. Many other mergers followed. 1960 has been described as 'the take-over year for the car industry'[103] with Jaguar buying up Daimler and Standard-Triumph being taken over by Leyland Motors. The obverse of the consolidation of the big firms was the increasing difficulty of survival of the smaller ones. In 1946 small independent firms enjoyed an 11 per cent share of the domestic market; in 1955 it was only 4·4 per cent.

In the meantime improvements in the motor car increased the ease and attractiveness of private motoring. In the 1950s came synchromesh gears and light trafficators. In the 1960s there were automatic gearboxes and seat safety belts.

By 1953 Britain's balance of payments had improved sufficiently for petrol rationing to be ended. With employment and real earnings increasing, domestic demand for motor cars rocketed and the car makers diverted a larger proportion of their output to the home market. From then onwards the problem raised by the 'mixed blessing'[104] of private car ownership in Britain loomed larger and larger with each year that passed.

The gigantic upsurge of car ownership took place when the road system of Great Britain still retained many of its nineteenth-century characteristics. The great improvement since the First World War had been in road surfaces rather than mileage, road widths or convenience for fast-moving traffic. Total road mileage in 1959 was only 16,769 miles more than in 1911, a rise of 9·5 per cent. Over the same period of time the number of motor vehicles rose from a quarter of a million to over eight and a half million, a rise of 3,400 per cent. The number of motor vehicles per mile of road rose sharply from 1·1 in 1911 to 44·8 in 1959 and 63·8 in 1970. Throughout these years Britain had the most crowded roads of any major country in the world.[105] It is scarcely surprising that with immense quantities of capital and labour invested in the motor industry and in motor transport a strong demand arose for radical improvements in Britain's roads. The campaign for greater expenditure on the modernisation of the road system was led by the British Road Federation, the Road Haulage Association, the Roads Campaign Council and the private car-owners' organisations the A.A. and the R.A.C. In the British Road Federation's *The Road to Recovery*, published in 1948,[106] it was claimed that a modernised road system would save the country £60 million a year, made up of £26 million through saving of time, £12 million through fuel economies, £3 million through decreased wear and tear of tyres, £9 million through decreased expenditure on repairs and £10 million from savings in insurance. The same organisation's cleverly designed booklet *No Road*, published in 1953, summarised the shortcomings of British roads as including 'bottlenecks, sharp turns. blind bends, inadequate sight lines, narrow and often humped-back bridges, low bridges, congested built up areas and a carriageway for the most part only wide enough for one line of traffic in each direction'. Among the carefully chosen illustrations was a photograph revealing that a pedal cycle parked against a kerb in East Retford on the A1 (Great North Road) reduced traffic to single line working. G. T. Brunner, one of the leading advocates of road improvement, summed up the viewpoint of the road interest in the mid-1950s when he wrote: 'It is surely time that this paralysis of will and endeavour in British road policy gave way to a more progressive outlook and a determination to give Britain a highway system equal to the best on the Continent'.[107]

It was not through lack of plans that Britain had to wait until November 1959 for its first major motorway—the first stage of the M1 linking London and Birmingham. As has been shown in the preceding chapter, the idea of a motorway was advanced at the very beginning of the twentieth century and carefully prepared blueprints were available at the Ministry of Transport before 1939. For the Ministry of War Transport, Mr P. J. Noel-Baker, announced on 21 May 1943 that work was well advanced on plans for the provision of motor roads and the segregation of fast motor traffic. Three years later motorways formed part of a ten-year programme announced by the Labour government's Minister of Transport, Alfred Barnes. Nine further years elapsed and two Conservative Ministers of Transport came and went before a third Conservative in the office, Mr Boyd Carpenter, on 2 February 1955 announced plans for a government expenditure of £147 million over four years on road improvements, including motorways between London and Yorkshire (the M1) and Birmingham and Preston.[108] Undoubtedly one of the main reasons why successive governments were slow to recognise the case for better roads was that while expenditure came direct from the taxpayer, the benefits, though they might affect millions of people indirectly, were far less tangible. But in addition, a motorway was a road of a completely new kind which broke completely with the age-long tradition of the Queen's Highway open for all to use by whatever means of locomotion took their fancy. There was understandably hesitation before making a major departure from this tradition. New legislation, the Special Roads Act 1949, was needed before roads of the new type could be constructed.

Although the London–Birmingham motorway was, strictly speaking, not the first road of this new kind to be opened in Britain, being preceded a year earlier by the eight-mile-long Preston by-pass, it was the first major undertaking. Seventy-five miles in length, it was an outstanding example of civil engineering completed at a rate of construction without parallel in Britain and seldom, if ever, achieved abroad. The motorway with its 183 bridges, was completed in 586 days, so that on average one bridge was completed every three days and a mile of dual carriageway every eight days.[109] Once this important first stage of the M1 had been completed the construction of other motorways gathered momentum so that at the beginning of the 1970s, as shown in Maps 18 and 19 and Fig. 31, more than 750 miles of motorway were completed.

The emergence of this radically different means of communication brought significant economic and social consequences. The most strikingly obvious economy was the saving of motorists' time. The estimate of the Ministry of Transport was that on the journey from London to Birmingham the saving of time through the switching of vehicles from the A5 and A45 to the M1 would be of the order of 2·7 million hours of driving a year. With the ten-fold increase in motorway mileage between 1959 and 1970 time-saving of a much greater order of magnitude was effected. The time-saving was of benefit not only to the joyriding motorist breaking the speed limit by

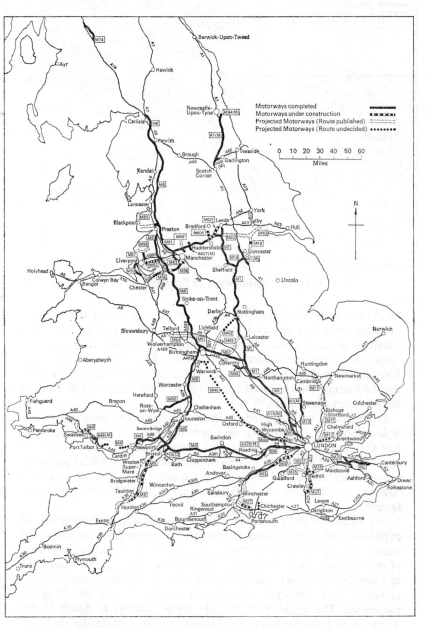

Map 18   Motorways in England and Wales 1971

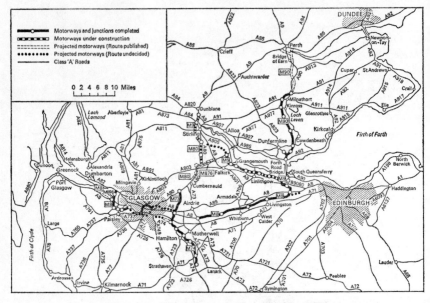

Map 19   Motorways in Scotland in 1971

racing down the third traffic lane at over 70 m.p.h., but also to businessmen, road hauliers and even the passenger travelling by motor coach. Immediately the M1 was opened the Midland Red company began an express coach service between the Digbeth Coach Station in Birmingham and Victoria, London, which, on the first day of running, cut the journey time between the two cities from five hours 20 minutes to two hours 51 minutes.[110]

When accidents happened on the motorways they were often multiple crashes of a magnitude and gruesomeness quite unprecedented. But the accident *rate* on motorways was well below that of ordinary roads. On each million of vehicle miles there were 0·15 fatal accidents on ordinary roads and 0·06 on motorways. The rate of non-fatal 'serious' accidents on the ordinary roads was double the motorway rate.[111]

For industrialists, especially those engaged in the manufacture of expensive and sophisticated goods such as motor cars, the improved roads, and especially the motorways, could be treated as an extension of the particular industry's conveyor belt. The car might be assembled in Coventry from parts manufactured in South Wales, Lancashire and elsewhere and conveyed speedily on massive trucks travelling by motorway. The opening of the M4 from London to South Wales offered new hope for industrial employment to replace the declining job opportunities in coal and steel.

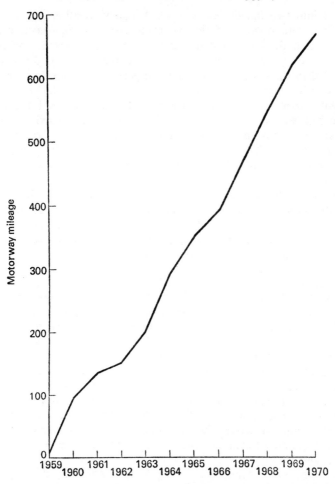

Sources: Annual Abstract of Statistics, 1970; British Road Federation, *Basic Road Statistics*, 1971.

Figure 31   Motorway Mileage in Great Britain 1959–70 (mileage open on March 31/April 1 of each year)

The opening of motorways sometimes brought a revival of social life and commerce in small towns hitherto plagued by the noise and fumes from through traffic. For example the opening of the M4 in 1971 was a boon to most of the citizens and shopkeepers in the old market town of Marlborough. When through traffic on the A4 clogged up the broad High Street it was difficult for people to talk to each other and hazardous to cross the road. The community tended to be divided into two halves between which communication was rapidly declining. And because of the inconvenience and unpleasantness of the situation the town was losing its attractiveness as a marketing centre for outlying villages. No sooner was the A4 traffic diverted to the M4 than the town became far more peaceful and civilised and its natural advantage as a marketing centre was revived. Motorways brought important shifts in property values. Before 1971 the commuter belt westwards of London did not stretch beyond Reading. But with fast movement possible on the new motorway, commuting spread to Calne, Chippenham and even further west. House prices in these towns immediately rose nearer the high levels of Greater London.[112]

For those who consider that the quality of life is more important than the maximisation of individual wealth and the Gross National Product, the transformation of Britain's roads is regarded as a menace rather than a blessing. Motorways do not merely transfer traffic from over-congested inferior roads; they generate new traffic. The Director of Road Research at the Department of Scientific and Industrial Research found, in a study of the M1, that 'generated' traffic formed as much as 30 per cent of the total of all vehicles passing along the motorway.[113] The crucial question of course is, what happened to this greatly increased volume of traffic before it entered and after it left the motorway? Inevitably as thousands of vehicles debouched from the broad traffic lanes of the motorway, congestion increased on the much narrower and far more overcrowded secondary roads. Flows of traffic between major conurbations were speeded up; but only at the expense of greater congestion and slower traffic flows within the urban areas. The same Midland Red Expressway coach which took only 59 minutes to cover the 65 miles between Birmingham and St Albans required a further 66 minutes to cover the 21 miles between St Albans and Victoria.

The Ministry of Transport when planning motorway development in the 1950s gave priority to the more straightforward rural motorways, such as the M1, rather than the more complicated and costly links through the more heavily built up areas. As the programme advanced through the 1960s the cost of construction rose from between £250,000 to £300,000 a mile to between £800,000 and £1 million a mile. The increase was only in part due to inflation. The first 75 miles of the M1 opened in 1959 was a relatively simple undertaking by comparison with the Midland links joining the M1, the M5 and the M6, a third of whose 66 miles is viaduct-carried urban motorway. For all their attractions to the motorist and the haulage contractor, motorways eat up far more land—a very scarce commodity in Britain —and are more costly to build than an electric railway, where average speeds of movement can exceed those of vehicles on an expressway.

And although, latterly, more attention has been given to the land-scaping of the motorways it is generally true that a modern railway is far less destructive of rural amenities than is a road.

As better roads generated more motor traffic so the finances of rural bus companies were increasingly threatened. The 1960s was a decade of bus closures. Services rapidly deteriorated; Maps 20 and 21 show

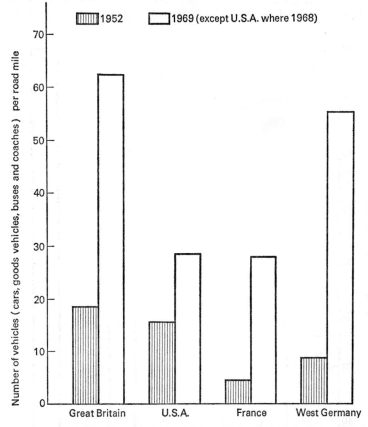

Note: An exact comparison of the vehicle/road mileage ratio between different countries is precluded by differing national definitions of what constitutes a road. The 1952 figures have been revised several times in succeeding annual editions of the publications of the British Road Federation and the International Road Federation—the latest revisions have been used here.

Source: British Road Federation, *Basic Road Statistics* (annually).

Figure 32   Cars, Goods Vehicles, Buses and Coaches (only) per Road Mile in Great Britain, USA, France and W. Germany in 1952 and in 1969 (latest USA figures are 1968)

the decline in services in one part of south-west England between 1960 and 1970, a decline made more serious because of contemporaneous rail closures. Nationally the number of bus and coach passenger journeys declined from 11,000 million in 1938 to 9,000 million in 1970, a year in which the accounts of the National Bus Company went into the red.[114] It was a decline which had begun in 1955-6—at the same time as the number of private motorists started to increase rapidly. Closures isolated and impoverished the lives of many persons. It was the view of the Jack Committee on Rural Bus Services in 1961

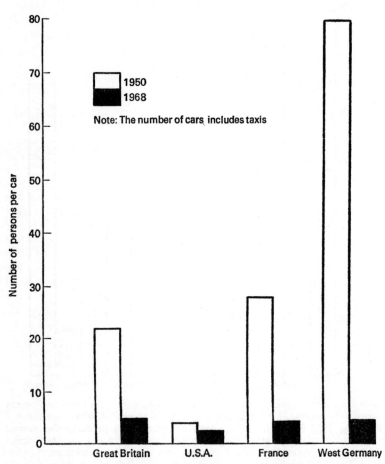

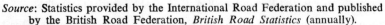

Source: Statistics provided by the International Road Federation and published by the British Road Federation, *British Road Statistics* (annually).

Figure 33   Persons per Car in Great Britain, USA, France and W. Germany in 1950 and in 1968

that 'while the number of persons who experience hardship or inconvenience may be decreasing the degree of hardship or inconvenience which they experience may tend to increase as services are
reduced'. The National Federation of Women's Institutes spelt out
the kind of hardships which were being experienced in many country
districts. The lack of public transport created

> difficulties for young people attending further education classes;
> difficulties for those working in towns, whose homes are in the
> country; difficulties for the elderly drawing pensions (a number
> of the sub Post Offices have closed in recent years); difficulties for
> the housewife who has to do her main shopping in the towns; diffi-
> culties for those attending doctors' or dentists' surgeries or needing
> to have prescriptions made up by the chemist; difficulties for those
> visiting patients in hospital or attending hospital for treatment.[115]

In Scotland many of the local bus services were only able to continue because they were subsidised directly or indirectly or because
the numerous one-man operators were able to carry a loss by combining bus operation with other paid employment.[116]

If the dominance of the motor car, the heavy lorry and the new
motor roads was something of a 'mixed blessing' to those living in the
country districts it was much more so to urban dwellers. A familiar
vicious circle—increasing numbers of private cars and lorries slowing
down and adding to the costs of operation of bus services; fares on
buses, trains and tubes being raised in a vain effort to meet rising
costs; these same fare increases persuading more commuters to provide their own means of transport: still greater road congestion combined with mounting costs and declining public support—appeared
in all of Britain's cities but most strikingly in London. On each
working day of 1959 some 926,000 persons (75 per cent of the total)
entered central London during the morning rush hour by tube or
suburban railway; 223,000 (18 per cent) came by bus and 85,000 (7 per
cent) by private car. On this basis a transfer of only one per cent
of the public transport commuters to private transport would lead
to a 12 per cent increase in private car journeys and, on the basis of
traffic composition, an increase of some 5 per cent in total traffic.[117]
Exactly this kind of transfer took place in the following decade. To
deal with what one Minister of Transport called the 'traffic thrombosis'
which was affecting the heart of London and other big cities the
first efforts were directed to speeding the flow of private vehicles and
providing inducements for their owners to park them off the main
streets. Every device of traffic engineering was mobilised in an attempt
to solve the problem. One-way streets multiplied and parking meters
sprang up like mushrooms in the principal city streets. But still the
traffic grew while its rate of movement declined. In central London

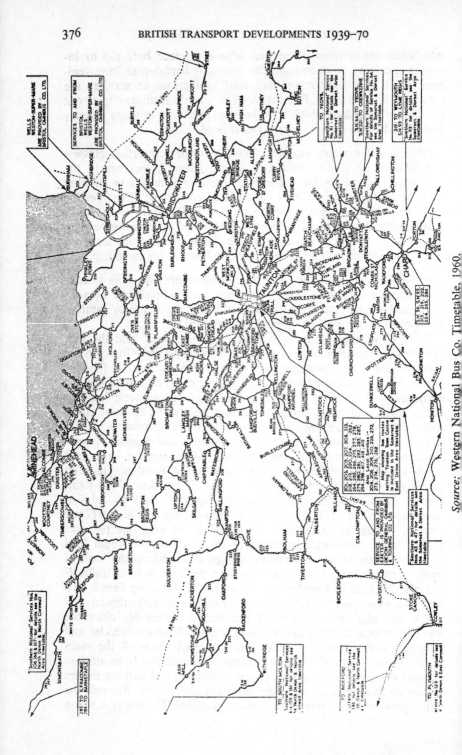

Source: Western National Bus Co. Timetable, 1960.

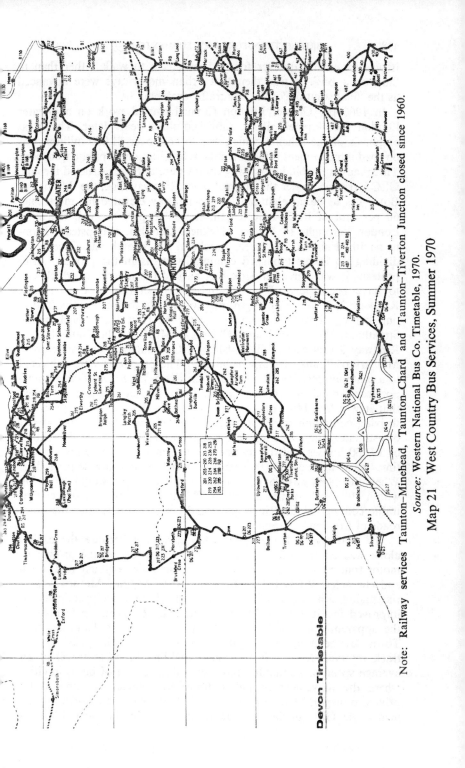

Note: Railway services Taunton–Minehead, Taunton–Chard and Taunton–Tiverton Junction closed since 1960.

Source: Western National Bus Co. Timetable, 1970.

Map 21 West Country Bus Services, Summer 1970

it was frequently quicker for the pedestrian to walk rather than to 'hop on a bus'. It was then that urban motorways were advanced as the 'final solution 'of the city traffic problem.

In 1966 the Greater London Council started work on a Greater London Development Plan, published three years later. The great emphasis of the scheme, which was to cost over £1,000 million, was on road improvement rather than the rehabilitation of public transport. Three massive orbital motorway routes were to be constructed through GLC territory. Under the original plan, Ringway One, the 'Motorway Box', was to be an eight-lane super-highway elevated for more than 60 per cent of its 30-mile length. It was to pass through the inner London boroughs of Poplar, Hackney, Camden, Hampstead, Hammersmith, Fulham, Battersea, Lambeth, Blackheath and Greenwich, dividing up long-established community areas in the process. After protests, it was agreed to sink that part of the motorway which was to have been elevated by cut-and-cover methods of construction. Ringway 2, 50 miles in length, was to encircle the metropolis further out, cutting through communities such as East Ham, Beckenham, Streatham, Wandsworth and Chiswick. Much of the 100-mile-long Ringway 3 was completely outside GLC boundaries and therefore a Ministry of Transport responsibility.[118] The proposals were subjected to a quite unprecedented volume of criticism. Even *The Times'* transport correspondent, who was generally favourable to them, conceded that it was 'the blow of a giant axe cutting a swath through living, thriving communities'.[119] Others emphasised that, even on the lowest of estimates, the execution of the plan would involve the demolition of 19,600 houses and the displacement of at least 60,000 people at a time when at least 250,000 persons were on housing waiting lists. When the plan was completed one million people would be living within 200 yards of the motorway.[120] There was every prospect that traffic coming off the Ringways would congest still further the other roads of London's boroughs.

The example of London has been cited, not because the capital alone was confronted with the problems created by the growth of motor transport, but because it reveals something of their magnitude and character. While the controversy over London's Motorway Box was raging, other communities were wisely giving more prominence to improved facilities for public transport and endeavouring to restrain the apparently insatiable demands of the motor car. Runcorn New Town devised a figure-of-eight roadway system with a 22-feet-wide track reserved for public transport, enabling buses to travel at an average speed of 22 m.p.h.—more than double that of buses in cities where the movement of public transport vehicles is impeded by private transport.[121] In part influenced by the success of such experiments, the GLC made two important moves in the early 1970s to prevent further erosion of its own transport services. One of these was the authorisation of a new underground railway extension—the Fleet Line—and the other was the adoption of bus freeways in some of the main roads of the city including Oxford Street. There was mounting evidence that the only real long-run economy was to make a massive investment in improved public transport services and to give these the right of way before the claims of the private motorist.

VIII

The three decades surveyed in this chapter began with two six-year periods, one of war and one of peace in which the direction of government policy was towards greater public ownership and control of the means of transport. But the peacetime experiment was scarcely allowed the necessary time and resources to prove its worth before there came a sharp reversal of policy after 1952. In the following 20 years the share of the public sector in both goods and passenger transport shrank rapidly because the emphasis of legislation and of capital investment was on the promotion of private enterprise. But by the end of the 1960s it was becoming more apparent that the policies which had encouraged the largely unrestrained growth in numbers of privately owned motor vehicles threatened to wreck much that was of value in the life of the community, while not providing the British people with as efficient or as economic a system of transport as might have emerged if fragmentation of ownership had not been resorted to in the early 1950s. In 1970 Britain possessed a much under-utilised railway system. British Rail had the capacity for carrying a much larger proportion of long-distance passenger and freight traffic than that actually carried. At the same time the nation's roads were the most congested in the world, with more than 62 vehicles per mile of road and accidents killing over 7,000 persons and costing £320 million annually.

The construction of motorways is an extremely expensive business in both financial and real terms. By 1970 the cost of construction had soared to £2 million a mile. The 100,000 tonnes of building aggregates (mostly cement) needed to complete one mile of a motorway are as much as is required for the building of no less than 2,000 detached three-bedroomed houses.

The costliness of the motorway alternative to a more fully utilised railway system underlines the serious consequences of the failure to invest in a modernised railway system in the inter-war years. In the light of the transport situation in the 1970s, the failure to implement the 1931 Weir Committee proposals for extensive railway electrification is seen as a major mistake of transport policy with profound consequences for the entire public transport sector in the following decades. If investment had been made in main line electrification in the 'cheap money' years 1932–9 British railways would have been in an exceptionally strong position to provide fast, reliable, and inexpensive freight and passenger services in postwar Britain. The present nonsensical situation of an under-utilised railway system existing alongside a grossly overcrowded road network need not have arisen.

In so far as there was a consistent philosophy behind the Transport Act of 1947 it was that a body such as the British Transport Commission was needed to strive for an optimum allocation of transport resources from the viewpoint of the national interest. Progress towards this objective was slow and punctuated by numerous mistakes; but at least in road haulage and in civil aviation there were outstanding successes in the publicly owned sector. The contrary philosophy, which prevailed in the years after 1952, was that of the 'unseen hand' of private interest so directing resources that the best interests of the nation would be served. But few, having in mind the 40-ton trucks roaring through the roads of Kentish villages or the growth of urban ghettos in the shadow of motorway viaducts, would claim unqualified success for the followers of this alternative philosophy.

The consequences of the neglect of public transport are plain for all to see. The disproportion between capital investment in railways and in roads, noted earlier in this chapter, has grown even greater in recent years. In 1971 British Rail spent a mere £26 million on maintaining or renewing the permanent way. At the same time no less than £687 million was spent on Britain's roads.

Great Britain has now reached a watershed in transport policy. The alternatives are either a blinkered policy of trying to make the railways pay—in the narrow accounting sense and with only the most cursory calculation of social costs—by constantly pruning back 'unprofitable' services, or a large expansion of investment in a thoroughly modern railway system based on the conviction that in the long run on both economic and social grounds this is an absolute necessity for civilised living.

It has frequently been asserted that a large part of the remaining railway passenger and freight traffic can be transferred, without undue inconvenience, to the nation's roads. New and improved roads, we are assured, could easily relieve any congestion resulting from railway closures. What tends to be forgotten is that road traffic invariably expands to fill any additional space provided. Furthermore, modern roads are becoming more and more regimented; with one way streets, 'no stopping' regulations and limited access and egress. Road transport's great asset, flexibility, is thereby reduced. Motorway traffic has been described as 'a railway system on rubber tyres'. When the time comes for even the new roads to fill up with traffic, the public will look round for railways—and find they are gone.

What is beyond dispute is the importance of transport both to the growth of the national economy and to the quality of life. With expenditure on transport absorbing as much as 14 per cent of the Gross National Product[122] it is manifestly important that there should be a wise and thrifty allocation of resources. In the densely populated Britain of the 1970s it was every bit as important that welfare and amenity consideration should influence transport policy. Whether or not life in Britain in the year 2000 will be pleasanter than it was in 1970 will depend very much on the wisdom of transport planners in the years which lie between.

Appendix

A   MINISTERS OF TRANSPORT

17 August	1919	Sir E. Geddes
7 November	1921	Viscount Peel
12 April	1922	Earl of Crawford
31 October	1922	Sir J. Baird
24 January	1924	H. Gosling
11 November	1924	W. Ashley
7 June	1924	H. Morrison
3 September	1931	J. Pybus
22 February	1933	O. Stanley
29 June	1934	L. Hore-Belisha
28 May	1937	L. Burgin
21 April	1939	E. Wallace
14 May	1940	Sir J. Reith
3 October	1940	J. Moore-Brabazon

MINISTER OF WAR TRANSPORT

1 May	1941	Lord Leathers

MINISTERS OF TRANSPORT

3 August	1945	A. Barnes
31 October	1951	J. Maclay
7 May	1952	A. Lennox-Boyd

MINISTERS OF TRANSPORT AND CIVIL AVIATION

1 October	1953	A. Lennox-Boyd
28 July	1954	J. Boyd Carpenter
20 December	1955	H. Watkinson

MINISTERS OF TRANSPORT

14 October	1959	E. Marples
16 October	1964	T. Fraser
23 December	1965	Mrs B. Castle
5 April	1968	R. Marsh
5 October	1969	F. Mulley

MINISTER OF TRANSPORT INDUSTRIES
(within the Department of the Environment)

15 October	1970	J. Peyton

B CHAIRMEN OF PUBLICLY OWNED TRANSPORT UNDERTAKINGS

British European Airways

1 August	1946	Sir H. Hartley
1 April	1947	G. d'Erlanger
14 March	1949	Lord Douglas
3 May	1956	Sir A. Milward

British Transport Commission

8 September	1947	Sir C. (later Lord) Hurcomb
15 September	1953	Sir B. Robertson
1 June 1961 to		
31 Dec. 1962		R. (later Lord) Beeching

EXECUTIVES OF THE BRITISH TRANSPORT COMMISSION

Railway Executive

1947–51	Sir E. Missenden
1951–3	J. (later Sir J.) Elliot

Road Passenger Executive

1948–52	G. Cardwell

Road Haulage Executive

1948–52	G. Russell

Docks and Inland Waterways

1947–53	Sir R. Hill

London Transport Executive

1948–53	Lord Latham
1953–9	Sir J. Elliot
1959–62	A. Valentine

Hotels Executive

1948–51	Lord Inman
1951–3	Sir H. Methuen

By the British Transport Commission (Executives) Order made by the Minister on 19 August 1953 (coming into effect on 1 October 1953) the Railway, Road Haulage, Docks and Inland Waterways and Hotels Executives were abolished and their functions became directly exercisable by the Commission.

Notes

Chapter 1: *Inland Navigation in Britain before 1830*

1. C. A. Pratt, *A History of Inland Transport and Communication in England*, 1912, p. 128.
2. Joseph Priestley, *An Historical Account of the Navigable Rivers, Canals and Railways of Great Britain*, 1831, p. 5.
3. Priestley, op. cit. pp. 448, 666, 661.
4. Sir Alexander Gibb, *The Story of Telford*, 1935, ch. 1.
5. *Gentleman's Magazine*, vol. 21. 1751, p. 282.
6. B. R. Mitchell and P. Deane, *Abstract of British Historical Statistics*, 1962, pp. 177–8.
7. W. B. Stephens, 'The Exeter Lighter Canal, 1566–1698', *Jnl Tspt Hist.*, vol. III, 1957.
8. T. C. Barker, 'The Beginnings of the Canal Age in the British Isles', in L. S. Presnell (ed.) *Studies in the Industrial Revolution*, 1960, p. 1.
9. F. Mullineux, *The Duke of Bridgewater's Canal*, 1959, p. 13.
10. C. Hadfield, *The Canals of Southern England*, 1955, p. 116.
11. C. Hadfield and G. Biddle, *The Canals of North West England*, vol. 2, p. 264.
12. C. Hadfield, *The Canals of the West Midlands*, 1966, p. 29.
13. C. Hadfield, *The Canals of South West England*, 1967, p. 67.
14. Jean Lindsay, *The Canals of Scotland*, 1968, pp. 29–30.
15. C. Hadfield, *The Canals of South Wales and the Border*, 1960, p. 18.
16. Gloucester R.O. H/C S.C., *South Wales and Great Western Direct Railway Bill*, 1865; evidence of W. B. Clegram, q. 3848.
17. C. Hadfield, *The Canals of the West Midlands*, 1966, p. 168.
18. J. Lindsay, op. cit., p. 117. G. E. Mingay, *English Landed Society in the Eighteenth Century*, 1963, p. 200.
19. C. Hadfield and G. Biddle, op. cit., vol. 2, pp. 267, 209.
20. C. Hadfield, *The Canals of Southern England*, 1955, pp. 109–12.
21. J. Lindsay, op. cit., pp. 143, 168.
22. C. Hadfield, *British Canals*, (4th edition) 1968, p. 55.
23. C. Hadfield, *The Canals of the West Midlands*, 1966, p. 35.
24. Ibid., p. 36.
25. G. R. Hawke, *Railways and Economic Growth in England and Wales, 1840–1870*, 1970, p. 86.
26. 'Canals: their cost, their dividends and their traffic', *Railway News*, 30 April 1864. C. Hadfield, *The Canals of South and South East England*, 1969, p. 28.
27. C. Hadfield, *The Canals of South Wales and the Border*, 1960, p. 218.
28. J. Lindsay, op. cit., App. IV, p. 220.
29. C. Hadfield, *The Canals of South West England*, 1967, passim.

30. C. Hadfield, *The Canals of the West Midlands*, 1966, p. 70.
31. J. Wesley, *Journal*, 1906 (Everyman) edition, vol. 2, p. 500; vol. 4, p. 202.
32. C. Hadfield and G. Biddle, op. cit., vol. 1, p. 176.
33. J. Lindsay, op. cit., Appendices III and IV.
34. C. Hadfield, *The Canals of South West England*, 1967, p. 72.
35. J. Lindsay, op. cit., p. 107.
36. C. Hadfield, *The Canals of South Wales and the Border*, 1960, p. 25.
37. C. Hadfield, *The Canals of the East Midlands*, 1966, p. 63.
38. J. Lindsay, op. cit., p. 28.
39. C. Hadfield, *The Canals of the West Midlands*, p. 202.
40. Gloucester R.O. D 149/A21.
41. J. Lindsay, op. cit., p. 80.
42. *Return Relating to Inland Navigation and Canal Companies in England and Wales*, P.P., 1870, LVI, p. 679.
43. HLRO H/C S.C., Minutes of Evidence, *Wiltshire, Somerset and Weymouth Railway Bill*, 1845, vol. 89; evidence of R. W. Carpenter.
44. C. Hadfield, *The Canals of Southern England*, 1955, p. 240.
45. Ibid., p. 312.
46. Sir A. Gibb, *The Story of Telford*, 1935, p. 35.
47. Ibid., pp. 115–35.
48. J. Lindsay, op. cit., p. 92.
49. Ibid., pp. 42–8.
50. C. Hadfield and G. Biddle, op. cit., vol. 1, p. 35, vol. 2, p. 360.
51. Ibid., pp. 254–6.
52. C. Hadfield, *The Canals of the West Midlands*, 1966, p. 169. Sir G. Head, *A Home Tour of the Manufacturing Districts of England*, 1836, pp. 8–11.
53. C. Hadfield, *The Canals of the East Midlands*, p. 119.
54. C. Hadfield, *The Canals of South Wales and the Border*, 1960, p. 27.
55. J. Lindsay, op. cit., App. III.
56. Ibid., p. 96.
57. C. Hadfield and G. Biddle, op. cit., vol. 2, pp. 254–6.
58. Ibid., vol. 1, p. 343.
59. C. Hadfield, *British Canals*, (4th edition) 1968, p. 161.
60. C. Hadfield and G. Biddle, op. cit., vol. 1, p. 170.
61. Ibid., vol. 2, p. 275.
62. C. Hadfield, *The Canals of South West England*, 1967, p. 72.
63. F. C. Mather, *After the Canal Duke*, 1970, passim.
64. S. R. Broadbridge, 'Living Conditions on Midland Canal Boats', *Tspt Hist.*, vol. 3, No. 1, March 1970, p. 36.
65. R. M. Macleod, 'Social Policy and the Floating Population', *Past and Present*, No. 35, Dec. 1966, p. 130.
66. Board of Education, *Annual Report*, 1938, p. 12.
67. Sir George Head, *A Home Tour of the Manufacturing Districts and other parts of England, Scotland, Ireland, including the Channel Islands and the Isle of Man*, 1836, vol. 1, p. 146.

Chapter 2: *Road Transport before the Railway Age*

1. Tobias Smollett, *Works,* 1916 edition, vol. 1. Roderick Random, ch. 8.
2. J. Crofts, *Packhorse, Waggon and Post,* 1967, pp. 3, 6.
3. S. and B. Webb, *The Story of the King's Highway,* 1963 edition, p. 71.
4. K.G., 'An Essay on the British Roads', *The Gentleman's Magazine,* Nov.–Dec. 1972, p. 519.
5. Gloucester Record Office, D.153/82.
6. John Copeland, *Roads and their Traffic, 1750–1850,* 1968, p. 13.
7. M. Searle, *Turnpikes and Toll Bars,* vol. 1, 1930, p. 86.
8. Webb, *The Story of the King's Highway,* 1963, p. 75.
9. Searle, op. cit., vol. 1, p. 116.
10. W. T. Jackman, *The Development of Transportation in Modern England,* 1962 edition, p. 73.
11. *S.C. on the General Turnpike Acts, P.P.* 1797–8, vol. XLV, p. 940.
12. Webb, *The Story of the King's Highway,* 1963, p. 64 et seq.
13. For examples of road haulage charges see Jackman, op. cit., App. 7, p. 718.
14. Copeland, *Roads and their Traffic, 1750–1850,* p. 23.
15. *R.C. on the state of the Roads in England and Wales, P.P.* 1840, vol. XXVII, p. 11.
16. G. Elliot, *Silas Marner,* 1861, ch. 1.
17. *P.P.* 1840, vol. XXVII, p. 11.
18. K.G., 'An Essay on the English Roads', *The Gentleman's Magazine,* Nov.–Dec. 1752, p. 519.
19. Robert H. Spiro (Jnr), 'John London McAdam, and the Metropolitan Turnpike Trust', *Jnl Tspt Hist.,* vol. II, No. 4, Nov. 1956.
20. Webb, *The Story of the King's Highway,* 1963, p. 124.
21. G. and A. Thrupp, *The History of Coaches,* 1877, p. 107.
22. W. T. Jackman, *The Development of Transportation in Modern England,* 1962, p. 685.
23. C. G. Harper, *The Brighton Road,* (3rd (revised) edition) 1922, p. 4.
24. H. W. Hart, 'Some Notes on Coach Travel, 1750–1848', *Jnl Tspt Hist.,* vol. IV, No. 3, May 1960, p. 147.
25. *Return of the Mail Coaches in England, Ireland and Scotland, P.P.* 1836, vol. XLV, p. 449.
26. This estimate is based on information contained in trade directories of the ten cities concerned.
27. Anthony Bird, *Roads and Vehicles,* 1969, p. 126.
28. B. R. Mitchell and P. Deane, *Abstract of British Historical Statistics,* pp. 225–6.
29. *1st Report of the Commissioners of Inland Revenue, P.P.* 1857, iv, App. 24.
30. HLRO H/C S.C. on the Bristol and Exeter Railway Bill 1836: evidence of W. Charman, employee of the Stamp Office.
31. HLRO H/C S.C. on Edinburgh and Northern Railway Bill, 1845, vol. 28: evidence of William Marshall.

32. HLRO H/C S.C. on South Devon Railway Bill, 1844, vol. 37, p. 189.
33. Cyril Noall, *A History of Cornish Mail and Stage Coaches,* Truro, 1963, p. 18.
34. P.O. Records, Post 10/1 Box 2, File 29.
35. G. A. Thrupp, *The History of Coaches,* 1877, p. 111.
36. P.O. Records, P.O. 10/4.
37. P.O. Records, P.O. 10/2.
38. Edmund Vale, *The Mail Coach men of the late eighteenth century,* 1967, p. 47.
39. P.O. Records, Post 10/5, *Instructions to Mail Guards,* vol. 1.
40. C. G. Harper, *Stage Coach and Mail in Days of Yore,* 1963, p. 67.
41, P.O. Records, Post 10/10.
42. P.O. Records, Post 10/1, Files 20 and 21.
43. John Philipson, *The Art and Craft of Coach Building,* 1897, p. 38; R. Strawn, *Carriages and Coaches, their History and their Evolution,* 1912, pp. 204–5; R. L. Edgeworth, *An Essay on the Construction of Roads and Carriages,* (2nd edition) 1817, p. 106.
44. P.O. Records, 10/10.
45. XLVI Geo. III Cap. 136. The earlier Act limiting the number of 'outsides' to four had been passed in 1790. (XXX Geo. III Cap. 36.)
46. C. G. Harper, *Stage Coach and Mail in Days of Yore,* 1903, vol. 1, p. 189. Estimates of the number of Chaplin's horses vary. S. Harris in *The Coaching Age,* 1885, p. 111, mentions '1,200 horses at work'.
47. Harper, op. cit., vol. II, p. 195.
48. S. Harris, *The Coaching Age,* 1885, p. 146.
49. C. G. Harper, *The Manchester and Glasgow Road,* (2nd (revised) edition) 1924, vol. 1, p. 29.
50. Ibid., pp. 156–7.
51. C. G. Harper, *The Great North Road,* (2nd (revised) edition) 1922, vol. 1, p. 37.
52. C. G. Harper, *Stage Coach and Mail in Days of Yore,* 1903, vol. II, p. 187. W. C. A. Blew, *Brighton and its Coaches,* 1894, passim.
53. Anthony Bird, *Roads and Vehicles,* 1969, p. 124.
54. P.O. Records, Post 10/1.
55. P.O. Records, Post 10/7, *Time Bills*
56. Thomas de Quincey, *The English Mail Coach (1849),* 1905 edition, p. 18.
57. C. Dickinson, 'Stage Coach Services in the West Riding of Yorkshire between 1830–40', *Jnl Tspt Hist.,* vol. iv, No. 1, May 1959.
58. Athol Maudslay, *Highways and Horses,* 1888, p. 110.
59. A. F. Robbins, *Launceston Past and Present,* p. 47.
60. R. B. Sheridan, *She Stoops to Conquer,* 1775, Act 1.
61. E. A. Pratt, *A History of Inland Transport and Communication,* 1912, p. 328.
62. A Schoyen, *The Chartist Challenge,* 1959, p. 41–2.
63. *Times,* March 4, 1812; *Annual Register,* pp. 31–2.
64. John Copeland, *Roads and their Traffic, 1750–1850,* 1968, pp. 154–5.
65. R. B. Sheridan, *A Trip to Scarborough,* 1781, Act 1, Scene 1.

66. *1st Report of the Commissioners of Inland Revenue*, P.P. 1857, iv. App. 25.
67. HLRO H/C S.C. 1) Bristol and Exeter Railway Bill, 1836, vol. 2, evidence of William Charman, employee of the Stamp Office, Inland Revenue.
    2) Edinburgh and Northern Railway Bill, 1845, vol. 28.
    3) Reading, Guildford and Reigate Railway Bill, 1846, vol. 26, 'Returns of present passenger traffic'.
    4) South Devon Railway Bill, 1844, vol. 37: evidence of Joseph Fisher.
68. C. B. Andrews, (ed.) *The Torrington Diaries; A selection from the tours of the Hon. John Byng, later fifth Viscount Torrington, 1781–94*, 1954, p. 233.
69. C. G. Harper, *The Exeter Road*, 1899, p. 9.
72. T. Steele, 'In the Coach to London', *Spectator*, No. 132, 1 August 1711.
71. C. G. Harper, *Stage Coach and Mail in Days of Yore*, 1903, vol. 1, p. 119.
72. Thomas Delaune, *The Present State of London*, 1681. I am grateful to Mr D. A. Baker for drawing my attention to this work.
73. *Universal British Directory*, 1791, pp. 614–20.
74. Pigot and Co's *London and Provincial Commercial Directory for 1823–4*, pp. 51–7.
75. *Exeter Pocket Journal*, 1792. *Exeter Itinerary and Directory, 1831*. I am grateful to Mrs J. Lawley for these two references.
76. Directories of Sheffield 1787 and 1833.
77. Universal British Directory 1790, Pigot and Co. Directories various dates. Bailey's London Directory, Gore's Liverpool Directories, Matthew's Directories of Bristol, etc.
78. HLRO H/C S.C., Minutes of Evidence on the Bristol and Exeter Railway Bill: evidence of Mr William Heming, vol. 2, p. 207.
79. HLRO H/C S.C., Minutes of Evidence on the Caledonian Railway Bill 1845: evidence of W. Dare.
80. HLRO H/C S.C., Minutes of Evidence on the Edinburgh and Northern Railway Bill 1845, vol. 28: evidence of Mr William Marshall, shore viewer at Leith.
81. Hull Directories 1806–7, 1826 and 1838.
82. Dean's and Co.'s *Manchester and Salford Directory*, 1804.
83. John Copeland, *Roads and their Traffic, 1750–1850*, 1968, p. 69.
84. Ibid., p. 67.
85. H. J. Dyos and D. H. Aldcroft, *British Transport*, 1969, p. 72.

Chapter 3: *Coastal Shipping*

1. Adam Smith, *The Wealth of Nations*, 1776, Bk II, ch. 5.
2. Cited in T. S. Willan, *The English Coasting Trade*, 1938, p. 61.
3. Ibid., p. 79.
4. Ibid., p. 80.
5. HLRO S.C. *On Ramsgate and Margate Harbours*, July, 1850.

6. C. Lamb, 'The Old Margate Hoy', *London Magazine,* July 1823; L. Hunt, *Autobiography,* 1859.
7. *The Kentish Companion for the Year of Our Lord 1792,* 1792, p. 160.
8. J. Nasmyth, *Autobiography,* 1885, p. 121.
9. *The Life and Struggles of William Lovett in his Pursuit of Bread, Knowledge, and Freedom,* 1920 edition, p. 24.
10. Cited in T. S. Ashton, *Economic Fluctuations in England, 1700–1800,* 1959, p. 5.
11. P.O. Records, *Irish Packet Delays,* Pkt 133c, 1818.
12. J. Swift, 'Holyhead Journal', in H. Davis (ed), *J. Swift: Miscellaneous and Autobiographical Pieces, Fragments and Marginalia,* 1962, p. 201.
13. J. Grant, *Old and New Edinburgh,* n.d. (1884?), vol. 3, pp. 210–11.
14. *P.P.,* 1843, LII, pp. 384–5, 398–9. Trade and Navigation Accounts, Board of Trade, Marine Library.
15. K. T. Rowland, *Steam at Sea: A History of Steam Navigation,* 1970, pp. 33–4, 48–50.
16. J. Williamson, *The Clyde Passenger Steamer, its Rise and Progress during the Nineteenth Century,* 1904, p. 22.
17. *House of Lords, Accounts and Papers, P.P.* 1830, vol. CCLXXVIII, p. 118; 1848, vol. XXI, p. 346.
18. R. P. Cruden, *The History of the town of Gravesend in the county of Kent and of the Port of London,* 1843, p. 484; and *An Account of the Origin of Steamboats in Spain, Great Britain and America,* 1831, p. 74; *Herapath's Railway Journal,* 28 May 1842, p. 535.
19. S. Middlebrook, *Newcastle on Tyne: its Growth and Achievement,* 1968, p. 184. W. Featherstone, 'How Steam came to the Tyne', *Sea Breezes,* Jan. 1965.
20. J. Williamson, op. cit., p. 59.
21. G. Chandler, *Liverpool Shipping,* 1960, p. 50. A. C. Wardle, 'Early Steamships on the Mersey, 1815–20'. *Trans. Hist. Soc. of Lancs. and Cheshire,* vol. XCII, 1940, p. 85.
22. G. Dodd, *An Historical and Explanatory Dissertation on Steam Engines and Steam Packets,* 1818.
23. D. B. McNeill, *Irish Passenger Steamship Services,* vol. 1: *North of Ireland,* 1969, p. 21.
24. *Edinburgh Evening Courant,* 25 June and 2 July 1821.
25. Ibid., 21 May 1821.
26. R. N. Worth, *History of Plymouth,* 1890, p. 341.
27. *The Hampshire County Newspaper and South West of England Pilot,* 3 June 1822.
28. W. I. Barry, *History of the Port of Cork Steam Navigation,* 1915.
29. Advertisements in the *Edinburgh Evening Courant,* various dates June 1821–March 1830.
30. P. S. Bagwell, 'The Post Office Steam Packets, 1821–36, and the Development of Shipping on the Irish Sea', *Maritime History,* vol. 1, No. 1, April 1971. D. B. McNeill, *Irish Passenger Steamship Services,* vol. 2: *South of Ireland,* 1971, pp. 13–21.
31. *Herapath's Railway Magazine,* 24 July 1841, p. 623.

NOTES

32. These estimates are based on an examination of the manuscript minutes of evidence of 39 railway and harbour bills, but principally the London and Cambridge, London and York, Bristol and Exeter, Edinburgh and Northern and Glasgow, Kilmarnock and Ayr railways kept in the House of Lords Record Office. Figure for 1849 Edinburgh–London traffic taken from J. Thomas, *The North British Railway*, vol. 1, 1969, p. 43.
33. G. Dodd, op. cit., p. xiii.
34. *New Statistical Account of Scotland*, vol. VI, 1845, p. 202.
35. G. R. Hawke in his *Railways and Economic Growth in England and Wales 1840–1870*, 1970, p. 43, incorrectly states that journeys were cheaper by coach.
36. Advert. in *Edinburgh Evening Courant*, 13 February 1832.
37. G. G. Harper, *The Great North Road*, (2nd revised edition) 1922, vol. 1, p. 37.
38. R. P. Cruden, *An Account of the origin of Steamboats in Spain, Great Britain and America*, 1831, p. 41. Anon., *The Steamboat Companion and Strangers Guide to the Western Islands and Highlands of Scotland*, Glasgow, 1820, p. 8.
39. J. S. Maclean, *The Newcastle and Carlisle Railway*, 1948, pp. 10, 24.
40. *Articles of Agreement* between C. W. Williams and others, 13 September 1823, Irish P.R.O., 1070–88.
41. *Deed of Settlement, City of Dublin Steam Packet Company*, 1828, Irish P.R.O. D5925.
42. *Edinburgh Evening Courant*, 13 August, 3 September 1832.
43. D. B. McNeil, *Irish Passenger Steamship Services*, vol. 2: *South of Ireland*, 1971, pp. 109–10.
44. J. Grant, *Old and New Edinburgh*, n.d., p. 211.
45. P.O. Records, Packet 549/D 1828.
46. E. E. Allen, 'On the Comparative Cost of Transit by Steam and Sailing Colliers and on the different modes of Ballasting', Inst. Civ. Eng., *Proceedings*, vol. XIV, 1854–5, p. 318.
47. H. S. Irvine, 'Some Aspects of Passenger Traffic between Britain and Ireland, 1820–50', *Jnl Tspt Hist.*, vol. 4, November 1960.
48. HLRO, Minutes of Evidence of H/C S.C. on North Midland Railway Bill, 26 February 1836.
49. HLRO, Minutes of Evidence H/C S.C. on York and North Midland Railway Bill, 20 April 1836.
50. I am indebted to Mr John Armstrong for abstracting the above information from the London Bills of Entry of 1824.
51. *R.C. on Canals and Inland Waterways, 4th Report, P.P.*, 1910, vol. XII, paras 293–4.
52. London Guildhall Library, mss. 1667/123.
53. F. G. G. Carr, *Sailing Barges*, 2nd edition 1951, pp. 8–11; H. Benham, *Down Tops'l*, 1951, p. 47.
54. HLRO, Minutes of Evidence of H/C S.C. on London and Cambridge Railway, evidence of Thomas Evans, meat salesman, 18 April 1836 and Robert Herbert, agricultural reporter, 20 April 1836. G. Channon, 'The Aberdeenshire Beef Trade with London: a study in Steamship and Railway Competition', *Transport History*, vol. 2,

No. 1, March 1969, p. 1. W. MacCombie, *Cattle and Cattle Breeders*, 1886, pp. 72, 73, 82.

55. James Wilson, *A Voyage round the Coasts of Scotland and the Isles*, vol. 1, 1842, p. 56.

56. Gloucester R.O. H/C S.C. on the South Wales and Great Western Direct Railway Bill, 22 May 1865, Minutes of Evidence of W. West, Agent for Risca Colliery. Cardiff Chamber of Commerce, *Annual Reports*. C. Hadfield, *Canals of South Wales and the Border*, 1960, p. 26.

57. Table compiled from returns in *P.P.* 1824, vol. XVII, pp. 90–99; 1828, vol. XVIII, pp. 318–25; 1830–31, vol. X, p. 393; 1837, vol. V, pp. 397–400; 1839, vol. XLV, p. 65; 1841, vol. XXIV, p. 60; and 1847, vol. L, p. 405.

58. G. R. Porter, *The Progress of the Nation*, 1851 edition, p. 346.

59. Numbers of Livestock shipped from Ireland to Great Britain, *P.P.* 1833, V, p. 630; 1870, LXI, p. 110.

60. G. R. Porter, op. cit., p. 344.

61. *S.C. on Taxation of Internal Communication, Minutes of Evidence, P.P.* 1837, vol. XX, qs. 484–6.

62. Ibid., evidence of C. Kemplay, coach proprietor, York, q. 475.

63. Ibid., evidence of Sir John Hall, Bart., q. 321.

64. *Petition of Mail Coach Contractors and Stage Coach Proprietors on the Great North Road*, 1838.

65. HLRO Minutes of Evidence of H/C S.C. on London and York Railway Bill, evidence of J. Duckworth, surveyor, of Barnet.

66. *Edinburgh Evening Courant*, 5 January 1846, 1 January 1849. *Edinburgh Courant*, 1 January 1885.

67. BTHR GN 1/319/19, Audit Office, Kings Cross, proposed reduction in fares, 5 April 1870.

68. *The New Statistical Account of Scotland*, 1845, vol. 5, pp. 804–5.

69. Anon., *Tales, Traditions and Antiquities of Leith*, 1865, p. 322. Leith Dock Commission, *The Port of Leith*, 1966.

70. J. W. Burrows, *Southend on Sea and District: Historical Notes*, 1909, p. 180. HLRO Minutes of Evidence of H/C S.C. on Southend Pier Bill, May 1835. Evidence of T. Ingram, Waterman of Southend.

71. A. H. John, *The Industrial Development of South Wales*, 1950, p. 120.

72. T. Gray, 'Fifty years of Legislation in relation to the Shipping Trade and the Safety of ships and seamen' in Worshipful Company of Shipwrights' *Lectures at the Mansion House, 1886–7*, 1887, p. 171.

73. 'Various Well Known Experts', *The Industrial Rivers of England*, 1891, p. 119.

74. S. Middlebrook, *Newcastle on Tyne: its Growth and Achievement*, 1968, p. 194. Earlier improvements in the area are examined in A. G. Kenwood, 'Capital Investment in Docks, Harbours and river improvements in N.E. England', 1825–50, *Jnl Tspt Hist.*, N.S., vol. 1, No. 2, September 1971.

75. J. Guthrie, *The River Tyne: its History and Resources*, 1880.

76. S. Middlebrook, op. cit., p. 235.

77. Blyth Harbour Commission, *Port of Blyth: Official Handbook*, 1954, p. 21.
78. *Journal* of R.M.S.P. *Prince Arthur*, National Library of Ireland, ms 2818.
79. W. Runciman, *Before the Mast—and After*, 1924, p. 85.
80. E. E. Allen, 'On the Comparative Cost of Transit by Steam and Sailing Colliers and on the different modes of Ballasting', Inst. Civ. Eng., *Proceedings*, vol. XIV, 1854, p. 321.
81. Journal of R.M.S.P. *Prince Arthur*, loc. cit.
82. W. Runciman wrote: 'Some of the owners of these colliers were more willing to spend money on paints and oils than others were on essential repairs. They had a sound belief in the efficiency of appearance', op. cit., p. 81.
83. H. Benham, *Last Stronghold of Sail*, 1948, p. 112.
84. W. Runciman, op. cit., p. 224.
85. Journal of the *St Columba*, 1861, contains, on the flyleaf, a list of names of the eight men headed with the statement 'Not to be employed any more in the CDSPCo.' National Library of Ireland, ms 2955.
86. L. H. Powell, *The Shipping Federation: a history of the first sixty years*, 1950, p. 6.
87. G. Alderman, 'Samuel Plimsoll and the Shipping Interest', *Maritime History*, vol. 1, No. 1, April 1971, p. 73.
88. J. C. Robertson and H. H. Hagan, 'A Century of Coaster Design and Operation', *Transactions of the Institution of Engineers and Shipbuilders in Scotland*, 1953.
89. H.L. *Enquiry on Steam Vessel Accidents*, P.P. 1839, vol. XXV, p. 642.
90. Committee of Privy Council for Trade, *Report on Steam Vessels Enquiry*, H/L Sessional Papers 1839, vol. V, p. 25.
91. *Hansard*, 3rd series, vol. VI, Col. 401, 22 August 1831.
92. D. O'Neill, 'Safety at Sea, 1850–1950', *Trans. Inst. Marine Engineers*, vol. LXII, No. 2, 1950.
93. T. Gray, '1836–1886: 50 years of Regulation in relation to the Shipping Trade', Worshipful Company of Shipwrights, *Lectures at the Mansion House, 1886–7*, 1881.
94. J. P. Bowen, *British Lighthouses*, 1947. W. J. Kelly, 'Irish Lights', *Sea Breezes*, vol. 31, January 1961.
95. Royal National Lifeboat Institution, *The Story of the Lifeboat*, 1957.
96. T. Gray, op. cit., p. 174.

Chapter 4: *The Foundation of the Railway System*

1. M. Robbins, *The Railway Age*, 1962, p. 12, citing C. E. Lee, *The Evolution of Railways*, 1937.
2. J. U. Nef, *The Rise of the British Coal Industry*, 1932, vol. 1, p. 80.
3. Ibid., vol. 1, p. 158.
4. M. J. T. Lewis, *Early Wooden Railways*, 1970, p. 90. R. B. Smith, 'England's First Rails: A Reconsideration', *Renaissance and Modern Studies*, vol. IV, 1960, p. 119.

5. Lewis, op. cit., p. 87.
6. Ibid., p. 130.
7. Ibid., p. 298.
8. H. W. Dickinson and A. Tilley, *Richard Trevithick, the Engineer and the Man*, 1934, p. 57.
9. Ibid., p. 108.
10. *Engineering*, 27 March 1868.
11. R. W. Kidner, *The Early History of the Railway Locomotive, 1804–1879*, 1946, p. 6. C. F. Dendy Marshall, *Early British Locomotives*, passim.
12. H. J. Dyos and D. H. Aldcroft, *British Transport*, 1969, p. 116.
13. W. T. Jackman, *The Development of Transportation in Modern England*, 1962 edition, pp. 514–17.
14. Prospectus of the Liverpool and Manchester Railway Company, quoted in R. E. Carlson, *The Liverpool and Manchester Railway Project 1821–1831*, 1969, pp. 81–4.
15. G. F. Westcott, *The British Railway Locomotive*, 1958, p. 5.
16. C. E. Lee, *The World's First Public Railway*, 1931.
17. *S.C. on Communications by Railway*, P.P. 1839, vol. X, App. 29, p. 410.
18. H. J. Dyos and D. H. Aldcroft, *British Transport*, p. 127.
19. Railway Shareholders' Association, *Report of the Proceedings at the National Conference of Railway Shareholders, Town Hall, Manchester, 14 and 15 April, 1868*, p. 36.
20. *S.C. on Railway and Canal Bills, Fifth Report*, p. 5, *P.P.* 1852–3, vol. XXXVIII, p. 451.
21. M. C. Reed, 'Railways and the Growth of the Capital Market', in M. C. Reed (ed.), *Railways in the Victorian Economy*, 1969, p. 164.
22. R. E. Carlson, *The Liverpool and Manchester Railway Project 1821–31*, 1969, p. 153. H. Pollins, 'The Finances of the Liverpool and Manchester Railway', *Ec. Hist. Rev.* 2nd series, vol. V, No. 1, 1952.
23. S. Broadbridge, *Studies in Railway Expansion and the Capital Market in England 1825–73*, 1970, p. 113.
24. R. B. Fellows, *History of the Canterbury and Whitstable Railway*, 1930, p. 28.
25. S. Broadbridge, op. cit., p. 161. E. T. MacDermot, *History of the Great Western Railway*, 1927, vol. I, pp. 11, 19, 147.
26. J. Melville and J. L. Hobbs, *Early Railway History of Furness*, 1951, p. 21.
27. J. Simmons, *The Maryport and Carlisle Railway*, 1947, p. 1.
28. Stephenson Locomotive Society, *The Highland Railway Company and its Constituents and Successors*, 1955, p. 4.
29. John Thomas, *The North British Railway*, 1969, vol. 1, p. 21.
30. S. Broadbridge, op. cit., pp. 136–50.
31. W. T. Jackman, *The Development of Transportation in Modern England*, p. 584.
32. S. Broadbridge, op. cit., pp. 146–50.
33. *Herapath's Railway Journal*, 24 November 1846, p. 1289.
34. Henry Ayres, *The Financial Position of Railways*, 1869, p. viii (cited in S. Broadbridge, op. cit., p. 159).

35. The above account is based on H. Pollins' article, 'Railway Contractors and the Finance of Railway Development in Britain', *Jnl Tspt Hist.* III, 1957, p. 41
36. R. J. Irving, 'British Railway Investment and Innovation 1900–1914', *Business History*, vol. XIII, No. 1, January 1971, p. 39.
37. G. D. Parkes, *The Hull and Barnsley Railway*, 1948, p. 2.
38. J. S. Jeans, *Railway Problems*, 1887, p. 32.
39. J. C. Jeaffreson, *Life of Robert Stephenson*, 1864, vol. 1, p. 269–70.
40. *S.C. on Railways, P.P.* 1839, vol. X, q. 2059; M. Robbins, *The Railway Age*, p. 38.
41. *S.C. on Railways, P.P.* 1839, vol. X, qs. 1234–7.
42. Ibid., q. 1447.
43. Ibid., q. 2059.
44. Ibid., q. 3940.
45. H. Pollins, 'A Note on Railway Constructional Costs 1825–1850', *Economica*, new series, vol. 19, Nov. 1952, p. 395.
46. HLRO, *House of Lords S.C. on Railways*, 1846, manuscript record of evidence of George Burke.
47. *S.C. on Railways, P.P.* 1839, vol. X, evidence of John Harman, qs. 1942–8.
48. J. S. Jeans, *Railway Problems*, p. 429.
49. J. Simmons, *The Railways of Britain*, 1965, p. 15.
50. J. S. Jeans, op. cit., p. 40.
51. M. Robbins, *The Railway Age*, p. 36.
52. Sir A. Helps, *Life and Labours of Mr. Brassey*, 1969 edition (with an introduction by Jack Simmons), p. 28.
53. *S.C. on Railway Labourers, P.P.* 1846, vol. XIII, evidence of I. K. Brunel, q. 2047.
54. C. Walker, *Thomas Brassey: Railway Builder*, 1969, p. 28.
55. J. R. Francis, *A History of the English Railway*, 1851, vol. 1, p. 269.
56. J. Simmons, Introduction to *Life and Labours of Mr. Brassey*, 1969, p. x.
57. Wages paid by Brassey are cited in Helps, op. cit., App. C.
58. *Select Committee on Emigration*, 1827, cited in J. A. Jackson, *The Irish in Britain*, 1965, p. 79.
59. J. R. Francis, op. cit., vol. 2, p. 67.
60. *S.C. on Railway Labourers, P.P.* 1846, vol. XIII, Minutes of Evidence, qs 1309, 2161.
61. J. A. Patmore, 'A Navvy Gang of 1851', *Jnl Tspt Hist.*, VIII, 1962, p. 183.
62. T. Coleman, *The Railway Navvies*, 1965, p. 79.
63. Ibid., p. 54. The machine cost £1,500.
64. Ibid., p. 212.

Chapter 5: *The Economic and Social Effects of Railways*

1. *S.C. on Railways, 1839, P.P.* 1839, Minutes of Evidence, vol. X, q. 3818.
2. *S.C. on Railways, 1840, P.P.* 1840, Minutes of Evidence, vol. XIII, q. 4860.

3. J. Simmons, 'Railways', *V.C.H. Leicestershire*, vol. 3, 1955, p. 113.
4. G. R. Hawke, *Railways and Economic Growth in England and Wales 1840–70*, 1970, p. 33.
5. *S.C. on Railways 1844, P.P.* 1844, Minutes of Evidence, vol. XI, q. 4290.
6. BTHR LVM, 1/2 Minute of the Board of Directors, 17 October 1831.
7. R. B. Fellows, *History of the Canterbury and Whitstable Railway*, 1930, p. 34.
8. *S.C. on Railways, 1839, P.P.* 1839, Minutes of Evidence, vol. X, q. 5844.
9. *S.C. on Railways, 1844, 5th Report*, App. 2, p. 605.
10. BTHR LY, 1/2 Minute 522 of the Board of Directors, 23 July 1838.
11. *S.C. on Railways, 1839, P.P.* 1839, Minutes of Evidence, vol. X, q. 4762.
12. Hawke, op. cit., p. 53.
13. E. Cleveland-Stevens, *English Railways, Their Development and Their Relation to the State*, 1915, p. 178.
14. P. S. Bagwell, *The Railway Clearing House in the British Economy 1842–1922*, 1968, ch. 4.
15. *Railway Returns*, 1847–53.
16. *Navigation and Canal Companies Returns, P.P.* 1870, vol. LVI.
17. B. R. Mitchell, 'The Coming of the Railways and United Kingdom Economic Growth', *Jnl Ec. Hist.*, XXIV, 1964, p. 318.
18. *Railway Returns.*
19. *Railway Returns 1912, P.P.* 1914–16, vol. LX, p. 680.
20. Ibid., p. 643.
21. Ibid., p. 680.
22. *R.C. on Canals, 4th Report*, 1910, para. 293–4.
23. Mitchell, op. cit., p. 325. G. R. Hawke, *Railways and Economic Growth in England and Wales*, 1840–70, 1970, ch. 9.
24. BTHR LSO 1/2, London and Southampton Railway Board Minutes, 29 October 1834. Dr Hawke's book includes two tables showing the rail orders of the London and Birmingham Railway between December 1835 and November 1837.
25. *L.M.S. Magazine*, July 1926, p. 199.
26. *Engineer*, 18 March 1864, p. 173.
27. *S.C. on Railways, 1839, P.P.* 1839, Minutes of Evidence, vol. X, q. 286.
28. D. E. C. Eversley, 'Engineering and Railway Works', in *V.C.H. Wiltshire*, vol. 4, p. 215.
29. S. B. Saul, 'The Market and the Development of Mechanical Engineering in Britain, 1860–1914', *Ec. Hist. Rev.*, April 1967, p. 114.
30. *Railway Returns, 1912, P.P.* 1914–16, vol. LX, pp. 148 and xiii.
31. J. M. Dunn, *The Chester and Holyhead Railway*, 1948, pp. 9–10.
32. B. R. Mitchell, 'The Coming of the Railways and United Kingdom Economic Growth', *Jnl Ec. Hist.*, vol. XXIV, 1964, p. 318.
33. M. Christy, 'Brickmaking and Tilemaking', in *V.C.H. Essex*, vol. 2, 1907, p. 457.

34. C. Jamison, 'Bricks, Tiles, Pottery', in *V.C.H. Buckinghamshire*, vol. 2, 1908, p. 114.
35. M. Christy, op. cit., p. 356.
36. J. H. Clapham, *Economic History of Modern Britain*, 1950, vol. 1, p. 463.
37. *S.C. on Railway Acts Enactments, 1846, P.P.* 1846, Minutes of Evidence, vol. XIV, qs. 3152–61.
38. J. D. Chambers and G. E. Mingay, *The Agricultural Revolution 1750–1880*, 1966, p. 174.
39. *S.C. of the House of Commons on the Taff Vale Railway Bill, 1857*, BTHR PYB, 1 48A.
40. HLRO H/C, *S.C. on London and Cambridge Railway Bill*, 22 April 1836, vol. 18, evidence of Mr G. Calthorpe, merchant and commission agent of Spalding.
41. C. S. Orwin and E. H. Whetham, *History of British Agriculture, 1846–1914*, 1964, p. 27.
42. Ibid., p. 99.
43. *The Times*, 19 July 1856.
44. J. D. Chambers and G. E. Mingay, *The Agricultural Revolution, 1750–1880*, 1966, p. 187–8.
45. W. W. Glenny, 'Sea Fisheries', in *V.C.H. Essex*, vol. 2, 1907, p. 439.
46. B. R. Mitchell, 'The Coming of the Railways and United Kingdom Economic Growth', *Jnl Ec. Hist.*, vol. XXIV, 1964, p. 331. G. R. Hawke, *Railways and Economic Growth in England and Wales 1840–1870*, 1970, pp. 197–212.
47. T. H. Green Papers, Balliol College, Oxford, cited in C. Harvie and others (ed.) *Industrialisation and Culture*, 1970, p. 86.
48. G. R. Hawke, op. cit., 404–5.
49. N. E. MacMunn, 'Social and Economic History', in *V.C.H. Essex*, vol. 2, 1907, p. 336.
50. *Isle of Wight Times*, 8 September and 3 November 1864.
51. BTHR LNW 1/20, Minute M20 of the Board of Directors, 10 January 1846.
52. J. M. Dunn, *The Chester and Holyhead Railway*, 1948, p. 46.
53. *Edinburgh Evening Courant*, 20 November 1847.
54. B. Disraeli, *Sybil*, 1845, p. 153.
55. Isle of Wight R.O., TPT 44, letter to the Editor of the *Hampshire Telegraph*, 1 July 1845.
56. A. Trollope, *Barchester Towers*, 1945 (Everyman edition), p. 34.
57. R. B. Fellows, *History of the Canterbury and Whitstable Railway*, 1930, p. 34.
58. BTHR LVM 1/2 Liverpool & Manchester Railway Board, 8 September 1830.
59. A. Trollope, loc. cit.
60. W. F. Rae, *The Business of Travel; A Fifty Year Record*, 1891, p. 20. J. Pudney, *The Thomas Cook Story*, 1953, pp. 53–9.
61. BTHR LVM 1/2, Liverpool & Manchester Railway Board, 9 May and 20 June 1831.
62. *Report of the Departmental Committee on Holidays with Pay*, 1938, p. 11.

63. H. Perkin, *The Age of the Railway*, 1970, p. 228.
64. *The Times*, 2 May 1867.
65. J. A. R. Pimlott, *The Englishman's Holiday*, 1947.
66. 'Railroads in Ireland', *Quarterly Review*, 1839, p. 30.
67. J. M. Dunn, *The Chester and Holyhead Railway*, 1948, App. 4, p. 33.
68. *The Times* Publishing Co., *A Newspaper History*, 1785–1935, p. 126.
69. BTHR LVM 1/2, Liverpool & Manchester Railway Board Minutes, 1 August 1831.
70. Minute 914, Superintendents' Conference, RCH, 25 January 1866, RCH 1/115.
71. *The Times* Publishing Co., op. cit., p. 176.
72. The following account of the town is based on Dr W. H. Chaloner's book, *The Social and Economic Development of Crewe, 1780–1923*, 1950.
73. P. Richards, 'The Influence of the Railways on the Growth of Wolverton, Buckinghamshire', *Records of Buckinghamshire*, vol. XVII, pt. 2, 1962. *V.C.H. Buckinghamshire*, vol. 2, pp. 126–7.
74. D. E. C. Eversley, 'Engineering and Railway Works', in *V.C.H. Wiltshire*, vol. 4, pp. 207–19.
75. B. J. Turton, 'The Railway Towns of Southern England', *Transport History*, vol. 2, No. 2, July 1969, p. 104–19. K. Jackson, 'The South Eastern Railway and its Workshops at Ashford', *Cantium*, 1971, pp. 93–101.
78. W. Ashworth, 'Metropolitan Essex since 1850', in *V.C.H. Essex*, vol. V, 1966, p. 23.
79. *Palmers Green Gazette*, 9 April 1971.
80. The account which follows is largely based on J. R. Kellett, *The Impact of Railways on Victorian Cities*, 1969.
81. *The Times*, 2 March 1861.
82. Ashworth, op. cit., p. 24. Kellett, op. cit., p. 379.
83. H. J. Dyos, 'Workmen's Fares in South London, 1860–1914', *Jnl Tspt Hist.*, vol. I, No. 1, May 1953, p. 5.
84. *S.C. on Metropolitan Communications*, P.P. 1854–5, vol. X, App. pp. 215–16.
85. *The Times*, 20 October 1863.
86. T. C. Barker and M. Robbins, *A History of London Transport*, vol. 1, 1963, p. 139. E. Course, *London Railways*, 1962, pp. 45–54.
87. E. Course, op. cit., p. 48.
88. T. C. Barker and M. Robbins, op. cit., p. 108.
89. Ibid., p. 134.
90. C. E. Lee, *Sixty years of the Northern*, 1967, p. 11.

Chapter 6: *Road and Water Transport in the Railway Age*

1. *S.C. on Railroad Communications*, P.P. 1838, vol. XVI, q. 1100. Another coach proprietor, Edward Sherman, declared that travelling on the turnpike roads between London and Birmingham would be 'completely annihilated as to animal power'. Ibid., q. 166.
2. M. Robbins, *The Railway Age*, 1965, p. 44.

3. C. C. Harper, *The Brighton Road,* (3rd revised edition) 1922, pp. 41–2.
4. HLRO H/C S.C., 17 May 1845, vol. 56, Minutes of Evidence on the London and York Railway Bill, evidence of T. Walker.
5. *Derby Mercury,* 9 September 1840.
6. *Report of R.C. for enquiring into the State of the Roads in England and Wales, P.P.* 1840, vol. XXVII, App. X
7. *S.C. on Turnpike Trusts, P.P.* 1839, vol. IX, qs 190–203.
8. *Derby Mercury,* 13 May 1840.
9. *The Leeds Times,* 23 April 1836.
10. *Leeds Intelligencer,* 10 October 1840.
11. *Report of R.C. for enquiring into the State of Roads in England and Wales, P.P.* 1840, vol. XXVII, App. X.
12. BTHR L and M 1/8.
13. BTHR LSO 1/3.
14. BTHR BDJ 1/2, Board Minutes, 29 July 1840.
15. T. May, 'Road Passenger Transport in Harrow in the Nineteenth and early Twentieth Centuries', *Jnl Tspt Hist.,* new series, vol. I, No. 1, 1971, pp. 18–38.
16. *The Norwich Mercury,* 3 January 1846.
17. *S.C. on Railroad Communication, P.P.* 1838, vol. XVI, q. 1097.
18. *S.C. on Internal Communication Taxation, Report, P.P.* 1837, vol. XX, p. 293.
19. *First Report of the Commissioners of Inland Revenue on the Inland Revenue, P.P.* 1857, vol. IV, App. 24.
20. *S.C. on Turnpike Trusts, P.P.* 1839. vol. IX, qs 190–199.
21. H/L *S.C. on Horses, P.P.* 1873, vol. XIV, evidence of Mr J. East, Dealer and Job Master, qs 71–2.
22. Ibid., qs 3633 and 3686–7.
23. F. M. L. Thompson, *Victorian England: the horse-drawn society,* 1970, p. 13.
24. Ibid., p. 15.
25. *Report of the R.C. for enquiring into the state of roads in England and Wales, P.P.* 1840, vol. XXVII, p. 8.
26. Ibid., App.
27. *Minutes of the Gloucester and Hereford Turnpike Trust,* Gloucester R.O., D 204/2/4.
28. C. Capper, *The Port and Trade of London, 1862,* p. 449. BTHR LVM 1/2, Liverpool and Manchester Railway Board Minutes, 4 November 1830.
29. *Report of the R.C. for enquiring into the state of the roads in England and Wales, P.P.* 1840, vol. XXVII, App.
30. S. and B. Webb, *The Story of the King's Highway,* 1963 edition, p. 215.
31. *S.C. on the Turnpike Trusts, P.P.* 1864, Minutes of Evidence, vol. IX, q. 162.
32. C. Dickens, *'The Uncommercial Traveller',* 1860 edition, ch. 24.
33. *Sunday Times,* 30 July, 1826.
34. *S.C. on the Turnpike Trusts, P.P.* 1864, Minutes of Evidence, vol. IX, q. 295.

35. Ibid., qs 2254, 2264.
36. Ibid., qs 2426–9.
37. T. C. Barker and M. Robbins, *A History of London Transport*, 1963, vol. I, p. 13. R. H. Spiro, Jn., 'John London McAdam and the Metropolitan Turnpike Trust', *Jnl Tspt Hist.*, vol. II, 1956, pp. 207–213.
38. David Williams, *The Rebecca Riots*, 1955, pp. 178, 291. The name of the uprising was taken from Genesis XXIV, 60, 'And they blessed Rebekah and said unto her, let thy seed possess the gates of those who hate them.'
39. *S.C. on the Turnpike Trusts, Report*, P.P. 1864, vol. IX, pp. iii–iv.
40. A Hacking, *The Story of the Roads*, 1927, p. 149.
41. Webb, op. cit., p. 222.
42. *S.C. of H/L on Highways Acts*, P.P. 1881, vol. X, 11.
43. Ibid., p. 47.
44. P. S. Bagwell, *The Railway Clearing House in the British Economy, 1842–1922*, 1968, p. 116. C. G. Harper, *The Norwich Road*, 1901, p. 54.
45. Webb, op. cit., p. 240.
46. H. O. Duncan, *The World on Wheels*, 1927, pp. 297–8.
47. Article on the 'Bicycle', *Chambers Encyclopaedia*, 1966 edition, vol. 2, p. 307.
48. P. S. Bagwell, *The Railway Interest: its organisation and influence, 1839–1914*, *Jnl Tspt Hist.*, vol. vii, 1965.
49. C. Klapper, *The Golden Age of Tramways*, 1961, p. 133.
50. G. C. Dickinson, 'The Development of Suburban Road Passenger Transport in Leeds 1840–1895', *Jnl Tspt Hist.*, vol. IV, 1960, No. 4, p. 214.
51. Ward's *North of England Directory*, 1861, pp. 63, 290. Ward's *Directory of Newcastle-upon-Tyne, Gateshead and Sunderland, 1873–4*, p. 59.
52. Klapper, op. cit., p. 16.
53. Ibid., pp. 16–20.
54. Board of Trade return: *Tramways and Light Railways, Street and Road and Trackless Trolley Undertakings: Annual Return of Capital*, P.P. 1914, vol. LXXVII, p. 949.
55. Klapper, op. cit., p. 61. W. H. Brett and J. C. Gillham, *Great British Tramway Networks*, (4th edition) 1962.
56. Number of train passenger journeys (including season ticket holders) 1,549·8 million. Number of tram journeys 3,426·5 million. Source, *Railway Returns*, Klapper, op. cit., p. 5.
57. Klapper, op. cit., p. 212.
58. E. Jackson-Stevens, *British Electric Tramways*, 1971, p. 47.
59. *P.P.* 1914, vol. LXXVII, p. 949.
60. I am grateful to Mr R. Fitzgerald for this information.
61. T. Boyle, *Hope for the Canals Showing the evil of Amalgamations with Railways to Public and Private Interest*, 1848, p. 20.
62. E. A. Pratt, *Canals and Traders*, 1910, pp. 89–91.
63. F. C. Mather, *After the Canal Duke*, 1970, p. 210.

64. *R.C. on Canals, 1906 Report,* App. 1, p. 499, *P.P.* 1906, vol. XXXII. *S.C. on Canals 1883,* evidence of W. H. Bartholomew, Engineer of Aire and Calder Canal, *P.P.* 1883, vol. XIII, qs 786–801.
65. E. L. Williams giving evidence before *S.C. on Railway Companies Amalgamation, P.P.* 1872, vol. XIII, q. 3595.
66. L. T. C. Rolt, *The Inland Waterways of England,* 1950, p. 62.
67. Evidence of Sir H. Jekyll (Board of Trade), *R.C. on Canals,* 1906, *P.P.* 1909, vol. XIII, q. 62.
68. *S.C. on Canals, 1883, Report, P.P.* 1883, vol. XIII, Minutes of Evidence. P.I. App. No. 2, pp. 206–9.
69. *2nd Report, P.P.* 1846, vol. XIII, pp. iii–iv.
70. Evidence of N. Robson, Civil Engineer of Glasgow, before S.C. on Railways and Canals Amalgamation, *P.P.* 1846, vol. XIII, q. 919.
71. *S.C. on Railways and Canals Amalgamation, P.P.* 1846, vol. XIII, qs. 555–8.
72. *S.C. on Railway Companies Amalgamation, P.P.* 1872, vol. XIII (i), q. 5041.
73. *R.C. on Canals, P.P.* 1910, vol. XII, Minutes of Evidence, qs 24242–5.
74. Ibid., *Report,* para. 410.
75. *R.C. on Railways, Minutes of Evidence, P.P.* 1867, vol. XXXVIII (i), q. 10046.
76. *R.C. on Canals, Minutes of Evidence, P.P.* 1909, vol. XIII, q. 934475.
77. Document signed by William Pratt at Brimscombe Port, 2 January 1856. Gloucester R.O. D 2169/15.
78. *S.C. on Railway Companies Amalgamation,* Minutes of Evidence, *P.P.* 1872, vol. XIII (i), q. 3604.
79. Ibid., q. 5032.
80. *S.C. on Railways and Canals Amalgamation,* Minutes of Evidence, *P.P.* 1846, vol. XIII, q. 941.
81. *R.C. on Canals,* Minutes of Evidence, *P.P.* 1909, vol. XIII, q. 4298.
82. Ibid., qs 40800–5.
83. Ibid., qs 23554.
84. C. Hadfield, *The Canals of Southern England,* 1955, pp. 269–70.
85. Gloucester R.O., 1180/5/36.
86. *S.C. on Railways and Canals Amalgamation,* Minutes of Evidence, *P.P.* 1846, vol. XIII, q. 338.
87. *S.C. on Railway Companies Amalgamation,* Minutes of Evidence, *P.P.* 1872, vol. XIII (i), q. 7532.
88. Ibid., q. 5021.
89. *R.C. on Railways,* Minutes of Evidence, *P.P.* 1867, vol. XXXVIII (i), q. 9900–9901.
90. *S.C. on Railway Companies Amalgamation,* Minutes of Evidence, *P.P.* 1872, vol. XIII (i), q. 5022. *S.C. on Canals,* Minutes of Evidence, *P.P.* 1883, vol. XIII, q. 313.
91. *S.C. on Canals,* Minutes of Evidence, *P.P.* 1883, vol. XIII, q. 3461.
92. *R.C. on Canals,* Minutes of Evidence, *P.P.* 1906, vol. XXXII, qs 9296–9297.
93. Ibid., *P.P.* 1910, vol. XII, App. 1.

94. E. A. Pratt, *Railways and their Rates*, 1905, p. 80.
95. *R.C. on Canals*, Report on the Waterways of France, *P.P.* 1909, vol. XIII. Report on the Waterways of Belgium, Germany and Holland, *P.P.* 1910, vol. XII. J. H. Clapham, *The Economic Development of France and Germany 1815–1914*, (4th edition) 1948, pp. 350–52.
96. *R.C. on Canals*, Minutes of Evidence, *P.P.* 1906, vol. XXXII, qs 8295–7.
97. Ibid. Final Report, *P.P.* 1910, vol. XII, para. 410.
98. Ibid., para. 415.
99. Ibid., para. 442.
100. Ibid., paras 486, 880.
101. British Transport Commission, Board of Survey, *Report*, November 1954, Canals in Group 1.
102. C. E. R. Hadfield, *British Canals*, 1950 edition, p. 233.

Chapter 7: *Government and the Railways 1830–1914*

1. D. Lardner, *Railway Economy*, 1850, p. 506.
2. J. H. Chapman, *The Economic Development of France and Germany 1815–1914*, (4th edition) 1936, pp. 140–46.
3. *Hansard*, 3rd series, vol. 132, 6 April 1854, Col. 588.
4. J. Morrison, *Speech on Railways*, 1836, pp. 7–17.
5. *S.C. on Railways, Second Report, P.P.* 1839, vol. X, p. v.
6. *Hansard*, 3rd series, vol. 72, 5 February 1844, Col. 236.
7. H. Pollins, *Britain's Railways: an industrial history*, 1971, p. 38.
8. *P.P.* 1839, vol. X.
9. J. R. Kellett, *The Impact of Railways on Victorian Cities*, 1969, p. 105.
10. Claim made by Mr Mangles in the House of Commons, 4 May 1854 (*Hansard*, 3rd series, vol. 132, Col. 1234).
11. H. Parris, *Government and the Railways in Nineteenth Century Britain*, 1965, p. 85.
12. *P.P.* 1844, vol. XI.
13. The words were those of Mr Gisborne, M.P., *Hansard*, 3rd series, vol. 76, 11 July 1844, Col. 662.
14. *Hansard*, 3rd series, vol. 74, Cols 480–508.
15. Mr Gisborne's words, ibid., Col. 466.
16. The above account is based on E. Cleveland-Stevens, *English Railways: their development and their relation to the state*, 1915, pp. 142–57, and H. Parris, op. cit., pp. 103–23.
18. *Hansard*, 3rd series, vol. 83, Col. 221, 26 January 1846.
19. Cited in J. R. Kellett, op. cit., p. 31.
20. These are Dr Kellett's own words, op. cit., p. 31. Even the classical economist J. R. McCulloch noted the drawbacks of the method of railway promotion when he wrote 'In the instance of railway legislation, the public interests have been overlooked to a degree that is not very excusable', *A Statistical Account of the British Empire*, 2nd edition, 1839, vol. 2, p. 59.
21. *Hansard*, 3rd series, vol. 132, Col. 585, 6 April 1854.

22. E. Cardwell, quoting the report of the S.C. on Railway and Canal Bills, *Hansard,* 3rd series, vol. 132, Col. 587, 6 April 1854.
23. *P.P.* 1852–3, vol. XXXVIII.
24. *The Economist,* 24 December 1864.
25. *Royal Commission on Railways, Report, P.P.* 1867, vol. XXXVIII i.
26. E. Cleveland-Stevens, op. cit., p. 238.
27. *S.C. on Railway Companies' Amalgamation: Report P.P.* 1872, vol. XIII.
28. *P.P.* 1872, vol. XIII ii, App. N., p. 823.
29. For an account of this episode see my 'The Rivalry and Working Union of the South Eastern and London, Chatham and Dover Railways', *Jnl Tspt Hist.,* vol. ii, No. 2, 1955.
30. C. I. Savage, *An Economic History of Transport,* 1959, p. 79.
31. *Departmental Committee on Railway Agreements and Amalgamations:* Minutes of Evidence, *P.P.* 1911, vol. XXIX, pt. 2, qs 118, 461–8.
32. *Hansard,* 3rd series, vol. 183, Col. 1632, 11 February 1908.
33. *Departmental Committee on Railway Agreements and Amalgamation Report,* Appendix X, *P.P* 1911, vol. XXIX, pt. 2.
34. Ibid., para. 185.
35. *Hansard,* 4th series, vol. 3, Col. 426, 31 March 1909.
36. A. T. Hadley, *Railroad Transportation,* 1886, p. 173.
37. *Royal Commission on Agricultural Depression,* Minutes of Evidence, *P.P.* 1881, vol. XV, qs 8096–8.
38. A. W. Kirkaldy and A. D. Evans, *The Economics and History of Transport,* 1927 edition, p. 176.
39. Letter from the Minister of Public Works to the Railway Council, October 1884, quoted in Kiekaldy and Evans, op. cit., App. XII, p. 407.
40. Cited in H. R. Wilson, *Railway Accidents: Legislation and Statistics, 1825–1924,* 1925, p. 5 .
41. *Hansard,* 3rd series, vol. 62, Col. 1045, 22 April 1842.
42. *S.C. on Railway and Canal Bills 5th Report, P.P.* 1852–3, vol. XXXVIII.
43. *Hansard,* 3rd series, vol. 145, Col. 1267, 24 February 1857.
44. *S.C. on Railway Accidents,* Minutes of Evidence, *P.P.* 1857–8, vol. XIV.
45. D. Galton and J. Brunless, *Railway Accidents,* reprinted from Institute of Civil Engineers, *Proceedings,* vol. XXI, 1861–2. Contribution to the discussion by C. W. Siemens.
46. H. R. Wilson, op. cit., p. 12.
47. *S.C. on Railways, P.P.* 1870, vol. X, p. v.
48. H. R. Wilson, op. cit., p. 12.
49. *Railway Companies Association: Sub-Committee Report,* 14 March 1871, Minute 565.
50. *Returns in pursuance of the Railway Returns (Continuous Brakes) Act, 1878.*
51. *S.C. on Railway Accidents, P.P.* 1857–8, vol. XIV, p. 195.
52. *Royal Commission on Railway Accidents, Report, P.P.* 1877, vol. XLV, 94. H. R. Wilson, op. cit., Table K.

53. *S.C. on Railways*, Minutes of Evidence, *P.P.* 1870, qs 472–6.
54. *Royal Commission on Railway Accidents, Report, P.P.* 1877, vol. XLVIII.
55. Ibid., p. 95.
56. Ibid., App. G.
57. G. Findlay, *The Working and Management of an English Railway*, 1889, p. 78. C. Edwards, *Railway Nationalisation*, (2nd edition) 1907, pp. 117–18.
58. A.S.R.S. *General Secretary's Reports*, 1885–1900.
59. *Hansard*, 3rd series, vol. 349, Col. 905 et seq., 23 January 1891.
60. *S.C. on Railway Servants Hours of Labour: Report, P.P.* 1890–1, v. XVI.
61. A.S.R.S., *General Secretary's Report*, 1900.
62. A representative viewpoint was that of G. Findlay, General Manager of the London and North Western Railway. He told the *Select Committee on Railway Servants Hours of Labour*: 'I say we will deal with our own men in our own way and give them every consideration, but I altogether object to deal with the leader of a trades union, however respectable he may be'. *P.P.* 1890–91, vol. XVI, q. 5402.

Chapter 8: *The Development of Motor Transport*

1. D. Scott-Moncrieff, *Veteran and Edwardian Motor Cars*, 1955, ch. 2. Society of Motor Manufacturers and Traders, *The Motor Industry of Great Britain*, 1939 edition, p. 7. St. John C. Nixon, *The Invention of the Automobile*, 1936.
2. Charles E. Lee claims that the Locomotives Act, 1865, 'effectually retarded developments for thirty years' (*The Early Motor Bus*, 1964, p. 5). G. Maxcy and A. Silberston wrote that the legislation 'throttled the development of the industry' (*The Motor Industry*, 1959. p. 11).
3. W. Plowden, *The Motor Car and Politics, 1896–1970*, 1971, pp. 25–8.
4. St. John C. Nixon, *Daimler 1896–1946*, 1948, p. 41.
5. W. Plowden, op. cit., p. 29.
6. BBC1 Television Programme, *The Car Makers*, 12 December 1971.
7. W. Plowden, op. cit., p. 28.
8. A. Bird, *The Motor Car, 1765–1914*, 1960, p. 107.
9. St. John C. Nixon, *The Simms Story from 1891*, 1955, p. 107.
10. G. Maxcy, 'The Motor Industry', in P. L. Cook and R. Cohen (ed.) *Effects of Mergers*, 1958, p. 358.
11. C. Wilson and W. W. Reader, *Men and Machines: A History of Napier and Sons, Engineers Ltd., 1808–1958*, 1958, p. 61.
12. K. Grahame, *The Wind in the Willows*, 1908, pp. 38, 42.
13. S. B. Saul, 'The Motor Industry in Britain to 1914', *Business History*, vol. V, December 1962, p. 41.
14. C. Wilson and W. Reader, op. cit., p. 86.
15. A. Bird, *The Motor Car, 1765–1914*, 1960, pp. 123, 132.
16. St. John C. Nixon, *Daimler 1896–1946*, 1948, p. 79.

17. D. J. Smith, 'The need for a wider outlook in automobile engineering', Institution of Automobile Engineers, *Proceedings,* vol. XVII, 1922–3, pp. 8–15.
18. G. Maxcy and A. Silbertson, *The Motor Industry,* 1959, p. 13.
19. P. W. S. Andrews and E. Brunner, *The Life of Lord Nuffield,* 1955, pp. 70–72.
20. S. B. Saul, op. cit., p. 4.
21. Institution of Automobile Engineers, *Proceedings,* vol. XIX, 1924–5, p. 467.
22. P. W. Kingsford, *F. W. Lanchester,* 1960, p. 47.
23. Andrews and Brunner, op. cit., pp. 43, 52, 61.
24. P. W. Kingsford, op. cit., p. 43.
25. St. John C. Nixon, *Wolseley: A Saga of the Motor Industry,* 1949, p. 43.
26. S. B. Saul, op. cit., p. 31.
27. Ibid.
28. P. W. Kingsford, *F. W. Lanchester,* p. 47.
29. G. Maxcy and A. Silberston, *The Motor Industry,* p. 12.
30. Society of Motor Manufacturers and Traders, *The British Motor Industry,* 1930 edition, p. 28. G. C. Allen estimated pre-war exports at a quarter of total output. *The British Motor Industry,* London and Cambridge Economic Service, Special Memorandum 18, 1926, p. 13.
31. Maxcy and Silberston, op. cit., p. 17.
32. Society of Motor Manufacturers and Traders, *The British Motor Industry,* 1926 edition, pp. 40–41. London and Cambridge Economic Service, *The British Economy: Key Statistics, 1900–1964,* 1964, p. 8.
33. C. Wilson and W. Reader, *Men and Machines: a history of D. Napier and Sons, Engineers, Ltd., 1808–1958,* 1958, p. 96.
34. St. John C. Nixon, *Wolseley: A Saga of the Motor Industry,* p. 47.
35. St. John C. Nixon, *Daimler, 1896–1946,* p. 135.
36. Nixon, *Wolseley,* p. 68.
37. P. W. S. Andrews and E. Brunner, *The Life of Lord Nuffield,* p. 72.
38. Guy Motors Ltd, *Forty Years of Achievement, 1914–1954,* 1954, p. 7.
39. A. J. P. Taylor, *English History 1914–45,* 1965, p. 122.
40. L. H. Seltzer, 'The Automobile Industry', *Encyclopaedia of the Social Sciences,* 1935 edition, vol. 2, p. 328.
41. Evidence of Sir Evan Jones, Chairman of the Road Transport Board, *S.C. on Transport, P.P.* 1918, vol. IV, q. 3293.
42. *The Economist,* 9 February 1925.
43. G. C. Allen, '*The British Motor Car Industry*', London and Cambridge Economic Service, Special Memorandum 18, June 1926, p. 23.
44. G. Maxcy, 'The Motor Industry', in P. L. Cook and R. Cohen (ed.) *Effects of Mergers,* 1958, p. 364.
45. P.E.P. *Engineering Reports II: Motor Vehicles, 1950,* p. 5.
46. G. Maxcy, op. cit., p. 5.
47. A. C. Armstrong, *Bouverie Street to Bowling Green Lane,* 1946, p. 209.
48. P.E.P., op. cit., p. 5.

49. H. G. Castle, *Britain's Motor Industry*, 1950, p. 157.
50. *The Times: Trade and Engineering Supplement*, 3 April 1926.
51. P. W. S. Andrews and E. Brunner, *The Life of Lord Nuffield*, p. 96.
52. G. Maxcy, 'The Motor Industry', in P. L. Cook and R. Cohen (ed.) *Effects of Mergers*.
53. G. Maxcy and A. Silberston, *The Motor Industry*, p. 13.
54. G. Maxcy, op. cit., p. 372.
55. Society of Motor Manufacturers and Traders, *The Motor Industry of Great Britain*, 1926 edition, p. 14.
56. Ibid.
57. Society of Motor Manufacturers and Traders, *The Motor Industry of Great Britain*, 1939 edition, p. 120–23.
58. Institution of Automobile Engineers, *Proceedings*, vol. XVI, pt. 2, 1923–4, p. 650.
59. G. Maxcy, op. cit., p. 393.
60. Institution of Automobile Engineers, *Proceedings*, vol. XVI, 1921–2, pt. 1, p. 19.
61. Society of Motor Manufacturers and Traders, *The Motor Industry of Great Britain*, 1926 edition, p. 48.
62. H. G. Castle, *Britain's Motor Industry*, p. 146.
63. *R.C. on Motor Cars, Minutes of Evidence, P.P.* 1906, vol. XLVIII, q. 8086.
64. Ibid., qs 10170–95.
65. Ibid., evidence of W. B. Mason, estate agent, qs 13,500–13,508 and Sir W. Vincent, landowner and county alderman of Surrey, q. 3374.
66. Evidence of Mr H. Hall of Exeter, q. 2646.
67. Ibid., q. 4462.
68. G. R. Askwith, *Industrial Problems and Disputes*, 1920, p. 70.
69. K. Grahame, *The Wind in the Willows*, 1908, p. 125.
70. W. Plowden, *The Motor Car and Politics, 1896–1970*, 1971, ch. 4. D. Keir and B. Morgan, *Golden Milestone*, 1955, pp. 32–43. Also information kindly provided by Mr J. W. L. Forge and by the Automobile Association.
71. *First Annual Report of the Road Board*, paras 24–28, *P.P.* 1911, vol. XL, p. 713.
72. J. B. F. Earle, *A Century of Road Materials: the History of the Roadstone Division of Tarmac Ltd.*, 1971. F. Wood, *Modern Road Construction*, 1920 edition, ch. 8.
73. *R.C. on Motor Cars*, evidence of Lord Montagu of Beaulieu, 16 November 1905. *P.P.* 1906, vol. XLVIII, q. 8099. J. C. Haller, County Surveyor of Notts, maintained that an experiment with tarmac was conducted as early as 1903. *Jnl Inst. Tspt*, vol. 2, No. 4, Feb. 1921, p. 157.
74. R. E. Crompton, 'Roads and Vehicle Maintenance', Institution of Automobile Engineers, *Proceedings*, vol. XV, 1920–21, p. 168.
75. J. C. Haller, 'Roads and Road Traffic', *Jnl Inst. Tspt*, vol. 2, No. 4, Feb. 1921, p. 157.
76. D. J. Smith, Presidential Address, Institution of Automobile Engineers, *Proceedings*, vol. XVII, 1922–3.
77. Cited in W. Plowden, *The Motor Car and Politics 1896–1970*, p. 91.

In November 1905 Lord Montagu of Beaulieu mentioned plans for toll motorways from London to Brighton and London to Bristol. *R.C. on the Motor Car*, Minutes of Evidence, *P.P.* 1906, vol. XLVIII, qs 8121–5.

78. *Road Board, Third Annual Report, P.P.* 1913, vol. XXXIX, Apps 10 & 11.
79. C. E. Lee, *The Early Motor Bus*, 1964, p. 25.
80. H. Wyatt, *The Motor Industry*, 1918, pp. 5–6.
81. Ibid.
82. *R.C. on the Motor Car*, Minutes of Evidence, *P.P.* 1906, vol. XLVIII, qs 1246–79.
83. Ibid., q. 12496.
84. Quoted by E. S. Shrapnell-Smith, 'Five decades of Commercial Road Transport with implications about its Future', *Jnl Inst. Tspt*, vol. 22, No. 6, Feb.–March 1946, p. 214.
85. *S.C. on Transport*, Minutes of Evidence, *P.P.* 1918, vol. IV, q. 3564.
86. E. S. Shrapnell-Smith, op. cit., p. 214.
87. D. MacGregor, *The National Way*, 1944, pp. 5–8.
88. E. S. Shrapnell-Smith, op. cit., pp. 221, 226.
89. *S.C. on Transport*, Minutes of Evidence, *P.P.* 1918, vol. IV, q. 1674. Messrs Whitbread, the brewers, reached the same conclusion as did the LNWR about transport in London according to their transport officer, S. Neville. *Jnl Inst. Tspt*, vol. 3, July 1922, p. 394.
90. Society of Motor Manufacturers and Traders, *The Motor Industry of Great Britain*, 1926 edition, p. 30.
91. G. A. Booth, 'Edinburgh Experimental Vehicles', in J. Hibbs (ed.), *The Omnibus*, 1971.
92. J. Hibbs, *The History of British Bus Services*, 1968, p. 47.
93. Ibid., p. 64.
94. W. J. Crosland-Taylor, *Crosville: the sowing and the harvest*, 1948, p. 4.
95. E. T. MacDermot, *History of the Great Western Railway*, 1927–31, vol. II, p. 427.
96. Earl Cawdor, Chairman of GWR, in *Great Western Railway Magazine*, vol. XV, Sept. 1903, p. 115.
97. BTHR GW 1/47, 8 October 1903.
98. *Great Western Railway Magazine*, vol. XVI, April 1904, p. 55.
99. Ibid., vol. XIX, March 1907, p. 61.
100. For a general picture of these services see C. E. Lee, 'One Hundred Years of Railway Associated Omnibus Services', in J. Hibbs (ed.), *The Omnibus*, 1971, pp. 147–180.
101. W. J. Crosland-Taylor, *Crosville: the sowing and the harvest*, p. 16.
102. *Modern Transport*, No. 2,000, 27 July 1957, pp. 9–10.
103. Guy Motors Ltd, *Forty years of Achievement, 1914–1954*, 1955.
104. H. G. Castle, *Britain's Motor Industry*, p. 198.
105. W. J. Crosland-Taylor, op. cit., p. 17.
106. Article 'The Growth of the Bus Industry', *Modern Transport*, 27 July, 1957, p. 13.
107. 'Bus War', *London Transport Magazine*, Oct. 1971.
108. W. J. Crosland-Taylor, op. cit., pp. 23–5.

109. See also chapter 9 for a fuller treatment of this subject.
110. D. MacGregor, *The National Way*, pp. 9–12.
111. C. E. R. Sherrington, *A Hundred Years of Inland Transport*, 1934, p. 342.
112. R. C. Anderson and G. Frankis, *History of Royal Blue Express Services*, 1970, p. 32.
113. Ibid., p. 37.
114. J. Hibbs, *The History of British Bus Services*, p. 163.
115. W. J. Crosland Taylor, *Crosville, the Sowing and the Harvest*, p. 143.
116. C. H. Feinstein, *Domestic Capital Formation in the U.K. 1920–38*, 1965, p. 44.
117. British Road Federation, *Basic Road Statistics*.
118. C. H. Feinstein, op. cit., p. 39.
119. G. R. Hawke, *Railways and Economic Growth in England and Wales, 1840–1870*, 1970, p. 209.
120. M. Beesley, 'Changing Locational Advantages in the British Motor Car Industry', *Jnl Ind. Econ.*, October 1957, p. 55.
121. G. Maxcy and A. Silberston, *The Motor Industry*, pp. 55–6.
122. Society of Motor Manufacturers and Traders, *The Motor Industry of Great Britain*, 1939, p. 50. B. R. Mitchell, 'The Coming of the Railway and United Kingdom Economic Growth', in M. C. Reed (ed.), *Railways in the Victorian Economy*, 1969.
123. Society of Motor Manufacturers and Traders, op. cit., 1929 edition, p. 18; 1939 edition, p. 146.
124. Ibid., 1939 edition, p. 50.
125. London and Cambridge Economic Service, *The British Economy: Key Statistics 1900–1964*, 1965, p. 14, and Society of Motor Manufacturers and Traders, op. cit., 1939 edition, p. 159.
126. C. H. Lee, *Regional Economic Growth in the U.K. since the 1880s*, 1971, p. 101.
127. British Road Federation, *Basic Road Statistics, 1971*, p. 2.
128. W. Ashworth, *An Economic History of England, 1870–1939*, 1960, p. 339.
129. Quoted in R. Graves and A. Hodge, *The Long Week-end*, 1940, p. 184.
130. G. M. Young, *Country and Town: a summary of the Scott and Uthwatt Reports*, 1943, p. 50.
131. A. J. P. Taylor, *English History 1914–45*, 1965, p. 304.

Chapter 9: *British Transport Policy 1914–39*

1. PRO MT 49/2.
2. D. H. Aldcroft, *British Railways in Transition*, 1968, p. 12.
3. F. H. Dixon and J. M. Parmelee, *War Administration of the Railways in the United States and Great Britain*, 1918, pp. 82–8.
4. S. J. Hurwitz, *State Intervention in Great Britain*, 1949, p. 69.
5. C. R. Fayle, *The War and the Shipping Industry*, 1927, p. 221.
6. E. A. Pratt, *British Railways and the Great War*, (2 vols) 1921. *Report of the S.C. on Transport*, 1918, HC 130/136. P. S. Bagwell, *The Railway Clearing House in the British Economy, 1842–1922*,

1968, p. 279. The War Cabinet, *Report for the Year 1918,* chap. 11, 'Transport'. Cmd 325 of 1919, *P.P.* 1919, vol. XXX.

7. C. Hadfield, *British Canals,* 1950 edition, pp. 233–4. The War Cabinet, *Report for the Year 1918,* chap. 11, Sect. E: 'Canals'. Cmd 3250/1919, *P.P.* 1919, vol. XXX.

8. M. Salt, 'Water Transport—Coastwise Shipping of the U.K.', *Jnl Inst. Tspt,* vol. 3, No. 1, Nov. 1921.

9. PRO MT 49/67.

10. S. Armitage, *The Politics of Decontrol of Industry: Britain and the United States,* 1969, p. 37.

11. *Hansard,* 5th series, vol. 130, Col. 2435. In 1919 the Ministry of Transport had lost all trace of Runciman's letter and had to write to the REC for a copy.

12. Extracts from a report of a deputation to the Rt. Hon. David Lloyd George from the TUC, Blackpool, Sept. 1917. 20 March 1918, PRO MT 49/2.

13. S. Armitage, op. cit., p. 65, and PRO MT 49/2.

14. *Report of the S.C. on Transport,* H.C. 130/136, 1918.

15. PRO MT 45/226.

16. Obituary notice, *The Times,* 23 June 1937.

17. PRO MT/45 234, 1919. Draft letter to Parliamentary Draughtsman from Sir Eric Geddes.

18. Note of appreciation of Sir Eric Geddes by Sir Ralph Wedgwood, *The Times,* 25 June 1937.

19. PRO MT/45 266.

20. Memorandum headed *Justification for a Ministry of Ways and Communications* in PRO MT/45 266.

21. PRO MT/45 225.

22. PRO MT/45 226.

23. War Cabinet 534, 19 February 1919, PRO MT/45 234.

24. PRO MT 45/234.

25. PRO MT 45/235.

26. *Hansard,* 5th series, vol. 112, 26 February 1919, Col. 1824.

27. *Hansard,* 5th series, vol. 113, 17 March 1919, Col. 1786.

28. *Hansard,* 5th series, vol. 117, 1 July 1919, Col. 809.

29. P. B. Johnson, *Land fit for Heroes,* 1968, p. 42.

30. *Hansard,* 5th series, vol. 117, 1 July 1919, Col. 2121.

31. Cited in S. Armitage, *The Politics of Decontrol of Industry: Britain and the United States,* 1969, p. 92.

32. *The Times,* 5 March 1919.

33. PRO MT 45/226.

34. *R.C. on Transport, Final Report,* 1930.

35. Note of a meeting between the Officers of the Ministry of Transport and the General Managers of the Railway Companies, 12 October 1920, PRO MT 49/2.

36. *Memorandum for the War Cabinet by the Ministry of Transport,* 13 October 1919, PRO 49/2.

37. PRO 49/2.

38. P. S. Bagwell, *The Railwaymen,* 1963, pp. 410–12.

39. *Memorandum on the Railways Bill,* Cmd 1292, 1921, p. 4.

40. G. Walker, *Road and Rail,* (2nd edition) 1947, p. 130.
41. PRO MT 49/2.
42. Cmd 1292 of 1921.
43. D. H. Aldercroft, *British Railways in Transition,* 1968, p. 44.
44. *Memorandum from the Consulting Mechanical Engineer, Ministry of Transport,* 7 May 1920, PRO MT 49/50.
45. *Engineering,* 5 May 1922, p. 569.
46. D. H. Aldcroft, *British Railways in Transition,* p. 62.
47. PRO MT 33/44. By the term 'Jitney' Mr Stirk meant freelance operators working on a shoestring budget.
48. G. Walker, 'The Economics of Road and Rail Competition', *Econ. Jnl,* vol. 33, 1933, p. 217.
49. D. R. Lamb, 'Coordination of Road and Rail Transport', *Jnl Inst. Tspt,* vol. 6, No. 9, July 1925, p. 471.
50. *Committee on the Road Conveyance of Goods by the Railway Companies,* Cmd 1228, 1921.
51. PRO CAB 23/94, 9 March 1922.
52. BTHR PYB 2514 A. S.C. Group F, qs 3837, 3842, 3846, 3905 and 3910.
53. PRO CAB 54 (27).
54. *Report of the Committee on Main Line Railway Electrification,* 1931.
55. Memorandum from Col. J. A. Pickard to Sir Philip Nash, 23 September 1919, PRO MT 33/168.
56. Letter (n.d.) from Sir Eric Geddes to Lord Inverforth, quoted in PRO MT 33/168.
57. *R.C. on London Traffic,* 1906.
58. PRO MT 31/1.
59. PRO MT 31/11.
60. Draft letter to the Secretary of the R.C. on London Government, 21 December 1921, in PRO MT 36/11.
61. Sir L. Macassey, 'The Problem of London Traffic', *Jnl Inst. Tspt,* vol. 6, No. 1, November 1924, p. 21.
62. *R.C. on Transport: Minutes of Evidence,* Sir H. Maybury, 15 November 1928, qs 504–7.
63. London Transport, *London General: the Story of the London Bus, 1856–1956,* 1956, pp. 51–4 (research conducted by A. L. Latchford and H. Pollins).
64. *Chairman:* 'You realise that it is very interesting to us to learn what you have been able to accomplish and in what respects you have not been able to accomplish in London as a very good example of what might take place in other areas'. *Sir H. Maybury:* 'Yes'. *R.C. on Transport: Minutes of Evidence,* 15 November 1928, q. 508.
65. PRO CP 39(28) in CAB 24/192.
66. Record of a Meeting of the Board of Trade Advisory Council, 17 February 1928. PRO CP 49/28 in CAB 24/192.
67. Memorandum by the Rt. Hon. H. Morrison, Minister of Transport, 9 July 1929. PRO CP 194(29) in CAB 24/204.
68. Cited in W. Plowden, *The Motorcar and Politics,* 1971, p. 142.
69. PRO MT 34/8.

70. Section 93, Road Traffic Act, 1930.
71. *Hansard,* 5th series, vol. 235, Col. 1207.
72. *Second Interim Report of the Departmental Committee on the Taxation and Regulation of Road Vehicles,* 1922, PRO MT 39/26. W. Plowden, op. cit., p. 255. *Hansard,* 5th series, vol. 235, Col. 1254.
73. *Royal Commission on Transport,* Minutes of Evidence, 14 November 1928, qs 71–84.
74. John Hibbs, *Transport for Passengers* (Hobart Paper 23, 1963), pp. 40, 45.
75. D. N. Chester, *Public Control of Road Passenger Transport,* 1936, ch. XI.
76. C. Hurcomb, 'Coordination of Transport in Great Britain during the years 1935–44', *Jnl Inst. Tspt,* vol. 22, No. 2, Feb.–March 1945, p. 90.
77. PRO MT 33/44.
78. *Hansard,* 5th series, vol. 335, 11 May 1935, Col. 1611.
79. PRO CAB 24/228.
80. PRO CAB 24/229 CP 150(32).
81. *The Times,* 24 April 1932.
82. *Transport Policy,* Memorandum by P. J. Pybus, Minister of Transport, 22 August 1932, PRO CAB 24/232 CP 286(32).
83. Salter Conference, *Report,* para. 89.
84. Ibid., para. 97.
85. *Transport Policy,* P. J. Pybus, PRO CAB 24/232 CP 286(32).
86. C. Hurcomb, op. cit., p. 94.
87. *R.C. on Transport, Minutes of Evidence,* Sir H. Maybury, qs 554–605 in PRO MT 42/32.
88. *London Passenger Transport Act,* 1933, Sect. 3.
89. Ministry of Reconstruction Report in PRO MT 29/30.
90. PRO MT 39/26 and 39/32.
91. H. H. Piggott, Memorandum to the R.C. on Transport, 14 November 1928, PRO MT 42/32.
92. PRO MT 39/619.
93. PRO MT 29/30.
94. Col. T. C. McLagan, S.C. of H.L. on Road Accidents, 24 May 1938, qs 4441–4576.
95. PRO MT 39/45.
96. Chamber of Shipping of the United Kingdom, *Annual Reports.*
97. Transport Advisory Council, *Coordination of Internal Goods Transport: Rail, Road, Canals and Coastwise Shipping,* PRO MT 43/61.
98. *Fairplay: Annual Summary of British Shipping Finance.* P.E.P. Transport Group, typescript *Coastwise Shipping,* 1937, in Institute of Transport Library, 80 Portland Place, London, W.1.
99. J. R. Cooper, 'British Coasting Trade and its National Importance', *Jnl Inst. Tspt,* vol. 15, No. 5, March 1934, p. 225.
100. P.E.P., op. cit.
101. J. R. Cooper, op. cit.
102. L. G. Hudson, 'A Review of the London Collier Trade', typescript in the Institute of Transport Library. On 6 July 1938 the Shipowners Parliamentary Committee informed the Merchant Marine

Department of the Board of Trade that the improvements in coastal carryings in recent years had been due mainly to increased coal traffic. 'The demand for coal by public utility companies is now enormously greater and their requirements are for coal produced in the Northumberland pits, which owing to their proximity to the ports, has led to a rational increase in coastal carryings.' PRO MT 9/2976.

103. J. R. Cooper, op. cit.
104. J. B. F. Earle, *A Century of Road Materials,* 1971, p. 135.
105. BTHR LMS 1/65, Shipping Committee Minutes, 28 May 1924.
106. Transport Advisory Council, Report on Services and Rates, Coastwise Shipping, 1938.
107. Ibid.
108. Joint Memorandum to the Transport Advisory Council upon the terms of agreement between railways and coastwise tramp shipping (n.d.), PRO MT 9/3021.
109. Chamber of Shipping of the U.K., *Financial Position of Coasting and Home Trade Tramps,* 1938, in PRO MT 9/9032.
110. H. Hopperton, 'Harbour Accommodation: Services and Charges in relation to Coasting and Overseas Trade', *Jnl Inst. Tspt,* vol. 19, No. 6, April 1938, p. 216. See also *Report of the Rates Advisory Committee on Coastwise Shipping and Exceptional Rates,* 1921, *P.P.* 1921, vol. XV.
111. T. W. Gattie, cited in D. H. Aldcroft, 'The Eclipse of British Coastal Shipping, 1913–21', *Jnl Tspt Hist.,* vol. VI, 1963–4, p. 31.
112. PRO MT 9/3032.
113. *Daily Express,* 5 July 1938.
114. *Motor Ship Reference Book for 1936,* p. 219.
115. Sir A. Read, 'Coastal Shipping in relation to Transport Planning', *Jnl Inst. Tspt,* vol. 18, No. 1, November 1936, p. 1.
116. Ministry of Health, Circular 1807 of 8 May 1939 in PRO MT 9/3032.
117. E. S. Shrapnell-Smith in discussion on S. E. Manning-Lewis's paper on 'Inland Waterways', *Jnl Inst. Tspt,* vol. 5, No. 4, February 1924, p. 162.
118. W. Fraser, 'The Future of Inland Water Transport', *Jnl Inst. Tspt,* vol. 22, No. 13, July–August 1947, p. 500.
119. G. Cadbury, 'The Economic Future of Canals', *Jnl Inst. Tspt,* vol. 19, No. 2, February 1938, p. 145.
120. F. C. Shelmerdine, 'Air Transport in Great Britain—some problems and needs', *Jnl Inst. Tspt,* vol. 17, No. 2, December 1935, p. 98.
121. J. Stroud, *Annals of British and Commonwealth Air Transport 1919–39,* 1960, p. 23.
122. R. Miller and D. Sawers, *The Technical Development of Modern Aviation,* 1968, p. 15.
123. G. E. W. Humphrey, 'A Review of Air Transport', *Jnl Inst. Tspt,* vol. 14, No. 5, March 1933, p. 284. Col. the Master of Sempill, 'Commercial and Civil Aviation, *United Empire,* vol. XXIII, April 1932, p. 195.
124. Col. the Master of Sempill, op. cit.

125. C. H. Gibbs-Smith, *The Aeroplane*, 1960, p. 104.
126. F. Handley-Page, 'The Achievements and Possibilities of Air Transport', *Jnl Inst. Tspt*, vol. 11, No. 8, June 1930, p. 371.
127. G. Holt Thomas, 'Air Transport and its Uses', *Jnl Inst. Tspt*, vol. 5, No. 6, April 1924, p. 245. Col. the Master of Sempill, op. cit.
128. F. C. Shelmerdine, 'Air Transport in Great Britain: Some Problems and Needs', *Jnl Inst. Tspt*, vol. 17, No. 2, December 1935, p. 103.
129. F. J. Field, *British Inland Air Posts*, 1934, p. 3.
130. F. Handley-Page, op. cit.
131. S. A. Hirst, 'The Development of Air Travel', *Jnl Inst. Tspt*, vol. 12, No. 2, December 1930, p. 92.
132. J. F. Leeming, 'The Development of Civil Air Transport since 1930', *Jnl Inst. Tspt*, vol. 16, No. 2, December 1934, p. 53.
133. G. Holt Thomas, 'Air Transport and its Uses', *Jnl Inst. Tspt*, vol. 5, No. 6, April 1924, p. 245.
134. F. C. Shelmerdine, op. cit., p. 103.
135. C. Birkhead, 'The Financial Failure of British Air Transport Companies, 1919–24', *Jnl Tspt. Hist.*, vol. IV, No. 3, May 1960, p. 143.
136. *Report of the Committee to Consider the Development of Civil Aviation in the UK*, (Maybury Committee) January 1937, *P.P.* 1936–7, vol. XVIII, paras 21–25.
137. G. S. Humphrey, 'A Review of Air Transport', *Jnl Inst. Tspt*, vol. 14, No. 5, March 1933.
138. *Report of the Committee of Enquiry into Civil Aviation*, (Cadman Committee) March 1938, *P.P.* 1937–8, vol. VIII, para. 7.
139. Ibid., paras 124–5.
140. D. H. Aldcroft, 'Britain's Internal Airways: The Pioneer Stage of the 1930s', *Business History*, vol. VI, 1964.
141. *Cadman Committee Report*, para. 80.
142. Cited in D. H. Aldcroft, op. cit., p. 117.
143. *Hansard*, 5th series, vol. 336, Cols 336 et seq.
144. The following account is based on D. H. Aldcroft's article 'The Railways and Air Transport in Great Britain, 1933–9', *Scottish Journal of Political Economy*, vol. XII, No. 1, February 1965, p. 50.
145. Committee of Inquiry into Civil Aviation (Cadman Committee), Report, 1938, *P.P.* 1937–8, vol. VIII, para. 74.

Chapter 10: *British Transport Developments 1939–70*

1. C. I. Savage, *Inland Transport* (History of the Second World War, UK Civil Series), 1957, p. 37.
2. R. Bell, *History of British Railways during the War, 1939–45*, 1946, p. 5.
3. C. I. Savage, op. cit., p. 69.
4. Ibid., pp. 73–75, 635.
5. A. Calder, *The People's War: Britain 1939–45*, 1969, p. 318.
6. D. H. Aldcroft, *British Railways in Transition*, 1968, p. 95.
7. British Railways Press Office, *British Railways in Peace and War*, 1944, p. 44.
8. A. Calder, op. cit., p. 232.

9. D. H. Aldcroft, op. cit., p. 102.
10. W. K. Hancock and M. M. Gowing, *British War Economy*, 1949, pp. 279, 487. C. I. Savage, *Inland Transport*, 1957, pp. 313, 317, 320–21, 619.
11. W. K. Hancock and M. M. Gowing, op. cit., p. 278.
12. E. C. R. Hadfield, *British Canals*, 1950 edition, p. 240.
13. Figures taken from C. I. Savage, *Inland Transport*, pp. 619, 621.
14. *The Economist*, 7 December 1946, p. 898.
15. The words are those of Sir Cyril (later Lord) Hurcombe, first Chairman of the British Transport Commission. *Jnl Inst. Tspt*, vol. 23, No. 2, January 1949, p. 33.
16. *The Times*, 16 December 1946, p. 5. *The Economist*, 7 December 1946, p. 898.
17. H. Morrison, *An Autobiography*, 1960, p. 259.
18. TUC, *Public Ownership: an Interim Report*. Presented to the 85th TUC, Douglas, I. of M., September 1953, p. 10. J. Elliot, 'An Act of Stewardship', *Jnl Inst. Tspt*, vol. 25, No. 7, November 1953, p. 245.
19. BTC, *Annual Report and Accounts*, 1961, p. 3.
20. R. Pryke, *Public Enterprise in Practice*, 1971, p. 42. BTC, *Annual Report and Accounts*, 1949, p. 19, 1951, p. 1, 1952, p. 3.
21. BTC, *Annual Report and Accounts*, 1952.
22. *S.C. on Nationalised Industries: Railways, Report*, 1960, paras 183, 180.
23. B. R. Williams, 'Nationalisation and After', *Jnl Inst. Tspt*, vol. 25, No. 1, November 1952.
24. M. R. Bonavia, *The Organisation of British Railways*, 1971, p. 55.
25. E. S. Cox, *Locomotive Panorama*, 1966, vol. 2, pp. 1–2.
26. M. R. Bonavia, op. cit., p. 52.
27. *British Transport Review*, 1950, p. 55.
28. Acton Society Trust, *Management Under Nationalisation*, p. 46.
29. *The Economist*, 25 November 1950, p. 899.
30. *Jnl Ind. Econ.*, 1953–4, p. 55.
31. R. Pryke, *Public Enterprise in Practice*, 1971, p. 29.
32. R. Wilson, 'Monopolies in Transport', *Jnl Inst. Tspt*, vol. 26, No. 10, May 1956, p. 368.
33. S. Wheatcroft, *Air Transport Policy*, 1964, p. 92.
34. *S.C. on the Nationalised Industries: the Air Corporations, Report*, *P.P.* 1958–9, vol. VII, pp. 104–117.
35. BEA, *Annual Report and Accounts*, 1951, App. 7.
36. BEA, *Annual Report and Accounts*, 1953.
37. S. Wheatcroft, *Air Transport Policy*, 1964, p. 33.
38. *Hansard* (Lords), 5th series, vol. CLX, Col. 351.
39. Air Transport Advisory Council, *Annual Report*, 1949, App. C, p. 13.
40. Air Transport Advisory Council, *Annual Reports*, 1949, 1951.
41. T. James, 'How Air Competes with Rail in Britain', *British Transport Review*, vol. 5, No. 4, August 1959, p. 267.
42. S. Wheatcroft, *Air Transport Policy*, 1964, p. 29.
43. BEA, *Annual Report and Accounts*, 1947, *P.P.* 1947–8, vol. X, p. 51.
44. BTC, *Annual Report and Accounts*, 1952.

45. *Modern Transport,* 10 May 1952.
46. R. Pryke, *Public Enterprise in Practice,* 1971, p. 29.
47. Ibid., p. 39.
48. Ibid., p. 37.
49. *Hansard,* 5th series, vol. 543, Col. 1701. G. W. Quick Smith in 'British Road Services in the Competitive Era', *British Transport Review,* vol. IV, No. 2, August 1956, considered the 1956 Act 'a standing tribute' to the success of BRS.
50. Figures for licences taken from British Road Federation, *Basic Road Statistics,* 1971, p. 15.
51. *Sunday Times,* 7 January 1968.
- 52. G. F. Allen, *British Railways after Beeching,* 1966, pp. 305–6.
53. A. J. Pearson, *The Railways and the Nation,* 1964, p. 78.
54. A. A. Harrison, 'Railway Freight Charges', *Jnl Inst. Tspt,* vol. 27, No. 5, July 1957, p. 143, and 'Reflections on the Railway Charges Scheme', *British Transport Review,* vol. IV, No. 5, August 1957, p. 399.
55. BTC, *Modernisation and Re-equipment of British Railways,* 1955.
56. D. H. Aldcroft, *British Railways in Transition,* 1968, p. 155.
57. Ministry of Transport, *Carriers' Licensing,* 1965, p. 28.
58. I am grateful to M. F. Moxley, Editor of the *Railway Review,* for this information.
59. BTC, *Annual Reports and Accounts.*
60. *S.C. on Nationalised Industries: Railways, Report,* 1960, pp. 350–52.
61. S. Joy, 'Intersystem comparison of Railway Productivity', *Peg,* No. 3, August 1972, p. 8 (Journal of the Public Enterprise Group).
62. Sir R. Hill, 'The Future of our Inland Waterways', *Jnl Inst. Tspt,* vol. 25, No. 9, March 1954, p. 344. Sir R. Hill was Chairman of the Docks and Inland Waterways Executive from 1947–53.
63. W. Fraser, 'Development of Inland Waterways', *Jnl Inst. Tspt,* vol. 26, No. 9, March 1956.
64. British Waterways Board, *The Future of the Waterways,* 1964, p. 6.
65. M. R. Bonavia, *The Organisation of British Railways,* 1971, p. 79.
66. *Hansard,* 5th series, vol. 619, 10 March 1960, Cols 642–4.
67. *S.C. on Nationalised Industries: Railways,* Report, 1960.
68. D. L. Munby, 'The Reshaping of British Railways', *Jnl Ind. Econ.,* vol. XI, July 1963, p. 161.
69. *Hansard,* 5th series, vol. 676, 30 April 1963, Col. 963.
70. *British Railways Year Book,* 1965, p. 15.
71. *BTC Annual Report and Accounts,* 1962, p. 36.
72. R. Pryke, *Public Enterprise in Practice,* 1971, p. 243.
73. G. F. Allen, *British Rail after Beeching,* 1966, p. 146 .
74. British Railways Board, *Annual Report and Accounts,* 1966, p. 3.
75. British Railways Board, *Annual Report and Accounts,* 1970.
76. B. Hinchcliff, *Railway Magazine,* August 1969, p. 442.
77. R. Pryke, *Public Enterprise in Practice,* 1971, p. 204. *Annual Abstract of Statistics,* 1961, pp. 209–17.
78. G. May, *The Challenge of BEA,* 1971, p. 116. *Annual Abstract of Statistics,* 1971, p. 231.

79. G. Walker, 'New Thinking in Transport', *Jnl Inst. Tspt*, vol. 26, No. 5, July 1955, p. 161. K. F. Glover and D. N. Miller, 'The Outlines of the Road Goods Transport Industry', *Jnl Roy. Stat. Socy*, vol. 117, Pt. 3, Ser. 'A', 1954, p. 300.

80. Ministry of Transport, *Carriers' Licensing*, 1965, p. 45.

81. Ministry of Transport, *Industrial Demand for Transport*, 1970.

82. *Hansard*, 5th series, vol. 756, December 1967, Col. 1281.

83. National Freight Corporation, *Annual Report and Accounts*, 1969, p. 4.

84. 'The Transport Bill', *Labour Research*, vol. LVII, No. 2, February 1968, p. 22.

85. S. Joy, 'Intersystem comparison of Railway Productivity', *Peg*, No. 3, p. 8.

86. *Hansard*, 5th series, vol. 756, December 1967, Col. 1281 .

87. Scottish Transport Group, *Annual Report and Accounts*, 1969.

88. A. H. Milward, 'Facts of Domestic Air Services', *The Times*, 28 February 1963.

89. *The Times*, 19 February 1963.

90. *The Times*, 18 November 1970.

91. Chamber of Shipping of the United Kingdom, *Annual Reports*.

92. *Board of Trade Journal*, various dates.

93. P. Ford and J. A. Bound, *Coastwise Shipping and the Small Ports*, 1951, p. 16.

94. *The Economist*, 1 April 1961, p. 49.

95. *Annual Abstract of Statistics*, 1971.

96. M. A. Robinson, 'Coastwise—Cross Channel', *Jnl Inst. Tspt*, vol. 26, No. 2, January 1955, p. 36.

97. *The Times, Container Transport Supplement*, 30 November 1966.

98. B. M. Deakin and T. Seward, *Productivity in Transport*, 1969, p. 218.

99. *The Financial Times, Pipes and Pipelines Supplement*, 2 June 1970, p. 25.

100. *The Times*, 20 June 1962. 'Ducks and Drakes', *Times Literary Supplement*, 11 June 1970, p. 625. R. McLeavy (ed.), *Jane's Surface Skimmer Systems*, 1970. 'Hovercraft and Hydrofoils', *The Times*, 21 October 1970.

101. C. Buchanan, *Traffic in Towns*, 1963, p. 10.

102. G. Turner, *The Car Makers*, 1964 edition, p. 35.

103. Ibid., p. 41.

104. C. Buchanan, *Mixed Blessing: the Motor in Britain*, 1958.

105. P.E.P. 'The Cost of Roads', *Planning*, vol. XXVII, No. 452, 15 May 1961, p. 114. British Road Federation, *Basic Road Statistics*, 1960, 1971, 1972.

106. Based on a lecture by C. T. Brunner, 'The Ideal Road System and its Economy', given to the Institute of Highway Engineers in January 1947.

107. C. T. Brunner, *Britain's Roads—Paralysis or Progress?*, 1954, p. 6.

108. J. F. A. Baker (Chief Engineer, Ministry of Transport), 'The General Motorway Plan', Institute of Civil Engineers, *Proceedings*, vol. 15, April 1960, paper no. 6442.

109. Ministry of Transport, *London–Yorkshire Motorway: first section, London–Birmingham,* 1959, p. 5. `

110. *The Times,* 3 November 1959.

111. W. H. Granville (Director of Road Research Department of Scientific and Industrial Research), 'Economic and Traffic Studies', Institute of Civil Engineers, *Proceedings,* vol. 15, April 1960, paper no. 6438, p. 333.

112. D. Hart-Davis, 'Sweeter for some with M4', *Sunday Telegraph,* 2 April 1972.

113. W. K. Granville, op. cit.

114. National Bus Company, *Annual Report and Accounts,* 1970, p. 13.

115. HMSO, *Rural Bus Services: Report,* 1961, pp. 19–20 .

116. Ministry of Transport, *Highland Transport Enquiry: Bus Services in the Highlands and Islands,* 1961, p. 10. Also *Transport Services in the Highlands and Islands,* Report, 1963.

117. D. J. Reynolds, 'Urban Motorways and Urban Congestion', *British Transport Review,* vol. VI, No. 4, August–December 1961.

118. J. M. Thomson, *Motorways in London,* 1969. J. Hillman, *Planning for London,* 1971.

119. *The Times,* 8 January 1969.

120. G. Hindley, *A History of Roads,* 1971, p. 144. T. Aldous, *Battle for the Environment,* 1972, chs 6 and 7.

121. *The Times,* 4 May 1972.

122. Estimated from *S.C. on Nationalised Industries, Report: British Railways,* July 1960, Annex to App. 8, p. 335. In 1962 the Ministry of Transport estimated an expenditure on transport of £2,100 million out of a GNP of 24,000 million. This would make transport expenditure just under 10 per cent of GNP. Ministry of Transport Statistical Paper No. 3, *Highway Statistics,* 1963.

Bibliography

The literature on the very large subject of transport history, even though the scope be confined to the post-industrial revolution era, is immense. No attempt will be made here to provide an exhaustive list of published works. Instead mention will be made of those books and articles which have been found of the greatest value in the writing of this book. The reader wishing to probe more deeply into any aspect of the subject will be given further guidance to bibliographical sources.

Of the general accounts of the history of British Transport the most recent and the most valuable is H. J. Dyos and D. H. Aldcroft, *British Transport* (1969). This is particularly useful for its coverage of urban transport, port and dock development and the birth of civil aviation. It has a remarkably extensive bibliography and is very well indexed. But the treatment of coastal shipping is sketchy and the account ends with the outbreak of the Second World War. Still very useful for the period from the sixteenth to the middle of the nineteenth century is W. T. Jackman's *The Development of Transportation in Modern England,* originally published in two volumes in 1916, but reprinted with a new bibliographical introduction by W. H. Chaloner in 1962. C. I. Savage, *An Economic History of Transport* (1959, revised edition 1966), gives an authoritative, if somewhat brief, account, principally of road and rail transport regulation in the past two centuries. E. A. Pratt's *A History of Inland Transport and Communication in England* (1912, new edition, with an introductory note by C. R. Clinker, 1970), though written from the viewpoint of a railway publicist, has a wider coverage than Jackman, carries the account forward to 1912, and also considers the impact of improved communications on economic life. C. E. R. Sherrington, *A Hundred Years of Inland Transport 1830–1933*, (1933 new edition, 1969) is a readable, popular, account of a more limited period of time. The best book with a geographical approach is J. H. Appleton, *The Geography of Communications in Great Britain* (1962).

The number of journals in the field of transport history is on the increase. The more important of these are *The Journal of Transport History, Transport History, The Institute of Transport Journal* and *Modern Transport.* For more specialised aspects of transport there are *The Railway Gazette, The Railway Magazine, Maritime History, Shipping World, Fairplay, Sea Breezes, Shipbuilding and Shipping Record, Aeroplane* and *Flight.*

For the very important area of government policy and Parliamentary enquiries the starting-off point is P. Ford and G. Ford, *A Guide to Parliamentary Papers* (1956). This may be followed up by the same authors' *Select List of British Parliamentary Papers, 1833–1899* (1953), *A Breviate of Parliamentary Papers, 1917–39* (1951). For government publications subsequent to 1939 the annual indexes, published by the Stationery Office, may be consulted.

There are some extremely helpful bibliographies. For railways the most comprehensive and valuable is G. Ottley, *A Bibliography of British Railway History* (1965), a very substantial work giving details of nearly 8,000 books arranged topically and with a first-class index. *The Journal of Transport History* has included bibliographical articles of value including R. C. Jarvis, 'Sources for the History of Ports', iii (1957); J. Simmons, 'Railway History in English Local Records', i (1954); D. B. Wardle, 'Sources for the History of Railways at the Public Record Office', ii (1956); M. Bond, 'Materials for Transport History among the Records of Parliament', iv (1964); C. Hadfield, 'Sources for the History of British Canals', ii (1955); J. A. B. Hibbs, 'Road Transport History in *Notices and Proceedings*', i (1954); and H. J. Dyos, 'Transport History in University Theses', iv (1960). Also of value is H. S. Cobb, 'Parliamentary Records Relating to Internal Navigation', *Archives,* vol. 9 (1969). Good bibliographical essays on railways are to be found in E. T. Bryant, *Railways: A Readers' Guide* (1968) and in J. Simmons, *The Railways of Britain,* (2nd edition 1968). A recent addition is C. R. Clinker, *Railway History: a hand list of the principal sources of original material, with notes and guidance on its use* (1969). For shipping the latest bibliographical essay is by N. Cox, 'The Records of the Registrar-General of Shipping and Seamen', *Maritime History,* vol. 2 (1972).

INLAND NAVIGATION IN BRITAIN BEFORE 1830

The outstanding study of river improvements in the pre-canal age is by T. S. Willan, *River Navigation in England, 1600–1750* (1936). Among the more important detailed studies by the same author are 'Yorkshire River Navigation, 1600–1750', *Geography,* xxii (1937); 'The River Navigation and Trade of the Severn Valley, 1600–1750', *Econ. Hist. Rev.,* iii (1937–8). 'The Navigation of the Great Ouse', Beds. Hist. Rec. Socy, *Publications,* vol. XXIV (1942); and 'River Navigation and Trade from the Witham to the Yare, 1600–1750', *Norfolk Archeology,* XXVI (1938). Other useful works include I. S. Beckwith, *The River Trade of Gainsborough, 1500–1850,* Lincs. Local Hist. Socy (1968); B. F. Duckham, *The Yorkshire Ouse: the History of a River Navigation* (1967); J. Tann, 'The Yorkshire Foss Navigation', *Tspt Hist.,* vol. 3 (1970); W. B. Stevens, 'The Exeter Lighter

Canal 1566–1698', *Jnl Tspt Hist.*, iii (1957); S. W. Skempton, 'The Engineers of the English River Navigations, 1620–1760', *Trans. Newcomen Socy*, vol. XXIX (1953); F. S. Thacker, *The Thames Highway* (1914); A. W. Goodfellow, 'Sheffield's Waterway to the Sea', *Trans. Hunter Archaeological Socy*, vol. V (1943) and G. G. Hopkinson, 'The Development of Inland Navigation in South Yorkshire and North Derbyshire, 1697–1850', ibid., vol. VII (1956). For the engineering side of river improvements there is A. G. Keller, *A Theatre of Machines* (1964).

Important contemporary accounts of inland navigations include J. Phillips, *General History of Inland Navigation* (1792, reprinted 1970); Joseph Priestley, *Historical Account of the Navigable Rivers, Canals and Railways of Britain* (1831, reprinted, with an introduction by E. C. R. Hadfield, 1969); T. Bentley, *A Short View of the General Advantages of Inland Navigation, 1781–1794* (1906) and Anon. (but probably T. Bentley), *The History of Inland Navigations* (1766, 1769 and 1779).

The most authoritative survey by a modern writer is E. C. R. Hadfield, *British Canals* (4th edition 1969), although L. T. C. Rolt, *The Inland Waterways of England* (1950) is most attractively produced and has the best general canal map. Hadfield's more recent general introduction is *The Canal Age* (1968). The regional history of canals is now much more adequately covered in E. C. R. Hadfield's *The Canals of South Wales and the Border* (1960); *The Canals of the East Midlands* (1966), *The Canals of South West England* (1967); *The Canals of South and South East England* (1969) and *The Canals of the West Midlands* (1969). For Scotland J. Lindsay, *The Canals of Scotland* (1968) is indispensable. Also important within the same series is E. C. R. Hadfield & G. Biddle, *The Canals of North West England* (1970). For the beginning of canal-building activity in the north-west the important works are T. C. Barker, 'The Beginnings of the Canal Age in the British Isles' in L. S. Pressnell (ed.), *Studies in the Industrial Revolution* (1960), and the same author's 'The Sankey Navigation: the first Lancashire Canal', *Trans. of the Historic Society of Lancashire and Cheshire*, vol. C (1948) and 'Lancashire Coal, Cheshire Salt and the Rise of Liverpool', ibid., vol. ciii (1951). Other specialist studies include F. Mullineux, *The Duke of Bridgewater's Canal* (1959); A. T. Patterson, 'The Making of the Leicestershire Canals, 1777–1814', *Trans. of the Leicestershire Archaeological Socy*, vol. xxvii (1951); H. Pollins, 'The Swansea Canal', *Jnl Tspt Hist.*, vol. i (1954); H. Clegg, 'The Third Duke of Bridgewater's Canal Works at Manchester', *Trans. of the Lancashire and Cheshire Antiquarian Soc.*, vol. xv (1955); and H. Household, 'The Thames and Severn Canal', *Jnl Tspt Hist.*, vol. vii (1966).

For contemporary impressions of the impact of canals on industry, society and the environment two entertaining accounts are G. Head, *A Home Tour of the Manufacturing Districts and other parts of England, Scotland, Ireland, including the Channel Islands and the Isle of Man* (1840), and J. Hassell, *A Tour of the Grand Junction Canal in 1819* (new edition with notes and introduction by J. Cranfield, 1968).

For the immense stimulus given by canal construction to the growth of civil engineering the leading works include S. Smiles, *Lives of the Engineers* (2nd edition, 5 vols, 1878) and A. Gibb, *The Story of Telford: the Rise of Civil Engineering* (1936), a reliable, well illustrated account of the engineer's work in Britain and in Sweden. It is supplemented by L. T. C. Rolt's *Thomas Telford* (1958). The work of other canal engineers is recorded in E. C. R. Hadfield, 'James Green and Canal Engineer', *Jnl Tspt Hist.*, i (1953); C. T. G. Boucher, *John Rennie, 1761–1821* (1963); H. G. W. Household, 'Early Engineering on the Thames and Severn Canal', *Trans. of the Newcomen Socy*, vol. xxvii (1949–51). W. H. Chaloner, *People and Industries* (1963) and J. Simmons, *Parish and Empire* (1952).

The plight of the canal-boat people was revealed by G. Smith, *Our Canal Population* (1875) and *Canal Adventures by Moonlight* (1881). More scholarly treatments of the problem are to be found in R. M. Macleod, 'Social Policy and the Floating Population', *Past and Present*, No. 35 (1966) and S. R. Broadbridge, 'Living Conditions on Midland Canal Boats', *Tspt Hist.*, vol. 3 (1970).

ROAD TRANSPORT BEFORE THE RAILWAY AGE

The two most important books of recent date on the British road system are J. Copeland, *Roads and their Traffic, 1750–1850* (1968) and W. Albert, *The Turnpike Road System in England 1663–1840* (1972), the former a very readable general account incorporating up-to-date knowledge and the latter a remarkably thorough analysis of the management and finances of the turnpike roads. Still very useful are S. and B. Webb, *The Story of the King's Highway* (1913, new edition, 1963) and W. T. Jackman, *The Development of Transportation in Modern England* (1916, new edition, with an up-to-date bibliography of W. H. Chaloner, 1962). For types of road haulage J. Crofts, *Packhorse, Waggon and Post* (1967) is of value.

Of the numerous books and articles on the local history of roads the following is a representative selection: P. L. Payne, 'The Bermondsey, Rotherhithe and Deptford Turnpike Trust 1776–1810', *Jnl Tspt Hist.*, vol. ii (1956); W. Harrison, 'The Development of the Turnpike System in Lancashire and Cheshire', *Transactions of the Lancashire and Cheshire Antiquarian Socy*, vol. iv (1886); G. H. Tupling, 'The Turnpike Trusts of Lancashire', *Memoirs and Proceedings of the Manchester Literary and Philosophical Socy*, vol. xciv

(1952–3); F. H. W. Sheppard, *Local Government in St Marylebone, 1688–1835* (1958); A. D. Anderson, 'The Development of the Road System in the Stewatry of Kircudbright 1590–1890', *Dumfrieshire and Galloway Natural History and Antiquarian Socy Transactions,* vol. 44 (1967) and 45 (1968); A. Cossons, *The Turnpike Roads of Nottinghamshire* (1934). Some of the county histories in the *Victoria History of the Counties of England* contain sub-sections on road communications. These include S. A. H. Burne, 'Roads', in *Staffordshire,* vol. 2 (1967); A. Cossons, 'Roads', in *Wiltshire,* vol. iv (1959) and C. R. Elrington, 'Communications', in *Warwickshire,* vol. vii, 'The City of Birmingham' (1964).

For the records of turnpike trusts there is a useful survey in B. F. Duckham, 'Turnpike Records', *History,* vol. 53 (1968). Other articles include F. A. Bailey, 'The Minutes of the Trustees of the Turnpike Roads from Liverpool to Prescot, St Helens, Warrington and Ashton-in-Makerfield, 1726–89', *Transactions N. Staffs. Field Club,* vols lxxxiii (1948) and lxxxiv (1949).

The social consequences of turnpike roads in south Wales are examined in masterly fashion by D. Williams in *The Rebecca Riots* (1955). In the lavishly produced and fascinating book by M. Searle, *Turnpikes and Toll Bars* (2 vols, 1930) there is a representative collection of prints, documents and contemporary accounts of life on the road. The literature on stage-coaching is very substantial, a great deal of it appearing at the time of revived interest in roads in late Victorian and in Edwardian times. The popular writer was C. G. Harper, whose books included *Stage-Coach and Mail in Days of Yore* (2 vols, 1903); *The Brighton Road* (1892); *The Dover Road* (1895); *The Exeter Road* (1899); *The Great North Road* (2 vols, 1901); *The Holyhead Road* (2 vols, 1902) and *Manchester and Glasgow Road* (2nd revised edition 1924), among numerous others. They recapture admirably the flavour of the times. Other products of the same period are W. Outram-Tristram, *Coaching Days and Coaching Ways* (1893); S. Harris, *The Coaching Age* (1885) and W. C. A. Blew, *Brighton and its Coaches* (1894). Among the more important books by modern scholars, E. W. Bovill's *The England of Nimrod and Surtees, 1815–54* (1959) and *English Country Life, 1780–1830* (1962) are outstanding. Valuable information on fares and itineraries is included in H. W. Hart, 'Some Notes on Coach Travel 1750–1848', *Jnl Tspt Hist.,* vol. iv (1960). Also useful is C. Dickinson on 'Stage Coach Services in the West Riding of Yorkshire, 1830–40', *Jnl Tspt Hist.,* vol. iv (1959).

Of contemporary travel books C. B. Andrews (ed.), *The Torrington Diaries: A Selection from the Tours of the Hon. John Byng, later fifth Viscount Torrington,* 1781–94 (1954) and C. Moritz, *Travels Chiefly on Foot, through Several Parts of England, in 1782* (included in J. Pinkerton's *A General Collection of the Best and Most Interest-*

ing Voyages and Travels in All Parts of the World (17 vols, 1808–14: vol. ii) are the best. A. Young, *A Six Months' Tour through the North of England* (1771) should be read in conjunction with E. F. Gay, 'Arthur Young on English Roads', *Qly Jnl Econ.*, xli (1927). For the role of the carrier in the eighteenth century G. Eland (ed.), *Purefoy Letters 1735–1753* (1931), is highly entertaining and instructive.

A valuable survey of coach services in their prime is given in A. Bates, *Directory of Stage Coach Services, 1836* (1969).

The part played by the Post Office in improving communications by road is dealt with in E. Vale, *The Mail Coach Men of the Late Eighteenth Century* (1960). There is also C. Noall, *A History of Cornish Mail and Stage Coaches* (1963) and C. R. Clear, *John Palmer, Mail Coach Pioneer* (1955).

The improvements in design of coaches and other road vehicles was considered by nineteenth-century writers including R. L. Edgeworth, *An Essay on the Construction of Roads and Carriages* (2nd edition 1817); G. A. Thrupp, *The History of Coaches* (1877), J. W. Burgess, *A Practical Treatise on Coach-Building, Historical and Descriptive* (1881) and J. Philipson, *The Art and Craft of Coach Building* (1897). Later writings include R. Strauss, *Carriages and Coaches, their History and their Evolution* (1912), H. McCausland *The English Carriage* (1948) and A. Bird, *Roads and Vehicles* (1969).

The history of road goods haulage in the days before commercial motors still awaits full treatment by an historian. Aspects of this important part of the British economy are dealt with by T. S. Willan, 'The Justices of the Peace and the Rates of Land Carriage, 1692–1827', *Jnl. Tspt. Hist.*, vol. v (1962) and by W. Albert, 'The Justices' Rates for Land Carriage 1748–1827, reconsidered', *Tspt Hist.*, vol. 1, No. 2 (1968). Other pointers on the use of land transport in industry are to be found in R. A. Lewis, 'Transport for Eighteenth Century Ironworks', *Economica*, vol. xviii (1951) and B. L. C. Johnson, 'The Foley Partnerships: the Iron Industry at the End of the Charcoal Era', *Econ. Hist. Rev.*, 2nd series, vol. iv (1951–2).

The progress of road-building techniques and of this branch of civil engineering and considered in R. H. Spiro (Jnr), 'John London McAdam and the Metropolitan Turnpike Trust', *Jnl Tspt Hist.*, vol. ii (1956). They are dealt with sketchily in G. Hindley, *A History of Roads* (1971), a work which attempts to summarise road development throughout the world in just over 150 pages. Contemporary accounts include J. L. McAdam's treatises, *Remarks on the Present System of Road Making* (1816) and *Observations on the Management of Trusts for the Care of Turnpike Roads* (1825). Historical facts are included in both T. Aitken, *Road Making and Maintenance* (1900) and H. Law and D. K. Clark, *The Construction of Roads and Streets* (1901). A very recent work of value is J. B. F. Earle, *A Century of Road*

Materials (1971). For Telford's part in the building of the Holyhead Road there is M. Hughes, 'Telford, Parnell, and the Great Irish Road', *Jnl Tspt Hist.*, vol. vi (1964).

COASTAL SHIPPING

For the first half of the eighteenth century the role of coastal shipping in British transport is given full treatment in T. S. Willan, *The English Coasting Trade, 1600–1750* (1938). There is no work of comparable excellence to cover the second half of the eighteenth century and the years before Bell's *Comet* appeared on the Clyde in 1812. The student is obliged to refer to early trade directories and contemporary literature to piece together the facts of packet services and coastal tramp-shipping. However, the most important component of the coastal shipping trade, the carriage of coal from the Tyne to London, is treated authoritatively in R. Smith, *Sea-Coal for London* (1961) and valuable information about the coastal trade of particular ports can be obtained from S. Middlebrook, *Newcastle on Tyne: its Growth and Achievement* (1968); G. Chandler, *Liverpool Shipping* (1960); C. N. Parkinson, *The Rise of the Port of Liverpool* (1952); G. Jackson, *Hull in the eighteenth century* (1872); J. Latimer, *Annals of Bristol in the Nineteenth Century* (1887, 1902); J. Latimer and J. G. Broodbank, *Annals of History of the Port of London* (2 vols, 1921).

The early history of the steamboat and its impact on passenger transport is recorded in G. Dodd, *An Historical and Explanatory Dissertation on Steam Engines and Steam Packets* (1818); H. P. Spratt, *The Birth of the Steamboat* (1958); A. C. Wardle, 'Early Steamships on the Mersey, 1815–1820', *Trans. of the Historic Society of Lancashire and Cheshire*, vol. xcii (1940); H. S. Irvine, 'Some Aspects of Passenger Traffic between Britain and Ireland, 1820–1850', *Jnl Tspt Hist.*, vol. iv (1960); M. Gray, *The Highland Economy, 1750–1850* (1957); *New Statistical Account of Scotland*, especially vols vi and vii (1854); *Topographical Statistical Gazeteer of Scotland* (2 vols 1842); R. P. Cruden, *The History of the town of Gravesend in the County of Kent and of the Port of London* (1843); J. W. Burrows, *Southend on Sea and District* (1909) and R. N. Worth, *History of Plymouth* (1890). J. Williamson, *The Clyde Passenger Steamer, its Rise and Progress during the Nineteenth Century* (1904) and D. B. McNeill, *Irish Passenger Steamship Services*, vol. 1, *North of Ireland* (1969), vol. 2, *South of Ireland* (1971). There is a very good outline of the development of steam navigation in R. T. Rowland, *Steam at Sea* (1971).

The carriage of freight coastwise in sailing vessels survived long after the steamboat dominated the carriage of passengers. Essential for an understanding of the east coast coal trade are W. Runciman's

Before the Mast and After (1924) and *Collier Brigs and their Sailors* (1926). Other accounts recording the survival of sailing ships include Slade, *Out of Appledore* (1959) and H. Benham, *Last Stronghold of Sail* (1948). For the east coast meat trade there is a valuable article by G. Channon, 'The Aberdeenshire Beef Trade with London: a study in Steamship and Railway Competition', *Tspt Hist.*, vol. 2 (1969). The eventual triumph of the screw collier over the collier brig in the coal trade is explained in S. Everard, *History of the Gas, Light and Coke Company* (1949) and in E. E. Allen, 'On the Comparative cost of transit by Steam and Sailing Colliers and on the different modes of Ballasting', *Institution of Civil Engineers, Proceedings*, vol. xiv (1854). There are some useful references to the role of coastal shipping in the industrial growth of South Wales in A. H. John, *The Industrial Development of South Wales* (1950).

The importance of port investments in the growth of the coastal trade is well brought out in A. G. Kenwood, 'Capital Investment in Docks, Harbours and river improvements in North East England, 1825–50', *Jnl Tspt Hist.*, N.S., vol. 1 (1971). There are shorter accounts of earlier developments in D. Swann, 'The Pace and Progress of Port Investment in England, 1660–1830', *Yorkshire Bulletin of Economic and Social Research*, vol. xii (1960) and 'The Engineers of English Port Improvements 1660–1830', *Tspt Hist.*, vol. 1 (1968). Other useful works on ports involved in coastal trade include R. Jones, 'Kingston-upon-Hull: A Study in Port Development', *Scottish Geographical Magazine*, vol. xxxv (1919); J. Guthrie, *The River Tyne: Its History and Resources* (1880); W. H. Jones, *History of the Port of Swansea* (1922). For port labour two books of outstanding merit are W. Stern, *The Porters of London* (1960) and J. Lovell, *Stevedores and Dockers* (1969). There is very little available on trade unionism amongst seamen in the coasting trade, but E. Tupper, *Seamen's Torch* (1938) and E. Taplin, *Liverpool Dockers and Seamen 1870–1890* (1973) provide some information. For organisations of shipowners see L. H. Powell, *The Shipping Federation* (1950).

On the fascinating subject of the seaworthiness of vessels and the safety of the men employed in them, T. Gray, 'Fifty years of Legislation in relation to the Shipping Trade and the safety of Ships and Seamen', *Worshipful Company of Shipwrights, Lectures at the Mansion House, 1886–7* (1887), provides a valuable survey of the legislation. A most authoritative recent account is by G. Alderman, 'Samuel Plimsoll and the Shipping Interest', *Maritime History*, vol. 1 (1971).

THE FOUNDATION OF THE RAILWAY SYSTEM

The outstanding work on the origins and early development of railways is M. J. T. Lewis, *Early Wooden Railways* (1970), a subject treated earlier in some of its aspects in R. B. Smith, 'England's First Rails: A Reconstruction', *Renaissance and Modern Studies*, vol. iv (1960). The beginnings of the railway system are also dealt with in C. E. Lee, *The Evolution of Railways* (1937, 2nd edition 1943); J. Simmons, *The Railways of Britain* (1961, 2nd edition 1968); J. B. Snell, *Early Railways* (1964); and C. E. R. Sherrington, *Economics of Rail Transport in Great Britain* (2 vols, 1928).

Two classics of the early development of the railway system are H. G. Lewin, *Early British Railways, 1801–44* (1925) and *The Railway Mania and its Aftermath, 1845–52* (1936, revised edition, with new introduction by C. R. Clinker, but without the maps, 1968). Other important books of the early years of railways include R. E. Carlson, *The Liverpool and Manchester Railway Project, 1821–31* (1969); C. F. Dendy Marshall, *History of British Railways down to the year 1830* (1938, 2nd edition, with a new introduction by W. H. Chaloner, 1971) and E. A. Forward, 'Report on Railways in England, 1826–7', *Trans. of the Newcomen Socy,* vol. xxix (1958).

Contemporary accounts of the greatest value are F. Whishaw, *The Railways of Great Britain and Ireland* (1840–41); J. Francis, *A History of the English Railway* (2 vols, 1851); F. S. Williams, *Our Iron Roads* (1852, new edition, with introduction by C. E. Lee, 1968); H. Spencer, *Railway Morals and Railway Policy* (1855) and D. Lardner, *Railway Economy* (1850), a work whose reputation has been enhanced in recent years.

Of great importance for understanding the sources of capital for the first 50 years of railways are S. R. Broadbridge, *Studies in Railway Expansion and the Capital Market in England, 1825–73* (1970); M. C. Reed (ed.), *Railways in the Victorian Economy: Studies in Finance and Economic Growth* (1969) and H. Pollins, *Britain's Railways: an Industrial History* (1971). For Scotland there are three articles by W. Vamplew, 'Sources of Scottish railway share capital before 1860' and 'The financing of Scottish railways before 1860: a reply', *Scottish Journal of Political Economy* (1970 and 1971) and 'Railway Investment in the Scottish Highlands', *Tspt Hist.,* vol. 3 (1970). See also T. R. Gourvish and M. C. Reed, 'The financing of Scottish railways before 1860: a Comment', *Scottish Journal of Political Economy* (1971).

Of recent years there has been a rapidly increasing output of regional histories of railways. These include E. Course, *London Railways* (1962) and the following volumes in the *Regional History of the Railways of Great Britain* series: D. St. J. Thomas, *The West Country* (1960); H. P. White, *Southern England* (1961) and *Greater London* (1963); K. Hoole, *The North East* (1965) and D. I. Gordon, *The Eastern Counties* (1968). *The Victoria Histories of the Counties of England* contain important articles on railway development. Among the best of these are those by H. C. Darby in *Cambridgeshire*, vol. ii (1948); J. Simmons in *Leicestershire*, vol. iii (1955); C. R. Clinker in *Wiltshire*, vol. iv (1959); H. W. Parris in *Yorkshire: The City of York* (1961); C. R. Elrington in *Warwickshire*, vol. vii (1964); W. Ashworth in *Essex*, vol. v (1966) and S. A. H. Bourne, W. J. Wise and P. L. Clark in *Staffordshire*, vol. ii (1967). A very good example of a local history is J. H. Lucking, *Railways of Dorset: an outline of their establishment, development and progress from 1825* (1968).

Histories of individual railway companies are so numerous that space does not permit the mention of all of them here. There are, however, larger companies whose histories form a very important part of railway literature. These include E. T. MacDermot, *History of the Great Western Railway* (3 vols, ed. C. R. Clinker, 1964); C. H. Grinling, *History of the Great Northern Railway* (3rd edition, 1966); G. Dow, *Great Central* (3 vols, 1959–65); C. J. Allen, *The Great Eastern Railway* (4th edition, 1967); W. W. Tomlinson, *The North Eastern Railway* (1915); H. Ellis, *The South Western Railway* (1956); H. Pollins, 'The Last Main Line to London', *Jnl Tspt Hist.*, vol. iv (1959); and F. Dendy Marshall, *A History of the Southern Railway* (new edition, revised by R. W. Kidner, 1968). For information on the histories of other railway companies the reader is referred to G. Ottley's *Bibliography of British Railway History* (1965).

For the railway engineers the best accounts are to be found in L. T. C. Rolt, *George and Robert Stephenson: the Railway Revolution* (1960) and the same author's *Isambard Kingdom Brunel* (1957) and *Railway Engineering* (1968); see also M. Jamieson, *The Railway Stephensons* (1970). Much less satisfactory are J. Devey, *The Life of Joseph Locke* (1862) and O. J. Vignoles, *Life of Charles Blacker Vignoles* (1889). In a class by itself for the insight it gives into the Stockton and Darlington Railway and the Stephensons is A. Pease (ed.) *The Diaries of Edward Pease, the Father of English Railways* (1907). The best account of a railway contractor is by A. Helps, *Life and Labours of Mr Brassey* (new edition, with an introduction by J. Simmons, 1969) although there is also a shorter account of Brassey in R. K. Middlemass, *The Master Builders* (1963) and a well illustrated, but somewhat disappointing, recent life by C. Walker, *Thomas Brassey: Railway Builder* (1969). Brassey's enlightened views on railway navvies are shown in the book of his son, T. Brassey, *Work and Wages* (1872). Also of value are T. R. Conder, *Personal Recollections of English Engineers* (1868); H. Peto, *Sir Morton Peto* (1893); F. McDermott, *Life of Joseph Firbank* (1887) and I. Thomas, *Top Sawyer* (1938), which is an account of the leading Welsh contractor, David Davies. For the early science of railway engineering there are two important accounts: N. Wood, *A Practical Treatise on Railways*

(1825) and L. Herbert, *A Practical Treatise on Railroads and Locomotive Engines* (1837).

The financing of railway works has been ably treated in two articles by H. Pollins, 'Railway Contractors and the Finance of Railway Development in Britain', *Jnl Tspt Hist.*, vol. iii (1957) and 'A Note on Railway Constructional Costs, 1825–1850', *Economica*, vol. xix (1952–3). For an assessment of the adequacy of later investment in railways the reader should consult R. J. Irving, 'British Railway Investment and Innovations 1900–14', *Business History*, vol. 13 (1971).

Of outstanding interest for the railway labourers is Terry Coleman, *The Railway Navvies* (revised, paperback, edition 1968). The special composition of a navvy gang employed in Yorkshire is analysed in J. A. Patmore, 'A Navvy Gang of 1851', *Jnl Tspt Hist.*, vol. v (1962); E. Chadwick's efforts to improve the working conditions and accommodation of the navvies are examined in R. A. Lewis, 'Edwin Chadwick and the Railway Labourers', *Econ. Hist. Rev.*, vol. iii (1950).

THE ECONOMIC AND SOCIAL EFFECTS OF RAILWAYS

The best general introduction, which covers a wide spectrum and is very readable, is H. Perkin, *The Age of the Railway* (1970). Another short introduction both perceptive and entertaining is M. Robbins, *The Railway Age* (1962), a book which gives some consideration to railway developments outside Great Britain. Representative of the new econometric school of economic history is G. R. Hawke's *Railways and Economic Growth in England and Wales* (1970), a book in which an attempt is made to measure more precisely the impact of railways on British industry. A pioneering assessment in this area was made by B. R. Mitchell, 'The Coming of the Railway and United Kingdom Economic Growth', *Jnl Econ. Hist.*, vol. xxiv (1964). From a completely different approach there is E. L. Waugh's 'Railroads and the Changing Face of Britain, 1825–1901', *Business History Review*, vol. xxx (1956).

The impact of railways on engineering is considered in relation to the Swindon works of the Great Western Railway in D. E. C. Eversley, 'Engineering and Railway Works', *Victoria Histories of the Counties of England, Wiltshire*, vol. iv (1959), and in S. B. Saul, 'The Market and the Development of Mechanical Engineering in Britain, 1860–1914', *Ec. Hist. Rev.*, 2nd series, vol. xx (1967).

The influence of the railways on the growth and structure of the capital market in Britain is dealt with in the above-mentioned works of H. Pollins, S. R. Broadbridge and M. C. Reed and in E. V. Morgan and W. A. Thomas, *The Stock Exchange: its History and Functions* (1962). For the frauds and malpractices in railway promotion and associated enterprises a contemporary survey is in D. Morier Evans, *Facts, Failures and Frauds* (1859). The classic biography of George Hudson is R. S. Lambert, *The Railway King, 1800–1871* (2nd impression 1964). Additional evidence is to be found in H. Spencer, *Railway Morals and Railway Policy* (1855) and in J. S. Jeans, *Railway Problems* (1887). The railways created new problems of management and of industrial organisation and these aspects are examined in T. R. Gourvish, *Mark Huish and the London and North Western Railway* (1972); G. Findlay, *The Working and Management of an English Railway* (1889); G. P. Neele, *Railway Reminiscences* (1904); G. H. Evans Jr, *British Corporation Finance 1775–1850: A Study of Preference Shares* (1936); and C. A. Cooke, *Corporation, Trust and Company* (1950).

The influence of railways on the spread of improved technology and on marketing in agriculture is considered in J. D. Chambers and G. E. Mingay, *The Agricultural Revolution, 1750–1880* and in C. S. Orwin and E. H. Whetham, *History of British Agriculture 1846–1914* (1964).

The exploitation of the railway passenger facilities in the growth of the holiday business is revealed in J. Pudney, *The Thomas Cook Story* (1953) and in W. E. Rae, *The Business of Travel; A Fifty Year Record* (1891). Also of value are J. A. R. Pimlott, *The Englishman's Holiday* (1947) and two books which reveal the major contribution made by railways to the growth of the seaside towns: E. W. Gilbert, *Brighton: Old Ocean's Bubble* (1954) and D. S. Young, *The Story of Bournemouth* (1957).

There is now an impressive literature on the railway towns. Of outstanding merit is W. H. Chaloner, *The Social and Economic Development of Crewe, 1780–1923* (1950). For Swindon, apart from the above-mentioned work by D. E. C. Eversley, there is K. Hudson, 'The Early Years of the Railway Community in Swindon', *Tspt Hist.*, vol. 1, No. 2 (1968) and H. B. Wells, 'Swindon in the 19th and 20th Centuries', in *Studies in the History of Swindon*, ed. L. V. Grinsell and others (1950). The growth of other railway towns is examined in P. Richards, 'The Influence of the Railways on the Growth of Wolverton, Buckinghamshire', *Records of Buckinghamshire*, vol. xvii, Pt. 2 (1962); B. J. Turton, 'The Railway Towns of Southern England', *Tspt Hist.*, vol. 2 No. 2 (1969); B. Barber, 'The Concept of the Railway Town and the Growth of Darlington, 1801–1911—a note', *Tspt Hist.*, vol. 3 (1970); and K. Jackson, 'The South-Eastern Railway and its workshops at Ashford', *Cantium* (1971). The railways also greatly changed the character of life in previously existing urban centres. Their voracious demand for land in the centre of big cities is demonstrated in an important book by J. R. Kellett, *The Impact of Railways on Victorian Cities* (1969). Other essential reading on this topic includes H. J. Dyos (ed.), *The Study of Urban History* (1968), and the same author's *Victorian Suburb: A Study of the Growth of Camberwell* (1961); 'Railways and Housing in Victorian London', *Jnl Tspt Hist.*, vol. ii (1955); 'Some Social Costs of Railway Building in London', ibid., vol. iii (1957); 'The Slums of Victorian London', *Victorian Studies*, vol. xi (1967) and 'Workmen's Fares in South London, 1860–1914', *Jnl Tspt Hist.*, vol. i (1953). See also P. N. Jones, 'Workmen's Trains in the South Wales Coalfield, 1870–1926', *Tspt Hist.*, vol. 3, 1970.

For the development of underground railway and other forms of transport in the metropolis the standard work, very readable and most aptly illustrated, is T. C. Barker and M. Robbins, *A History of London Transport*, vol. 1: *The Nineteenth Century* (1963). A compact account written by J. R. Day, *The Story of London's Underground*, was published by London Transport in 1963. For the same organisation C. E. Lee wrote *Sixty Years of the Northern* (1967); *100 Years of the District* (1968) and *Seventy Years of the Central* (1970).

The impact of the railway on the development of the electric telegraph has recently been given full treatment in J. L. Kieve, *The Electric Telegraph: A Social and Economic History* (1973).

ROAD AND WATER TRANSPORT IN THE RAILWAY AGE

The popular image of Victorian England is of a society whose members travelled by train. There is an excellent corrective of this view in F. M. L. Thompson, *Victorian England: the horse drawn society* (Bedford College, London, 1970). It was the main road traffic which suffered most and for this W. Sheardown, *The Great North Road and the Great Northern Railway* (1863) and H. Wilson, *Hints to Road Speculators, together with the Influence Railroads will have upon Society* (1845) are instructive reading. T. May in 'Road Passenger Transport in Harrow in the Nineteenth and Early Twentieth Centuries', *Jnl Tspt Hist.*, new series, vol. 1 (1971), shows how poor siting of railway stations brought expanding business to horse-drawn buses. Coach and wagon services in the early railway age are considered in J. Copeland, *Roads and their Traffic, 1750–1850* (1968) and in the same author's 'Coach Horse versus Steam Engine: the stage and mail transport revolution', *Country Life*, vol. 146 (4 December 1969). For the ramifications of railway expansion on the business of an old-established road and canal haulage firm see G. L. Turnbull, 'The Railway Revolution and the Carriers' Response: Messrs Pickford and Company, 1830–50', *Tspt Hist.*, vol. 2 (1969) and for the effects of railway developments on other forms of transport north of the Tweed, W. Vamplew, 'Railways and the Scottish Transport system in the Nineteenth Century', *Jnl Tspt Hist.*, new series, vol. 1 (1971–2).

The changing fortunes of turnpike roads during the railway age are examined in S. and B. Webb, *The Story of the King's Highway* (1913, new edition 1963); and in R. H. Spiro, Jnr, 'John London McAdam and the Metropolitan Turnpike Trust', *Jnl Tspt Hist.*, vol. ii (1956).

The development of alternative forms of road transport to the horse-drawn vehicle is covered in its various aspects in J. Woodforde, *The Story of the Bicycle* (1970); H. O. Duncan, *The World on Wheels* (1927) and C. St. C. B. Davison, *History of Steam Road Vehicles* (HMSO, 1953).

There is a rapidly growing literature on commuting and the expansion of tramway and bus services. Among the most informative are G. C. Dickinson, 'The Development of Road Passenger Transport in Leeds', *Jnl Tspt Hist.*, vol. iv (1960); C. F. Klapper, *The Golden Age of Tramways* (1961); W. H. Bett and J. C. Gillham, *Great British Tramway Networks* (4th edition, 1962); W. Jackson-Stevens, *British Electric Tramways* (1971); S. A. Munro, 'Tramway Companies of Liverpool, 1859–1897', *Historic Society of Lancashire and Cheshire, Transactions* (1967); C. E. Lee, 'The English Street Tramways of George Francis Train', *Jnl Tspt Hist.*, vol. i (1953); A. B. Hopkins, *Tramway Legislation in England* (1891); S. E. Harrison, *The Tramways of Portsmouth* (1955); P. W. Gentry, *The Tramways of the West of England* (1952); J. S. Webb, *The Tramways of the Black Country* (1954); I. Yearsley, *The Manchester Tram* (1962); 'Rodinglea', *The Tramways of East London* (1967); and D. L. G. Hunter, *Edinburgh's Transport* (1964). J. Hibbs, *The History of British Bus Services* (1968) and C. E. Lee, *The Horse Bus as a Vehicle* (1962). J. Hibbs (ed.) *The Omnibus* (1971), though mainly concerned with motor buses, is also of value. R. Bean's 'Working conditions, labour agitation and the origins of unionism on the Liverpool tramways', *Tspt Hist.*, vol. 5 (1972) is a brief sketch of labour problems. The early history of London transport has been well covered in T. C. Barker and M. Robbins, *A History of London Transport:* vol. 1, *The Nineteenth Century* (1963).

The consequences to canal transport of the growth of the railway system are best examined in the Parliamentary Papers referred to in the footnotes to chapter 6, but there is a great deal of incidental information in the above-mentioned regional canal histories by C. Hadfield, J. Lindsay and G. Biddle. The railway companies' viewpoint is given in E. A. Pratt, *Railways and their Rates* (1905) and comparisons with canal development in France, Belgium and Germany may be made by reference to J. Clapham, *The Economic Development of France and Germany, 1818–1914* (4th edition 1948) and in the special reports on the inland waterways of the continent presented to the Royal Commission on Canals, 1906–10. Also of value, though primarily concerned with the canal system after 1918, is G.

Cadbury and S. P. Dobbs, *Canals and Inland Waterways* (1928). An outstanding recent study of a canal which prospered after the coming of the railways is F. C. Mather, *After the Canal Duke* (1970).

The railway companies' development of their own steam packet services is considered in E. W. P. Veale, *Gateway to the Continent* (1955); R. Bucknall, *Boat Trains and Channel Packets* (1957); J. H. Lucking, *The Great Western at Weymouth: a railway and shipping history* (1971); *The Jubilee of the Railway News* (1914) and B. F. Duckham, 'Railway Steamship Enterprise; the Lancashire and York-shire Railway's East Coast Fleet, 1904–14', *Business History*, vol. x (1968). A number of railway company histories deal with steamboat services. A particularly good example is John Thomas, *The North British Railway*, vol. 1 (1969).

GOVERNMENT AND THE RAILWAYS, 1830–1914

The controversies on state versus private ownership of railways, the regulation of freight charges, the control of monopoly and the prevention of railway accidents have led to a spate of publications from the 1820s onwards. Among the more important contemporary contributions to the discussion are J. Morrison, *Speech on Railways* (1836) and the same author's *Observations Illustrative of the Defects of the English System of Railway Legislation* (1846); D. Lardner, *Railway Economy* (1850); W. Galt, *Railway Reform; its Importance and Practicability* (1865); J. Hole, *National Railways* (1893) and A. E. Davies, *The Nationalisation of Railways* (2nd revised edition, 1911). Of later works, exceptionally good for the early development of monopoly is E. Cleveland-Stevens, *English Railways, their development and their relation to the State* (1915). The role of the Board of Trade in the regulation of railways particularly before 1868, is dealt with very ably in H. W. Parris, *Government and the Railways in Nine-teenth Century Britain* (1968). That Britain escaped a greater degree of public control of the railways in the nineteenth century is partly due to the railway companies' cooperation through the Railway Clearing House. This aspect of the situation is the subject of P. S. Bagwell's *The Railway Clearing House in the British Economy, 1842–1922* (1968). It is also in part due to effective lobbying by the large number of railway directors in Parliament. G. Alderman's *The Railway Interest* (1973) is the first detailed study of a nineteenth-century interest group. It supersedes the much shorter essay by P. S. Bagwell, 'The Railway Interest: its organisation and influence 1839–1914', *Jnl Tspt Hist.*, vol. vii (1965). For the later development of monopoly there is a useful article by D. Broke, 'Railway Consolida-tion and competition in N.E. England, 1854–80', *Tspt Hist.*, vol. 5, No. 1 (1972) and two soundly written books: W. A. Robertson, *Com-*

bination among railway companies (1912) and W. E. Simnett, *Railway Amalgamation in Great Britain* (1923).

On the vexed question of railway charges the outstanding works are W. M. Acworth, *Elements of Railway Economics* (new edition 1924) and the same author's *The Railways and the Traders* (1891).

The leading Victorian authority on railway accidents was C. E. Stretton, whose *Safe Railway Working* went into three editions between 1887–93. His *A Few Remarks on Railway Accidents; their cause and prevention,* was another best-seller with four editions in 1881–2. Also authoritative for the period are H. R. Wilson, *Railway Accidents: Legislation and Statistics, 1814–1924* (1925) and C. Manby and J. Forrest (ed.), *Railway Accidents* (1864), a work which includes a valuable contribution by Douglas Galton. The two best recent accounts are by O. S. Nock, *Historic Railway Accidents* (1966) and L. T. C. Rolt, *Red for Danger* (2nd edition 1966).

The recruitment and early organisation of the labour force is well treated in a pioneering study by P. W. Kingsford, *Victorian Railwaymen: the emergence and growth of railway labour, 1830–70* (1971). On later labour relations there is G. Alderman, 'The Railway companies and the growth of trade unionism in the late nineteenth and early twentieth centuries', *Historical Journal,* vol. 14 (1971). The jubilee of the Amalgamated Society of Railway Servants was commemorated in G. W. Alcock, *Fifty Years of Railway Trade Unionism* (1922), a book of value because written by a participant in labour relations, but marred by a very poor index. The official history of the National Union of Railwaymen was written by P. S. Bagwell, *The Railwaymen* (1963). For the Associated Society of Locomotive Engineers and Firemen there is the well-written book by J. R. Raynes, *Engines and Men* (1921), and the later, but in many ways less adequate, account by N. McKillop, *The Lighted Flame* (1950). Pending the publication of a history of the organisation of the clerical grades the account of the Railway Clerks Association given in G. D. H. Cole and R. P. Arnot, *Trade Unionism on the Railways* (1917) is still of value. An interesting account of how railways and railwaymen were employed to quell labour unrest is by F. C. Mather, 'The Railways, the Electric Telegraph, and Public Order during the Chartist Period, 1837–48', *History,* vol. xxxviii (1953).

THE DEVELOPMENT OF MOTOR TRANSPORT

There is no fully adequate history of the growth of the motor industry in Great Britain, but the story, in its different phases, can be pieced together through reading the following books: St. John C. Nixon, *The Invention of the Automobile* (1936); D. Scott-Moncrieff, *Veteran and Edwardian Motor Cars* (1955); G. Maxcy and A. Silberston, *The*

Motor Industry (1959); G. Maxcy, 'The Motor Industry' in P. L. Cook and R. Cohen (ed.), *Effects of Mergers* (1958); S. B. Saul, 'The Motor Industry in Britain to 1914', *Business History,* vol. v (1962); A. Bird, *The Motor Car, 1765–1914* (1960); H. Wyatt, *The Motor Industry* (1918); G. C. Allen, *The British Motor Industry* (Lond. & Cambs. Econ. Studies 18, 1926); H. G. Castle, *Britain's Motor Industry* (1950); and G. Turner, *The Car Makers* (1963). Technical progress in the industry may be traced through the *Proceedings* of the Incorporated Institution of Automobile Engineers (1906–) and the commercial progress through the annual publication of the Society of Motor Manufacturers and Traders, *The Motor Industry of Great Britain* (1926–). There are a number of histories of motor manufacturing firms which give insight into the conditions of the market and of production in the early years of the industry. These include St. John C. Nixon, *Daimler, 1896–1946* (1948); the same author's *Wolseley: A Saga of the Motor Industry* (1949); C. Wilson and W. W. Reader, *Men and Machines: A History of Napier and Sons, Engineers Ltd., 1808–1958* (1958); P. W. Kingsford, *F. W. Lanchester* (1960); and P. W. S. Andrews and E. Brunner, *The Life of Lord Nuffield* (1955). The most famous of Britain's small cars is the subject of R. J. Wyatt, *The Motor for the Million: the Austin Seven, 1922–39* (1968).

For the early development of commercial motor transport St. John C. Nixon in *The Simms Story from 1891* (1955) tells of the growth of demand for heavy commercial vehicles and how it was met. For public passenger transport there is C. E. Lee, *The Early Motor Bus* (1964). J. Hibbs's *The History of British Bus Services* is a disappointing survey which fails to place the industry in the perspective of the development of transport as a whole and makes no attempt to measure the scale of its progress. For the extent of investment in road motor transport the reader should turn to C. H. Feinstein, *Domestic Capital Formation in the United Kingdom, 1920–38* (1965). J. Hibbs (ed.) *The Omnibus: Readings in the History of Road Passenger Transport* (1971) gives some insight into the conditions of operation before and after the legislation of 1930 and 1933. There is a brilliant survey of the progress of commercial motoring by E. S. Shrapnell-Smith, 'Five Decades of Commercial Road Transport with implications about its future', *Jnl Inst. Tspt,* vol. 22 (1946). For the growth of an important bus company the reader should consult W. J. Crossland-Taylor, *Crosville: the sowing and the harvest* (1948).

Exhaustive treatment has recently been given to the whole subject of government regulation and taxation of the private motor car in W. Plowden, *The Motor Car and Politics, 1896–1970* (1971). It is to be regretted that there is no comparable account of government policy for commercial vehicles and the road haulage industry. The origins and growth of the Automobile Association are recorded in D. Kier and B. Morgan, *Golden Milestone* (1955). The comparable work for the rival organisation is D. Noble (ed.), *The Jubilee Book of the Royal Automobile Club, 1897–1947* (1947). There is also a brief account by P. Fleetwood-Hesketh, 'The Royal Automobile Club' in *Country Life*, vol. 150 (1971).

The problems of road improvement are considered by J. C. Haller, 'Roads and Road Traffic', *Jnl Inst. Tspt*, vol. 2 (1921) and in subsequent volumes of the same journal. Also of great value are F. Wood, *Modern Road Construction* (1920) and J. B. F. Earle, *A Century of Road Materials: the History of Roadstone Division of Tarmac Ltd* (1971).

Statistical information on road mileage, the growth of automobile production and registration, road accidents and their cost, the taxation of road vehicles and many other aspects of the motor industry is provided in *Basic Road Statistics*, produced annually by the British Road Federation.

BRITISH TRANSPORT POLICY 1914–39

The standard work on wartime railway operation is E. A. Pratt, *British Railways and the Great War* (2 vols, 1921), but there is a valuable comparative study by F. H. Dixon and J. M. Parmelee, *War Administration of the Railways in the United States and Great Britain* (1918). The general significance of growing state involvement in the economy is discussed in S. J. Hurwitz, *State Intervention in Great Britain* (1949). D. H. Aldcroft, *British Railways in Transition* (1968) is invaluable for the whole period from World War I to the Beeching era of the 1960s. The effect of the war on the shipping industry is given full treatment in C. R. Fayle, *The War and the Shipping Industry* (1927), but the best account for coastal shipping is D. H. Aldcroft, 'The Eclipse of British Coastal Shipping 1913–21', *Jnl Tspt Hist.*, vol. vi (1963). There is no specific wartime history of the inland waterways but E. C. R. Hadfield, *British Canals* (1960 ed.) explains, briefly, the reasons for falling traffic.

Plans for transport in the Ministry of Reconstruction and decontrol in the immediate post-war years are examined in S. Armitage, *The Politics of Decontrol of Industry: Britain and the United States* (1969) and in P. D. Johnson, *Land Fit for Heroes* (1968). Two articles by D. H. Aldcroft: 'The Decontrol of British Shipping and Railways after the First World War', *Jnl Tspt. Hist.*, vol. v (1961) and 'Port Congestion and the Shipping Boom of 1919–20', *Business History*, vol. iii (1961) deal with other aspects of decontrol. For railway reorganisation, culminating in the Railways Act of 1921, there is information in the above-mentioned work of S. Armitage and in W. M. Acworth, 'Grouping under the Railways Act, 1921', *Econ. Jnl*, vol.

xxxiii (1923); C. E. R. Sherrington, 'Some Economic Results of the British Railways Act of 1921', *American Economic Review*, vol. xiv (1920); W. E. Simnett, *Railway Amalgamation in Britain* (1923); H. C. Kidd, *A New Era for British Railways* (1929) and W. G. Scott, 'An Aspect of the British Railways Act, 1921', in H. A. Innis (ed.) *Essays in Transportation in Honour of W. T. Jackman* (1941).

For the later development of railways there is a useful statistical analysis in K. G. Fenelon, 'British Railways Since the War', *Jnl Roy. Stat. Socy*, vol. xcvi (1933), while the same author's *Railway Economics* (1932) is a valuable guide to the outstanding characteristics of railway operation. Other worthwhile accounts include A. Brown, *The Railway Problem* (1932) and W. V. Wood and J. Stamp, *Railways* (1928). The two most important books on costs and charges are G. Walker, *Road and Rail* (2nd edition, 1947) and A. M. Milne and A. Laing, *The Obligation to Carry* (1956). The effect of booms and slumps in industry on the profitability of railways is examined in C. D. Campbell, *British Railways in Boom and Depression: An Essay in Trade Fluctuations and their effects, 1878–1930* (1932). Technical progress on British railways is covered in S. H. Fisher, 'Acceleration of Railway Services', *Jnl Inst. Tspt*, vol. xix (1939); G. T. Moody, *Southern Electric: the History of the World's largest suburban and electrified system* (4th edition 1968); and C. J. Allen, *Locomotive Practice and Performance in the Twentieth Century* (1949).

For road transport, essential reading includes the Royal Commission on Transport, *Reports:* 'Control of Traffic on Roads' (1929); 'The Licensing and Regulation of Public Service Vehicles' (1929); and 'The Co-ordination and Development of Transport' (1930). A critical view of these reports and of the legislation which followed them is contained in J. Hibbs, *Transport for Passengers* (Hobart Paper 23, 1963). Still of great value as an analysis of the Road Traffic Act, 1930 and its effects is D. N. Chester, *Public Control of Road Passenger Transport* (1936). A more recent interpretation is to be found in P. E. Hart, 'The Restriction of Road Haulage', *Scottish Journal of Political Economy*, vol. vi (1959). The aspect of transport coordination is surveyed in C. Hurcomb, 'Coordination of Transport in Great Britain during the years 1935–44', *Jnl Inst. Tspt*, vol. 22 (1945); by G. J. Ponsonby, 'Freight Charges by Road in Competition', *Economic Journal*, vol. xlviii (1938); and by H. O. Mance, *The Road and Rail Transport Problem* (1940). The situation in the capital is ably surveyed in L. Magassey, 'The Problem of London Traffic', *Jnl Inst. Tspt*, vol. 6 (1924). London Transport's *London General: the Story of the London Bus 1856–1956* (1956) tells of the development of an important part of the transport services of the metropolis. For some of the developments in the provinces R. Fulford, *Five Decades of B.E.T.: The Story of the British Electric Traction Company* (1946) is of interest.

The principal sources for the development of the highway system are R. Jeffreys, *The King's Highway* (1949); A. Day, *Roads* (1963); G. Walker, 'Highway Finance', *Journal of Industrial Economics* (1956) and G. C. Gurnock, *New Roads for Britain* (1944).

The best account of the composition of coastwise shipping and its role in the inter-war years is contained in the P.E.P. Transport Group's typescript *Coastwise Shipping* (1937). The importance of the trade in the general context of transport is discussed in J. R. Cooper, 'British Coasting Trade and its National Importance', *Jnl Inst. Tspt*, vol. 15 (1934) and A. Read, 'Coastal Shipping in Relation to Transport Planning', *Jnl Inst. Tspt*, vol. 18 (1936). The importance of good harbour facilities and realistic charges is discussed in H. Hopperton, 'Harbour Accommodation: Services and Charges in relation to Coasting and Overseas Trade', *Jnl Inst. Tspt*, vol. 19 (1938).

The declining fortunes of British canals in the inter-war years was the subject of an address by G. Cadbury, 'The Economic Future of the Canals', *Jnl Inst. Tspt*, vol. 22 (1938). Ten years earlier the same author, in collaboration with S. P. Dobbs, wrote more fully on the same subject in *Canals and Inland Waterways* (1928). The situation reached at the end of the Second World War is outlined in W. Fraser, 'The Future of Inland Water Transport', *Jnl Inst. Tspt*, vol. 22 (1947).

The beginnings of civil aviation are considered in E. Birkhead, 'The Financial Failure of British Air Transport Companies', 1919–24, *Jnl Tspt Hist.*, vol. iv (1960) and the same author's 'The Daimler Airway', ibid., vol. iii (1958). F. C. Shelmerdine, 'Air transport in Great Britain—some problems and needs', *Jnl Inst. Tspt*, vol. 17 (1935) is of great value. Technical progress in aviation is the subject of C. H. Gibbs-Smith, *The Aeroplane* (1960) and of R. Miller and D. Sawers, *The Technical Development of Modern Aviation* (1968); D. H. Aldcroft has provided two very useful articles, 'Britain's Internal Airways: the Pioneer Stage of the 1930s', *Business History*, vol. vi (1964); and 'Railways and Air Transport in Great Britain, 1933–39', *Scottish Journal of Political Economy*, vol. xii (1965).

BRITISH TRANSPORT DEVELOPMENTS 1939–70

The official history of British transport in the years 1939–45 is C. I. Savage, *Inland Transport* (1957), a comprehensive survey of the mobilisation of both land and water transport in all their different forms. More colourfully A. Calder, *The People's War: Britain 1939–45* (1969) recalls episodes such as the evacuation of schoolchildren from the big cities at the beginning of the war. R. Bell, *History of British Railways during the War, 1939–45* (1946) is a strictly railway history with little examination of the economies of railway working. For the trained economist's approach the reader should turn to D. H. Aldcroft, *British Railways in Transition* (1968) and for a consideration of the role of transport in the wartime economy to W. K. Hancock and M. M. Gowing, *British War Economy* (1949).

B. R. Williams, 'Nationalisation and After', *Jnl Inst. Tspt*, vol. 25 (1952), surveys the progress of British transport under the Transport Act, 1947, while J. Elliot, 'An Act of Stewardship', *Jnl Inst. Tspt*, vol. 25, No. 7 (1953) assesses the management of the railways over the same span of time. M. R. Bonavia, *The Organisation of British Railways* (1971) looks principally at the management side of railway operation and has penetrating observations on the conflict between the Railway Executive and the British Transport Commission, 1948–1962. The monthly publication *British Transport Review* has importance as reflecting contemporary concerns. R. Pryke, *Public Enterprise in Practice* (1971) is a masterly assessment of the achievements and shortcomings of all major publicly owned industries after 1946. The work is of importance for understanding the economic problems of a nationalised road haulage and airways as well as the railways. The various reports of the *Select Committee on Nationalised Industries* are a mine of information on the principal problems of business organisation. The National Union of Railwaymen's point of view is given in *Planning Transport for you* (1959).

A standard work on postwar air transport is S. Wheatcroft, *Air Transport Policy* (1964). The threat to long-distance rail passenger services is examined in T. James, 'How air competes with rail in Britain', *British Transport Review*, vol. 5 (1959). The story of one of the great air corporations is told, with lavish illustrations, in G. May, *The Challenge of BEA: the story of a great airline's first twenty-five years* (1971). R. S. Doganis in *A National Airport Plan* (Fabian Tract 377, 1967) makes a valuable contribution to the understanding of British airport development after 1939.

A transport economist's standpoint is given in C. D. Foster, *The Transport Problem* (1963) while the same author's essay (written in conjunction with M. E. Beesley), 'The Victoria Line', is reprinted in D. L. Munby (ed.) *Transport: Selected Readings* (1968). Other important contributions to the general discussion of transport policy in the last two decades include K. M. Gwilliam's *Transport and Public Policy* (1964) and J. R. Sargent, *British Transport Policy* (1958).

The background to the Beeching Plan is traced in A. J. Pearson, *The Railways and the Nation* (1964) and its character and immediate aftermath examined in G. F. Allen, *British Railways after Beeching* (1966). H. Pollins, *British Railways: an Industrial History* (1971) is also of value for this period. An interesting comparison is made between the post-Beeching efficiency of British Railways with the railways of some other European countries by S. Joy, 'Intersystem comparison of Railway productivity', *Peg*, No. 3 (August 1972). H. Johnson, 'Twenty Years of Nationalised Railways', *National Pro-*

vincial Bank Review, No. 863 (1968) gives the viewpoint of a main participant, while B. M. Deakin and T. Seward, *Productivity in Transport: a study of employment, capital, productivity and technical change* (1969) analyses the changes over the period 1952–65. A valuable regional study of the progress and benefits of railway modernisation is K. Hoole, 'Railway electrification on Tyneside, 1902–1967', *Tspt Hist.* (1969).

The declining commercial importance of Britain's inland waterways is revealed in H. D. Watts, 'Inland Waterways of the United Kingdom in the 1960s', *Economic Geography*, vol. 43, 1967, and in R. Hill, 'The Future of Inland Waterways', *Jnl Inst. Tspt*, vol. 25 (1954) and W. Fraser, 'Development of Inland Waterways', *Jnl Inst. Tspt*, vol. 26 (1956).

Coastwise shipping was subject to investigation soon after the Second World War by P. Ford and J. A. Bound, *Coastwise Shipping and the Small Ports* (1951). The passenger services are examined in M. A. Robinson, 'Coastwise—Cross Channel', *Jnl Inst. Tspt*, vol. 26 (1955).

There is a valuable survey of the road haulage industry in K. F. Glover and D. N. Miller, 'The Outlines of the Road Goods Transport Industry', *Jnl Roy. Stat. Socy*, vol. 117 (1954) and authoritative articles by S. Joy, 'Unregulated road haulage: the Australian experience', *Oxford Economic Papers*, vol. 16 (1964) and D. L. Munby, 'The Economics of Road Haulage Licensing', *Oxford Economic Papers*, vol. 17 (1965). The Ministry of Transport Report, *Carriers' Licensing* (1965) is essential reading for this phase of the history of the industry.

PEP's 'The Cost of Roads', *Planning*, vol. xxvii, No. 452 (1961) contains a great deal of valuable information and analysis within a small compass. C. T. Brunner's *Britain's Roads—Paralysis or Progress?* (1954) is representative of the arguments for greater expenditure on roads in the 1950s. A. Day, *Roads* (1963) deals with the growth of traffic, parking, accidents and the costs and benefits of new road construction. G. Roth, *Paying for Roads* (1967) is an enquiry into the economics of traffic congestion. Two classic statements of the social and environmental problems of the motor car are C. Buchanan, *Mixed Blessing: the Motor in Britain* (1958) and the same author's *Traffic in Towns* (1963). These (and other) issues are also considered in T. Aldous, *Battle for the Environment* (1972). For urban motorways the reader should consult J. M. Thomson, *Motorways in London* (1969); J. Hillman, *Planning for London* (1971) and D. J. Reynolds, 'Urban Motorways and Urban Congestion', *British Transport Review*, vol. vi (1961). Among very many critical studies of the damaging consequences of the proliferation of private motor transport in the urban environment F. Hope, 'A car-owning democracy: Sombre reflections on a twentieth century plague', *New Statesman* (21 February 1969) is worthy of mention.

Indexes

Index to Bibliography

General Index

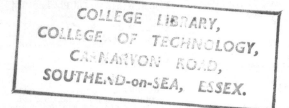